THE RAILS WAY

Addison-Wesley Professional Ruby Series

Obie Fernandez, Series Editor

The Addison-Wesley Professional Ruby Series provides readers with practical, people-oriented, and in-depth information about applying the Ruby platform to create dynamic technology solutions. The series is based on the premise that the need for expert reference books, written by experienced practitioners, will never be satisfied solely by blogs and the Internet.

Books currently in the series

The Ruby Way: Solutions and Techniques in Ruby Programming, Second Edition
Hal Fulton, ISBN 13: 9780672328848, ©2007

RailsSpace: Building a Social Networking Website with Ruby on Rails™
Michael Hartl & Aurelius Prochazka, ISBN 13: 9780321480798, ©2008

The Rails Way
Obie Fernandez, ISBN 13: 9780321445612, ©2008

Design Patterns in Ruby
Russ Olsen, ISBN 13: 9780321490452, ©2008

Short Cuts

Rails Routing
David A. Black • 0321509242 • ©2007

Rails Refactoring to Resources: Using CRUD and REST in Your Rails Application
Trotter Cashion • 0321501748 • ©2007

Mongrel: Serving, Deploying and Extending Your Ruby Applications
Matt Pelletier and Zed Shaw • 0321483502 • ©2007

Rails Plugins: Extending Rails Beyond the Core
James Adam • 0321483510 • ©2007

Rubyism in Rails
Jacob Harris • 0321474074 • ©2007

Troubleshooting Ruby Processes: Leveraging System Tools when the Usual Ruby Tricks Stop Working
Philippe Hanrigou • 0321544684 • ©2008

Writing Efficient Ruby Code
Dr. Stefan Kaes • 0321540034 • ©2008

Video

RailsSpace Ruby on Rails Tutorial (Video LiveLessons)
Aurelius Prochazka • 0321517067 • ©2008

www.awprofessional.com/ruby

THE RAILS WAY

Obie Fernandez

✦✦Addison-Wesley

Upper Saddle River, NJ • Boston • Indianapolis • San Francisco
New York • Toronto • Montreal • London • Munich • Paris • Madrid
Capetown • Sydney • Tokyo • Singapore • Mexico City

Many of the designations used by manufacturers and sellers to distinguish their products are claimed as trademarks. Where those designations appear in this book, and the publisher was aware of a trademark claim, the designations have been printed with initial capital letters or in all capitals.

The author and publisher have taken care in the preparation of this book, but make no expressed or implied warranty of any kind and assume no responsibility for errors or omissions. No liability is assumed for incidental or consequential damages in connection with or arising out of the use of the information or programs contained herein.

The publisher offers excellent discounts on this book when ordered in quantity for bulk purchases or special sales, which may include electronic versions and/or custom covers and content particular to your business, training goals, marketing focus, and branding interests. For more information, please contact:

U.S. Corporate and Government Sales
(800) 382-3419
corpsales@pearsontechgroup.com

For sales outside the United States please contact:

International Sales
international@pearsoned.com

 This Book Is Safari Enabled

The Safari® Enabled icon on the cover of your favorite technology book means the book is available through Safari Bookshelf. When you buy this book, you get free access to the online edition for 45 days.

Safari Bookshelf is an electronic reference library that lets you easily search thousands of technical books, find code samples, download chapters, and access technical information whenever and wherever you need it.

To gain 45-day Safari Enabled access to this book:

- Go to http://www.awprofessional.com/safarienabled
- Complete the brief registration form
- Enter the coupon code 52GH-T7VF-4T1U-ATFQ-DMJH

If you have difficulty registering on Safari Bookshelf or accessing the online edition, please e-mail customer-service@safaribooksonline.com.

Visit us on the Web: www.awprofessional.com

Library of Congress Cataloging-in-Publication Data:

Fernandez, Obie.

The Rails way / Obie Fernandez.

p. cm.

Includes index.

ISBN 0-321-44561-9 (pbk. : alk. paper)

1. Ruby on rails (Electronic resource) 2. Object-oriented programming (Computer science) 3. Ruby (Computer program language) 4. Web site development . 5. Application softare--Development. I. Title.

QA76.64F47 2007

005.1'17--dc22

2007039880

ISBN-13: 978-0-321-44561-9
ISBN-10: 0-321-44561-9
Text printed in the United States on recycled paper at R.R. Donnelly in Crawfordsville, IN.
First printing November 2007

Associate Publisher
Mark Taub

Acquisitions Editor
Debra Williams Cauley

Development Editor
Songlin Qiu

Managing Editor
Patrick Kanouse

Senior Project Editor
San Dee Phillips

Indexer
Tim Wright

Publishing Coordinator
Cindy Teeters

Book Designer
Chuti Prasertsith

Composition
Mark Shirar

Copy Editor
Margaret Berson

Proofreader
Kathy Ruiz

Technical Reviewer
Francis Hwang
Sebastian Delmont
Wilson Bilkovich
Courtenay Gasking
Sam Aaron
Nola Stowe
Susan Potter
Jon Larkowski

To Desi, my love, my companion, my muse.

Contents

❖

Foreword

Rails is more than programming framework for creating web applications. It's also a framework for thinking about web applications. It ships not as a blank slate equally tolerant of every kind of expression. On the contrary, it trades that flexibility for the convenience of "what most people need most of the time to do most things." It's a designer straightjacket that sets you free from focusing on the things that just don't matter and focuses your attention on the stuff that does.

To be able to accept that trade, you need to understand not just how to do something in Rails, but also why it's done like that. Only by understanding the why will you be able to consistently work with the framework instead of against it. It doesn't mean that you'll always have to agree with a certain choice, but you will need to agree to the overachieving principle of conventions. You have to learn to relax and let go of your attachment to personal idiosyncrasies when the productivity rewards are right.

This book can help you do just that. Not only does it serve as a guide in your exploration of the features in Rails, it also gives you a window into the mind and soul of Rails. Why we've chosen to do things the way we do them, why we frown on certain widespread approaches. It even goes so far as to include the discussions and stories of how we got there—straight from the community participants that helped shape them.

Learning how to do Hello World in Rails has always been easy to do on your own, but getting to know and appreciate the gestalt of Rails, less so. I applaud Obie for trying to help you on this journey. Enjoy it.

—David Heinemeier Hansson
    Creator of Ruby on Rails

Acknowledgments

A very heartfelt and special thank you goes to my editor, Debra Williams Cauley, for recognizing my potential and ever-patiently guiding me through the all of the ups and downs of getting this book finished over the course of a year and a half. She's also one of the sweetest, smartest women I know, and I look forward to a long and productive friendship with her. The rest of my team at Addison-Wesley was also phenomenally helpful, patient, and always encouraging: San Dee Phillips, Songlin Qiu, Mandie Frank, Marie McKinley, and Heather Fox.

Of course, my family bore the brunt of my preoccupation with working on the book, especially during the last six months (once the deadline pressure started getting really intense). Taylor, Liam, and Desi: I love you so much. Thank you for giving me the time and tranquility to write. I'll never be able to thank my longtime partner (and favorite Rails developer) Desi McAdam enough for taking over practically all of my domestic duties during this time. I also have to thank my dad Marco, for insightfully suggesting that I propose a whole Ruby series instead of just this book.

Writing a book of this scope and magnitude is by no means a solo effort—I owe a tremendous debt of gratitude to my extended team of contributors and reviewers. David Black helped kickstart my early progress by contributing material about routing and controllers. Fellow series authors James Adam, Trotter Cashion, and Matt Pelletier also chipped in, with contributions about plugins, `ActiveRecord`, and production deployment, respectively. Matt Bauer helped me finish the Ajax and XML chapters, and Jodi Showers wrote the Capistrano chapter. Pat Maddox rescued me during a particularly bad case of writer's block and helped me finish the RSpec chapter, for which David Chelimsky later provided an expert review. Charles Brian Quinn and Pratik Naik provided timely advice and contributions on background processing. Diego Scataglini also helped with review of some of the later chapters.

Francis Hwang and Sebastian Delmont provided accurate technical review, starting early in the life of the book. They were later joined by Wilson Bilkovich and Courtenay Gasking, who, in addition to contributing original writing and sidebar content, did a lot of work helping me to meet final deadlines. Wilson in particular kept me laughing the whole time with his witty comedic timing, and even rewrote the background processing chapter to incorporate his expert knowledge of the subject. Other valued reviewers include Sam Aaron, Nola Stowe, and Susan Potter. In the last few weeks, my newest friend and programming pair Jon "Lark" Larkowski has picked out a number of remaining errors that other reviewers somehow overlooked.

The infamous Zed Shaw was my roommate during a significant amount of time I spent working on the book and was a constant source of inspiration and motivation. Also a huuu-uge thank you to my friends on the #caboose IRC channel for consistently providing expert insights and opinions. Some I've already mentioned—others are (in no particular order): Josh Susser (hasmanyjosh), Rick Olson (technoweenie), Ezra Zygmuntovich (ezmobius), Geoffrey Grosenbach (topfunky), Robby Russel (robbyonrails), Jeremy Hubert, Dave Fayram (kirindave), Matt Lyon (mattly), Joshua Sierles (corp), Dan Peterson (danp), Dave Astels (dastels), Trevor Squires (protocool), David Goodlad (dgoodlad), Amy Hoy (eriberri), Josh Goebel (Dreamer3), Evan Phoenix (evan), Ryan Davis (zenspider), Michael Schubert, Cristi Balan (evilchelu), Jamie van Dyke (fearoffish), Nic Williams (drnick), Eric Hodel (drbrain), James Cox (imajes), Kevin Clark (kevinclark), Thomas Fuchs (madrobby), Manfred Stienstra (manfred-s), Pastie Paste Bot (pastie), Evan Henshaw-Plath (rabble), Rob Orsini (rorsini), Adam Keys (therealadam), John Athayde (boborishi), Robert Bousquet, Bryan Helkamp (brynary), and Chad Fowler. I should also mention that David Heinemeier Hansson (nextangler) himself was always encouraging, and even answered a few sticky questions I had along the way.

Plenty of former colleagues from ThoughtWorks indirectly helped this book happen. First and foremost, Martin Fowler is not only a role model and inspiration—he also helped me secure the relationship with Addison-Wesley, and offered much personal advice and support in the early days of the project, when I really had no idea what I was getting myself into. ThoughtWorks CEO Roy Singham recognized the potential of Rails in early 2005, once I introduced him to David Hansson, and was subsequently steadfast in his support of my Ruby evangelism (including doing quite a bit of it himself around the world). That was especially important in the early times, when many other respected people at ThoughtWorks thought Rails was nothing but hype and wouldn't last.

There are so many others at ThoughtWorks that I must acknowledge and thank. First of all, I'm proud to have mentored Jay Fields in Ruby, and point to him as living proof that students can exceed their teachers. Carlos Villela is part of the reason I got interested in Ruby again after my initial dislike of it. My buddy Upendra Kanda and I spent long solitary months working on the first paid Rails client projects at ThoughtWorks. Hacker extraordinaire Michael Granger taught me much about the creative possibilities with Ruby. Fred George is a mentor and inspiration. Steve Wilkins and Fern Schiff were some of the initial supporters of Rails on the business development side. Other enthusiastic Rails supporters at ThoughtWorks who helped me in some way or another include Badri Janakiraman, Rohan Kini, Kartik C, Paul Hammant, Robin Gibson, Nick Drew, Srihari Srinivasan, Julian Boot, Jon Tirsen, Chris Stevenson, Alex Verkhovsky, Patrick Farley, Neal Ford, Ron Campbell, Julias Shaw, David Rice, Jeff Patton (finish your book!), Kent Spillner, John Hume, Jake Scruggs, and Stephen Chu.

My paid work with Rails has involved some pretty progressive thinkers and risk-takers on the client side, good people who trusted me and my teams to deliver solutions with unproven technology. I can't possibly name everyone who fits into this category, but some stand out: I have to thank Hank Roark, Tom Horsley, Howard Todd, Jeff Elam, and Carol Rinauro for their unwavering support and trust at Deere. I must thank Robert Brown at Barclays for being forward-thinking, a friend, and source of encouragement. Dirk and Brett Elmendorf at Rackspace were terrific to work with.

InfoQ.com has also been very cooperative and understanding of my time constraints while finishing the book. A very special thank you to Floyd Marinescu and Diana Plesa for being so patient, as well as my team of Ruby writers, including Werner Schuster and Sebastien Auvray.

As of the beginning of January 2007, my friend Mark Smith has given me the distinct pleasure of working with a group of brilliant people on interesting Web 2.0 projects, based in sunny Atlantic Beach, Florida. The First Street Live team has been incredibly supportive 100% of the time: Marian Phelan, Ryan Poland, Nick Strate, Joe Hunt, Clay Kromberg, Dena Freeman, and everyone else… (Mark, I love you man, and we're gonna be friends forever. Thanks for the fun work environment, the book party, and constant intellectual stimulation. I really don't believe I would have been able to finish this book so successfully if I hadn't come down here to work for you.)

Last, but not least, I owe a heartfelt thanks to PragDave Thomas, who was quoted as saying: *"Obie writing a book about Rails would be like the Marquis de Sade writing a book about table manners."*

About the Author

Obie Fernandez is a recognized tech industry leader and independent consultant. He has been hacking computers since he got his first Commodore VIC-20 in the eighties, and found himself in the right place and time as a programmer on some of the first Java enterprise projects of the mid-nineties. He moved to Atlanta, Georgia, in 1998 and gained prominence as lead architect of local startup success MediaOcean. He also founded the Extreme Programming (later Agile Atlanta) User Group and was that group's president and organizer for several years. In 2004, he made the move back into the enterprise, tackling high-risk, progressive projects for world-renowned consultancy ThoughtWorks.

He has been evangelizing Ruby and Rails online via blog posts and publications since early 2005, and earned himself quite a bit of notoriety (and trash talking) from his old friends in the Java open-source community. Since then, he has presented on a regular basis at numerous industry events and user group meetings, and even does the occasional training gig for corporations and groups wanting to get into Rails development.

Nowadays, Obie specializes in the development and marketing of large-scale, web-based applications. He still posts almost daily on various topics to his popular technology weblog, http://obiefernandez.com.

Introduction

In late 2004, I was consulting at one of the big American auto makers, alongside a good friend of mine, Aslak Hellesoy.[1] It was a challenging assignment, chock full of difficult political situations, technical frustration, and crushing deadlines. Not your ordinary deadlines either; they were the type of deadline where the client would get fined a million dollars a day if we were late. The pressure was on!

In a moment of questionable judgment, the team agreed to base our continuous integration system on a pet project of Aslak's named DamageControl. It was a Ruby-based version of the venerable CruiseControl server produced by our employer, ThoughtWorks.

The problem was that DamageControl wasn't quite what you'd call a finished product. And like many other Ruby-related things, it just didn't work very well on Windows. Yet for some reason I can't quite remember today, we had to deploy it on an old Windows 2000 server that also hosted the StarTeam source repository (yikes!).

Aslak needed help—over the course of several weeks we pair-programmed extensively on both the application code of DamageControl and C-based internals of the Win32 process libraries for Ruby. At the time I had eight years of serious enterprise Java programming experience under my belt and a deep love of the brilliant IntelliJ IDE. I really cannot convey how much I hated Ruby at that point in my career.

So what changed? Well, for starters I eventually made it out of that stressful assignment alive, and took on a relatively easy assignment overseas out of the London office of ThoughtWorks. Within a month or so, Ruby caught my attention again, this time via considerable blogsphere excitement about an up-and-coming web framework named Ruby on Rails. I decided to give Ruby another chance. Perhaps it wasn't so bad after all? I quickly built an innovative social networking system for internal use at ThoughtWorks.

That first Rails experience, over the course of a few weeks in February 2005, was life-altering. All of the best practices I had learned over the years about building web apps had been distilled into a single framework, written in some of the most elegant and concise code that I had ever seen in my life. My interest in Java died a sudden death (although it took me almost another year to stop using IntelliJ). I began avidly blogging about Ruby and Rails and evangelizing it heavily both inside and out of ThoughtWorks. The rest, as they say, is history.

As I write this in 2007, the Rails business I pioneered at ThoughtWorks accounts for almost half of their global revenue, and they've established a large product division churning out Ruby-based commercial software. Among them is CruiseControl.rb, which I suspect is what Aslak wanted to build all along—it has the honor of being the official continuous integration server of the Ruby on Rails core team.

Ruby and Rails

Why do experienced enterprise folks like me fall in love with Ruby and Rails? Given a set of requirements to fulfill, the complexity of solutions created using Java and Microsoft technology is simply unacceptable. Excess complexity overwhelms individual understanding of the project and dramatically increases communications overhead for the team. The emphasis on following design patterns, as well as the obsession with performance, wears down the pure joy of application development with those platforms.

> There's no peer pressure to do anything in the Rails community. DHH (David Heinemeier Hansson) picked a language that made him happy. Rails was born from code that he felt was beautiful. That kind of set the tone for the Rails community. So much about Rails is subjective. People either "get it" or they don't. But there's no malice from those who do towards those who don't, just gentle encouragement.
> —Pat Maddox

Ruby is beautiful. Coding in Ruby is beautiful. Everyone I've known who makes the move into Ruby says they are happier than before. For this reason more than any other, Ruby and Rails are shaking up the status quo, especially in enterprise computing. Prior to getting involved with Rails, I was accustomed to working on projects based on fuzzy requirements bearing no relation to real-world needs. I was tired of mind-boggling arrays of competing frameworks to choose from and integrate, and I was tired of ugly code.

In contrast, Ruby is a beautiful, dynamic, high-level language. Ruby code is easier to read and write because it more closely maps to the problem domains we tackle, in a style that is closer to human language. The enhanced readability yields many benefits, both short-term and long-term, as code moves into production and must be understood by maintenance programmers.

My experience has shown me that programs written in Ruby have fewer lines of code than comparable programs in Java and C#. Smaller codebases are easier to maintain and long-term maintenance is widely cited as the biggest cost of successful software projects. Smaller codebases are also faster to debug when things go wrong, even without fancy debugging tools.

The Rise of Rails and Mainstream Acceptance

In ways similar to the Agile movement that helped birth it, Rails is all about catering to our needs as application developers—not as software engineers, and certainly not as computer scientists. By aggressively attacking unneeded complexity, Rails shines brightest in the people-oriented aspects of development that really matter to the ultimate success of our projects. We have fun when we're programming in Rails, and that makes us want to succeed!

The tools and technical infrastructure provided by Rails are comprehensive, encouraging us to focus on delivering business value. Ruby's Principle of Least Surprise is embodied in the simple and elegant design of the Rails. Best of all, Rails is completely free open-source software, which means that when all else fails, browsing the source code can yield answers to even the most difficult of problems.

David has occasionally mentioned that he is not particularly excited about Rails reaching mainstream acceptance, because the competitive edge enjoyed by early adopters would be diminished. Those early adopters have primarily been individuals and small groups of web designers and programmers, with legions of them coming out of the PHP world.

Enterprise Adoption

Call me an idealist if you like, but I believe that even enterprise developers at large and conservative corporations will act to become more effective and innovative at their jobs if they are given the tools and encouragement to do so. That's why it seems like they're jumping on the Rails bandwagon in ever-greater numbers with every year that passes.

Perhaps enterprise developers will ultimately be the most vocal and enthusiastic adopters of Ruby and Rails, because right now they are the ones who as a group stand to lose the most from the status quo. They're consistently the targets of mass layoffs and misguided outsourcing efforts, based on assumptions such as "specification is more important than implementation" and "implementation should be mechanical and trivial."

Is specification actually more important than the implementation? Not for most projects. Is implementation of all but the simplest projects trivial? Of course not! There are significant underlying reasons for the difficulties of software development, especially in enterprise environments:[2]

- Hard-to-understand legacy systems.

- Highly complex business domains such as investment banking.

- Stakeholders and business analysts who don't actually know what they want.

- Managers resistant to productivity because it shrinks their yearly budgets.

- End users who actively sabotage your project.

- Politics! Sticking your head out means worrying that it'll get chopped off.

As a consultant to Fortune 1000 companies, I lived and breathed those situations on an everyday basis for almost 10 years, eventually stumbling upon a powerful concept. There is a viable alternative to playing it safe, an alternative so powerful that it transcends politics and is guaranteed to bring you acclaim and open new doors of opportunity.

That alternative is being exceptional! It starts with productivity. I'm talking about becoming so obviously effective at your job that nobody will ever be able to scapegoat you, to the extent that it would be political suicide to try. I'm talking about cultivating practices that make your results stand out so brilliantly that they bring tears of joy to even the most cynical and hardened stakeholders of your projects. I mean regularly having time to polish your applications to a state of wonderfulness that consistently breeds passionate end users.

By simply being exceptional, you can be that individual (or team) that keeps clients happy and paying their invoices on time, or that survives layoffs year after year, because the decision-makers say: "Oh, there's no way we can afford to lose them."

Let me pause for a second. I wouldn't blame you for regarding my words with skepticism, but none of what I'm saying is idle hype. I'm describing my own life since moving to Ruby on Rails. This book is intended to help you make Ruby on Rails your secret (or not-so-secret) weapon for thriving in the treacherous world of software development.

Delivering Results

My contributors and I draw on our collective experience and industry knowledge to show you how to deliver practical results using Ruby on Rails on your projects, giving you the ammunition needed to justify your choice of technology and even defeat objections that will undoubtedly come your way. Since we know there are never any silver bullets, we'll also warn you about situations where choosing Rails would be a mistake.

Along the way, we'll analyze each of the components of Rails in depth and discuss how to extend them when the need arises. Ruby is an extremely flexible language, which means there are myriad ways to customize the behavior of Rails yourself. As you will learn, the Ruby way is all about giving you the freedom to find the optimal solution to the problem at hand.

As a reference work, this book functions as a guide to the Rails API and the wealth of Ruby idioms, design approaches, libraries, and plugins useful to the Ruby on Rails enterprise developer.

About Opinionated Software

Before going on, I should mention that part of what makes Rails exceptional is that it is opinionated software, written by opinionated programmers. Likewise, this is an opinionated book, written by opinionated writers.

Here are some of the opinions about development that influence this book. You don't have to agree with all of them—just be aware of their influence:

- Developer motivation and productivity trump all other factors for project success.

- The best way to keep motivated and productive is to focus on delivering business value.

- Performance means "executing as fast as possible, on a given set of resources."

- Scalability means "executing as fast as needed, on as many resources as needed."

- Performance is irrelevant if you can't scale.

- If you can scale cheaply, milking every ounce of performance from your processors should never be your first priority.

- Linking scalability to choice of development tools is a pervasive mistake in the industry and most software does not have extreme scalability requirements.

- Performance *is* related to choice of language and tools because higher-level languages are easier to write and understand. There is wide consensus that the performance problems in most applications are caused by poorly written application code.

- Convention over configuration is a better way to write software. Huge XML configuration files must be eliminated!

- Code portability, the ability to take code and run it on a different hardware platform, is not particularly important.

- It's better to solve a problem *well* even if the solution only runs on one platform. Portability is irrelevant if your project fails.

- Database portability, the ability to run the same code on different relational database systems is rarely important and is almost never achieved.

- Presentation is very important, even for small projects. If your application looks bad, everyone will assume it is written badly.

- Allowing technology to dictate the approach to solving a business problem is usually a bad idea; however, that advice shouldn't be used as an excuse to stick with inferior technology.

- The benefits of generalized application components are dubious. Individual projects usually have very particular business needs and wildly different infrastructure requirements, making parameterized reuse very difficult to achieve in practice.

Phew, that's a lot of opinions. But don't worry, *The Rails Way* is primarily a reference work, and this list is the only one of its kind in the book. Speaking of which….

About This Book

This book is not a tutorial or basic introduction to Ruby or Rails. It is meant as a day-to-day reference for the full-time Rails developer. At times we delve deep into the Rails codebase to illustrate why Rails behaves the way that it does, and present snippets of actual Rails code. The more confident reader might be able to get started in Rails using just this book, extensive online resources, and his wits, but there are other publications that are more introductory in nature and might be a wee bit more appropriate for beginners.

I am a fulltime Rails application developer and so is every contributor to this book. We do not spend our days writing books or training other people, although that is certainly something that we enjoy doing on the side.

I started writing this book mostly for myself, because I hate having to use online documentation, especially API docs, which need to be consulted over and over again. Since the API documentation is liberally licensed (just like the rest of Rails), there are a few sections of the book that reproduce parts of the API documentation. In practically all cases, the API documentation has been expanded and/or corrected, supplemented with additional examples and commentary drawn from practical experience.

Hopefully you are like me—I really like books that I can keep next to my keyboard, scribble notes in, and fill with bookmarks and dog-ears. When I'm coding, I want to be able to quickly refer to both API documentation, in-depth explanations, and relevant examples.

Book Structure

I attempted to give the material a natural structure while meeting the goal of being the best-possible Rails reference book. To that end, careful attention has been given to presenting holistic explanations of each subsystem of Rails, including detailed API information where appropriate. Every chapter is slightly different in scope, and I suspect that Rails is now too big a topic to cover the whole thing in depth in just one book.

Believe me, it has not been easy coming up with a structure that makes perfect sense for everyone. Particularly, I have noted surprise in some readers when they notice that `ActiveRecord` is not covered first. Rails is foremost a web framework and at least to me, the controller and routing implementation is the most unique, powerful, and effective feature, with `ActiveRecord` following a close second.

Therefore, the flow of the book is as follows:

- The Rails environment, initialization, configuration, and logging
- The Rails dispatcher, controllers, rendering, and routing
- REST, Resources, and Rails
- `ActiveRecord` basics, associations, validation, and advanced techniques
- `ActionView` templating, caching, and helpers
- Ajax, Prototype, and Scriptaculous JavaScript libraries, and RJS
- Session management, login, and authentication
- XML and `ActiveResource`
- Background processing and `ActionMailer`
- Testing and specs (including coverage of RSpec on Rails and Selenium)
- Installing, managing, and writing your own plugins
- Rails production deployment, configurations, and Capistrano

Sample Code and Listings

The domains chosen for the code samples should be familiar to almost all professional developers. They include time and expense tracking, regional data management, and blogging applications. I don't spend pages explaining the subtler nuances of the business logic for the samples or justify design decisions that don't have a direct relationship to the topic at hand. Following in the footsteps of my series colleague Hal Fulton and *The Ruby Way*, most of the snippets are not full code listings—only the relevant code is shown. Ellipses (...) denote parts of the code that have been eliminated for clarity.

Whenever a code listing is large and significant, and I suspect that you might want to use it verbatim in your own code, I supply a listing heading. There are not too many of those. The whole set of code listings will not add up to a complete working system, nor are there 30 pages of sample application code in an appendix. The code listings should serve as inspiration for your production-ready work, but keep in mind that it often lacks touches necessary in real-world work. For example, examples of controller code are often missing pagination and access control logic, because it would detract from the point being expressed.

Plugins

Whenever you find yourself writing code that feels like *plumbing*, by which I mean completely unrelated to the business domain of your application, you're probably doing too much work. I hope that you have this book at your side when you encounter that feeling. There is almost always some new part of the Rails API or a third-party plugin for doing exactly what you are trying to do.

As a matter of fact, part of what sets this book apart is that I never hesitate in calling out the availability of third-party plugins, and I even document the ones that I feel are most crucial for effective Rails work. In cases where a plugin is better than the built-in Rails functionality, we don't cover the built-in Rails functionality (pagination is an example).

An average developer might see his productivity double with Rails, but I've seen serious Rails developers achieve gains that are much, much higher. That's because we follow the Don't Repeat Yourself (DRY) principle religiously, of which Don't Reinvent The Wheel (DRTW) is a close corollary. Reimplementing something when an existing implementation is *good enough* is an unnecessary waste of time that nevertheless can be very tempting, since it's such a joy to program in Ruby.

Ruby on Rails is actually a vast ecosystem of core code, official plugins, and third-party plugins. That ecosystem has been exploding rapidly and provides all the raw technology you need to build even the most complicated enterprise-class web applications. My goal is to equip you with enough knowledge that you'll be able to avoid continuously reinventing the wheel.

Recommended Reading and Resources

Readers may find it useful to read this book while referring to some of the excellent reference titles listed in this section.

Most Ruby programmers always have their copy of the "Pickaxe" book nearby, *Programming Ruby* (ISBN: 0-9745140-5-5), because it is a good language reference. Readers interested in really understanding all of the nuances of Ruby programming should acquire *The Ruby Way, Second Edition* (ISBN: 0-6723288-4-4).

I highly recommend *Peepcode Screencasts*, in-depth video presentations on a variety of Rails subjects by the inimitable Geoffrey Grosenbach, available at http://peepcode.com.

Regarding David Heinemeier Hansson a.k.a. DHH

I had the pleasure of establishing a friendship with David Heinemeier Hansson, creator of Rails, in early 2005, before Rails hit the mainstream and he became an *International Web 2.0 Superstar*. My friendship with David is a big factor in why I'm writing this book today. David's opinions and public statements shape the Rails world, which means he gets quoted a lot when we discuss the nature of Rails and how to use it effectively.

David has told me on a couple of occasions that he hates the "DHH" moniker that people tend to use instead of his long and difficult-to-spell full name. For that reason, in this book I try to always refer to him as "David" instead of the ever-tempting "DHH." When you encounter references to "David" without further qualification, I'm referring to the one-and-only David Heinemeier Hansson.

Rails is by and large still a small community, and in some cases I reference core team members and Rails celebrities by name. A perfect example is the prodigious core-team member, Rick Olson, whose many useful plugins had me mentioning him over and over again throughout the text.

Goals

As stated, I hope to make this your primary working reference for Ruby on Rails. I don't really expect too many people to read it through end to end unless they're expanding their basic knowledge of the Rails framework. Whatever the case may be, over time I hope this book gives you as an application developer/programmer greater confidence in making design and implementation decisions while working on your day-to-day tasks. After spending time with this book, your understanding of the fundamental concepts of Rails coupled with hands-on experience should leave you feeling comfortable working on real-world Rails projects, with real-world demands.

If you are in an architectural or development lead role, this book is not targeted to you, but should make you feel more comfortable discussing the pros and cons of Ruby on Rails adoption and ways to extend Rails to meet the particular needs of the project under your direction.

Finally, if you are a development manager, you should find the practical perspective of the book and our coverage of testing and tools especially interesting, and hopefully get some insight into why your developers are so excited about Ruby and Rails.

Prerequisites

The reader is assumed to have the following knowledge:

- Basic Ruby syntax and language constructs such as blocks
- Solid grasp of object-oriented principles and design patterns
- Basic understanding of relational databases and SQL
- Familiarity with how Rails applications are laid out and function
- Basic understanding of network protocols such as HTTP and SMTP
- Basic understanding of XML documents and web services
- Familiarity with transactional concepts such as ACID properties

As noted in the section "Book Structure," this book does not progress from easy material in the front to harder material in the back. Some chapters do start out with fundamental, almost introductory material, and push on to more advanced coverage. There are definitely sections of the text that experienced Rails developer will gloss over. However, I believe that there is new knowledge and inspiration in every chapter, for all skill levels.

Required Technology

A late-model Apple *MacBookPro* with 4GB RAM, running OSX 10.4. Just kidding, of course. Linux is pretty good for Rails development also. Microsoft Windows—well, let me just put it this way—your mileage may vary. I'm being nice and diplomatic in saying that. We specifically *do not* discuss Rails development on Microsoft platforms in this book.[3] To my knowledge, most working Rails professionals develop and deploy on non-Microsoft platforms.

References

1. Aslak is a well-known guy in Java open-source circles, primarily for writing XDoclet.

2. I'm not saying startups are much easier, but they usually have less dramatic problems.

3. For that information, try the Softies on Rails blog at http://softiesonrails.com.

CHAPTER 1

Rails Environments and Configuration

[Rails] gained a lot of its focus and appeal because I didn't try to please people who didn't share my problems. Differentiating between production and development was a very real problem for me, so I solved it the best way I knew how.
—David Heinemeier Hansson

Rails applications are preconfigured with three standard modes of operation: *development*, *test*, and *production*. These modes are basically execution environments and have a collection of associated settings that determine things such as which database to connect to, and whether or not the classes of your application are reloaded with each request. It is also simple to create your own custom environments if necessary.

The current environment is always specified in the environment variable RAILS_ENV, which names the desired mode of operation and corresponds to an environment definition file in the config/environment folder. Since the environment settings govern some of the most fundamental aspects of Rails, such as classloading, in order to really understand the Rails way you should really understand its environment settings.

In this chapter, we get familiar with how Rails starts up and handles requests, by examining scripts such as boot.rb and environments.rb and the settings that make up the three standard environment settings (modes). We also cover some of the basics of defining your own environments, and why you might choose to do so.

Startup

Whenever you start a process to handle requests with Rails (such as a Webrick server), one of the first things that happens is that `config/environment.rb` is loaded. For instance, take a look at the top of `public/dispatch.rb`:

```
require File.dirname(__FILE__) + "/../config/environment"
```

Other processes that need the *whole* Rails environment, such as the console and your tests, also require `config/environment.rb`, hence you'll notice the `require` statement at the top files such as `test/test_helper.rb`.

Default Environment Settings

Let's go step by step through the settings provided in the default `environment.rb` file that you get when bootstrapping a Rails 1.2 application.

Mode Override

The first setting is only applicable to people deploying on shared hosting environments. It is commented out, since it should be unusual to need to set the Rails mode here:

```
# Uncomment below to force Rails into production mode when
# you don't control web/app server and can't set it the proper way
# ENV['RAILS_ENV'] ||= 'production'
```

A word of caution: If you were to set the `RAILS_ENV` environment variable to `production` here, or the constant variable `RAILS_ENV` for that matter, it would cause *everything* you did in Rails to run in production mode. For instance, your test suite would not work correctly, since `test_helper.rb` sets `RAILS_ENV` to test right before loading the environment.

Rails Gem Version

Remember that at this point, the Rails framework hasn't been loaded—in fact, the script has to find the framework and load it before anything else happens. This setting tells the script which version of Rails to load:

```
# Specifies gem version of Rails to use when vendor/rails is not
present
RAILS_GEM_VERSION = '1.2.3'
```

As you can see, at the time that I'm writing this chapter the latest released version of Rails (that I have installed as a gem, anyway) is 1.2.3. This setting is meaningless if you're running *edge*, which is the community-accepted term meaning that you're running a frozen snapshot of Rails out of the vendor/rails directory of your project. You can invoke the `rake rails:freeze:edge` command in your project to copy the latest repository version of Rails into vendor/rails.

Bootstrapping

The next lines of environment.rb are where the wheels really start turning, once config/boot.rb is loaded:

```
# Bootstrap the Rails environment, frameworks, and default
configuration
require File.join(File.dirname(__FILE__), 'boot')
```

Note that the boot script is generated as part of your Rails application, but it is not meant to be edited. I'll briefly describe what it does, since it may help you troubleshoot a broken Rails installation.

First of all, the boot script ensures that the RAILS_ROOT environment variable is set: It holds the path to the root of the current Rails project. RAILS_ROOT is used all over the place in the Rails codebase for finding files, such as view templates. If it isn't set already, the folder one level up is specified (remember that we're currently in the config folder).

On non-Windows platforms, the useful standard Ruby library pathname is used to clean up the path string by removing consecutive slashes and useless dots:

```
unless RUBY_PLATFORM =~ /mswin32/
  require 'pathname'
  root_path = Pathname.new(root_path).cleanpath(true).to_s
end
```

Now the boot script has to figure out which version of Rails to use. The first thing it does is to check for the existence of vendor/rails in your project, which would mean that you're running edge:

```
File.directory?("#{RAILS_ROOT}/vendor/rails")
```

That is essentially the easiest case. Unless you're not running edge, and I'd guess that most Rails developers do not, then the boot script has to do a little bit more work to find Rails as a *RubyGem*.

Edge Rails

There's an expression, "If you're not on the edge, you're taking up too much room." Well, for many Rails developers, being on the edge means using the latest (and hopefully, greatest) version of Ruby on Rails that's available.

The core team of developers that maintain the Rails codebase check their files into a publicly available Subversion repository. Since the early days, running your application on nonreleased Rails code in order to take advantage of new features and bug fixes became known as *running edge rails*. All you had to do was to check out the Rails codebase into the vendor/rails directory of your application:

```
svn co http://dev.rubyonrails.org/svn/rails/trunk
vendor/rails
```

In October of 2005, tasks were added to the standard Rails rakefile to automate the process of *freezing* and *unfreezing* your application on a particular version of edge rails. Those Rake tasks are rails:freeze:edge and rails:unfreeze.

Unless you're familiar with the phenomenon already, you might be wondering why anyone in their right mind would want to develop their application using what is essentially an unstable dependency. The motivation for most of us is to stay as current as possible with new features, and luckily, it's usually not a crazy decision at all.

Historically the trunk version of Rails remains quite stable. During 2005, as Rails made the march toward a 1.0

release, I developed a project on edge for a large enterprise client. Despite the perceived risks, there were certain critical new features and bug fixes in edge that we could not live without. Over the course of several months, updating our version of Rails up to a couple of times a week, there was only one occasion on which an unexpected error cropped up and was traced back to a problem in the Rails codebase.

The stability of edge is primarily due to Rails' extensive test coverage, which effectively prevents major regressions from creeping into the codebase. Ever since I can remember, all patches submitted to the core team must include adequate unit and functional test coverage to even be considered. Agile practices are not simply a guideline in the Rails world; they are orthodoxy.

Particularly after the release of Rails 1.2, it hasn't really made *that* much sense to go through the trouble of developing on edge, and the core team members actively discourage mainstream Rails developers from doing so. The officially released versions are generally good enough for the vast majority of developers. However, edge Rails still comes in handy sometimes. For example, it allowed us to extensively cover Rails 2.0 features in this book prior to the actual, official 2.0 release.

RubyGems

First, the boot script requires `rubygems`. You probably know about RubyGems already, since you had to install it in order to install Rails, by invoking `gem install rails` from the command line.

For reasons outside of the scope of this discussion, sometimes Rails is loaded with *just the boot script*. So the next thing the boot script does is read the `config/environment.rb` file as text (minus the commented lines) and parse out the `RAILS_GEM_VERSION` setting with a `regexp`.

Once the boot script determines which version of Rails to load, it requires the Rails gem. At this point, if the Rails version specified in your particular `environment.rb` file is out of synch with the versions available on your workstation, you'll have a problem, indicated by an error message similar to the following one when you try to start a Rails server or console:

```
Cannot find gem for Rails =1.1.5:
   Install the missing gem with 'gem install -v=1.1.5 rails', or

   change environment.rb to define RAILS_GEM_VERSION with your
   desired version.
```

Initializer

The boot script then requires the Rails script `initializer.rb`, which is responsible for configuration and will be used next by the environment script.

Finally, the boot script tells the initializer to set up default load paths (in other words, it constructs the classpath). The load path is assembled from the list of component frameworks that make up Rails and the folders of your Rails application that contain code. Remember that load paths in Ruby just specify where the `require` method should look for code when invoked. Until this point, the load path was only the current working directory.

Default Load Paths

The Rails code that specifies the load paths is pretty readable and well-commented, so I'll copy it instead of explaining it. See Listing 1.1.

Listing 1.1 Some of the Methods in `railties/lib/initializer.rb`

```
def default_frameworks
  [ :active_record, :action_controller, :action_view,
    :action_mailer, :action_web_service ]
end

def default_load_paths
  paths = ["#{root_path}/test/mocks/#{environment}"]
```

```ruby
  # Add the app's controller directory
  paths.concat(Dir["#{root_path}/app/controllers/"])

  # Then components subdirectories.
  paths.concat(Dir["#{root_path}/components/[_a-z]*"])

  # Followed by the standard includes.
  paths.concat %w(
    app
    app/models
    app/controllers
    app/helpers
    app/services
    app/apis
    components
    config
    lib
    vendor
  ).map { |dir| "#{root_path}/#{dir}" }.select { |dir|
  File.directory?(dir) }

  paths.concat Dir["#{root_path}/vendor/plugins/*/lib/"]
  paths.concat builtin_directories
end

def builtin_directories
  # Include builtins only in the development environment.
  (environment == 'development') ?
   Dir["#{RAILTIES_PATH}/builtin/*/"] :  []
end
```

Rails, Modules, and Auto-Loading Code

Normally in Ruby, when you want to include code from another file in your application, you have to include a require statement. However, Rails enhances Ruby's default behavior by establishing a simple convention that enables Rails to automatically load your code in most cases.

If you've used the Rails console at all, you've already seen this behavior in action: You never have to explicitly load anything!

This is how it works: If Rails encounters a class or module in your code that is not already defined, Rails uses the following convention to guess which files it should require to load that module or class:

- If the class or module is not nested, insert an underscore between the constant's names and require a file of this name. For example:

  - EstimationCalculator becomes require 'estimation_calculator'

  - KittTurboBoost becomes require 'kitt_turbo_boost'

- If the class or module is nested, Rails inserts an underscore between each of the containing modules and requires a file in the corresponding set of subdirectories. For example:

  - MacGyver::SwissArmyKnife becomes require 'mac_gyver/swiss_army_knife'

- `Some::ReallyRatherDeeply::NestedClass` becomes require `'some/really_rather_deeply/nested_class'` and if not already loaded, Rails would expect to find it in a file called `nested_class.rb`, in a directory called `really_rather_deeply`, itself in the directory `some` of which can be found somewhere in Ruby's load path (e.g., one of the `app` subdirectories, `lib`, or a plugin's `lib` directory).

The bottom line is that you should rarely need to explicitly load Ruby code in your Rails applications (using `require`) if you follow the naming conventions.

Builtin Rails Info

You might be wondering what that `builtin_directories` method in Listing 1.1 is all about in the `default_load_paths` method. It is the place for Rails to include application behavior (meaning models, helpers, and controllers). You can think about it as kind of like a framework-provided plugin mechanism.

The only builtin that exists at this time is in `railties/builtin/rails_info` and it isn't particularly well-known, other than as the target of the "About your application's environment" link on the default "Welcome Aboard" `index.html` page that can be seen in a newly created Rails application.

To check it out, fire up any Rails application in development mode and go to http://localhost:3000/rails/info/properties via your browser. You'll see a diagnostic screen with a dump of significant version numbers and settings that looks something like this:

```
Ruby version                  1.8.5 (i686-darwin8.8.1)
RubyGems version              0.9.0
Rails version                 1.2.0
Active Record version         1.14.4
Action Pack version           1.12.5
Action Web Service version    1.1.6
Action Mailer version         1.2.5
Active Support version        1.3.1
Edge Rails revision           33
Application root              /Users/obie/prorails/time_and_expenses
Environment                   development
Database adapter              mysql
Database schema version       8
```

Configuration

Back to the environment script, where we're about to get into developer-defined settings. The next couple of lines read as follows:

```
Rails::Initializer.run do |config|
  # Settings in config/environments/* take precedence over
  # those specified here
```

The comment reminds you that the settings in the mode-specific environment files will take precedence over settings in environment.rb, which is essentially because they are loaded afterward and will overwrite your settings.

Skipping Frameworks

The first setting gives you the option of *not* loading parts of the Rails that you might not be using. (Ruby is, of course, interpreted, and if you can get away with a smaller-sized codebase for the interpreter to parse, you should do so, simply for performance reasons.) Quite a few Rails applications do not use email or Web services, which is why they are given as examples:

```
# Skip frameworks you're not going to use (only works if
# using vendor/rails)
config.frameworks -= [ :action_web_service, :action_mailer ]
```

Additional Load Paths

In the rare case of needing to add to the default load paths, the option is given to do so next:

```
# Add additional load paths for your own custom dirs
config.load_paths += %W( #{RAILS_ROOT}/extras )
```

In case you didn't know, the `%W` functions as a whitespace-delimited array literal and is used quite often in the Rails codebase for convenience. (I do admit it was a little off-putting for me at first as a long-time Java programmer.)

I'm tempted to say that the additional load paths option is not really needed, since you'll want to extend Rails by writing plugins, which have their own convention for load paths. Chapter 19, "Extending Rails with Plugins," covers the subject, and a companion book to this one in the Addison-Wesley Professional Ruby Series, *Rails Plugins: Extending Rails Beyond the Core* (ISBN: 0-321-48351-0) by James Adam, is an exhaustive reference about authoring plugins.

Notice how the last two settings were not settings in the traditional sense of plain assignment of an option value to a property. Rails takes full advantage of Ruby in letting you remove and add from an array in its configuration object.

Log-Level Override

The default log level is `:debug` and you can override it if necessary.

```
# Force all environments to use the same logger level
# (by default production uses :info, the others :debug)
config.log_level = :debug
```

This book covers use of the Rails logger in-depth later on in this chapter.

ActiveRecord Session Store

If you want to store user sessions in the database (and you definitely do in almost all production scenarios), this is where to set that option:

```
# Use the database for sessions instead of the file system
# (create the session table with 'rake db:sessions:create')
config.action_controller.session_store = :active_record_store
```

This book covers configuration and implications of `ActiveRecord` session store in Chapter 13, "Session Management."

Schema Dumper

Every time you run tests, Rails dumps the schema of your development database and copies it to the test database using an autogenerated `schema.rb` script. It looks very similar to an `ActiveRecord` migration script; in fact, it uses the same API.

You might find it necessary to revert to the older style of dumping the schema using SQL, if you're doing things that are incompatible with the schema dumper code (see the comment).

```
# Use SQL instead of Active Record's schema dumper when creating the
# test database. This is necessary if your schema can't be completely
# dumped by the schema dumper, for example, if you have constraints
# or db-specific column types
config.active_record.schema_format = :sql
```

Observers

`ActiveRecord` observers are first-class objects in your Rails applications that perform specific tasks such as clearing caches and managing denormalized data. The examples in the default `environment.rb` are just that, examples of classes that you might theoretically be writing in your application as observers. (There aren't actually `cacher` or `garbage_collector` observers provided by Rails, but don't take that to mean that Ruby doesn't do garbage collection!)

```
# Activate observers that should always be running
# config.active_record.observers = :cacher, :garbage_collector
```

This book covers `ActiveRecord` observers in-depth in Chapter 9, "Advanced `ActiveRecord`."

Time Zones

The default time zone for Rails is local time (using `Time.local`), that is, the same time zone as your server. You can change the time zone that Rails picks up as your local time zone by modifying the `TZ` environment variable.

The list of time zones is typically in your /usr/share/zoneinfo folder. If you're on a Mac, check the contents of /usr/share/zoneinfo/zone.tab for a list of valid zone names. Keep in mind that this solution, and particularly what values to use, is operating system-specific and said operating system might have already set it to the appropriate value on your behalf.

You can set the value of TZ code anywhere, but if you want to change it for your entire web application, you might as well put it in environment.rb, near the other time zone settings.

```
ENV['TZ'] = 'US/Eastern'
```

What if you want to support user-specific time zones? The first step is to tell ActiveRecord to record time in the database as UTC (using Time.utc).

```
# Make Active Record use UTC-base instead of local time
config.active_record.default_timezone = :utc
```

Then you'll need a way to convert back and forth to a time zone specified in association with your user. Unfortunately, the standard Rails TimeZone class doesn't handle Daylight Saving Time (DST), which frankly makes it quite useless.

There is a pure-Ruby gem called TZInfo[1] with a TimeZone class that does correctly handle DST and can be dropped in as a replacement to the one in Rails. To use it in your application you will need to install both the tzinfo gem and the tzinfo_timezone plugin. However, that solution is pure Ruby and reportedly quite slow (although it might be fast enough for your needs).

Wait a minute—doesn't Ruby's Time class already understand how to deal with DST correctly?

```
>> Time.now
=> Mon Nov 27 16:32:51 -0500 2006
>> Time.now.getgm
=> Mon Nov 27 21:32:56 UTC 2006
```

The output in the console listing is in fact correct. So writing our own conversion routine shouldn't be too hard, should it?

In a post to the rails-mailing-list in August 2006[2], Grzegorz Daniluk gives us an example of how to do just that (and benchmarks it at seven to nine times faster than

TZInfo). You would add the following code to one of your application's helper modules or put it in its own class within the lib folder:

```
# to convert posted date/time to UTC and save to DB
def user2utc(t)
  ENV["TZ"] = current_user.time_zone_name
  res = Time.local(t.year, t.month, t.day, t.hour, t.min, t.sec).utc
ENV["TZ"] = "UTC"
  res
end

# to display date/time in a view
def utc2user(t)
  ENV["TZ"] = current_user.time_zone_name
  res = t.getlocal
  ENV["TZ"] = "UTC"
  res
end
```

In a detailed response to the mailing list, the author of TZInfo, Philip Ross, informs us that the preceding solution does not work for Windows users.[3] He also comments about the handling of invalid times: "Another area TZInfo improves upon using the TZ environment variable is in its handling of invalid and ambiguous local times (i.e., during the transitions to and from daylight savings). Time.local always returns a time regardless of whether it was invalid or ambiguous. TZInfo reports invalid times and allows the ambiguity to be resolved by specifying whether to use the DST or non-DST time or running a block to do the selection."

To summarize, don't use Windows. No, just kidding. The real lesson from this issue is that handling time zones correctly is not an easy affair and should be considered very carefully.

Additional Configuration

That does it for the configuration options for which we get examples in the default environment.rb. There are additional options, which I suspect that you will rarely need to use or know about. If you want to see the whole list, look at the source code and docs for the Configuration class starting around line 400 of the file railties/lib/initializer.rb.

Remember we said that the value of the RAILS_ENV environment variable dictates which additional environment settings are loaded next? So now let's review the default settings for each of Rails' standard modes.

Development Mode

Development is Rails' default mode and the one in which you will spend most of your time as a developer:

```
# Settings specified here will take precedence over those in
# config/environment.rb

# In the development environment your application's code is reloaded on

# every request.  This slows down response time but is perfect for
# development since you don't have to restart the webserver when you
# make code changes.
config.cache_classes = false

# Log error messages when you accidentally call methods on nil.
config.whiny_nils = true

# Enable the breakpoint server that script/breakpointer connects to
config.breakpoint_server = true

# Show full error reports and disable caching
config.action_controller.consider_all_requests_local = true
config.action_controller.perform_caching            = false
config.action_view.cache_template_extensions        = false
config.action_view.debug_rjs                        = true

# Don't care if the mailer can't send
config.action_mailer.raise_delivery_errors = false
```

In the following sections I cover the important settings in depth, starting with the caching of classes: the setting that makes Rails' dynamic class reloading possible.

Automatic Class Reloading

One of the signature benefits of using Rails is the quick feedback cycle whenever you're working in development mode. Make changes to your code, hit Reload in the browser, and *Shazam!* Magically, the changes are reflected in your application. This behavior is governed by the `config.cache_classes` setting, which you see is set to `false` at the top of `config/environments/development.rb`.

Without getting into too much nitty-gritty detail, when the `config.cache_classes` setting is `true`, Rails will use Ruby's `require` statement to do its class loading, and when it is `false`, it will use `load` instead.

When you require a Ruby file, the interpreter executes and caches it. If the file is required again (as in subsequent requests), the interpreter ignores the request statement and moves on. When you load a Ruby file, the interpreter executes the file again, no matter how many times it has been loaded before.

Now it's time to examine the Rails class-loading behavior a bit more in depth, because sometimes you won't be able to get certain things to reload automatically and it will drive you crazy *unless* you understand how class loading works!

The Rails Class Loader

In plain old Ruby, a script file doesn't need to be named in any particular way that matches its contents. In Rails, however, you'll notice that there's almost always a direct correlation between the name of a Ruby file and the class contained within. Rails takes advantage of the fact that Ruby provides a callback mechanism for missing constants. When Rails encounters an undefined constant in the code, it uses a classloader routine based on file-naming conventions to find and require the needed Ruby script.

How does the classloader know where to search? We already covered it earlier in the chapter where we discussed the role of `initializer.rb` in the Rails startup process. Rails has the concept of load paths, and the default load paths include the base directories of just about anywhere you would think of adding code to your Rails application.

The `default_load_paths` method shows you the order in which Rails searches the directories in its load path. We'll dissect the source of this method here and explain the reason behind each part of the load path.

The test/mocks directory (covered more extensively in Chapter 17, "Testing,") is provided to give you the ability to override the behavior of standard Rails classes.

```
paths = ["#{root_path}/test/mocks/#{environment}"]

# Add the app's controller directory
paths.concat(Dir["#{root_path}/app/controllers/"])

# Then components subdirectories.
paths.concat(Dir["#{root_path}/components/[_a-z]*"])

# Followed by the standard includes.
paths.concat %w(
  app
  app/models
  app/controllers
  app/helpers
  app/services
  app/apis
  components
  config
  lib
  vendor
).map { |dir| "#{root_path}/#{dir}" }.select { |dir|
  File.directory?(dir) }

  paths.concat Dir["#{root_path}/vendor/plugins/*/lib/"]
  paths.concat builtin_directories
end
```

Want to see the contents of your project's load path? Just fire up the console and type $: as follows:

```
$ console
Loading development environment.
>> $:
=> ["/usr/local/lib/ruby/gems/1.8/gems/ ... # about 20 lines of output
```

I snipped the console output to save space. A typical Rails project load path will usually have 30 or more items in its load path. Try it and see.

Test Mode

Whenever you run Rails in test mode, that is, the value of the RAILS_ENV environment value is test, then the following settings are in effect:

```
# Settings specified here will take precedence over those in
# config/environment.rb

# The test environment is used exclusively to run your application's
# test suite.  You never need to work with it otherwise.  Remember that
# your test database is "scratch space" for the test suite and is wiped
# and recreated between test runs.  Don't rely on the data there!
config.cache_classes = true

# Log error messages when you accidentally call methods on nil.
config.whiny_nils = true

# Show full error reports and disable caching
config.action_controller.consider_all_requests_local = true
config.action_controller.perform_caching            = false

# Tell ActionMailer not to deliver emails to the real world.
# The :test delivery method accumulates sent emails in the
# ActionMailer::Base.deliveries array.
config.action_mailer.delivery_method = :test
```

Most people get by without ever needing to modify their test environment settings.

Production Mode

Finally, production mode is what you want your Rails application running in whenever it is deployed to its hosting environment and serving public requests. There are a number of significant ways that production mode differs from the other modes, not least of which is the speed boost you get from not reloading all of your application classes for every request.

```
# Settings specified here will take precedence over those
# in config/environment.rb
```

```
# The production environment is meant for finished, "live" apps.
# Code is not reloaded between requests
config.cache_classes = true

# Use a different logger for distributed setups
# config.logger = SyslogLogger.new
# Full error reports are disabled and caching is turned on
config.action_controller.consider_all_requests_local = false
config.action_controller.perform_caching            = true

# Enable serving of images, stylesheets, and javascripts
# from an asset server
# config.action_controller.asset_host = "http://assets.example.com"

# Disable delivery errors, bad email addresses will be ignored
# config.action_mailer.raise_delivery_errors = false
```

Custom Environments

If necessary, you can create additional environments for your Rails app to run by cloning one of the existing environment files in the config/environments directory of your application. The most common use case for custom environments is in setting up additional production configurations, such as for staging and QA deployments.

Do you have access to the production database from your development workstation? Then a *triage* environment might make sense. Use the normal environment settings for development mode, but point its database connection to a production database server. It's a potentially life-saving combination when you need to quickly diagnose issues in production.

Logging

Most programming contexts in Rails (models, controllers, view templates) have a logger attribute, which holds a reference to a logger conforming to the interface of Log4r or the default Ruby 1.8+ Logger class. Can't get a reference to logger somewhere in your code? The RAILS_DEFAULT_LOGGER global variable has a reference to the logger that you can use anywhere. It even has its own TextMate shortcut (**rdb** →).

It's really easy to create a new `Logger` in Ruby, as shown in the following example:

```
$ irb
> require 'logger'
=> true

irb(main):002:0> logger = Logger.new STDOUT
=> #<Logger:0x32db4c @level=0, @progname=nil, @logdev=
#<Logger::LogDevice:0x32d9bc ... >

> logger.warn "do not want!!!"
W, [2007-06-06T17:25:35.666927 #7303]  WARN -- : do not want!!!
=> true

> logger.info "in your logger, giving info"
I, [2007-06-06T17:25:50.787598 #7303]  INFO -- : in your logger, giving
your info
=> true
```

Typically, you add a message to the log using the logger whenever the need arises, using a method corresponding to the severity of the log message. The standard logger's severities are (in increasingly severe order):

- **debug** Use the debug level to capture data and application state useful for
  debugging problems later on. This level is not usually captured in production
  logs.

- **info** Use info level to capture informational messages. I like to use this log level
  for time-stamping non-ordinary events that are still within the bounds of good
  application behavior.

- **warn** Use the warn level to capture things that are out of the ordinary and might
  be worth investigating. Sometimes I'll throw in a logged warning when guard
  clauses in my code keep a client from doing something they weren't supposed to
  do. My goal is to alert whoever's maintaining the application about a malicious
  user or bug in the user interface, as in the following example:

```
def create
  begin
    @group.add_member(current_user)
    flash[:notice] = "Successfully joined #{@scene.display_name}"
```

```
    rescue ActiveRecord::RecordInvalid
      flash[:error] = "You are already a member of #{@group.name}"
      logger.warn "A user tried to join a group twice. UI should
                       not have allowed it."
    end

    redirect_to :back
  end
```

- **error**   Use the error log level to capture information about error conditions that don't require a server restart.

- **fatal**   The worst-case imaginable has happened—your application is now dead and manual intervention is necessary to restart it.

Rails Log Files

The log folder of your Rails application holds three log files corresponding to each of the standard environments, plus a log and pid file for Mongrel. Log files can grow very large over time. A rake task is provided for easily clearing the log files:

```
rake log:clear  # Truncates all *.log files in log/ to zero bytes
```

The contents of log/development.log are very useful while you're working. Many Rails coders leave a terminal window open with a continuous tail of the development log open while they're coding:

```
$ tail -f log/development.log

  User Load (0.000522)   SELECT * FROM users WHERE (users.`id` = 1)
  CACHE (0.000000)   SELECT * FROM users WHERE (users.`id` = 1)
```

All sorts of valuable information are available in the development log. For instance, every time you make a request, a bunch of useful information about it shows up in the log. Here's a sample from one of my projects, followed by a list of all the data items it contains:

```
Processing UserPhotosController#show (for 127.0.0.1 at 2007-06-06
17:43:13) [GET]
  Session ID: b362cf038810bb8dec076fcdaec3c009
```

```
Parameters: {"/users/8-Obie-Fernandez/photos/406"=>nil,
"action"=>"show", "id"=>"406", "controller"=>"user_photos",
"user_id"=>"8-Obie-Fernandez"}
User Load (0.000477)   SELECT * FROM users WHERE (users.`id` = 8)
Photo Columns (0.003182)   SHOW FIELDS FROM photos
Photo Load (0.000949)   SELECT * FROM photos WHERE (photos.`id` = 406
AND (photos.resource_id = 8 AND photos.resource_type = 'User'))
Rendering template within layouts/application
Rendering photos/show
CACHE (0.000000)   SELECT * FROM users WHERE (users.`id` = 8)
Rendered adsense/_medium_rectangle (0.00155)
User Load (0.000541)   SELECT * FROM users WHERE (users.`id` = 8)
LIMIT 1
Message Columns (0.002225)   SHOW FIELDS FROM messages
SQL (0.000439)   SELECT count(*) AS count_all FROM messages WHERE
(messages.receiver_id = 8 AND (messages.`read` = 0))
Rendered layouts/_header (0.02535)
Rendered adsense/_leaderboard (0.00043)
Rendered layouts/_footer (0.00085)
Completed in 0.09895 (10 reqs/sec) | Rendering: 0.03740 (37%) | DB:
0.01233 (12%) | 200 OK [http://localhost/users/8-Obie-
Fernandez/photos/406]
User Columns (0.004578)   SHOW FIELDS FROM users
```

- The controller and action that were invoked
- The remote IP address of the computer making the request
- A timestamp indicating when the request happened
- The session ID associated with the request
- The hash of parameters associated with the request
- Database request information including the time and the SQL statement executed
- Query cache hit info including time and the SQL statement triggering results from the cache instead of a roundtrip to the database
- Rendering information for each template involved in rendering the view output and time consumed by each

- Total time used in completing the request with corresponding request-per-second figures

- Analysis of the time spent in database operations versus rendering

- The HTTP status code and URL of the response sent back to the client

Log File Analysis

A number of informal analyses can be easily performed using just the development log output and some common sense.

- **Performance** One of the more obvious analyses would be a study of the performance of your application. The faster your requests execute, the more requests you can serve with a given Rails process. That's why performance figures are often expressed in terms of *requests per second*. Find the queries and rendering sections that are taking a long time and figure out why.

  It's important to realize that the times reported by the logger are *not superaccurate*. In fact, they're wrong more often than not, if simply for the reason that it's very difficult to measure the timing of something from within itself. Add up the percentage of rendering and database times for any given request and it will not always be close to 100%.

  However, despite not being accurate in a purely objective sense, the reported times are perfect for making subjective comparisons within the same application. They give you a way of gauging whether an action is taking longer than it used to, or whether it is relatively faster or slower than another action, and so on.

- **SQL queries** `ActiveRecord` not behaving as expected? The fact that SQL generated by `ActiveRecord` is logged can often help you debug problems caused by complicated queries.

- **Identification of N+1 select problems** Whenever you are displaying a record along with an associated collection of records, there's a chance that you will have a so-called *N+1 select* problem. You'll recognize the problem by a series of many SELECT statements, with the only difference being the value of the primary key.

For example, here's a snippet of some log output from a real Rails application showing an N+1 select issue in the way that `FlickrPhoto` instances are being loaded:

```
FlickrPhoto Load (0.001395)   SELECT * FROM flickr_photos WHERE
(flickr_photos.resource_id = 15749 AND flickr_photos.resource_type =
'Place' AND (flickr_photos.`profile` = 1)) ORDER BY updated_at desc
LIMIT 1
FlickrPhoto Load (0.001734)   SELECT * FROM flickr_photos WHERE
(flickr_photos.resource_id = 15785 AND flickr_photos.resource_type =
'Place' AND (flickr_photos.`profile` = 1)) ORDER BY updated_at desc
LIMIT 1
FlickrPhoto Load (0.001440)   SELECT * FROM flickr_photos WHERE
(flickr_photos.resource_id = 15831 AND flickr_photos.resource_type =
'Place' AND (flickr_photos.`profile` = 1)) ORDER BY updated_at desc
LIMIT 1
```

… and so on and so forth, for pages and pages of log output. Look familiar?

Luckily, each of those database queries is executing very quickly, around 0.0015 seconds each. That's because 1) MySQL is extraordinarily fast for small `SELECT` statements and 2) my Rails process is on the same physical machine as the database.

Still, accumulate enough of those N queries and they add up quickly to eat away at performance. Absent the mitigating factors I mentioned, I would have a serious performance problem to address. The problem would be especially severe if the database was on a separate machine, giving me network latency to deal with on each of those queries.

N+1 select issues are not the end of the world. A lot of times all it takes is proper use of an `:include` option on a particular `find` method call to alleviate the problem.

- **Separation of concerns** A well-designed model-view-controller application follows certain protocols related to which logical tier does database operations (that would be the model) versus rendering tasks (the view). Generally speaking, you want your controller to cause the loading of all of the data that is going to be needed for rendering from the database. In Rails, it is accomplished by controller code that queries the model for needed data and stores that data in instance variables to be consumed by the view.

Database access during rendering is usually considered a bad practice. Calling
find methods directly from template code violates proper separation of concerns and
is a maintainability nightmare.[4]

However, there are plenty of opportunities for implicit database access during
view rendering to creep into your codebase, encapsulated by the model, and perhaps
triggered by lazy loading of associations. Can we conclusively call it a bad practice? It's
hard to say so definitively. There are cases (such as usage of fragment caching) where
it makes sense to have database operations happening during view rendering.

> ### Using Alternate Logging Schemes
>
> It's easy! Just assign a class compatible with Ruby's Logger
> to one of the various `logger` class variables, such as
> `ActiveRecord::Base.logger`.
>
> A quick hack based on the ability to swap loggers is one
> demonstrated by David at various events, including his
> keynote at Railsconf 2007. During a console session,
> assign a new `Logger` instance pointing to `STDOUT` to
> `ActiveRecord::Base.logger` in order to see the SQL
> being generated right in your console. Jamis has a com-
> plete write-up of the technique and more at http://
> weblog.jamisbuck.org/2007/1/31/more-on-watching-
> activerecord.

Syslog

UNIX-like systems have a system service called `syslog`. For various reasons, it might
be a better choice for production logging of your Rails applications.

- Finer-grained control over logging levels and content.

- Consolidation of logger output for multiple Rails applications.

- If you're using remote syslog capabilities of many systems, consolidation of logger
  output for multiple Rails application servers is possible. Contrast with having to
  handle individual log files on each application server box separately.

You can use Eric Hodel's SyslogLogger[5] to interface your Rails application to `sys-`
`log`. Setup will involve downloading the library, requiring it in your `environ-`
`ment.rb` file, and replacing the `RAILS_DEFAULT_LOGGER` instance.

Conclusion

We've kicked off our Rails journey by reviewing the different environments in which Rails executes and how it loads its dependencies, including your application code. An in-depth look at `environment.rb` and its per-mode variants revealed how we can customize Rails behavior to our taste. In discussing the version of Rails libraries used for a particular project, we also had an opportunity to discuss running edge and whether it might make sense for your project.

We also learned about the Rails startup process by actually taking a peek at some of its source code. (Throughout the rest of the book, we'll dive into Rails source code wherever it makes sense to do so.)

In Chapter 2, "Working with Controllers," we continue our journey by delving into the Rails dispatcher and the `ActionController` framework.

References

1.   http://tzinfo.rubyforge.org/

2.   www.ruby-forum.com/topic/79431

3.   http://article.gmane.org/gmane.comp.lang.ruby.rails/75790

4.   Practically every PHP application ever written has this problem.

5.   http://seattlerb.rubyforge.org/SyslogLogger/

CHAPTER 2

Working with Controllers

Remove all Business Logic from your Controllers and put it in the model. Your Controllers are only responsible for mapping between URLs (including other HTTP Request data), coordinating with your Models and your Views, and channeling that back to an HTTP response. Along the way, Controllers may do Access Control, but little more. These instructions are precise, but following them requires intuition and subtle reasoning.
—Nick Kallen, Pivotal Labs
http://www.pivotalblabs.com/articles/2007/07/16/the-controller-formula

Like any computer program, your Rails application involves the flow of control from one part of your code to another. The flow of program control gets pretty complex with Rails applications. There are many bits and pieces in the framework, many of which execute each other. And part of the framework's job is to figure out, on the fly, what your application files are called and what's in them, which of course varies from one application to another.

The heart of it all, though, is pretty easy to identify: It's the *controller*. When someone connects to your application, what they're basically doing is asking the application to execute a *controller action*. Yes, there are different flavors of how this can happen, and edge cases where it doesn't exactly happen at all… but if you know how controllers fit into the application life cycle, you can anchor everything else around that knowledge. That's why we're covering controllers first, before the rest of the Rails APIs.

Controllers are the "C" in "MVC." They're the first port of call, after the dispatcher, for the incoming request. They're in charge of the flow of the program: They pull information out of the database (generally through the use of the `ActiveRecord` interface), and they make that information available to the views.

Controllers are also very closely linked to views—more closely than they're linked to models. It's possible to write the entire model layer of an application before you create a single controller, or to have different people working on the controller and model layers who never meet or talk to each other. Views and controllers, however, are more tightly coupled. They share a lot of information, mainly through instance variables. That means that the names you choose for your variables in the controller will have an effect on what you do in the view.

In this chapter, we're going to look at what happens on the way to a controller action being executed, and what happens as a result. In the middle, we'll take a long look at how controller classes themselves are set up, particularly in regard to the many different ways that we can render views. We'll wrap up the chapter with a couple of additional topics related to controllers: filters and streaming.

The Dispatcher: Where It All Begins

Rails is used to build web-based applications, so before anything else happens, and for anything that does happen, a web server—Apache, Lighttpd, Nginx, and so on—handles a *request*. The server then forwards that request to the Rails application, where it is handled by the *dispatcher*.

Request Handling

As the request is handled, the server passes off some information to the dispatcher, principally

- The request URI (http://localhost:3000/timesheets/show/3, or whatever)
- The CGI environment (bindings of CGI parameter names to values)

  The dispatcher's job is to

- Figure out which controller is involved in the request
- Figure out which action should be executed

- Load the appropriate controller file, which will contain a Ruby class definition for a controller class (`TimesheetsController`, for example)

- Create an instance of the controller class

- Tell that instance to execute the appropriate action

All of this happens quickly, behind the scenes. It's unlikely that you would ever need to dig into the source code for the dispatcher; it's the sort of thing that you can take for granted to just work. However, to really understand the Rails way, it is important to know what's going on with the dispatcher. In particular, it's important to remember that the various parts of your application are just bits (sometimes long bits) of Ruby code, and that they're getting loaded into a running Ruby interpreter.

Getting Intimate with the Dispatcher

For instructional purposes let's trigger the Rails dispatching mechanism manually. It will give you a good feel for the flow of program control in Rails.

We'll do this little exercise from the ground up, starting with a new Rails application:

```
$ rails dispatch_me
```

Now, create a single controller, with an `index` action:

```
$ cd dispatch_me/
$ ruby ./script/generate controller demo index
```

If you look at the controller you just generated, in `app/controllers/demo_controller.rb`, you'll see that it has an `index` action:

```
class DemoController < ApplicationController
  def index
  end
end
```

There's also a view template file, `app/views/demo/index.rhtml`, corresponding to the action, and also created automatically, courtesy of the `generate` script.

That template file contains some placeholder language. Just to see things more clearly, let's replace it with something we'll definitely recognize when we see it again. Delete the lines in index.rhtml and enter the following:

```
Hello!
```

Not much of a design accomplishment, but it will do the trick. Now that we've got a set of dominos lined up, it's just a matter of pushing over the first one: the dispatcher. To do that, start by firing up the Rails console from your Rails application directory. Type **ruby script/console** from a command prompt:

```
$ ruby script/console
Loading development environment.
>>
```

We're now inside the beating heart of a Rails application and it's waiting to receive instructions.

There are a pair of environment variables that would normally be set by the web server passing the request to the Rails dispatcher. Since we're going to be invoking the dispatcher manually, we have to set those environment variables manually:

```
>> ENV['REQUEST_URI'] = "/demo/index"
=> "/demo/index"
>> ENV['REQUEST_METHOD'] = "get"
=> "get"
```

We're now ready to fool the dispatcher into thinking it's getting a request. Actually, it *is* getting a request. It's just that it's coming from someone sitting at the console, rather than from a web server.

Here's the command:

```
>> Dispatcher.dispatch
```

And here's the response from the Rails application:

```
Content-Type: text/html; charset=utf-8
Set-Cookie: _dispatch_me_session_id=336c1302296ab4fa1b0d838d; path=/
Status: 200 OK
Cache-Control: no-cache
```

```
Content-Length: 7

Hello!
```

We've executed the `dispatch` class method of the Ruby class `Dispatcher`, and as a result, the `index` action got executed and the index template (such as it is) got rendered and the results of the rendering got wrapped in some HTTP headers and returned.

Just think: If you were a web server, rather than a human, and you had just done the same thing, you could now return that document, headers and "Hello!" and all, to a client. And that's exactly what happens. Have a look in the `public` subdirectory of `dispatch_me` (or any other Rails application). Among other things, you'll see these dispatcher files:

```
$ ls dispatch.*
dispatch.cgi  dispatch.fcgi  dispatch.rb
```

Every time a Rails request comes in, the web server hands control to one of those files. *Which* file depends on the exact server configuration. Ultimately, they all do the same thing: They call `Dispatcher.dispatch`, just as you did from the console.

You can follow the trail of bread crumbs even further, if you look at `public/.htaccess` and your server configuration. But for purposes of understanding the chain of events in a Rails request, and the role of the controller, the peek under the hood we've just done is sufficient.

Render unto View...

The goal of the typical controller action is to render a view template—that is, to fill out the template and hand the results, usually an HTML document, back to the server for delivery to the client.

Oddly—at least it might strike you as a bit odd, though not illogical—you don't actually need to define a controller action, *as long as you've got a template that matches the action name.*

You can try this out in under-the-hood mode. Go into `app/controller/demo_controller.rb`, and delete the `index` action so that the file will look empty, like this:

```
class DemoController < ApplicationController
end
```

Don't delete `app/views/demo/index.rhtml`, and then try the console exercise (`Dispatcher.dispatch` and all that) again. You'll see the same result.

By the way, make sure you reload the console when you make changes—it doesn't react to changes in source code automatically. The easiest way to reload the console is simply to type `reload!`. But be aware that any existing instances of `ActiveRecord` objects that you're holding on to will also need to be reloaded (using their individual `reload` methods). Sometimes it's simpler to just exit the console and start it up again.

When in Doubt, Render

Rails knows that when it gets a request for the `index` action of the demo controller, what *really* matters is handing something back to the server. So if there's no `index` action in the controller file, Rails shrugs and says, "Well, let's just assume that if there *were* an `index` action, it would be empty anyway, and I'd just render `index.rhtml`. So that's what I'll do."

You can learn something from an empty controller action, though. Let's go back to this version of the demo controller:

```
class DemoController < ApplicationController
  def index
  end
end
```

What you learn from seeing the empty action is that, at the end of every controller action, *if nothing else is specified*, the default behavior is to render the template whose name matches the name of the controller and action. In this case, that means `app/views/demo/index.rhtml`.

In other words, every controller action has an implicit `render` command in it. And `render` is actually a real method. You could write the preceding example like this:

```
def index
  render :template => "demo/index"
end
```

You don't have to, though, because it's assumed that that's what you want, and that is part of what Rails people are talking about when they discuss *convention over configuration*. Don't force the developer to add code that could simply be assumed by convention.

The `render` command, however, does more than just provide a way of telling Rails to do what it was going to do anyway.

Explicit Rendering

Rendering a template is like putting on a shirt: If you don't like the first one you find in your closet—the default, so to speak—you can reach for another one and put it on instead.

If a controller action doesn't want to render its default template, it can render a different one by calling the `render` method explicitly. Any template file in the `app/views` directory tree is available. (Actually, that's not exactly true. Any template on the whole system is available!) But why would you want your controller action to render a template other than its default? There are several reasons, and by looking at some of them, we can cover all of the handy features of the controller's `render` method.

Rendering Another Action's Template

A common reason for rendering an entirely different template is to redisplay a form, when it gets submitted with invalid data and needs correction. In such circumstances, the usual web strategy is to redisplay the form with the submitted data, and trigger the simultaneous display of some error information, so that the user can correct the form and resubmit.

The reason that process involves rendering another template is that the action that *processes* the form and the action that *displays* the form may be—and often are—different from each other. Therefore, the action that processes the form needs a way to redisplay the original (form) template, instead of treating the form submission as successful and moving on to whatever the next screen might be.

Wow, that was a mouthful of an explanation. Here's a practical example:

```
class EventController < ActionController::Base

  def new
    # This (empty) action renders the new.rhtml template, which
    # contains the form for inputting information about the new

    # event record and is not actually needed.
  end
```

```
def create
  # This method processes the form input. The input is available via
  # the params hash, in the nested hash hanging off the :event key.
  @event = Event.new(params[:event])
  if @event.save
    flash[:notice] = "Event created!"
    redirect_to :controller => "main"  # ignore this line for now
  else
    render :action => "new" # doesn't execute the new method!
  end
end

end
```

On failure, that is, if `@event.save` does not return `true`, we render the `"new"` template, `new.rhtml`, again. Assuming `new.rhtml` has been written correctly, this will automatically include the display of error information embedded in the new (but unsaved) `Event` object, `@event`.

Note that the template itself, `new.rhtml`, doesn't "know" that it's been rendered by the `create` action rather than the `new` action. It just does its job: It fills out and expands and interpolates, based on the instructions it contains and the data (in this case, `@event`) that the controller has passed to it.

Rendering a Different Template Altogether

In a similar fashion, if you are rendering a template for a different action, it is possible to render any template in the system by calling `render` with either a `:template` or `:file` option pointing to the desired template file.

The `:template` option takes a path relative to the template root (`app/views`, unless you changed it, which would be extremely unusual), whereas `:file` takes an absolute filesystem path.

Admittedly, the `:template` option is rarely used by the majority of Rails developers.

```
render :template => "abuse/report" # renders
app/views/abuse/report.rhtml
render :file => "/railsapps/myweb/app/views/templates/common.rhtml"
```

Rendering a Partial Template

Another option is to render a *partial* template (usually referred to simply as a "partial"). In general, usage of partial templates allows you to organize your template code into small files, which helps you to avoid clutter and encourages you to break your template code up into reusable modules.

Partial rendering from a controller is mostly used in conjunction with AJAX calls that need to dynamically update segments of an already displayed page. The technique, along with generic use of partials in views, is covered in greater detail in Chapter 10, "`ActionView`."

Rendering Inline Template Code

Occasionally, you need to send the browser the result of translating a snippet of template code, too small to merit its own partial. I admit that this practice is contentious, because it is a flagrant violation of proper separation of concerns between the MVC layers.

One common use case for inline rendering, and probably the only reason it was introduced to begin with, is when using one of the Rails AJAX view helpers, such as `auto_complete_result` (covered in Chapter 12, "Ajax on Rails").

```
render :inline => "<%= auto_complete_result(@headings, 'name') %>"
```

Rails treats the inline code exactly as if it were a view template.

> **Courtenay Says...**
>
> If you were one of my employees, I'd reprimand you for using view code in the controller, even if it is only one line.
>
> Try to keep your view-related code in the views!

Rendering Text

What if you simply need to send plain text back to the browser, particularly when responding to AJAX and certain types of web service requests?

```
render :text => 'Submission accepted'
```

Rendering Other Types of Structured Data

The `render` command also accepts a series of (convenience) options for returning structured data such as JSON or XML. The content-type of the response will be set appropriately and additional options apply.

:json

JSON[1] is a small subset of JavaScript selected for its usability as a lightweight data-interchange format. It is mostly used as a way of sending data down to JavaScript code running in a rich web application via AJAX calls. `ActiveRecord` has built-in support for conversion to JSON, which makes Rails an ideal platform for serving up JSON data, as in the following example:

```
render :json => @record.to_json
```

:xml

`ActiveRecord` also has built-in support for conversion to XML, as in the following example:

```
render :xml => @record.to_xml
```

We cover XML-related topics like this one extensively in Chapter 15, "XML and `ActiveResource`."

Rendering Nothing

On rare occasions, you don't want to render anything at all. (To avoid a bug in Safari, rendering nothing actually means sending a single space character back to the browser.)

```
render :nothing => true, :status => 401 # Unauthorized
```

It's worth noting that, as illustrated in this snippet, `render :nothing => true` is often used in conjunction with an HTTP status code (as covered in the next section, "Rendering Options").

Rendering Options

Most calls to the `render` method accept additional options. Here they are in alphabetical order.

`:content_type`

All content flying around the web is associated with a MIME type[2]. For instance, HTML content is labeled with a content-type of `text/html`. However, there are occasions where you want to send the client something other than HTML. Rails doesn't validate the format of the MIME identifier you pass to the `:content_type` option, so make sure it is valid.

`:layout`

By default, Rails has conventions regarding the layout template it chooses to wrap your response in, and those conventions are covered in detail in Chapter 10, "`ActionView`." The `:layout` option allows you to specify whether you want a layout template to be rendered or not.

`:status`

The HTTP protocol includes many standard status codes[3] indicating a variety of conditions in response to a client's request. Rails will automatically use the appropriate status for most common cases, such as `200 OK` for a successful request.

The theory and techniques involved in properly using the full range of HTTP status codes would require a dedicated chapter, perhaps an entire book. For your convenience, Table 2.1 demonstrates a couple of codes that I've occasionally found useful in my day-to-day Rails programming.

Table 2.1 Common HTTP Status Codes

Status Code	Description
307 Temporary Redirect The requested resource resides temporarily under a different URI.	Occasionally, you need to temporarily redirect the user to a different action, perhaps while some long-running process is happening or while the account of a particular resource's owner is suspended.
	This particular status code dictates that an HTTP response header named `Location` contain the URI of the resource that the client redirects to. Since the `render` method doesn't take a hash of response header fields, you have to set them manually prior to invoking `render`. Luckily, the `response` hash is in scope within controller methods, as in the following example:

	<pre>def paid_resource
	  if current_user.account_expired?
	    response.headers['Location'] =
	      account_url(current_user)
	    render :text => "Account expired", :status => 307
	  end
	end</pre>

401 Unauthorized	Sometimes a user will not provide credentials to view a restricted resource or their authentication and/or authorization will fail. Assuming using a Basic or Digest HTTP Authentication scheme, when that happens you should probably return a `401`.
403 Forbidden The server understood the request, but is refusing to fulfill it.	I like to use `403` in conjunction with a short `render :text` message in situations where the client has requested a resource that is not normally available via the web application's interface. In other words, the request appears to have happened via artificial means. A human or robot, for reasons innocent or guilty (it doesn't matter) is trying to trick the server into doing something it isn't supposed to do.
	For example, my current Rails application is public-facing and is visited by the GoogleBot on a daily basis. Probably due to a bug existing at some point, the URL `/favorites` was indexed. Unfortunately, `/favorites` is only supposed to be available to logged-in users. However, once Google knows about a URL it will keep coming back for it in the future. This is how I told it to stop:

	<pre>def index
	  return render :nothing => true,
	                :status => 403 unless logged_in?
	  @favorites = current_user.favorites.find(:all)
	end</pre>

Status Code	Description
404 Not Found The server cannot find the resource you requested.	You may choose to use `404` when a resource of a specific given ID does not exist in your database (whether due to it being an invalid ID or due to the resource having been deleted).
	For example, "GET /people/2349594934896107" doesn't exist in our database at all, so what do we display? Do we render a show view with a flash message saying no person with that ID exists? Not in our RESTful world—a 404 would be better.
	Moreover, if we happen to be using something like `acts_as_paranoid` and we know that the resource *used* to exist in the past, we could respond with `410 Gone`.
503 Service Unavailable The server is temporarily unavailable.	The 503 code comes in very handy when taking a site down for maintenance, particularly when upgrading RESTful web services. One of this book's reviewers, Susan Potter, shares the following suggestion:
	For my projects, I create a stub Rails application that responds with a 503 for each valid type of request that comes in. Clients of my services are usually services themselves or other applications, so this helps client developers that consume my web services know that this is a temporary blip and should be due to scheduled maintenance (and a good reminder for them to check the emails I sent them over the weekend instead of ignoring them).

Redirecting

The life cycle of a Rails application is divided into requests. Every time there's a new request, we're starting again.

Rendering a template, whether the default one or an alternate one—or, for that matter, rendering a partial or some text or anything—is the final step in the handling of a request. *Redirecting*, however, means terminating the current request and initiating a new one.

Look again at the example of the form-handling `create` method:

```
def create
  @event = Event.new(params[:event])
  if @event.save
    flash[:notice] = "Event created!"
```

```
    redirect_to :controller => "main"
  else
    render :action => "new"
  end
end
```

If the save operation succeeds, we store a message in the flash hash and redirect_to a completely new action. In this case, it's the index action (not specified, but that's the default) of the *main* controller.

The logic here is that if the new Event record gets saved, the next order of business is to take the user back to the top-level view. Why not just render the main/index.rhtml template?

```
if @event.save
  flash[:notice] = "Event created!"
  render :controller => "main", :action => "index"
  ...
```

Courtenay Says...

Remember that code after a redirect or render call will still be run, and the application will wait until it's complete before sending that data to the browser.

If you have complex logic, you'll often want to return after a redirect or render nested inside a series of if statements to prevent a DoubleRenderError:

```
def show
  @user = User.find(params[:id])
  if @user.activated?
    render :action => 'activated' and return
  end
  case @user.info
  ...
  end
end
```

The result of this would be that main/index.rhtml template would, indeed, be rendered. But there are some pitfalls. For instance, let's say that the main/index action looks like this:

```
def index
  @events = Event.find(:all)
end
```

If you render the `index.rhtml` from the `event/create` action, the `main/index` action *will not be executed.* So `@events` won't be initialized. That means that `index.rhtml` will blow up, because (presumably) it's planning to make use of `@events`:

```
<h1>Schedule Manager</h1>
<p>Here are your current events:</p>
<% @events.each do |event| %>
  some kind of display HTML would go here
<% end %>
```

That's why you have to redirect to `main/index`, instead of just borrowing its template. The `redirect_to` command clears the decks: It creates a new request, triggers a new action, and starts from scratch in deciding what to render.

Sebastian Says...

Which redirect is the right one?

When you use Rails' `redirect_to` method, you tell the user agent (i.e., the browser) to perform a new request for a different URL. That response can actually mean different things, and it's why modern HTTP has four different status codes for redirection.

The old HTTP 1.0 had two codes: 301, aka "Moved Permanently," and 302, aka "Moved Temporarily." A permanent redirect meant that the user agent should forget about the old URL and use the new one from now on, updating any references it might have kept (i.e., a bookmark, or in the case of Google, its search databases). A temporary redirect was a "one-time only" affair. The original URL was still valid, but for this particular request the user agent should fetch a new resource from the redirection URL.

But there was a problem: If the original request had been a POST, what method should be used for the redirected request? For permanent redirects it was safe to assume the new request should be a GET, since that was the case in all usage scenarios. But temporary redirects were used both for redirecting to a view of a resource that had just been modified in the original POST request (which happens to be the most common usage pattern), and also for redirecting the entire original POST request to a new URL that would take care of it.

HTTP 1.1 solved this problem with the introduction of two new status codes: 303, meaning "See Other," and 307 meaning "Temporary Redirect." A 303 redirect would tell the user agent to perform a GET request, regardless of what the original verb was, whereas a 307 would *always* use the same method used for the original request.

These days, most browsers handle 302 redirects *the same way as 303*, with a GET request, which is the argument used by the Rails Core team to keep using 302 in `redirect_to`. A 303 status would be the better alternative, because it leaves no room for interpretation (or confusion), but I guess nobody has found it annoying enough to push for a patch.

If you ever need a 307 redirect, say, to continue processing a POST request in a different action, you can always accomplish your own custom redirect by assigning a path to `response.header["Location"]` and then rendering with `render :status => 307`.

Controller/View Communication

When a view template is rendered, it generally makes use of data that the controller has pulled from the database. In other words, the controller gets what it needs from the model layer, and hands it off to the view.

The way Rails implements controller-to-view data handoffs is through instance variables. Typically, a controller action initializes one or more instance variables. Those instance variables can then be used by the view.

There's a bit of irony (and possible confusion for newcomers) in the choice of instance variables to share data between controllers and views. The main reason that instance variables exist is so that objects (whether `Controller` objects, `String` objects, and so on) can hold on to data that they *don't* share with other objects. When your controller action is executed, everything is happening in the context of a controller object—an instance of, say, `DemoController` or `EventController`. "Context," here, includes the fact that every instance variable in the code belongs to the controller instance.

When the view template is rendered, the context is that of a different object, an instance of `ActionView::Base`. That instance has its own instance variables, and does not have access to those of the controller object.

So instance variables, on the face of it, are about the worst choice for a way for two objects to share data. However, it's possible to make it happen—or make it appear to happen. What Rails does is to loop through the controller object's variables and, for each one, create an instance variable for the view object, with the same name and containing the same data.

It's kind of labor-intensive, for the framework: It's like copying over a grocery list by hand. But the end result is that things are easier for you, the programmer. If you're a Ruby purist, you might wince a little bit at the thought of instance variables serving to connect objects, rather than separate them. On the other hand, being a Ruby purist should also include understanding the fact that you can do *lots* of different things in Ruby—such as copying instance variables in a loop. So there's nothing really un-Ruby-like about it. And it does provide a seamless connection, from the programmer's perspective, between a controller and the template it's rendering.

Filters

Filters enable controllers to run shared pre- and post-processing code for its actions. These filters can be used to do authentication, caching, or auditing before the intended action is performed. Filter methods are *macro-style*, that is, they appear at the top of your controller method, inside the class context, before method definitions. We also leave off the parentheses around the method arguments, to emphasize their declarative nature, like this:

```
before_filter :require_authentication
```

As with many other *macro-style* methods in Rails, you can pass as many symbols as you want to the filter method:

```
before_filter :security_scan, :audit, :compress
```

Or you can break them out into separate lines, like this:

```
before_filter :security_scan
before_filter :audit
before_filter :compress
```

In contrast to the somewhat similar callback methods of `ActiveRecord`, you can't implement a filter method on a controller by adding a method named `before_filter` or `after_filter`.

You should make your filter methods `protected` or `private`; otherwise, they might be callable as public actions on your controller (via the default route).

Importantly, filters have access to the request, response, and all the instance variables set by other filters in the chain or by the action (in the case of `after` filters). Filters can set instance variables to be used by the requested action, and often do so.

> **Courtenay Says...**
>
> Some of us like to use `before` filters to load the records for single-record operations, where there is some kind of complex logic. Instance variables set in a filter are of course available to any actions.
>
> This is a contentious issue; some developers believe that database actions should stay out of filters and be specified in the `action` method.
>
> ```
> before_filter :load_product, :only => [ :show,
> :edit, :update, :destroy ]
> def load_product
>     @product =
> current_user.products.find_by_permalink(params[:id]
> )
>     redirect_to :action => 'index' and return false
> unless @product.active?
> end
> ```

Filter Inheritance

Controller inheritance hierarchies share filters downward. Your average Rails application has an `ApplicationController` from which all other controllers inherit, so if you wanted to add filters that are always run no matter what, that would be the place to do so.

```
class ApplicationController < ActionController::Base
  after_filter :compress
```

Subclasses can also add and/or skip already defined filters without affecting the superclass. For example, consider the two related classes in Listing 2.1, and how they interact.

Listing 2.1 A Pair of Cooperating before Filters

```
class BankController < ActionController::Base

  before_filter :audit

  private

    def audit
      # record this controller's actions and parameters in an audit log
    end

end

class VaultController < BankController

  before_filter :verify_credentials

  private

    def verify_credentials
      # make sure the user is allowed into the vault
    end

end
```

Any actions performed on BankController (or any of its subclasses) will cause the audit method to be called before the requested action is executed. On the VaultController, first the audit method is called, followed by the verify_credentials method, because that's the order in which the filters were specified.

(Filters are executed in the class context where they're declared, and the `BankController` has to be loaded before `VaultController`, since it's the parent class.)

If the audit method happens to return `false` for whatever reason, `verify_credentials` and the requested action are never called. This is called *halting the filter chain* and when it happens, if you look in your development log, you'll see a message to the effect that such-and-such a filter halted request processing.

Filter Types

A filter can take one of three forms: method reference (symbol), external class, or inline method (proc). The first is by far the most common and works by referencing a protected or private method somewhere in the inheritance hierarchy of the controller. In the bank example in Listing 2.1, both `BankController` and `VaultController` use this form.

Filter Classes

Using an external class makes for more easily reused generic filters, such as output compression. External filter classes are implemented by having a static filter method on any class and then passing this class to the filter method, as in Listing 2.2.

Listing 2.2   An Output Compression Filter

```
class OutputCompressionFilter
  def self.filter(controller)
    controller.response.body = compress(controller.response.body)
  end
end

class NewspaperController < ActionController::Base
  after_filter OutputCompressionFilter
end
```

The `self.filter` method of the `Filter` class is passed the controller instance it is filtering, which gives it access to all aspects of the controller and can manipulate them as it sees fit.

Inline Filter Method

The inline method (using a block parameter to the filter method) can be used to quickly do something small that doesn't require a lot of explanation, or just as a quick test. It works like this:

```
class WeblogController < ActionController::Base
  before_filter {|controller| false if controller.params["stop"]}
end
```

As you can see, the block expects to be passed the controller after it has assigned the request to the internal variables. This means that the block has access to both the request and response objects complete with convenience methods for params, session, template, and assigns. Note that the inline method doesn't strictly have to be a block—any object that responds to `call` such as a `Proc` or an `Method` object will do.

Around filters behave a little differently than normal `before` and `after` filters with regard to filter types. The section dedicated to `around_filters` elaborates on the topic.

Filter Chain Ordering

Using `before_filter` and `after_filter` appends the specified filters to the existing *chain*. That's usually just fine, but sometimes you care more about the order in which the filters are executed. When that's the case, you can use `prepend_before_filter` and `prepend_after_filter`. Filters added by these methods will be put at the beginning of their respective chain and executed before the rest, like the example in Listing 2.3.

Listing 2.3   An Example of Prepending `before` Filters

```
class ShoppingController < ActionController::Base
  before_filter :verify_open_shop

class CheckoutController < ShoppingController
  prepend_before_filter :ensure_items_in_cart, :ensure_items_in_stock
```

The filter chain for the `CheckoutController` is now `:ensure_items_in_cart`, `:ensure_items_in_stock`, `:verify_open_shop`. So if either of the `ensure` filters returns `false`, we'll never get around to seeing if the shop is open or not; the filter chain will be halted.

You may pass multiple filter arguments of each type as well as a filter block. If a block is given, it is treated as the last argument.

Around Filters

`Around` filters wrap an action, executing code both before and after the action that they wrap. They may be declared as method references, blocks, or objects responding to filter or to both `before` and `after`.

To use a method as an `around_filter`, pass a symbol naming the Ruby method. Use `yield` (or `block.call`) within the method to run the action.

For example, Listing 2.4 has an `around` filter that logs exceptions (not that you need to do anything like this in your application; it's just an example).

Listing 2.4 An `around` Filter to Log Exceptions

```
around_filter :catch_exceptions

private

  def catch_exceptions
    yield
  rescue => exception
    logger.debug "Caught exception! #{exception}"
    raise
  end
```

To use a block as an `around_filter`, pass a block taking as args both the controller and the action block. You can't call `yield` directly from an `around_filter` block; explicitly call the action block instead:

```
around_filter do |controller, action|
  logger.debug "before #{controller.action_name}"
  action.call
  logger.debug "after #{controller.action_name}"
end
```

To use a filter object with `around_filter`, pass an object responding to `:filter` or both `:before` and `:after`. With a filter method, yield to the block like this:

```
around_filter BenchmarkingFilter

class BenchmarkingFilter
  def self.filter(controller, &block)
    Benchmark.measure(&block)
  end
end
```

A filter object with `before` and `after` methods is peculiar in that you must explicitly return `true` from the `before` method if you want the `after` method to run.

```
around_filter Authorizer

class Authorizer
  # This will run before the action. Returning false aborts the action
  def before(controller)
    if user.authorized?
      return true
    else
      redirect_to login_url
      return false
    end
  end

  def after(controller)
    # runs after the action only if the before returned true
  end
end
```

Filter Chain Skipping

Declaring a filter on a base class conveniently applies to its subclasses, but sometimes a subclass should skip some of the filters it inherits from a superclass:

```
class ApplicationController < ActionController::Base
  before_filter :authenticate
  around_filter :catch_exceptions
end

class SignupController < ApplicationController
```

```
    skip_before_filter :authenticate
end

class ProjectsController < ApplicationController
  skip_filter :catch_exceptions
end
```

Filter Conditions

Filters may be limited to specific actions by declaring the actions to include or exclude. Both options accept single actions (like :only => :index) or arrays of actions (:except => [:foo, :bar]).

```
class Journal < ActionController::Base
  before_filter :authorize, :only => [:edit, :delete]

  around_filter :except => :index do |controller, action_block|
    results = Profiler.run(&action_block)
    controller.response.sub! "</body>", "#{results}</body>"
  end

  private

    def authorize
      # Redirect to login unless authenticated.
    end

end
```

Filter Chain Halting

The before_filter and around_filter methods may halt the request before the body of a controller action method is run. This is useful, for example, to deny access to unauthenticated users.

As mentioned before, all you have to do to halt the filter chain is to return false from the filter. Calling render or redirect_to will also halt the filter chain.

After filters will not be executed if the filter chain is halted. Around filters halt the request unless the action block is called.

If an `around` filter returns before yielding, it is effectively halting the chain and any `after` filters will not be run.

If a `before` filter returns false, the second half of any `around` filters will still run, but the action method itself will not run, and neither will any `after` filters.

Streaming

It's a little-known fact that Rails has some built-in support for streaming binary content back to the browser, instead of rendering view templates. Streaming comes in handy whenever you need to send dynamically generated files to the browser (e.g., images, PDF files) and Rails supports it with two methods in the `ActionController::Streaming` module: `send_data` and `send_file`.

One of these methods is useful, but the other one should not be used under almost any circumstance. Let's cover the useful one first.

send_data(data, options = {})

The `send_data` method allows you to send textual or binary data to the user as a named file. You can set options that affect the content type and apparent filename, and alter whether an attempt is made to display the data inline with other content in the browser or the user is prompted to download it as an attachment.

Options for send_data

The `send_data` method has the following options:

- `:filename` Suggests a filename for the browser to use.

- `:type` Specifies an HTTP content type. Defaults to `application/octet-stream`.

- `:disposition` Specifies whether the file will be shown inline or downloaded. Valid values are `inline` and `attachment` (default).

- `:status` Specifies the status code to send with the response. Defaults to `200 OK`.

Usage Examples

Creating a download of a dynamically generated tarball might look like this:

```
send_data generate_tgz('dir'), :filename => 'dir.tgz'
```

Listing 2.5 has an example of sending a dynamic image to the browser—it's a partial implementation of a *captcha* system, used to prevent malicious bots from abusing your web application.

Listing 2.5 A Captcha Controller Using RMagick and send_data

```
require 'RMagick'

class CaptchaController < ApplicationController

  def image
    # create an RMagic canvas and render difficult to read text on it
    ...
    image = canvas.flatten_images
    image.format = "JPG"

    # send it to the browser
    send_data(image.to_blob, :disposition => 'inline',
                             :type => 'image/jpg')
  end
end
```

send_file(path, options = {})

The send_file method streams a file 4096 bytes at a time down to the client. The API docs say, "This way the whole file doesn't need to be read into memory at once, which makes it feasible to send even very large files."

Unfortunately, *that isn't true.* When you use send_file in a Rails app that runs on Mongrel, which most people do nowadays, *the whole file is indeed read into memory!* Therefore, using send_file to send big files will give you big headaches. The following section discusses how you can get your web server to serve files directly.

> **Security Alert**
>
> Note that the `send_file` method can be used to read any file accessible to the user running the Rails server process, so be extremely careful to sanitize[4] the `path` parameter if it's in any way coming from an untrusted web page.

Options for `send_file`

In case you do decide to use `send_file` (and don't say I didn't warn you), here are the options that it understands:

- `:filename` suggests a filename for the browser to use. Defaults to `File.basename(path)`.

- `:type` specifies an HTTP content type. Defaults to `'application/octet-stream'`.

- `:disposition` specifies whether the file will be shown inline or downloaded. Valid values are `'inline'` and `'attachment'` (default).

- `:stream` specifies whether to send the file to the user agent as it is read (`true`) or to read the entire file before sending (`false`). Defaults to `true`.

- `:buffer_size` specifies size (in bytes) of the buffer used to stream the file. Defaults to 4096.

- `:status` specifies the status code to send with the response. Defaults to `'200 OK'`.

- `:url_based_filename` should be set to `true` if you want the browser to guess the filename from the URL, which is necessary for i18n filenames on certain browsers (setting `:filename` overrides this option).

Most of these options are processed and set on the response object by the private method `send_file_headers!` of the `ActionController::Streaming` module, so if you're using the web server to send files, you might want to crack open the Rails source code and take a look at it. There's also a lot more to read about the other Content-* HTTP headers[5] if you'd like to provide the user with more information that Rails doesn't natively support (such as `Content-Description`).

Courtenay Says…

There are very few legitimate reasons to serve static files through Rails.

Very, very few.

If you simply must use `send_data` or `send_file`, I strongly recommend you cache the file after sending it. There are a few ways to do this. (Remember that a correctly configured web server will serve files in `public/` and bypass `rails`.)

You can just copy the file to the `public` directory:

```
public_dir = File.join(RAILS_ROOT, 'public',
controller_path)
FileUtils.mkdir_p(public_dir)

FileUtils.cp(filename, File.join(public_dir,
filename))
```

All subsequent views of this resource will be served by the web server.

Alternatively, you can try using the `caches_page` directive, which will automatically do something similar for you. (Caching is covered in Chapter 10.

Finally, be aware that the document may be cached by proxies and browsers. The Pragma and Cache-Control headers declare how the file may be cached by intermediaries. They default to require clients to validate with the server before releasing cached responses.[6]

More Reasons to Hate Internet Explorer

The default Content-Type and Content-Disposition headers are set to support downloads of arbitrary binary files in as many browsers as possible. As if you needed more reasons to hate Internet Explorer, versions 4, 5, 5.5, and 6 of that godforsaken browser are all known to have a variety of download-handling quirks, especially when downloading via HTTPS.

Usage Examples

Here's the simplest example, just a simple zip file download:

```
send_file '/path/to.zip'
```

Sending a JPG to be displayed inline requires specification of the MIME content-type:

```
send_file '/path/to.jpg',
          :type => 'image/jpeg',
          :disposition => 'inline'
```

This will show a 404 HTML page in the browser. We append a charset declaration to the MIME type information:

```
send_file '/path/to/404.html,
          :type => 'text/html; charset=utf-8',
          :status => 404
```

How about streaming an FLV file to a browser-based Flash video player?

```
send_file @video_file.path,
          :filename => video_file.title + '.flv',
          :type => 'video/x-flv',
          :disposition => 'inline'
```

Letting the Web Server Send Files

The solution to the memory-consumption problems inherent to send_file is to leverage functionality provided by Apache, Lighttpd, and Nginx that allows you to serve files directly from the web server, even if they're not in a public document directory. The technique works by setting a special HTTP request header with the path to the file you want the web server to send along to the client.

Here's how you do it in Apache and Lighttpd:

```
response.headers['X-Sendfile'] = path
```

And here's how you do it with Nginx:

```
response.headers['X-Accel-Redirect'] = path
```

In both cases, you want to end your controller action method by telling Rails to not bother sending anything, since the web server will handle it.

```
render :nothing => true
```

Regardless of how you do it, you may wonder *why* you would need a mechanism to send files to the browser anyway, since it already has one built in—requesting files from the `public` directory. Well, lots of times a web application will front files that need to be protected from public access.[7] (That's practically every porn site in existence!)

Conclusion

In this chapter, we covered some concepts at the very core of how Rails works: the dispatcher and how controllers render views. Importantly, we covered the use of controller action filters, which you will use constantly, for all sorts of purposes. The `ActionController` API is fundamental knowledge, which you need to understand well along your way to becoming an expert Rails programmer.

Moving on, we'll continue with another subject that is closely related to the dispatcher and controllers, in fact it's how Rails figures out how to respond to requests: the Routing system.

References

1. For more information on JSON go to http://www.json.org/.

2. MIME is specified in *five* RFC documents, so it is much more convenient to point you to a rather good description of MIME provided by Wikipedia at http://en.wikipedia.org/wiki/MIME.

3. For a full list of HTTP status codes, consult the spec at http://www.w3.org/Protocols/rfc2616/rfc2616-sec10.html.

4. Heiko Webers has the best write-up about sanitizing filenames at http://www.rorsecurity.info/2007/03/27/working-with-files-in-rails/.

5. See the official spec at http://www.w3.org/Protocols/rfc2616/rfc2616-sec14.html.

6. See http://www.mnot.net/cache_docs/ for an overview of web caching.

7. Ben Curtis writes up an excellent approach to securing downloads at http://www.bencurtis.com/archives/2006/11/serving-protected-downloads-with-rails/.

CHAPTER 3
Routing

I dreamed a thousand new paths. . . I woke and walked my old one.
—Chinese proverb

The routing system in Rails is the system that examines the URL of an incoming request and determines what action should be taken by the application. And it does a good bit more than that. Rails routing can be a bit of a tough nut to crack. But it turns out that most of the toughness resides in a small number of concepts. After you've got a handle on those, the rest falls into place nicely.

This chapter will introduce you to the principal techniques for defining and manipulating routes. The next chapter will build on this knowledge to explore the facilities Rails offers in support of writing applications that comply with the principles of Representational State Transfer (REST). As you'll see, those facilities can be of tremendous use to you even if you're not planning to scale the heights of REST theorization.

Many of the examples in these two chapters are based on a small auction application. The examples are kept simple enough that they should be comprehensible on their own. The basic idea is that there are auctions; each auction involves auctioning off an item; there are users; and users submit bids. That's most of it.

The triggering of a controller action is the main event in the life cycle of a connection to a Rails application. So it makes sense that the process by which Rails determines *which* controller and *which* action to execute must be very important. That process is embodied in the routing system.

The routing system maps URLs to actions. It does this by applying rules—rules that you specify, using Ruby commands, in the configuration file `config/routes.rb`. If you don't override the file's default rules, you'll get some reasonable behavior. But it doesn't take much work to write some custom rules and reap the benefits of the flexibility of the routing system.

Moreover, the routing system actually does two things: It maps requests to actions, and it writes URLs for you for use as arguments to methods like `link_to`, `redirect_to`, and `form_tag`. The routing system knows how to turn a visitor's request URL into a controller/action sequence. It also knows how to manufacture URL strings based on your specifications.

When you do this:

```
<%= link_to "Items", :controller => "items", :action => "list" %>
```

the routing system provides the following URL to the `link_to` helper:

```
http://localhost:3000/items/list
```

The routing system is thus a powerful, two-way routing complex. It *recognizes* URLs, routing them appropriately; and it *generates* URLs, using the routing rules as a template or blueprint for the generated string. We'll keep an eye on both of these important purposes of the routing system as we proceed.

The Two Purposes of Routing

Recognizing URLs is useful because it's how your application decides what it's supposed to do when a particular request comes in:

```
http://localhost:3000/myrecipes/apples    What do we do now?!
```

Generating URLs is useful because it allows you to use relatively high-level syntax in your view templates and controllers when you need to insert a URL—so you don't have to do this:

```
<a href="http://localhost:3000/myrecipes/apples">My Apple Recipes</a>
Not much fun having to type this out by hand!
```

The routing system deals with both of these issues: how to interpret (recognize) a request URL and how to write (generate) a URL. It performs both of these functions based on rules that you provide. The rules are inserted into the file `config/routes.rb`, using a special syntax. (Actually it's just Ruby program code, but it uses special methods and parameters.)

Each rule—or, to use the more common term, simply each *route*—includes a pattern string, which will be used both as a template for matching URLs and as a blueprint for writing them. The pattern string contains a mixture of static substrings, forward slashes (it's mimicking URL syntax), and wildcard positional parameters that serve as "receptors" for corresponding values in a URL, for purposes of both recognition and generation.

A route can also include one or more bound parameters, in form of key/value pairs in a hash. The fate of these key/value pairs depends on what the key is. A couple of keys (`:controller` and `:action`) are "magic," and determine what's actually going to happen. Other keys (`:blah`, `:whatever`, etc.) get stashed for future reference.

Putting some flesh on the bones of this description, here's a sample route, related to the preceding examples:

```
map.connect 'myrecipes/:ingredient',
            :controller => "recipes",
            :action => "show"
```

In this example, you can see:

- A static string (`myrecipes`)

- A wildcard URL component (`:ingredient`)

- Bound parameters (`:controller => "recipes"`, `:action => "show"`)

Routes have a pretty rich syntax—this one isn't by any means the most complex (nor the most simple)—because they have to do so much. A single route, like the one in this example, has to provide enough information both to match an existing URL *and* to manufacture a new one. The route syntax is engineered to address both of these processes.

It's actually not hard to grasp, if you take each type of field in turn. We'll do a run-through using the "ingredient" route. Don't worry if it doesn't all sink in the first time through. We'll be unpacking and expanding on the techniques and details throughout the chapter.

As we go through the route anatomy, we'll look at the role of each part in both URL recognition and URL generation. Keep in mind that this is just an introductory example. You can do lots of different things with routes, but examining this example will give you a good start in seeing how it all works.

Bound Parameters

If we're speaking about route recognition, the bound parameters—key/value pairs in the hash of options at the end of the route's argument list—determine what's going to happen if and when this route matches an incoming URL. Let's say someone requests this URL from their web browser:

```
http://localhost:3000/myrecipes/apples
```

This URL will match the ingredient route. The result will be that the show action of the recipes controller will be executed. To see why, look at the route again:

```
map.connect 'myrecipes/:ingredient',
            :controller => "recipes",
            :action => "show"
```

The :controller and :action keys are *bound*: This route, when matched by a URL, will always take the visitor to exactly that controller and that action. You'll see techniques for matching controller and action based on *wildcard* matching shortly. In this example, though, there's no wildcard involved. The controller and action are hard-coded.

Now, when you're generating a URL for use in your code, you provide values for all the necessary bound parameters. That way, the routing system can do enough match-ups to find the route you want. (In fact, Rails will complain by raising an exception if you don't supply enough values to satisfy a route.)

The parameters are usually bundled in a hash. For example, to generate a URL from the ingredient route, you'd do something like this:

```
<%= link_to "Recipe for apples",
    :controller => "recipes",
    :action     => "show",
    :ingredient => "apples" %>
```

The values "recipes" and "show" for :controller and :action will match the ingredient route, which contains the same values for the same parameters. That means that the pattern string in that route will serve as the template—the blueprint— for the generated URL.

The use of a hash to specify URL components is common to all the methods that produce URLs (link_to, redirect_to, form_for, etc.). Underneath, these methods are making their own calls to url_for, a lower-level URL generation method that we'll talk about more a little further on.

We've left :ingredient hanging. It's a wildcard component of the pattern string.

Wildcard Components ("Receptors")

The symbol :ingredient inside the quoted pattern in the route is a wildcard parameter (or variable). You can think of it as a *receptor*. Its job is to be latched onto by a value. Which value latches onto which wildcard is determined positionally, lining the URL up with the pattern string:

```
http://localhost:3000/myrecipes/apples       Someone connects to this URL...
                       'myrecipes/:ingredient'   which matches this pattern string
```

The :ingredient receptor, in this example, receives the value apples from the URL. What that means for you is that the value params[:ingredient] will be set to the string "apples". You can access that value inside your recipes/show action. When you generate a URL, you have to supply values that will attach to the receptors—the wildcard symbols inside the pattern string. You do this using key => value syntax. That's the meaning of the last line in the preceding example:

```
<%= link_to "My Apple Recipes",
      :controller => "recipes",
      :action     => "show",
      :ingredient => "apples" %>
```

In this call to link_to, we've provided values for three parameters. Two of them are going to match hard-coded, bound parameters in the route; the third, :ingredient, will be assigned to the slot in the URL corresponding to the :ingredient slot in the pattern string.

But they're all just hash key/value pairs. The call to `link_to` doesn't "know" whether it's supplying hard-coded or wildcard values. It just knows (or hopes!) that these three values, tied to these three keys, will suffice to pinpoint a route—and therefore a pattern string, and therefore a blueprint for a URL.

Static Strings

Our sample route contains a static string inside the pattern string: `recipes`.

```
map.connect 'myrecipes/:ingredient',
            :controller => "recipes",
            :action => "show"
```

This string anchors the recognition process. When the routing system sees a URL that starts `/recipes`, it will match that to the static string in the ingredient route. Any URL that does not contain the static string `recipes` in the leftmost slot will not match this route.

As for URL generation, static strings in the route simply get placed, positionally, in the URL that the routing system generates. Thus the `link_to` example we've been considering

```
<%= link_to "My Apple Recipes",
      :controller => "recipes",
      :action     => "show",
      :ingredient => "apples" %>
```

will generate the following HTML:

```
<a href="http://localhost:3000/myrecipes/apples">My Apple Recipes</a>
```

The string `myrecipes` did not appear in the `link_to` call. The *parameters* of the `link_to` call triggered a match to the ingredients route. The URL generator then used that route's pattern string as the blueprint for the URL it generated. The pattern string stipulates the substring `myrecipes`.

URL *recognition* and URL *generation*, then, are the two jobs of the routing system. It's a bit like the address book stored in a cell phone. When you select "Gavin" from your contact list, the phone looks up the phone number. And when Gavin calls you, the phone figures out *from* the number provided by caller ID that the caller is

Gavin; that is, it recognizes the number and maps it to the value "Gavin", which is displayed on the phone's screen.

Rails routing is a bit more complex than cell phone address book mapping, because there are variables involved. It's not just a one-to-one mapping. But the basic idea is the same: recognize what comes in as requests, and generate what goes into the code as HTML.

We're going to turn next to the routing rules themselves. As we go, you should keep the dual purpose of recognition/generation in mind. There are two principles that are particularly useful to remember:

- *The same rule* governs both recognition and generation. The whole system is set up so that you don't have to write rules twice. You write each rule once, and the logic flows through it in both directions.

- The URLs that are generated by the routing system (via `link_to` and friends) *only make sense to the routing system.* The path `recipes/apples`, which the system generates, contains not a shred of a clue as to what's supposed to happen— except insofar as it maps to a routing rule. The routing rule then provides the necessary information to trigger a controller action. Someone looking at the URL without knowing the rules won't know what the URL means.

You'll see how these play out in detail as we proceed.

The `routes.rb` File

Routes are defined in the file `config/routes.rb`, as shown (with some extra comments) in Listing 3.1. This file is created when you first create your Rails application. It comes with a few routes already written and in most cases you'll want to change and/or add to the routes defined in it.

Listing 3.1   The Default `routes.rb` File

```
ActionController::Routing::Routes.draw do |map|
  # The priority is based upon order of creation
  # First created gets highest priority.

  # Sample of regular route:
  # map.connect 'products/:id', :controller => 'catalog',
                                :action => 'view'
```

```
        # Keep in mind you can assign values other than
        # :controller and :action

        # Sample of named route:
        # map.purchase 'products/:id/purchase', :controller => 'catalog',
                                                :action => 'purchase'
        # This route can be invoked with purchase_url(:id => product.id)

        # You can have the root of your site routed by hooking up ''
        # -- just remember to delete public/index.html.
        # map.connect '', :controller => "welcome"

        # Allow downloading Web Service WSDL as a file with an extension

        # instead of a file named 'wsdl'
        map.connect ':controller/service.wsdl', :action => 'wsdl'

        # Install the default route as the lowest priority.
        map.connect ':controller/:action/:id.:format'
        map.connect ':controller/:action/:id'
    end
```

The whole thing consists of a single call to the method `ActionController:
:Routing::Routes.draw`. That method takes a block, and everything from the second line of the file to the second-to-last line is body of that block.

Inside the block, you have access to a variable called `map`. It's an instance of the class `ActionController::Routing::RouteSet::Mapper`. Through it you configure the Rails routing system: You define routing rules by calling methods on your mapper object. In the default `routes.rb` file you see several calls to `map.connect`. Each such call (at least, those that aren't commented out) creates a new route by registering it with the routing system.

The routing system has to find a pattern match for a URL it's trying to recognize, or a parameters match for a URL it's trying to generate. It does this by going through the rules—the routes—in the order in which they're defined; that is, the order in which they appear in `routes.rb`. If a given route fails to match, the matching routine falls through to the next one. As soon as any route succeeds in providing the necessary match, the search ends.

> **Courtenay Says...**
>
> Routing is probably one of the most complex parts of Rails. In fact, for much of Rails' history, only one person could make any changes to the source, due to its labrynthine implementation. So, don't worry too much if you don't grasp it immediately. Most of us still don't.
>
> That being said, the `routes.rb` syntax is pretty straightforward if you follow the rules. You'll likely spend less than 5 minutes setting up routes for a vanilla Rails project.

The Default Route

If you look at the very bottom of `routes.rb` you'll see the *default route*:

```
map.connect ':controller/:action/:id'
```

The default route is in a sense the end of the journey; it defines what happens when nothing else happens. However, it's also a good place to start. If you understand the default route, you'll be able to apply that understanding to the more intricate examples as they arise.

The default route consists of just a pattern string, containing three wildcard "receptors." Two of the receptors are `:controller` and `:action`. That means that this route determines what it's going to do based entirely on wildcards; there are no bound parameters, no hard-coded controller or action.

Here's a sample scenario. A request comes in with the URL:

```
http://localhost:3000/auctions/show/1
```

Let's say it doesn't match any other pattern. It hits the last route in the file—the default route. There's definitely a congruency, a match. We've got a route with three receptors, and a URL with three values, and therefore three positional matches:

```
:controller/:action/:id
 auctions  / show / 1
```

We end up, then, with the auctions controller, the `show` action, and "1" for the id value (to be stored in `params[:id]`). The dispatcher now knows what to do.

The behavior of the default route illustrates some of the specific default behaviors of the routing system. The default action for any request, for example, is index. And, given a wildcard like :id in the pattern string, the routing system prefers to find a value for it, but will go ahead and assign it *nil* rather than give up and conclude that there's no match.

Table 3.1 shows some examples of URLs and how they will map to this rule, and with what results.

Table 3.1 Default Route Examples

URL	Result		Value of `id`
	Controller	Action	
/auctions/show/3	auctions	show	3
/auctions/index	auctions	index	*nil*
/auctions	auctions	index (default)	*nil*
/auctions/show	auctions	show	*nil*—probably an error!

The *nil* in the last case is probably an error because a show action with no id is usually not what you'd want!

Spotlight on the :id Field

Note that the treatment of the :id field in the URL is not magic; it's just treated as a value with a name. If you wanted to, you could change the rule so that :id was :blah—but then you'd have to remember to do this in your controller action:

```
@auction = Auction.find(params[:blah])
```

The name :id is simply a convention. It reflects the commonness of the case in which a given action needs access to a particular database record. The main business of the router is to determine the controller and action that will be executed. The id field is a bit of an extra; it's an opportunity for actions to hand a data field off to each other.

The `id` field ends up in the `params` hash, which is automatically available to your controller actions. In the common, classic case, you'd use the value provided to dig a record out of the database:

```ruby
class ItemsController < ApplicationController
  def show
    @item = Item.find(params[:id])
  end
end
```

Default Route Generation

In addition to providing the basis for recognizing URLs, and triggering the correct behavior, the default route also plays a role in URL generation. Here's a `link_to` call that will use the default route to generate a URL:

```erb
<%= link_to item.description,
    :controller => "item",
    :action => "show",
    :id => item.id %>
```

This code presupposes a local variable called `item`, containing (we assume) an `Item` object. The idea is to create a hyperlink to the `show` action for the item controller, and to include the `id` of this particular item. The hyperlink, in other words, will look something like this:

```html
<a href="localhost:3000/item/show/3">A signed picture of Houdini</a>
```

This URL gets created courtesy of the route-generation mechanism. Look again at the default route:

```ruby
map.connect ':controller/:action/:id'
```

In our `link_to` call, we've provided values for all three of the fields in the pattern. All that the routing system has to do is plug in those values and insert the result into the URL:

```
item/show/3
```

When someone clicks on the link, that URL will be recognized—courtesy of the other half of the routing system, the recognition facility—and the correct controller and action will be executed, with params[:id] set to 3.

The generation of the URL, in this example, uses wildcard logic: We've supplied three symbols, :controller, :action, and :id, in our pattern string, and those symbols will be replaced, in the generated URL, by whatever values we supply. Contrast this with our earlier example:

```
map.connect 'recipes/:ingredient',
            :controller => "recipes",
            :action => "show"
```

To get the URL generator to choose this route, you have to specify "recipes" and "show" for :controller and :action when you request a URL for link_to. In the default route—and, indeed, any route that has symbols embedded in its pattern—you still have to match, but you can use any value.

Modifying the Default Route

A good way to get a feel for the routing system is by changing things and seeing what happens. We'll do this with the default route. You'll probably want to change it back… but changing it will show you something about how routing works.

Specifically, swap :controller and :action in the pattern string:

```
# Install the default route as the lowest priority.
map.connect ':action/:controller/:id'
```

You've now set the default route to have actions first. That means that where previously you might have connected to http://localhost:3000/auctions/show/3, you'll now need to connect to http://localhost:3000/show/auctions/3. And when you generate a URL from this route, it will come out in the /show/auctions/3 order.

It's not particularly logical; the original default (the default default) route is better. But it shows you a bit of what's going on, specifically with the magic symbols :controller and :action. Try a few more changes, and see what effect they have. (And then put it back the way it was!)

The Ante-Default Route and `respond_to`

The route just before the default route (thus the "ante-default" route) looks like this:

```
map.connect ':controller/:action/:id.:format'
```

The `.:format` at the end matches a literal dot and a wildcard "format" value after the id field. That means it will match, for example, a URL like this:

```
http://localhost:3000/recipe/show/3.xml
```

Here, `params[:format]` will be set to `xml`. The `:format` field is special; it has an effect inside the controller action. That effect is related to a method called `respond_to`.

The `respond_to` method allows you to write your action so that it will return different results, depending on the requested format. Here's a `show` action for the items controller that offers either HTML or XML:

```
def show
  @item = Item.find(params[:id])
  respond_to do |format|
    format.html
    format.xml { render :xml => @item.to_xml }
  end
end
```

The `respond_to` block in this example has two clauses. The HTML clause just consists of `format.html`. A request for HTML will be handled by the usual rendering of the RHTML view template. The XML clause includes a code block; if XML is requested, the block will be executed and the result of its execution will be returned to the client.

Here's a command-line illustration, using `wget` (slightly edited to reduce line noise):

```
$ wget http://localhost:3000/items/show/3.xml -O -
Resolving localhost... 127.0.0.1, ::1
Connecting to localhost|127.0.0.1|:3000... connected.
HTTP request sent, awaiting response... 200 OK
Length: 295 [application/xml]
<item>
```

```
    <created-at type="datetime">2007-02-16T04:33:00-05:00</created-at>
    <description>Violin treatise</description>
    <id type="integer">3</id>
    <maker>Leopold Mozart</maker>
    <medium>paper</medium>
    <modified-at type="datetime"></modified-at>
    <year type="integer">1744</year>
</item>
```

The .xml on the end of the URL results in respond_to choosing the "xml" branch, and the returned document is an XML representation of the item.

respond_to and the HTTP-Accept Header

You can also trigger a branching on respond_to by setting the HTTP-Accept header in the request. When you do this, there's no need to add the .:format part of the URL.

Here's a wget example that does not use .xml but does set the Accept header:

```
wget http://localhost:3000/items/show/3 -O - —header="Accept:
  text/xml"
Resolving localhost... 127.0.0.1, ::1
Connecting to localhost|127.0.0.1|:3000... connected.
HTTP request sent, awaiting response...
200 OK
Length: 295 [application/xml]
<item>
  <created-at type="datetime">2007-02-16T04:33:00-05:00</created-at>
  <description>Violin treatise</description>
  <id type="integer">3</id>
  <maker>Leopold Mozart</maker>
  <medium>paper</medium>
  <modified-at type="datetime"></modified-at>
  <year type="integer">1744</year>
</item>
```

The result is exactly the same as in the previous example.

The Empty Route

Except for learning-by-doing exercises, you're usually safe leaving the default route alone. But there's another route in `routes.rb` that plays something of a default role and you will probably want to change it: the empty route.

A few lines up from the default route (refer to Listing 3.1) you'll see this:

```
# You can have the root of your site routed by hooking up ''
# -- just remember to delete public/index.html.
# map.connect '', :controller => "welcome"
```

What you're seeing here is the empty route—that is, a rule specifying what should happen when someone connects to

```
http://localhost:3000      Note the lack of "/anything" at the end!
```

The empty route is sort of the opposite of the default route. Instead of saying, "I need any three values, and I'll use them as controller, action, and id," the empty route says, "I don't want *any* values; I want *nothing*, and I already know what controller and action I'm going to trigger!"

In a newly generated `routes.rb` file, the empty route is commented out, because there's no universal or reasonable default for it. You need to decide what this "nothing" URL should do for each application you write.

Here are some examples of fairly common empty route rules:

```
map.connect '', :controller => "main", :action => "welcome"
map.connect '', :controller => "top", :action => "login"
map.connect '', :controller => "main"
```

That last one will connect to `main/index`—index being the default action when there's none specified.

Note that Rails 2.0 introduces a mapper method named `root` which becomes the proper way to define the empty route for a Rails application, like this:

```
map.root :controller => "homepage"
```

Defining the empty route gives people something to look at when they connect to your site with nothing but the domain name.

Writing Custom Routes

The default route is a very general one. Its purpose is to catch all routes that haven't matched already. Now we're going to look at that *already* part: the routes defined earlier in the `routes.rb` file, routes that match more narrowly than the general one at the bottom of the file.

You've already seen the major components that you can put into a route: static strings, bound parameters (usually including `:controller` and often including `:action`), and wildcard "receptors" that get their values either positionally from a URL, or key-wise from a URL hash in your code.

When you write your routes, you have to think like the routing system.

- On the recognition side, that means your route has to have enough information in it—either hard-coded or waiting to receive values from the URL—to decide which controller and action to choose. (Or at least a controller; it can default to `index` if that's what you want.)

- On the generation side, your need to make sure that your hard-coded parameters and wildcards, taken together, provide you with enough values to pinpoint a route to use.

As long as these things are present—and as long as your routes are listed in order of priority ("fall-through" order)—your routes should work as desired.

Using Static Strings

Keep in mind that there's no necessary correspondence between the number of fields in the pattern string, the number of bound parameters, and the fact that every connection needs a controller and an action.

For example, you *could* write a route like this:

```
map.connect ":id",  :controller => "auctions", :action => "show"
```

which would recognize a URL like this:

```
http://localhost:3000/8
```

The routing system would set `params[:id]` to 8 (based on the position of the `:id` "receptor," which matches the position of "8" in the URL), and it would execute the `show` action of the `auctions` controller. Of course, this is a bit of a stingy route, in terms of visual information. You might want to do something more like Listing 2.2, which is a little richer semantically-speaking:

```
map.connect "auctions/:id", :controller => "auctions", :action => "show"
```

This version of the route would recognize this:

```
http://localhost:3000/auctions/8
```

In this route, "auctions" is a static string. It will be looked for in the URL, for recognition purposes; and it will be inserted into the URL when you generate it with the following code:

```
<%= link_to "Auction details",
    :controller => "auctions",
    :action => "show",
    :id => auction.id %>
```

Using Your Own "Receptors"

So far, we've used the two magic parameters, `:controller` and `:action`, and the nonmagic but standard `:id`. It is also possible to use your own parameters, either hard-coded or wildcard. Doing this can help you add some expressiveness and self-documentation to your routes, as well as to your application code.

The main reason you'd want to use your own parameters is so that you can use them as handles in your code. For example, you might want a controller action to look like this:

```
def show
  @auction = Auction.find(params[:id])
  @user = User.find(params[:user_id])
end
```

Here we've got the symbol `:user_id` showing up, along with `:id`, as a key to the params hash. That means it got there, somehow. In fact, it got there the same way as the :id parameter: It appears in the pattern for the route by which we got to the show action in the first place.

Here's that route:

```
map.connect 'auctions/:user_id/:id',
    :controller => "auctions",
    :action => "show"
```

This route, when faced with a URL like this

```
/auctions/3/1
```

will cause the auctions/show action to run, and will set both :user_id and :id in the params hash. (:user_id matches 3 positionally, and :id matches 1.)

On the URL generation side, all you have to do is include a :user_id key in your URL specs:

```
<%= link_to "Auction",
    :controller => "auctions",
    :action => "show",
    :user_id => current_user.id,
    :id => ts.id %>
```

The :user_id key in the hash will match the :user_id receptor in the route pattern. The :id key will also match, and so will the :controller and :action parameters. The result will be a URL based on the blueprint 'auctions/:user_id/:id'.

You can actually arbitrarily add many specifiers to a URL hash in calls to link_to and other similar methods. Any parameters you define that aren't found in a routing rule will be added to the URL as a query string. For example, if you add:

```
:some_other_thing => "blah"
```

to the hash in the link_to example above, you'll end up with this as your URL:

```
http://localhost:3000/auctions/3/1?some_other_thing=blah
```

A Note on Route Order

Routes are consulted, both for recognition and for generation, in the order they are defined in `routes.rb`. The search for a match ends when the first match is found, which means that you have to watch out for false positives.

For example, let's say you have these two routes in your `routes.rb`:

```
map.connect "users/help", :controller => "users"
map.connect ":controller/help", :controller => "main"
```

The logic here is that if someone connects to `/users/help`, there's a `users/help` action to help them. But if they connect to `/any_other_controller/help`, they get the `help` action of the main controller. Yes, it's tricky.

Now, consider what would happen if you reversed the order of these two routes:

```
map.connect ":controller/help", :controller => "main"
map.connect "users/help", :controller => "users"
```

If someone connects to `/users/help`, that first route is going to match—because the more specific case, handling `users` differently, is defined later in the file.

It's very similar to other kinds of matching operations, like `case` statements:

```
case string
when /./
  puts "Matched any character!"
when /x/
  puts "Matched 'x'!"
end
```

The second *when* will never be reached, because the first one will match `x`. You always want to go *from* the specific or special cases, *to* the general case:

```
case string
when /x/
  puts "Matched 'x'!"
when /./
  puts "Matched any character!"
end
```

These `case` examples use regular expressions—`/x/` and so forth—to embody patterns against which a string can be tested for a match. Regular expressions actually play a role in the routing syntax too.

Using Regular Expressions in Routes

Sometimes you want not only to recognize a route, but to recognize it at a finergrained level than just what components or fields it has. You can do this through the use of regular expressions.[1]

For example, you could route all "show" requests so that they went to an error action if their `id` fields were non-numerical. You'd do this by creating two routes, one that handled numerical ids, and a fall-through route that handled the rest:

```
map.connect ':controller/show/:id',
   :id => /\d+/, :action => "show"

map.connect ':controller/show/:id',
   :action => "alt_show"
```

If you want to do so, mainly for clarity, you can wrap your regular expression-based constraints in a special hash parameter named `:requirements`, like this:

```
map.connect ':controller/show/:id',
   :action => "show", :requirements => { :id => /\d+/ }
```

Regular expressions in routes can be useful, especially when you have routes that differ from each other *only* with respect to the patterns of their components. But they're not a full-blown substitute for data-integrity checking. A URL that matches a route with regular expressions is like a job candidate who's passed a first interview. You still want to make sure that the values you're dealing with are usable and appropriate for your application's domain.

Default Parameters and the `url_for` Method

The URL generation techniques you're likely to use—`link_to`, `redirect_to`, and friends—are actually wrappers around a lower-level method called `url_for`. It's worth looking at `url_for` on its own terms, because you learn something about how

Rails generates URLs. (And you might want to call url_for on its own at some point.)

The url_for method's job is to generate a URL from your specifications, married to the rules in the route it finds to be a match. This method abhors a vacuum: In generating a URL, it likes to fill in as many fields as possible. To that end, if it can't find a value for a particular field from the information in the hash you've given it, it looks for a value in the current request parameters.

In other words, in the face of missing values for URL segments, url_for defaults to the current values for :controller, :action, and, where appropriate, other parameters required by the route.

This means that you can economize on repeating information, if you're staying inside the same controller. For example, inside a show view for a template belonging to the auctions controller, you could create a link to the edit action like this:

```
<%= link_to "Edit auction", :action => "edit", :id => @auction.id %>
```

Assuming that this view is only ever rendered by actions in the auctions controller, the current controller at the time of the rendering will always be auctions. Because there's no :controller specified in the URL hash, the generator will fall back on auctions, and based on the default route (:controller/:action/:id), it will come up with this (for auction 5):

```
<a href="http://localhost:3000/auctions/edit/5">Edit auction</a>
```

The same is true of the action. If you don't supply an :action key, then the current action will be interpolated. Keep in mind, though, that it's pretty common for one action to render a template that belongs to another. So it's less likely that you'll want to let the URL generator fall back on the current action than on the current controller.

What Happened to :id?

Note that in that last example, we defaulted on :controller but we had to provide a value for :id. That's because of the way defaults work in the url_for method. What happens is that the route generator marches along the template segments, from left to right—in the default case like this:

```
:controller/:action/:id
```

And it fills in the fields based on the parameters from the current request until it hits one where you've provided a value:

```
:controller/:action/:id
  default!            provided!
```

When it hits one that you've provided, it checks to see whether what you've provided is the default it would have used anyway. Since we're using a show template as our example, and the link is to an edit action, we're not using the default value for :action.

Once it hits a non-default value, url_for stops using defaults entirely. It figures that once you've branched away from the defaults, you want to keep branching. So the nondefault field and *all fields to its right* cease to fall back on the current request for default values.

That's why there's a specific value for :id, even though it may well be the same as the params[:id] value left over from the previous request.

Pop quiz: What would happen if you switched the default route to this?

```
map.connect ':controller/:id/:action'
```

And then you did this in the show.rhtml template:

```
<%= link_to "Edit this auction", :action => "edit" %>
```

Answer: Since :id is no longer to the right of :action, but to its left, the generator would happily fill in both :controller and :id from their values in the current request. It would then use "edit" in the :action field, since we've hard-coded that. There's nothing to the right of :action, so at that point everything's done.

So if this is the show view for auction 5, we'd get the same hyperlink as before—*almost*. Since the default route changed, so would the ordering of the URL fields:

```
<a href="http://localhost:3000/auctions/5/edit">Edit this auction</a>
```

There's no advantage to actually doing this. The point, rather, is to get a feel for how the routing system works by seeing what happens when you tweak it.

Using Literal URLs

You can, if you wish, hard-code your paths and URLs as string arguments to `link_to`, `redirect_to`, and friends. For example, instead of this:

```
<%= link_to "Help", :controller => "main", :action => "help" %>
```

You can write this:

```
<%= link_to "Help", "/main/help" %>
```

However, using a literal path or URL bypasses the routing system. If you write literal URLs, you're on your own to maintain them. (You can of course use Ruby's string interpolation techniques to insert values, if that's appropriate for what you're doing, but really stop and think about whether you are reinventing Rails functionality if you go down that path.)

Route Globbing

In some situations, you might want to grab one or more components of a route without having to match them one by one to specific positional parameters. For example, your URLs might reflect a directory structure. If someone connects to

```
/files/list/base/books/fiction/dickens
```

you want the `files/list` action to have access to all four remaining fields. But sometimes there might be only three fields:

```
/files/list/base/books/fiction
```

or five:

```
/files/list/base/books/fiction/dickens/little_dorrit
```

So you need a route that will match (in this particular case) *everything after the second URI component.*

You can do that with a *route glob*. You "glob" the route with an asterisk:

```
map.connect 'files/list/*specs'
```

Now, the `files/list` action will have access to an array of URI fields, accessible via `params[:specs]`:

```
def list
  specs = params[:specs] # e.g, ["base", "books", "fiction", "dickens"]
end
```

The glob has to come at the end of the pattern string in the route. You *cannot* do this:

```
map.connect 'files/list/*specs/dickens'  # Won't work!
```

The glob sponges up all the remaining URI components, and its semantics therefore require that it be the last thing in the pattern string.

Globbing Key-Value Pairs

Route globbing might provide the basis for a general mechanism for fielding queries about items up for auction. Let's say you devise a URI scheme that takes the following form:

```
http://localhost:3000/items/field1/value1/field2/value2/...
```

Making requests in this way will return a list of all items whose fields match the values, based on an unlimited set of pairs in the URL.

In other words, `http://localhost:3000/items/year/1939/medium/wood` would generate a list of all wood items made in 1939.

The route that would accomplish this would be:

```
map.connect 'items/*specs', :controller => "items", :action => "specify"
```

Of course, you'll have to write a `specify` action like the one in Listing 3.2 to support this route.

Listing 3.2 The `specify` Action

```
def specify
  @items = Item.find(:all, :conditions => Hash[params[:specs]])
  if @items.any?
    render :action => "index"
  else
    flash[:error] = "Can't find items with those properties"
    redirect_to :action => "index"
  end
end
```

How about that square brackets class method on `Hash`, eh? It converts a one-dimensional array of key/value pairs into a hash! Further proof that in-depth knowledge of Ruby is a prerequisite for becoming an expert Rails developer.

Next stop: Named routes, a way to encapsulate your route logic in made-to-order helper methods.

Named Routes

The topic of named routes almost deserves a chapter of its own. What you learn here will feed directly into our examination of REST-related routing in Chapter 4.

The idea of naming a route is basically to make life easier on you, the programmer. There are no outwardly visible effects as far as the application is concerned. When you name a route, a new method gets defined for use in your controllers and views; the method is called *name*`_url` (with *name* being the name you gave the route), and calling the method, with appropriate arguments, results in a URL being generated for the route. In addition, a method called *name*`_path` also gets created; this method generates just the path part of the URL, without the protocol and host components.

Creating a Named Route

The way you name a route is by calling a method on your mapper object with the name you want to use, instead of the usual connect:

```
map.help 'help',
  :controller => "main",
  :action     => "show_help"
```

In this example, you'll get methods called `help_url` and `help_path`, which you can use wherever Rails expects a URL or URL components:

```
<%= link_to "Help!", help_path %>
```

And, of course, the usual recognition and generation rules are in effect. The pattern string consists of just the static string component "help". Therefore, the path you'll see in the hyperlink will be

```
/help
```

When someone clicks on the link, the `show_help` action of the `main` controller will be invoked.

The Question of Using *name*_path Versus *name*_url

When you create a named route, you're actually creating at least two route helper methods. In the preceding example, those two methods are `help_url` and `help_path`. The difference is that the `_url` method generates an entire URL, including protocol and domain, whereas the `_path` method generates just the path part (sometimes referred to as a *relative* path).

According to the HTTP spec, redirects should specify a URI, which can be interpreted (by some people) to mean a fully-qualified URL[2]. Therefore, if you want to be pedantic about it, you probably *should* always use the `_url` version when you use a named route as an argument to `redirect_to` in your controller code.

The `redirect_to` method seems to work perfectly with the relative paths generated by `_path` helpers, which makes arguments about the matter kind of pointless. In fact, other than redirects, permalinks, and a handful of other edge cases, it's the *Rails way* to use `_path` instead of `_url`. It produces a shorter string and the user agent (browser or otherwise) should be able to infer the fully qualified URL whenever it needs to do so, based on the HTTP headers of the request, a base element in the document, or the URL of the request.

As you read this book, and as you examine other code and other examples, the main thing to remember is that `help_url` and `help_path` are basically doing the same thing. I tend to use the `_url` style in general discussions about named route techniques, but to use `_path` in examples that occur inside view templates (for example, with `link_to` and `form_for`). It's mostly a writing-style thing, based on the theory that the URL version is more general and the path version more specialized. In any case, it's good to get used to seeing both and getting your brain to view them as very closely connected.

Considerations

Named routes save you some effort when you need a URL generated. A named route zeros in directly on the route you need, bypassing the matching process. That means you don't have to provide as much detail as you otherwise would. You have to provide a value for any wildcard parameter in the route's pattern string, but you don't have to go down the laundry list of hard-coded, bound parameters. The only reason for doing that when you're trying to generate a URL is to steer the routing system to the correct route. But when you use a named route, the system already knows which rule you want to apply, and there is a (slight) corresponding performance boost.

What to Name Your Routes

The best way to figure out what named routes you'll need is to think top-down; that is, think about what you want to write in your application code, and then create the routes that will make it possible.

Take, for example, this call to `link_to`:

```
<%= link_to "Auction of #{h(auction.item.description)}",
    :controller => "auctions",
    :action     => "show",
    :id         => auction.id %>
```

The routing rule to match that path is this (generic type of route):

```
map.connect "auctions/:id",
  :controller => "auctions",
  :action     => "show"
```

It seems a little heavy-handed to spell out all the routing parameters again, just so that the routing system can figure out which route we want. And it sure would be nice to shorten that `link_to` code. After all, the routing rule already specifies the controller and action.

This is a good candidate for a named route. We can improve the situation by introducing `auction_path`:

```
<%= link_to "Auction for #{h(auction.item.description)}",
       auction_path(:id => auction.id) %>
```

Giving the route a name is a shortcut; it takes us straight to that route, without a long search and without having to provide a thick description of the route's hard-coded parameters.

> **Courtenay Says...**
>
> Remember to escape your item descriptions!
>
> Links such as `#{auction.item.description}` should always be wrapped in an `h()` method to prevent *cross-site scripting hacks* (XSS). That is, unless you have some clever way of validating your input.

The named route will be the same as the plain route—except that we replace "connect" with the name we want to give the route:

```
map.auction "auctions/:id",
  :controller => "auctions",
  :action     => "show"
```

In the view, we can now use the more compact version of `link_to`; and we'll get (for auction 3, say) this URL in the hyperlink:

```
http://localhost:3000/auctions/show/3
```

Argument Sugar

In fact, we can make the argument to `auction_path` even shorter. If you need to supply an id number as an argument to a named route, you can just supply the number, without spelling out the `:id` key:

```
<%= link_to "Auction for #{h(auction.item.description)}",
       auction_path(auction.id) %>
```

And the syntactic sugar goes even further: You can just provide objects and Rails will grab the id automatically.

```
<%= link_to "Auction for #{h(auction.item.description)}",
    auction_path(auction) %>
```

This principle extends to other wildcards in the pattern string of the named route. For example, if you've got a route like this:

```
map.item 'auction/:auction_id/item/:id',
  :controller => "items",
  :action     => "show"
```

you'd be able to call it like this:

```
<%= link to item.description, item_path(@auction, item) %>
```

and you'd get something like this as your path (depending on the exact id numbers):

```
/auction/5/item/11
```

Here, we're letting Rails infer the ids of both an auction object and an item object. As long as you provide the arguments in the order in which their ids occur in the route's pattern string, the correct values will be dropped into place in the generated path.

A Little More Sugar with Your Sugar?

Furthermore, it doesn't have to be the id value that the route generator inserts into the URL. You can override that value by defining a to_param method in your model.

Let's say you want the description of an item to appear in the URL for the auction on that item. In the item.rb model file, you would override to_params; here, we'll override it so that it provides a "munged" (stripped of punctuation and joined with hyphens) version of the description:

```
def to_param
 description.gsub(/\s/, "-").gsub([^\W-], '').downcase
end
```

Subsequently, the method call `item_path(@item)` will produce something like this:

```
/auction/3/item/cello-bow
```

Of course, if you're putting things like "cello-bow" in a path field called `:id`, you will need to make provisions to dig the object out again. Blog applications that use this technique to create "slugs" for use in permanent links often have a separate database column to store the "munged" version of the title that serves as part of the path. That way, it's possible to do something like

```
Item.find_by_munged_description(params[:id])
```

to unearth the right item. (And yes, you can call it something other than `:id` in the route to make it clearer!)

> **Courtenay Says...**
>
> Why shouldn't you use numeric IDs in your URLs?
>
> First , your competitors can see just how many auctions you create. Numeric consecutive IDs also allow people to write automated spiders to steal your content. It's a window into your database. And finally, words in URLs just look better.

The Special Scope Method `with_options`

Sometimes you might want to create a bundle of named routes, all of which pertain to the same controller. You can achieve this kind of batch creation of named routes via the `with_options` mapping method.

Let's say you've got the following named routes:

```
map.help '/help', :controller => "main", :action => "help"
map.contact '/contact', :controller => "main", :action => "contact"
map.about '/about', :controller => "main", :action => "about"
```

You can consolidate these three named routes like this:

```
map.with_options :controller => "main" do |main|
  main.help '/help', :action => "help"
  main.contact '/contact', :action => "contact"
  main.about '/about', :action => "about"
end
```

The three inner calls create named routes that are scoped—constrained—to use "main" as the value for the :controller parameter, so you don't have to write it three times.

Note that those inner calls use main, not map, as their receiver. After the scope is set, map calls upon the nested mapper object, main, to do the heavy lifting.

Courtenay Says...

The advanced Rails programmer, when benchmarking an application under load, will notice that routing, route recognition, and the url_for, link_to and related helpers are often the slowest part of the request cycle. (Note: This doesn't become an issue until you are at least into the thousands of pageviews per hour, so you can stop prematurely optimizing now.)

Route recognition is slow because everything stops while a route is calculated. The more routes you have, the slower it will be. Some projects have hundreds of custom routes.

Generating URLs is slow because there are often many occurances of link_to in a page, and it all adds up.

What does this mean for the developer? One of the first things to do when your application starts creaking and groaning under heavy loads (lucky you!) is to cache those generated URLs or replace them with text. It's only milliseconds, but it all adds up.

Conclusion

The first half of the chapter helped you to fully understand generic routing based on `map.connect` rules and how the routing system has two purposes:

- Recognizing incoming requests and mapping them to a corresponding controller action, along with any additional variable receptors

- Recognizing URL parameters in methods such as `link_to` and matching them up to a corresponding route so that proper HTML links can be generated

We built on our knowledge of generic routing by covering some advanced techniques such as using regular expressions and globbing in our route definitions.

Finally, before moving on, you should make sure that you understand how named routes work and why they make your life easier as a developer by allowing you to write more concise view code. As you'll see in the next chapter, when we start defining batches of related named routes, we're on the cusp of delving into REST.

References

1. For more on regular expressions in Ruby, see *The Ruby Way* by Hal Fulton, part of this series.

2. Zed Shaw, author of the Mongrel web server and expert in all matters HTTP-related, was not able to give me a conclusive answer, which should tell you something. (About the looseness of HTTP that is, not Zed.)

CHAPTER 4

REST, Resources, and Rails

Before REST came I (and pretty much everyone else) never really knew where to put stuff.
—Jonas Nicklas on the Ruby on Rails mailing list

With version 1.2, Rails introduced support for designing APIs consistent with the REST style. Representational State Transfer (REST) is a complex topic in information theory, and a full exploration of it is well beyond the scope of this chapter.[1] We'll touch on some of the keystone concepts, however. And in any case, the REST facilities in Rails can prove useful to you even if you're not a REST expert or devotee.

The main reason is that one of the inherent problems that all web developers face is deciding how to name and organize the resources and actions of their application. The most common actions of all database-backed applications happen to fit well into the REST paradigm—we'll see what that means in a moment.

REST in a Rather Small Nutshell

REST is described by its creator, Roy T. Fielding, as a network "architectural style," specifically the style manifested in the architecture of the World Wide Web. Indeed, Fielding is not only the creator of REST but also one of the authors of the HTTP protocol itself—REST and the web have a very close relationship.

Fielding defines REST as a series of constraints imposed upon the interaction between system components: Basically, you start with the general proposition of machines that can talk to each other, and you start ruling some practices in and others out by imposing constraints.

The REST constraints include (among others)

- Use of a client-server architecture

- Stateless communication

- Explicit signaling of response cacheability

The World Wide Web allows for REST-compliant communication. It also allows for violations of REST principles; the constraints aren't always all there unless you put them there. But Fielding is one of the authors of the HTTP protocol; and while he has some criticisms of the protocol from the REST point of view (as well as criticisms of widespread non-REST-compliant practices, such as the use of cookies), the overall fit between REST and the web is not a coincidence.

REST is designed to help you provide services, and to provide them using the native idioms and constructs of HTTP. You'll find, if you look for it, lots of discussion comparing REST to, for example, SOAP—the thrust of the pro-REST argument being that HTTP already enables you to provide services, so you don't need a semantic layer on top of it. Just use what HTTP already gives you.

One of the payoffs of REST is that it scales relatively well for big systems, like the web. Another is that it encourages—mandates, even—the use of stable, long-lived identifiers (URIs). Machines talk to each other by sending requests and responses labeled with these identifiers. Those requests and responses also contain *representations* (manifestations in text, XML, graphic format, and so on) of *resources* (high-level, conceptual descriptions of content). Ideally at least, when you ask a machine for an XML representation of a resource—say, *Romeo and Juliet*—you'll use the same identifier every time and the same request metadata indicating that you want XML, and you'll get the same response. And if it's not the same response, there's a reason—like, the resource you're retrieving is a changeable one ("*The current transcript for Student #3994*," for example).

We'll look at resources and representations further a little later on. For now, though, let's bring Rails back into the picture.

REST in Rails

The REST support in Rails consists of helper methods and enhancements to the routing system, designed to impose a particular style and order and logic on your controllers and, consequently, on the way the world sees your application. There's more to it than just a set of naming conventions (though there's that too). We'll get to details shortly. In the large scheme of things, the benefits that accrue to you when you use Rails' REST support fall into two categories:

- Convenience and automatic best practices for you
- A REST interface to your application's services, for everyone else

You can reap the first benefit even if you're not concerned with the second. In fact, that's going to be our focus here: what the REST support in Rails can do for you in the realm of making your code nicer and your life as a Rails developer easier.

This isn't meant to minimize the importance of REST itself, nor the seriousness of the endeavor of providing REST-based services. Rather, it's an expedient; we can't talk about everything, and this section of the book is primarily about routing and how to do it, so we're going to favor looking at REST in Rails from that perspective.

Moreover, the relationship between Rails and REST, while a fruitful one, is not free of difficulties. Much Rails practice is noncompliant with the precepts of REST from the beginning. REST involves stateless communication; every request has to contain everything necessary for the recipient to generate the correct response. But pretty much every nontrivial Rails program in the world uses server state to track sessions. To the extent that they do, they are not adhering to the REST design. On the client side, cookies—also used by many Rails applications—are singled out by Fielding as a non-REST-compliant practice.

Untangling all the issues and dilemmas is beyond our scope here. Again, the focus will be on showing you how the REST support works, and opening the door to further study and practice—including the study of Fielding's dissertation and the theoretical tenets of REST. We won't cover everything here, but what we do cover will be "onward compatible" with the wider topic.

The story of REST and Rails starts with CRUD…

Routing and CRUD

The acronym CRUD (Create Read Update Delete) is the classic summary of the spectrum of database operations. It's also a kind of rallying cry for Rails practitioners. Because we address our databases through abstractions, we're prone to forget how simple it all is. This manifests itself mainly in excessively creative names for controller actions. There's a temptation to call your actions `add_item` and `replace_email_address` and things like that. But we needn't, and usually shouldn't, do this. True, the controller does not map to the database, the way the model does. But things get simpler when you name your actions after CRUD operations, or as close to the names of those operations as you can get.

The routing system is not wired for CRUD. You can create a route that goes to any action, whatever the action's name. Choosing CRUD names is a matter of discipline. Except... when you use the REST facilities offered by Rails, it happens automatically.

REST in Rails involves standardization of action names. In fact, the heart of the Rails' REST support is a technique for creating bundles of named routes automatically—named routes that are hard-programmed to point to a specific, predetermined set of actions.

Here's the logic. It's good to give CRUD-based names to your actions. It's convenient and elegant to use named routes. The REST support in Rails gives you named routes that point to CRUD-based action names. Therefore, using the REST facilities gives you a shortcut to some best practices.

"Shortcut" hardly describes how little work you have to do to get a big payoff. If you put this:

```
map.resources :auctions
```

into your `routes.rb` files, you will have created four named routes, which, in a manner to be described in this chapter, actually allow you to connect to *seven* controller actions. And those actions have nice CRUD-like names, as you will see.

The term "resources" in `map.resources` deserves some attention.

Resources and Representations

The REST style characterizes communication between system *components* (where a component is, say, a web browser or a server) as a series of requests to which the responses are *representations* of *resources*.

A resource, in this context, is a "conceptual mapping" (Fielding). Resources themselves are not tied to a database, a model, or a controller. Examples of resources include

- The current time of day
- A library book's borrowing history
- The entire text of *Little Dorrit*
- A map of Austin
- The inventory of a store

A resource may be singular or plural, changeable (like the time of day) or fixed (like the text of *Little Dorrit*). It's basically a high-level description of the thing you're trying to get hold of when you submit a request.

What you actually do get hold of is never the resource itself, but a *representation* of it. This is where REST unfolds onto the myriad content types and actual deliverables that are the stuff of the web. A resource may, at any given point, be available in any number of representations (including zero). Thus your site might offer a text version of *Little Dorrit*, but also an audio version. Those two versions would be understood as the same resource, and would be retrieved via the same *identifier* (URI). The difference in content type—one representation vs. another—would be negotiated separately in the request.

REST Resources and Rails

Like most of what's in Rails, the Rails support for REST-compliant applications is "opinionated"; that is, it offers a particular way of designing a REST interface, and the more you play in its ballpark, the more convenience you reap from it. Rails applications are database-backed, and the Rails take on REST tends to associate a resource very closely with an `ActiveRecord` model, or a model/controller stack.

In fact, you'll hear people using the terminology fairly loosely—for instance, saying that they have created "a Book resource." What they really mean, in most cases, is that they have created a `Book` model, a book controller with a set of CRUD actions, and some named routes pertaining to that controller (courtesy of `map.resources :books`). You can have a `Book` model and controller, but what you actually present to the world as your resources, in the REST sense, exists at a higher level of abstraction: *Little Dorrit*, borrowing history, and so on.

The best way to get a handle on the REST support in Rails is by going from the known to the unknown—in this case, from the topic of named routes to the more specialized topic of REST.

From Named Routes to REST Support

When we first looked at named routes, we saw examples where we consolidated things into a route name. By creating a route like this...

```
map.auction 'auctions/:id',
  :controller => "auction",
  :action     => "show"
```

you gain the ability to use nice helper methods in situations like this:

```
<%= link_to h(item.description), auction_path(item.auction) %>
```

The route ensures that a path will be generated that will trigger the `show` action of the auctions controller. The attraction of this kind of named route is that it's concise and readable.

By associating the `auction_path` method with the `auction/show` action, we've done ourselves a service in terms of standard database operations. Now, think in terms of CRUD. The named route `auction_path` is a nice fit for a `show` (the, um, R in CRUD) action. What if we wanted similarly nicely named routes for the `create`, `update`, and `delete` actions?

Well, we've used up the route name `auction_path` on the `show` action. We could make up names like `auction_delete_path` and `auction_create_path`... but those are cumbersome. We really want to be able to make a call to `auction_path` and have it mean different things, depending on which action we want the URL to point to.

So we need a way to differentiate one `auction_path` call from another. We could differentiate between the singular (`auction_path`) and the plural (`auctions_path`). A singular URL makes sense, semantically, when you're doing something with a single, existing auction object. If you're doing something with auctions in general, the plural makes more sense.

The kinds of things you do with auctions in general include creating. The `create` action will normally occur in a form:

```
<% form_tag auctions_path do |f| %>
```

It's plural because we're not saying *Perform an action with respect to a particular auction*, but rather *With respect to the whole world of auctions, perform the action of creation*. Yes, we're creating one auction, not many. But at the time we make the call to our named route, `auctions_path`, we're addressing auctions in general.

Another case where you might want a plural named route is when you want an overview of all of the objects of a particular kind—or, at least, some kind of general view, rather than a display of a particular object. This kind of general view is usually handled with an `index` action. `Index` actions typically load a lot of data into one or more variables, and the corresponding view displays it as a list or table (possibly more than one).

Here again, we'd like to be able to say:

```
<%= link_to "Click here to view all auctions", auctions_path %>
```

Already, though, the strategy of breaking `auction_path` out into singular and plural has hit the wall: We've got two places where we want to use the plural named route. One is create; the other is index. But they're both going to look like this:

```
http://localhost:3000/auctions
```

How is the routing system going to know that when we click on one, we mean the `create` action, and when we click on the other, we mean `index`? We need another data-slot, another flag, another variable on which to branch.

Luckily, we've got one.

Reenter the HTTP Verb

Form submissions are POSTs. Index actions are GETs. That means that we need to get the routing system to realize that

```
/auctions     submitted in a GET request!
```

versus

```
/auctions     submitted in a POST request!
```

are two different things. We also have to get it to generate one and the same URL—/auctions—but with a different HTTP request method, depending on the circumstances.

This is what the REST facility in Rails does for you. It lets you stipulate that you want /auctions routed differently, depending on the HTTP request method. It lets you define named routes with the same name, but with intelligence about their HTTP verbs. In short, it uses HTTP verbs to provide that extra data slot necessary to achieve everything you want to achieve in a concise way.

The way you do this is by using a special form of routing command: map.resources. Here's what it would look like for auctions:

```
map.resources :auctions
```

That's it. Making this one call inside routes.rb is the equivalent of defining four named routes (as you'll see shortly). And if you mix and match those four named routes with a variety of HTTP request methods, you end up with seven useful—very useful—permutations.

The Standard RESTful Controller Actions

Calling map.resources :auctions involves striking a kind of deal with the routing system. The system hands you four named routes. Between them, these four routes point to seven controller actions, depending on HTTP request method. In return, you agree to use very specific names for your controller actions: index, create, show, update, destroy, new, edit.

It's not a bad bargain, since a lot of work is done for you and the action names you have to use are nicely CRUD-like.

Table 4.1 summarizes what happens. It's a kind of "multiplication table" showing you what you get when you cross a given RESTful named route with a given HTTP request method. Each box (the nonempty ones, that is) shows you, first, the URL that the route generates and, second, the action that gets called when the route is recognized. (The table uses _url rather than _path, but you get both.)

Table 4.1   RESTful Routes Table Showing Helpers, Paths, and the Resulting Controller Action

Helper Method	GET	POST	PUT	DELETE
client_url(@client)	/clients/1 *show*		/clients/1 *update*	/clients/1 *destroy*
clients_*url*	/clients *index*	/clients *create*		
edit_client_url(@client)	/clients/1/edit *edit*			
new_client_url	/clients/new *new*			

(The edit and new actions have unique named routes, and their URLs have a special syntax. We'll come back to these special cases a little later.)

Since named routes are now being crossed with HTTP request methods, you'll need to know how to specify the request method when you generate a URL, so that your GET'd clients_url and your POST'd clients_url don't trigger the same controller action. Most of what you have to do in this regard can be summed up in a few rules:

1. The default request method is GET.

2. In a form_tag or form_for call, the POST method will be used automatically.

3. When you need to (which is going to be mostly with PUT and DELETE operations), you can specify a request method along with the URL generated by the named route.

An example of needing to specify a DELETE operation is a situation when you want to trigger a destroy action with a link:

```
<%= link_to "Delete this auction",:url => auction(@auction),
     :method => :delete %>
```

Depending on the helper method you're using (as in the case of `form_for`), you might have to put the method inside a nested hash:

```
<% form_for "auction", :url => auction(@auction),
        :html => { :method => :put } do |f| %>
```

That last example, which combined the singular named route with the PUT method, will result in a call to the `update` action (as per row 2, column 4 of the table).

The PUT and DELETE Cheat

Web browsers generally don't handle request methods other than GET and POST. Therefore, in order to send them PUT and DELETE requests, it's necessary for Rails to do a little sleight of hand. It's not anything you need to worry about, other than to be aware of what's going on.

A PUT or DELETE request, in the context of REST in Rails, is actually a POST request with a hidden field called `_method` set to either "put" or "delete". The Rails application processing the request will pick up on this, and route the request appropriately to the `update` or `destroy` action.

You might say, then, that the REST support in Rails is ahead of its time. REST components using HTTP *should* understand all of the request methods. They don't— so Rails forces the issue. As a developer trying to get the hang of how the named routes map to action names, you don't have to worry about this little cheat. And hopefully some day it won't be necessary any more.

Singular and Plural RESTful Routes

Some of the RESTful routes are singular; some are plural. The logic is as follows.

1. The routes for `show`, `new`, `edit`, and `destroy` are singular, because they're working on a particular resource.

2. The rest of the routes are plural. They deal with collections of related resources.

The singular RESTful routes require an argument, because they need to know the id of the particular member of the collection that you're operating on. You can use either a straightforward argument-list syntax:

```
item_url(@item)  # show, update, or destroy, depending on HTTP verb
```

or you can do it hash style:

```
item_url(:id => @item)
```

You don't have to call the `id` method on `@item` (though you can), as Rails will figure out that that's what you want.

The Special Pairs: `new/create` and `edit/update`

As Table 4.1 shows, `new` and `edit` obey somewhat special RESTful naming conventions. The reason for this actually has to do with `create` and `update`, and how `new` and `edit` relate to them.

Typically, `create` and `update` operations involve submitting a form. That means that they really involve two actions—two requests—each:

1. The action that results in the display of the form

2. The action that processes the form input when the form is submitted

The way this plays out with RESTful routing is that the `create` action is closely associated with a preliminary `new` action, and `update` is associated with `edit`. These two actions, `new` and `edit`, are really assistant actions: All they're supposed to do is show the user a form, as part of the process of creating or updating a resource.

Fitting these special two-part scenarios into the landscape of resources is a little tricky. A form for editing a resource is not, itself, really a resource. It's more like a pre-resource. A form for creating a new resource is sort of a resource, if you assume that "being new"—that is, nonexistent—is something that a resource can do, and still be a resource...

Yes, it gets a bit philosophical. But here's the bottom line, as implemented in RESTful Rails.

The new action is understood to be giving you a new, single (as opposed to plural) resource. However, since the logical verb for this transaction is GET, and GETting a single resource is already spoken for by the show action, new needs a named route of its own.

That's why you have to use

```
<%= link_to "Create a new item", new_item_path %>
```

to get a link to the items/new action.

The edit action is understood not to be giving you a full-fledged resource, exactly, but rather a kind of edit "flavor" of the show resource. So it uses the same URL as show, but with a kind of modifier, in the form of /edit, hanging off the end, which is consistent with the URL form for new:

```
/items/5/edit
```

It's worth mentioning that prior to Rails 2.0, the edit action was set off by semicolons like this: /items/5;edit, a choice that may have had more to do with the limitations of the routing system than any other loftier motives. However, the semicolon scheme caused more problems than it solved,[2] and was scrapped in Edge Rails right after the release of Rails 1.2.3.

The corresponding named route is edit_item_url(@item). As with new, the named route for edit involves an extra bit of name information, to differentiate it from the implied show of the existing RESTful route for GETting a single resource.

Singular Resource Routes

In addition to map.resources, there's also a singular (or "singleton") form of resource routing: map.resource. It's used to represent a resource that only exists once in its given context.

A singleton resource route at the top level of your routes can be appropriate when there's only one resource of its type for the whole application, or perhaps per user session.

For instance, an address book application might give each logged-in user an address book, so you could write:

```
map.resource :address_book
```

You would get a subset of the full complement of resource routes, namely the singular ones: GET/PUT `address_book_url`, GET `edit_address_book_url`, and PUT `update_address_book_url`.

Note that the method name `resource`, the argument to that method, and all the named routes are in the singular. It's assumed that you're in a context where it's meaningful to speak of "the address book"—the one and only—because there's a user to which the address book is scoped. The scoping itself is not automatic; you have to authenticate the user and retrieve the address book from (and/or save it to) the database explicitly. There's no real "magic" or mind-reading here; it's just an additional routing technique at your disposal if you need it.

Nested Resources

Let's say you want to perform operations on bids: create, edit, and so forth. You know that every bid is associated with a particular auction. That means that whenever you do anything to a bid, you're really doing something to an auction/bid pair—or, to look at it another way, an auction/bid nest. Bids are at the bottom of a "drill-down" that always passes through an auction.

What you're aiming for here is a URL that looks like this:

```
/auctions/3/bids/5
```

What it does depends on the HTTP verb it comes with, of course. But the semantics of the URL itself are: the resource that can be identified as bid 5, belonging to auction 3.

Why not just go for `bids/5` and skip the auction? For a couple of reasons. First, the URL is more informative—longer, it's true, but longer in the service of telling you something about the resource. Second, thanks to the way RESTful routes are engineered in Rails, this kind of URL gives you immediate access to the auction id, via `params[:auction_id]`.

To created nested resource routes, put this in `routes.rb`:

```
map.resources :auctions do |auction|
  auction.resources :bids
end
```

Note that in the inner call to resources, the receiver of the call is `auction`, not `map`. That's an easy thing to forget.

What that tells the mapper is that you want RESTful routes for auction resources; that is, you want `auctions_url`, `edit_auction_url`, and all the rest of it. You also want RESTful routes for bids: `auction_bids_url`, `new_auction_bid_url`, and so forth.

However, the nested resource command also involves you in making a promise: You're promising that whenever you use the bid named routes, you will provide a auction resource in which they can be nested. In your application code, that translates into an argument to the named route method:

```
<%= link_to "See all bids", auction_bids_path(@auction) %>
```

When you make that call, you enable the routing system to add the `/auctions/3` part before the `/bids` part. And, on the receiving end—in this case, in the action `bids/index`, which is where that URL points, you'll find the id of `@auction` in `params[:auction_id]`. (It's a plural RESTful route, using GET. See Table 4.1 again if you forgot.)

You can nest to any depth. Each level of nesting adds one to the number of arguments you have to supply to the nested routes. This means that for the singular routes (`show`, `edit`, `destroy`), you need at least two arguments, as in Listing 4.1.

Listing 4.1 Passing Two Parameters to Identify a Nested Resource Using `link_to`

```
<%= link_to "Delete this bid",
    auction_bid_path(@auction, @bid), :method => :delete %>
```

This will enable the routing system to get the information it needs (essentially `@auction.id` and `@bid.id`) in order to generate the route.

If you prefer, you can also make the same call using hash-style method arguments, but most people don't because it's longer code:

```
auction_bid_path(:auction => @auction, :bid => @bid)
```

Setting `:path_prefix` Explicitly

You can also achieve the nested route effect by specifying the `:path_prefix` option to your resource mapping call explicitly. Here's how you'd do this for the auctions/bids nest:

```
map.resources :auctions
map.resources :bids, :path_prefix => "auctions/:auction_id"
```

What you're saying here is that you want all of the bids URLs to include the static string "auctions" and a value for `auction_id`—in other words, to contain the contextual information necessary to associate the bid collection or member with a particular auction.

The main difference between this technique and regular nesting of resources has to do with the naming of the helper methods that are generated. Nested resources automatically get a name prefix corresponding to their parent resource. (See `auction_bid_path` in Listing 4.1.)

You're likely to see the nesting technique more often than the explicit setting of `:path_prefix`, because it's usually easier just to let the routing system figure it out from the way you've nested your resources. Plus, as we'll see in a moment, it's easy to get rid of the extra prefixes if you want to do so.

Setting `:name_prefix` Explicitly

Sometimes you might want to nest a particular resource inside more than one other resource. Or you might want to access a resource through a nested route sometimes, and directly other times. You might even want your named route helpers to point to different resources depending on the context in which they are executed.[3] The `:name_prefix` makes it all possible, since it lets you control the way that named route helper methods are generated.

Let's say you want to get at bids through auctions, as in the preceding examples, but also just by themselves. In other words, you want to be able to recognize and generate both:

`/auctions/2/bids/5` and `/bids/5`

The first thought might be `bid_path(@auction, @bid)` for the first helper, and `bid_path(@bid)` for the second. It seems logical to assume that if you want a route to bid that doesn't pass through the auction nest, you'd just leave out the auction parameter.

Given the automatic name-prefixing behavior of the routing system, you'd have to override the `name_prefix` of bids to make it all work as desired, as in Listing 4.2.

Listing 4.2 Overriding *name_prefix* in a Nested Route

```
map.resources :auctions do |auction|
  auction.resources :bids, :name_prefix => nil
end
```

I will warn you, as someone who has used this technique extensively in real applications, that when you eliminate name prefixing, debugging route problems gets an order of magnitude harder. As they say, *your mileage may vary*.

As an example, what if we wanted a different way to access bids, via the person who made them, instead of in the context of auctions? See Listing 4.3.

Listing 4.3 Overriding *name_prefix* in a Nested Route

```
map.resources :auctions do |auction|
  auction.resources :bids, :name_prefix => nil
end

map.resource :people do |people|
  people.resources :bids, :name_prefix => nil # are you sure?
end
```

Amazingly, the code in Listing 4.3 should[4] work just fine, and generate the following route helpers:

```
bid_path(@auction, @bid) # /auctions/1/bids/1
bid_path(@person, @bid)  # /people/1/bids/1
```

The thing is that your controller and view code might start getting a wee bit complex if you go down this route (pardon the pun).

First of all, your controller code would have to check for the presence of `params[:auction_id]` versus `params[:person_id]` and load the context accordingly. The view templates would probably need to do similar checking, in order to display correctly. At worst your code would end up with tons of `if/else` statements cluttering things up!

Whenever you're programming dual functionality like that, you're probably doing something wrong. Luckily, we can also specify which controller we would like to be involved in each of our routes explicitly.

Specifying RESTful Controllers Explicitly

Something we haven't yet discussed is how RESTful routes are mapped to a given controller. It was just presented as something that happens automatically, which in fact it does, based on the name of the resource.

Going back to our recurring example, given the following nested route:

```
map.resources :auctions do |auction|
  auction.resources :bids
end
```

...there are two controllers that come into play, the `AuctionsController` and the `BidsController`.

You could explicitly specify which controller to use with the `:controller_name` option of the `resources` method. Having the option means you can name the (user-facing) resource whatever you want, and keep the name of your controller aligned with different naming standards, for example:

```
map.resources :my_auctions, :controller => :auctions do |auction|
  auction.resources :my_bids, :controller => :bids
end
```

All Together Now

Now that we know about the `:name_prefix`, `:path_prefix`, and `:controller` options, we can bring it all together to show why having such fine-grained control over RESTful routes is useful.

For example, we can improve what we were trying to do in Listing 4.3, by using the `:controller` option. See Listing 4.4.

Listing 4.4   Multiple Nested Bids Resources, with Explicit Controller

```
map.resources :auctions do |auction|
  auction.resources :bids, :name_prefix => nil,
                          :controller => :auction_bids
end

map.resource :people do |people|
  people.resources :bids, :name_prefix => nil,
                         :controller => :person_bids
end
```

Realistically, the `AuctionBidsController` and `PersonBidsController` would extend the same parent class `BidsController`, as in Listing 4.5, and leverage `before` filters to load things correctly.

Listing 4.5   Subclassing Controllers for Use with Nested Routes

```
class BidsController < ApplicationController
  before_filter :load_parent
  before_filter :load_bid

  protected

    def load_parent
      # overriden in subclasses
    end

    def load_bid
      @bids = @parent.bids
    end
end

class AuctionBidsController < BidsController

  protected

    def load_parent
      @parent = @auction = Auction.find(params[:auction_id])
    end
```

```
    end

    class PersonBidsController < BidsController

      protected

        def load_parent
          @parent = @person = Person.find(params[:person_id])
        end

    end
```

Note that that although it is customary to provide name-style options as symbols, the `:controller` option does understand strings, as you would need to use if you were specifying a *namespaced controller*, like this example, which sets up an administrative route for auctions:

```
    map.resources :auctions,
               :controller => 'admin/auctions', # Admin::AuctionsController
               :name_prefix => 'admin_',
               :path_prefix => 'admin'
```

Considerations

Is nesting worth it? For single routes, a nested route usually doesn't tell you anything you wouldn't be able to figure out anyway. After all, a bid belongs to an auction. That means you can access `bid.auction_id` just as easily as you can `params[:auction_id]`, assuming you have a bid object already.

Furthermore, the bid object doesn't depend on the nesting. You'll get `params[:id]` set to 5, and you can dig that record out of the database directly. You don't need to know what auction it belongs to.

```
    Bid.find(params[:id])
```

A common rationale for judicious use of nested resources, and the one most often issued by David, is the ease with which you can enforce permissions and context-based constraints. Typically, a nested resource should only be accessible in the context of its parent resource, and it's really easy to enforce that in your code based on the way that you load the nested resource using the parent's `ActiveRecord` association (see Listing 4.6).

Listing 4.6   Loading a Nested Resource Using the Parent's `has_many` Association

```
@auction = Auction.find(params[:auction_id])
@bid = @auction.bids.find(params[:id]) # prevents auction/bid mismatch
```

If you want to add a bid to an auction, your nested resource URL would be:

```
http://localhost:3000/auctions/5/bids/new
```

The auction is identified in the URL rather than having to clutter your new bid form data with hidden fields, name your action `add_bid` and stash the user in `:id`, or any other non-RESTful practice.

Deep Nesting?

Jamis Buck is a very influential figure in the Rails community, almost as much as David himself. In February 2007, via his blog,[5] he basically told us that deep nesting was a *bad* thing, and proposed the following rule of thumb: *Resources should never be nested more than one level deep.*

That advice is based on experience and concerns about practicality. The helper methods for routes nested more than two levels deep become long and unwieldy. It's easy to make mistakes with them and hard to figure out what's wrong when they don't work as expected.

Assume that in our application example, bids have multiple comments. We could nest comments under bids in the routing like this:

```
map.resources :auctions do |auctions|
  auctions.resources :bids do |bids|
    bids.resources :comments
  end
end
```

However, we'd have to start resorting to all sort of options to avoid having a `auction_bid_comments_path` helper to deal with. (Actually, that's not *too* bad, but I've seen and written much worse.)

Instead, Jamis would have us do the following:

```
map.resources :auctions do |auctions|
  auctions.resources :bids
end

map.resources :bids do |bids|
  bids.resources :comments
end

map.resources :comments
```

Notice that each resource (except auction) is defined twice, once in the top-level namespace, and one in its context. The rationale? When it comes to parent-child scope, you really only need two levels to work with. The resulting URLs are shorter, and the helper methods are easier to work with.

```
auctions_path             # /auctions
auctions_path(1)          # /auctions/1
auction_bids_path(1)      # /auctions/1/bids
bid_path(2)               # /bids/2
bid_comments_path(3)      # /bids/3/comments
comment_path(4)           # /comments/4
```

I personally don't follow Jamis' guideline all the time in my projects, but I have noticed something about limiting the depth of your nested resources—it makes it all the more palatable to keep those handy-dandy name prefixes in place, instead of lopping them off with `:name_prefix => nil`. And trust me, those name prefixes do help with maintainability of your codebase in the long run.

> **Courtenay Says...**
>
> Many of us disagree with the venerable Jamis. Want to get into fisticuffs at a Rails conference? Ask people whether they believe routes should be nested more than one layer deep.

RESTful Route Customizations

Rails' RESTful routes give you a pretty nice package of named routes, hard-wired to call certain very useful and common controller actions—the CRUD superset you've already learned about. Sometimes, however, you want to customize things a little more, while still taking advantage of the RESTful route naming conventions and the "multiplication table" approach to mixing named routes and HTTP request methods.

The techniques for doing this are useful when, for example, you've got more than one way of viewing a resource that might be described as "showing." You can't (or shouldn't) use the *show* action itself for more than one such view. Instead, you need to think in terms of different perspectives on a resource, and create URLs for each one.

Extra Member Routes

For example, let's say we want to make it possible to retract a bid. The basic nested route for bids looks like this:

```
map.resources :auctions do |a|
  a.resources :bids
end
```

We'd like to have a `retract` action that shows a form (and perhaps does some screening for retractability). The `retract` isn't the same as `destroy`; it's more like a portal to `destroy`. It's similar to `edit`, which serves as a form portal to `update`.

Following the parallel with `edit`/`update`, we want a URL that looks like this:

```
/auctions/3/bids/5/retract
```

and a helper method called `retract_bid_url`. The way you achieve this is by specifying an extra `:member` route for the `bids`, as in Listing 4.7.:

Listing 4.7   Adding an Extra Member Route

```
map.resources :auctions do |a|
  a.resources :bids, :member => { :retract => :get }
end
```

Then you can add a retraction link to your view with the following code:

```
<%= link_to "Retract", retract_bid_path(auction, bid) %>
```

and the URL generated will include the /retract modifier. That said, you should probably let that link pull up a retraction form (and not trigger the retraction process itself!). The reason I say that is because, according to the tenets of HTTP, GET requests should not modify the state of the server—that's what POST requests are for.

Is it enough to add a :method option to link_to?

```
<%= link_to "Retract", retract_bid_path(auction,bid), :method=>:post
%>
```

Not quite. Remember that in Listing 4.7 we defined the retract route as a :get, so a POST will not be recognized by the routing system. The solution is to define the extra member route as mapping to any HTTP verb, like this:

```
map.resources :auctions do |a|
  a.resources :bids, :member => { :retract => :any }
end
```

Extra Collection Routes

You can also use this routing technique to add routes that conceptually apply to an entire collection of resources:

```
map.resources :auctions, :collection => { :terminate => :any }
```

This example will give you a terminate_auctions_path method, which will produce a URL mapping to the terminate action of the auctions controller. (A slightly bizarre example, perhaps, but the idea is that it would enable you to end all auctions at once.)

Thus you can fine-tune the routing behavior—even the RESTful routing behavior—of your application, so that you can arrange for special and specialized cases while still thinking in terms of resources.

Considerations

During a discussion of RESTful routing on the Rails mailing list,[6] Josh Susser proposed *flipping* the syntax for custom actions so that they would be keyed on the HTTP verb and accept an array of action names, like this:

```
map.resources :comments,
              :member => { :get => :reply,
                           :post => [:reply, :spawn, :split] }
```

Among other reasons, Josh cited how it would simplify the practice of writing so-called *post-backs*, dual-purpose controller actions that handle both GET and POST requests in one method.

The response from David was not a positive one. After expressing his position against post-backs, he said: "I'm starting to think that explicitly ignoring [post-backs] with `map.resources` is a feature."

Later in the thread, continuing to defend the API, David added, "If you're writing so many additional methods that the repetition is beginning to bug you, you should revisit your intentions. *You're probably not being as RESTful as you could be.*" (italics mine)

The last sentence is key. Adding extra actions corrupts the elegance of your overall RESTful application design, because it leads you away from finding all of the resources lurking in your domain.

Keeping in mind that *real* applications are more complicated than code examples in a reference book, let's see what would happen if we had to model retractions strictly using resources. Rather than tacking a `retract` action onto the `BidsController`, we might feel compelled to introduce a retraction resource, associated with bids, and write a `RetractionController` to handle it.

```
map.resources :bids do |bids|
  bids.resource :retraction
end
```

`RetractionController` could now be in charge of everything having to do with retraction activities, rather than having that functionality mixed into `BidsController`. And if you think about it, something as weighty as bid retraction would eventually accumulate quite a bit of logic. Some would call breaking it out into its own controller *proper separation of concerns* or even just good *object-orientation*.

I can't help but continue the story of that fateful mailing list thread, because it led to a priceless moment in Rails community history, which added to our reputation as an opinionated bunch!

Josh replied, "Just checking... You think that code that is less readable and more tedious to write is an advantage? I guess from the perspective of macro-optimization versus micro-optimization I wouldn't argue with you, but I think that's a hell of a way to encourage people to do the right thing. If going RESTful is all that, you shouldn't need to rely on *syntactic vinegar* to force people to do it the right way. Now, if you were to say that organizing the actions hash as `{:action => method, ...}` is desirable because it guarantees an action only is used once, then sure, that makes sense." (italics mine)

David did indeed see the less readable and more tedious code as an advantage in this particular case, and he latched on to the *syntactic vinegar* term with enthusiasm. About two months later, he wrote one of his most famous blog entries about the concept (excerpted here):

> Syntactic sugar has long hogged the spotlight in discussions of framework and language design. It holds the power to turn idioms into conventions, to promote a common style through beauty, brevity, and ease of use. We all love syntactic sugar—and we want it all: the terrifying lows, the dizzying highs, the creamy middles. It's what makes languages such as Ruby taste ever so sweet in comparison to the plain alternatives.
>
> But sugar is not all we need. Good design lies not only in emphasizing the proper, but de-emphasizing the improper too. Just as we can sprinkle syntactic sugar across a certain style or approach to promote its use, we can add syntactic vinegar to discourage it as well. It's more sparingly used, but that makes it no less important. ... http://www.loudthinking.com/arc/2006_10.html

Controller-Only Resources

The word "resource" has a substantive, noun-like flavor that puts one in mind of database tables and records. However, a REST resource does not have to map directly to an `ActiveRecord` model. Resources are high-level abstractions of what's available through your web application. Database operations just happen to be one of the ways that you store and retrieve the data you need to generate representations of resources.

A REST resource doesn't necessarily have to map directly to a controller, either, at least not in theory. As we learned in relation to the `:path_prefix` and `:controller` options of `map.resources`, you could, if you wanted to, provide REST services whose public identifiers (URIs) did not match the names of your controllers at all.

What all of this adds up to is that you might have occasion to create a set of resource routes, and a matching controller, that don't correspond to any model in your application at all. There's nothing wrong with a full resource/controller/model stack where everything matches by name. But you may find cases where the resources you're representing can be encapsulated in a controller but not a model.

An example in the auction application is the sessions controller. Assume a `routes.rb` file containing this line:

```
map.resource :session
```

It maps the URL `/session` to a `SessionController` as a singleton resource, yet there's no `Session` model. (By the way, it's properly defined as a singleton resource because from the user's perspective there is only *one* session.)

Why go the RESTful style for authentication? If you think about it, user sessions can be created and destroyed. The creation of a session takes place when a user logs in; when the user logs out, the session is destroyed. The RESTful Rails practice of pairing a `new` action and view with a `create` action can be followed! The user login form can be the session-creating form, housed in the template file such as `session/new.rhtml` (see Listing 4.8).

Listing 4.8   A RESTful Login Screen

```
<h1>Log in</h1>

<% form_for :user, :url => session_path do |f| %>
  <p>Login: <%= f.text_field :login %></p>
  <p>Password: <%= f.password_field :password %></p>
  <%= submit_tag "Log in" %>
<% end %>
```

When the form is submitted, the input is handled by the `create` method of the sessions controller in Listing 4.9.

Listing 4.9 A RESTful Login Action

```
def create
  @user = User.find_by_login(params[:user][:login])
  if @user and @user.authorize(params[:user][:password])
    flash[:notice] = "Welcome, #{@user.first_name}!"
    redirect_to home_url
  else
    flash[:notice] = "Login invalid."
    redirect_to :action => "new"
  end
end
```

Nothing is written to any database table in this action, but it's worthy of the name `create` by virtue of the fact that it creates a session. Furthermore, if you *did* at some point decide that sessions should be stored in the database, you'd already have a nicely abstracted handling layer.

It pays to remain open-minded, then, about the possibility that CRUD as an action-naming philosophy and CRUD as actual database operations may sometimes occur independently of each other—and the possibility that the resource-handling facilities in Rails might usefully be associated with a controller that has no corresponding model. Creating a session isn't the most shining example of REST-compliant practices, since REST mandates stateless transfers of representations of resources… But it's a good illustration of why, and how, you might make design decisions involving routes and resources that don't implicate the whole application stack.

Sticking to CRUD-like action names is, in general, a good idea. As long as you're doing lots of creating and destroying anyway, it's easier to think of a user logging in as the creation of a session, than to come up with a whole new semantic category for it. Rather than the new concept of "user logs in," just think of it as a new occurrence of the old concept, "session gets created."

Different Representations of Resources

One of the precepts of REST is that the components in a REST-based system exchange *representations* of resources. The distinction between resources and their representations is vital.

As a client or consumer of REST services, you don't actually retrieve a resource from a server; you retrieve representations of that resource. You also provide representations: A form submission, for example, sends the server a representation of a resource, together with a request—for example, PUT—that this representation be used as the basis for updating the resource. Representations are the exchange currency of resource management.

The `respond_to` Method

The ability to return different representations in RESTful Rails practice is based on the `respond_to` method in the controller, which, as you've seen, allows you to return different responses depending on what the client wants. Moreover, when you create resource routes you automatically get URL recognition for URLs ending with a dot and a `:format` parameter.

For example, assume that you have `map.resources :auctions` in your routes file and some `respond_to` logic in the `AuctionsController` like this:

```
def index
  @auctions = Auction.find(:all)
  respond_to do |format|
    format.html
    format.xml { render :xml => @auctions.to_xml }
  end
end
```

Now, you'll now be able to connect to this URL: `http://localhost:3000/auctions.xml`

The resource routing will ensure that the `index` action gets executed. It will also recognize the `.xml` at the end of the route and interact with `respond_to` accordingly, returning the XML representation.

Of course, all of this is URL recognition. What if you want to generate a URL ending in `.xml`?

Formatted Named Routes

The resource routing facility also gives you `.:format`-flavored versions of its named routes. Let's say you want a link to the XML representation of a resource. You can achieve this by using the `formatted_` version of the RESTful named route:

```
<%= link_to "XML version of this auction",
       formatted_auction_path(@auction, "xml") %>
```

This will generate the following HTML:

```
<a href="/auctions/1.xml">XML version of this auction</a>
```

When followed, this link will trigger the XML clause of the `respond_to` block in the `show` action of the auctions controller. The resulting XML may not look like much in a browser, but the named route is there if you want it.

The circuit is now complete: You can generate URLs that point to a specific response type, and you can honor requests for different types by using `respond_to`. And if the request wants to specify its desired response by using the `Accept` header instead, it can do that too. All told, the routing system and the resource routing facilities built on top of it give you quite a set of powerful, concise tools for differentiating among requests and, therefore, being able to serve up different representations.

The RESTful Rails Action Set

Rails' REST facilities, ultimately, are about named routes and the controller actions to which they point. The more you use RESTful Rails, the more you get to know each of the seven RESTful actions. How they work across different controllers (and different applications) is of course somewhat different. Still, perhaps because there's a finite number of them and their roles are fairly well-delineated, each of the seven tends to have fairly consistent properties and a characteristic "feel" to it.

We're going to take a look at each of the seven actions, with examples and comments. You've encountered all of them already, particularly in Chapter 2, "Working with Controllers," but here you'll get some "backstory" and start to get a sense of the characteristic usage of them and issues and choices associated with them.

Index

Typically, an `index` action provides a representation of a plural (or *collection*) resource. The index representation will usually be generic and public. The `index` action shows the world the most neutral representation possible.

A typical `index` action looks like this:

```
class AuctionsController < ApplicationController

  def index
    @auctions = Auction.find(:all)
  end

  ...


end
```

The view template will display public information about each auction, with links to specific information about each one, and to public profiles of the sellers.

Although `index` is best thought of as public, you'll certainly encounter situations where you want to display a representation of a collection, but in a restricted way. For example, users should be able to see a listing of all their bids. But you don't want everyone seeing everyone else's lists.

The best strategy here is to slam down the gate at the latest possible point. You can use RESTful routing to help you.

Let's say we want each user to see his or her bid history. We could decide that the `index` action of the bids controller will be filtered through the current user (`@user`). The problem with that, though, is that it rules out a more public use of that action. What if we want a public collection view that shows all the current highest bids? Maybe even a redirect to the auction index view. The point is to keep things as public as possible for as long as possible.

There are a couple of ways to do this. One way is to test for the presence of a logged-in user, and decide what to show based on that. But that's not going to work here. For one thing, the logged-in user might want to see the more public view. For another, the more dependence on server-side state we can eliminate or consolidate, the better.

So let's look at the two bid lists, not as a public and private version of the same resource, but as different resources. We can encapsulate the difference directly in the routing:

```
map.resources :auctions do |auctions|
  auctions.resources :bids, :collection => { :manage => :get }
end
```

We can now organize the bids controller in such a way that access is nicely layered, using filters only where necessary and eliminating conditional branching in the actions themselves:

```
class BidsController < ApplicationController

  before_filter :load_auction
  before_filter :check_authorization, :only => :manage

  def index
    @bids = Bid.find(:all)
  end

  def manage
    @bids = @auction.bids
  end

  ...

  protected

    def load_auction
      @auction = Auction.find(params[:auction_id])
    end

    def check_authorization
      @auction.authorized?(current_user)
    end
end
```

There's now a clear distinction between /bids and /bids/manage and the role that they play in your application.

Courtenay Says...

Some developers believe that using filters to load data *is a travesty against all that is good and pure.* If your coworker or boss is of this persuasion, make sure your finds are within the action like this:

```
def show
  @auction = Auction.find(params[:id])
  unless auction.authorized?(current_user)
    ... # access_denied
  end
end
```

An alternate way of doing this is to add a method to the `User` class, because the user object should be responsible for authorization:

```
class User < ActiveRecord::Base

  def find_authorized_auction(auction_id)
    auction = Auction.find(auction_id)
    return auction.authorized?(self) && auction
  end

end
```

And call it from the `AuctionController` like this:

```
def show
  @auction = current_user.find_authorized_auction
(params[:id])  else
    raise ActiveRecord::RecordNotFound
  end
end
```

You could even add a method to the `Auction` model, since it's this model that controls access to its data.

```
def self.find_authorized(id, user)
  auction = find(id)
  return auction.authorized?(user) && auction
end
```

On the named route side, we've now got `bids_url` and `manage_bids_url`. We've thus preserved the public, stateless face of the `/bids` resource, and quarantined as much stateful behavior as possible into a discrete subresource, `/bids/manage`. Don't fret if this mentality doesn't come to you naturally—it's part of the REST learning curve.

If I were dogmatic about REST, I might find it ironic, even distasteful, to discuss REST-related techniques in the context of quarantining stateful behavior, since RESTful requests are not supposed to depend on session state to begin with. It goes to show, however, that the REST facilities available to you in Rails can, so to speak, gracefully degrade, in situations where you need to depart from a strictly REST-compliant interface.

Show

The RESTful `show` action is the singular flavor of a resource. That generally translates to a representation of information about one object, one member of a collection. Like `index`, `show` is triggered by a GET request.

A typical—one might say classic—`show` action looks like this:

```
class AuctionController < ApplicationController
  def show
    @auction = Auction.find(params[:id])
  end
end
```

Of course, the `show` action might depend on `before_filters` as a way of not having to load the shown resource explicitly in the `show` action. You might want to differentiate between publicly available profiles, perhaps based on a different route, and the profile of the current user, which might include modification rights and perhaps different information.

As with index actions, it's good to make your show actions as public as possible, and offload the administrative and privileged views into either a different controller or a different action.

Destroy

Destroy actions are good candidates for administrative safeguarding, though of course it depends on what you're destroying. You might want something like the code in Listing 4.10 to protect the `destroy` action.

Listing 4.10 Safeguarding the *destroy* Action

```
class UsersController < ApplicationController
  before_filter :admin_required, :only => :destroy
```

A typical `destroy` action might look like this, assuming that `@user` was already loaded by a `before` filter:

```
def destroy
  @user.destroy
  flash[:notice] = "User deleted!"
  redirect_to users_url
end
```

This approach might be reflected in a simple administrative interface like this:

```
<h1>Users</h1>
<% @users.each do |user| %>
  <p><%= link_to h(user.whole_name), user_path(user) %>
  <%= link_to("delete", user_path(user), :method => :delete) if
  current_user.admin? %></p>
<% end %>
```

That delete link appears, depending on the whether current user is an admin.

In fact, the most striking thing about the RESTful destroy sequence in Rails is what happens in the view that contains the links *to* the action. Here's the HTML from one time through the loop. Be warned: It's longer than you might think.

```
<p><a href="http://localhost:3000/users/2">Emma Knight Peel</a>
 <a href="http://localhost:3000/users/2" onclick="var f =
document.createElement('form'); f.style.display = 'none';
this.parentNode.appendChild(f); f.method = 'POST'; f.action =
this.href;var m = document.createElement('input');
m.setAttribute('type', 'hidden'); m.setAttribute('name', '_method');
m.setAttribute('value', 'delete'); f.appendChild(m);f.submit();return
false;">Delete</a>)</p>
```

Why so much code—JavaScript, yet!—for two little links? The first link is handled quickly; it's just a link to the show view for the user. The reason the second link is so long is this. DELETE submissions are dangerous. Rails wants to make them as hard as possible to spoof or trigger accidentally—for instance, by a crawler or bot sending requests to your site. So when you specify the DELETE method, a whole JavaScript script is generated inside your HTML document. This script actually wraps your link in a form. Since bots don't submit forms, this gives a layer of protection to your code.

New and Create

As you've already seen, the `new` and `create` actions go together in RESTful Rails. A "new resource" is really just a virtual entity waiting to be created. Accordingly, the `new` action customarily presents a form, and `create` creates a new record, based on the form input.

Let's say you want a user to be able to create (that is, start) an auction. You're going to need

1. A `new` action, which will display a form

2. A `create` action, which will create a new `Auction` object based on the form input, and proceed to a view (`show` action) of that auction.

The `new` action doesn't have to do much. In fact, it has to do nothing. Like any empty action, it can even be left out. Rails will still figure out that you want to render the `new.erb.html` view.

The `new.erb.html` template might look like Listing 4.11. Notice that some of the input fields are namespaced to `:item` (courtesy of the `fields_for` helper method) and some are namespaced to `:auction` (courtesy of `form_for`). That's because an item and an auction really get created in tandem.

Listing 4.11 A New Auction Form

```
<h1>Create a new auction</h1>
<%= error_messages_for :auction %>

<% form_for :auction, :url => auctions_path do |f| %>
  <% fields_for :item do |i| %>
    <p>Item description: <%= i.text_field "description" %></p>
    <p>Item maker: <%= i.text_field "maker" %></p>
    <p>Item medium: <%= i.text_field "medium" %></p>
    <p>Item year: <%= i.text_field "year" %></p>
  <% end %>
  <p>Reserve: <%= f.text_field "reserve" %></p>
  <p>Bid increment: <%= f.text_field "incr" %></p>
  <p>Starting bid: <%= f.text_field "starting_bid" %></p>
  <p>End time: <%= f.datetime_select "end_time" %></p>
  <%= submit_tag "Create" %>
<% end %>
```

The form action here is expressed by the named route auctions, coupled with the fact that this is a form and will therefore automatically generate a POST request.

Once the information is filled out, it's time for the main event: the create action. Unlike new, this action has something to do.

```
def create
  @auction = current_user.auctions.build(params[:auction])
  @item = @auction.build_item(params[:item])

  if @auction.save
    flash[:notice] = "Auction started!"
    redirect_to auction_url(@auction)
  else
    render :action => "new"
  end
end
```

Having used both an "auction" namespace and an "item" namespace for our input fields, we can piggyback on both, via the params hash, to instantiate a new Auction object from the current user's auctions association and hang an Item object off it with build_item. This is a convenient way to operate on two associated objects at once. If @auction.save fails for any reason, the associated item will not be created, so we don't have to worry about cleaning up after a failure.

When the save succeeds, both auction and item will be created.

Edit and Update

Like new and create, the edit and update actions go together: edit provides a form, and update processes the form input.

The form for editing a record is very similar to the form for creating one. (In fact, you can put much of it in a partial template and use it for both; that's left as an exercise for the reader.) Here's what edit.html.erb might look like for editing an item:

```
<h1>Edit Item</h1>

<% form_for :item, :url => item_path(@item),
            :html => { :method => :put } do |item| %>
```

```
    <p>Description: <%= item.text_field "description" %></p>
    <p>Maker: <%= item.text_field "maker" %></p>
    <p>Medium: <%= item.text_field "medium" %></p>
    <p>Year: <%= item.text_field "year" %></p>
    <p><%= submit_tag "Save Changes" %></p>

<% end %>
```

The main difference between this form and the form for specifying a new item (Listing 4.11) is which named RESTful route you use, and the fact that for the `update` action, you have to specify the PUT request method. That will have the effect of steering the dispatcher to the update method.

Conclusion

In this chapter, we tackled the tough subject of using REST principles to guide the design of our Rails applications, mainly as they apply to the routing system and controller actions. We learned how the foundation of RESTful Rails is the `map.resources` method in your routes file, and how to use the numerous options available to make sure that you can structure your application exactly how it needs to be structured. We also learned how in some cases, David and Rails core team apply syntactic vinegar to keep us from straying down the wrong path.

One of the challenges of writing and maintaining serious Rails applications is the routing system, namely understanding it and being able to figure out mistakes that you will undoubtedly make during the course of day-to-day development. It's such a crucial topic for the Rails developer that we have an entire chapter devoted to it.

Reference

1. For those interested in REST, the canonical text is Roy Fielding's dissertation, which you can find at http://www.ics.uci.edu/~fielding/pubs/dissertation/top.htm. In particular, you'll probably want to focus on Chapters 5 and 6 of the dissertation, which cover REST and its relation to HTTP. You'll also find an enormous amount of information, and links to more, on the REST wiki at http://rest.blueoxen.net/cgi-bin/wiki.pl.

2. In addition to being *weird*, the semicolon had a number of significant problems. For instance, it wreaked havoc on caching. Safari users were not able to authenticate URLs with semicolons in them. Also, various web servers (most damningly Mongrel) correctly consider the semicolon to be part of the query string, since that character is reserved for delimiting the start of path parameters (specific to a path element in between slashes, as opposed to request parameters that come after a '?' character).

3. Trevor Squires has a great plugin called ResourceFu that makes this technique possible, which is available at http://agilewebdevelopment.com/plugins/resource_fu.

4. I can only say *should work*, because routing code is historically some of the most volatile in the entire Rails codebase, so whether it works depends on your version of Rails. I know for a fact that it *doesn't* work in Rails 1.2.3.

5. http://weblog.jamisbuck.org/2007/2/5/nesting-resources

6. Read the full thread at http://www.ruby-forum.com/topic/75356.

CHAPTER 5

Reflecting on Rails Routing

> You are in a maze of twisty little passages, all alike.
> —Adventure (late 70s-era computer game)

In this context, reflecting doesn't mean pondering; it means examining, testing, and troubleshooting. The routing system gives you numerous points of entry for reflection of this kind—and there are some handy plugins that can help you further.

We're not going to look at every technique and/or plugin, but in this chapter you'll become acquainted with several important facilities that will help you make sure your routes are doing what you think they're doing, and how to figure out why they're not if they're not.

We'll also take a look at the source code for the routing system, including the RESTful routing facilities.

Examining Routes in the Application Console

Coming full circle to the approach we took at the beginning of the book with respect to the dispatcher, you can examine the workings of the routing system in the application console. This can help with troubleshooting, and can also help you learn about the routing system.

Dumping Routes

Let's start by examining all the available routes. To do this, you need to get hold of the current `RouteSet` object:

```
$ ruby script/console
Loading development environment.
>> rs = ActionController::Routing::Routes
```

You'll see a rather huge amount of output—a screen dump of all the defined routes. You can, however, get this dump in a more readable form:

```
>> puts rs.routes
```

This will give you a kind of chart of all the defined routes:

```
GET    /bids/                 {:controller=>"bids", :action=>"index"}
GET    /bids.:format/         {:controller=>"bids", :action=>"index"}
POST   /bids/                 {:controller=>"bids", :action=>"create"}
POST   /bids.:format/         {:controller=>"bids", :action=>"create"}
GET    /bids/new/             {:controller=>"bids", :action=>"new"}
GET    /bids/new.:format/     {:controller=>"bids", :action=>"new"}
GET    /bids/:id;edit/        {:controller=>"bids", :action=>"edit"}
GET    /bids/:id.:format;edit {:controller=>"bids", :action=>"edit"}

# etc.
```

The amount of information may be greater than you need, but it can be enlightening to see it in this form. You get a graphic sense of the fact that each route includes a request method, a URL pattern, and parameters specifying the controller/action sequence.

You can also look at named routes in a similar format. With named routes it pays to neaten up the format a bit. As you iterate through the routes, you get a name and a route for each one. You can use this information to output a chart:

```
rs.named_routes.each {|name, r| printf("%-30s  %s\n", name, r) }; nil
```

The `nil` at the end is to stop `irb` from outputting the actual return value of the call to each, which would push the interesting stuff off the screen.

The result looks like this (modified to look decent on this page):

```
history   ANY     /history/:id/   {:controller=>"auctions",
                                    :action=>"history"}
new_us    GET     /users/new/     {:controller=>"users", :action=>"new"}
new_auction GET /auctions/new/ {:controller=>"auctions",
:action=>"new"}

# etc.
```

The upshot of this is that you can get a lot of routing information in the console, and slice and dice it any way you need. But what about the "raw" information? That original screen dump contained some important elements too:

```
#<ActionController::Routing::Route:0x275bb7c
@requirements={:controller=>"bids", :action=>"create"},

@to_s="POST    /bids.:format/ {:controller=>\"bids\",
:action=>\"create\"}",
@significant_keys=[:format, :controller, :action],
@conditions={:method=>:post},
@segments=[#<ActionController::Routing::DividerSegment:0x275d65c
@raw=true, @is_optional=false, @value="/">,
#<ActionController::Routing::StaticSegment:0x275d274
@is_optional=false, @value="bids">,
#<ActionController::Routing::DividerSegment:0x275ce78 @raw=true,
@is_optional=false, @value=".">,
#<ActionController::Routing::DynamicSegment:0x275cdc4
@is_optional=false, @key=:format>,
#<ActionController::Routing::DividerSegment:0x275c798 @raw=true,
@is_optional=true, @value="/">]>
```

Anatomy of a Route Object

The best way to see what's going on here is to look at a YAML (Yet Another Markup Language) representation of this particular route. Here's the output of a to_yaml operation, together with some comments. There's a lot of information here, but you can learn a lot by looking it over. You're seeing a kind of X-ray of how a route is constructed.

```
# The whole thing is a Route object

-- !ruby/object:actionController::Routing::Route

# This route only recognizes PUT requests.
conditions:
  :method: :put

# The basic chain of events upon recognition, and the hooks for
# matching when generating.
requirements:
  :controller: bids
  :action: update

# The segments. This is the formal definition of the pattern string.
# Everything is accounted for, including the dividers (the forward
# slashes).

# Note that each segment is an instance of a particular class:
# DividerSegment, StaticSegment, or DynamicSegment.

# If you read along, you can reconstruct the possible values
# of the pattern.

# Note the regexp field, automatically inserted, constraining the
# possible values of the :id segment.
segments:
- !ruby/object:actionController::Routing::DividerSegment
  is_optional: false
  raw: true
  value: /
- !ruby/object:actionController::Routing::StaticSegment
  is_optional: false
  value: auctions
- !ruby/object:actionController::Routing::DividerSegment
  is_optional: false
  raw: true
  value: /
- !ruby/object:actionController::Routing::DynamicSegment
  is_optional: false
  key: :auction_id
```

```
    - !ruby/object:actionController::Routing::DividerSegment
      is_optional: false
      raw: true
      value: /
    - !ruby/object:actionController::Routing::StaticSegment
      is_optional: false
      value: bids
    - !ruby/object:actionController::Routing::DividerSegment
      is_optional: false
      raw: true
      value: /
    - !ruby/object:actionController::Routing::DynamicSegment
      is_optional: false
      key: :id
      regexp: !ruby/regexp /[^\/;.,?]+/
    - !ruby/object:actionController::Routing::DividerSegment
      is_optional: true
      raw: true
      value: /
  significant_keys:
  - :auction_id
  - :id
  - :controller
  - :action

  # (This should be on one line; it's split here for formatting
  reasons.)
  to_s: PUT /auctions/:auction_id/bids/:id/
            {:controller=>"bids" :action=>"update"}
```

The storage of segments in a collection enables the routing system to perform recognition and generation, since the segments can be traversed both in an attempt to match the segments from a candidate URL, and to output a URL using the segments as a template or blueprint.

You can, of course, find out more about the inner workings of routes by looking in the routing source code. We're not going to go into it in depth here, but have a look at the files routing.rb and resources.rb in the ActionController source tree. You'll see the definitions of Routing, RouteSet, the various Segment classes, and more. If you want to learn more about how the source code functions, there's a series of blog posts by Jamis Buck, Rails core team member, which will give you a good guided tour.[1]

There's more you can do in the console: You can directly execute recognition and generation of URLs.

Recognition and Generation in the Console

To do manual recognition and generation in the console, let's first scope our console session to the `RouteSet` object. (If you've never seen this technique, you'll be learning a nice IRB trick along the way.)

```
$ ./script/console
Loading development environment.
>> irb ActionController::Routing::Routes
>>
```

By giving the `irb` command *inside* IRB, we've set the default object—`self`—to the route set. This saves some typing as we proceed to give commands.

To see a route generated from parameters, feed the parameters to the `generate` method. Here are some annotated examples.

Here's a nested resource routes for bids. The create action generates a collection URL; there's no `:id` field. But there is an `:auction_id` field, to achieve the nesting.

```
>> generate(:controller => "bids", :auction_id => 3, :action =>
   "create")
=> "/auctions/3/bids"
```

Here are our two custom action routes for `bids`, nested inside `users`. In each case (`retract` and `manage`), providing the appropriate action name is enough to trigger the use of the extra path segment in the URL.

```
>> generate(:controller => "bids", :user_id => 3, :id => 4, :action =>
   "retract")
=> "/users/3/bids/4/retract"
>> generate(:controller => "bids", :user_id => 3, :action => "manage")
=> "/users/3/bids/manage"
```

Remember the bid history action "history" in the auctions controller? Here's how to generate the URL for it.

```
>> generate(:controller => "auctions", :action => "history", :id => 3)
=> "/history/3"
```

These next two examples use the `item_year` route that requires a year parameter consisting of four digits. Note that the generation fails when the year doesn't match this pattern; the year value is *added to the query string*, rather than included as a URL segment.

```
>> generate(:controller => "items", :action => "item_year", :year =>
1939)
=> "/item_year/1939"
>> generate(:controller => "items", :action => "item_year", :year =>
19393)
=> "/items/item_year?year=19393"
```

You can go in the other direction too, starting with paths and seeing how they play out in terms of controller, action, and parameters, according to the route recognition system.

The top-level path, as defined by us in `routes.rb`:

```
>> recognize_path("/")
=> {:controller=>"auctions", :action=>"index"}
```

Similar results come from the auctions resource, called in the plural with the GET request method.

```
>> recognize_path("/auctions", :method => :get)
=> {:controller=>"auctions", :action=>"index"}
```

With the POST method, the result is different: It's routed to the create action.

```
>> recognize_path("/auctions", :method => :post)
=> {:controller=>"auctions", :action=>"create"}
```

The same logic applies to a plural POST request in a nested route.

```
>> recognize_path("/auctions/3/bids", :method => :post)
=> {:controller=>"bids", :action=>"create", :auction_id=>"3"}
```

The custom actions are recognized and broken down into the appropriate controller and action parameters.

```
>> recognize_path("/users/3/bids/1/retract", :method => :get)
=> {:controller=>"bids", :user_id=>"3", :action=>"retract", :id=>"1"}
```

Here's our history route, bound to the auctions controller.

```
>> recognize_path("/history/3")
=> {:controller=>"auctions", :action=>"history", :id=>"3"}
```

The `item_year` route only recognizes paths with four-digit numbers in the `:year` position. In the second of these two examples, the system reports failure: there's no appropriate route.

```
>> recognize_path("/item_year/1939")
=> {:controller=>"items", :action=>"item_year", :year=>"1939"}
>> recognize_path("/item_year/19393")
ActionController::RoutingError: no route found to match
"/item_year/19393" with {}
```

Named Routes in the Console

You can also execute named routes in the console. The easiest way to do this is to include the module `ActionController::UrlWriter`, and then set the default host value to anything (just to suppress errors):

```
>> include ActionController::UrlWriter
=> Object
>> default_url_options[:host] = "example.com"
=> "example.com"
```

Now you can call named routes and see their return values—that is, the URLs they generate.

```
>> auction_url(1)
=> "http://example.com/auctions/1"
>> formatted_auction_url(1,"xml")
=> "http://example.com/auctions/1.xml"
>> formatted_auctions_url("xml")
=> "http://example.com/auctions.xml"
```

As always, the application console can help you both learn and debug. If you keep your `routes.rb` file open in one window and the console in another, you'll make rapid progress in getting a feel for how the recognition and generation of routes dovetail with each other. Sadly, the console doesn't seem to reload the routing table automatically. Not even the `reload!` method seems to force it to be read again.

The console is good for learning and ad-hoc testing, but there are also facilities for the more systematic process of testing routes.

Testing Routes

The testing system gives you some facilities for testing routes:

- `assert_generates`
- `assert_recognizes`
- `assert_routing`

The third of these, `assert_routing`, is really the first two rolled into one: You give it a path and some parameters, and it tests both the recognition of the path, making sure it resolves to the parameters you've given, and the generation of the path from the parameters. Testing and specifying of routing is covered in detail in Chapters 17, "Testing," and 18, "RSpec on Rails," of this book.

Exactly which tests you write for your routes, and how many tests, is up to you. Ideally, of course, your test suite would include at least every permutation that you're actually using in your application. If you want to see a rather thorough set of routing tests, have a look at the file `routing.rb`, in the test subdirectory of your `ActionPack` installation. At last count it was 1881 lines long. It's testing the actual framework, so you're not expected (or advised!) to duplicate it in your own tests—but, like the other Rails framework test files, it might give you some ideas and will certainly illustrate the process of test-driven development for you.

A Word about Argument Syntax

Don't forget Ruby's rule about hashes in argument lists:

If the last argument in the list is a hash, you can omit the curly braces.

That's why you can do this:

```
assert_generates(user_retract_bid_path(3,1),
                 :controller => "bids",
                 :action => "retract",
              :id => "1", :user_id => "3")
```

If you use a hash anywhere except in the last position, you have to wrap it in curly braces. That's why you *must* do this:

```
assert_recognizes({:controller => "auctions",
                   :action => "show",
                   :id => auction.id.to_s },
                  auction_path(auction))
```

Here, `auction_path(auction)` is the last argument, so the hash has to use the curly braces.

If you ever get slightly mysterious syntax errors pertaining to your argument lists, make sure you're not violating the hash rule.

The Routing Navigator Plugin

Rick Olson, one of the Rails core developers, has written a plugin called Routing Navigator that gives you a deluxe version of the kind of information you can get by examining routes in the console—right in your browser.

To install the Routing Navigator plugin, give this command from the top level of your Rails application directory:

```
./script/plugin install
    http://svn.techno-weenie.net/projects/plugins/routing_navigator/
```

Now, you have to tell one or more controllers that you want them to show you the route information you crave. In `auction_controller.rb`, for example, put this line:

```
routing_navigator :on
```

at the beginning of the controller class definition (right where you'd put `before_filters` and other class methods). This is definitely something that you want to do on an occasional basis during development; you don't want to leave routing navigation on in a production application.

The Recognize and Generate buttons give you input boxes where you can put paths (for recognition) or parameters (for generation) and have the operations performed for you. It's similar to doing the same thing in the application console, but a lot slicker.

The last button is Routing Navigator. This takes you to a new page, which includes every single route, named or not, defined for your application. Above the list of routes is the Routing Viewer utility. You can input paths and/or route parameters, and perform recognition and generation operations.

The list of all available routes at the bottom of the viewer can get quite long. But you can filter it, using another of the input windows—the one labeled "YAML to filter routes by requirements." For example, if you put `controller: bids` into this window, and hit the Filter button, the list at the bottom will be refreshed to include only those routes that pertain to the bids controller.

The Routing Navigator is a fine debugging tool, and it's worthwhile to spend some time working with it just for learning.

Conclusion

This brings us to the end of our tour of Rails routing, RESTful and otherwise. As you develop Rails applications, you're sure to find some favorites among the various idioms and techniques available to you; and there's a whole world of existing code to which you can look for examples. If you keep the fundamentals in mind, you'll find that your routing skills will develop nicely and will greatly enhance the look and logic of your code.

Happy routing!

References

1. http://weblog.jamisbuck.org/2006/10/4/under-the-hood-route-recognition-in-rails.

CHAPTER 6
Working with ActiveRecord

An object that wraps a row in a database table or view, encapsulates the database access, and adds domain logic on that data.
– Martin Fowler, P of EA

The Active Record pattern, identified by Martin Fowler in his seminal work, *Patterns of Enterprise Architecture,* maps one domain class to one database table, and one instance of that class to each row of that database. It is a simple approach that, while not perfectly applicable in all cases, provides a powerful framework for database access and object persistence in your application.

Rails' ActiveRecord framework includes mechanisms for representing models and their relationships, CRUD (Create, Read, Update and Delete) operations, complex searches, validation, callbacks, and many more features. It relies heavily on "convention over configuration," so it's easiest to use when you're creating a new database schema that can follow those conventions. However, ActiveRecord also provides configuration settings that let you adapt it to work well with legacy database schemas that don't necessarily conform to Rails conventions.

According to Martin Fowler, delivering the keynote address at the inaugural Rails conference in 2006, Ruby on Rails has successfully taken the Active Record pattern much further than anyone imagined it could go. It shows you what you can achieve when you have a single-minded focus on a set of ideals, which in the case of Rails is simplicity.

The Basics

For the sake of completeness, let's begin with the real basics of how ActiveRecord works. In order to create a new model class, the first thing you do is to declare it as a subclass of `ActiveRecord::Base`, using Ruby's class extension syntax:

```
class Client < ActiveRecord::Base
end
```

By convention, an ActiveRecord class named `Client` will be mapped to the `clients` table. Rails understands pluralization, as covered in the section "Pluralization" in this chapter. Also by convention, ActiveRecord will expect an `id` column to use as primary key. It should be an integer and incrementing of the key should be managed automatically by the database server when creating new records. Note how the class itself makes no mention of the table name, columns, or their datatypes.

Each instance of an ActiveRecord class provides access to the data from one row of the backing database table, in an object-oriented manner. The columns of that row are represented as attributes of the object, using straightforward type conversions (i.e. ruby strings for varchars, Ruby dates for dates, and so on), and with no default data validation. Attributes are inferred from the column definition pertaining to the tables with which they're linked. Adding, removing, and changing attributes and their types are done by changing the columns of the table in the database.

When you're running a Rails server in *development mode*, changes to the database schema are reflected in the Active Record objects immediately, via the web browser. However, if you make changes to the schema while you have your Rails console running, the changes will *not* be reflected automatically, although it is possible to pick up changes manually by typing `Dispatcher.reset_application!` at the console.

The Rails way of doing things is to use code generation to produce boilerplate code. As a result, you'll hardly ever create a file for your model class and enter the class declaration yourself. It's just so much easier to use the Rails model generator instead.

For instance, let's use the model generator to create our Client class and review the resulting files that are created:

```
$ script/generate model client
      exists   app/models/
      exists   test/unit/
```

```
exists   test/fixtures/
create   app/models/client.rb
create   test/unit/client_test.rb
create   test/fixtures/clients.yml
exists   db/migrate
create   db/migrate/002_create_clients.rb
```

The file containing our new model class is **client.rb**:

```
class Client < ActiveRecord::Base
end
```

Nice and simple. Let's see what else was created. There's a unit test skeleton in **client_test.rb**:

```
require File.dirname(__FILE__) + '/../test_helper'

class ClientTest < Test::Unit::TestCase
  fixtures :clients

  # Replace this with your real tests.
  def test_truth
    assert true
  end
end
```

It asks us to replace the `test_truth` method with real tests. Right now we're just taking a glance at the generated code, so we'll move on. Notice `ClientTest` references a *fixture* file, **clients.yml**:

```
# Read about fixtures at
http://ar.rubyonrails.org/classes/Fixtures.html
one:
  id: 1
two:
  id: 2
```

Not much there at all, just some ids. Unit tests and fixtures are covered in Chapter 17, "Testing."

Finally, there is a migration file named **002_create_clients.rb**:

```ruby
class CreateClients < ActiveRecord::Migration
  def self.up
    create_table :clients do |t|
      # t.column :name, :string
    end
  end

  def self.down
    drop_table :clients
  end
end
```

Migrations is the mechanism used in Rails to create and evolve your database schema, without which you wouldn't have ActiveRecord models. (Well, they'd be very boring.) That being the case, let's go ahead and examine migrations in depth.

> **Courtenay Says.....**
>
> ActiveRecord is a great example of the Rails "Golden Path"—that is, if you keep within its limitations, you can go far. Stray from the path, and you'll probably get stuck in the mud. This Golden Path involves many conventions, like naming your tables in the plural form ("users").
>
> It's common for new developers to Rails and rival web-framework evangelists to complain about how tables must be named in a particular manner, how there are no constraints in the database layer, that foreign keys are handled all wrong, enterprise systems must have composite primary keys, and more.
>
> Get the complaining out of your system now, because all these defaults are simply defaults, and in most cases can be overridden with a single line of code or a plugin.

Migrations

It's a fact of life that the database schema of your application will evolve over the course of development. Tables are added, names of columns are changed, things are dropped—you get the picture. Without strict conventions and process discipline for the application developers to follow, keeping the database schema in proper lock-step with application code is traditionally a very troublesome job.

Migrations are Rails' way of helping you to evolve the database schema of your application (also known as its DDL) without having to drop and re-create the database each time you make a change. And not having to drop and recreate the database each time a change happens means that you don't lose your development data—which may or may not be that important, but is usually very convenient. The only changes made when you execute a migration are those necessary to move the schema from one version to another, whether that move is forward *or backward* in time.

Creating Migrations

Rails provides a generator for creating migrations. Here is its help text at the command line:

```
$ script/generate migration
Usage: script/generate migration MigrationName [options]


Rails Info:
    -v, --version               Show the Rails version and quit.
    -h, --help                  Show this help message and quit.


General Options:
    -p, --pretend               Run but do not make any changes.
    -f, --force                 Overwrite files that already
exist.
    -s, --skip                  Skip files that already exist.
    -q, --quiet                 Suppress normal output.
    -t, --backtrace             Debugging: show backtrace on
errors.
    -c, --svn                   Modify files with subversion.
                                (Note: svn must be in path)


Description:
    The migration generator creates a stub for a new database
migration.

    The generator takes a migration name as its argument.  The
migration
    name may be given in CamelCase or under_score.
```

```
    The generator creates a migration class in db/migrate prefixed by
    its number in the queue.

Example:
    ./script/generate migration AddSslFlag

    With 4 existing migrations, this will create an AddSslFlag
migration
    in the file db/migrate/005_add_ssl_flag.rb
```

As you can see, all you have to do is provide a descriptive name for the migration in CamelCase, and the generator does the rest. We only invoke this generator directly when we want to change attributes of an existing table.

As we discussed earlier in the chapter, other generators, such as the model generator, also create migration scripts for you, unless you specify the `--skip-migration` option.

Naming Migrations

The sequential aspect of migrations is accomplished via a simple numbering scheme baked into the name of the migration file, and automatically handled by the migration generator.

By convention, the file name begins with a three-digit version number (padded with zeros) followed by the name of the migration class, separated with underscores. (Note: The name of the file *does* need to match the name of the class or the migration will fail.)

The migrations generator handles checking to see what the next sequence number should be, based on the value of a special table in the database that Rails maintains. It is named `schema_info` and it is very simple:

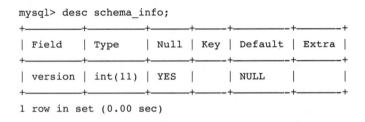

```
mysql> desc schema_info;
+---------+--------+------+-----+---------+-------+
| Field   | Type   | Null | Key | Default | Extra |
+---------+--------+------+-----+---------+-------+
| version | int(11)| YES  |     | NULL    |       |
+---------+--------+------+-----+---------+-------+
1 row in set (0.00 sec)
```

It only contains one column, and one row—the current migration version of your application.

The descriptive part of the migration name is up to you, but most Rails developers that I know try to make it match the schema operation (in simple cases) or at least allude to what's going on inside (in more complex cases).

Migration Pitfalls

If you only ever write Rails programs by yourself, there are no pitfalls to the sequentially numbered naming scheme, and you should skip this little section. Problems can and do crop up when you're working together with other programmers on the same project, especially big teams with lots of other developers. I'm not talking about problems with the migrations API of Rails itself; it's just that the overall problem of maintaining and evolving database schemas is hard and not completely solved yet.

My old ThoughtWorks partner-in-crime Jay Fields has been leading big Rails teams and writes in his blog about the troubles faced with Rails migrations on his team:

> Migrations are great, but they do come at a cost. When working with a large team (my current team size is 14 and growing) migration conflicts happen. This can be mitigated with communication, but migrations can definitely be a bottleneck. Also, the process of creating a migration can be painful on a large team. Before creating a migration you should always update from source control to ensure you get all the migrations checked in by your teammates. Then, the best case scenario is when you can create a migration that doesn't change anything and immediately check it in. Checking in a new migration immediately helps ensure you don't block other teammates from creating migrations; however, it's not always as simple as adding a new table. Migrations that alter the database structure often break several tests. Obviously, you can't check those migrations in until you fix all the breaking tests, which can take time. During this time, database changes are blocked for the entire team.[1]

Another manifestation of the same problem happens when you have development happening in multiple code branches that need to be updated, and has been described as nightmarish (see the comments to Jay's blog entry for more on that subject).

Unfortunately there is no straightforward solution to this problem, other than designing the entire database up-front prior to implementing your application, and that would have its own big set of problems (too big to broach here). I can tell you from experience that doing enough analysis up-front to have at least a rough, but fairly complete database schema ready before diving into application code is quite useful.

It's also useful to call out to your fellow developers whenever you're about to embark on the creation of a new migration, so that two of you don't inadvertently try to commit the same migration number later on, which would lead to drama.

Sebastian Says.....

One trick we use (based on Conor Hunt's idea) is to have an svn hook script check new migrations being added to the repository and prevent duplicate numbers.

Another trick is to have a single member of the team be responsible for migrations. Developers would create and test migrations locally and then email them to the "coordinator" for checking (and proper numbering).

Courtenay Says.....

Keeping your database schema in revision control far outweighs the difficulties that arise when a team changes the schema in an ad-hoc fashion. Pipelining database changes through code revisions prevents the dreaded question "Who added this field?"

As usual, there are multiple Rails plugins related to this issue. One, which I wrote, is called IndependentMigrations. Simply put, it lets you have multiple migrations with the same number. Other plugins allow migrations keyed by timestamp. Read more about my plugin and alternatives at http://blog.caboo.se/articles/2007/3/27/independent-migrations-plugin.

Migration API

Getting back to the Migration API itself, here is the **002_create_clients.rb** file again, from earlier in the chapter, after adding four column definitions for the `clients` table:

```
class CreateClients < ActiveRecord::Migration
  def self.up
    create_table :clients do |t|
```

```
      t.column :name, :string
      t.column :code, :string
      t.column :created_at, :datetime
      t.column :updated_at, :datetime
    end
  end

  def self.down
    drop_table :clients
  end
end
```

As you can see in the example, migration directives happen within two class method definitions, `self.up` and `self.down`. If we go to the command line in our project folder and type `rake db:migrate`, the `clients` table will be created. Rails gives us informative output during the migration process so that we see what is going on:

```
$ rake db:migrate
(in /Users/obie/prorails/time_and_expenses)

== 2 CreateClients: migrating
==========================================
-- create_table(:clients)
   -> 0.0448s
== 2 CreateClients: migrated (0.0450s)
=================================
```

Normally, only the code in the up method is run, but if you ever need to *rollback* to an earlier version of the schema, the down method specifies how to undo what happened in up.

To execute a rollback, use the migrate task, but pass it a version number to rollback to, as in `rake db:migrate VERSION=1`.

create_table(name, options)

The `create_table` method needs at minimum a name for the table and a block containing column definitions. Why do we specify identifiers with symbols instead of strings? Both will work, but symbols require one less keystroke.[2]

The `create_table` method makes a huge, but usually true assumption that we want an autoincrementing, integer-typed, primary key. That is why you don't see it declared in the list of columns. If that assumption happens to be wrong, it's time to pass `create_table` some options in a hash.

For example, how would you define a simple join table consisting of two foreign key columns and not needing its own primary key? Just pass the `create_table` method an `:id` option set to `false`, as a boolean, not a symbol! It will stop the migration from autogenerating a primary key altogether:

```
create_table :ingredients_recipes, :id => false do |t|
  t.column :ingredient_id, :integer
  t.column :recipe_id, :integer
end
```

If all you want to do is change the name of the primary key column from its default of 'id', pass the `:id` option a symbol instead. For example, let's say your corporation mandates that primary keys follow the pattern *tablename_id*. Then the earlier example would look as follows:

```
create_table :clients, :id => :clients_id do |t|
  t.column :name, :string
  t.column :code, :string
  t.column :created_at, :datetime
  t.column :updated_at, :datetime
end
```

The `:force => true` option tells the migration to *go ahead and drop the table being defined if it exists*. Be careful with this one, since it will produce (possibly unwanted) data loss when run in production. As far as I know, the `:force` option is mostly useful for making sure that the migration puts the database in a known state, but isn't all that useful on a daily basis.

The `:options` option allows you to append custom instructions to the SQL CREATE statement and is useful for adding database-specific commands to your migration. Depending on the database you're using, you might be able to specify things such as character set, collation, comments, min/max sizes, and many other properties using this option.

The `:temporary => true` option specifies creation of a temporary table that will only exist during the current connection to the database. In other words, it only exists during the migration. In advanced scenarios, this option might be useful for migrating big sets of data from one table to another, but is not commonly used.

> **Sebastian Says...**
>
> A little known fact is that you can remove files from your migration directories (while still keeping the higher-numbered ones) to keep the `db/migrate` folder to a manageable size. You can move the older migrations to a `db/archived_migrations` folder or something like that.
>
> If you want to make absolutely sure your code is deployable from scratch, you can replace the lowest-numbered migration with a "recreate all" migration based on the contents of `schema.rb`.

Defining Columns

Columns can be added to a table using either the `column` method, inside the block of a `create_table` statement, or with the `add_column` method. Other than taking the name of the table to add the column to as its first argument, the methods work identically.

```
create_table :clients do |t|
  t.column :name, :string
end

add_column :clients, :code, :string
add_column :clients, :created_at, :datetime
```

The first (or second) parameter obviously specifies the name of the column, and the second (or third) obviously specifies its type. The SQL92 standard defines fundamental data types, but each database implementation has its own variation on the standards.

If you're familiar with database column types, when you examine the preceding example it might strike you as a little weird that there is a database column declared as type `string`, since databases don't have string columns—they have char or varchars types.

Column Type Mappings

The reason for declaring a database column as type string is that Rails migrations are meant to be database-agnostic. That's why you could (as I've done on occasion) develop using Postgres as your database and deploy in production to Oracle.

A complete discussion of how to go about choosing the right data type for your application needs is outside the scope of this book. However, it is useful to have a reference of how migration's generic types map to database-specific types. The mappings for the databases most commonly used with Rails are in Table 6.1.

Table 6.1   Column Mappings for the Databases Most Commonly Used with Rails

Migration type Ruby class	MySQL	Postgres	SQLite	Oracle
:binary String	blob	bytea	blob	blob
:boolean Boolean	tinyint(1)	boolean	boolean	number(1)
:date Date	date	date	date	date
:datetime Time	datetime	timestamp	datetime	date
:decimal BigDecimal	decimal	decimal	decimal	decimal
:float Float	float	float	float	number
:integer Fixnum	int(11)	integer	integer	number(38)
:string String	varchar(255)	character varying (255)	varchar(255)	varchar2(255)
:text String	text	clob(32768)	text	clob
:time Time	time	time	time	date
:timestamp Time	datetime	timestamp	datetime	date

Each connection adapter class has a `native_database_types` hash which establishes the mapping described in Table 6.1. If you need to look up the mappings for a database not listed in Table 6.1, you can pop open the adapter Ruby code and find the `native_database_types` hash, like the following one inside the `SQLServerAdapter` class within **sqlserver_adapter.rb**:

```
def native_database_types
  {
    :primary_key => "int NOT NULL IDENTITY(1, 1) PRIMARY KEY",
    :string      => { :name => "varchar", :limit => 255  },
    :text        => { :name => "text" },
    :integer     => { :name => "int" },
    :float       => { :name => "float", :limit => 8 },
    :decimal     => { :name => "decimal" },
    :datetime    => { :name => "datetime" },
    :timestamp   => { :name => "datetime" },
    :time        => { :name => "datetime" },
    :date        => { :name => "datetime" },
    :binary      => { :name => "image"},
    :boolean     => { :name => "bit"}
  }
end
```

Column Options

For many column types, just specifying type is not enough information. All column declarations accept the following options:

`:default => value`

Sets a default to be used as the initial value of the column for new rows. You don't ever need to explicitly set the default value to `null`. Just leave off this option to get a null default value.

`:limit => size`

Adds a size parameter to string, text, binary, or integer columns. Its meaning varies depending on the column type that it is applied to. Generally speaking, limits for string types refers to number of characters, whereas for other types it specifies the number of bytes used to store the value in the database.

`:null => true`

Makes the column required at the database level by adding a `not null` constraint.

Decimal Precision

Columns declared as type `:decimal` accept the following options:
`:precision => number`

Precision is the total number of digits in a number.
`:scale => number`

Scale is the number of digits to the *right* of the decimal point. For example, the number 123.45 has a precision of 5 and a scale of 2. Logically, the scale cannot be larger than the precision.

> **NOTE**
>
> Decimal types pose a serious opportunity for data loss during migrations of production data between different kinds of databases. For example, the default precisions between Oracle and SQL Server can cause the migration process to truncate and change the value of your numeric data. It's always a good idea to specify precision details for your data.

Column Type Gotchas

The choice of column type is not necessarily a simple choice and depends on both the database you're using and the requirements of your application.

- **:binary**   Depending on your particular usage scenario, storing binary data in the database can cause big performance problems. Rails isn't choosy when it loads objects from the database, and putting large binary attributes on commonly used models will increase the load on your database server significantly.

- **:boolean**   The way that boolean values are stored varies from database to database. Some use 1 and 0 integer values to represent true and false, respectively. Others use characters such as T and F. Rails handles the mapping between Ruby's `true` and `false` very well, so you don't need to worry about the underlying scheme yourself. Setting attributes directly to database values such as 1 or F may work correctly, but is considered an anti-pattern.

- **:date, :datetime and :time**   Trying to store dates on databases that don't have a native date type, such as Microsoft SQL Server, can be problematic. The Ruby class that Rails maps to `datetime` columns is `Time`, which has the limitation of not working with year values prior to 1970. Ruby's `DateTime` class *does* work with year values prior to 1970, so why doesn't Rails just use `DateTime` instead? The answer has to do with performance. Under the covers, `Time` is implemented in C and is very fast, whereas `DateTime` is written in pure Ruby and is comparatively slow.

To make ActiveRecord map to `DateTime` instead of `Time`, drop the code from Listing 6.1 into a file in your **lib/** directory and require it from **config/ environment.rb**.

Listing 6.1   Map Dates to `DateTime` Instead of `Time`

```
require 'date'
# It's necessary to do this, because Time doesn't
# support dates before 1970...

class ActiveRecord::ConnectionAdapters::Column
  def self.string_to_time(string)
    return string unless string.is_a?(String)
    time_array = ParseDate.parsedate(string)[0..5]
    begin
      Time.send(Base.default_timezone, *time_array)
    rescue
      DateTime.new(*time_array) rescue nil
    end
  end
end
```

- **:decimal**   Older versions of Rails (prior to 1.2) did not support the fixed-precision `:decimal` type and as a result many old Rails applications incorrectly used `:float` datatypes. Floating-point numbers are by nature imprecise, so it is important to choose **:decimal** instead of **:float** for most business-related applications.

- **:float**   Don't use floats to store currency[3] values, or more accurately, any type of data that needs fixed precision. Since floating-point numbers are pretty much approximations, any single representation of a number as a float is probably okay. However, once you start doing mathematical operations or comparisons with float values, it is ridiculously easy to introduce difficult to diagnose bugs into your application.

- **:integer and :string**   There aren't many gotchas that I can think of when it comes to integers and strings. They are the basic data building blocks of your application, and many Rails developers leave off the size specification, which results in the default maximum sizes of 11 digits and 255 characters, respectively.

You should keep in mind that you won't get an error if you try to store values that exceed the maximum size defined for the database column, which again, is 255 characters by default. Your string will simply get truncated. Use validations to make sure that user-entered data does not exceed the maximum size allowed.

- **:text**   There have been reports of text fields slowing down query performance, enough to be a consideration for applications that need to scale to high loads. If you must use a text column in a performance-critical application, put it in a separate table.

- **:timestamp**   As of Rails 1.2, when creating new records, ActiveRecord may not work very well with default database values that are generated with functions, as in the case of timestamp columns on Postgres. The issue is that instead of leaving those columns out of the `insert` statement, Rails supplies a `null` value, which may cause the default value to be ignored.

Custom Data Types

If use of database-specific datatypes (such as `:double`, for higher precision than `:float`) is critical to your project, use the `config.active_record.schema_format = :sql` setting in **config/environment.rb** to make Rails dump schema information in native SQL DDL format rather than its own cross-platform compatible Ruby code, via the **schema.rb** file.

"Magic" Timestamp Columns

Rails does *magic* with datetime columns, if they're named a certain way. Active Record will automatically timestamp *create* operations if the table has columns named `created_at` or `created_on`. The same applies to *updates* when there are columns named `updated_at` or `updated_on`.

Note that `created_at` and `updated_at` should be defined as `datetime`-type columns not timestamps in your migration.

Automatic timestamping can be turned off globally, by setting the following variable in **config/environment.rb**

```
ActiveRecord::Base.record_timestamps = false
```

Via inheritance, the preceding code turns off timestamps for all models, but you can also do it on a case-by-case basis by setting `record_timestamps` to false in specific models. Timestamps are in the local timezone by default, but can use UTC by setting `ActiveRecord::Base.default_timezone = :utc`.

Macro-Style Methods

Most of the important classes you write while coding a Rails application are configured using what I call *macro-style* method invocations (also known in some circles as a *domain-specific language* or *DSL*). Basically, the idea is to have a highly readable block of code at the top of your class that makes it immediately clear how it is configured.

Macro-style invocations are usually placed at the top of the file, and for good reason. Those methods *declaratively* tell Rails how to manage instances, perform data validation and callbacks, and relate with other models. Many of them do some amount of *metaprogramming*, meaning that they participate in adding behavior to your class at runtime, in the form of additional instance variables and methods.

Relationship Declarations

For example, look at the `Client` class with some relationships declared. Don't worry about the meaning of those declarations just yet, because we'll talk about them extensively in Chapter 7, "ActiveRecord Associations." All I want to do right now is to illustrate what I'm talking about when I say *macro-style*:

```
class Client < ActiveRecord::Base
  has_many :billing_codes
  has_many :billable_weeks
  has_many :timesheets, :through => :billable_weeks

end
```

As a result of those three `has_many` declarations, the `Client` class gains at least three new attributes, proxy objects that let you manipulate the associated collections interactively.

I still remember the first time I sat with an experienced Java programmer friend of mine to teach him some Ruby and Rails. After minutes of profound confusion, an almost visible light bulb appeared over his head as he proclaimed, "Oh! They're methods!"

Indeed, they're regular old method calls, in the context of the class object. We leave the parentheses off to emphasize the declarative intention. That's a style issue, but it just doesn't feel right to me with the parentheses in place, as in the following code snippet:

```
class Client < ActiveRecord::Base
  has_many(:billing_codes)
  has_many(:billable_weeks)
  has_many(:timesheets, :through => :billable_weeks)
end
```

When the Ruby interpreter loads **client.rb**, it executes those has_many methods, which, again, are defined as *class methods* of ActiveRecord's `Base` class. They are executed in the context of the `Client` *class*, adding attributes that are subsequently available to `Client` *instances*. It's a programming model that is potentially strange to newcomers, but quickly becomes second-nature to the Rails programmer.

Convention over Configuration

Convention over configuration is one of Rails' guiding principles. If we follow Rails conventions, very little explicit configuration is needed, which stands in stark contrast to the reams of configuration that are required to get even a simple application running in other technologies.

It's not that a newly bootstrapped Rails application comes with *default* configuration in place already, reflecting the conventions that will be used. It's that the conventions are *baked into* the framework, actually hard-coded into its behavior, and you need to override the default behavior with explicit configuration when applicable.

It's also worth mentioning that most configuration happens in close proximity to what you're configuring. You will see *associations*, *validations*, and *callback* declarations at the top of most ActiveRecord models.

I suspect that the first explicit configuration (over convention) that many of us deal with in ActiveRecord is the mapping between class name and database table, since by default Rails assumes that our database name is simply the pluralized form of our class name. And since the issue of pluralization trips up so many beginning Rails developers, we'll cover it here before going further with ActiveRecord.

Pluralization

Rails has a class named `Inflector` whose responsibility is to transform strings (words) from singular to plural, class names to table names, modularized class names to ones without, and class names to foreign keys, etc. (Some of its operations have funny names, such as `dasherize`.)

The default inflections for pluralization and singularization of uncountable words are kept in an interesting file inside your Rails installation, named **inflections.rb**.

Most of the time the `Inflector` class does a decent job of figuring out the pluralized table name for a given class, but occasionally it won't. This is one of the first stumbling blocks for many new Rails users, but it is not necessary to panic. With a little ad-hoc testing beforehand, it's easy to find out how `Inflector` will react to certain words. We just need to use the Rails console, which by the way is one of the *best* things about working in Rails.

You fire up the console from your command prompt using the executable Ruby script located at **script/console** in your project directory.

```
$ script/console
>> Inflector.pluralize "project"
=> "projects"
>> Inflector.pluralize "virus"
=> "viri"
>> Inflector.pluralize "pensum"
=> "pensums"
```

As you can see in the example, `Inflector` is pretty smart, pluralizing "virus" as "viri"; but if you know your Latin you have already noticed that the plural "pensum" should actually be "pensa". Needless to say, the inflector does *not* know Latin.

However, you *can* teach the inflector new tricks either by adding new pattern rules, by pointing out an exception, or by declaring certain words un-pluralizable. The preferred place to do that is inside the **config/environment.rb** file, where a commented example is already provided.

```
Inflector.inflections do |inflect|
  inflect.plural /^(.*)um$/i, '\1a'
  inflect.singular /^(.*)a/i, '\1um'
  inflect.irregular 'album', 'albums'
  inflect.uncountable %w( valium )
end
```

By the way, as of Rails 1.2 the pluralizer takes *already pluralized* strings and...does nothing with them, which is probably best. Older versions of Rails were not as smart about that.

```
>> "territories".pluralize
=> "territories"
>> "queries".pluralize
=> "queries"
```

For a long list of pluralizations correctly handled by `Inflector`, take a look inside **activesupport/test/inflector_test.rb**. I found some of them pretty interesting, such as:

```
"datum"       => "data",
"medium"      => "media",
"analysis"    => "analyses"
```

Should I Report INFLECTOR Bugs to the Core Team?

According to Michael Koziarski, one of the members of the Rails core team, you shouldn't report issues with `Inflector`: "The inflector is basically frozen, prior to 1.0 we'd add lots of new rules to fix bugs, and just end up enraging people who looked at the old output and named their tables accordingly. You can add those exceptions yourself in environment.rb."

Setting Names Manually

Now that we understand inflection, let's get back to configuration of ActiveRecord model classes. The `set_table_name` and `set_primary_key` methods let you bypass Rails conventions and explicitly define the table name for the model, and the column name for its primary key.

For example purposes (only!), let's say I had some icky naming convention that I was forced to follow for my database tables, that differed from ActiveRecord's convention. I might have to do the following:

```
class Client < ActiveRecord::Base
  set_table_name "CLIENT"
  set_primary_key "CLIENT_ID"
end
```

The `set_table_name` and `set_primary_key` methods let you use any table and primary names you'd like, but you'll have to specify them explicitly in your model class. It's only a couple of extra lines per model, but on a large application it adds unnecessary complexity, so don't do it if you don't absolutely have to.

When you're not at liberty to dictate the naming guidelines for your database schema, such as when a separate DBA group controls all database schemas, then you probably don't have a choice. But if you have flexibility, you should really just follow Rails' conventions. They might not be what you're used to, but following them will save you time and unnecessary headaches.

Legacy Naming Schemes

If you are working with legacy schemas, you may be tempted to automatically `set_table_name` everywhere, whether you need it or not. Before you get accustomed to doing that, learn the additional options available that might just be more DRY and make your life easier.

Let's assume you need to turn off table pluralization altogether; you would set the following attribute to false at the bottom of **config/environment.rb**:

```
ActiveRecord::Base.pluralize_table_names = false
```

There are various other useful attributes of `ActiveRecord::Base`, provided for configuring Rails to work with legacy naming schemes.

- `primary_key_prefix_type` Accessor for the prefix type that will be prepended to every primary key column name. If `:table_name` is specified, the ActiveRecord will look for "tableid" instead of "id" as the primary column. If `:table_name_with_underscore` is specified, ActiveRecord will look for "table_id" instead of "id".

- `table_name_prefix` Some departments prefix table names with the name of the database. Set this attribute accordingly to avoid having to include the prefix in all of your model class names.

- `table_name_suffix` Similar to prefix, but adds a common ending to all table names.

- `underscore_table_names` Set to `false` to prevent ActiveRecord from underscoring compound table names.

Defining Attributes

The list of attributes associated with an ActiveRecord model class is not coded explicitly. At runtime, the ActiveRecord model examines the database schema directly from the server. Adding, removing, and changing attributes and their type is done by manipulating the database itself, either directly using SQL commands or GUI tools, but ideally via ActiveRecord migrations.

The practical implication of the ActiveRecord pattern is that you have to define your database table structure and make sure it actually exists in the database prior to working with your persistent models. Some people may have issues with that design philosophy, especially if they're coming from a background in top-down design.

The Rails way is undoubtedly to have model classes that map closely to your database schema. On the other hand, remember you can have models that are simple Ruby classes and do not extend ActiveRecord::Base. Among other things, it is common to use non-ActiveRecord model classes to encapsulate data and logic for the view layer.

Default Attribute Values

Migrations let you define default attribute values by passing a `:default` option to the `column` method, but most of the time you'll want to set default attribute values at the model layer, not the database layer. Default values are part of your domain logic and should be kept together with the rest of the domain logic of your application, in the model layer.

A common example is the case when your model should return the string 'n/a' instead of a nil (or empty) string for an attribute that has not been populated yet. Seems simple enough and it's a good place to start looking into how attributes exist at runtime.

To begin, let's whip up a quick test case describing the desired behavior.

```
class SpecificationTest < Test::Unit::TestCase
  def test_default_string_for_tolerance_should_be_na
    spec = Specification.new
    assert_equal 'n/a', spec.tolerance
  end
end
```

We run that test and it fails, as expected. ActiveRecord doesn't provide us with any class-level methods to define default values for models declaratively. So it seems we'll have to create an explicit attribute accessor that provides a default value.

Normally, attribute accessors are handled magically by ActiveRecord's internals, but in this case we're overriding the magic with an explicit *getter*. All we need to do is to define a method with the same name as the attribute and use Ruby's or operator, which will short-circuit if @tolerance is not nil.

```
class Specification < ActiveRecord::Base
  def tolerance
    @tolerance or 'n/a'
  end
end
```

Now we run the test and it passes. Great. Are we done? Not quite. We should test a case when the real tolerance value should be returned. I'll add another test for a specification with a not-nil tolerance value and also go ahead and make my test method names a little more descriptive.

```
class SpecificationTest < Test::Unit::TestCase
  def test_default_string_for_tolerance_should_return_na_when_nil
    spec = Specification.new
    assert_equal 'n/a', spec.tolerance
  end

  def test_tolerance_value_should_be_returned_when_not_nil
    spec = Specification.new(:tolerance => '0.01mm')
    assert_equal '0.01mm', spec.tolerance
  end
end
```

Uh-oh. The second test fails. Seems our default 'n/a' string is being returned no matter what. That means that @tolerance must not get set. Should we even know that it is getting set or not? It is an implementation detail of ActiveRecord, is it not?

The fact that Rails does not use instance variables like @tolerance to store the model attributes is in fact an implementation detail. But model instances have a couple of methods, write_attribute and read_attribute, conveniently provided by ActiveRecord for the purposes of overriding default accessors, which is exactly what we're trying to do. Let's fix our Specification class.

```
class Specification < ActiveRecord::Base
  def tolerance
    read_attribute(:tolerance) or 'n/a'
  end
end
```

Now the test passes. How about a simple example of using `write_attribute`?

```
class SillyFortuneCookie < ActiveRecord::Base
  def message=(txt)
    write_attribute(:message, txt + ' in bed')
  end
end
```

Alternatively, both of these examples could have been written with the shorter forms of reading and writing attributes, using square brackets.

```
class Specification < ActiveRecord::Base
  def tolerance
    self[:tolerance] or 'n/a'
  end
end


class SillyFortuneCookie < ActiveRecord::Base
  def message=(txt)
    self[:message] =  txt + ' in bed'
  end
end
```

Serialized Attributes

One of ActiveRecord's coolest features (IMO) is the ability to mark a column of type "text" as being *serialized*. Whatever object (more accurately, graph of objects) that you assign to that attribute should be represented in the database as YAML, which is Ruby's native serialization format.

Sebastian Says...

TEXT columns usually have a maximum size of 64K and if your serialized attributes exceeds the size constraints, you'll run into a lot of errors.

On the other hand, if your serialized attributes are that big, you might want to rethink what you're doing—At least move them into a separate table and use a larger column type if your server allows it.

CRUD: Creating, Reading, Updating, Deleting

The four standard operations of a database system combine to form a popular acronym: CRUD.

It sounds somewhat negative, because as a synonym for 'garbage' or 'unwanted accumulation' the word 'crud' in English has a rather bad connotation. However, in Rails circles, use of the word CRUD is benign. In fact, as we'll see in later chapters, designing your app to function primarily as CRUD operations is considered a best practice!

Creating New ActiveRecord Instances

The most straightforward way to create a new instance of an ActiveRecord model is by using a regular Ruby constructor, the class method new. New objects can be instantiated as either empty (by omitting parameters) or pre-set with attributes, but not yet saved. Just pass a hash with key names matching the associated table column names. In both instances, valid attribute keys are determined by the column names of the associated table—hence you can't have attributes that aren't part of the table columns.

Newly constructed, unsaved ActiveRecord objects have a `@new_record` attribute that can be queried using the method `new_record?`:

```
>> c = Client.new
=> #<Client:0x2515584 @new_record=true, @attributes={"name"=>nil,
"code"=>nil}>
>> c.new_record?
=> true
```

ActiveRecord constructors take an optional block, which can be used to do additional initialization. The block is executed after any passed-in attributes are set on the instance:

```
>> c = Client.new do |client|
?> client.name = "Nile River Co."
>> client.code = "NRC"
>> end
=> #<Client:0x24e8764 @new_record=true, @attributes={"name"=>"Nile
River Co.", "code"=>"NRC"}>
```

ActiveRecord has a handy-dandy `create` class method that creates a new instance, persists it to the database, and returns it in one operation:

```
>> c = Client.create(:name => "Nile River, Co.", :code => "NRC")
=> #<Client:0x4229490 @new_record_before_save=true, @new_record=false,
@errors=#<ActiveRecord::Errors:0x42287ac @errors={},
@base=#<Client:0x4229490 ...>>, @attributes={"name"=>"Nile River,
Co.", "updated_at"=>Mon Jun 04 22:24:27 UTC 2007, "code"=>"NRC",
"id"=>1, "created_at"=>Mon Jun 04 22:24:27 UTC 2007}>
```

The `create` method doesn't take a block. It probably should, as it feels like a natural place for a block to initialize the object before saving it, but alas it doesn't.

Reading ActiveRecord Objects

Reading data from the database into ActiveRecord object instances is very easy and convenient. The primary mechanism is the `find` method, which hides SQL SELECT operations from the developer.

find

Finding an existing object by its primary key is very simple, and is probably one of the first things we all learn about Rails when we first pick up the framework. Just invoke `find` with the key of the specific instance you want to retrieve. Remember that if an instance is not found, a `RecordNotFound` exception is raised.

```
>> first_project = Project.find(1)
>> boom_client = Client.find(99)
ActiveRecord::RecordNotFound: Couldn't find Client with ID=99
        from
/vendor/rails/activerecord/lib/active_record/base.rb:1028:in
`find_one'
        from
/vendor/rails/activerecord/lib/active_record/base.rb:1011:in
`find_from_ids'
        from
/vendor/rails/activerecord/lib/active_record/base.rb:416:in `find'
        from (irb):
```

The `find` method also understands a pair of specially designated Ruby symbols, `:first` and `:all`:

```
>> all_clients = Client.find(:all)
=> [#<Client:0x250e004 @attributes={"name"=>"Paper Jam Printers",
"code"=>"PJP", "id"=>"1"}>, #<Client:0x250de88
@attributes={"name"=>"Goodness Steaks", "code"=>"GOOD_STEAKS",
"id"=>"2"}>]

>> first_client = Client.find(:first)
=> #<Client:0x2508244 @attributes={"name"=>"Paper Jam Printers",
"code"=>"PJP", "id"=>"1"}>
```

Somewhat surprisingly to me, there is no `:last` parameter, but you can do a last query pretty easily using the `:order` option:

```
>> all_clients = Client.find(:first, :order => 'id desc')
=> #<Client:0x2508244 @attributes={"name"=>"Paper Jam Printers",
"code"=>"PJP", "id"=>"1"}>
```

By the way, it is entirely common for methods in Ruby to return different types depending on the parameters used, as illustrated in the example. Depending on how `find` is invoked, you will get either a single ActiveRecord object or an array of them.

Finally, the `find` method also understands arrays of keys, and throws a `RecordNotFound` exception if it can't find all of the keys specified:

```
>> first_couple_of_clients = Client.find(1, 2)
[#<Client:0x24d667c @attributes={"name"=>"Paper Jam Printers",
"code"=>"PJP", "id"=>"1"}>, #<Client:0x24d65b4 @attributes={"name"=>
"Goodness Steaks", "code"=>"GOOD_STEAKS", "id"=>"2"}>]

>> first_few_clients = Client.find(1, 2, 3)
ActiveRecord::RecordNotFound: Couldn't find all Clients with IDs
(1,2,3)
  from /vendor/rails/activerecord/lib/active_record/base.rb:1042:in
 `find_some'
  from /vendor/rails/activerecord/lib/active_record/base.rb:1014:in
 `find_from_ids'
  from /vendor/rails/activerecord/lib/active_record/base.rb:416:in
 `find'
  from (irb):9
```

Reading and Writing Attributes

After you have retrieved a model instance from the database, you can access each of its columns in several ways. The easiest (and clearest to read) is simply with dot notation:

```
>> first_client.name
=> "Paper Jam Printers"
>> first_client.code
=> "PJP"
```

The private `read_attribute` method of ActiveRecord, covered briefly in an earlier section, is useful to know about, and comes in handy when you want to override a default attribute accessor. To illustrate, while still in the Rails console, I'll go ahead and *reopen* the `Client` class on the fly and override the `name` accessor to return the value from the database, but *reversed*:

```
>> class Client
>>   def name
>>     read_attribute(:name).reverse
>>   end
>> end
=> nil
>> first_client.name
=> "sretnirP maJ repaP"
```

Hopefully it's not too painfully obvious for me to demonstrate *why* you need `read_attribute` in that scenario:

```
>> class Client
>> def name
>>   self.name.reverse
>> end
>> end
=> nil
>> first_client.name
SystemStackError: stack level too deep
        from (irb):21:in `name'
        from (irb):21:in `name'
        from (irb):24
```

As can be expected by the existence of a `read_attribute` method, there is a `write_attribute` method that lets you change attribute values.

```
project = Project.new
project.write_attribute(:name, "A New Project")
```

Just as with attribute getter methods, you can override the setter methods and provide your own behavior:

```
class Project
  # The description for a project cannot be changed to a blank string
  def description=(new_value)
    self[:description] = new_value unless new_value.blank?
  end
end
```

The preceding example illustrates a way to do basic validation, since it checks to make sure that a value is not blank before allowing assignment. However, as we'll see later in the book, there are better ways to do this.

Hash Notation

Yet another way to access attributes is using the `[attribute_name]` operator, which lets you access the attribute as if it were a regular hash.

```
>> first_client['name']
=> "Paper Jam Printers"
>> first_client[:name]
=> "Paper Jam Printers"
```

String Versus Symbol

Many Rails methods accept symbol and string parameters interchangeably, and that is potentially very confusing. Which is more correct?

The general rule is to use symbols when the string is a name for something, and a string when it's a value. You should probably be using symbols when it comes to keys of options hashes and the like.

> Common sense dictates picking one convention and sticking to it in your application, but most Rails people will use symbols everywhere possible.

The `attributes` Method

There is also an `attributes` method that returns a hash with each attribute and its corresponding value as returned by `read_attribute`. If you use your own custom attribute reader and writer methods, it's important to remember that `attributes` will *not* use custom attribute readers when accessing its values, but `attributes=` (which lets you do mass assignment) *does* invoke custom attribute writers.

```
>> first_client.attributes
=> {"name"=>"Paper Jam Printers", "code"=>"PJP", "id"=>1}
```

Being able to grab a hash of all attributes at once is useful when you want to iterate over all of them or pass them in bulk to another function. Note that the hash returned from `attributes` is *not* a reference to an internal structure of the ActiveRecord object—it is copied, which means that changing its values will have no effect on the object it came from:

```
>> atts = first_client.attributes
=> {"name"=>"Paper Jam Printers", "code"=>"PJP", "id"=>1}
>> atts["name"] = "Def Jam Printers"
=> "Def Jam Printers"
>> first_client.attributes
=> {"name"=>"Paper Jam Printers", "code"=>"PJP", "id"=>1}
```

To make changes to an ActiveRecord object's attributes in bulk, it is possible to pass a hash to the `attributes` writer.

Accessing and Manipulating Attributes Before They Are Typecast

The ActiveRecord connection adapters fetch results as strings and Rails takes care of converting them to other datatypes if necessary, based on the type of the database column. For instance, integer types are cast to instances of Ruby's `Fixnum` class, and so on.

Even if you're working with a new instance of an ActiveRecord object, and have passed in constructor values as strings, they will be typecast to their proper type when you try to access those values as attributes.

Sometimes you want to be able to read (or manipulate) the raw attribute data without having the column-determined typecast run its course first, and that can be done by using the `<attribute>_before_type_cast` accessors that are automatically created in your model.

For example, consider the need to deal with currency strings typed in by your end users. Unless you are encapsulating currency values in a currency class (highly recommended, by the way) you need to deal with those pesky dollar signs and commas. Assuming that our `Timesheet` model had a rate attribute defined as a `:decimal` type, the following code would strip out the extraneous characters before typecasting for the save operation:

```
class Timesheet < ActiveRecord::Base
  before_save :fix_rate

  def fix_rate
    rate_before_type_cast.tr!('$,','')
  end
end
```

Reloading

The `reload` method does a query to the database and resets the attributes of an ActiveRecord object. The optional options argument is passed to find when reloading so you may do, for example, `record.reload(:lock => true)` to reload the same record with an exclusive row lock. (See the section "Database Locking" later in this chapter.)

Dynamic Attribute-Based Finders

Since one of the most common operations in many applications is to simply query based on one or two columns, Rails has an easy and effective way to do these queries without having to resort to the conditions parameter of `find`. They work thanks to the magic of Ruby's `method_missing` callback, which is executed whenever you invoke a method that hasn't been defined yet.

Dynamic finder methods begin with `find_by_` or `find_all_by_`, indicating whether you want a single value or array of results returned. The semantics are similar to calling find with the `:first` versus the `:all` option.

```
>> City.find_by_name("Hackensack")
=> #<City:0x3205244 @attributes={"name" => "Hackensack", "latitude" =>
"40.8858330000", "id" => "15942", "longitude" => "-74.0438890000",
"state" => "NJ" }>

>> City.find_all_by_name("Atlanta").collect(&:state)
=> ["GA", "MI", "TX"]
```

It's also possible to use multiple attributes in the same find by separating them with "and", so you get finders like `Person.find_by_user_name_and_password` or even `Payment.find_by_purchaser_and_state_and_country`.

Dynamic finders have the benefits of being shorter and easier to read and understand. Instead of writing `Person.find(:first, ["user_name = ? AND password = ?", user_name, password])`, try writing `Person.find_by_user_name_and_password(user_name, password)`.

```
>> City.find_by_name_and_state("Atlanta", "TX")
=> #<City:0x31faeac @attributes={ "name" => "Atlanta", "latitude" =>
"33.1136110000", "id" => "25269", "longitude" => "-94.1641670000",
"state" => "TX"}>
```

You can even customize dynamic finder calls with options, just like regular finder methods! `Payment.find_all_by_amount` is actually `Payment.find_all_by_amount(amount, options)`. And the full interface to `Person.find_by_user_name` is actually `Person.find_by_user_name(user_name, options)`. So you can call `Payment.find_all_by_amount(50, :order => "created_on")`.

The same dynamic finder style can be used to create the object if it doesn't already exist. This dynamic finder is called with `find_or_create_by_` and will return the object if it already exists and otherwise creates it, then returns it. Use the `find_or_initialize_by_` finder if you want to return a new record without saving it first.

Custom SQL Queries

The `find_by_sql` class method takes a SQL select query and returns an array of ActiveRecord objects based on the results. Here's a barebones example, which you would never actually need to do in a real application:

```
>> Client.find_by_sql("select * from clients")
=> [#<Client:0x4217024 @attributes={"name"=>"Nile River, Co.",
"updated_at"=>"2007-06-04 22:24:27", "code"=>"NRC", "id"=>"1",
"created_at"=>"2007-06-04 22:24:27"}>, #<Client:0x4216ffc
@attributes={"name"=>"Amazon, Co.", "updated_at"=>"2007-06-04
22:26:22",
"code"=>"AMZ", "id"=>"2", "created_at"=>"2007-06-04 22:26:22"}>]
```

I can't stress this enough: You should take care to use `find_by_sql` *only when you really need it!* For one, it reduces database portability—when you use ActiveRecord's normal find operations, Rails takes care of handling differences between the underlying databases for you.

Also, ActiveRecord already has a ton of built-in functionality abstracting SELECT statements—functionality that it would be very unwise to reinvent. There are lots of cases where at first glance it might seem that you might *need* to use `find_by_sql`, but you actually don't. A common case is when doing a LIKE query:

```
>> Client.find_by_sql("select * from clients where code like 'A%'")
=> [#<Client:0x4206b34 @attributes={"name"=>"Amazon, Inc.", ...}>]
```

Turns out that you can easily put that LIKE clause into a conditions option:

```
>> param = "A"
>> Client.find(:all, :conditions => ["code like ?", "#{param}%"])
=> [#<Client:0x41e3594 @attributes={"name"=>"Amazon, Inc...}>] #
Right!
```

Under the covers, Rails *sanitizes*[4] your SQL code, provided that you parameterize your query. ActiveRecord executes your SQL using the `connection.select_all` method, iterating over the resulting array of hashes, and invoking your ActiveRecord's `initialize` method for each row in the result set. What would the last example look like *un-parameterized?*

```
>> param = "A"
```

```
>> Client.find(:all, :conditions => ["code like '#{param}%'"])
=> [#<Client:0x41e3594 @attributes={"name"=>"Amazon, Inc...}>] #
NOOOOO!
```

Notice the missing question mark as a variable placeholder. Always remember that interpolating user-supplied values into a SQL fragment of any type is very unsafe! Just imagine what would happen to your project if a malicious user called that unsafe find with a param like this:

```
"Amazon'; DELETE FROM users;'
```

Sadly, very few people actually understand what SQL injection means. Google can be one of your best friends in this case.

The Query Cache

By default, Rails attempts to optimize performance by turning on a simple *query cache*. It is a hash stored on the current thread, one for every active database connection. (Most Rails processes will have just one.)

Whenever a `find` (or any other type of select operation) happens and the query cache is active, the corresponding result set is stored in a hash with the SQL that was used to query for them as the key. If the same SQL statement is used again in another operation, the cached result set is used to generate a new set of model objects instead of hitting the database again.

You can enable the query cache manually by wrapping operations in a `cache` block, as in the following example:

```
User.cache do
  puts User.find(:first)
  puts User.find(:first)
  puts User.find(:first)
end
```

Check your `development.log` and you should see the following entries:

```
Person Load (0.000821)   SELECT * FROM people LIMIT 1
   CACHE (0.000000)   SELECT * FROM people LIMIT 1
   CACHE (0.000000)   SELECT * FROM people LIMIT 1
```

The database was queried only once. Try a similar experiment in your own console without the `cache` block, and you'll see that three separate `Person Load` events are logged.

Save and delete operations result in the cache being cleared, to prevent propagation of instances with invalid states. If you find it necessary to do so for whatever reason, call the `clear_query_cache` class method to clear out the query cache manually.

> ### The ActiveRecord Context Plugin
>
> Rick Olson extracted a plugin from his popular Lighthouse application that allows you to easily *seed* the query cache with sets of objects that you know you will need. It's a powerful complement to ActiveRecord's built-in caching support.
>
> Learn more about it at http://activereload.net/2007/5/23/spend-less-time-in-the-database-and-more-time-outdoors.

Logging

The log file indicates when data is being read from the query cache instead of the database. Just look for lines starting with CACHE instead of a Model Load.

```
Place Load (0.000420)   SELECT * FROM places WHERE (places.`id` =
15749)
CACHE (0.000000)   SELECT * FROM places WHERE (places.`id` = 15749)
CACHE (0.000000)   SELECT * FROM places WHERE (places.`id` = 15749)
```

Default Query Caching in Controllers

For performance reasons, ActiveRecord's query cache is turned on by default for the processing of controller actions. The module `SqlCache`, defined in **caching.rb** of ActionController, is mixed into `ActionController::Base` and wraps the `perform_action` method using `alias_method_chain`:

```
module SqlCache
  def self.included(base) #:nodoc:
    base.alias_method_chain :perform_action, :caching
  end
```

```
def perform_action_with_caching
  ActiveRecord::Base.cache do
    perform_action_without_caching
  end
end
end
```

Limitations

The ActiveRecord query cache was purposely kept very simple. Since it literally keys cached model instances on the SQL that was used to pull them out of the database, it can't connect multiple find invocations that are phrased differently but have the same semantic meaning and results.

For example, "select foo from bar where id = 1" and "select foo from bar where id = 1 limit 1" are considered different queries and will result in two distinct cache entries. The **active_record_context** plugin[5] by Rick Olson is an example of a query cache implementation that is a little bit smarter about identity, since it keys cached results on primary keys rather than SQL statements.

Updating

The simplest way to manipulate attribute values is simply to treat your ActiveRecord object as a plain old Ruby object, meaning via direct assignment using myprop=(some_value)

There are a number of other different ways to update ActiveRecord objects, as illustrated in this section. First, let's look at how to use the update class method of ActiveRecord::Base

```
class ProjectController < ApplicationController
  def update
    Project.update(params[:id], params[:project])
    redirect_to :action=>'settings', :id => project.id
  end

  def mass_update
    Project.update(params[:projects].keys, params[:projects].values)
    redirect_to :action=>'index'
  end
```

```
end
```

The first form of update takes a single numeric id and a hash of attribute values, while the second form takes a list of ids and a list of values and is useful in scenarios where a form submission from a web page with multiple updateable rows is being processed.

The update class method does invoke validation first and will not save a record that fails validation. However, it returns the object whether or not the validation passes. That means that if you want to know whether or not the validation passed, you need to follow up the call to update with a call to valid?

```
class ProjectController < ApplicationController
  def update
    @project = Project.update(params[:id], params[:project])
    if @project.valid? # uh-oh, do we want to run validate again?
      redirect_to :action=>'settings', :id => project.id
    else
      render :action => 'edit'
    end
  end
end
```

A problem is that now we are calling valid? twice, since the update call also called it. Perhaps a better option is to use the update_attributes instance method:

```
class ProjectController < ApplicationController
  def update
    @project = Project.find(params[:id]
    if @project.update_attributes(params[:project])
      redirect_to :action=>'settings', :id => project.id
    else
      render :action => 'edit'
    end
  end
end
```

And of course, if you've done some basic Rails programming, you'll recognize that idiom since it is used in the generated scaffolding code. The update_attributes method takes a hash of attribute values, and returns true or false depending on whether the save was successful or not, which is dependent on validation passing.

Updating by Condition

ActiveRecord has another class method useful for updating multiple records at once: `update_all`. It maps closely to the way that you would think of using a SQL update..where statement. The `update_all` method takes two parameters, the set part of the SQL statement and the conditions, expressed as part of a where clause. The method returns the number of records updated[5].

I think this is one of those methods that is generally more useful in a scripting context than in a controller method, but you might feel differently. Here is a quick example of how I would reassign all the Rails projects in the system to a new project manager.

```
Project.update_all("manager = 'Ron Campbell'", "technology = 'Rails'")
```

Updating a Particular Instance

The most basic way to update an ActiveRecord object is to manipulate its attributes directly and then call `save`. It's worth noting that `save` will insert a record in the database if necessary *or* update an existing record with the same primary key.

```
project = Project.find(1)
project.manager = 'Brett M.'
assert_equal true, project.save
```

The `save` method will return true if it was successful or false if it failed for any reason. There is another method, `save!`, that will use exceptions instead. Which one to use depends on whether you plan to deal with errors right away or delegate the problem to another method further up the chain.

It's mostly a matter of style, although the non-bang save and update methods that return a boolean value are often used in controller actions, as the clause for an if condition:

```
class StoryController < ApplicationController

  def points
    @story = Story.find(params[:id])
    if @story.update_attribute(:points, params[:value])
      render :text => "#{@story.name} updated"
    else
      render :text => "Error updating story points"
    end
  end
end
```

Updating Specific Attributes

The instance methods `update_attribute` and `update_attributes` take one key/value pair or hash of attributes, respectively, to be updated on your model and saved to the database in one operation.

The `update_attribute` method updates a single attribute and saves the record. Updates made with this method *are not subjected to validation checks!* In other words, this method allows you to persist an ActiveRecord model *to the database* even if the full object isn't valid. According to the Rails core team that behavior is by design. Internally, this method does exactly the same as `model.attribute = some_value` and then `model.save(false)`.

On the other hand, `update_attributes` *is subject to validation checks* and is often used on update actions and passed the params hash containing updated values.

> **Courtenay Says.....**
>
> If you have associations on a model, ActiveRecord automatically creates convenience methods for mass assignment. In other words, a `Project` model that `has_many` `:users` will expose a `user_ids` attribute writer, which gets used by its `update_attributes` method.
>
> This is an advantage if you're updating associations with checkboxes, because you just name the checkboxes `project[user_ids][]` and Rails will handle the magic.
>
> In some cases, allowing the user to set associations this way would be a security risk. You definitely want to consider using `attr_accessible` to prevent mass-assignment whenever there's a possibility that your application will get abused by malicious users.

Convenience Updaters

Rails provides a number of convenience update methods in the form of `increment`, `decrement`, and `toggle`, which do exactly what their names suggest with numeric and boolean attributes. Each has a bang variant (such as `toggle!`) that additionally invokes save after modifying the attribute.

Controlling Access to Attributes

Constructors and update methods that take hashes to do mass assignment of attribute values are susceptible to misuse by hackers when they are used in conjunction with parameter hashes available in a controller method.

When you have attributes in your ActiveRecord class that you want to protect from inadvertent or mass assignment, use one of the following two class methods to control access to your attributes:

The `attr_accessible` method takes a list of attributes that will be accessible for mass assignment. This is the more conservative choice for mass-assignment protection.

If you'd rather start from an all-open default and restrict attributes as needed, then use `attr_protected`. Attributes passed to this method will be protected from mass-assignment. Their assignment will simply be ignored. You will need to use direct assignment methods to assign values to those attributes, as illustrated in the following code example:

```
class Customer < ActiveRecord::Base
  attr_protected :credit_rating
end

customer = Customer.new(:name => "Abe", :credit_rating => "Excellent")
customer.credit_rating # => nil

customer.attributes = { "credit_rating" => "Excellent" }
customer.credit_rating # => nil

# and now, the allowed way to set a credit_rating
customer.credit_rating = "Average"
customer.credit_rating # => "Average"
```

Deleting and Destroying

Finally, if you want to remove a record from your database, you have two choices. If you already have a model instance, you can destroy it:

```
>> bad_timesheet = Timesheet.find(1)

>> bad_timesheet.destroy
```

```
=> #<Timesheet:0x2481d70 @attributes={"updated_at"=>"2006-11-21
05:40:27", "id"=>"1", "user_id"=>"1", "submitted"=>nil, "created_at"=>
"2006-11-21 05:40:27"}>
```

The `destroy` method will both remove it from the database and freeze it (make it read-only) so you won't be able to save it again:

```
>> bad_timesheet.save
TypeError: can't modify frozen hash
        from activerecord/lib/active_record/base.rb:1965:in `[]='
```

Alternatively, you can call `destroy` and `delete` as class methods, passing the id(s) to delete. Both variants accept a single parameter or array of ids:

```
Timesheet.delete(1)
Timesheet.destroy([2, 3])
```

The naming might seem inconsistent, but it isn't. The `delete` method uses SQL directly and does not load any instances (hence it is faster). The `destroy` method does load the instance of the ActiveRecord object and then calls `destroy` on it as an instance method. The semantic differences are subtle, but come into play when you have assigned `before_destroy` callbacks or have *dependent* associations—child objects that should be deleted automatically along with their parent object.

Database Locking

Locking is a term for techniques that prevent concurrent users of an application from overwriting each other's work. ActiveRecord doesn't normally use any type of database locking when loading rows of model data from the database. If a given Rails application will only ever have one user updating data at the same time, then you don't have to worry about locking.

When more than one user may be accessing and updating the same data simultaneously, then it is vitally important for you as the developer to think about *concurrency*. Ask yourself, what types of *collisions* or *race conditions* could happen if two users were to try to update a given model at the same time?

There are a number of approaches to dealing with concurrency in database-backed applications, two of which are natively supported by ActiveRecord: *optimistic* and *pessimistic* locking. Other approaches exist, such as locking entire database tables.

Every approach has strengths and weaknesses, so it is likely that a given application will use a combination of approaches for maximum reliability.

Optimistic Locking

Optimistic locking describes the strategy of detecting and resolving collisions if they occur, and is commonly recommended in multi-user situations where collisions should be infrequent. Database records are never actually locked in optimistic locking, making it a bit of a misnomer.

Optimistic locking is a fairly common strategy, because so many applications are designed such that a particular user will mostly be updating with data that conceptually *belongs* to him and not other users, making it rare that two users would compete for updating the same record. The idea behind optimistic locking is that since collisions should occur infrequently, we'll simply deal with them only if they happen.

If you control your database schema, optimistic locking is really simple to implement. Just add an integer column named **lock_version** to a given table, with a default value of zero.

```
class AddLockVersionToTimesheets < ActiveRecord::Migration

  def self.up
    add_column :timesheets, :lock_version, :integer, :default => 0
  end

  def self.down
    remove_column :timesheets, :lock_version
  end

end
```

Simply adding that `lock_version` column changes ActiveRecord's behavior. Now if the same record is loaded as two different model instances and saved differently, the first instance will *win* the update, and the second one will cause an `ActiveRecord::StaleObjectError` to be raised.

We can illustrate optimistic locking behavior with a simple unit test:

```
class TimesheetTest < Test::Unit::TestCase

  fixtures :timesheets, :users
```

```
def test_optimistic_locking_behavior
  first_instance = Timesheet.find(1)
  second_instance = Timesheet.find(1)

  first_instance.approver = users(:approver)
  second_instance.approver = users(:approver2)

  assert first_instance.save, "First instance save succeeded"

  assert_raises ActiveRecord::StaleObjectError do
    second_instance.save
  end
end

end
```

The test passes, because calling save on the second instance raises the expected `ActiveRecord::StaleObjectError` exception. Note that the save method (without the bang) returns false and does not raise exceptions if the save fails *due to validation*, but other problems such as locking in this case, can indeed cause it to raise exceptions.

To use a database column named something other than **lock_version** change the setting using `set_locking_column`. To make the change globally, add the following line to **environment.rb:**

```
ActiveRecord::Base.set_locking_column 'alternate_lock_version'
```

Like other ActiveRecord settings, you can also change it on a per-model basis with a declaration in your model class:

```
class Timesheet < ActiveRecord::Base
  set_locking_column 'alternate_lock_version'
end
```

Handling `StaleObjectError`

Now of course, after adding optimistic locking, you don't want to just leave it at that, or the end user who is on the losing end of the collision would simply see an application error screen. You should try to handle the `StaleObjectError` as gracefully as possible.

Depending on the criticality of the data being updated, you might want to spend a lot of time crafting a user-friendly solution that somehow preserves the changes that the loser was trying to make. At minimum, if the data for the update is easily re-creatable, let the user know why their update failed with controller code that looks something like the following:

```
def update
  begin
    @timesheet = Timesheet.find(params[:id])
    @timesheet.update_attributes(params[:timesheet])
    # redirect somewhere
  rescue ActiveRecord::StaleObjectError
    flash[:error] = "Timesheet was modified while you were editing
it."
    redirect_to :action => 'edit', :id => @timesheet
  end
end
```

There are some advantages to optimistic locking. It doesn't require any special feature in the database, and it is fairly easy to implement. As you saw in the example, very little code is required to handle the `StaleObjectError`.

The disadvantages to optimistic locking are mainly that update operations are a bit slower because the lock version must be checked, and there is the potential for a bad user experience, since they don't find out about the failure until *after* they've submitted potentially painful-to-lose data.

Pessimistic Locking

Pessimistic locking requires special database support (built into the major databases) and locks down specific database rows during an update operation. It prevents another user from reading data that is about to be updated, in order to prevent them from working with stale data.

Pessimistic locking is a fairly new addition to Rails, and works in conjunction with transactions as in the following example:

```
Timesheet.transaction do
  t = Timesheet.find(1, :lock=> true)
  t.approved = true
  t.save!
end
```

It's also possible to call `lock!` on an existing model instance, which simply calls `reload(:lock => true)` under the covers. You wouldn't want to do that on an instance with attribute changes since it would cause them to be discarded by the reload.

Pessimistic locking takes place at the database level. The SELECT statement generated by ActiveRecord will have a FOR UPDATE (or similar) clause added to it, causing all other connections to be blocked from access to the rows returned by the select statement. The lock is released once the transaction is committed. There are theoretically situations (Rails process goes boom mid-transaction?!) where the lock would not be released until the connection is terminated or times out.

Considerations

Web applications scale best with optimistic locking, which as we've discussed doesn't really use any locking at all. However, you have to add application logic to handle failure cases. Pessimistic locking is a bit easier to implement, but can lead to situations where one Rails process is waiting on another to release a database lock, that is, waiting and *not serving any other incoming requests*. Remember that Rails processes are single-threaded.

In my opinion, pessimistic locking should not be super dangerous as it is on other platforms, since in Rails we don't ever persist database transactions across more than a single HTTP request. In fact, I'm pretty sure it would be impossible to do that given the shared-nothing architecture.

A situation to be wary of would be one where you have many users competing for access to a particular record that takes a long time to update. For best results, keep your pessimistic-locking transactions small and make sure that they execute quickly.

Advanced Finding

In our first review of ActiveRecord's `find` method, we didn't look at the wealth of options available in addition to finding by primary key and the `:first` and `:all` keyword parameters.

Conditions

It's very common to need to filter the result set of a find operation (just a SQL SELECT under the covers) by adding conditions (to the WHERE clause).

ActiveRecord gives you a number of ways to do just that in the options hash optionally passed to the `find` method.

Conditions are specified in the options hash as `:conditions` and can be specified as a string, array, or hash representing the WHERE-part of a SQL statement. The array form should be used when the input data is coming from the outside world, a web form for instance, and should be *sanitized* prior to being sent to the database. Insecure, outside data is called *tainted*.

The simple string form can be used for statements that don't involve tainted data. Finally, the hash form works much like the array form, except only equality is possible. If all you need is equality, versus, say LIKE criteria, I advise you to use the hash notation, since it's safe and arguably the most readable of the bunch.

The Rails API docs examples do a pretty good job illustrating usage of the `:conditions` option:

```
class User < ActiveRecord::Base
  def self.authenticate_unsafely(login, password)
    find(:first,
         :conditions => "login='#{login}' AND password='#{password}'")
  end

  def self.authenticate_safely(login, password)
    find(:first,
         :conditions => ["login= ? AND password= ?", login, password])
  end

  def self.authenticate_safely_simply(login, password)
    find(:first,
         :conditions => {:login => login, :password => password})
  end
end
```

The `authenticate_unsafely` method inserts the parameters directly into the query and is thus susceptible to *SQL-injection attacks* if the user_name and password parameters come directly from a HTTP request. A malicious end user could supply his own evil SQL query inside the string that was intended to just be a login or password.

The `authenticate_safely` and `authenticate_safely_simply` methodsboth will *sanitize* the user_name and password before inserting them in the query, which will ensure that an attacker can't escape the query and fake the login (or worse).

When using multiple parameters in the conditions, it can easily become hard to read exactly what the fourth or fifth question mark is supposed to represent. In those cases, you can resort to named bind variables instead. That's done by replacing the question marks with symbols and supplying a hash with values for the matching symbol keys.

Again, the Rails API docs give us a pretty good example (modified for brevity):

```
Company.find(:first, [
    " name = :name AND division = :div AND created_at > :date",
    {:name => "37signals", :div => "First", :date => '2005-01-01' }
])
```

During a quick discussion on IRC about this final form, Robby Russell gave me the following clever snippet:

```
:conditions => ['subject LIKE :foo OR body LIKE :foo', {:foo =>
'woah'}]
```

In other words, when you're using named placeholders (versus question mark characters) you can use the same bind variable more than once. Cool!

Simple hash conditions like this are very common and useful:

```
:conditions => {:login => login, :password => password})
```

They will only generate conditions based on equality with SQL's AND operator. If you want something other than AND, you'll have to use one of the other forms available.

Boolean Conditions

It's particularly important to take care in specifying conditions that include boolean values. Databases have various different ways of representing boolean values in columns. Some have native boolean datatypes, and others use a single character, often '1' and '0' or 'T' and 'F' (or even 'Y' and 'N').

Rails will transparently handle the data conversion issues for you if you use arrayed or hash conditions and use a Ruby boolean value as your parameter:

```
Timesheet.find(:all, :conditions => ['submitted=?', true])
```

Ordering of Find Results

The :order option takes a fragment of SQL specifying the ordering of columns:

```
Timesheet.find(:all, :order => 'created_at desc')
```

The SQL spec defaults to ascending order if the ascending/descending option is omitted.

> **Wilson Says.....**
> The SQL spec doesn't prescribe any particular ordering if no 'order by' clause is specified in the query. That seems to trip people up, since the common belief is that 'ORDER BY id AS' is the default.

Random Ordering

The value of the :order option is not validated by Rails, which means you can pass any code that is understood by the underlying database, not just column/direction tuples. An example of why that is useful is when wanting to fetch a random record:

```
# MySQL
Timesheet.find(:first, :order => 'RAND()')

# Postgres
Timesheet.find(:first, :order => 'RANDOM()')

# Microsoft SQL Server
Timesheet.find(:first, :order => 'NEWID()')

# Oracle
Timesheet.find(:first, :order => 'dbms_random.value')
```

Remember that ordering large datasets randomly is known to perform terribly on most databases, particularly MySQL.

Limit and Offset

The :limit parameter takes an integer value establishing a limit on the number of rows to return from the query. The :offset parameter specifies the offset from where the rows should be fetched in the result set and is 1-indexed. Together these options are used for paging results.

For example, a find for the second page of 10 results in a list of timesheets is:

```
Timesheet.find(:all, :limit => 10, :offset => 11)
```

Depending on the particulars of your application's data model, it may make sense to always put *some* limit on the maximum amount of ActiveRecord objects fetched in any one specific query. Letting the user trigger unbounded queries pulling thousands of ActiveRecord objects into Rails at one time is a recipe for disaster.

Select Option

By default, the `:select` option is '*' as in SELECT * FROM, but it can be changed if, for example, you want to do a join, but not include the joined columns. Or you might want to include calculated columns in the result set:

```
>> b = BillableWeek.find(:first, :select => "monday_hours +
   tuesday_hours + wednesday_hours as three_day_total")
=> #<BillableWeek:0x2345fd8 @attributes={"three_day_total"=>"24"}>
```

When using `:select`, as in the preceding example, keep in mind that columns not specified in the query, whether by * or explicitly, *will not be populated in the resulting objects!* So, for instance, continuing the preceding example, trying to access monday_hours on b has unexpected results:

```
>> b.monday_hours
NoMethodError: undefined method `monday_hours' for
 #<BillableWeek:0x2336f74 @attributes={"three_day_total"=>"24"}>
   from activerecord/lib/active_record/base.rb:1850:in
`method_missing'
     from (irb):38
```

To get the object's normal columns *plus* the calculated column, add a *, to the `:select` parameter:

```
:select => '*, monday_hours + tuesday_hours + wednesday_hours as
three_day_total'
```

From Option

The :from option specifies the table name portion of the generated SQL statement. You can provide a custom value if you need to include extra tables for joins, or reference a database view.

Here's an example of usage from an application that features tagging:

```
def find_tagged_with(list)
  find(:all,
       :select => "#{table_name}.*",
       :from => "#{table_name}, tags, taggings",
       :conditions =>
  ["#{table_name}.#{primary_key}=taggings.taggable_id
         and taggings.taggable_type = ?
         and taggings.tag_id = tags.id and tags.name IN (?)",
         name, Tag.parse(list)])
  end
```

If you're wondering why table_name is used instead of a an explicit value, it's because this code is mixed into a target class using Ruby modules. That subject is covered in Chapter 9, "Advanced ActiveRecord."

Group By Option

An attribute name by which the result should be grouped. Uses the GROUP BY SQL-clause. Generally you'll want to combine :group with the :select option, since valid SQL requires that all selected columns in a grouped SELECT be either aggregate functions or columns.

```
>> users = Account.find(:all,
                          :select => 'name, SUM(cash) as money',
                          :group => 'name')
=> [#<User:0x26a744 @attributes={"name"=>"Joe", "money"=>"3500"}>,
    #<User:0xaf33aa @attributes={"name"=>"Jane", "money"=>"9245"}>]
```

Keep in mind that those extra columns you bring back are strings—ActiveRecord doesn't try to typecast them. You'll have to use to_i and to_f to explicitly convert to numeric types.

```
>> users.first.money > 1_000_000
ArgumentError: comparison of String with Fixnum failed
  from (irb):8:in '>'
```

Locking Option

Specifying the :lock => true option on a find operation, *within the scope of a transaction*, establishes an exclusive lock on the rows selected. This option is covered in detail earlier in this chapter, in the section "Database Locking".

Joining and Including Associations

The :joins option can be useful when you're performing GROUP BY and aggregating data from other tables, but you *don't* want to load the associated objects.

```
Buyer.find(:all,
           :select => 'buyers.id, count(carts.id) as cart_count',
           :joins  => 'left join carts on carts.buyer_id=buyers.id',
           :group  => 'buyers.id')
```

However, the most common usages of the :joins and :include options are to allow you to *eager-fetch* additional objects in a single SELECT statement. We cover the subject in Chapter 7.

Read Only

Specifying the :readonly => true option marks returned objects as read-only. You can change their attributes, you just can't save them back to the database.

```
>> c = Comment.find(:first, :readonly => true)
=> #<Comment id: 1, body: "Hey beeyotch!">
>> c.body = "Keep it clean!"
=> "Keep it clean!"
>> c.save
ActiveRecord::ReadOnlyRecord: ActiveRecord::ReadOnlyRecord
        from /vendor/rails/activerecord/lib/active_record/base.rb:1958
```

Connections to Multiple Databases in Different Models

Connections are usually created through ActiveRecord::Base.establish_connection and retrieved by ActiveRecord::Base.connection. All classes inheriting from ActiveRecord::Base will use this connection. What if you want some of your models to use a different connection? ActiveRecord allows you to add class-specific connections.

For example, let's say you have a subclass of `ActiveRecord::Base` named `LegacyProject` with data residing in a database apart from the one used by the rest of your Rails application. Begin by adding details for the additional database under its own key in `database.yml`. Then call `LegacyProject.establish_connection` to make LegacyProject *and all its subclasses* use the alternate connection instead.

Incidentally, to make this example work, you must specify `self.abstract_class = true` in the class context. Otherwise, Rails considers the subclasses of `LegacyProject` to be using single-table inheritance (STI), which we discuss at length in Chapter 9.

```
class LegacyProject < ActiveRecord::Base
  establish_connection :legacy_database
  self.abstract_class = true
  ...
end
```

The `establish_connection` method takes a string (or symbol) key pointing to a configuration already defined in `database.yml`. Alternatively, you can pass it a literal hash of options, although it seems kind of messy to put this sort of configuration data right into your model file instead of `database.yml`

```
class TempProject < ActiveRecord::Base
  establish_connection(:adapter => 'sqlite3', :database =>
':memory:')
  ...
end
```

Rails keeps database connections in a connection pool inside the `ActiveRecord::Base` class instance. The connection pool is simply a `Hash` object indexed by ActiveRecord class. During execution, when a connection is needed, the `retrieve_connection` method walks up the class-hierarchy until a matching connection is found.

Using the Database Connection Directly

It is possible to use ActiveRecord's underlying database connections directly, and sometimes it is useful to do so from custom scripts and for one-off or ad-hoc testing. Access the connection using the `connection` attribute of any ActiveRecord class. If all your models use the same connection, then use the connection attribute of `ActiveRecord::Base`.

The most basic operation that can be done with a connection is simply an `execute`, from the `DatabaseStatements` module (detailed in the following section). For example, Listing 6.2 shows a method that executes a SQL file statement by statement.

Listing 6.2   Execute a SQL File Line by Line Using ActiveRecord's Connection

```
def execute_sql_file(path)
  File.read(path).split(';').each do |sql|
    begin
      ActiveRecord::Base.connection.execute(#{sql}\n") unless
sql.blank?
    rescue ActiveRecord::StatementInvalid
      $stderr.puts "warning: #{$!}"
    end
  end
end
```

The `DatabaseStatements` Module

The `ActiveRecord::ConnectionAdapters::DatabaseStatements` module mixes a number of useful methods into the connection object that make it possible to work with the database directly instead of using ActiveRecord models. I've purposely left out some of the methods of this module (such as `add_limit!` and `add_lock`) because they are used internally by Rails to construct SQL statements dynamically and I don't think they're of much use to application developers.

```
begin_db_transaction()
```

Begins a database transaction manually (and turns off ActiveRecord's default autocommitting behavior).

`commit_db_transaction()`

Commits the transaction (and turns on ActiveRecord's default autocommitting behavior again).

`delete(sql_statement)`

Executes a SQL DELETE statement provided and returns the number of rows affected.

`execute(sql_statement)`

Executes the SQL statement provided in the context of this connection. This method is abstract in the `DatabaseStatements` module and is overridden by specific database adapter implementations. As such, the return type is a result set object corresponding to the adapter in use.

`insert(sql_statement)`

Executes an SQL INSERT statement and returns the last autogenerated ID from the affected table.

`reset_sequence!(table, column, sequence = nil)`

Used in Oracle and Postgres; updates the named sequence to the maximum value of the specified table's column.

`rollback_db_transaction()`

Rolls back the currently active transaction (and turns on auto-committing). Called automatically when a transaction block raises an exception or returns false.

`select_all(sql_statement)`

Returns an *array* of record hashes with the column names as keys and column values as values.

```
ActiveRecord::Base.connection.select_all("select name from businesses
order by rand() limit 5")
=> [{"name"=>"Hopkins Painting"}, {"name"=>"Whelan & Scherr"},
{"name"=>"American Top Security Svc"}, {"name"=>"Life Style Homes"},
{"name"=>"378 Liquor Wine & Beer"}]
```

```
select_one(sql_statement)
```

Works similarly to `select_all`, but returns only the first row of the result set, as a single Hash with the column names as keys and column values as values. Note that this method does not add a limit clause to your SQL statement automatically, so consider adding one to queries on large datasets.

```
>> ActiveRecord::Base.connection.select_one("select name from
businesses
order by rand() limit 1")
=> {"name"=>"New York New York Salon"}
```

```
select_value(sql_statement)
```

Works just like `select_one`, except that it returns a *single* value: the first column value of the first row of the result set.

```
>> ActiveRecord::Base.connection.select_value("select * from
businesses
order by rand() limit 1")
=> "Cimino's Pizza"
```

```
select_values(sql_statement)
```

Works just like `select_value`, except that it returns an array of the values of the first column in all the rows of the result set.

```
>> ActiveRecord::Base.connection.select_values("select * from
businesses
order by rand() limit 5")
=> ["Ottersberg Christine E Dds", "Bally Total Fitness", "Behboodikah,
Mahnaz Md", "Preferred Personnel Solutions", "Thoroughbred Carpets"]
```

```
update(sql_statement)
```

Executes the update statement provided and returns the number of rows affected. Works exactly like `delete`.

Other Connection Methods

The full list of methods available on `connection`, which returns an instance of the underlying database adapter, is fairly long. Most of the Rails adapter implementations define their own custom versions of these methods, which makes sense, since all databases have slight variations in how they handle SQL and very large variations in how they handle extended commands, such as for fetching metadata.

A peek at **abstract_adapter.rb** shows us the default method implementations:

```
...

  # Returns the human-readable name of the adapter.  Use mixed case -
one
  # can always use downcase if needed.
  def adapter_name
    'Abstract'
  end

  # Does this adapter support migrations?  Backend specific, as the
  # abstract adapter always returns +false+.
  def supports_migrations?
    false
  end

  # Does this adapter support using DISTINCT within COUNT?  This is
+true+
  # for all adapters except sqlite.
  def supports_count_distinct?
    true
  end

...
```

In the following list of method descriptions and code samples, I'm accessing the connection of our sample **time_and_expenses** application in the Rails console, and I've assigned `connection` to a local variable named `conn`, for convenience.

`active?`

Indicates whether the connection is active and ready to perform queries.

```
adapter_name
```

Returns the human-readable name of the adapter, as in the following example:

```
>> conn.adapter_name
=> "SQLite"
```

disconnect! and reconnect!

Closes the active connection or closes and opens a new one in its place, respectively.

```
raw_connection
```

Provides access to the underlying database connection. Useful for when you need to execute a proprietary statement or you're using features of the Ruby database driver that aren't necessarily exposed in ActiveRecord. (In trying to come up with a code sample for this method, I was able to crash the Rails console with ease—there isn't much in the way of error checking for exceptions that you might raise while mucking around with `raw_connection`.)

```
supports_count_distinct?
```

Indicates whether the adapter supports using DISTINCT within COUNT in SQL statements. This is `true` for all adapters except SQLite, which therefore requires a workaround when doing operations such as calculations.

```
supports_migrations?
```

Indicates whether the adapter supports migrations.

```
tables
```

Produces a list of tables in the underlying database schema. It includes tables that aren't usually exposed as ActiveRecord models, such as `schema_info` and `sessions`.

```
>> conn.tables
=> ["schema_info", "users", "timesheets", "expense_reports",
"billable_weeks", "clients", "billing_codes", "sessions"]
```

```
verify!(timeout)
```

Lazily verify this connection, calling `active?` only if it hasn't been called for `timeout` seconds.

Other Configuration Options

In addition to the configuration options used to instruct ActiveRecord on how to handle naming of tables and primary keys, there are a number of other settings that govern miscellaneous functions. Set them in **config/environment.rb.**

`ActiveRecord::Base.colorize_logging`   Tells Rails whether or not to use ANSI codes to colorize the logging statements committed by the ActiveRecord connection adapter. The colors make it much easier to read the logs (except on Windows) and may complicate matters if you use software like syslog. Defaults to `true`. Change to `false` if you view your logs with software that doesn't understand the ANSI color codes.

Here's a snippet of log output with the ANSI codes visible:

```
^[[4;36;1mSQL (0.000000)^[[0m   ^[[0;1mMysql::Error: Unknown table
'expense_reports': DROP TABLE expense_reports^[[0m
  ^[[4;35;1mSQL (0.003266)^[[0m   ^[[0mCREATE TABLE expense_reports
(`id`
int(11) DEFAULT NULL auto_increment PRIMARY KEY, `user_id` int(11))
ENGINE=InnoDB^[[0m
```

> **Wilson Says...**
>
> Almost nobody I meet seems to know how to display colorized logs in a pager. The `-R` option tells `less` to output "raw" control characters to the screen.

`ActiveRecord::Base.default_timezone` Tells Rails whether to use `Time.local` (using `:local`) or `Time.utc` (using `:utc`) when pulling dates and times from the database. Defaults to `:local`

`ActiveRecord::Base.allow_concurrency`   Determines whether or not to create a database connection for each thread, or to use a single shared connection for all threads. Defaults to `false` and given the number of warnings and horror-stories[6] that follow any mention of this option online, it would be prudent to leave it in its default setting. Setting this option to **true** is known to cause excessive use of database connections.

ActiveRecord::Base.generate_read_methods Determines whether to speed up access by generating optimized reader methods to avoid expensive calls to method_missing when accessing attributes by name. Defaults to **true**.

ActiveRecord::Base.schema_format Specifies the format to use when dumping the database schema with certain default rake tasks. Use the **:sql** option to have the schema dumped as potentially database-specific SQL statements. Just beware of incompatibilities if you're trying to use the **:sql** option with different databases for development and testing.

The default option is **:ruby**, which dumps the schema as an `ActiveRecord::Schema` file that can be loaded into any database that supports migrations.

Conclusion

This chapter covered the fundamentals of ActiveRecord, the framework included with Ruby on Rails for creating database-bound model classes. We've learned how ActiveRecord expresses the *convention over configuration* philosophy that is such an important part of the Rails way, and how to make settings manually, which override the conventions in place.

We've also looked at the methods provided by `ActiveRecord::Base`, the parent class of all persistent models in Rails, which include everything you need to do basic CRUD operations: Create, Read, Update, and Delete. Finally, we reviewed how to drill through ActiveRecord to use the database connection whenever you need to do so.

In the following chapter, we continue our coverage of ActiveRecord by learning about how related model objects interact via associations.

References

1. http://jayfields.blogspot.com/2006/12/rails-migrations-with-large-team-part.html

2. If you find it annoying that strings and symbols are used pretty much interchangeably throughout Rails, welcome to the club.

3. A recommended open-source Money class is available at http://dist.leetsoft.com/api/money/.

4. Sanitization prevents SQL injection attacks. For more information about SQL injection and Rails see http://www.rorsecurity.info/2007/05/19/sql-injection/.

5. http://activereload.net/2007/5/23/spend-less-time-in-the-database-and-more-time-outdoors.

6. Microsoft's ADO library doesn't support reporting back the number of affected rows, so `update_all` does not work with the SQLServer adapter.

7. Read http://permalink.gmane.org/gmane.comp.lang.ruby.mongrel.general/245 for Zed Shaw's explanation of the dangers of `allow_concurrency` on the Mongrel mailing list.

CHAPTER 7

ActiveRecord Associations

Any time you can rarefy something, you can create something that embodies a
concept, it gives you leverage to work with it more powerfully. That's exactly
what's going on with has_many :through.
—Josh Susser

Active Record *associations* let you declaratively express relationships between model
classes. The power and readability of the Associations API is an important part of what
makes working with Rails so special.

This chapter covers the different kinds of `ActiveRecord` associations available
while highlighting use cases and available customizations for each of them. We also
take a look at the classes that give us access to relationships themselves.

The Association Hierarchy

Associations typically appear as methods on ActiveRecord model objects. For example, the method `timesheets` might represent the timesheets associated with a given
`user`.

```
>> user.timesheets
```

However, people might get confused about the type of objects that are returned
by association with these methods. This is because they have a way of masquerading
as plain old Ruby objects and arrays (depending on the type of association we're considering). In the snippet, the `timesheet` method may appear to return an array of
project objects.

The console will even confirm our thoughts. Ask any association collection what its return type is and it will tell you that it is an `Array`:

```
>> obie.timesheets.class
=> Array
```

It's actually lying to you, albeit very innocently. Association methods for has_many associations are actually instances of `HasManyAssociation`, shown within its class hierarchy in Figure 7.1.

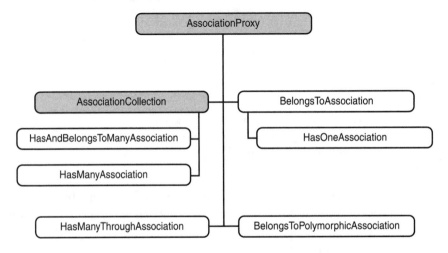

Figure 7.1   The Association proxies in their class hierarchy

The parent class of all associations is `AssociationProxy`. It contains the basic structure and functionality of all assocation proxies. If you look near the top of its source code excerpted in Listing 7.1, you'll notice that it undefines a bunch of methods.

Listing 7.1   Excerpt from lib/active_record/associations/association_proxy.rb

```
instance_methods.each { |m|
  undef_method m unless m =~ /(^__|^nil\?$|^send$|proxy_)/ }
```

As a result, most normal instance methods aren't actually defined on the proxy anymore, but are instead delegated to the target of the proxy via `method_missing`. That means that a call to `timesheets.class` returns the class of the underlying array rather than the proxy. You can prove that `timesheet` is actually a proxy by asking it if it responds to one of `AssociationProxy`'s public methods, such as `proxy_owner`:

```
>> obie.timesheets.respond_to? :proxy_owner
=> true
```

Fortunately, it's not the Ruby way to care about the actual class of an object. What messages an object responds to is a lot more significant. That's why I think it would be a mistake to make your code depend on working with an array instead of an association proxy. If absolutely necessary, you can always call `to_a` to get an actual `Array` object:

```
>> obie.timesheets.to_a # make absolutely sure we're working with an
Array
=> []
```

The parent class of all `has_many` associations is AssociationCollection and most of the methods that it defines work similarly regardless of the options declared for the relationship. Before we get much further into the details of the association proxies, let's delve into the most fundamental type of association that is commonly used in Rails applications: the `has_many` / `belongs_to` pair.

One-to-Many Relationships

In our recurring sample application, an example of a one-to-many relationship is the association between the `User`, `Timesheet`, and `ExpenseReport` classes:

```
class User < ActiveRecord::Base
  has_many :timesheets
  has_many :expense_reports
end
```

Timesheets and expense reports should be linked in the opposite direction as well, so that it is possible to reference the `user` to which a timesheet or expense report belongs.

```
class Timesheet < ActiveRecord::Base
  belongs_to :user
end
```

```
class ExpenseReport < ActiveRecord::Base
  belongs_to :user
end
```

When these relationship declarations are executed, Rails uses some *metaprogram-ming* magic to dynamically add code to your models. In particular, *proxy* collection objects are created that let you manipulate the relationship easily.

To demonstrate, let's play with these relationships in the console. First, I'll create a user.

```
>> obie = User.create :login => 'obie', :password => '1234',
:password_confirmation => '1234', :email => 'obiefernandez@gmail.com'
=> #<User:0x2995278 ...}>
```

Now I'll verify that I have collections for timesheets and expense reports.

```
>> obie.timesheets
ActiveRecord::StatementInvalid:
SQLite3::SQLException: no such column: timesheets.user_id:
SELECT * FROM timesheets WHERE (timesheets.user_id = 1)
from /.../connection_adapters/abstract_adapter.rb:128:in `log'
```

As David might say, "Whoops!" I forgot to add the foreign key columns to the `timesheets` and `expense_reports` tables, so in order to go forward I'll generate a migration for the changes:

```
$ script/generate migration add_user_foreign_keys
      exists  db/migrate
      create  db/migrate/004_add_user_foreign_keys.rb
```

Then I'll open `db/migrate/004_add_user_foreign_keys.rb` and add the missing columns.

```
class AddUserForeignKeys < ActiveRecord::Migration
  def self.up
    add_column :timesheets, :user_id, :integer
    add_column :expense_reports, :user_id, :integer
  end

  def self.down
```

```
      remove_column :timesheets, :user_id
      remove_column :expense_reports, :user_id
   end
end
```

Running `rake db:migrate` applies the changes:

```
$ rake db:migrate
(in /Users/obie/prorails/time_and_expenses)
== AddUserForeignKeys: migrating
================================================
-- add_column(:timesheets, :user_id, :integer)
   -> 0.0253s
-- add_column(:expense_reports, :user_id, :integer)
   -> 0.0101s
== AddUserForeignKeys: migrated (0.0357s)
================================================
```

Now I should be able to add a new blank timesheet to my user and check `timesheets` again to make sure it's there:

```
>> obie = User.find(1)
=> #<User:0x29cc91c ... >
>> obie.timesheets << Timesheet.new
=> [#<Timesheet:0x2147524 @new_record=true, @attributes={}>]
>> obie.timesheets
=> [#<Timesheet:0x2147524 @new_record=true, @attributes={}>]
```

Adding Associated Objects to a Collection

According to the Rails documentation, adding an object to a `has_many` collection automatically saves that object, unless the parent object (the owner of the collection) is not yet stored in the database. Let's make sure that's the case using `ActiveRecord`'s `reload` method, which re-fetches the attributes of an object from the database:

```
>> obie.timesheets.reload
=> [#<Timesheet:0x29b3804 @attributes={"id"=>"1", "user_id"=>"1"}>]
```

There it is. The foreign key, `user_id`, was automatically set by the `<<` method.

The << method takes one or more association objects to add to the collection, and since it flattens its argument list and inserts each record, push and concat behave identically.

In the blank timesheet example, I could have used the create method on the association proxy, and it would have worked essentially the same way:

```
>> obie.timesheets.create
=> #<Timesheet:0x248d378 @new_record=false ... >
```

However, be careful when deciding between << and create!. Even though at first glance << and create do the same thing, there are several very important differences in how they're implemented and you need to be aware of them (see the next subsection "AssociationCollection Methods" for more information).

AssociationCollection Methods

As illustrated in Figure 7.1, AssociationCollection has the following subclasses: HasManyAssociation and HasAndBelongsToManyAssociation. The following methods are inherited by and available to both of these subclasses. (HasManyThroughAssociation defines its own very similar set methods, covered later in the chapter.)

<<(*records) and create(attributes = {})

In Rails 1.2.3 and earlier versions, the first thing that the << method did was to load *the entire contents of the collection* from the database, an operation that could be very expensive! On the other hand, create simply invoked its counterpart on the association's model class, passing along the value of the foreign key, so that the link is established in the database. Thankfully, Rails 2.0 corrects the behavior of << in that it doesn't load the entire collection, making it similar in function to create.

However, this is an area of Rails where you can really hurt yourself if you're not careful. For instance, both methods will add either a single associated object or many, depending on whether you pass them an array or not. However, << is transactional, and create is not.

Yet another difference has to do with association callbacks (covered in this chapter's options section for has_many). The << method triggers the :before_add and :after_add callbacks, but the create method does not.

Finally, the return value behavior of both methods varies wildly. The `create` method returns the new instance created, which is what you'd expect given its counterpart in `ActiveRecord::Base`. The `<<` method returns the association proxy (ever masquerading as an array), which allows chaining and is also natural behavior for a Ruby array.

However, `<<` will return `false` and not itself *if any of the records being added causes the operation to fail.* Therefore you shouldn't really depend on its return value being an array that you can continue operating on in a chained fashion.

clear

Removes all records from this association by clearing the foreign key field (see `delete`). If the association is configured with the `:dependent` option set to `:delete_all`, then `clear` iterates over all the associated objects and invokes `destroy` on each one.

The `clear` method is *transactional.*

delete(*records) and delete_all

The `delete` and `delete_all` methods are used to sever specified associations, or all of them, respectively. Both methods operate *transactionally.*

It's worth noting, for performance reasons, that calling `delete_all` first loads the entire collection of associated objects into memory in order to grab their ids. Then it executes a `SQL UPDATE` that sets foreign keys for all currently associated objects to nil, effectively disassociating them from their parent. Since it loads the entire association into memory, it would be ill-advised to use this method with an extremely large collection of associated objects.

> **NOTE**
> The names of the `delete` and `delete_all` methods can be misleading. By default, they don't delete anything from the database—they only sever associations by clearing the foreign key field of the associated record. This behavior is related to the `:dependent` option, which defaults to `:nullify`. If the association is configured with the `:dependent` option set to `:delete_all` or `:destroy`, then the associated records will actually be deleted from the database.

destroy_all

The `destroy_all` method takes no parameters; it's an all or nothing affair. When called, it begins a transaction and invokes `destroy` on each object in the association, causing them all to be deleted from the database with individual DELETE SQL statements. Again, there are load issues to consider if you plan to use this method with large association collections, since many objects will be loaded into memory at once.

length

Returns the size of the collection by loading it and calling `size` on the array. If you want to use this method to check whether the association collection is empty, use `length.zero?` instead of just `empty?`. It's more efficient.

replace(other_array)

Replaces the collection with `other_array`. Works by deleting objects that exist in the current collection, but not in `other_array` and inserting (using `concat`) objects that don't exist in the current collection, but do exist in `other_array`.

size

If the collection has already been loaded, the `size` method returns its size. Otherwise a SELECT COUNT(*) query is executed to get the size of the associated collection without having to load any objects.

When starting from an unloaded state where it's likely that the collection is not actually empty and you will need to load the collection no matter what, it'll take one less SELECT query if you use `length`.

The `:uniq` setting, which removes duplicates from association collections, comes into play when calculating size—basically it will force all objects to be loaded from the database so that Rails can remove duplicates in Ruby code.

sum(column, *options)

Calculates a summed value in the database using SQL. The first parameter should be a symbol identifying the column to be summed. You have to provide a `:group` option, so that a summation actually takes place.

```
total = person.accounts.sum(:credit_limit, :group => 'accounts.firm_id')
```

Depending on the way your association is structured, you may need to disambiguate the query by prefixing the name of the table to the value you pass to :group.

uniq

Iterates over the target collection and populates a Set with the unique values present. Keep in mind that equality of ActiveRecord objects is determined by identity, meaning that the value of the id attribute is the same for both objects being compared.

> **A Warning About Association Names**
>
> Don't create associations that have the same name as instance methods of ActiveRecord::Base. Since the association adds a method with that name to its model, it will override the inherited method and break things.
>
> For instance, attributes and connection would make really bad choices for association names.

The `belongs_to` Association

The belongs_to class method expresses a relationship from one ActiveRecord object to a single associated object for which it has a foreign key attribute. The trick to remembering whether a class "belongs to" another one is determining where the foreign key column will reside.

Assigning an object to a belongs_to association will set its foreign key attribute to the owner object, but will not save the record to the database automatically, as in the following example:

```
>> timesheet = Timesheet.create
=> #<Timesheet:0x248f18c ... @attributes={"id"=>1409, "user_id"=>nil,
"submitted"=>nil} ...>
>> timesheet.user = obie
=> #<User:0x24f96a4 ...>
>> timesheet.user.login
=> "obie"
>> timesheet.reload
=> #<Timesheet:0x248f18c @billable_weeks=nil, @new_record=false,
@user=nil...>
```

Defining a `belongs_to` relationship on a class establishes an attribute of the same name on instances of that class. As mentioned earlier, the attribute is actually a proxy to the related `ActiveRecord` object and adds capabilities useful for manipulating the relationship.

Reloading the Association

Just invoking the attribute will query the database (if necessary) and return an instance of the related object. The accessor method actually takes a `force_reload` parameter that tells `ActiveRecord` whether to reload the related object, if it happens to have been cached already by a previous access.

In the following capture from my console, I look up a timesheet and take a peek at the `object_id` of its related user object. Notice that the second time I invoke the association via `user`, the `object_id` remains the same. The related object has been cached. However, passing `true` to the accessor reloads the relationship and I get a new instance.

```
>> ts = Timesheet.find :first
=> #<Timesheet:0x3454554 @attributes={"updated_at"=>"2006-11-21
05:44:09", "id"=>"3", "user_id"=>"1", "submitted"=>nil,
"created_at"=>"2006-11-21 05:44:09"}>
>> ts.user.object_id
=> 27421330
>> ts.user.object_id
=> 27421330
>> ts.user(true).object_id
=> 27396270
```

Building and Creating Related Objects via the Association

The `belongs_to` method does some metaprogramming and adds factory methods for creating new instances of the related class and attaching them via the foreign key automatically.

The `build_association` method does not save the new object, but the `create_association` method does. Both methods take an optional hash of attribute parameters with which to initialize the newly instantiated objects. Both are essentially one-line conveniences, which I don't find particularly useful, because it just doesn't usually make sense to create instances in that direction!

To illustrate, I'll simply show the code for building a User from a Timesheet or creating a Client from a BillingCode, neither of which would ever happen in real code because it just doesn't make sense to do so:

```
>> ts = Timesheet.find :first
=> #<Timesheet:0x3437260 @attributes={"updated_at"=>"2006-11-21
05:44:09", "id"=>"3", "user_id"=>"1", "submitted"=>nil, "created_at"
=>"2006-11-21 05:44:09"}>

>> ts.build_user
=> #<User:0x3435578 @attributes={"salt"=>nil, "updated_at"=>nil,
"crypted_password"=>nil, "remember_token_expires_at"=>nil,
"remember_token"=>nil, "login"=>nil, "created_at"=>nil, "email"=>nil},
@new_record=true>

>> bc = BillingCode.find :first
=> #<BillingCode:0x33b65e8 @attributes={"code"=>"TRAVEL", "client_id"
=>nil, "id"=>"1", "description"=>"Travel expenses of all sorts"}>

>> bc.create_client
=> #<Client:0x33a3074 @new_record_before_save=true,
@errors=#<ActiveRecord::Errors:0x339f3e8 @errors={},
@base=#<Client:0x33a3074 ...>>, @attributes={"name"=>nil, "code"=>nil,
"id"=>1}, @new_record=false>
```

You'll find yourself creating instances of belonging objects from the has_many side of the relationship much more often.

belongs_to Options

The following options can be passed in a hash to the belongs_to method.

:class_name

Assume for a moment that we wanted to establish *another* belongs_to relationship from the Timesheet class to User, this time modeling the relationship to the approver of the timesheet. You might start by adding an approver_id column to the timesheets table and an authorized_approver column to the users table:

```
class AddApproverInfo < ActiveRecord::Migration

  def self.up
```

```
    add_column :timesheets, :approver_id, :integer
    add_column :users, :authorized_approver, :boolean
  end

  def self.down
    remove_column :timesheets, :approver_id
    remove_column :users, :authorized_approver
  end

end
```

Then you would add a `belongs_to` that looks like the following:

```
class Timesheet < ActiveRecord::Base
  belongs_to :approver
  ...
```

The thing is that Rails can't figure out what class you're trying to connect to with just the information provided, because you've (legitimately) acted against the Rails convention of naming a relationship according to the related class. It's time for a `:class_name` parameter.

```
class Timesheet < ActiveRecord::Base
  belongs_to :approver, :class_name => 'User'
  ...
```

:conditions

What about adding conditions to the `belongs_to` association? Rails allows us to add conditions to a relationship that must be satisfied in order for it to be valid. The `:conditions` option allows you to do just that, with the same syntax that is used when you add conditions to a `find` invocation.

In the last migration, I added an `authorized_approver` column to the `users` table and we'll make use of it here:

```
class Timesheet < ActiveRecord::Base
  belongs_to :approver,
             :class_name => 'User',
             :conditions => ['authorized_approver = ?', true]
  ...
end
```

Now in order for the assignment of a user to the approver field to work, that user must be authorized. I'll go ahead and add a test that both indicates the intention of my code and shows it in action.

First I need to ensure that my users fixture (users.yml) makes an authorized approver available to my test methods. For good measure, I go ahead and add a non-authorized user too. The following markup appears at the bottom of test/fixtures/users.yml:

```
approver:
  id: 4
  login: "manager"
  authorized_approver: true
joe:
  id: 5
  login: "joe"
  authorized_approver: false
```

Then I turn my attention to test/unit/timesheet_test.rb, where I add a test to make sure that my application code works and is correct:

```
require File.dirname(__FILE__) + '/../test_helper'

class TimesheetTest < Test::Unit::TestCase

  fixtures :users

  def test_only_authorized_user_may_be_associated_as_approver
    sheet = Timesheet.create
    sheet.approver = users(:approver)
    assert_not_nil sheet.approver, "approver assignment failed"
  end

end
```

It's a good start, but I also want to make sure something happens to prevent the system from assigning a nonauthorized user to the approver field, so I add another test:

```
def test_non_authorized_user_cannot_be_associated_as_approver
  sheet = Timesheet.create
  sheet.approver = users(:joe)
```

```
   assert sheet.approver.nil?, "approver assignment should have
failed"
   end
```

I have my suspicions about the validity of that test, though, and as I half-expected, it doesn't really work the way I want it to work:

```
1) Failure:
test_non_authorized_user_cannot_be_associated_as_approver(TimesheetTest
)
[./test/unit/timesheet_test.rb:16]:
approver assignment should have failed.
<false> is not true.
```

The problem is that `ActiveRecord` (for better or worse, probably worse) allows me to make the invalid assignment. The `:conditions` option only applies during the query to get the association back from the database. I'll have some more work ahead of me to achieve the desired behavior, but I'll go ahead and prove out Rails' actual behavior by fixing my tests:

```
def test_only_authorized_user_may_be_associated_as_approver
  sheet = Timesheet.create
  sheet.approver = users(:approver)
  assert sheet.save
  assert_not_nil sheet.approver(true), "approver assignment failed"
end

def test_non_authorized_user_cannot_be_associated_as_approver
  sheet = Timesheet.create
  sheet.approver = users(:joe)
  assert sheet.save
  assert sheet.approver(true).nil?, "approver assignment should fail"
end
```

Those two tests do pass. I went ahead and made sure to save the `sheet`, since just assigning a value to it will not save the record. Then I took advantage of the `force_reload` parameter to make Rails reload `approver` from the database, and not just simply give me the same instance I originally assigned to it.

The lesson to learn is that `:conditions` on relationships never affect the assignment of associated objects, only how they're read back from the database. To enforce the rule that a timesheet approver must be authorized, you'd need to add a before_save callback to the Timesheet class itself. Callbacks are covered in detail at the beginning of Chapter 9, "Advanced ActiveRecord," and since I've gotten us a little bit off on a tangent, we'll go back to the list of options available for the belongs_to association.

:foreign_key

Specifies the name of the foreign key column that should be used to find the associated object. Rails will normally infer this setting from the name of the association, by adding _id . You can override the inferred foreign key name with this option if necessary.

```
# without the explicit option, Rails would guess administrator_id
belongs_to :administrator, :foreign_key => 'admin_user_id'
```

:counter_cache

Use this option to make Rails automatically update a counter field on the associated object with the number of belonging objects. The option value can be true, in which case the *pluralized* name of the belonging class plus _count is used, or you can supply your own column name to be used:

```
:counter_cache => true
:counter_cache => 'number_of_children'
```

If a significant percentage of your association collections will be empty at any given moment, you can optimize performance at the cost of some extra database storage by using counter caches liberally. The reason is that when the counter cache attribute is at zero, Rails *won't even try* to query the database for the associated records!

> **NOTE**
> The value of the counter cache column *must be set to zero by default* in the database! Otherwise the counter caching *won't work at all.* It's because the way that Rails implements the counter caching behavior is by adding a simple callback that goes directly to the database with an UPDATE command and increments the value of the counter.

If you're not careful, and neglect to set a default value of 0 for the counter cache column on the database, or misspell the column name, the counter cache will still seem to work! There is a magic method on all classes with `has_many` associations called *collection*_count, just like the counter cache. It will return a correct count value if you don't have a counter cache option set or the counter cache column value is null!

:include

Takes a list of second-order association names that should be eager-loaded when this object is loaded. A SELECT statement with the necessary LEFT OUTER JOINS will be constructed on the fly so that all the data needed to construct a whole object graph is queried in one database request.

With judicious use of `:include` and careful benchmarking, you can sometimes improve the performance of your application dramatically, mostly by eliminating N+1 queries. On the other hand, since doing huge multijoin queries and instantiating large object trees can also get very costly, certain usages of `:include` can actually make your application perform much more slowly. As they say, *your mileage may vary.*

Wilson Says...

If `:include` speeds your app up, it's too complicated and you should redesign it.

:polymorphic => true

Use the `:polymorphic` option to specify that an object is related to its association in a *polymorphic* way, which is the Rails way of saying that the type of the related object is stored in the database along with its foreign key. By making a `belongs_to` relationship polymorphic, you abstract out the association so that any other model in the system can fill it.

Polymorphic associations let you trade some measure of relational integrity for the convenience of implementation in child relationships that are reused across your application. Common examples are models such as photo attachments, comments, notes, line items, and so on.

Let's illustrate by writing a `Comment` class that attaches to its subjects polymorphically. We'll associate it to both expense reports and timesheets. Listing 7.2 has the schema information in migration code, followed by the code for the classes involved.

Notice the :subject_type column, which stores the class name of the associated class.

Listing 7.2   Comment Class Using Polymorphic `belongs_to` Relationship

```
create_table :comments do |t|
  t.column :subject,      :string
  t.column :body,         :text
  t.column :subject_id,   :integer
  t.column :subject_type, :string
  t.column :created_at,   :datetime
end

class Comment < ActiveRecord::Base
  belongs_to :subject, :polymorphic => true
end

class ExpenseReport < ActiveRecord::Base
  belongs_to :user
  has_many :comments, :as => :subject
end

class Timesheet < ActiveRecord::Base
  belongs_to :user
  has_many :comments, :as => :subject
end
```

As you can see in the ExpenseReport and Timesheet classes of Listing 7.2, there is a corresponding syntax where you give ActiveRecord a clue that the relationship is polymorphic by specifying :as => :subject. We haven't even covered has_many relationships yet, and polymorphic relationships have their own section in Chapter 9. So before we get any further ahead of ourselves, let's take a look at has_many relationships.

The **has_many** Association

Just like it sounds, the has_many association allows you to define a relationship in which one model *has many* other models that *belong to* it. The sheer readability of code constructs such as has_many is a major reason that people fall in love with Rails.

The `has_many` class method is often used without additional options. If Rails can guess the type of class in the relationship from the name of the association, no additional configuration is necessary. This bit of code should look familiar by now:

```
class User
  has_many :timesheets
  has_many :expense_reports
```

The names of the associations can be singularized and match the names of models in the application, so everything works as expected.

`has_many` Options

Despite the ease of use of `has_many`, there is a surprising amount of power and customization possible for those who know and understand the options available.

`:after_add`

Called after a record is added to the collection via the `<<` method. Is not triggered by the collection's `create` method, so careful consideration is needed when relying on association callbacks.

Add callback method options to a `has_many` by passing one or more symbols corresponding to method names, or `Proc` objects. See Listing 7.3 in the `:before_add` option for an example.

`:after_remove`

Called after a record has been removed from the collection with the `delete` method. Add callback method options to a `has_many` by passing one or more symbols corresponding to method names, or `Proc` objects. See Listing 7.3 in the `:before_add` option for an example.

`:as`

Specifies the polymorphic `belongs_to` association to use on the related class. (See Chapter 9 for more about polymorphic relationships.)

:before_add

Triggered when a record is added to the collection via the << method. (Remember that concat and push are aliases of <<.) Raising an exception in the callback will stop the object from getting added to the collection. (Basically, because the callback is triggered right after the type mismatch check, and there is no rescue clause to be found inside <<.)

Add callback method options to a has_many by passing one or more symbols corresponding to method names, or Proc objects. You can set the option to either a single callback (as a Symbol or Proc) or to an array of them.

Listing 7.3 A Simple Example of :before_add Callback Usage

```
has_many :unchangable_posts,
         :class_name => "Post",
         :before_add => :raise_exception

private                         •

  def raise_exception(object)
    raise "You can't add a post"
  end
```

Of course, that would have been a lot shorter code using a Proc since it's a one liner. The owner parameter is the object with the association. The record parameter is the object being added.

```
has_many :unchangable_posts,
  :class_name => "Post",
  :before_add => Proc.new {|owner, record| raise "Can't do it!"}
```

One more time, with a lambda, which doesn't check the *arity* of block parameters:

```
has_many :unchangable_posts,
  :class_name => "Post",
  :before_add => lamda {raise "You can't add a post"}
```

:before_remove

Called before a record is removed from a collection with the delete method. See before_add for more information.

:class_name

The :class_name option is common to all of the associations. It allows you to specify, as a string, the name of the class of the association, and is needed when the class name cannot be inferred from the name of the association itself.

:conditions

The :conditions option is common to all of the associations. It allows you to add extra conditions to the ActiveRecord-generated SQL query that bring back the objects in the association.

You can apply extra :conditions to an association for a variety of reasons. How about approval?

```
has_many :comments, :conditions => ['approved = ?', true]
```

Plus, there's no rule that you can't have more than one has_many association exposing the same two related tables in different ways. Just remember that you'll probably have to specify the class name too.

```
has_many :pending_comments, :conditions => ['approved = ?', true],
                            :class_name => 'Comment'
```

:counter_sql

Overrides the ActiveRecord-generated SQL query that would be used to count the number of records belonging to this association. Not necessarily needed in conjunction with the :finder_sql option, since ActiveRecord will automatically generate counter SQL code based on the custom finder SQL statement.

As with all custom SQL specifications in ActiveRecord, you must use single-quotes around the entire string to prevent premature interpolation. (That is, you don't want the string to get interpolated in the context of the class where you're declaring the association. You want it to get interpolated at runtime.)

```
has_many :things, :finder_sql => 'select * from t where id = #{id}'
```

:delete_sql

Overrides the ActiveRecord-generated SQL statement that would be used to break associations. Access to the associated model is provided via the record method.

:dependent => :delete_all

All associated objects are deleted in fell swoop using a single SQL command. Note: While this option is *much* faster than :destroy_all, it doesn't trigger any destroy callbacks on the associated objects—you should use this option very carefully. It should only be used on associations that depend solely on the parent object.

:dependent => :destroy_all

All associated objects are destroyed along with the parent object, by iteratively calling their destroy methods.

:dependent => :nullify

The default behavior for deleting associated records is to *nullify*, or clear, the foreign key that joins them to the parent record. You should never have to specify this option explicitly, it is only here for reference.

:exclusively_dependent

Deprecated; equivalent to :dependent => :delete_all.

:extend => ExtensionModule

Specifies a module with methods that will extend the association collection proxy. Used as an alternative to defining additional methods in a block passed to the has_many method itself. Discussed in the section "Association Extensions".

:finder_sql

Specifies a complete SQL statement to fetch the association. This is a good way to load complex associations that depend on multiple tables for their data. It's also quite rare to need to go this route.

Count operations are done with a SQL statement based on the query supplied via the :finder_sql option. If ActiveRecord botches the transformation, it might be necessary to supply an explicit :counter_sql value also.

:foreign_key

Overrides the convention-based foreign key name that would normally be used in the SQL statement that loads the association.

:group

An attribute name by which the result should be grouped. Uses the GROUP BY SQL clause.

:include

Takes an array of second-order association names (as an array) that should be eager-loaded when this collection is loaded. As with the :include option on belongs_to associations, with judicious use of :include and careful benchmarking you can sometimes improve the performance of your application dramatically.

To illustrate, let's analyze how :include affects the SQL generated while navigating relationships. We'll use the following simplified versions of Timesheet, BillableWeek, and BillingCode:

```
class Timesheet < ActiveRecord::Base
  has_many :billable_weeks
end

class BillableWeek < ActiveRecord::Base
  belongs_to :timesheet
  belongs_to :billing_code
end

class BillingCode < ActiveRecord::Base
  belongs_to :client
  has_many :billable_weeks
end
```

First, I need to set up my test data, so I create a timesheet instance and add a couple of billable weeks to it. Then I assign a billable code to each billable week, which results in an object graph (with four objects linked together via associations).

Next I do a fancy one-line collect, which gives me an array of the billing codes associated with the timesheet:

```
>> Timesheet.find(3).billable_weeks.collect{ |w| w.billing_code.code }
=> ["TRAVEL", "DEVELOPMENT"]
```

Without the :include option set on the billable_weeks association of Timesheet, that operation cost me the following four database hits (copied from log/development.log, and prettied up a little):

```
Timesheet Load (0.000656)     SELECT * FROM timesheets
                              WHERE (timesheets.id = 3)


BillableWeek Load (0.001156) SELECT * FROM billable_weeks
                              WHERE (billable_weeks.timesheet_id = 3)


BillingCode Load (0.000485)   SELECT * FROM billing_codes
                              WHERE (billing_codes.id = 1)


BillingCode Load (0.000439)   SELECT * FROM billing_codes
                              WHERE (billing_codes.id = 2)
```

This is demonstrates the so-called "N+1 select" problem that inadvertently plagues many systems. Anytime I need *one* billable week, it will cost me *N* select statements to retrieve its associated records.

Now let's add :include to the billable_weeks association, after which the Timesheet class looks as follows:

```
class Timesheet < ActiveRecord::Base
  has_many :billable_weeks, :include => [:billing_code]
end
```

Simple! Rerunning our test statement yields the same results in the console:

```
>> Timesheet.find(3).billable_weeks.collect{ |w| w.billing_code.code }
=> ["TRAVEL", "DEVELOPMENT"]
```

But look at how different the generated SQL is:

```
Timesheet Load (0.002926)    SELECT * FROM timesheets LIMIT 1

BillableWeek Load Including Associations (0.001168)   SELECT
billable_weeks."id" AS t0_r0, billable_weeks."timesheet_id" AS t0_r1,
billable_weeks."client_id" AS t0_r2, billable_weeks."start_date" AS
t0_r3, billable_weeks."billing_code_id" AS t0_r4,
billable_weeks."monday_hours" AS t0_r5, billable_weeks."tuesday_hours"
AS t0_r6, billable_weeks."wednesday_hours" AS t0_r7,
```

```
billable_weeks."thursday_hours" AS t0_r8,
billable_weeks."friday_hours"
AS t0_r9, billable_weeks."saturday_hours" AS t0_r10,
billable_weeks."sunday_hours" AS t0_r11, billing_codes."id" AS t1_r0,
billing_codes."client_id" AS t1_r1, billing_codes."code" AS t1_r2,
billing_codes."description" AS t1_r3 FROM billable_weeks LEFT OUTER
JOIN
billing_codes ON billing_codes.id = billable_weeks.billing_code_id
WHERE
(billable_weeks.timesheet_id = 3)
```

Rails has added a LEFT OUTER JOIN clause so that billing code data is loaded along with billable weeks. For larger datasets, the performance improvement can be quite dramatic!

It's generally easy to find N+1 select issues just by watching the log scroll by while clicking through the different screens of your application. (Of course, make sure that you're looking at realistic data or the exercise will be pointless.) Screens that might benefit from eager loading will cause a flurry of single-row SELECT statements, one for each record in a given association being used.

If you're feeling particularly daring (perhaps masochistic is a better term) you can try including a deep hierarchy of associations, by mixing hashes into your eager :include array:

```
Post.find(:all, :include=>[:author, {:comments=>{:author=>:gravatar }}])
```

That example snippet will grab not only all the comments for a Post, but all the authors and gravatar pictures as well. You can mix and match symbols, arrays and hashes in any combination to describe the associations you want to load.

Frankly, deep :includes are not well-documented functionality and are probably more trouble than what they're worth. The biggest problem is that pulling too much data in one query can really kill your performance. You should always start out with the simplest solution that will work, then use benchmarking and analysis to figure out if optimizations such as eager-loading help improve your performance.

> **Wilson Says...**
> Let people learn eager loading by crawling across broken
> glass, like we did. It builds character!

:insert_sql

Overrides the ActiveRecord-generated SQL statement that would be used to create associations. Access the associated model via the record method.

:limit

Appends a LIMIT clause to the SQL generated for loading this association.

:offset

An integer determining the offset from where the rows should be fetched.

:order

Specifies the order in which the associated objects are returned via an "ORDER BY" sql fragment, such as "last_name, first_name DESC".

:select

By default, this is * as in SELECT * FROM, but can be changed if you for example want to add additional calculated columns or "piggyback" additional columns from joins onto the associated object as its loaded.

:source and :source_type

Used exclusively as additional options to assist in using has_many :through associations with polymorphic belongs_to and is covered in detail later in the chapter.

:table_name

The :table_name option lets you override the table names (FROM clause) that will be used in SQL statements generated for loading the association.

:through

Creates an association collection via another association. See the section in this chapter entitled "has_many :through" for more information.

:uniq => true

Strips duplicate objects from the collection. Useful in conjunction with has_many :through.

Proxy Methods

The has_many class method creates an association collection proxy, with all the methods provided by AssociationCollection and a few more methods defined in HasManyAssociation.

build(attributes = {})

Instantiates a new object in the associated collection, and links it to the owner by specifying the value of the foreign key. Does not save the new object in the database and the new object is not added to the association collection. As you can see in the following example, unless you capture the return value of build, the new object will be lost:

```
>> obie.timesheets
=> <timesheets not loaded yet>
>> obie.timesheets.build
=> #<Timesheet:0x24c6b8c @new_record=true, @attributes={"user_id"=>1,
"submitted"=>nil}>
>> obie.timesheets
=> <timesheets not loaded yet>
```

As the online API documents point out, the build method is exactly the same as constructing a new object and passing in the foreign key value as an attribute:

```
>> Timesheet.new(:user_id => 1)
=> #<Timesheet:0x24a52fc @new_record=true, @attributes={"user_id"=>1,
"submitted"=>nil}>
```

`count(*args)`

Counts the number of associated records in the database using SQL.

`find(*args)`

Not much different here than the normal `ActiveRecord find` method, other than that the scope is constrained to associated records and any additional conditions specified in the declaration of the relationship.

Remember the `has_one` example shown earlier in the chapter? It was somewhat contrived, since it would have been easier to look up the last modified timesheet using `find:`.

Many-to-Many Relationships

Associating persistent objects via a join table can be one of the trickier aspects of object-relational mapping to implement correctly in a framework. Rails has a couple of techniques that let you represent many-to-many relationships in your model. We'll start with the older and simpler `has_and_belongs_to_many` and then cover the newer `has_many :through`.

has_and_belongs_to_many

The `has_and_belongs_to_many` method establishes a link between two associated `ActiveRecord` models via an intermediate join table. Unless the join table is explicitly specified as an option, Rails guesses its name by concatenating the table names of the joined classes, in alphabetical order and separated with an underscore.

For example, if I was using `has_and_belongs_to_many` (or `habtm` for short) to establish a relationship between `Timesheet` and `BillingCode`, the join table would be named `billing_codes_timesheets` and the relationship would be defined in the models. Both the migration class and models are listed:

```
class CreateBillingCodesTimesheets < ActiveRecord::Migration
  def self.up
    create_table :billing_codes_timesheets, :id => false do |t|
      t.column :billing_code_id, :integer, :null => false
      t.column :timesheet_id, :integer, :null => false
    end
  end
```

```ruby
  def self.down
    drop_table :billing_codes_timesheets
  end
end

class Timesheet < ActiveRecord::Base
  has_and_belongs_to_many :billing_codes
end

class BillingCode < ActiveRecord::Base
 has_and_belongs_to_many :timesheets
end
```

Note that an `id` primary key is not needed, hence the `:id => false` option was passed to the `create_table` method. Also, since the foreign key columns are both needed, we pass them a `:null => false` option. (In real code, you would also want to make sure both of the foreign key columns were indexed properly.)

Self-Referential Relationship

What about *self-referential* many-to-many relationships? Linking a model to itself via a `habtm` relationship is easy—you just have to provide explicit options.

In Listing 7.4, I've created a join table and established a link between related `BillingCode` objects. Again, both the migration and model class are listed:

Listing 7.4   Related Billing Codes

```ruby
class CreateRelatedBillingCodes < ActiveRecord::Migration
  def self.up
    create_table :related_billing_codes, :id => false do |t|
      t.column :first_billing_code_id, :integer, :null => false
      t.column :second_billing_code_id, :integer, :null => false
    end
  end

  def self.down
    drop_table :related_billing_codes
  end
end

class BillingCode < ActiveRecord::Base
```

```
has_and_belongs_to_many :related,
  :join_table => 'related_billing_codes',
  :foreign_key => 'first_billing_code_id',
  :association_foreign_key => 'second_billing_code_id',
:class_name => 'BillingCode'
end
```

Bidirectional Relationships

It's worth noting that the `related` relationship of the `BillingCode` in Listing 7.4 is not *bidirectional*. Just because you associate two objects in one direction does not mean they'll be associated in the other direction. But what if you need to automatically establish a bidirectional relationship?

First let's write a test for the `BillingCode` class to prove our solution. We'll start by writing a couple of sample records to work with in `test/fixtures/billing_codes.yml`:

```
travel:
  code: TRAVEL
  client_id:
  id: 1
  description: Travel expenses of all sorts
development:
  code: DEVELOPMENT
  client_id:
  id: 2
  description: Coding, etc
```

When we add bidirectional, we don't want to break the normal behavior, so at first my test method establishes that the normal `habtm` relationship works:

```
require File.dirname(__FILE__) + '/../test_helper'

class BillingCodeTest < Test::Unit::TestCase
  fixtures :billing_codes

  def test_self_referential_habtm_association
    billing_codes(:travel).related << billing_codes(:development)
    assert BillingCode.find(1).related.include?(BillingCode.find(2))
  end
end
```

I run the test and it passes. Now I can modify the test method to add proof that the bidirectional behavior that we're going to add works. It ends up looking very similar to the original method. (Normally I would lean toward only having one assertion per test method, but in this case it makes more sense to keep them together.) The second `assert` statement checks to see that the newly associated class also has its related `BillingCode` in its `related` collection.

```ruby
require File.dirname(__FILE__) + '/../test_helper'

class BillingCodeTest < Test::Unit::TestCase

  fixtures :billing_codes

  def setup
    @travel = billing_codes(:travel)
    @development = billing_codes(:development)
  end

  def test_self_referential_bidirectional_habtm_association
    @travel.related << @development
    assert @travel.related.include?(@development)
    assert @development.related.include?(@travel)
  end
end
```

Of course, the new test fails, since we haven't added the new behavior yet. I'm not entirely happy with this approach, since it involves bringing hand-coded SQL into my otherwise beautiful Ruby code. However, the Rails way is to use SQL when it makes sense to do so, and this is one of those cases.

> **Wilson Says...**
> If only `<<` and `create` both triggered association callbacks, we could implement this bidirectional mayhem without writing any SQL code. Unfortunately, they don't. You could still do it... but as soon as someone used `create`, it would miss the other side of the relationship.

Custom SQL Options

To get our bidirectional, we'll be using the `:insert_sql` option of `has_and_belongs_to_many` to override the normal INSERT statement that Rails would use to associate objects with each other.

Here's a neat trick so that you don't have to figure out the syntax of the INSERT statement from memory. Just copy and paste the normal INSERT statement that Rails uses. It's not too hard to find in `log/test.log` if you tail the file while running the unit test we wrote in the previous section:

```
INSERT INTO related_billing_codes (`first_billing_code_id`,
`second_billing_code_id`) VALUES (1, 2)
```

Now we just have to tweak that INSERT statement so that it adds two rows instead of just one. You might be tempted to just add a semicolon and a second, full INSERT statement. That won't work, because it is invalid to stuff two statements into one using a semicolon. Try it and see what happens if you're curious.

After some quick googling, I found the following method of inserting multiple rows with one SQL statement that will work for Postgres, MySQL, and DB2 databases.[1] It is valid according to the SQL-92 standard, just not universally supported:

```
:insert_sql => 'INSERT INTO related_billing_codes
                (`first_billing_code_id`, `second_billing_code_id`)
                VALUES (#{id}, #{record.id}), (#{record.id}, #{id})'
```

There are some very important things to remember when trying to get custom SQL options to work. The first is to *use single quotes* around the entire string of custom SQL. If you were to use double quotes, the string would be interpolated in the context of the class where it is being declared, not at the time of your query like you need it to be.

Also, while we're on the subject of quotation marks and how to use them, note that when I copied the INSERT query over from my log, I ended up with backtick characters around the column names, instead of single quotes. Trying to use single-quotes around values instead of backtick characters will fail, because the database adapter will escape the quotes, producing invalid syntax. Yes, it's a pain in the neck—luckily you shouldn't need to specify custom SQL very often.

Another thing to remember is that when your custom SQL string is interpolated, it will happen in the context of the object holding the association. The object being associated will be made available as `record`. If you look closely at the code listing, you'll notice that to establish the bidirectional link, we just added two rows in the `related_billing_codes` table, one in each direction.

A quick test run confirms that our `:insert_sql` approach did indeed work. We should also use the `:delete_sql` option to make sure that the relationship can be broken bidirectionally as well. Again, I'll drive the implementation in a TDD fashion, adding the following test to `BillingCodeTest`:

```ruby
def test_that_deletion_is_bidirectional_too
  billing_codes(:travel).related << billing_codes(:development)
  billing_codes(:travel).related.delete(billing_codes(:development))
  assert !BillingCode.find(1).related.include?(BillingCode.find(2))
  assert !BillingCode.find(2).related.include?(BillingCode.find(1))
end
```

It's similar to the previous test method, except that after establishing the relationship, it immediately deletes it. I expect that the first assertion will pass right away, but the second should fail:

```
$ ruby test/unit/billing_code_test.rb
Loaded suite test/unit/billing_code_test
Started
.F
Finished in 0.159424 seconds.

  1) Failure:
test_that_deletion_is_bidirectional_too(BillingCodeTest)
[test/unit/billing_code_test.rb:16]:
<false> is not true.

2 tests, 4 assertions, 1 failures, 0 errors
```

Yep, just as expected. Let's peek at `log/test.log` and grab the SQL DELETE clause that we'll work with:

```sql
DELETE FROM related_billing_codes WHERE first_billing_code_id = 1 AND
second_billing_code_id IN (2)
```

Hmph! This might be a little trickier than the insert. Curious about the IN operator, I take a peek inside the `active_record/associations/has_and_belongs_to_many_association.rb` file and find the following relevant method:

```
def delete_records(records)
  if sql = @reflection.options[:delete_sql]
    records.each { |record|
      @owner.connection.execute(interpolate_sql(sql, record))
    }
  else
    ids = quoted_record_ids(records)
    sql = "DELETE FROM #{@reflection.options[:join_table]}
           WHERE #{@reflection.primary_key_name} = #{@owner.quoted_id}
           AND #{@reflection.association_foreign_key} IN (#{ids})"
    @owner.connection.execute(sql)
  end
end
```

The final `BillingCode` class now looks like this:

```
class BillingCode < ActiveRecord::Base
  has_and_belongs_to_many :related,
    :join_table => 'related_billing_codes',
    :foreign_key => 'first_billing_code_id',
    :association_foreign_key => 'second_billing_code_id',
    :class_name => 'BillingCode',
    :insert_sql => 'INSERT INTO related_billing_codes
                    (`first_billing_code_id`,
`second_billing_code_id`)
                    VALUES (#{id}, #{record.id}), (#{record.id},
#{id})'
end
```

Linking Two Existing Objects Efficiently

Prior to Rails 2.0, the << method loads *the entire contents of the associated collection* from the database into memory—which, depending on how many associated records you have in your database, could take a really long time!

Extra Columns on `has_and_belongs_to_many` Join Tables

Rails won't have a problem with you adding as many extra columns as you want to `habtm`'s join table. The extra attributes will be read in and added onto model objects accessed via the `habtm` association. However, speaking from experience, the severe annoyances you will deal with in your application code make it really unattractive to go that route.

What kind of annoyances? For one, records returned from join tables with additional attributes will be marked as read-only, because it's not possible to save changes to those additional attributes.

You should also consider that the way that Rails makes those extra columns of the join table available might cause problems in other parts of your codebase. Having extra attributes appear magically on an object is kind of cool, but what happens when you try to access those extra properties on an object that *wasn't* fetched via the `habtm` association? Kaboom! Get ready for some potentially bewildering debugging exercises.

Other than the deprecated `push_with_attributes`, methods of the `habtm` proxy act just as they would for a `has_many` relationship. Similarly, `habtm` shares options with `has_many`; only its `:join_table` option is unique. It allows customization of the join table name.

To sum up, `habtm` is a simple way to establish a many-to-many relationship using a join table. As long as you don't need to capture additional data about the relationship, everything is fine. The problems with `habtm` begin once you want to add extra columns to the join table, after which you'll want to upgrade the relationship to use `has_many :through` instead.

"Real Join Models" and `habtm`

Rails 1.2 documentation advises readers that: "It's strongly recommended that you upgrade any [habtm] associations with attributes to a real join model." Use of `habtm`, which was one of the original innovative features in Rails, fell out of favor once the ability to create *real* join models was introduced via the `has_many :through` association.

Realistically, `habtm` is not going to be removed from Rails, for a couple of sensible reasons. First of all, plenty of legacy Rails applications need it. Second, `habtm` provides a way to join classes without a primary key defined on the join table, which is occasionally useful. But most of the time you'll find yourself wanting to model many-to-many relationships with `has_many :through`.

has_many :through

Well-known Rails guy and fellow cabooser Josh Susser is considered the expert on ActiveRecord associations, even his blog is called *has_many :through*. His description of the :through association[2], written back when the feature was originally introduced in Rails 1.1, is so concise and well-written that I couldn't hope to do any better. So here it is:

> The has_many :through association allows you to specify a one-to-many relationship indirectly via an intermediate join table. In fact, you can specify more than one such relationship via the same table, which effectively makes it a replacement for has_and_belongs_to_many. The biggest advantage is that the join table contains full-fledged model objects complete with primary keys and ancillary data. No more push_with_attributes; join models just work the same way all your other ActiveRecord models do.

Join Models

To illustrate the has_many :through association, we'll set up a Client model so that it has many Timesheet objects, through a normal has_many association named billable_weeks.

```
class Client < ActiveRecord::Base
  has_many :billable_weeks
  has_many :timesheets, :through => :billable_weeks
end
```

The BillableWeek class was already in our sample application and is ready to be used as a join model:

```
class BillableWeek < ActiveRecord::Base
  belongs_to :client
  belongs_to :timesheet
end
```

We can also set up the inverse relationship, from timesheets to clients, like this.

```
class Timesheet < ActiveRecord::Base
  has_many :billable_weeks
  has_many :clients, :through => :billable_weeks
end
```

Notice that `has_many :through` is always used in conjunction with a normal `has_many` association. Also, notice that the normal `has_many` association will often have the same name on both classes that are being joined together, which means the `:through` option will read the same on both sides.

```
:through => :billable_weeks
```

How about the join model; will it always have two `belongs_to` associations? *No.* You can also use `has_many :through` to easily aggregate `has_many` or `has_one` associations on the join model. Forgive me for switching to completely nonrealistic domain for a moment—it's only intended to clearly demonstrate what I'm trying to describe:

```
class Grandparent < ActiveRecord::Base
  has_many :parents
  has_many :grand_children, :through => :parents, :source => :childs
end

class Parent < ActiveRecord::Base
  belongs_to :grandparent
  has_many    :childs
end
```

For the sake of clarity in later chapters, I'll refer to this usage of `has_many :through` as *aggregating*.

Courtenay Says...

We use `has_many :through` so much! It has pretty much replaced the old `has_and_belongs_to_many`, because it allows your join models to be upgraded to full objects.

It's like when you're just dating someone and they start talking about the Relationship (or, eventually, Our Marriage). It's an example of an association being promoted to something more important than the individual objects on each side.

Usage Considerations and Examples

You can use nonaggregating `has_many` `:through` associations in almost the same ways as any other `has_many` associations. The limitations have to do with handling of unsaved records.

```
>> c = Client.create(:name => "Trotter's Tomahawks", :code => "ttom")
=> #<Client:0x2228410...>

>> c.timesheets << Timesheet.new
ActiveRecord::HasManyThroughCantAssociateNewRecords: Cannot associate
new records through 'Client#billable_weeks' on '#'. Both records must
have an id in order to create the has_many :through record associating
them.
```

Hmm, seems like we had a hiccup. Unlike a normal `has_many`, ActiveRecord won't let us add an object to the the `has_many` `:through` association if both ends of the relationship are unsaved records.

The `create` method saves the record before adding it, so it does work as expected, provided the parent object isn't unsaved itself.

```
>> c.save
=> true

>> c.timesheets.create
=> [#<Timesheet:0x2212354 @new_record=false, @new_record_before_save=
true, @attributes={"updated_at"=>Sun Mar 18 15:37:18 UTC 2007,
"id"=>2,
"user_id"=>nil, "submitted"=>nil, "created_at"=>Sun Mar 18 15:37:18
UTC
2007}, @errors=#<ActiveRecord::Errors:0x2211940 @base=
#<Timesheet:0x2212354 ...>, @errors={}>> ]
```

The main benefit of `has_many` `:through` is that ActiveRecord takes care of managing the instances of the join model for you. If we call `reload` on the `billable _weeks` association, we'll see that there was a billable week object created for us:

```
>> c.billable_weeks.reload
=> [#<BillableWeek:0x139329c @attributes={"tuesday_hours"=>nil,
"start_date"=>nil, "timesheet_id"=>"2", "billing_code_id"=>nil,
"sunday_hours"=>nil, "friday_hours"=>nil, "monday_hours"=>nil,
```

```
"client_id"=>"2", "id"=>"2", "wednesday_hours"=>nil,
"saturday_hours"=>nil, "thursday_hours"=>nil}> ]
```

The `BillableWeek` object that was created is properly associated with both the client and the `Timesheet`. Unfortunately, there are a lot of other attributes (e.g., `start_date`, and the hours columns) that were not populated.

One possible solution is to use `create` on the `billable_weeks` association instead, and include the new `Timesheet` object as one of the supplied properties.

```
>> bw = c.billable_weeks.create(:start_date => Time.now,
                                 :timesheet => Timesheet.new)
=> #<BillableWeek:0x250fe08 @timesheet=#<Timesheet:0x2510100
@new_record=false, ...>
```

Aggregating Associations

When you're using `has_many :through` to aggregate multiple child associations, there are more significant limitations—essentially you can query to your hearts content using `find` and friends, but you can't append or create new records through them.

For example, let's add a `billable_weeks` association to our sample `User` class:

```
class User < ActiveRecord::Base
  has_many :timesheets
  has_many :billable_weeks, :through => :timesheets
  ...
```

The `billable_weeks` association aggregates all the billable week objects belonging to all of the user's timesheets.

```
class Timesheet < ActiveRecord::Base
  belongs_to :user
  has_many :billable_weeks, :include => [:billing_code]
  ...
```

Now let's go into the Rails console and set up some example data so that we can use the new `billable_weeks` collection (on `User`).

```
>> quentin = User.find :first
=> #<User id: 1, login: "quentin" ...>
```

```
>> quentin.timesheets
=> []

>> ts1 = quentin.timesheets.create
=> #<Timesheet id: 1 ...>

>> ts2 = quentin.timesheets.create
=> #<Timesheet id: 2 ...>

>> ts1.billable_weeks.create(:start_date => 1.week.ago)
=> #<BillableWeek id: 1, timesheet_id: 1 ...>

>> ts2.billable_weeks.create :start_date => 2.week.ago
=> #<BillableWeek id: 2, timesheet_id: 2 ...>

>> quentin.billable_weeks
=> [#<BillableWeek id: 1, timesheet_id: 1 ...>, #<BillableWeek id: 2,
timesheet_id: 2 ...>]
```

Just for fun, let's see what happens if we try to create a `BillableWeek` with a
`User` instance:

```
>> quentin.billable_weeks.create(:start_date => 3.weeks.ago)
NoMethodError: undefined method `user_id=' for
#<BillableWeek:0x3f84424>
```

There you go... `BillableWeek` doesn't belong to a user, it belongs to a timesheet,
so it doesn't have a `user_id` field.

Join Models and Validations

When you append to a non-aggregating `has_many :through` association with `<<`,
ActiveRecord will always create a new join model, even if one already exists for the
two records being joined. You can add `validates_uniqueness_of` constraints on
the join model to keep duplicate joins from happening.

This is what such a constraint might look like on our `BillableWeek` join model.

```
validates_uniqueness_of :client_id, :scope => :timesheet_id
```

That says, in effect: "There should only be one of each client per timesheet."

If your join model has additional attributes with their own validation logic, then there's another important consideration to keep in mind. Adding records directly to a `has_many` `:through` association causes a new join model to be automatically created *with a blank set of attributes*. Validations on additional columns of the join model will probably fail. If that happens, you'll need to add new records by creating join model objects and associating them appropriately through their own association proxy.

```
timesheet.billable_weeks.create(:start_date => 1.week.ago)
```

has_many `:through` Options

The options for `has_many` `:through` are the same as the options for `has_many`—remember that `:through` is just an option on `has_many`! However, the use of some of `has_many`'s options change or become more significant when `:through` is used.

First of all, the `:class_name` and `:foreign_key` options are no longer valid, since they are implied from the target association on the join model.

Here are the rest of the options that have special significance together with `has_many` `:through`.

:source

The `:source` option specifies *which* association to use on the associated class. This option is not mandatory because normally ActiveRecord assumes that the target association is the singular (or plural) version of the `has_many` association name. If your association names don't match up, then you have to set `:source` explicitly.

For example, the following code will use the `BillableWeek`'s `sheet` association to populate `timesheets`.

```
has_many :timesheets, :through => :billable_weeks, :source => :sheet
```

:source_type

The `:source_type` option is needed when you establish a `has_many` `:through` to a polymorphic `belongs_to` association on the join model.

Consider the following example of clients and contacts:

```
class Client < ActiveRecord::Base
  has_many :contact_cards
```

```
    has_many :contacts, :through => :contact_cards
end

class ContactCard < ActiveRecord::Base
  belongs_to :client
  belongs_to :contacts, :polymorphic => true
end
```

The most important fact here is that a `Client` has many `contacts`, which can be any kind of model since they are declared polymorphically on the join model, `ContactCard`. For example purposes, let's associate people and businesses to contact cards:

```
class Person < ActiveRecord::Base
  has_many :contact_cards, :as => :contact
end

class Business < ActiveRecord::Base
  has_many :contact_cards, :as => :contact
end
```

Now take a moment to consider the backflips that ActiveRecord would have to perform in order to figure out which tables to query for a client's contacts. It would theoretically need to be aware of every model class that is linked to the other end of the contacts polymorphic association.

In fact, it can't do those kinds of backflips, which is probably a good thing as far as performance is concerned:

```
>> Client.find(:first).contacts
ArgumentError: /.../active_support/core_ext/hash/keys.rb:48:
in `assert_valid_keys': Unknown key(s): polymorphic
```

The only way to make this scenario work (somewhat) is to give ActiveRecord some help by specifying which table it should search when you ask for the `contacts` collection, and you do that with the `source_type` option. The value of the option is the name of the target class, symbolized:

```
class Client < ActiveRecord::Base
  has_many :people_contacts, :through => :contact_cards,
           :source => :contacts, :source_type => :person
```

```
  has_many :business_contacts, :through => :contact_cards,
           :source => :contacts, :source_type => :business
end
```

After the `:source_type` is specified, the association will work as expected.

```
>> Client.find(:first).people_contacts.create!
[#<Person:0x223e788 @attributes={"id"=>1}, @errors=
#<ActiveRecord::Errors:0x223dc0c @errors={}, @base=
#<Person: 0x...>>, @new_record_before_save=true, @new_record=false>]
```

The code is a bit longer and less magical, but it works. If you're upset that you cannot associate `people_contacts` and `business_contacts` together in a contacts association, you could try writing your own accessor method for a client's contacts:

```
class Client < ActiveRecord::Base
  def contacts
    people_contacts + business_contacts
  end
end
```

Of course, you should be aware that calling that `contacts` method will result in at least two database requests and will return an `Array`, without the association proxy methods that you might expect it to have.

:uniq

The `:uniq` option tells the association to include only unique objects. It is especially useful when using `has_many` `:through`, since two different `BillableWeeks` could reference the same `Timesheet`.

```
>> client.find(:first).timesheets.reload
[#<Timesheet:0x13e79dc @attributes={"id"=>"1", ...}>,
 #<Timesheet:0x13e79b4 @attributes={"id"=>"1", ...}>]
```

It's not extraordinary for two distinct model instances of the same database record to be in memory at the same time—it's just not usually desirable.

```
class Client < ActiveRecord::Base
  has_many :timesheets, :through => :billable_weeks, :uniq => true
end
```

After adding the `:uniq` option, only one instance per record is returned.

```
>> client.find(:first).timesheets.reload
[#<Timesheet:0x22332ac ...>]
```

The implementation of `uniq` on `AssociationCollection` is a neat little example of how to build a collection of unique values in Ruby, using a `Set` and the `inject` method. It also proves that the record's primary key (and nothing else) is what's being used to establish uniqueness:

```ruby
def uniq(collection = self)
  seen = Set.new
  collection.inject([]) do |kept, record|
    unless seen.include?(record.id)
      kept << record
      seen << record.id
    end
    kept
  end
end
```

One-to-One Relationships

One of the most basic relationship types is a one-to-one object relationship. In `ActiveRecord` we declare a one-to-one relationship using the `has_one` and `belongs_to` methods together. As in the case of a `has_many` relationship, you call `belongs_to` on the model whose database table contains the foreign key column linking the two records together.

has_one

Conceptually, `has_one` works almost exactly like `has_many` does, except that when the database query is executed to retrieve the related object, a `LIMIT 1` clause is added to the generated SQL so that only one row is returned.

The name of a `has_one` relationship should be singular, which will make it read naturally, for example: `has one :last_timesheet`, `has one :primary_account`, `has one :profile_photo`, and so on.

Let's take a look at `has_one` in action by adding avatars for our users.

```
class Avatar < ActiveRecord::Base
  belongs_to :user
end

class User < ActiveRecord::Base
  has_one :avatar
  # ... the rest of our User code ...
end
```

That's simple enough. Firing this up in `script/console`, we can look at some of the new methods that `has_one` adds to `User`.

```
>> u = User.find(:first)
>> u.avatar
=> nil

>> u.build_avatar(:url => '/avatars/smiling')
#<Avatar:0x2266bac @new_record=true, @attributes={"url"=>
"/avatars/smiling", "user_id"=>1}>

>> u.avatar.save
=> true
```

As you can see, we can use `build_avatar` to build a new avatar object and associate it with the user. While it's great that `has_one` will associate an avatar with the user, it isn't really anything that `has_many` doesn't already do. So let's take a look at what happens when we assign a new avatar to the user.

```
>> u = User.find(:first)
>> u.avatar
=> #<Avatar:0x2266bac @attributes={"url"=>"/avatars/smiling",
"user_id"=>1}>

>> u.create_avatar(:url => '/avatars/frowning')

=> #<Avatar:0x225071c @new_record=false, @attributes={"url"=>
"/avatars/4567", "id"=>2, "user_id"=>1}, @errors=
#<ActiveRecord::Errors:0x224fc40 @base=#<Avatar:0x225071c ...>,
@errors={}>>
```

```
>> Avatar.find(:all)
=> [#<Avatar:0x22426f8 @attributes={"url"=>"/avatars/smiling",
"id"=>"1", "user_id"=>nil}>, #<Avatar:0x22426d0
@attributes={"url"=>"/avatars/frowning", "id"=>"2", "user_id"=>"1"}>]
```

The last line from that `script/console` session is the most interesting, because it shows that our initial avatar is now no longer associated with the user. Of course, the previous avatar was not removed from the database, which is something that we want in this scenario. So, we'll use the `:dependent => :destroy` option to force avatars to be destroyed when they are no longer associated with a user.

```
class User
  has_one :avatar, :dependent => :destroy
end
```

With some fiddling around in the console, we can verify that it works as intended.

```
>> u = User.find(:first)
>> u.avatar
=> #<Avatar:0x22426d0 @attributes={"url"=>"/avatars/frowning",
"id"=>"2", "user_id"=>"1"}>

>> u.avatar = Avatar.create(:url => "/avatars/jumping")
=> #<Avatar:0x22512ac @new_record=false,
@attributes={"url"=>"avatars/jumping", "id"=>3, "user_id"=>1},
@errors=#<ActiveRecord::Errors:0x22508e8 @base=#<Avatar:0x22512ac
...>,
@errors={}>>

>> Avatar.find(:all)
=> [#<Avatar:0x22426f8 @attributes={"url"=>"/avatars/smiling", "id"
=>"1", "user_id"=>nil}>, #<Avatar:0x2245920 @attributes={"url"=>
"avatars/jumping","id"=>"3", "user_id"=>"1"}>]
```

As you can see, adding `:dependent => :destroy` got rid of the frowning avatar, but not the smiling avatar. Rails only destroys the avatar that was just removed from the user, so bad data that is in your database from before will still remain. Keep this in mind when you decide to add `:dependent => :destroy` and remember to manually clear any bad data from before.

As I alluded to earlier, has_one is often used to single out one record of signifi-cance alongside an already established has_many relationship. For instance, let's say we want to easily be able to access the last timesheet a user was working on:

```
class User < ActiveRecord::Base
  has_many :timesheets
  has_one  :latest_timesheet, :class_name => 'Timesheet'
end
```

I had to specify a :class_name, so that ActiveRecord knows what kind of object we're associating. (It can't figure it out based on the name of the association, :latest _timesheet.)

When adding a has_one relationship to a model that already has a has_many defined to the same related model, it is *not* necessary to add another belongs_to method call to the target object, just for the new has_one. That might seem a little counterintuitive at first, but if you think about it, the same foreign key value is being used to read the data from the database.

What happens when you replace an existing has_one target object with another? A lot depends on whether the newly related object was created before or after the object that it is replacing, because ActiveRecord doesn't add any additional ordering parameters to its has_one query.

has_one Options

The options for has_one associations are similar to the ones for has_many.

:as

Allows you to set up a polymorphic association, covered in Chapter 9.

:class_name

Allows you to specify the class this association uses. When you're doing has_one :latest_timesheet, :class_name => 'Timesheet', :class_name => 'Timesheet' specifies that latest_timesheet is actually the last Timesheet object in the database that is associated with this user. Normally, this option is inferred by Rails from the name of the association.

:conditions

Allows you to specify conditions that the object must meet to be included in the association. The conditions are specified the same as if you were using ActiveRecord#find.

```
class User
  has_one :manager,
          :class_name => 'Person',
          :conditions => ["type = ?", "manager"]
end
```

Here manager is specified as a person object that has type = "manager". I tend to almost always use :conditions in conjunction with has_one. When ActiveRecord loads the association, it's grabbing one of potentially many rows that have the right foreign key. Absent some explicit conditions (or perhaps an order clause), you're leaving it in the hands of the database to pick a row.

:dependent

The :dependent option specifies how ActiveRecord should treat associated objects when the parent object is deleted. There are a few different values that you can pass and they work just like the :dependent option of has_many.

If you pass :destroy to it, you tell Rails to destroy the associated object when it is no longer associated with the primary object. Passing :delete will destroy the associated object without calling any of Rails' normal hooks. Finally, the default (:nullify) will simply set the foreign key values to null so that the connection is broken.

:foreign_key

Specifies the name of the foreign key column on the association's table.

:include

Allows you to "eagerload" additional association objects when your associated object is loaded. See the :include option of the has_many and belongs_to associations for more details.

:order

Allows you to specify a SQL fragment that will be used to order the results. This is an especially useful option with `has_one` when trying to associate the latest of something or another.

```
class User
  has_one :latest_timesheet,
          :class_name => 'Timesheet',
          :order => 'created_at desc'
end
```

Unsaved Objects and Associations

You can manipulate objects and associations before they are saved to the database, but there is some special behavior you should be aware of, mostly involving the saving of associated objects. Whether an object is considered unsaved is based on the result of calling `new_record?`

One-to-One Associations

Assigning an object to a `has_one` association automatically saves that object *and* the object being replaced (if there is one), so that their foreign key fields are updated. The exception to this behavior is if the parent object is unsaved, since that would mean that there is no foreign key value to set.

If save fails for either of the objects being updated (due to one of them being invalid) the assignment operation returns false *and the assignment is cancelled.* That behavior makes sense (if you think about it), but it can be the cause of much confusion when you're not aware of it. If you have an association that doesn't seem to work, check the validation rules of the related objects.

If you happen to want to assign an object to a `has_one` association *without* saving it, you can use the association's `build` method:

```
user.profile_photo.build(params[:photo])
```

Assigning an object to a `belongs_to` association does not save the parent or the associated object.

Collections

Adding an object to `has_many` and `has_and_belongs_to_many` collections automatically saves it, unless the parent object (the owner of the collection) is not yet stored in the database.

If objects being added to a collection (via << or similar means) fail to save properly, then the addition operation will return `false`. If you want your code to be a little more explicit, or you want to add an object to a collection without automatically saving it, then you can use the collection's `build` method. It's exactly like `create`, except that it doesn't `save`.

Members of a collection are automatically saved (or updated) when their parent is saved (or updated).

Association Extensions

The proxy objects that handle access to associations can be extended with your own application code. You can add your own custom finders and factory methods to be used specifically with a particular association.

For example, let's say you wanted a concise way to refer to an account's people by name. You might wrap the `find_or_create_by_first_name_and_last_name` method of a `people` collection in the following neat little package as shown in Listing 7.5.

Listing 7.5 An Association Extension on a People Collection

```
class Account < ActiveRecord::Base

  has_many :people do
    def named(name)
      first_name, last_name = name.split(" ", 2)
      find_or_create_by_first_name_and_last_name(first_name,
last_name)
    end
  end

end
```

Now we have a `named` method available to use on the `people` collection.

```
person = Account.find(:first).people.named("David Heinemeier Hansson")
person.first_name # => "David"
person.last_name  # => "Heinemeier Hansson"
```

If you need to share the same set of extensions between many associations, you can use specify an extension module, instead of a block with method definitions.

Here is the same feature shown in Listing 7.5, except broken out into its own Ruby module:

```
module ByNameExtension
  def named(name)
    first_name, last_name = name.split(" ", 2)
    find_or_create_by_first_name_and_last_name(first_name, last_name)
  end
end
```

Now we can use it to extend many different relationships, as long as they're compatible. (Our contract in the example consists of the `find_or_create_by_first_name_and_last_name` method.)

```
class Account < ActiveRecord::Base
  has_many :people, :extend => ByNameExtension
end

class Company < ActiveRecord::Base
  has_many :people, :extend => ByNameExtension
end
```

If you need to use multiple named extension modules, you can pass an array of modules to the `:extend` option instead of a single module, like this:

```
has_many :people, :extend => [ByNameExtension, ByRecentExtension]
```

In the case of name conflicts, methods contained in modules added later in the array supercede those earlier in the array.

The `AssociationProxy` Class

`AssociationProxy`, the parent of all association proxies (refer to Figure 7.1 if needed), contributes a number of useful methods that apply to most kinds of associations and can come into play when you're writing association extensions.

`reload` and `reset`

The `reset` method puts the association proxy back in its initial state, which is unloaded (cached association objects are cleared). The `reload` method invokes `reset`, and then loads associated objects from the database.

`proxy_owner`, `proxy_reflection`, and `proxy_target`

References to the internal `owner`, `reflection`, and `target` attributes of the association proxy, respectively.

The `proxy_owner` method provides a reference to the parent object holding the association.

The `proxy_reflection` object is an instace of `ActiveRecord::Reflection::AssociationReflection` and contains all of the configuration options for the association. That includes both default settings and those that were passed to the association method when it was declared.[3]

The `proxy_target` is the associated array (or associated object itself in the case of `belongs_to` and `has_one`).

It might not appear sane to expose these attributes publicly and allow their manipulation. However, without access to them it would be much more difficult to write advanced association extensions. The `loaded?`, `loaded`, `target`, and `target=` methods are public for similar reasons.

The following code sample demonstrates the use of `proxy_owner` within a `published_prior_to` extension method contributed by Wilson Bilkovich:

```ruby
class ArticleCategory < ActiveRecord::Base

  acts_as_tree

  has_many :articles do

    def published_prior_to(date, options = {})
```

```
      if proxy_owner.top_level?
        Article.find_all_published_prior_to(date, :category =>
proxy_owner)
      else
        # self is the `articles' association here so we inherit its
scope
        self.find(:all, options)
      end
    end

  end # has_many :articles extension

  def top_level?
    # do we have a parent, and is our parent the root node of the tree?
    self.parent && self.parent.parent.nil?
  end

end
```

The `acts_as_tree` ActiveRecord plugin extension creates a self-referential association based on a `parent_id` column. The `proxy_owner` reference is used to check
if the parent of this association is a "top-level" node in the tree.

Conclusion

The ability to model associations is what make ActiveRecord more than just a data-
access layer. The ease and elegance with which you can declare those associations are
what make ActiveRecord more than your ordinary object-relational mapper.

In this chapter, we covered the basics of how ActiveRecord associations work. We
started by taking a look at the class hierarchy of associations classes, starting with
`AssociationProxy`. Hopefully, by learning about how associations work under the
hood, you've picked up some enhanced understanding about their power and flexibility.

Finally, the options and methods guide for each type of association should be a
good reference guide for your day-to-day development activities.

References

1. http://en.wikipedia.org/wiki/Insert_(SQL)#Multirow_inserts

2. http://blog.hasmanythrough.com/articles/2006/02/28/association-goodness

3. To learn more about how the reflection object can be useful, including an explanation on how to establish `has_many :through` associations via other `has_many :through` associations, check out the must-read article: http://www.pivotalblabs.com/articles/2007/08/26/ten-things-i-hate-about-proxy-objects-part-i.

CHAPTER 8

ActiveRecord Validations

Computers are like Old Testament gods; lots of rules and no mercy.
—Joseph Campbell

The Validations API in `ActiveRecord` allows you to declaratively define valid states for your model objects. The validation methods hook into the life cycle of an `ActiveRecord` model object and are able to inspect the object to determine whether certain attributes are set, have values in a given range, or pass any other logical hurdles that you specify.

In this chapter, we'll describe the validation methods available and how to use them effectively. We'll explore how those validation methods interact with your model's attributes and how the built-in error-messaging system messages can be used effectively in your application's user interface to provide descriptive feedback.

Finally, we'll also cover an important RubyGem named `Validatable`, which goes beyond Rails' native capabilities by allowing you to define different sets of validation criteria for a given model object, depending on the role it is currently playing in your system.

Finding Errors

Validation problems are also known as (drumroll please...): errors! Every `ActiveRecord` model object contains a collection of errors, accessible (unsurprisingly) as the `errors` attribute. It's an instance of the class `ActiveRecord::Errors` and it's defined in the file `lib/active_record/validations.rb` along with the rest of the validation code.

When a model object is valid, the `errors` collection is empty. In fact, when you call `valid?` on a model object, a series of steps to find errors is taken as follows (slightly simplified):

1. Clear the `errors` collection.

2. Run validations.

3. Return whether the model's `errors` collection is now empty or not.

If the `errors` collection ends up empty, the object is valid. Simple as that.

In some of the validation methods described in this chapter, the ones where you have to write the actual validation logic yourself, you mark an object invalid by adding items to the `errors` collection using its `add` methods.

We'll cover the methods of the `Errors` class in some more detail later on. It makes more sense to look at the validation methods themselves first.

The Simple Declarative Validations

Whenever possible, you should set validations for your models declaratively by using one or more of the following class methods available to all `ActiveRecord` classes. Unless otherwise noted, all of the `validates` methods accept a variable number of attributes, plus options. There are some options for these validation methods that are common to all of them, and we'll cover them at the end of the section.

validates_acceptance_of

Many web applications have screens in which the user is prompted to agree to terms of service or some similar concept, usually involving a check box. No actual database column matching the attribute declared in the validation is required; when you call this method, it will create virtual attributes automatically for each named attribute you specify. I see this validation as a type of *syntax sugar* since it is so specific to web application programming.

```
class Account < ActiveRecord::Base
  validates_acceptance_of :privacy_policy, :terms_of_service
end
```

Error Message

When the `validates_acceptance_of` validation fails, an error message is stored in the model object reading "*attribute* must be accepted."

The `accept` Option

The `:accept` option makes it easy to change the value considered acceptance. The default value is "1", which matches the value supplied by check boxes generated using Rails helper methods.

```
class Cancellation < ActiveRecord::Base
  validates_acceptance_of :account_cancellation, :accept => 'YES'
end
```

If you use the preceding example in conjunction with a text field connected to the `account_cancellation` attribute, the user would have to type the word *YES* in order for the cancellation object to be valid.

validates_associated

When a given model has associated model objects that also need to be valid when it is saved, you use the `validates_associated` method, which works with any kind of association. When the validation is invoked (on save, by default), the `valid?` method of each associated object will be called.

```
class Invoice < ActiveRecord::Base
  has_many :line_items
  validates_associated :line_items
end
```

It's worth noting that careless use of `validates_associated` can result in a circular dependency and cause infinite recursion. Well, not *infinite*, but it will blow up. Given the preceding example, do not do the following on the `LineItem` class:

```
class LineItem < ActiveRecord::Base
  belongs_to :invoice
  validates_associated :invoice
end
```

This validation will not fail if the association is nil because it hasn't been set yet. If you want to make sure that the association is populated *and* valid, you have to use `validates_associated` in conjunction with `validates_presence_of` (covered later in this chapter).

validates_confirmation_of

The `validates_confirmation_of` method is another case of syntactic sugar for web applications, since it is so common to include dual-entry text fields to make sure that the user entered critical data such as passwords and e-mail address correctly. This validation will create a virtual attribute for the confirmation value and compare the two attributes to make sure they match in order for the model to be valid.

Here's an example, using our fictional `Account` model again:

```
class Account < ActiveRecord::Base
  validates_confirmation_of :email, :password
end
```

The user interface used to set values for the `Account` model would need to include extra text fields named with a `_confirmation` suffix, and when submitted, the value of those fields would have to match in order for this validation to pass.

validates_each

The `validates_each` method is a little more free-form than its companions in the validation family in that it doesn't have a predefined validation function. Instead, you give it an array of attribute names to check, and supply a Ruby block to be used in checking each attribute's validity.

The block function designates the model object as valid or not by merit of adding to its `errors` array or not. *The return value of the block is ignored.*

There aren't too many situations where this method is necessary, but one plausible example is when interacting with external services for validation. You might wrap the external validation in a *façade* specific to your application, and then call it using a `validates_each` block:

```
class Invoice < ActiveRecord::Base
  validates_each :supplier_id, :purchase_order do |record, attr,
  value|
```

```
        record.errors.add(attr) unless PurchasingSystem.validate(attr,
    value)
      end
  end
```

Notice that parameters for the model instance (`record`), the name of the attribute, and the value to check are passed as block parameters.

validates_inclusion_of and validates_exclusion_of

The `validates_inclusion_of` method and its complement, `validates_exclusion_of`, are pretty cool, but unless you're super-thorough with your application requirements, I'll bet a small sum that you haven't realized yet why you need them.

These methods take a variable number of attribute names and an `:in` option. When they run, they check to make sure that the value of the attribute is included (or excluded, respectively) in the enumerable object passed as the `:in` option.

The examples in the Rails docs are probably some of the best illustrations of their use, so I'll take inspiration from them:

```
class Person < ActiveRecord::Base
  validates_inclusion_of :gender, :in => ['m','f'],
                         :message => 'O RLY?'

class Account
  validates_exclusion_of :login,
                         :in => ['admin', 'root', 'superuser'],
                         :message => 'Borat says "Naughty, naughty!"'
end
```

Notice that in the examples I've introduced usage of the `:message` option, common to all validation methods, to customize the error message constructed and added to the `Errors` collection when the validation fails. We'll cover the default error messages and how to effectively customize them a little further along in the chapter.

validates_existence_of

This validation is provided by a plugin, but I've found it so useful in day-to-day work that I had to include it. It checks that a foreign key in a `belongs_to` association references an exisiting record in the database. You can think of it as a foreign-key constraint, except in your Rails code. It also works fine with polymorphic `belongs_to` associations.

```
class Person < ActiveRecord::Base
  belongs_to :address
  validates_existence_of :address
end
```

Josh Susser came up with the idea and the plugin and described it on his blog:

The thing that's always frustrated me is that there isn't a validation to enforce that a foreign key references a record that exists. Sure, `validates_presence_` `of` will make sure you have a foreign key that isn't nil. And `validates_` `associated` will tell you if the record referenced by that key passes its own validations. But that is either too little or too much, and what I want is in the middle ground. So I decided it was time to roll my own. http://blog.hasmanythrough.com/2007/7/14/validate-your-existence

To install the plugin just type the following in your project directory:

```
$ script/plugin install
http://svn.hasmanythrough.com/public/plugins/validates_existence/
```

As for options, if `:allow_nil => true`, then the key itself may be `nil` and no validation will occur. A non-nil key will cause a query to be issued to make sure that the foreign object exists in the database. The default error message is "does not exist", but can be overriden just like other validations using the `:message` option.

validates_format_of

To use `validates_format_of`, you'll have to know how to use Ruby regular expressions. Pass the method one or more attributes to check, and a regular expression as the (required) `:with` option. A good example, as shown in the Rails docs, is checking for a valid e-mail address format:

```
class Person < ActiveRecord::Base
  validates_format_of :email,
    :with => /\A([^@\s]+)@((?:[-a-z0-9]+\.)+[a-z]{2,})\Z/i
end
```

By the way, that example is totally *not* an RFC-compliant email address format checker[1].

Courtenay Says...

Regular expressions are awesome but can get very complex, particularly when validating domain names or email addresses.

You can use #{} inside regular expressions, so split up your regex into chunks like this:

```
validates_format_of :name, :with =>
/^((localhost)|#{DOMAIN}|#{NUMERIC_IP})#{PORT}$/
```

That expression is pretty straightforward and easy to understand.

The constants themselves are not so easy to understand but easier than if they were all jumbled in together:

```
PORT = /(([:]\d+)?)/
DOMAIN = /([a-z0-9\-]+\.?)*([a-z0-9]{2,})\.[a-z]{2,}/
NUMERIC_IP = /(?>(?:1?\d?\d|2[0-4]\d|25[0-
5])\.){3}(?:1?\d?\d|2[0-4]\d|25[0-
5])(?:\/(?:[12]?\d|3[012]))|-(?> (?:1?\d?\d|2[0-
4]\d|25[0-5])\.){3}(?:1?\d?\d|2[0-4]\d|25[0-5]))?/
```

---

validates_length_of

The `validates_length_of` method takes a variety of different options to let you concisely specify length constraints for a given attribute of your model.

```
class Account < ActiveRecord::Base
  validates_length_of :login, :minimum => 5
end
```

Constraint Options

The `:minimum` and `:maximum` options work as expected, but don't use them together. To specify a range, use the `:within` option and pass it a Ruby range, as in the following example:

```
class Account < ActiveRecord::Base
  validates_length_of :login, :within => 5..20
end
```

To specify an exact length of an attribute, use the `:is` option:

```
class Account < ActiveRecord::Base
  validates_length_of :account_number, :is => 16
end
```

Error Message Options

Rails gives you the ability to generate detailed error messages for `validates_length_of`
via the `:too_long`, `:too_short`, and `:wrong_length` options. Use `%d` in your custom
error message as a placeholder for the number corresponding to the constraint.

```
class Account < ActiveRecord::Base
  validates_length_of :account_number, :is => 16,
                      :wrong_length => "should be %d characters long"
end
```

validates_numericality_of

The somewhat clumsily named `validates_numericality_of` method is used to
ensure that an attribute can only hold a numeric value. The `:integer_only` option
lets you further specify that the value should only be an integral value and defaults to
false.

```
class Account < ActiveRecord::Base
  validates_numericality_of :account_number, :integer_only => true
end
```

validates_presence_of

Last but not least is one of the more common validation methods, `:validates_presence_of`, which is used to denote mandatory attributes. This method checks whether the attribute is blank via Rails' `blank?` method, defined on `Object`, which returns `true` for values that are `nil` or a blank string `""`.

```
class Account < ActiveRecord::Base
  validates_presence_of :login, :email, :account_number
end
```

Validating the Presence of Associated Objects

When you're trying to ensure that an association is present, write your association against its foreign key attribute, not the association variable itself. Note that the validation will fail in cases when both the parent and child object are unsaved (since the foreign key will be blank).

validates_uniqueness_of

The `validates_uniqueness_of` method ensures that the value of an attribute is unique for all models of the same type. This validation does *not* work by adding a uniqueness constraint at the database level. It does work by constructing and executing a query looking for a matching record in the database. If any record is returned when this method does its query, the validation fails.

```
class Account < ActiveRecord::Base
  validates_uniqueness_of :login
end
```

By specifying a `:scope` option, additional attributes can be used to determine uniqueness. You may pass `:scope` one or more attribute names as symbols (putting multiple symbols in an array).

```
class Address < ActiveRecord::Base
  validates_uniqueness_of :line_two, :scope => [:line_one, :city,
  :zip]
end
```

It's also possible to specify whether to make the uniqueness constraint case-sensitive or not, via the `:case_sensitive` option (ignored for nontextual attributes).

Enforcing Uniqueness of Join Models

In the course of using join models (with `has_many :through`), it seems pretty common to need to make the relationship unique. Consider an application that models students, courses, and registrations with the following code:

```ruby
class Student < ActiveRecord::Base
  has_many :registrations
  has_many :courses, :through => :registrations
end

class Registration < ActiveRecord::Base
  belongs_to :student
  belongs_to :course
end

class Course < ActiveRecord::Base
  has_many :registrations
  has_many :students, :through => :registrations
end
```

How do you make sure that a student is *not registered more than once* for a particular course? The most concise way is to use `validates_uniqueness_of` with a `:scope` constraint. The important thing to remember with this technique is to reference the foreign keys, not the names of the associations themselves:

```ruby
class Registration < ActiveRecord::Base
  belongs_to :student
  belongs_to :course

  validates_uniqueness_of :student_id, :scope => :course_id,
                          :message => "can only register once per
course"
end
```

Notice that since the default error message generated when this validation fails would not make sense, I've provided a custom error message that will result in the expression: "Student can only register once per course."

`RecordInvalid`

Whenever you do so-called bang operations (such as `save!`) or operations that save behind the scenes, and a validation fails, you should be prepared to rescue `ActiveRecord::RecordInvalid`. Validation failures will cause `RecordInvalid` to be raised and its message will contain a description of the failures.

Here's a quick example from one of my applications that has pretty restrictive validations on its `User` model:

```
>> u = User.new
=> #<User ...>
>> u.save!
ActiveRecord::RecordInvalid: Validation failed: Name can't be blank,
Password confirmation can't be blank, Password is too short (minimum
is 5 characters), Email can't be blank, Email address format is bad
```

Common Validation Options

The following options apply to all of the validation methods.

`:allow_nil`

In many cases, you only want to trigger a validation if a value is present and the absence of a value is not a problem. The `:allow_nil` option skips the validation if the value of the attribute is `nil`. Remember that this option only checks for `nil`, and empty strings `""` are not considered nil.

`:if`

The `:if` option is covered in the next section, "Conditional Validation."

`:message`

As we've discussed earlier in the chapter, the way that the validation process registers failures is by adding items to the `Errors` collection of the model object being checked. Part of the error item is a specific message describing the validation failure. All of the validation methods accept a `:message` option so that you can override the default error message format.

```
class Account < ActiveRecord::Base
  validates_uniqueness_of :login, :message => "is already taken"
end
```

:on

By default, validations are run on save (both create and update operations). If you need to do so, for whatever reason, you can limit a given validation to just one of those operations by passing the :on option either :create or :update.

One good use for :on => :create is in conjunction with validates_uniqueness_of, since checking uniqueness with a query on large datasets can be time-consuming.

```
class Account < ActiveRecord::Base
  validates_uniqueness_of :login, :on => :create
end
```

But wait a minute—wouldn't that pose a problem if the account model was updated later on with a nonunique value? That's where attr_protected comes in. Sensitive attributes of your model should be protected from mass assignment using the attr_protected method. In your controller action that creates new accounts, you'll have to grab the login parameter and set it manually.

Conditional Validation

All validation methods also accept an :if option, to determine at runtime (and *not* during the class definition) whether the validation needs to be run or not.

The following evaluate_condition method, from ActiveRecord::Validations, is called with the value of the :if option as the condition parameter and the model object to be validated as record:

```
# Determine from the given condition whether or not to validate the
# record, (whether a block, procedure, method or string.)
def evaluate_condition(condition, record)
  case condition
    when Symbol: record.send(condition)
    when String: eval(condition, binding)
    else
      if condition_block?(condition)
```

```
            condition.call(record)
        else
          raise ActiveRecordError,
            "Needs to be a symbol, string (to be eval'ed), or a proc"
        end
      end
  end
```

As can be discerned by the `case` statement in the implementation of the method, the following three types of arguments can be supplied as an `:if` option:

- `Symbol`   The name of a method to invoke as a symbol. This is probably the most common option, and offers the best performance.

- `String`   A snippet of Ruby code to `eval` might be useful when the condition is really short, but keep in mind that eval'ing statements is relatively slow.

- `Block`   A proc to be `call`'d. Perhaps the most elegant choice for one-line conditionals.

Usage and Considerations

When does it make sense to use conditional validations? The answer is: whenever an object can be validly persisted in more than one state.

A very common example, since it is used by the `acts_as_authenticated` plugin, involves the `User` (or `Person`) model, used for login and authentication.

```
validates_presence_of :password, :if => :password_required?
validates_presence_of :password_confirmation, :if =>
:password_required?
validates_length_of :password, :within => 4..40,
:if=>:password_required?
validates_confirmation_of :password, :if => :password_required?
```

This code is not DRY (meaning that it is repetitive). You can learn how to refactor it using the `with_options` method described in Chapter 14, "Login and Authentication." Usage and implementation of the `acts_as_authenticated` plugin is covered in greater detail in Chapter 14.

There are only two cases when a (plaintext) password field should be required in order for the model to be valid.

```
protected

  def password_required?
    crypted_password.blank? || !password.blank?
  end
```

The first case is if the `crypted_password` attribute is blank, because that means we are dealing with a new `User` instance that has not been given a password yet. The other case is when the `password` attribute itself is not blank; perhaps this is happening during an update operation and the user is attempting to reset her password.

Working with the `Errors` Object

Here's a quick reference of the default wording for error messages, pulled straight out of the Rails codebase:

```
@@default_error_messages = {
  :inclusion => "is not included in the list",
  :exclusion => "is reserved",
  :invalid => "is invalid",
  :confirmation => "doesn't match confirmation",
  :accepted  => "must be accepted",
  :empty => "can't be empty",
  :blank => "can't be blank",
  :too_long => "is too long (maximum is %d characters)",
  :too_short => "is too short (minimum is %d characters)",
  :wrong_length => "is the wrong length (should be %d characters)",
  :taken => "has already been taken",
  :not_a_number => "is not a number"
}
```

As we stated previously, the name of the attribute is capitalized and prepended to the beginning of those default error messages to create the validation failure message. Remember, you can override the default message by using the `:message` option.

Manipulating the `Errors` Collection

Some methods are provided to allow you to add validation errors to the collection manually and alter the state of the `Errors` collection.

`add_to_base(msg)`

Adds an error message related to the object state *itself* and not the value of any particular attribute. Make your error messages complete sentences, because Rails does not do any additional processing of them to make them readable.

`add(attribute, msg)`

Adds an error message related to a particular attribute. The message should be a sentence fragment that reads naturally when prepended with the capitalized name of the attribute.

`clear`

As you might expect, the `clear` method clears the `Errors` collection.

Checking for Errors

It's also possible to check the `Errors` object for validation failures on specific attributes with a couple of methods.

`invalid?(attribute)`

Returns true or false depending on whether there are validation errors associated with `attribute`.

`on(attribute)`

Has multiple return types depending on the state of the errors collection for an `attribute`. Returns `nil` if no errors are associated with the specified attribute. Returns an error message string if only one error is associated with the specified attribute. Finally, returns an array of error message strings if more than one error is associated with the specified attribute.

Custom Validation

We've now reached the matter of custom validation methods, which you might choose to employ if the normal declarative validation methods are not cutting it for you.

Earlier in the chapter, I described the process used to find validation errors, with a disclaimer that my explanation was slightly simplified. Here is the real implementation, since it is quite elegant and readable in my opinion, and helps illuminate where custom validation logic can be added.

```
def valid?
  errors.clear

  run_validations(:validate)
  validate

  if new_record?
    run_validations(:validate_on_create)
    validate_on_create
  else
    run_validations(:validate_on_update)
    validate_on_update
  end

  errors.empty?
end
```

There are three calls to `run_validations`, which is where your declarative validations have been lined up, ready to check your object, if you've defined any. Then there are those three callback (abstract?) methods, that is, methods that are purposely left without an implementation in the `Validations` module. They are intended to be overwritten in your own `ActiveRecord` model if you need them.

Custom validation methods are useful for checking the state of your object *holistically*, not just based on individual attributes. For lack of a better example, let's assume that you are dealing with a model object with a set of three integer attributes (`:attr1`, `:attr2`, and `:attr3`) and a precalculated total attribute (`:total`). The total must always equal the sum of the three attributes:

```
class CompletelyLameTotalExample < ActiveRecord::Base
  def validate
    if total != (attr1 + attr2 + attr3)
```

```
        errors.add_to_base("The total doesn't add up!")
    end
  end
end
```

Remember: The way to mark an object as invalid is to add to its `Errors` collection. The return value of a custom validation method is not used.

Skipping Validations

The `Validations` module mixed into `ActiveRecord::Base` affects three instance methods, as you can see in the following code snippet (from `activerecord/lib/active_record/validations.rb` in the Rails codebase):

```
def self.included(base) # :nodoc:
  base.extend ClassMethods
  base.class_eval do
    alias_method_chain :save, :validation
    alias_method_chain :save!, :validation
    alias_method_chain :update_attribute, :validation_skipping
  end
end
```

The methods `save`, `save!`, and `update_attribute` are affected. The validation process on `save` and `save!` can be skipped by passing in `false` as a method parameter.

The first time I came across `save(false)` in Rails code, it drove me a little batty. I thought to myself, "I don't remember `save` having a parameter," and when I checked the API docs, that was indeed the case! Figuring the docs must be lying, I dove into the codebase and checked the implementation of the `save` method in `ActiveRecord::Base`. No parameter. "WTF, welcome to the wonderful world of Ruby," I thought to myself. "How the heck am I not getting a 1 for 0 argument error here?"

Eventually I figured it out, or maybe some kind #cabooser clued me in: the regular `Base#save` method is replaced when the validations module is mixed in, which it is by default. As a result of using `alias_method_chain`, you end up with a public, yet undocumented, `save_without_validation` method, which is probably a lot more maintainable than `save(false)`.

What about `update_attribute`? The validations module overwrites the default implementation and makes it call `save(false)`. It's short, so I'll include it here:

```
def update_attribute_with_validation_skipping(name, value)
  send(name.to_s + '=', value)
  save(false)
end
```

That's why `update_attribute` doesn't invoke validations, yet its companion method `update_attributes` does, a question that comes up quite often on the mailing list. Whoever wrote the API docs believes that this behavior is "especially useful for Boolean flags on existing records."

I don't know if that is entirely true or not, but I do know that it is the source of ongoing contention in the community. Unfortunately, I don't have much more to add other than some simple common-sense advice: Be very careful using the `update_attribute` method. It can easily persist your model objects in invalid states.

Conclusion

In this (relatively speaking) short chapter, we covered the ActiveRecord Validations API in-depth. One of the most appealing aspects of Rails is how we can declaratively specify the criteria for determining the validity of model objects.

Reference

1. If you need to validate addresses try the plugin at http://code.dunae.ca/validates_email_format_of.

CHAPTER 9

Advanced `ActiveRecord`

`ActiveRecord` is a simple object-relational mapping (ORM) framework compared to other popular ORM frameworks, such as Hibernate in the Java world. Don't let that fool you, though: Under its modest exterior, `ActiveRecord` has some pretty advanced features. To really get the most effectiveness out of Rails development, you need to have more than a basic understanding of `ActiveRecord`—things like knowing when to break out of the one-table/one-class pattern, or how to leverage Ruby modules to keep your code clean and free of duplication.

In this chapter, we wrap up this book's comprehensive coverage of `ActiveRecord` by reviewing callbacks, observers, single-table inheritance (STI), and polymorphic models. We also review a little bit of information about metaprogramming and Ruby domain-specific languages (DSLs) as they relate to `ActiveRecord`.

Callbacks

This advanced feature of `ActiveRecord` allows the savvy developer to attach behavior at a variety of different points along their model's life cycle, such as after initialization, before database records are inserted, updated or removed, and so on.

Callbacks can do a variety of tasks, ranging from simple things such as logging and massaging of attribute values prior to validation, to complex calculations. Callbacks can halt the execution of the life-cycle process taking place. Some callbacks can even modify the behavior of the model class on the fly. We'll cover all of those scenarios in this section, but first let's get a taste of what a callback looks like. Check out the following silly example:

```
class Beethoven < ActiveRecord::Base

  before_destroy :last_words
  ...

  protected

    def last_words
      logger.info "Friends applaud, the comedy is over"
    end

end
```

So prior to dying (ehrm, being `destroy`'d), the last words of the `Beethoven` class will always be logged for posterity. As we'll see soon, there are 14 different opportunities to add behavior to your model in this fashion. Before we get to that list, let's cover the mechanics of registering a callback.

Callback Registration

Overall, the most common way to register a callback method is to declare it at the top of the class using a typical Rails macro-style class method. However, there's a less verbose way to do it also. Simply implement the callback as a method in your class. In other words, I could have coded the prior example as follows:

```
class Beethoven < ActiveRecord::Base
  ...

  protected

    def before_destroy
      logger.info "Friends applaud, the comedy is over"
    end

end
```

This is a rare case of the less-verbose solution being bad. In fact, it is almost always preferable, dare I say it is the Rails way, to use the callback macros over implementing callback methods, for the following reasons:

- Macro-style callback declarations are added near the top of the class definition, making the existence of that callback more evident versus a method body later in the file.

- Macro-style callbacks add callback methods to a queue. That means that more than one method can be hooked into the same slot in the life cycle. Callbacks will be invoked in the order in which they were added to the queue.

- Callback methods for the same hook can be added to their queue at different levels of an inheritance hierarchy and still work—they won't override each other the way that methods would.

- Callbacks defined as methods on the model are always called last.

One-Liners

Now, if (and only if) your callback routine is really short,[1] you can add it by passing a block to the callback macro. We're talking one-liners!

```
class Napoleon < ActiveRecord::Base
  before_destroy {|r| logger.info "Josephine..." }
  ...
end
```

Protected or Private

Except when you're using a block, the access level for callback methods should always be protected or private. It should never be public, since callbacks should never be called from code outside the model.

Believe it or not, there are even more ways to implement callbacks, but we'll cover those techniques further along in the chapter. For now, let's look at the lists of callback hooks available.

Matched `before`/`after` Callbacks

In total, there are 14 types of callbacks you can register on your models! Twelve of them are matching `before`/`after` callback pairs, such as `before_validation` and `after_validation`. (The other two, `after_initialize` and `after_find`, are special, and we'll discuss them later in this section.)

List of Callbacks

This is the list of callback hooks available during a `save` operation. (The list varies slightly depending on whether you're saving a new or existing record.)

- `before_validation`

- `before_validation_on_create`

- `after_validation`

- `after_validation_on_create`

- `before_save`

- `before_create` (for new records) and `before_update` (for existing records)

- `ActiveRecord` talks to the database and actually does an `INSERT` or `UPDATE`

- `after_create` (for new records) and `before_update` (for existing records)

- `after_save`

  `Delete` operations have their own two callbacks:

- `before_destroy`

- `ActiveRecord` talks to the database and actually does a `DELETE`

- `after_destroy` is called after all attributes have been frozen (read-only)

Halting Execution

If you return a Boolean `false` (not `nil`) from a callback method, `ActiveRecord` halts the execution chain. No further callbacks are executed. The `save` method will return `false`, and `save!` will raise a `RecordNotSaved` error.

Keep in mind that since the last expression of a Ruby method is returned implicitly, it is a pretty common bug to write a callback that halts execution unintentionally. If you have an object with callbacks that mysteriously fails to save, make sure you aren't returning `false` by mistake.

Callback Usages

Of course, the callback you should use for a given situation depends on what you're trying to accomplish. The best I can do is to serve up some examples to inspire you with your own code.

Cleaning Up Attribute Formatting with `before_validate_on_create`

The most common examples of using `before_validate` callbacks have to do with cleaning up user-entered attributes. For example, the following `CreditCard` class (as cited in the Rails API docs) cleans up its `number` attribute so that false negatives don't occur on validation:

```
class CreditCard < ActiveRecord::Base
  ...
  private

    def before_validation_on_create
      # Strip everything in the number except digits
      self.number = number.gsub(/[^0-9]/, "")
    end

end
```

Geocoding with `before_save`

Assume that you have an application that tracks addresses and has mapping features. Addresses should always be geocoded *before saving*, so that they can be displayed rapidly on a map later.[2]

As is often the case, the wording of the requirement itself points you in the direction of the `before_save` callback:

```
class Address < ActiveRecord::Base
  include GeoKit::Geocoders
```

```
before_save :geolocate
validates_presence_of :line_one, :state, :zip
...

private

  def geolocate
    res = GoogleGeocoder.geocode(to_s)
    self.latitude = res.lat
    self.longitude = res.lng
  end
end
```

Before we move on, there are a couple of additional considerations. The preceding code works great if the geocoding succeeds, but what if it doesn't? Do we still want to allow the record to be saved? If not, we should halt the execution chain:

```
def geolocate
  res = GoogleGeocoder.geocode(to_s)
  return false if not res.success       # halt execution

  self.latitude = res.lat
  self.longitude = res.lng
end
```

The only problem remaining is that we give the rest of our code (and by extension, the end user) no indication of why the chain was halted. Even though we're not in a validation routine, I think we can put the errors collection to good use here:

```
def geolocate
  res = GoogleGeocoder.geocode(to_s)
  if res.success
    self.latitude = res.lat
    self.longitude = res.lng
  else
    errors.add_to_base("Geocoding failed. Please check address.")
    return false
  end
end
```

If the geocoding fails, we add a base error message (for the whole object) and halt execution, so that the record is not saved.

Paranoia with `before_destroy`

What if your application has to handle important kinds of data that, once entered, should never be deleted? Perhaps it would make sense to hook into ActiveRecord's destroy mechanism and somehow mark the record as deleted instead?

The following example depends on the accounts table having a deleted_at datetime column.

```
class Account < ActiveRecord::Base
  ...
  def before_destroy
    update_attribute(:deleted_at, Time.now) and return false
  end

end
```

I chose to implement it as a callback method so that I am guaranteed it will execute last in the before_destroy queue. It returns false so that execution is halted and the underlying record is not actually deleted from the database.[3]

It's probably worth mentioning that there are ways that Rails allows you to unintentionally circumvent before_destroy callbacks:

- The `delete` and `delete_all` class methods of ActiveRecord::Base are almost identical. They remove rows directly from the database without instantiating the corresponding model instances, which means no callbacks will occur.

- Model objects in associations defined with the option :dependent => :delete_all will be deleted directly from the database when removed from the collection using the association's `clear` or `delete` methods.

Cleaning Up Associated Files with `after_destroy`

Model objects that have files associated with them, such as attachment records and uploaded images, can clean up after themselves when deleted using the

`after_destroy` callback. The following method from Rick Olson's excellent
AttachmentFu[4] plugin is a good example:

```
# Destroys the file.  Called in the after_destroy callback
def destroy_file
  FileUtils.rm(full_filename)
  ...
rescue
  logger.info "Exception destroying  #{full_filename ... }"
  logger.warn $!.backtrace.collect { |b|  " > #{b}" }.join("\n")
end
```

Special Callbacks: `after_initialize` and `after_find`

The `after_initialize` callback is invoked whenever a new `ActiveRecord` model
is instantiated (either from scratch or from the database). Having it available prevents
you from having to muck around with overriding the actual `initialize` method.

The `after_find` callback is invoked whenever `ActiveRecord` loads a model
object from the database, and is actually called *before* `after_initialize`, if both are
implemented. Because `after_find` and `after_initialize` are called for each
object found and instantiated by finders, performance constraints dictate that they can
only be added as methods, and not via the callback macros.

What if you want to run some code only the first time that a model is ever instantiated, and not after each database load? There is no native callback for that scenario,
but you can do it using the `after_initialize` callback. Just add a condition that
checks to see if it is a new record:

```
def after_initialize
 if new_record?
    ...
 end
end
```

In a number of Rails apps that I've written, I've found it useful to capture user
preferences in a serialized hash associated with the `User` object. The `serialize` feature of `ActiveRecord` models makes this possible, since it transparently persists Ruby

object graphs to a text column in the database. Unfortunately, you can't pass it a default value, so I have to set one myself:

```
class User < ActiveRecord::Base
  serialize :preferences # defaults to nil
  ...

  private

    def after_initialize
      self.preferences ||= Hash.new
    end
end
```

Using the `after_initialize` callback, I can automatically populate the `preferences` attribute of my user model with an empty hash, so that I never have to worry about it being `nil` when I access it with code such as `user.preferences [:show_help_text] = false`. Of course, you would only want to store data in serialized columns that you had no interest in querying with SQL in the future.

Ruby's metaprogramming capabilities combined with the ability to run code whenever a model is loaded using the `after_find` callback are a powerful mix. Since we're not done learning about callbacks yet, we'll come back to uses of `after_find` later on in the chapter, in the section "Modifying `ActiveRecord` Classes at Runtime."

Callback Classes

It is common enough to want to reuse callback code for more than one object that Rails gives you a way to write callback *classes*. All you have to do is pass a given callback queue an object that responds to the name of the callback and takes the model object as a parameter.

Here's our paranoid example from the previous section as a callback class:

```
class MarkDeleted
  def self.before_destroy(model)
    model.update_attribute(:deleted_at, Time.now) and return false
  end
end
```

The behavior of MarkDeleted is stateless, so I added the callback as a *class* method. Now you don't have to instantiate MarkDeleted objects for no good reason. All you do is pass the class to the callback queue for whichever models you want to have the mark-deleted behavior:

```
class Account < ActiveRecord::Base
  before_destroy MarkDeleted
  ...
end

class Invoice < ActiveRecord::Base
  before_destroy MarkDeleted
  ...

end
```

Multiple Callback Methods in One Class

There's no rule that says you can't have more than one callback method in a callback class. For example, you might have special audit log requirements to implement:

```
class Auditor
  def initialize(audit_log)
    @audit_log = audit_log
  end

  def after_create(model)
    @audit_log.created(model.inspect)
  end

  def after_update(model)
    @audit_log.updated(model.inspect)
  end

  def after_destroy(model)
    @audit_log.destroyed(model.inspect)
  end
end
```

To add audit logging to an `ActiveRecord` class, you would do the following:

```
class Account < ActiveRecord::Base
  after_create Auditor.new(DEFAULT_AUDIT_LOG)
  after_update Auditor.new(DEFAULT_AUDIT_LOG)
  after_destroy Auditor.new(DEFAULT_AUDIT_LOG)
  ...
end
```

Wow, that's kind of ugly, having to add three `Auditors` on three lines. We could extract a local variable called `auditor`, but it would still be repetitive. This might be an opportunity to take advantage of Ruby's *open classes*, the fact that you can modify classes that aren't part of your application.

Wouldn't it be better to simply say `acts_as_audited` at the top of the model that needs auditing? We can quickly add it to the `ActiveRecord::Base` class, so that it's available for all our models.

On my projects, the file where "quick and dirty" code like the method in Listing 9.1 would reside is `lib/core_ext/active_record_base.rb`, but you can put it anywhere you want. You could even make it a plugin (as detailed in Chapter 19, "Extending Rails with Plugins"). Just make sure to require it from `config/environment.rb` or it'll never get loaded.

Listing 9.1 A Quick-and-Dirty "Acts As Audited" Method

```
class ActiveRecord::Base
  def self.acts_as_audited(audit_log=DEFAULT_AUDIT_LOG)
    auditor = Auditor.new(audit_log)
    after_create auditor
    after_update auditor
    after_destroy auditor
  end
end
```

Now, the top of `Account` is a lot less cluttered:

```
class Account < ActiveRecord::Base
  acts_as_audited
  ...
end
```

Testability

When you add callback methods to a model class, you pretty much have to test that they're functioning correctly in conjunction with the model to which they are added. That may or may not be a problem. In contrast, callback classes are super-easy to test in isolation.

The following test method verifies correct operation of our `Auditor` callback class (using the Mocha mocking library available at http://mocha.rubyforge.org/):

```
def test_auditor_logs_created
  (model = mock).expects(:inspect).returns('foo')
  (log = mock).expects(:created).with('foo')

  Auditor.new(log).after_create(model)
end
```

Chapter 17, "Testing," and Chapter 18, "RSpec on Rails," cover testing with `Test::Unit` and `RSpec`, respectively.

Observers

The *single responsibility principle* is a very important tenet of object-oriented programming. It compels us to keep a class focused on a single concern. As you've learned in the previous section, callbacks are a useful feature of `ActiveRecord` models that allow us to hook in behavior at various points of a model object's life cycle. Even if we pull that extra behavior out into callback classes, the hook still requires code changes in the model class definition itself. On the other hand, Rails gives us a way to hook in that is completely transparent to the model class: `Observers`.

Here is the functionality of our old `Auditor` callback class as an observer of `Account` objects:

```
class AccountObserver < ActiveRecord::Observer
  def after_create(model)
    DEFAULT_AUDIT_LOG.created(model.inspect)
  end

  def after_update(model)
    DEFAULT_AUDIT_LOG.updated(model.inspect)
  end

  def after_destroy(model)
```

```
      DEFAULT_AUDIT_LOG.destroyed(model.inspect)
    end
  end
```

Naming Conventions

When `ActiveRecord::Observer` is subclassed, it breaks down the name of the subclass by stripping off the "Observer" part. In the case of our `AccountObserver` in the preceding example, it would know that you want to observe the `Account` class. However, that's not always desirable behavior. In fact, with general-purpose code such as our `Auditor`, it's positively a step backward, so it's possible to overrule the naming convention with the use of the `observe` macro-style method. We still extend `ActiveRecord::Observer`, but we can call the subclass whatever we want and tell it explicitly what to observe:

```
class Auditor < ActiveRecord::Observer
  observe Account, Invoice, Payment

  def after_create(model)
    DEFAULT_AUDIT_LOG.created(model.inspect)
  end

  def after_update(model)
    DEFAULT_AUDIT_LOG.updated(model.inspect)
  end

  def after_destroy(model)
    DEFAULT_AUDIT_LOG.destroyed(model.inspect)
  end
end
```

Registration of Observers

If there weren't a place for you to tell Rails which observers to load, they would never get loaded at all, since they're not referenced from any other code in your application. As mentioned in Chapter 1, "Rails Environments and Configuration," your application's boilerplate `config/environment.rb` has a commented-out line where you should define the observers to be loaded:

```
# Activate observers that should always be running
config.active_record.observers = [:auditor]
```

Timing

Observers are notified before the in-object callbacks are triggered. Otherwise, it wouldn't be possible to act on the whole object in something like a before_destroy observer without having the object's own callbacks executed first.

Single-Table Inheritance (STI)

A lot of applications start out with a User model of some sort. Over time, as different kinds of users emerge, it might make sense to make a greater distinction between them. Admin and Guest classes are introduced, as subclasses of User. Now, the shared behavior can reside in User, and subtype behavior can be *pushed down* to subclasses. However, all user data can still reside in the users table—all you need to do is introduce a type column that will hold the name of the class to be instantiated for a given row.

To continue explaining single-table inheritance, let's turn back to our example of a recurring Timesheet class. We need to know how many billable_hours are outstanding for a given user. The calculation can be implemented in various ways, but in this case we've chosen to write a pair of class and instance methods on the Timesheet class:

```ruby
class Timesheet < ActiveRecord::Base
  ...

  def billable_hours_outstanding
    if submitted?
      billable_weeks.map(&:total_hours).sum
    else
      0
    end
  end

  def self.billable_hours_outstanding_for(user)
    user.timesheets.map(&:billable_hours_outstanding).sum
  end

end
```

I'm not suggesting that this is good code. It works, but it's inefficient and that `if/else` condition is a little fishy. Its shortcomings become apparent once requirements emerge about marking a `Timesheet` as paid. It forces us to modify `Timesheet`'s `billable_hours_outstanding` method again:

```
def billable_hours_outstanding
  if submitted? and not paid?
    billable_weeks.map(&:total_hours).sum
  else
    0
  end
end
```

That latest change is a clear violation of the *open-closed principle,*[5] which urges you to write code that is open for extension, but closed for modification. We know that we violated the principle, because we were forced to change the `billable_hours_outstanding` method to accommodate the new `Timesheet` status. Though it may not seem like a large problem in our simple example, consider the amount of conditional code that will end up in the `Timesheet` class once we start having to implement functionality such as `paid_hours` and `unsubmitted_hours`.

So what's the answer to this messy question of the constantly changing conditional? Given that you're reading the section of the book about single-table inheritance, it's probably no big surprise that we think one good answer is to use object-oriented inheritance. To do so, let's break our original `Timesheet` class into four classes.

```
class Timesheet < ActiveRecord::Base
  # non-relevant code ommitted

  def self.billable_hours_outstanding_for(user)
    user.timesheets.map(&:billable_hours_outstanding).sum
  end
end

class DraftTimesheet < Timesheet
  def billable_hours_outstanding
    0
  end
end
```

```
class SubmittedTimesheet < Timesheet
  def billable_hours_outstanding
    billable_weeks.map(&:total_hours).sum
  end
end
```

Now when the requirements demand the ability to calculate partially paid timesheets, we need only add some behavior to a `PaidTimesheet` class. No messy conditional statements in sight!

```
class PaidTimesheet < Timesheet
  def billable_hours_outstanding
    billable_weeks.map(&:total_hours).sum - paid_hours
  end
end
```

Mapping Inheritance to the Database

Mapping object inheritance effectively to a relational database is not one of those problems with a definitive solution. We're only going to talk about the one mapping strategy that Rails supports natively, which is *single-table inheritance*, called *STI* for short.

In STI, you establish one table in the database to holds all of the records for any object in a given inheritance hierarchy. In `ActiveRecord` STI, that one table is named after the top parent class of the hierarchy. In the example we've been considering, that table would be named `timesheets`.

Hey, that's what it was called before, right? Yes, but to enable STI we have to add a `type` column to contain a string representing the type of the stored object. The following migration would properly set up the database for our example:

```
class AddTypeToTimesheet < ActiveRecord::Migration
  def self.up
    add_column :timesheets, :type, :string
  end

  def self.down
    remove_column :timesheets, :type
  end
end
```

No default value is needed. Once the type column is added to an `ActiveRecord` model, Rails will automatically take care of keeping it populated with the right value. Using the console, we can see this behavior in action:

```
>> d = DraftTimesheet.create
>> d.type
=> 'DraftTimesheet'
```

When you try to find an object using the `find` methods of a base STI class, Rails will automatically instantiate objects using the appropriate subclass. This is especially useful in cases such as the timesheet example we've been describing, where we retrieve all the records for a particular user and then call methods that behave differently depending on the object's class.

```
>> Timesheet.find(:first)
=> #<DraftTimesheet:0x2212354...>
```

Sebastian Says...

The word "type" is a very common column name and you might have plenty of uses for it not related to STI—which is why it's very likely you've experienced an `ActiveRecord::SubclassNotFound` error. Rails will read the "type" column of your `Car` class and try to find an "SUV" class that doesn't exist.

The solution is simple: Tell Rails to use another column for STI with the following code:

```
set_inheritance_column "not_sti"
```

Rails won't complain about the missing column; it will simply ignore it.

Recently, the error message was reworded with a better explanation, but too many developers skim error messages and then spend an hour trying to figure out what's wrong with their models. (A lot of people skim sidebar columns too when reading books, but hey, at least I am doubling their chances of learning about this problem.)

STI Considerations

Although Rails makes it extremely simple to use single-table inheritance, there are a few caveats that you should keep in mind.

To begin with, *you cannot have an attribute on two different subclasses with the same name but a different type.* Since Rails uses one table to store all subclasses, these attributes with the same name occupy the same column in the table. Frankly, there's not much of a reason why that should be a problem unless you've made some pretty bad data-modeling decisions.

More importantly, *you need to have one column per attribute on any subclass and any attribute that is not shared by all the subclasses must accept nil values.* In the recurring example, `PaidTimesheet` has a `paid_hours` column that is not used by any of the other subclasses. `DraftTimesheet` and `SubmittedTimesheet` will not use the `paid_hours` column and leave it as null in the database. In order to validate data for columns not shared by all subclasses, you must use `ActiveRecord` validations and not the database.

Third, it is *not a good idea to have subclasses with too many unique attributes.* If you do, you will have one database table with many null values in it. Normally, a tree of subclasses with a large number of unique attributes suggests that something is wrong with your application design and that you should refactor. If you have an STI table that is getting out of hand, it is time to reconsider your decision to use inheritance to solve your particular problem. Perhaps your base class is too abstract?

Finally, legacy database constraints may require a different name in the database for the `type` column. In this case, you can set the new column name using the class method `set_inheritance_column` in the base class. For the `Timesheet` example, we could do the following:

```
class Timesheet < ActiveRecord::Base
  set_inheritance_column 'object_type'
end
```

Now Rails will automatically populate the `object_type` column with the object's type.

STI and Associations

It seems pretty common for applications, particularly data-management ones, to have models that are very similar in terms of their data payload, mostly varying in their behavior and associations to each other. If you used object-oriented languages prior to

Rails, you're probably already accustomed to breaking down problem domains into hierarchical structures.

Take for instance, a Rails application that deals with the population of states, counties, cities, and neighborhoods. All of these are places, which might lead you to define an STI class named `Place` as shown in Listing 9.2. I've also included the database schema for clarity:[6]

Listing 9.2   The Places Database Schema and the `Place` Class

```
# == Schema Information
#
# Table name: places
#
# id              :integer(11)   not null, primary key
# region_id       :integer(11)
# type            :string(255)
# name            :string(255)
# description     :string(255)
# latitude        :decimal(20, 1)
# longitude       :decimal(20, 1)
# population      :integer(11)
# created_at      :datetime
# updated_at      :datetime

class Place < ActiveRecord::Base
end
```

`Place` is in essence an abstract class. It should not be instantiated, but there is no foolproof way to enforce that in Ruby. (No big deal, this isn't Java!) Now let's go ahead and define concrete subclasses of `Place`:

```
class State < Place
  has_many :counties, :foreign_key => 'region_id'
  has_many :cities, :through => :counties
end

class County < Place
  belongs_to :state, :foreign_key => 'region _id'
  has_many :cities, :foreign_key => 'region _id'
end

class City < Place
  belongs_to :county, :foreign_key => 'region _id'
end
```

You might be tempted to try adding a `cities` association to `State`, knowing that
`has_many :through` works with both `belongs_to` and `has_many` target associations. It would make the `State` class look something like this:

```
class State < Place
  has_many :counties, :foreign_key => 'region_id'
  has_many :cities, :through => :counties
end
```

That would certainly be cool, if it worked. Unfortunately, in this particular case,
since there's only one underlying table that we're querying, there simply isn't a way to
distinguish among the different kinds of objects in the query:

```
Mysql::Error: Not unique table/alias: 'places': SELECT places.* FROM
places INNER JOIN places ON places.region_id = places.id WHERE
((places.region_id = 187912) AND ((places.type = 'County'))) AND
((places.`type` = 'City' ))
```

What would we have to do to make it work? Well, the most realistic would be to
use specific foreign keys, instead of trying to overload the meaning of `region_id` for
all the subclasses. For starters, the `places` table would look like the example in Listing
9.3.

Listing 9.3 The Places Database Schema, Revised

```
# == Schema Information
#
# Table name: places
#
#  id                 :integer(11)      not null, primary key
#  state_id           :integer(11)
#  county_id          :integer(11)
#  type               :string(255)
#  name               :string(255)
#  description         :string(255)
#  latitude           :decimal(20, 1)
#  longitude          :decimal(20, 1)
#  population         :integer(11)
#  created_at         :datetime
#  updated_at         :datetime
```

The subclasses would be simpler without the `:foreign_key` options on the associations. Plus you could use a regular `has_many` relationship from `State` to `City`, instead of the more complicated `has_many :through`.

```
class State < Place
  has_many :counties
  has_many :cities
end

class County < Place
  belongs_to :state
  has_many :cities
end

class City < Place
  belongs_to :county
end
```

Of course, all those null columns in the places table won't win you any friends with relational database purists. That's nothing, though. Just a little bit later in this chapter we'll take a second, more in-depth look at polymorphic `has_many` relationships, which will make the purists positively hate you.

Abstract Base Model Classes

In contrast to single-table inheritance, it is possible for `ActiveRecord` models to share common code via inheritance and still be persisted to different database tables. The technique involves creating an abstract base model class that persistent subclasses will extend. It's actually one of the simpler techniques that we broach in this chapter.

Let's take the `Place` class from the previous section (refer to Listing 9.3) and revise it to be an abstract base class in Listing 9.4. It's simple really—we just have to add one line of code:

Listing 9.4   The Abstract `Place` Class

```
class Place < ActiveRecord::Base
  self.abstract = true
end
```

As I said, quite simple. Marking an `ActiveRecord` model abstract is essentially the opposite of making it an STI class with a type column. You're telling Rails: "Hey, I *don't* want you to assume that there is a table named `places`."

In our running example, it means we would have to establish tables for states, counties, and cities, which might be exactly what we want. Remember though, that we would no longer be able to query across subtypes with code like `Place.find(:all)`.

Abstract classes is an area of Rails where there aren't too many hard-and-fast rules to guide you—experience and gut feeling will help you out.

In case you haven't noticed yet, both class and instance methods are shared down the inheritance hierarchy of `ActiveRecord` models. So are constants and other class members brought in through module inclusion. That means we can put all sorts of code inside `Place` that will be useful to its subclasses.

Polymorphic `has_many` Relationships

Rails gives you the ability to make one class `belong_to` more than one type of another class, as eloquently stated by blogger Mike Bayer:

> The "polymorphic association," on the other hand, while it bears some resemblance to the regular polymorphic union of a class hierarchy, is not really the same since you're only dealing with a particular association to a single target class from any number of source classes, source classes which don't have anything else to do with each other; i.e. they aren't in any particular inheritance relationship and probably are all persisted in completely different tables. In this way, the polymorphic association has a lot less to do with object inheritance and a lot more to do with aspect-oriented programming (AOP); a particular concept needs to be applied to a divergent set of entities which otherwise are not directly related. Such a concept is referred to as a cross-cutting concern, such as, all the entities in your domain need to support a history log of all changes to a common logging table. In the AR example, an Order and a User object are illustrated to both require links to an Address object.[7]

In other words, this is not polymorphism in the typical object-oriented sense of the word; rather, it is something unique to Rails.

In the Case of Models with Comments

In our recurring Time and Expenses example, let's assume that we want both BillableWeek and Timesheet to have many comments (a shared Comment class). A naive way to solve this problem might be to have the Comment class belong to both the BillableWeek and Timesheet classes and have billable_week_id and timesheet_id as columns in its database table.

```
class Comment < ActiveRecord::Base
  belongs_to :timesheet
  belongs_to :expense_report
end
```

That approach is naive because it would be difficult to work with and hard to extend. Among other things, you would need to add code to the application to ensure that a Comment never belonged to both a BillableWeek and a Timesheet *at the same time.* The code to figure out what a given comment is attached to would be cumbersome to write. Even worse, every time you want to be able to add comments to another type of class, you'd have to add another nullable foreign key column to the comments table.

Rails solves this problem in an elegant fashion, by allowing us to define what it terms *polymorphic associations,* which we covered when we described the :polymorphic => true option of the belongs_to association in Chapter 7, "ActiveRecord Associations."

The Interface

Using a polymorphic association, we need define only a single belongs_to and add a pair of related columns to the underlying database table. From that moment on, any class in our system can have comments attached to it (which would make it *commentable*), without needing to alter the database schema or the Comment model itself.

```
class Comment < ActiveRecord::Base
  belongs_to :commentable, :polymorphic => true
end
```

There isn't a Commentable class (or module) in our application. We named the association :commentable because it accurately describes the interface of objects that will be associated in this way. The name :commentable will turn up again on the other side of the association:

```
class Timesheet < ActiveRecord::Base
  has_many :comments, :as => :commentable
end

class BillableWeek < ActiveRecord::Base
  has_many :comments, :as => :commentable
end
```

Here we have the friendly has_many association using the :as option. The :as marks this association as polymorphic, and specifies which interface we are using on the other side of the association. While we're on the subject, the other end of a polymorphic belongs_to can be either a has_many or a has_one and work identically.

The Database Columns

Here's a migration that will create the comments table:

```
class CreateComments < ActiveRecord::Migration
  def self.up
    create_table :comments do |t|
      t.column :text,             :text
      t.column :commentable_id,   :integer
      t.column :commentable_type, :string
    end
  end
end
```

As you can see, there is a column called commentable_type, which stores the class name of associated object. We can see how this works using the Rails console:

```
>> c = Comment.create(:text => "I could be commenting anything.")
>> t = TimeSheet.create
>> b = BillableWeek.create
>> c.update_attribute(:commentable, t)
=> true
>> "#{c.commentable_type}: #{c.commentable_id}"
```

```
=> "Timesheet: 1"
>> c.update_attribute(:commentable, b)
=> true
>> "#{c.commentable_type}: #{c.commentable_id}"
=> "BillableWeek: 1"
```

As you can tell, both the `Timesheet` and the `BillableWeek` that we played with in the console had the same id (1). Thanks to the `commentable_type` attribute, stored as a string, Rails can figure out which is the related object.

Has_many :through and Polymorphics

There are some logical limitations that come into play with polymorphic associations. For instance, since it is impossible for Rails to know the tables necessary to join through a polymorphic association, the following hypothetical code will not work.

```
class Comment < ActiveRecord::Base
  belongs_to :user
  belongs_to :commentable, :polymorphic => true
end

class User < ActiveRecord::Base
  has_many :comments
  has_many :commentables, :through => :comments
end
```

```
>> User.find(:first).comments
ActiveRecord::HasManyThroughAssociationPolymorphicError: Cannot have
a has_many :through association 'User#commentables' on the polymorphic
object 'Comment#commentable'.
```

If you really need it, `has_many :through` is possible with polymorphic associations, but only by specifying exactly what type of polymorphic associations you want. To do so, you must use the `:source_type` option. In most cases, you will also need to use the `:source` option, since the association name will not match the interface name used for the polymorphic association:

```
class User < ActiveRecord::Base
  has_many :comments
  has_many :commented_timesheets, :through => :comments,
          :source => :commentable, :source_type => 'Timesheet'
```

```
has_many :commented_billable_weeks, :through => :comments,
         :source => :commentable, :source_type => 'BillableWeek'
end
```

It's verbose, and the whole thing is arguably starting to lose its elegance if you go this route, but it works:

```
>> User.find(:first).commented_timesheets
=> [#<Timesheet:0x575b98 @attributes={}> ]
```

Considerations about `has_many`

As we work toward the end of this book's coverage of `ActiveRecord`, you might have noticed that we haven't really touched on a subject of particular importance to many programmers: foreign-key constraints in the database. That's mainly because use of foreign-key constraints simply isn't the Rails way to tackle the problem of relational integrity. To put it mildly, that opinion is controversial and some developers have written off Rails (and its authors) for expressing it.

There really isn't anything stopping you from adding foreign-key constraints to your database tables, although you'd do well to wait until after the bulk of development is done. The exception, of course, is those polymorphic associations, which are probably the most extreme manifestation of the Rails opinion against foreign-key constraints. Unless you're armed for battle, you might not want to broach that particular subject with your DBA.

Modules for Reusing Common Behavior

In this section, we'll talk about one strategy for breaking out functionality that is shared between disparate model classes. Instead of using inheritance, we'll put the shared code into modules.

In the section "Polymorphic `has_many` Relationships," we described how to add a commenting feature to our recurring sample Time and Expenses application. We'll continue fleshing out that example, since it lends itself to factoring out into modules.

The requirements we'll implement are as follows: Both users and approvers should be able to add their comments to a `Timesheet` or `ExpenseReport`. Also, since comments are indicators that a timesheet or expense report requires extra scrutiny or processing time, administrators of the application should be able to easily view a list of recent comments. Human nature being what it is, administrators occasionally gloss over the comments without actually reading them, so the requirements specify that a mechanism should be provided for marking comments as "OK" first by the approver, then by the administrator.

Again, here is the polymorphic has_many :as that we used as the foundation for this functionality:

```ruby
class Timesheet < ActiveRecord::Base
  has_many :comments, :as => :commentable
end

class ExpenseReport < ActiveRecord::Base
  has_many :comments, :as => :commentable
end

class Comment < ActiveRecord::Base
  belongs_to :commentable, :polymorphic => true
end
```

Next we create a controller and action for the administrator that list the 10 most recent comments with links to the item to which they are attached.

```ruby
class RecentCommentsController < ApplicationController
  def show
    @recent_comments = Comment.find( :all, :limit => 10,
        :order => 'created_at DESC' )
  end
end
```

Here's some of the simple view template used to display the recent comments.

```erb
<ul>
  <% @recent_comments.each do |comment| %>
    <li>
      <h4><%= comment.created_at -%></h4>
      <%= comment.text %>
      <div class="meta">
        Comment on:
        <%= link_to comment.commentable.title,
          content_url( comment.commentable ) -%>
      </div>
```

```
    </li>
  <% end %>
</ul>
```

So far, so good. The polymorphic association makes it easy to access all types of comments in one listing. But remember each comment needs to be marked "OK" by the approver and/or administrator. Comments should not appear once they've been marked as reviewed.

We won't go into the comment approval interface here. Suffice it to say that a Comment has a reviewed attribute that returns true after it has been marked "OK."

In order to find all of the unreviewed comments for an item, we can use an association extension by modifying the model class definitions as follows:

```
class Timesheet < ActiveRecord::Base
  has_many :comments, :as => :commentable do
    def approved
      find(:all, :conditions => {:reviewed => false })
    end
  end
end

class ExpenseReport < ActiveRecord::Base
  has_many :comments, :as => :commentable do
    def approved
      find(:all, :conditions => {:reviewed => false })
    end
  end
end
```

I'm not happy with this code and I hope by now you know why. It's not DRY! Both Timesheet and ExpenseReport currently have their own identical methods for finding unreviewed comments. Essentially, they both share a common interface. They're *commentable!*

The way that we define common interfaces that share code in Ruby is to include a module in each of those classes, where the module contains the code common to all implementations of the common interface.

So let's go ahead and define a `Commentable` module to do just that, and include it in our model classes:

```
module Commentable
  has_many :comments, :as => :commentable do
    def approved
      find( :all,
        :conditions => ['approved = ?', true ] )
    end
  end
end


class Timesheet < ActiveRecord::Base
  include Commentable
end

class ExpenseReport < ActiveRecord::Base
  include Commentable
end
```

Whoops, this code doesn't work! To fix it, we need to understand an essential aspect of the way that Ruby interprets our code dealing with open classes.

A Review of Class Scope and Contexts

In many other interpreted, OO programming languages, you have two phases of execution—one in which the interpreter loads the class definitions and says "this is the definition of what I have to work with," followed by the phase in which it executes the code. This makes it difficult (though not necessarily impossible) to add new methods to a class dynamically during execution.

In contrast, Ruby lets you add methods to a class at any time. In Ruby, when you type `class MyClass`, you're doing more than simply telling the interpreter to define a class; you're telling it to "execute the following code in the scope of this class."

Let's say you have the following Ruby script:

```
1  class Foo < ActiveRecord::Base
2    has_many :bars
3  end

4  class Foo
5    belongs_to :spam
6  end
```

When the interpreter gets to line 1, you are telling it to execute the following code (up to the matching end) in the context of the Foo class object. Because the Foo class object doesn't exist yet, it goes ahead and creates the class. At line 2, we execute the statement has_many :bars in the context of the Foo class object. Whatever the has_many message does, it does right now.

When we again say class Foo at line 4, we are once again telling the interpreter to execute the following code in the context of the Foo class object, but this time, the interpreter already knows about class Foo; it doesn't actually create another class. Therefore, on line 5, we are simply telling the interpreter to execute the belongs_to :spam statement in the context of that same Foo class object.

In order to execute the has_many and belongs_to statements, those methods need to exist in the context in which they are executed. Because these are defined as class methods in ActiveRecord::Base, and we have previously defined class Foo as extending ActiveRecord::Base, the code will execute without a problem.

However, when we defined our Commentable module like this:

```
module Commentable
  has_many :comments, :as => :commentable do
    def approved
      find( :all,
        :conditions => ['approved = ?', true ] )
    end
  end
end
```

...we get an error when it tries to execute the has_many statement. That's because the has_many method is not defined in the context of the Commentable module object.

Given what we now know about how Ruby is interpreting the code, we now realize that what we really want is for that has_many statement to be executed in the context of the including class.

The included Callback

Luckily, Ruby's Module class defines a handy callback that we can use to do just that. If a Module object defines the method included, it gets run whenever that module is included in another module or class. The argument passed to this method is the module/class object into which this module is being included.

We can define an `included` method on our `Commentable` module object so that it executes the `has_many` statement in the context of the including class (`Timesheet`, `ExpenseReport`, and so on):

```
module Commentable
  def self.included(base)
    base.class_eval do
      has_many :comments, :as => :commentable do
        def approved
          find(:all, :conditions => ['approved = ?', true ])
        end
      end
    end
  end
end
```

Now, when we include the Commentable module in our model classes, it will execute the `has_many` statement just as if we had typed it into each of those classes' bodies.

Courtenay Says...

There's a fine balance to strike here. Magic like `include Commentable` certainly saves on typing and makes your model look less complex, but it can also mean that your association code is doing things you don't know about. This can lead to confusion and hours of head-scratching while you track down code in a separate module.

My personal preference is to leave all associations in the model, and extend them with a module. That way you can quickly get a list of all associations just by looking at the code.

```
has_many :comments, :as => :commentable, :extend =>
Commentable
```

Modifying `ActiveRecord` Classes at Runtime

The metaprogramming capabilities of Ruby, combined with the `after_find` callback, open the door to some interesting possibilities, especially if you're willing to blur your perception of the difference between code and data. I'm talking about modifying the behavior of model classes *on the fly*, as they're loaded into your application.

Listing 9.5 is a drastically simplified example of the technique, which assumes the presence of a `config` column on your model. During the `after_find` callback, we get a handle to the unique *singleton* class[8] of the model instance being loaded. Then we execute the contents of the `config` attribute belonging to this particular `Account` instance, using Ruby's `class_eval` method. Since we're doing this using the singleton class for this instance, rather than the global `Account` class, other account instances in the system are completely unaffected.

Listing 9.5 Runtime Metaprogramming with `after_find`

```
class Account < ActiveRecord::Base
  ...
  private

    def after_find
      singleton = class << self; self; end
      singleton.class_eval(config)
    end
end
```

I used powerful techniques like this one in a supply-chain application that I wrote for a large industrial client. A *lot* is a generic term in the industry used to describe a shipment of product. Depending on the vendor and product involved, the attributes and business logic for a given lot vary quite a bit. Since the set of vendors and products being handled changed on a weekly (sometimes daily) basis, the system needed to be reconfigurable without requiring a production deployment.

Without getting into too much detail, the application allowed the maintenance programmers to easily customize the behavior of the system by manipulating Ruby code stored in the database, associated with whatever product the lot contained.

For example, one of the business rules associated with lots of butter being shipped for Acme Dairy Co. might dictate a strictly integral product code, exactly 10 digits in length. The code, stored in the database, associated with the product entry for Acme Dairy's butter product would therefore contain the following two lines:

```
validates_numericality_of :product_code, :only_integer => true
validates_length_of       :product_code, :is => 10
```

Considerations

A relatively complete description of everything you can do with Ruby metaprogramming, and how to do it correctly, would fill its own book. For instance, you might realize that doing things like executing arbitrary Ruby code straight out of the database is inherently dangerous. That's why I emphasize again that the examples shown here are very simplified. All I want to do is give you a taste of the possibilities.

If you do decide to begin leveraging these kinds of techniques in real-world applications, you'll have to consider security and approval workflow and a host of other important concerns. Instead of allowing arbitrary Ruby code to be executed, you might feel compelled to limit it to a small subset related to the problem at hand. You might design a compact API, or even delve into authoring a domain-specific language (DSL), crafted specifically for expressing the business rules and behaviors that should be loaded dynamically. Proceeding down the rabbit hole, you might write custom parsers for your DSL that could execute it in different contexts —some for error detection and others for reporting. It's one of those areas where the possibilities are quite limitless.

Ruby and Domain-Specific Languages

My former colleague Jay Fields and I pioneered the mix of Ruby metaprogramming, Rails, and *internal*[9] domain-specific languages while doing Rails application development for ThoughtWorks clients. I still occasionally speak at conferences and blog about writing DSLs in Ruby.

Jay has also continued writing and speaking about his evolution of Ruby DSL techniques, which he calls Business Natural Languages (or BNL for short[10]). When developing BNLs, you craft a domain-specific language that is not necessarily valid Ruby syntax, but is close enough to be transformed easily into Ruby and executed at runtime, as shown in Listing 9.6.

Listing 9.6   Example of Business Natural Language

```
employee John Doe
compensate 500 dollars for each deal closed in the past 30 days
compensate 100 dollars for each active deal that closed more than
365 days ago
compensate 5 percent of gross profits if gross profits are greater
than
1,000,000 dollars
compensate 3 percent of gross profits if gross profits are greater
than
2,000,000 dollars
compensate 1 percent of gross profits if gross profits are greater
than
3,000,000 dollars
```

The ability to leverage advanced techniques such as DSLs is yet another powerful tool in the hands of experienced Rails developers.

Courtenay Says...

DSLs suck! Except the ones written by Obie, of course.

The only people who can read and write most DSLs are their original authors. As a developer taking over a project, it's often quicker to just reimplement instead of learning the quirks and exactly which words you're allowed to use in an existing DSL.

In fact, a lot of Ruby metaprogramming sucks too. It's common for people gifted with these new tools to go a bit overboard. I consider metaprogramming, `self.included`, `class_eval`, and friends to be a bit of a code smell on most projects.

If you're making a web application, future developers and maintainers of the project will appreciate your using simple, direct, granular, and well-tested methods, rather than monkeypatching into existing classes, or hiding associations in modules.

That said, if you can pull it off... your code will become more powerful than you can possibly imagine.

Conclusion

With this chapter we conclude our coverage of `ActiveRecord`, one of the most significant and powerful Rails frameworks. We examined how callbacks and observers let us factor our code in a clean and object-oriented fashion. We also expanded our modeling options by considering single-table inheritance and `ActiveRecord`'s distinctive polymorphic relationships.

At this point in the book, we've covered two parts of the MVC pattern: the model and the controller. It's now time to delve into the third and final part: the view.

References

1. If you are browsing old Rails source code, you might come across callback macros receiving a short string of Ruby code to be eval'd in the binding of the model object. That way of adding callbacks was deprecated in Rails 1.2, because you're always better off using a block in those situations.

2. I recommend the excellent GeoKit for Rails plugin available at http://geokit.rubyforge.org/.

3. Real-life implementation of the example would also need to modify all finders to include `deleted_at` is NULL conditions; otherwise, the records marked deleted would continue to show up in the application. That's not a trivial undertaking, and luckily you don't need to do it yourself. There's a Rails plugin named ActsAsParanoid by Rick Olson that does exactly that, and you can find it at http://svn.techno-weenie.net/projects/plugins/acts_as_paranoid.

4. Get AttachmentFu at http://svn.techno-weenie.net/projects/plugins/attachment_fu.

5. http://en.wikipedia.org/wiki/Open/closed_principle has a good summary.

6. For autogenerated schema information added to the top of your model classes, try Dave Thomas's annotate_models plugin at http://svn.pragprog.com/Public/plugins/annotate_models.

7. http://techspot.zzzeek.org/?p=13

8. I don't expect this to make sense to you, unless you are familiar with Ruby's singleton classes, and the ability to evaluate arbitrary strings of Ruby code at runtime. A good place to start is http://whytheluckystiff.net/articles/seeingMetaclassesClearly.html.

9. The qualifier internal is used to differentiate a domain-specific language hosted entirely inside of a general-purpose language, such as Ruby, from one that is completely custom and requires its own parser implementation.

10. Googling BNL will give you tons of links to the Toronto-based band Barenaked Ladies, so you're better off going directly to the source at http://bnl.jayfields.com.

CHAPTER 10

ActionView

The very powerful and the very stupid have one thing in common. Instead of altering their views to fit the facts, they alter the facts to fit their views...which can be very uncomfortable if you happen to be one of the facts that needs altering. —Doctor Who

Controllers are the skeleton and musculature of your Rails application. In which case, models form the heart and mind, and your view templates (based on `ActionView`, the third major component of Rails) are your application's skin—the part that is visible to the outside world.

`ActionView` is the Rails API for putting together the visual component of your application, namely the HTML and associated content that will be rendered in a web browser whenever someone uses your Rails application. Actually, in this brave new world of REST resources, `ActionView` is involved in generating any sort of output you want to pour out of your app.

`ActionView` contains a full-featured templating system based on a Ruby library named ERb. It takes data prepared by the controller layer and interleaves it with view code to create a presentation layer for the end user.

In this chapter, we cover the fundamentals of the ActionView framework, from the basics of templating, to effective use of partials, to the significant performance boosts possible via caching.

ERb Basics

Inside standard Rails view template files, you're writing code in a kind of Ruby dialect, namely *Embedded Ruby*, or ERb, which is not unique to Rails. ERb is a standard library of the Ruby distribution.

An ERb document typically contains static HTML together with Ruby code that will be executed dynamically when the template is rendered. As I'm sure you know if you've done any Rails programming at all, to insert Ruby code into an ERb document, you place the code inside a pair of delimiters.

There are two different types of template delimiters available, which serve different purposes, and work identically to their counterparts in JSP and ASP technologies, which you might be familiar with already:

```
<% %> and <%= %>
```

The code between the delimiters will be executed in either case. The difference is that the return value of the first expression is discarded, while that of the second is inserted into the template's output.

A very common bug during everyday Rails coding is to *accidentally use the non-outputting delimiter where you actually needed one that produces output.* You'll tear your hair out trying to figure out why a certain value is not showing up on your screen, and yet no errors are being generated.

ERb Practice

You can get a feel for ERb outside of Rails since the ERb interpreter is a standard part of Ruby, and you can write and process ERb templates for practice using that interpreter. You simply use the command-line command `erb`.

For example, put the following template code in a file (`demo.erb`, perhaps):

```
Let's list all the methods of a Ruby string.

First we need a string.

<% str = "I am a string!" %>

We've got one: here it is:

  <%= str %>

Now, let's see its methods:
```

```
<% str.methods.sort[0...10].each_with_index do |m,i| %>
  <%= i+1 %>. <%= m %>
<% end %>
```

Now, run the file through `erb`:

```
$ erb demo.erb
```

You'll see the following output:

```
Let's list all the methods of a Ruby string.

First we need a string.


We've got one: here it is:

  I am a string!

Now, let's see its methods -- or maybe just a few, so they don't
scroll off the screen:


  1. %

  2. *

  3. +

  4. <

  5. <<

  6. <=

  7. <=>

  8. ==

  9. ===

  10. =~
```

As you can see, all of the Ruby code inside the delimiters has been executed, including the assignment to `str` and the iteration with `each`. Only the code inside the equal-sign delimiters, however, has contributed to the output from the execution of the template.

You may also notice a lot of blank lines in the output. The presence of delimited code in the template has no special effect, one way or the other, on the line count. A line is a line, so the following line comes through as a blank line:

```
<% end %>
```

Tightening Up ERb Output

Rails gives you a way to remove at least some of the extra blank lines, by using modified delimiters:

```
<%- str.methods.sort[0...10].each_with_index do |m,i| -%>
  <%= i+1 %>. <%= m %>
<%- end -%>
```

Note the minus signs in the delimiters; they will suppress *leading whitespace* and *extra newlines* in the output of the template. Used judiciously, they can pretty up your template output significantly. It isn't something that the end user cares about, but it might help you out whenever you're examining the HTML source code of your application.

Commenting Out ERb Delimiters

Ruby's commenting symbol # will work to cancel an ERb delimiter. Just insert it right after the percent sign of the opening delimiter tag.

```
<%#= str %>
```

The contents of the commented ERb tag will be ignored. You don't want to leave commented-out code littering your template, but it's useful for temporarily disabling something.

Conditional Output

One of the most common idioms you'll use when coding Rails views is to conditionally output content to the view. The most elementary way to control conditional output is to use if/else statements in conjunction with <% %> as follows:

```
<% if @show_subtitle %>
  <h2><%= @subtitle %></h2>
<% end %>
```

A lot of times you can use inline if conditions and shorten your code, since the <%= tag doesn't care if you feed it a nil value. Just add a postfix if condition to the statement:

```
<h2><%= @subtitle if @show_subtitle %></h2>
```

Of course, there's a potential problem with the preceding example. The first, more verbose, conditional output will eliminate the <h2> tags entirely, but the second example does not.

There are a couple of ways to deal with the problem and keep it a one-liner.

First, there's the butt-ugly solution that I've occasionally seen in some Rails applications, which is the only reason why I'm mentioning it here!

```
<%= "<h2>#{@subtitle}</h2>" if @show_subtitle %>
```

Aaargh! Ugly! The more elegant solution involves Rails' content_tag helper method.

```
<%= content_tag('h2', @subtitle) if @show_subtitle %>
```

Helper methods, both the ones included in Rails and the ones that you'll write on your own, are your main tool for building elegant view templates. Helpers are covered extensively in Chapter 11, "All About Helpers."

RHTML? RXML? RJS?

As of Rails 2.0 the standard naming practice is to suffix ERb template files with .erb, but in earlier versions of Rails, we used .rhtml.

There are two other standard formats and suffixes for templates:

- `.builder` (formerly `.rxml`) signals Rails to execute the template with Jim Weirich's `Builder::XmlMarkup` library, used to easily create XML-based output. Use of Builder is covered in Chapter 15, "XML and `ActiveResource`."

- `.rjs` (unchanged) triggers Rails' built-in JavaScript generation facilities, covered in Chapter 12, "Ajax on Rails."

Note that at the end of this chapter, we do a quick survey of third-party templating languages available that integrate nicely with Rails, and why you might want to try them. For now, let's continue with a review of layout and template usage.

Layouts and Templates

Rails has easy conventions for template usage, related to the location of templates with the Rails project directories.

The `app/views` directory, shown in Figure 10.1, contains subdirectories matching the name of each controller in the application. Within each controller's view subdirectory, you place a template named to match its corresponding action.

Figure 10.1   A typical `app/views` directory

The special `app/views/layout` directory holds layout templates, intended to be reusable containers for your views. Again, naming conventions are used to determine which templates to render, except this time it is the name of the controller that is used for matching.

In the case of layouts, the inheritance hierarchy of controllers comes into play. Most Rails applications have an `application.rhtml` file in their layout directory. It shares its name with the `ApplicationController`, which is typically extended by all the other controllers in an application; therefore it is picked up as the default layout for all views.

It is picked up, unless of course, a more specific layout template is in place, but most of the time it makes sense to use just one application-wide template, such as the simple one shown in Listing 10.1.

Listing 10.1 A Simple, General-Purpose *application.rhtml* Layout Template

```
<!DOCTYPE HTML PUBLIC "-//W3C//DTD HTML 4.01//EN"
"http://www.w3.org/TR/html4/strict.dtd">

<html>
 <head>
  <meta http-equiv="Content-Type" content="text/html; charset=UTF-8">
  <title>My Rails Application</title>
  <%= stylesheet_link_tag 'scaffold', :media => "all" %>
  <%= javascript_include_tag :defaults %>
 </head>
 <body>
  <%= yield :layout %>
 </body>
</html>
```

The `stylesheet_link_tag` and `javascript_include_tag` methods are helpers that automatically insert standard LINK and SCRIPT tags into your document, for CSS and JavaScript files, respectively. The only other interesting part of that template is the call to `yield :layout`, which we discuss next.

Yielding Content

The Ruby language's built-in `yield` keyword is put to good use in making layout and action templates collaborate. Notice the use of `yield` in the middle of the layout template:

```
<body>
  <%= yield :layout %>
</body>
```

In this case, the :layout symbol is a special message to the rendering system. It marks where to insert the output of the action's rendered output, which is usually the template corresponding to that action.

You can add extra places in your layout where you want to be able to yield content, by including additional yield invocations—just make sure to use a unique identifier. A good example is a layout that has left and right sidebar content (simplified, of course):

```
<body>
  <div class="left sidebar">
    <%= yield :left %>
  </div>
  <div id="main_content">
    <%= yield :layout %>
  </div>
  <div class="right sidebar">
    <%= yield :right %>
  </div>
</body>
```

The center DIV element receives the main template content generated. But how do you give Rails content for the left and right sidebars? Easy—just use the content_for method in your template code in the following way:

```
<% content_for(:left) do %>
<h2>Navigation</h2>
<ul>
  <li>...
</ul>
<% end %>

<% content_for(:right) do %>
<h2>Help</h2>
<p>Lorem ipsum dolor sit amet, consectetur adipisicing elit,
    sed do eiusmod tempor incididunt ut labore et dolore magna
    aliqua. Ut enim ad minim veniam, quis nostrud ...
<% end %>

<h1>Page Heading</h1>
<p>The normal template content that will get yielded
  to :layout</p>

  ...
```

Besides sidebars and other types of visible content blocks, I suggest you yield for additional content to be added to the HEAD element of your page, as shown in Listing 10.2. It's a super-useful technique, because Internet Explorer can occasionally get very ill-tempered about SCRIPT tags appearing outside of the HEAD element.

Listing 10.2 Yielding Additional Head Content

```
<!DOCTYPE HTML PUBLIC "-//W3C//DTD HTML 4.01//EN"
"http://www.w3.org/TR/html4/strict.dtd">

<html>
 <head>
  <meta http-equiv="Content-Type" content="text/html; charset=UTF-8">
  <title>My Rails Application</title>
  <%= stylesheet_link_tag 'scaffold', :media => "all" %>
  <%= javascript_include_tag :defaults %>
  <%= yield :head %>
 </head>
 <body>
  <%= yield :layout %>
 </body>
</html>
```

Template Variables

We've seen how layouts and yielding content blocks work, but other than that, how does data get from the controller layer to the view? During preparation of the template, instance variables set during execution of the controller action will be copied over as instance variables of the template context.

Instance Variables

Copying of instance variables is the main form of communication from controller to view, and frankly, that behavior is one of the most basic facts about Rails and I'm sure that you know it:

```
class HelloWorldController < ActionController::Base
  def index
    @msg = "Hello, world!"
  end
end
```

```
# template file /app/views/hello_world/index.html.erb
<%= @msg %>
```

What you might not be aware of is that a lot more than just instance variables from the controller are copied over to the template. It's not a good idea to depend on some of the following objects directly, and especially not to use them to do data operations. Remember that MVC standard practice is to let the controller layer prepare data for rendering, not the view!

assigns

Want to see everything that comes across the controller-view boundary? Throw `<%= debug(assigns) %>` into your template and take a look at the output. The `assigns` attribute is essentially internal to Rails and you should not use it directly in your production code.

base_path

Local filesystem path pointing to the base directory of your application where templates are kept.

controller

The current controller instance is made available via `controller`, before it goes out of scope at the end of request processing. You can take advantage of the controller's knowledge of its name (via the `controller_name` attribute) and the action that was just performed (via the `action_name` attribute), in order to structure your CSS more effectively, as shown in Listing 10.3.

Listing 10.3 Controller and Action Names as Body CSS Classes

```
<html>
  ...
  <body class="<%= controller.controller_name %>
               <%= controller.action_name %>">
    ...
  </body>
</html>
```

That would result in a BODY tag looking something like this, depending on the action executed:

```
<body class="timesheets index">
```

Hopefully you already know that the C in CSS stands for *cascading*, which refers to the fact that class names cascade down the tree of elements in your markup code and are available for creation of rules. Our trick in Listing 10.3 is to automatically include the controller and action name as classnames of your BODY element, so that you can use them to customize look and feel of the page very flexibly later on in the development cycle.

Here's an example of how the technique would be used to vary the background of header elements depending on the controller path:

```
body.timesheets .header {
    background: url(../images/timesheet-bg.png) no-repeat left top
}

body.expense_reports .header {
    background: url(../images/expense-reports-bg.png) no-repeat left top
}
```

flash

The flash is a view variable that you'll definitely use on a regular basis. It has popped up in larger code samples throughout the book so far, whenever you want to send the user a message from the controller layer, but only for the duration of the next request.

A common Rails practice is to use flash[:notice] to hold benign notice messages, and flash[:error] for communication of a more serious nature. Personally, I like to conditionally output both of them in DIV elements, right at the top of my layout, and use CSS to position them, as shown in Listing 10.4.

Listing 10.4   Standardized Flash Notice and Error Placement in *application.html.erb*

```
<html>
  ...
  <body>
    <%= content_tag 'div', h(flash[:notice]),
        :class => 'notice', :id => 'notice' if flash[:notice] %>
    <%= content_tag 'div', h(flash[:error]),
        :class => 'notice error', :id => 'error' if flash[:error] %>

    <%= yield :layout %>
  </body>
</html>
```

Using the `content_tag` helper facilitates making the entire output conditional. Otherwise, I'd need an `if` block around the HTML markup and the scheme would get pretty messy.

headers

The `headers` variable holds the values of HTTP headers that accompanied the request being processed. Not much you can do with `headers` in your view, other than occasionally view them for debugging reasons. Put `<%= debug(headers) %>` somewhere in your layout and you'll see output similar to the following in your browser, after refreshing the page of course:

```
--
Status: 200 OK
cookie:
- - adf69ed8dd86204d1685b6635adae0d9ea8740a0
Cache-Control: no-cache
```

logger

Have something to record for posterity in the logs while you're rendering the view? Use the `logger` method to get the view's `Logger` instance, `RAILS_DEFAULT_LOGGER` unless you've changed it.

params

This is the same `params` hash that is available in your controller, containing the key/value pairs of your request. I'll occasionally use a value from the `params` hash directly in the view, particularly when I'm dealing with pages that are subject to filtering or row sorting.

```
<p>Filter by month:
  <%= select_tag(:month_filter,
        options_for_select(@month_options, params[:month_filter])) %>
```

It's very dangerous from a security perspective to put unfiltered parameter data into the output stream of your template. The following section, "Protecting the Integrity of Your View from User-Submitted Content," covers that topic in depth.

request **and** *response*

The HTTP `request` and `response` objects are exposed to the view, but other than for debugging purposes, I can't think of any reason why you would want to use them directly from your template.

session

The `session` variable is the user's session hash. There might be situations where it'd be okay to pull values out to affect rendering, but I shudder to think that you might try to set values in the session from the view layer. Use with care, and primarily for debugging, just like `request` and `response`.

Protecting the Integrity of Your View from User-Submitted Content

If any data in your application is user-submitted, or in any way originates from a source that you don't trust completely, then you need to keep in mind the need to escape and sanitize template content. Otherwise, you leave yourself wide open to a variety of malicious hacker attacks.

For example, consider the following template snippet, which copies the value of `params[:page_number]` into its output quite innocently:

```
<h1>Search Results</h1>
<h2>Page <%= params[:page_number] %></h2>
```

Easy way to include the page number, right? Sure. But consider what happens if someone submits a request to that page that embeds a `SCRIPT` tag and some malicious code as the value of the `page_number` request parameter? Bingo! The malicious code goes right into your template!

Fortunately, there is a very simple way to prevent this form of attack and the Rails core developers expect you to use it very often, so they named the method with one character: `h`.

```
<h1>Search Results</h1>
<h2>Page <%=h(params[:page_number]) %></h2>
```

The `h` method *escapes* HTML content—instead of passing it through as markup, it will convert the less-than and greater-than characters into their respective character entities, and in so doing, cripple malicious injection attacks. Of course, it doesn't do anything to content that doesn't have markup.

But what if you are trying to display user-submitted HTML, as is often the case with web applications that feature blog-style commenting facilities? In those cases, you can try using the `sanitize` method of `ActionView::Helpers::TextHelper`. It'll strip out the tags most commonly used in attacks: `FORM` and `SCRIPT`, but leave others intact. The `sanitize` method is covered in depth in Chapter 11.

Partials

A partial is a fragment of template code. The Rails way is to use partials to factor view code into modular chunks that can be assembled in layouts with as little repetition as possible. The syntax for including a partial within a template starts with `render :partial => "name"`. Partial template names must begin with an underscore, which serves to set them apart visually within a given view template directory. However, *you leave the underscore out when you refer to them.*

Simple Use Cases

The simplest partial use case is simply to extract a portion of template code. Some developers divide their templates into logical parts by using partial extraction. Sometimes it is easier to understand the structure of a screen if the significant parts are factored out of it. For instance, Listing 10.5 is a simple user registration screen that has its parts factored out into partials.

Listing 10.5 Simple User Registration Form with Partials

```
<h1>User Registration</h1>
<%= error_messages_for :user %>
<% form_for :user, :url => users_path do -%>
  <table class="registration">
   <tr>
    <td class="details demographics">
     <%= render :partial => `details' %>
     <%= render :partial => `demographics' %>
    </td>
    <td class="location">
     <%= render :partial => `location' %>
    </td>
   </tr>
   <tr>
    <td colspan="2"><%= render :partial => `opt_in' %></td>
   </tr>
   <tr>
    <td colspan="2"><%= render :partial => `terms' %></td>
   </tr>
  </table>
  <p><%= submit_tag `Register' %></p>
<% end -%>
```

While we're at it, let me pop open one of those partials. To conserve space, we'll take a look at one of the smaller ones, the partial containing the opt-in check boxes of this particular app. The source is in Listing 10.6; notice that its name begins with an underscore.

Listing 10.6 The Opt-In Partial in the File *app/views/users/_opt_in.html.erb*

```
<fieldset id="opt_in">
  <legend>Spam Opt In</legend>
  <p><%= check_box :user, :send_event_updates %>
     Send me updates about events!<br/>
  <%= check_box :user, :send_site_updates%>
     Notify me about new services</p>
</fieldset>
```

Personally, I like partials to be entirely contained inside a semantically significant markup container. In the case of the opt-in partial in Listing 10.6, both check box controls are contained inside a single `<fieldset>` element, which I've given an `id` attribute. Following that rule, more as a loose guideline than anything else, helps me to mentally identify how the contents of this partial are going to fit inside the parent template. If we were dealing with other markup, perhaps outside of a form, I might choose to wrap the partial markup inside a well-identified `<div>` container, instead of a `<fieldset>`.

Why not include the `<td>` markup inside the partial templates? It's a matter of style—I like to be able to see the complete markup skeleton in one piece. In this case, the skeleton is the table structure that you see in Listing 10.5. If portions of that table were inside the partial templates, it would obfuscate the layout of the page. I do admit that this is one of those areas where personal style and preference should take precedence and I can only advise you as to what has worked for me, personally.

Reuse of Partials

Since the registration form is neatly factored out into its component parts, it is easy to create a simple edit form using some of its partials, as in Listing 10.7.

Listing 10.7 Simple User Edit Form Reusing Some of the Same Partials

```
<h1>Edit User</h1>
<%= error_messages_for :user %>
<% form_for :user, :url => user_path(@user),
                    :html => { :method => :put } do -%>
  <table class="settings">
   <tr>
    <td class="details">
     <%= render :partial => 'details' %>
    </td>
    <td class="demographics">
     <%= render :partial => 'demographics' %>
    </td>
   </tr>
   <tr>
    <td colspan="2" class="opt_in">
      <%= render :partial => 'opt_in' %>
    </td>
   </tr>
  </table>
  <p><%= submit_tag 'Save Settings' %></p>
<% end -%>
```

If you compare Listings 10.5 and 10.7, you'll notice that the structure of the table changed a little bit in the Edit form, and it has less content than the registration form. Perhaps the location is handled in greater detail on another screen, and certainly you don't want to require agreement of terms every time the user changes her settings.

Shared Partials

Until now we've been considering the use of partials that reside in the same directory as their parent template. However, you can easily refer to partials that are in other directories, just by prefixing the directory name. You still leave off the underscore, which might feel a little weird.

Let's add a `captcha` partial to the bottom of the registration form from Listing 10.5, to help prevent spammers from invading our web application:

```
...
<tr>
  <td colspan="2"><%= render :partial => 'terms' %></td>
</tr>
<tr>
  <td colspan="2"><%= render :partial => 'shared/captcha' %></td>
</tr>
</table>
<p><%= submit_tag 'Register' %></p>
<% end -%>
```

Since the `captcha` partial is used in various different parts of the application, it makes sense to let it reside in a shared folder rather than any particular view folder. However, you do have to be a little bit careful when you move existing template code into a shared partial. It's quite possible to inadvertently craft a partial that depends implicitly on where it's rendered.

For example, take the case of the Rails-talk mailing list member with a troublesome partial defined in `login/_login.rhtml`:

```
<% form_tag do %>
 <label>Username:</label>
 <%= text_field_tag :username, params[:username] %>
 <br />
 <label>Password:</label>
 <%= password_field_tag :password, params[:password] %>
 <br />
 <%= submit_tag "Login" %>
<% end %>
```

The login form submission worked when he rendered this partial as part of the login controller's `login` action ("the login page"), but not when it was included as part of the view for any other section of his website. The problem is that `form_tag` (covered in the next chapter) normally takes an optional action parameter telling it where to post its information. If you leave out the action, the form will post back to its current URL, which will vary for shared partials, depending on where they're being used from.

Passing Variables to Partials

Partials inherit the instance variables available to their parent templates. That's why the form helpers used in the partials of Listings 10.5 and 10.7 work: They rely implicitly on an `@user` variable to be in scope. I feel it's fine to use this implicit variable sharing in some cases, particularly when the partials are tightly bound to their parent templates. It would be especially true in cases where the only reason you broke out partials in the first place was to reduce the size and complexity of a particularly large template.

However, once you get into the practice of breaking out partial templates for application-wide reuse, depending on implicitly passed variables gets a lot more dicey. That's why Rails supports the passing of locally scoped variables to partial templates, as a hash parameter named `:locals`, as in the following snippet:

```
render :partial => 'shared/address', :locals => { :form => form }
```

The names and values of the `:locals` hash are converted into locally scoped variables (no @ sign) in the partial. Listing 10.8 is a variation on the registration template. This time we're using the version of `form_for` that yields a block parameter representing the form to its form helper methods. We'll pass that form parameter on, too.

Listing 10.8 Simple User Registration Template Passing Form as Local Variable

```
<h1>User Registration</h1>
<%= error_messages_for :user %>
<% form_for :user, :url => users_path do |form| -%>
  <table class="registration">
   <tr>
    <td class="details address demographics">
     <%= render :partial => 'details',
                :locals => {:form => form } %>
     <%= render :partial => 'shared/address',
                :locals => {:form => form } %>
    </td>
   </tr>
  </table>
  <p><%= submit_tag 'Register' %></p>
<% end -%>
```

And finally, in Listing 10.9 we have the shared address form.

Listing 10.9 A Simple Shared Address Partial Using Local Variable

```
<fieldset class="address">
  <legend>Address</legend>
  <p><label>Street</label><br/>
    <%= form.text_area :street, :rows => 2, :cols => 40 %></p>
  <p><label>City</label><br/>
    <%= form.text_field :city %></p>
  <p><label>State</label><br/>
    <%= form.text_field :state, :size => 2 %></p>
  <p><label>Zip</label><br/>
      <%= form.text_field :zip, :size => 15 %></p>
</fieldset>
```

The form helper methods, which we'll cover in Chapter 11, have a variation in which they are called on the `form` variable yielded by the `form_for` method. That is exactly what we passed on to these partials via the `:locals` hash.

The `local_assigns` Hash

If you need to check for the presence of a certain local variable, you need to do it by checking the `local_assigns` hash that is part of every template. Using `defined? variable` won't work due to limitations of the rendering system.

```
<% if local_assigns.has_key? :special %>
<%= special %>
<% end %>
```

Render Collections

One of the best uses of partials is to render collections. Once you get into the habit of rendering collections with partials, you won't want to go back to the relative ugliness of cluttering your templates with `for` loops and `each`.

```
render :partial => 'entry', :collection => @entries
```

Simple and precise, and dependent on a naming convention. The most important is how the object being rendered is exposed to the partial template. It is set as a local variable named the same as the partial template itself. The partial corresponding to the last code snippet would reference a local variable named `entry`.

```
<%= div_for(entry) do %>
  <%= h(entry.description) %>
  <%= distance_of_time_in_words_to_now entry.created_at %> ago
<% end %>
```

The `partial_counter` Variable

There's another variable set for collection-rendered partials that doesn't get much attention. It's a 0-indexed counter variable that tracks the number of times the partial has gotten rendered. It's useful for rendering numbered lists of things.

The name of the variable is the name of the partial, plus _counter.

```
<%= div_for(entry) do %>
  <%= entry_counter %>:
  <%= h(entry.description) %>
  <%= distance_of_time_in_words_to_now entry.created_at %> ago
<% end %>
```

Sharing Collection Partials

If you wanted to use the same partial that you use with a collection, execpt with a single entry object, you'd have to pass it that single instance via the `:locals` hash described in the preceding section, like this:

```
render :partial => 'entry', :locals => {:entry => @entry }
```

I've also seen the following hack done as a way to avoid needing that `locals` parameter:

```
<% entry = @entry if @entry %>
<% div_for(entry) do %>
  <%= h(entry.description) %>
  <%= distance_of_time_in_words_to_now entry.created_at %> ago
<% end %>
```

That works, but it's nasty, repetitive, and introduces an implicit optional dependency on @entry. Don't do stuff like that. Use the :locals parameter, as intended.

Logging

If you take a look at your development log, you'll notice that it shows which partials have been rendered and how long they took.

```
Rendering template within layouts/application
Rendering listings/index
Rendered listings/_listing (0.00663)
Rendered listings/_listing (0.00296)
Rendered listings/_listing (0.00173)
Rendered listings/_listing (0.00159)
Rendered listings/_listing (0.00154)
Rendered layouts/_login (0.02415)
Rendered layouts/_header (0.03263)
Rendered layouts/_footer (0.00114)
```

Caching

The Rails caching mechanism can make your production-deployed application very responsive. Caching lets you specify that anything from entire pages down to fragments of the page should be captured to disk as HTML files and sent along by your web server on future requests with minimal involvement from Rails itself.

There are three types of caching in Rails:

- Page caching   The output of an entire controller action is cached to disk, with no further involvement by the Rails dispatcher.

- Action caching   The output of an entire controller action is cached to disk, but the Rails dispatcher is still involved in subsequent requests, and controller filters are executed.

- Fragment caching   Arbitrary bits and pieces of your page's output can be cached to disk to save the time of having to render them in the future.

Caching in Development Mode?

I wanted to mention up front that caching is disabled in development mode. If you want to play with caching, you'll need to edit the following setting in the `config/environments/development.rb` file:

```
config.action_controller.perform_caching          = false
```

Of course, remember to change it back before checking it back into your project repository, or you might face some very confusing errors down the road.[1]

Page Caching

The simplest form of caching is page caching, triggered by use of the `caches_page` macro-style method in a controller. It tells Rails to capture the entire output of the request to disk so that it is served up directly by the web server on subsequent requests without the involvement of the dispatcher. Nothing will be logged to the Rails log, nor will controller filters be triggered—absolutely nothing to do with Rails will happen, just like the static HTML files in your project's `public` directory.

Action Caching

By definition, if there's anything that has to change on every request or specific to an end user's view of that page, page caching is not an option. On the other hand, if all we need to do is run some filters that check conditions before displaying the page requested, the `caches_action` method will work. It's almost like page caching, except that controller filters are executed prior to serving the cached HTML file. That gives you the option to do some extra processing or even redirect if necessary.

Action caching is implemented with fragment caching (covered later in this chapter) and an `around` filter (covered in Chapter 2, "Working with Controllers"). The cached action content is keyed based on the current host and the path, which means that it will still work even with Rails applications serving multiple subdomains using a DNS wildcard. Also, different representations of the same resource, such as HTML and XML, are treated like separate requests and cached separately.

We'll use our `lil_journal`[2] sample application as the basis for our code snippets in this section. The application should have public versus private entries, so for default requests, we should run a filter that figures out whether the visitor is logged in and redirects them to the `public` action if necessary. Listing 10.10 has the `EntriesController` code.

Listing 10.10 The *EntriesController* of *lil_journal*

```
class EntriesController < ApplicationController

  before_filter :check_logged_in, :only => [:index]

  caches_page :public
  caches_action :index

  def public
    @entries = Entry.find(:all,
                          :limit => 10,
                          :conditions => {:private => false})

    render :action => 'index'
  end

  def index
    @entries = Entry.find(:all, :limit => 10)
  end

  private

    def check_logged_in
      redirect_to :action => 'public' unless logged_in?
    end

end
```

The `public` action displays only the public entries and is visible to anyone, which makes it a candidate for page caching. However, since it doesn't require its own template, we just call `render :action => 'index'` explicitly at the end of the `public` action.

Design Considerations

Knowing that your application will eventually require caching should influence your design decisions. Projects with optional authentication often have controller actions that are impossible to page or action-cache, because they handle both login states internally. That would have been the case in Listing 10.10 if we had written the `index` action to handle both public and private display:

```
def index
  opts = {}
  opts[:limit] = 10
```

```
  opts[:conditions] = {:private => false } unless logged_in?
  @posts = Entry.find(:all, opts)
end
```

Most of the time, you won't have too many pages with completely static content that can be cached using `cache_page` or `cache_action`, and that's where fragment caching comes into play.

Fragment Caching

Users are accustomed to all sorts of dynamic content on the page, and your application layout will be filled with things like welcome messages and notification counts. Fragment caching allows us to capture parts of the rendered page on disk and serve them up on subsequent requests without needing to render their content again. The performance improvement is not as dramatic as with page or action caching, since the Rails dispatcher is still involved. However, you can still give your application a blazing speed boost by using fragment caching.

The `cache` Method

Fragment caching is by nature something you specify in your view template rather than at the controller level. You do so using the `cache` method of `ActionView`. It takes a block, which lets you wrap content that should be cached.

Once we log in to our Lil' Journal sample application, the header section should really display information about the logged-in user, so action-caching the index page is out of the question. We'll remove the `action_cache` directive from the `EntriesController`, but leave `cache_page` in place for the `public` action. Then we'll go into the `entries/index.html.erb` template and add fragment caching, as shown in Listing 10.11.

Listing 10.11 Lil' Journal's `entries/index.html.erb` Template with Fragment Caching

```
<%= content_tag :h1, "#{@user.name}'s Journal" %>
<% cache do %>
  <%= render :partial => 'entry', :collection => @entries %>
<% end %>
```

Easy as that—the HTML output of rendering the collection of entries is stored in the fragment cache associated with the entries/index page. That's fine if we're only caching one fragment of the page, but most of the time we'll need to give the fragment some extra identification.

Named Fragments

The cache method takes an optional name parameter.

```
<% cache "my_fragment" do %>
```

If you leave it blank, as we have in Listing 10.11, it caches its content keyed to the URL of its parent page. That's an acceptable solution as long as there is only one fragment on the page.

If we're caching more than one fragment on the page, we need to add an extra identifier, so that we don't suffer name collisions. Listing 10.12 is an enhanced version of the entries page, where we've added the display of recent comments in the sidebar.

Listing 10.12 The Entries Page with Two Fragment Cache Directives

```
<%= content_tag :h1, "#{@user.name}'s Journal" %>

<% cache(:fragment => 'entries') do %>
  <%= render :partial => 'entry', :collection => @entries %>
<% end %>

<%- content_for :sidebar -%>

  <% cache(:fragment => 'recent_comments') do %>
    <%= render :partial => 'comment', :collection => @recent_comments
%>
  <% end %>

<% end %>
```

After the code in Listing 10.12 is rendered, there will be two fragments stored in the cache, keyed as follows:

- /entries/index?fragment=entries
- /entries/index?fragment=recent_comments

The fact that Rails uses the page's URL scheme to key fragments in the cache is an elegant solution to a somewhat difficult problem. Consider for instance, what would happen if you added pagination to the Lil' Journal application and pulled up the second page of entries. Without further work, a pair of additional fragments would be correctly cached for future use:

- `/entries/index?page=2&fragment=entries`

- `/entries/index?page=2&fragment=recent_comments`

> **Note**
>
> Rails uses the `url_for` mechanism to construct unique identifiers for fragments out of convenience. *There's no requirement that your fragment keys correspond to actual working URLs in your application.*

Global Fragments

Sometimes, you'll want to fragment-cache content that is not specific to a single URL of your application. To add globally keyed fragments to the cache, we'll again use the name parameter of the `cache` helper method, but this time we'll give it a string identifier instead of a hash.

To demonstrate, let's add a requirement that our Lil' Journal application should display user statistics on every page. In Listing 10.13, we cache the stats partial for every user, using their name and a "`_stats`" suffix as the key.

Listing 10.13   The Entries Page with Global User Stats

```
<%= content_tag :h1, "#{@user.name}'s Journal" %>

<% cache(:fragment => 'entries') do %>
  <%= render :partial => 'entry', :collection => @entries %>
<% end %>

<%- content_for :sidebar -%>

  <% cache(@user.name + "_stats") do %>
    <%= render :partial => 'stats' %>
  <% end %>

  <% cache(:fragment => 'recent_comments') do %>
    <%= render :partial => 'comment', :collection => @recent_comments %>
  <% end %>

<% end %>
```

There's one part we've left out of our caching discussion so far, and that is the subject of expiring cached content once it is *stale*—once the data it is reflecting has become out of date.

Avoiding Extra Database Activity

Once you have fragments of your view cached, it no longer makes sense to do the database queries that supply those fragments with their data. After all, the results of those database queries will never be used until the cached fragments are expired. The read_fragment method lets you check for the existence of cached content, and takes the same parameters that you used with the associated cache method.

Here's how we would modify the index action accordingly:

```
def index
  unless read_fragment(:fragment => 'entries')
    @entries = Entry.find(:all, :limit => 10)
  end
end
```

Now the finder method will only get executed if the cache needs to be refreshed.

Expiration of Cached Content

Whenever you use caching, you need to consider any and all situations that will cause the cache to become stale, out of date. Then you need to write code that sweeps away the old content, so to speak, making room for new content to be cached in its place.

Expiring Pages and Actions

The expire_page and expire_action methods let you explicitly delete content from the cache, so that it is regenerated on the next request. You identify the content to expire using the url_for conventions used elsewhere in Rails. Listing 10.14 shows how we've added expiration to the create method of the entries controller.

Listing 10.14 The Entries *create* Action

```
1  def create
2    @entry = @user.entries.build(params[:entry])
3    if @entry.save
4      expire_page :action => 'public'
5      redirect_to entries_path(@entry)
6    else
7      render :action => 'new'
8    end
9  end
```

Notice how line 4 of Listing 10.14 explicitly expires the page associated with the public action. If you think about it, though, it's not only the `create` action that invalidates the cache. The `update` and `destroy` actions would invalidate it too.

In your applications, particularly if you're doing REST-style resources, remember that different representations of the same resource are treated like separate requests and cached separately. If you've cached the XML response of an action, you'll have to expire it by appending `:format => :xml` to the action specification.

Expiring Fragments

Whoops! I almost forgot (seriously) that we also have cached fragments to clear out, using the `expire_fragment` method. Now the `create` action looks like this:

```
def create
  @entry = @user.entries.build(params[:entry])
  if @entry.save
    expire_page :action => 'public'
    expire_fragment(:fragment => 'entries')
    expire_fragment(:fragment => (@user.name + "_stats"))
    redirect_to entries_path(@entry)
  else
    render :action => 'new'
  end
end
```

Using *regular expressions* in *expiration calls*

There's actually still (!) a serious problem with the expiration routine that we put in the `create` action. Remember we said that the fragment caching of entries would

work with pagination, and that we'd have cached fragments keyed like this:
`'/entries/index?page=2&fragment=entries'`

As a result, just doing `expire_fragment(:fragment => 'entries')` will only clear the first page from the cache. For that reason, the `expire_fragment` method understands regular expressions, and we'll need to use them in our code:

```
expire_fragment(r%{entries/.*})
```

There has to be a better way to handle invalidation than remembering to stick a bunch of complicated expiration statements in all your action methods. Besides, caching is a unique concern, which seems to indicate that it should be applied in a more aspect-oriented fashion.

Automatic Cache Expiry with Sweepers

A `Sweeper` class is kind of like an `ActiveRecord Observer` object, except that it's specialized for use in expiring cached content. When you write a sweeper, you tell it which of your models to observe for changes, just as you would with callback classes and observers.

Listing 10.15 is a sweeper to keep the caching of Lil' Journal's entries in order.

Listing 10.15   An Entries Sweeper for Lil' Journal

```
class EntrySweeper < ActionController::Caching::Sweeper
  observe Entry

  def expire_cached_content(entry)
    expire_page :controller => 'entries', :action => 'public'
    expire_fragment(r%{entries/.*})
    expire_fragment(:fragment => (entry.user.name + "_stats"))
  end

  alias_method :after_save, :expire_cached_content
  alias_method :after_destroy, :expire_cached_content

end
```

Once you have a `Sweeper` class (put it in your `app/models` directory), you need to tell your controller to use that sweeper in conjunction with its actions. Here's the top of the revised entries controller for Lil' Journal:

```
class EntriesController < ApplicationController

  before_filter :check_logged_in, :only => [:index]
  caches_page :public
  cache_sweeper :entry_sweeper, :only => [:create, :update, :destroy]

  ...
```

Like many other controller macros, the `cache_sweeper` method takes `:only` and `:except` options. There's no need to bother the sweeper for actions that can't modify the state of the application, so we do indeed include the `:only` option in our example.

Like the related `observers`, sweepers are not limited to observing just one model. The main thing to remember if we go down that route is that our callback methods will need to know how to handle all of them. Ruby's `case` statement may come in handy, as shown in Listing 10.16, a full revision of the `EntrySweeper`, which may now observe `Comment` as well as `Entry` objects.

Listing 10.16 The `EntrySweeper` Revised to Observe and Handle Both Entries and Comments

```
class EntrySweeper < ActionController::Caching::Sweeper
  observe Entry, Comment

  def expire_cached_content(record)
    expire_page :controller => 'entries', :action => 'public'
    expire_fragment(r%{entries/.*})

    user = case entry
      when Entry then record.user
      when Comment then record.entry.user
    end

    expire_fragment(:fragment => (user.name + "_stats"))
  end

  alias_method :after_save, :expire_cached_content
  alias_method :after_destroy, :expire_cached_content

end
```

Cache Logging

If you've turned on caching during development, you can actually monitor the Rails log for messages about caching and expiration.

```
Processing Entries#index (for 127.0.0.1 at 2007-07-20 23:07:09) [GET]
  ...
Cached page: /entries.html (0.03949)


Processing Entries#create (for 127.0.0.1 at 2007-07-20 23:10:50)
[POST]
  ...
Expired page: /entries.html (0.00085)
```

It's a good way to see whether your caching is actually working as expected.

Action Cache Plugin

The Action Cache plugin by Tom Fakes and Scott Laird is a recommended drop-in replacement for the built-in Rails caching facilities. It doesn't change the Caching API at all, only the underlying implementation.

```
script/plugin install http://craz8.com/svn/trunk/plugins/action_cache
```

These are the major features of the Action Cache plugin:

- Stores cached entries as YAML streams (instead of just HTML) so that the Response headers from the original response can be returned along with cached content.

- Adds a last-modified header to the response so that clients use a get-if-modified HTTP request. If the client already has cached content, sends a 304 Not Modified response.

- Ensures that only requests with a 200 OK status are cached. Otherwise, error pages and empty content can get stuck in the cache (and cause difficult-to-diagnose problems.)

- Allows developers to override Rails with their own implementation of cache key generation.

- Allows an action to specify an optional Time To Live value for a response, before cached content associated with the response will be automatically expired.

- Allows control over whether caching occurs for an action at runtime based on request parameters. (For instance, never cache content for site administrators.)

- A new method, `expire_all_actions`, clears out the entire action cache contents.

- Changes the `expire_action` implementation to actually use the `Regexp` fragment expiry call, causing all matching cache items to be cleared. For those of you using REST, and providing HTML, JS, and XML for the same action, all three will be expired when you expire one of them with code like this: `expire_action :controller => 'foo', :action => 'bar'`

Cache Storage

Unlike session data, fragment-cached data can grow to be quite large. Rails gives you four different options for cache storage:

- `FileStore`   Keeps the fragments on disk in the `cache_path`, which works well for all types of environments and shares the fragments for all the web server processes running off the same application directory.

- `MemoryStore`   Keeps the fragments in the memory, and can potentially consume an unacceptable amount of memory per process.

- `DRbStore`   Keeps the fragments in the memory of a separate, shared DRb process. This option only keeps one cache around for all processes, but requires that you run and manage a separate DRb process as part of your deployment process.

- `MemCacheStore`   Works like DRbStore, but uses a proven cache server named `memcached`. I informally surveyed a bunch of Rails professionals about cache storage, and all of them suggested that `memcache` is the best option.[3]

Configuration Example

The `:memory_store` option is enabled by default.

```
ActionController::Base.fragment_cache_store = :memory_store

ActionController::Base.fragment_cache_store = :file_store,
"/path/to/cache/directory"
ActionController::Base.fragment_cache_store = :drb_store,
"druby://localhost:9192"
ActionController::Base.fragment_cache_store = :mem_cache_store,
"localhost"
```

Limitations of File-Based Storage

As long as you're hosting your Rails application on a single server, setting up caching is fairly straightforward and easy to implement (of course, coding it is a different story).

If you think about the implications of running a cached application on a cluster of distinct physical servers, you might realize that cache invalidation is going to be painful. Unless you set up the file storage to point at a shared filesystem such as NFS or GFS, it won't work.

Manual Sweeping with *rake*

If you do choose file-based storage, you probably want to give yourself a way to manually clear your application's cached content. It's not difficult to do using Rake. Just add a file to the `lib/tasks` folder named `cache.rake`. You'll be creating a task similar to the one shown in Listing 10.17.

Listing 10.17 A *cache_sweeper* Custom Rake Task

```
desc "Manually sweep the cache"
task :cache_sweeper do
  FileUtils.rm_rf Dir[File.join(RAILS_ROOT, "public", "entries*")]
#pages
  FileUtils.rm_rf Dir[File.join(RAILS_ROOT, "tmp", "cache*")]
#fragments
end
```

I used `entries` in the example task, but remember that you may have to add one or more of your own `FileUtils.rm_rf` statements corresponding to the pages that *your* application is caching.

As a final note, keep in mind, that it's common to use the `FileUtils.rm_rf` brute-force approach in sweepers instead of the `expire_*` methods, mostly because a lot of times it's just easier to blow away entire cached directories and let them be rebuilt as needed.

Conclusion

In this chapter, we've covered the `ActionView` framework with a detailed explanation of ERb templating and how the Rails rendering system works. We've also covered the use of partials in-depth, since their use is essential for effective Rails programming.

From the relatively simple principles of templating, we jumped into a complicated subject: caching. Knowing how to implement caching will save you the day you work on Rails application that really need to perform. Indeed, developers of high-traffic Rails websites tend to see Rails as a very fancy HTML generation platform, which helps them create content for caching.

Now it's time to cover the mechanism whereby you can inject a whole bunch of smarts into your view layer without cluttering up your templates: Helpers.

References

1. In his great screencast on the subject, Geoffrey Grosenback suggests adding another environment mode to your project named `development_with_caching`, with caching turned on just for experimentation (http://peepcode.com/products/page-action-and-fragment-caching).

2. Subversion URL: http://obiefernandez.com/svn/projects/awruby/prorails/lil_journal.

3. If you go the memcache route, definitely consider using Err the Blog's CacheFu plugin, available at http://require.errtheblog.com/plugins/browser/cache_fu.

CHAPTER 11

All About Helpers

"Thank you for helping Helpers Helping the Helpless. Your help was very... helpful!"
—Mrs. Duong in the movie *The Weekenders*

We've already covered some of the helper methods provided by Rails to help you assemble the user interface of your web application. This chapter lists and explains all of the helper modules and their methods, followed by instructions on effectively creating your own helpers.

`PrototypeHelper` and `ScriptaculousHelper` were demoted out of Rails core and are now packaged as plugins in Rails 2.0. They are used to easily add Ajax functionality to your Rails application and are covered in-depth within Chapter 12, "Ajax on Rails."

> **NOTE**
>
> This chapter is essentially reference material. Although every effort has been made to make it readable straight through, you will notice that coverage of `ActionView`'s helper modules is arranged alphabetically, starting with `ActiveRecordHelper` and ending with `UrlHelper`. Within each module's section, the methods are broken up into logical groups whenever appropriate.

ActiveRecordHelper

The `ActiveRecordHelper` module contains helper methods for quickly creating forms from `ActiveRecord` models. The `form` method is able to create an entire form for all the basic content types of a given record. However, it does not know how to assemble user-interface components for manipulating associations. Most Rails developers assemble their own forms from scratch using methods from `FormHelper`, instead of using this module.

Reporting Validation Errors

The `error_message_on` and `error_messages_for` methods help you to add formatted validation error information to your templates in a consistent fashion.

error_message_on(object, method, prepend_text = "",

append_text = "", css_class = "formError")

Returns a `DIV` tag containing the error message attached to the specified method on the object, if one exists. The contents can be specialized with parameters for pre- and post-text and custom CSS class, as shown in the signature.

Use of this method is common when the user-interface requirements specify individual validation messages per input field of a form, as in the following real-life example:

```
<div class="form_field">
  <div class="field_label">
    <span class="required">*</span>
    <label>First Name</label>
  </div>
  <div class="textual">
    <%= form.text_field :first_name, :maxlength => 34, :tabindex => 1
%>
    <%= error_message_on :user, :first_name %>
  </div>
</div>
```

error_messages_for(*params)

Returns a DIV tag containing all of the error messages for all of the objects held in instance variables identified as parameters. This method is used by Rails scaffolding, but rarely in real production applications. The Rails API documentation advises you to use this method's implementation as inspiration to meet your own requirements:

> This is a prepackaged presentation of the errors with embedded strings and a certain HTML structure. If what you need is significantly different from the default presentation, it makes plenty of sense to access the object.errors instance yourself and set it up. View the source of this method to see how easy it is.

In fact, we'll go ahead and reproduce the source of the method here with the warning that you should *not* try to use it as inspiration unless you have a good grasp of Ruby! On the other hand, if you have time to study the way that this method is implemented, it will definitely teach you a lot about the way that Rails is implemented, which is its own distinctive flavor of Ruby.

```ruby
def error_messages_for(*params)
  options = params.last.is_a?(Hash) ? params.pop.symbolize_keys : {}
  objects = params.collect { |object_name|
              instance_variable_get("@#{object_name}")
            }.compact

  count = objects.inject(0) {|sum, object| sum + object.errors.count }
  unless count.zero?
    html = {}
    [:id, :class].each do |key|
      if options.include?(key)
        value = options[key]
        html[key] = value unless value.blank?
      else
        html[key] = 'errorExplanation'
      end
    end

    header_message = "#{pluralize(count, 'error')} prohibited this
    #{(options[:object_name] || params.first).to_s.gsub('_', ' ')}
    from being saved"

    error_messages = objects.map {|object|
      object.errors.full_messages.map {|msg| content_tag(:li, msg)}
    }
```

```
    content_tag(:div,
      content_tag(options[:header_tag] || :h2, header_message) <<
      content_tag(:p, 'There were problems with the following fields:') <<
      content_tag(:ul, error_messages), html )
  else
    ''
  end
end
```

Later on in the chapter we'll talk extensively about writing your own helper methods.

Automatic Form Creation

The next couple of methods are used for automatic field creation by the scaffolding code. You can try using them too, but I suspect that their usefulness is somewhat limited in real applications.

form(name, options)

Returns an entire form with input tags and everything for a named ActiveRecord model object. Here are the code examples given in the Rails API documentation, using a hypothetical Post object from a bulletin-board application as an example:

```
> form("post")

=> <form action='/post/create' method='post'>
     <p>
       <label for="post_title">Title</label><br/>
       <input id="post_title" name="post[title]"
              size="30" type="text" value="Hello World" />
     </p>
     <p>
       <label for="post_body">Body</label><br/>
       <textarea cols="40" id="post_body" name="post[body]"
rows="20">
         Back to the hill and over it again!
       </textarea>
     </p>
     <input type='submit' value='Create' />
   </form>
```

Internally, the method calls `record.new_record?` to infer whether the action for the form should be `create` or `update`. It is possible to explicitly specify the action of the form (and the value of the submit button along with it) by using the `:action` option.

If you need the form to have its `enctype` set to `multipart`, useful for file uploads, set the `options[:multipart]` to true.

You can also pass in an `:input_block` option, using Ruby's `Proc.new` idiom to create a new anonymous code block. The block you supply will be invoked for each *content column* of your model, and its return value will be inserted into the form.

```
> form("entry", :action => "sign",
    :input_block => Proc.new { |record, column|
      "#{column.human_name}: #{input(record, column.name)}<br/>" })

=> <form action='/post/sign' method='post'>
    Message:
    <input id="post_title" name="post[title]" size="30"
           type="text" value="Hello World" /><br />
    <input type='submit' value='Sign' />
   </form>
```

That example's *builder block*, as it is referred to in the Rails API docs, uses the `input` helper method, which is also part of this module, and is covered in the next section of this chapter.

Finally, it's also possible to add additional content to the form by giving the call to `form` a block, as in the following snippet:

```
form("entry", :action => "sign") do |s|
  s << content_tag("b", "Department")
  s << collection_select("department", "id", @departments, "id",
"name")
end
```

The block is yielded a string accumulator (named `s` in the example), to which you append any additional content that you want to appear between the main input fields and the submit tag.

`input(name, method, options)`

The appropriately named `input` method takes some identifying information, and automatically generates an HTML input tag based on an attribute of an `ActiveRecord` model. Going back to the `Post` example used in the explanation of `form`, here is the code snippet given in the Rails API docs:

```
input("post", "title")

=> <input id="post_title" name="post[title]" size="30"
         type="text" value="Hello World" />
```

To quickly show you the types of input fields generated by this method, I'll simply reproduce a portion of the code from the `ActiveRecordHelper` module itself:

```
def to_tag(options = {})
  case column_type
    when :string
      field_type = @method_name.include?("password") ? "password" :
"text"
      to_input_field_tag(field_type, options)
    when :text
      to_text_area_tag(options)
    when :integer, :float, :decimal
      to_input_field_tag("text", options)
    when :date
      to_date_select_tag(options)
    when :datetime, :timestamp
      to_datetime_select_tag(options)
    when :time
      to_time_select_tag(options)
    when :boolean
      to_boolean_select_tag(options)
  end
end
```

Customizing the Way Validation Errors Are Highlighted

By default, when Rails marks a field in your form that failed a validation check, it does so by wrapping that field in a `DIV` element, with the class name `fieldWithErrors`.

This behavior is actually customizable, since it is accomplished via a `Proc` object stored as a configuration property of the `ActionView::Base` class:

```
module ActionView
  class Base
    @@field_error_proc = Proc.new { |html_tag, instance|
      "<div class=\"fieldWithErrors\">#{html_tag}</div>"
    }
    cattr_accessor :field_error_proc
  end

  . . .
```

Armed with this knowledge, changing the validation error behavior is as simple as overriding `ActionView`'s `field_error_proc` attribute with your own custom `Proc`. I would suggest doing so either in `config/environment.rb` or your `ApplicationController` class.

In Listing 11.1, I changed the setting so that the input fields with validation errors are prefixed with a red ERR message.

Listing 11.1 Custom Validation Error Display

```
ActionView::Base.field_error_proc =
  Proc.new do |html_tag,instance|
    %(<div style="color:red">ERR</div>) + html_tag
  end
```

It has been suggested by many people that it would have been a much better default solution to simply add a `fieldWithErrors` CSS class to the input tag itself, instead of wrapping it with an extra `DIV` tag. Indeed, that would have made many of our lives easier, since an extra `DIV` often breaks pixel-perfect layouts. However, since `html_tag` is already constructed at the time when the `field_error_proc` is invoked, it is not trivial to modify its contents.

There are some solutions out there that use regular expressions and modify the `html_tag` string, for instance this one, found at http://snippets.dzone.com/tag/field_error_proc:

```
ActionView::Base.field_error_proc = Proc.new do |html_tag, instance|
  error_style = "background-color: #ffff80"
  if html_tag =~ /<(input|textarea|select)[^>]+style=/
```

```
      style_attribute = html_tag =~ /style=['"]/
      html_tag.insert(style_attribute + 7, "#{error_style}; ")
   elsif html_tag =~ /<(input|textarea|select)/
      first_whitespace = html_tag =~ /\s/
      html_tag[first_whitespace] = " style='#{error_style}' "
   end
   html_tag
end
```

Ugly! This is certainly an area of `ActionView` that could use improvement.

AssetTagHelper

According to the Rails API docs, this module

> Provides methods for linking an HTML page together with other assets such as
> images, javascripts, stylesheets, and feeds. You can direct Rails to link to assets
> from a dedicated assets server by setting `ActionController::Base.asset_`
> `host` in your `environment.rb`. These methods do not verify the assets exist
> before linking to them.

The `AssetTagHelper` module includes some methods that you will use on a
daily basis during active Rails development, particularly `image_tag`.

Head Helpers

Most of the helper methods in this module help you add content to the HEAD of your
HTML document.

auto_discovery_link_tag(type = :rss, url_options = {}, tag_options = {})

Returns a link tag that browsers and newsreaders can use to autodetect an RSS or
ATOM feed. The type can either be `:rss` (default) or `:atom`. Control the link options
in `url_for` format using the `url_options`.

You can modify the LINK tag itself using the `tag_options` parameter:

- `:rel`   Specify the relation of this link; defaults to "`alternate`".

- `:type`   Override MIME type (such as "`application/atom+xml`") that Rails
  would otherwise generate automatically for you.

- `:title`   Specify the title of the link; defaults to a capitalized type.

Here are examples of usages of `auto_discovery_link_tag` as shown in the Rails API docs:

```
auto_discovery_link_tag # =>
  <link rel="alternate" type="application/rss+xml" title="RSS"
  href="http://www.curenthost.com/controller/action" />

auto_discovery_link_tag(:atom) # =>
  <link rel="alternate" type="application/atom+xml" title="ATOM"
  href="http://www.curenthost.com/controller/action" />

auto_discovery_link_tag(:rss, {:action => "feed"}) # =>
  <link rel="alternate" type="application/rss+xml" title="RSS"
  href="http://www.curenthost.com/controller/feed" />

auto_discovery_link_tag(:rss, {:action => "feed"}, {:title => "My
RSS"}) # =>
  <link rel="alternate" type="application/rss+xml" title="My RSS"
  href="http://www.curenthost.com/controller/feed" />
```

The Lesson of the Favorite Icon

Because of the options provided, you could theoretically use `auto_discovery_link_tag` to generate a LINK tag for a favorite icon, the little image that displays in the browser's address bar and bookmarks:

```
auto_discovery_link_tag('image/x-icon', 'favicon.ico',
  :rel => 'shortcut icon', :title => '')
```

```
<link rel="shortcut icon" href="favicon.ico"
type="image/x-icon" title="">
```

That said, there is very little reason, if any, to use the `auto_discovery_link_tag` to generate a favorite icon link in this way, since the Rails incantation is actually longer and more complicated than typing the actual HTML code! Neither is there anything dynamic about the construction of this tag that requires helper logic.

I made a point of including this example to reinforce the lesson that it is not the Rails way to use helpers to generate markup that you could otherwise go ahead and write yourself.

`image_path(source)`

Computes the path to an image asset in the `public/images` directory. Full paths from the document root (beginning with a "/") will be passed through. This method is used internally by `image_tag` to build the image path. Passing a filename without an extension, as was practiced in early versions of Rails, is no longer supported.

```
image_path("edit.png")  # => /images/edit.png
image_path("icons/edit.png")  # => /images/icons/edit.png
image_path("/icons/edit.png")  # => /icons/edit.png
```

`image_tag(source, options = {})`

Returns an IMAGE tag for use in a template. The `source` parameter can be a full path or a file that exists in your public images directory. You can add additional arbitrary attributes to the IMAGE tag using the options parameter.

The following two options are treated specially:

- `:alt`   If no alternate text is given, the filename part of the source is used, after being capitalized and stripping off the extension.

- `:size`   Supplied as *widthxheight* so "30x45" becomes the attributes `width="30"` and `height="45"`. The `:size` option will fail silently if the value is not in the correct format.

```
image_tag("icon.png")  # =>
  <img src="/images/icon.png" alt="Icon" />

image_tag("icon.png", :size => "16x10", :alt => "Edit Entry")  # =>
  <img src="/images/icon.png" width="16" height="10" alt="Edit Entry"
/>

image_tag("/photos/dog.jpg", :class => 'icon')  # =>
  <img src="/photos/icon.gif" alt="Dog" class="icon"/>
```

> **Courtenay Says...**
>
> The `image_tag` method makes use of an internal method
> called `image_path`. This helpful method determines the
> path to use in the tag. Unfortunately, it also means you
> can't call a controller "image" and have it work as a
> resource, due to the conflicting name.

javascript_include_tag(*sources)

Returns a SCRIPT tag for each of the sources provided. You can pass in the filename
(the `.js` extension is optional) of JavaScript files that exist in your
`public/javascripts` directory for inclusion into the current page, or you can pass
their full path, relative to your document root.

To include the Prototype and Scriptaculous JavaScript libraries in your application,
pass `:defaults` as the source. When you're using `:defaults`, if an `application.js`
file exists in your `public/javascripts` directory, it will be included as well. You can
modify the attributes of the SCRIPT tag by passing a hash *as the last argument*.

```
javascript_include_tag "xmlhr", :defer => 'defer' # =>
  <script type="text/javascript" src="/javascripts/xmlhr.js"
  defer="defer"></script>

javascript_include_tag "common.javascript", "/elsewhere/cools" # =>
  <script type="text/javascript"
src="/javascripts/common.javascript"></script>
  <script type="text/javascript" src="/elsewhere/cools.js"></script>

javascript_include_tag :defaults # =>
  <script type="text/javascript"
src="/javascripts/prototype.js"></script>
  <script type="text/javascript"
src="/javascripts/effects.js"></script>
  ...
  <script type="text/javascript"
src="/javascripts/application.js"></script>
```

`javascript_path(source)`

Computes the path to a JavaScript asset in the public/javascripts directory. If the source filename has no extension, `.js` will be appended. Full paths from the document root will be passed through. Used internally by `javascript_include_tag` to build the script path.

`stylesheet_link_tag(*sources)`

Returns a stylesheet `LINK` tag for the sources specified as arguments. If you don't specify an extension, `.css` will be appended automatically. Just like other helper methods that take a variable number of arguments plus options, you can pass a hash of options as the last argument and they will be added as attributes to the tag.

```
stylesheet_link_tag "style" # =>
  <link href="/stylesheets/style.css" media="screen"
      rel="Stylesheet" type="text/css" />

stylesheet_link_tag "style", :media => "all" # =>
  <link href="/stylesheets/style.css" media="all"
      rel="Stylesheet" type="text/css" />

stylesheet_link_tag "random.styles", "/css/stylish" # =>
  <link href="/stylesheets/random.styles" media="screen"
      rel="Stylesheet" type="text/css" />
  <link href="/css/stylish.css" media="screen"
      rel="Stylesheet" type="text/css" />
```

`stylesheet_path(source)`

Computes the path to a stylesheet asset in the `public/stylesheets` directory. If the source filename has no extension, `.css` will be appended. Full paths from the document root will be passed through. Used internally by `stylesheet_link_tag` to build the stylesheet path.

For Plugins Only, Add Default JavaScript Includes

The `register_javascript_include_default` class method of `ActionView::Helpers::AssetTagHelper` lets plugin authors register one or more additional JavaScript files to be included when `javascript_include_tag` `:defaults` is called. This method is only intended to be called from plugin initialization to register additional `.js` files that the plugin installed in `public/javascripts`. You can find more details about this method in Chapter 19, "Extending Rails with Plugins."

BenchmarkHelper

One of the less frequently mentioned innovations in Rails is the usefulness of its built-in logging facilities. The `BenchmarkHelper` module adds the ability to time arbitrary bits of template code, and is useful when analyzing an application, looking for performance bottlenecks.

benchmark(message = "Benchmarking", level = :info)

Measures the execution time of a block in a template and reports the result to the log.

```
<% benchmark "Notes section" do %>
  <%= expensive_notes_operation %>
<% end %>
```

The preceding example will add something like "Notes section (0.34523)" to the log when the template is executed. It's possible to give an optional logger level as the second argument (`:debug`, `:info`, `:warn`, `:error`), but the default is `:info`.

CacheHelper

This module only contains one method, named `cache`. It is used to perform fragment caching of blocks within templates, without caching the output of an entire action as a whole. Rails also features page caching using the `caches_page` method of controllers, where the entire output of an action is stored as a HTML file that the web server can serve without going through the Action Pack.

In contrast, fragment caching is useful when certain elements of an action change frequently or depend on complicated state, while other parts rarely change or can be shared among multiple parties. The boundaries of a fragment to be cached are defined within a view template using the `cache` helper method. The topic was covered in detail in the caching section of Chapter 2, "Working with Controllers."

CaptureHelper

One of the great features of Rails views is that you are not limited to rendering a single "flow" of content. Along the way, you can define blocks of template code that should be inserted into other parts of the page during rendering using `yield`. The technique is accomplished via a pair of methods from the `CaptureHelper` module.

capture(&block)

The `capture` method lets you capture part of a template's output (inside a block) and assign it to an instance variable. The value of that variable can subsequently be used anywhere else on the template.

```
<% @message_html = capture do %>
<div>This is a message</div>
<% end %>
```

I don't think that the `capture` method is really that useful on its own in a template. It's a lot more useful when you use it in your own custom helper methods. It gives you the ability to write your own helpers that grab template content wrapped using a block. We cover that technique later on in this chapter in the section "Writing Your Own Helpers."

content_for(name, &block)

We mentioned the `content_for` method in Chapter 10 in the section "Yielding Content." It allows you to designate a part of your template as content for another part of the page. It works similarly to its sister method `capture` (in fact, it uses `capture` itself). Instead of returning the contents of the block provided to it, it stores the content to be retrieved using `yield` elsewhere in the template (or most commonly, in the surrounding layout).

A common example is to insert "sidebar" content into a layout. In the following example, the link will not appear in the "flow" of the view template—it will appear elsewhere in the template, wherever `<%= yield :navigation_sidebar %>` appears.

```
<% content_for :navigation_sidebar do %>
  <%= link_to 'Detail Page', item_detail_path(item) %>
<% end %>
```

DateHelper

The `DateHelper` module is used primarily to create HTML `select` tags for different kinds of calendar data. It also features one of the longest-named helper methods, a beast peculiar to Rails, called `distance_of_time_in_words_to_now`.

The Date and Time Selection Helpers

The following methods help you create form field input tags dealing with date and time data. All of them are prepared for multiparameter assignment to an `ActiveRecord` object. That's a fancy way of saying that even though they appear in the HTML form as separate input fields, when they are posted back to the server, it is understood that they refer to a single attribute of the model. That's some Rails magic for you!

date_select(object_name, method, options = {})

Returns a matched set of three `select` tags (one each for year, month, and day) preselected for accessing a specified date-based attribute (identified by the `method` parameter) on an object assigned to the template (identified by the `object_name` parameter).

It's possible to tailor the selects through the options hash, which accepts all the keys that each of the individual select builders do (like `:use_month_numbers` for `select_month`).

The `date_select` method also takes `:discard_year`, `:discard_month`, and `:discard_day` options, which drop the corresponding `select` tag from the set of three. Based on common sense, discarding the month select will also automatically discard the day select. If the day is omitted, but not the month, Rails will assume that the day should be the first of the month.

It's also possible to explicitly set the order of the tags using the `:order` option with an array of symbols `:year`, `:month`, and `:day` in the desired order. Symbols may be omitted and the respective `select` tag is not included.

Passing `:disabled => true` as part of the options will make elements inaccessible for change (see Listing 11.2).

Listing 11.2 Examples of `date_select`

```
date_select("post", "written_on")

date_select("post", "written_on", :start_year => 1995,
                                   :use_month_numbers => true,
                                   :discard_day => true,
                                   :include_blank => true)

date_select("post", "written_on", :order => [:day, :month, :year])

date_select("user", "birthday",   :order => [:month, :day])
```

`datetime_select(object_name, method, options = {})`

Works exactly like `date_select`, except for the addition of hour and minute `select` tags. Seconds may be added with the option `:include_seconds`. Along with the addition of time information come additional discarding options: `:discard_hour`, `:discard_minute`, and `:discard_seconds`.

`time_select(object_name, method, options = {})`

Returns a set of `select` tags (one for hour, minute, and optionally second) preselected for accessing a specified time-based attribute (identified by `method`) on an object assigned to the template (identified by `object_name`). You can include the seconds with `:include_seconds`.

```
time_select("post", "sunrise")
time_select("post", "start_time", :include_seconds => true)
```

The Individual Date and Time Select Helpers

Sometimes you need just a particular element of a date or time, and Rails obliges you with a comprehensive set of individual date and time select helpers. In contrast to the date and time helpers that we just looked at, the following helpers are not bound to an instance variable on the page. Instead, they all take a date or time Ruby object as their first parameter. (All of these methods have a set of common options, covered in the following subsection.)

select_date(date = Date.today, options = {})

Returns a set of `select` tags (one each for year, month, and day) preselected with the date provided (or the current date). It's possible to explicitly set the order of the tags using the `:order` option with an array of symbols `:year`, `:month`, and `:day` in the desired order.

select_datetime(datetime = Time.now, options = {})

Returns a set of `select` tags (one each for year, month, day, hour, and minute) preselected with the datetime. Optionally add a seconds field using the `:include_seconds => true` option. It's also possible to explicitly set the order of the tags using the `:order` option with an array of symbols `:year`, `:month`, and `:day`, `:hour`, `:minute`, and `:seconds` in the desired order. You can also add character values for the `:date_separator` and `:time_separator` options to control visual display of the elements (they default to "/" and ":").

select_day(date, options = {})

Returns a `select` tag with options for each of the days 1 through 31 with the current day selected. The date can also be substituted for an hour number. Override the field name using the `:field_name` option. It defaults to `day`. The `date` parameter may be substituted by a value from 1 to 31.

select_hour(datetime, options = {})

Returns a `select` tag with options for each of the hours 0 through 23 with the current hour selected. The `datetime` parameter can be substituted with an hour number from 0 to 23.

select_minute(datetime, options = {})

Returns a `select` tag with options for each of the minutes 0 through 59 with the current minute selected. Also can return a `select` tag with options by `minute_step` from 0 through 59 with the 00 minute selected. The `datetime` parameter can be substituted by a seconds value of 0 to 59.

select_month(date, options = {})

Returns a `select` tag with options for each of the months January through December with the current month selected. By default, the month names are presented as user options in the drop-down selection and the month numbers (1–12) are used as values submitted to the server.

It's also possible to use month numbers for the presentation instead of names, by setting `:use_month_numbers => true`. If you happen to want both numbers and names, set the `:add_month_numbers => true`. If you would prefer to show month names as abbreviations, set the `:use_short_month key => true`. Finally, if you want to use your own month names, set the value of the `:use_month_names` key in your options to an array of 12 month names.

```
# Will use keys like "January", "March"
select_month(Date.today)

# Will use keys like "1", "3"
select_month(Date.today, :use_month_numbers => true)

# Will use keys like "1 - January", "3 - March"
select_month(Date.today, :add_month_numbers => true)

# Will use keys like "Jan", "Mar"
select_month(Date.today, :use_short_month => true)

# Will use keys like "Januar", "Marts"
select_month(Date.today, :use_month_names => %w(Januar Februar
Marts ...))
```

Override the field name using the `:field_name` option. It defaults to `month`.

select_second(datetime, options = {})

Returns a `select` tag with options for each of the seconds 0 through 59 with the current second selected. The `datetime` parameter can either be a `DateTime` object or a second given as a number.

select_time(datetime, options = {})

Returns a set of HTML `select` tags (one for hour and minute). You can set `:add_separator` key to format the output.

select_year(date, options = {})

Returns a `select` tag with options for *each of the five years on each side of the current year*, which is selected. The five-year radius can be changed using the `:start_year` and `:end_year` options. Both ascending and descending year lists are supported by making `:start_year` less than or greater than `:end_year`. The date parameter can either be a `Date` object or a year given as a number.

```
# ascending year values
select_year(Date.today, :start_year => 1992, :end_year => 2007)

# descending year values
select_year(Date.today, :start_year => 2005, :end_year => 1900)
```

Common Options for Date Selection Helpers

All of the select-type methods share a number of common options that are as follows:

- `:discard_type`   Set to `true` if you want to discard the type part of the select name. If set to `true`, the `select_month` method would use simply `date` (which can be overwritten using `:prefix`) instead of `date[month]`.

- `:field_name`   Allows you to override the natural name of a `select` tag (from day, minute, and so on).

- `:include_blank`   Set to `true` if it should be possible to set an empty date.

- `:prefix`   Overwrites the default prefix of `date` used for the names of the `select` tags. Specifying `birthday` would result in a name of `birthday[month]` instead of `date[month]` when passed to the `select_month` method.

- `:use_hidden`   Set to `true` to embed the value of the datetime into the page as an HTML hidden input, instead of a `select` tag.

distance_in_time Methods with Complex Descriptive Names

Some `distance_in_time` methods have really long, complex descriptive names that nobody can ever remember without looking them up. Well, at least for the first dozen times or so you might not remember.

I find the following methods to be a perfect example of the Rails way when it comes to API design. Instead of going with a shorter and necessarily more cryptic alternative, the framework author decided to keep the name long and descriptive. It's one of those cases where a nonprogrammer can look at your code and understand what it's doing. Well, probably.

I also find these methods remarkable in that they are part of why people sometimes consider Rails part of the Web 2.0 phenomenon. What other web framework would include ways to *humanize* the display of timestamps?

distance_of_time_in_words(from_time, to_time = 0, include_seconds = false)

Reports the approximate distance in time between two Time or Date objects or integers as seconds. Set the include_seconds parameter to true if you want more detailed approximations when the distance is less than one minute.

Want to know how the times map out to expressions? Here is the implementation, which I think is some pretty cool Ruby code:

```
def distance_of_time_in_words(from_time, to_time = 0, include_seconds =
false)

  from_time = from_time.to_time if from_time.respond_to?(:to_time)
  to_time = to_time.to_time if to_time.respond_to?(:to_time)

  d_minutes = (((to_time - from_time).abs)/60).round
  d_seconds = ((to_time - from_time).abs).round

  case d_minutes
    when 0..1
      unless include_seconds
        return (d_minutes==0) ? 'less than a minute' : '1 minute'
      end

      case d_seconds
        when 0..4   then 'less than 5 seconds'
        when 5..9   then 'less than 10 seconds'
        when 10..19 then 'less than 20 seconds'
        when 20..39 then 'half a minute'
        when 40..59 then 'less than a minute'
        else             '1 minute'
```

```
      end

  when 2..44        then "#{d_minutes} minutes"
  when 45..89       then 'about 1 hour'
  when 90..1439     then "about #{(d_minutes.to_f/60.0).round} hours"
  when 1440..2879     then '1 day'
  when 2880..43199    then "#{(d_minutes / 1440).round} days"
  when 43200..86399   then 'about 1 month'
  when 86400..525599  then "#{(d_minutes / 43200).round} months"
  when 525600..1051199 then 'about 1 year'
  else                       "over #{(d_minutes / 525600).round}
years"
    end
end
```

The Rails API docs ask you to note that Rails calculates one year as 365.25 days.

distance_of_time_in_words_to_now(from_time, include_seconds = false)

Works exactly like `distance_of_times_in_words` except that the `to_time` is hard-coded to the current time. Usually invoked on `created_at` or `updated_at` attributes of your model, followed by the string `ago` in your template, as in the following example:

```
<strong><%= comment.user.name %></strong><br/>
<small><%= distance_of_time_in_words_to_now review.created_at %>
ago</small>
```

DebugHelper

The `DebugHelper` module only contains one method, named `debug`. Output it in your template, passing it an object that you want dumped to YAML and displayed in the browser inside PRE tags. Useful for debugging during development, but not much else.

FormHelper

The `FormHelper` module provides a set of methods for working with HTML forms, especially as they relate to `ActiveRecord` model objects assigned to the template. Its methods correspond to each type of HTML input fields (such as text, password, select, and so on) available. When the form is submitted, the value of the input fields are bundled into the `params` that is passed to the controller.

There are two types of form helper methods. The types found in this module are meant to work specifically with `ActiveRecord` model attributes, and the similarly named versions in the `FormTagHelper` module are not.

Creating Forms for `ActiveRecord` Models

The core method of this helper is called `form_for`, and we covered it to some extent in Chapter 4, "REST, Resources, and Rails." You pass it the name of the model you want to create a form for (or the model instance itself), as its first parameter, followed by URL information for the HTML form's action attribute. The helper method yields a `form` object, on which you can invoke input helper methods, omitting their first argument.

Assume we want a form for the user to create a new `Person` record and additionally assume that `@person = Person.new` happened in the action of the controller that is rendering this template code:

```
<% form_for :person, @person, :url => { :action => "create" } do
|form| %>
  <%= form.text_field :first_name %>
  <%= form.text_field :last_name %>
  <%= submit_tag 'Create' %>
<% end %>
```

This is the equivalent (old-school) version of `form_for`, which doesn't use a yielded form object and explicitly names the object being used in the input fields:

```
<% form_for :person, @person, :url => { :action => "create" } do %>
  <%= text_field :person, :first_name %>
  <%= text_field :person, :last_name %>
  <%= submit_tag 'Create' %>
<% end %>
```

The first version has less repetition (remember your DRY principle), but don't forget the more verbose style entirely—it's necessary in some circumstances.

Variables Are Optional

If you explicitly specify the object name parameter for input fields rather than letting them be supplied by the form, keep in mind that it doesn't have to match a "live" object instance in scope for the template. Rails won't complain if the object is not there—it will simply put blank values in the resulting form.

Rails-Generated Form Conventions

The HTML generated by the `form_for` invocations in the preceding example is characteristic of Rails forms, and follows specific naming conventions:

```
<form action="/persons/create" method="post">
  <input id="person_first_name" name="person[first_name]" size="30"
type="text" />
  <input id="person_last_name" name="person[last_name]" size="30"
type="text" />
  <input name="commit" type="submit" value="Create" />
</form>
```

When this form is submitted, the `params` hash will look like the following example (using the format reflected in your development log for every request):

```
Parameters: {"commit"=>"Create", "action"=>"create",
"controller"=>"persons",
 "person"=> {"first_name"=>"William", "last_name"=>"Smith"}}
```

As you can see, the `params` hash has a nested "person" value, which is accessed using `params[:person]` in the controller. That's pretty fundamental Rails knowledge, and I'd be surprised if you didn't know it already. I promise we won't rehash much more basic knowledge after the following section.

Displaying Existing Values

If you were editing an existing instance of `Person`, that object's attribute values would have been filled into the form, making the resulting HTML look something like this:

```
<form action="/persons/create" method="post">
  <input id="person_first_name" name="person[first_name]" size="30"
type="text" value="Obie"/>
  <input id="person_last_name" name="person[last_name]" size="30"
type="text" value="Fernandez"/>
  <input name="commit" type="submit" value="Create" />
</form>
```

Okay, that's also pretty fundamental Rails knowledge. What about if you want to edit a new model object instance, prepopulated with certain values? Do you have to pass the values as options to the input helper methods? No. Since the form helpers display the values of the model's attributes, it would simply be a matter of initializing the object with the desired values in the controller, as follows:

```
def new
  @person = Person.new(:first_name => 'First', :last_name => 'Last')
end
```

Since you're only using `new`, no record is persisted to the database, and your default values magically appear in the input fields.

Updating Multiple Objects at Once

That's all well and good for editing one object at a time. What if you want to edit multiple records at the same time? When the attribute name passed to `form_for` or individual input field helper methods contains a set of square brackets, the id for the object will be included in the autogenerated `name` and `id` attributes of the input tag.

I find this technique potentially challenging, on a couple of levels. First of all, we usually identify attribute names using symbols, but tacking a pair of square brackets onto a symbol (like `:name[]`) is invalid. We're forced to use a string to name the object instead:

```
<% form_for "person[]" do |form| %>
 <% for @person in @people %>
  <%= form.text_field :name %>

  ...
```

Secondly, it generates HTML for the input tags looking something like this:

```
<input type="text" id="person_8_name" name="person[8][name]"
 value="Obie Fernandez"/>
```

Whoa! The structure of the hash submitted to the controller is significantly different than what we're used to seeing. That nested params hash will now be three levels deep when it comes to the "person" and to make it more confusing, the ids of the objects are being used as has keys:

```
Parameters: {"person"=>{"8"=>{"name"=>"Obie Fernandez"},
                        "9"=>{"name"=>"Jodi Showers"}, ...}, ... }
```

Now the controller code to handle the form needs to change, or you're likely to see a stack trace like the following one:

```
NoMethodError (undefined method `8=' for #<User:0x8762174>):
    /vendor/rails/activerecord/lib/active_record/base.rb:2032:in
`method_missing'
```

The good news is that the way that you handle that nested hash structure in your controller's update method is probably one of the nicest examples of how Rails is well integrated across its MVC layers:

```
Person.update(params[:person].keys, params[:person].values)
```

Beautiful! This is the sort of thing that makes the Rails way so enjoyable.

Square Brackets with New Records?

If you have a way of inserting HTML into your document dynamically, via JavaScript and/or AJAX techniques, you can leverage Rails' behavior with regard to empty square brackets.

When you're using the square-brackets naming, Rails will happily generate HTML for new model objects that looks like this:

```
<input type="text" id="person__name" name="person[][name]"/>
```

If you were dynamically adding rows of child record entry forms to a parent form, you could replicate that convention easily. Just make sure the names of your input fields have the empty square brackets.

When you submit the form, the Rails request dispatcher will assume that the value of the :person key in the params hash is supposed to be an Array, and that is what you will have to deal with in the controller action as the value of params[:person], an array!

Considering that the create class method of ActiveRecord models takes an array or hashes to do multiple inserts, we have yet another one of those beautiful examples of Rails cross-layer integration:

```
def add_people
  Person.create(params[:person])
  ...
end
```

However, there are some drawbacks to this technique, because it only works when *all* of the input fields in the person namespace have empty square brackets. Stick any other input fields on the same object without the empty square brackets, and the Rails dispatcher will get very, very unhappy about it:

```
DISPATCHER FAILSAFE RESPONSE (has cgi) Sun Jul 15 14:36:35 -0400 2007
  Status: 500 Internal Server Error
  Conflicting types for parameter containers. Expected an instance of
  Hash but found an instance of Array. This can be caused by colliding
  Array and Hash parameters like qs[]=value&qs[key]=value.
```

Indexed Input Fields

Okay, moving forward, here is a slightly more verbose and less magical way to define multiple sets of input fields—use the :index option of the input field methods themselves. It lets you explicitly provide an identifier that will be inserted into the field names, and in doing so opens up some interesting possibilities.

First, it lets you replicate the square brackets technique that we just discussed in the preceding section. For example, here's a set of name fields for a collection of people:

```
<% for @person in @people %>
<%= text_field :person, :name, :index => @person.id %>
...
```

The id attribute of the person will be inserted into the parameter hash in the way we've already discussed with the square brackets, and we'll get the same nesting behavior.

Now to make it more interesting, notice that the :index option is not picky about the type of identifier that you supply it, which makes it pretty useful for defining enumerated sets of records! That is exactly what sets it apart from the square-brackets technique, and I'm sure I need to explain it a little more.

Consider the template code in Listing 11.3, part of a basketball tournament application (or in a more generalized guise, any application that stores people in well-defined roles):

Listing 11.3   Basketball Team Entry Form

```
<% form_for :team do |f|%>
  <h2>Team Name</h2>
  Name: <%= f.text_field :name %><br/>
  Coach: <%= f.text_field :coach %>
  <% ["guard_1", "guard_2", "forward_1", "forward_2", "center"].each
{|role| %>
    <h3><%= role.humanize %></h3>
    Name: <%= text_field :players, :name, :index => role %>
  <% } %>
<% end %>
```

That code produces the following HTML output when you run it:

```
<form method="post" action="/homepage/team">
  <h2>Team Name</h2>
  Name: <input id="team_name" type="text" size="30"
name="team[name]"/><br/>
  Coach: <input id="team_coach" type="text" size="30"
name="team[coach]"/>
  <h3>Guard 1</h3>
  Name: <input id="players_guard_1_name" type="text" size="30"
name="players[guard_1][name]"/>
  <h3>Guard 2</h3>
  Name: <input id="players_guard_2_name" type="text" size="30"
name="players[guard_2][name]"/>
  <h3>Forward 1</h3>
  Name: <input id="players_forward_1_name" type="text" size="30"
name="players[forward_1][name]"/>
  <h3>Forward 2</h3>
  Name: <input id="players_forward_2_name" type="text" size="30"
```

```
name="players[forward_2][name]"/>
<h3>Center</h3>
Name: <input id="players_center_name" type="text" size="30"
name="players[center][name]"/>
</form>
```

Now when you submit that form (as I just did, using one of my favorite basketball teams of all time), your controller action would receive the following parameters hash. I took the liberty of formatting the log output nicely, to make sure the structure is clear:

```
Parameters: {"team"=>{
                  "name"=>"Chicago Bulls",
                  "coach"=>"Phil Jackson"},
              {"players"=> {
                  "forward_1"=>{"name"=>"Scottie Pippen"},
                  "forward_2"=>{"name"=>"Horace Grant"},
                  "center"=>{"name"=>"Bill Cartwright"},
                  "guard_1"=>{"name"=>"Michael Jordan"},
                  "guard_2"=>{"name"=>"John Paxson"}}, ... }
```

I made it a point to give those text field inputs for the player's names and ages their own :players identifier, rather than linking them to the form's team object. You don't even need to worry about initializing an @players variable for the form to work. Form helper methods do not complain if the variable they're supposed to reflect is nil, *provided you identify it using a symbol and not by passing the instance variable directly to the method.*

For the sake of completeness, I'll give you some simplistic controller action code in Listing 11.4 that is capable of handling the form submission.

Listing 11.4   Controller Action to Create Team

```
def create
  @team = Team.create(params[:team])
  params[:players].keys.each do |role|
    @team.add_player(role, Player.new(params[:players][role]))
  end
  ...
end
```

Taking into account the nested parameters hash, we can take it apart in a loop based on `params[:players].keys` and do operations per role. Of course, this code assumes that the team has an instance method `add_player(role, player)`, but I think you should get my drift.

Faux Accessors

"Now hold on a second," you are probably saying to yourself. If our example `Team` model knew how to handle the setting of a `players` hash as part of its attributes, the controller code could be dramatically simpler. In fact, we could knock it down to just one line (excluding error checking and redirection):

```
def create
  @team = Team.create(params[:team])
  ...
end
```

Impressive, huh? (It is to me!) What we need is to *cheat* with what Josh Susser calls *faux accessors*[1]—setters that let you initialize parts of a model that aren't (database-backed) attributes. Our example `Team` model would need a `players` writer method that understood how to add those players to itself. Perhaps it would look like the example in Listing 11.5.

Listing 11.5 Adding Writer Methods That Understand `Params` Hashes

```
class Team < ActiveRecord::Base
  has_many :positions
  has_many :players, :through => :positions

  def players=(players_hash)
    players_hash.keys.each do |role|
      positions.create(:role => role,
                       :player => Player.new(players_hash[role]))
    end
  end
end

class Position < ActiveRecord::Base
  belongs_to :player
  belongs_to :team
end

class Player < ActiveRecord::Base
  has_many :positions
  has_many :teams, :through => :positions
end
```

To recap, the `players=` writer method gets invoked as a result of calling `Team.create` with the full `params` hash structure, which includes a nested hash of `:players`. I must warn you, that your mileage may, as they say, *vary* with this kind of technique. It's perfect for the example, with its `has_many :through` relationship connecting the `Team`, `Position`, and `Player` classes, but it may not be perfect for your domain model. The most important idea is to keep your mind open to the possibility of writing code that is *this clean*. It's the Rails way.

> **Courtenay Says...**
>
> Hiding your code behind a method like this will make your code both simpler, and more powerful. You can now test this method in isolation, and can stub it in a controller test. Stubbing in this case allows you to focus on testing the logic of the controller action, and not the behavior of the database.
>
> It also means you or another team member can change the implementation without breaking unrelated tests, and it keeps the database code where it belongs, in the model.

I've gotten us off on a bit of a tangent—we were talking about form helpers, so let's cover one more important aspect of them before moving forward.

How Form Helpers Get Their Values

A rather important lesson to learn about Rails form helper methods is that the value they display comes directly from the database prior to "meddling" by the developer. Unless you know what you're doing, you may get some unexpected results if you try to override the values to be displayed in a form.

Let's illustrate with a `LineItem` model, which has a decimal `rate` attribute (by merits of a `rate` column in its database table). We'll override its *implicit* rate accessor with one of our own:

```ruby
class LineItem < ActiveRecord::Base
  def rate
    "A RATE"
  end
end
```

In normal situations, the overridden accessor is hiding access to the real rate attribute, as we can illustrate using the console.

```
>> li = LineItem.new
=> #<LineItem:0x34b5d18>
>> li.rate
=> "A RATE"
```

However, suppose you were to compose a form to edit line items using form helpers:

```
<%- form_for :line_item do |f| -%>
  <%= f.text_field :rate %>
<%- end -%>
```

You would find that it works normally, as if that overridden `rate` accessor doesn't exist. The behavior is intentional, yet confusing enough that it has been reported multiple times as a bug.[2]

The fact is that Rails form helpers use special methods named *attribute*_before_type_cast (which are covered in Chapter 6, "Working with `ActiveRecord`"). The preceding example would use the method `rate_before_type_cast`, and bypass the overriding method we defined.

FormOptionsHelper

The methods in the `FormOptionsHelper` module are all about helping you to work with HTML `select` elements, by giving you ways to turn collections of objects into `option` tags.

Select Helpers

The following methods help you to create `select` tags based on a pair of `object` and `attribute` identifiers.

collection_select(object, attribute, collection, value_method, text_method, options = {}, html_options = {})

Return both `select` and `option` tags for the given `object` and `attribute` using `options_from_collection_for_select` (also in this module) to generate the list of `option` tags from the `collection` parameter.

country_select(object, attribute, priority_countries = nil, options = {}, html_options = {})

Return `select` and `option` tags for the given object and method, using `country_options_for_select` to generate the list of `option` tags. Note: The country values inserted by Rails do not include standard 2-character country codes.

The `priority_countries` argument allows you to specify an array of country names to display at the top of the drop-down selection for the user's convenience:

```
<%= form.country_select :billing_country, ["United States"] %>
```

select(object, attribute, choices, options = {}, html_options = {})

Create a `select` tag and a series of contained `option` tags for the provided `object_name` and attribute. The value of the attribute currently held by the object (if any) will be selected, provided that the object is available (not nil). See `options_for_select` section for the required format of the choices parameter.

Here's a small example where the value of `@person.person_id` is 1:

```
select("post", "person_id", Person.find(:all).collect {|p|
[ p.name, p.id ] }, { :include_blank => true })
```

Executing that helper code would generate the following HTML output:

```
<select name="post[person_id]">
  <option value=""></option>
  <option value="1" selected="selected">David</option>
  <option value="2">Sam</option>
  <option value="3">Tobias</option>
</select>
```

If necessary, specify `:selected => `*`value`* to explicitly set the selection or `:selected => nil` to leave all options unselected. The `:include_blank => true` option inserts a blank `option` tag at the beginning of the list, so that there is no pre-selected value.

time_zone_select(object, method, priority_zones = nil, options = {}, html_options = {})

Return `select` and `option` tags for the given object and method, using `time_zone_options_for_select` to generate the list of `option` tags.

In addition to the `:include_blank` option documented in the preceding section, this method also supports a `:model` option, which defaults to `TimeZone`. This may be used by users to specify a different timezone model object. (See `time_zone_options_for_select` section for more information.)

Option Helpers

For all of the following methods, only `option` tags are returned, so you have to invoke them from within a select helper or otherwise wrap them in a `select` tag.

country_options_for_select(selected = nil, priority_countries = nil)

Returns a string of `option` tags for pretty much any country in the world. Supply a country name as selected to have it marked as the selected `option` tag. You can also supply an array of countries as `priority_countries`, so that they will be listed above the rest of the (long) list.

option_groups_from_collection_for_select(collection, group_method, group_label_method, option_key_method, option_value_method, selected_key = nil)

Returns a string of `option` tags, like `options_from_collection_for_select`, but surrounds them with OPTGROUP tags. The `collection` should return a subarray of items when calling `group_method` on it. Each group in the `collection` should return its own name when calling `group_label_method`. The `option_key_method` and `option_value_method` parameters are used to calculate `option` tag attributes.

It's probably much easier to show in an example than to explain in words.

```
>> html_option_groups_from_collection(@continents, "countries",
   "continent_name", "country_id", "country_name",
@selected_country.id)
```

This example could output the following HTML:

```
<optgroup label="Africa">
 <select>Egypt</select>
 <select>Rwanda</select>
 ...
</optgroup>
<optgroup label="Asia">
 <select>China</select>
 <select>India</select>
 <select>Japan</select>
 ...
</optgroup>
```

For the sake of clarity, here are the model classes reflected in the example:

```
class Continent
  def initialize(p_name, p_countries)
    @continent_name = p_name; @countries = p_countries
  end

  def continent_name
    @continent_name
  end

  def countries
    @countries
  end
end

class Country
  def initialize(id, name)
    @id, @name = id, name
  end

  def country_id
```

```
    @id
  end

  def country_name
    @name
  end
end
```

options_for_select(container, selected = nil)

Accepts a container (hash, array, or anything else enumerable) and returns a string of option tags.

Given a container where the elements respond to first and last (such as a two-element array), the "lasts" serve as option values and the "firsts" as option text. It's not too hard to put together an expression that constructs a two-element array using the map and collect iterators.

For example, assume you have a collection of businesses to display, and you're using a select field to allow the user to filter based on the category of the businesses. The category is not a simple string; in this example, it's a proper model related to the business via a belongs_to association:

```
class Business < ActiveRecord::Base
  belongs_to :category
end

class Category < ActiveRecord::Base
  has_many :businesses

  def <=>(other)
end
```

A simplified version of the template code for displaying that collection of businesses might look like this:

```
<% opts = @businesses.map(&:category).sort.collect {|c| [[c.name],
[c.id]]} %>
<% select_tag(:filter, options_for_select(opts, params[:filter])) %>
```

The first line puts together the `container` expected by `options_for_select` by first aggregating the `category` attributes of the `businesses` collection using `map` and the nifty `&:method` syntax supported by Rails. The second line generates the `select` tag using those options (covered later in the chapter). Realistically you want to massage that category list a little more, so that it is ordered correctly and does not contain duplicates:

```
... @businesses.map(&:category).uniq.sort.collect {...
```

Particularly with smaller sets of data, it's perfectly acceptable to do this level of data manipulation in Ruby code. And of course, you probably don't want to ever shove hundreds or even thousands of rows in a `select` tag, which means this technique is quite useful. Remember to implement the *spaceship* method in your model if you need it to be sortable by the `sort` method.

Also, it's worthwhile to experiment with eager loading in these cases, so you don't end up with an individual database query for each of the objects represented in the `select` tag. In the case of our example, the controller would populate the businesses collection using code like this:

```
@businesses = Business.find(:conditions => ..., :include => :category)
```

Hashes are turned into a form acceptable to `options_for_select` automatically—the keys become "firsts" and values become "lasts."

If `selected` parameter is specified (with either a value or array of values for multiple selections), the matching "last" or element will get the selected attribute:

```
>> options_for_select([["Dollar", "$"], ["Kroner", "DKK"]])
   <option value="$">Dollar</option>
   <option value="DKK">Kroner</option>

>> options_for_select([ "VISA", "MasterCard" ], "MasterCard")
   <option>VISA</option>
   <option selected="selected">MasterCard</option>

>> options_for_select({ "Basic" => "$20", "Plus" => "$40" }, "$40")
   <option value="$20">Basic</option>
   <option value="$40" selected="selected">Plus</option>

>> options_for_select([ "VISA", "MasterCard", "Discover" ],
                      ["VISA", "Discover"])
```

```
<option selected="selected">VISA</option>
<option>MasterCard</option>
<option selected="selected">Discover</option>
```

A lot of people have trouble getting this method to correctly display their selected item—make sure that the value you pass to `selected` matches the type contained in the object collection of the `select`; otherwise, it won't work. In the following example, assuming `price` is a numeric value, without the `to_s`, selection would be broken, since the values passed as options are all strings:

```
>> options_for_select({ "Basic" => "20", "Plus" => "40" }, price.to_s)
   <option value="20">Basic</option>
   <option value="40" selected="selected">Plus</option>
```

options_from_collection_for_select(collection, value_method, text_method, selected=nil)

Returns a string of `option` tags that have been compiled by iterating over the collection and assigning the result of a call to the `value_method` as the option value and the `text_method` as the option text. If selected is specified, the element returning a match on `value_method` will get preselected.

time_zone_options_for_select(selected = nil, priority_zones = nil, model = TimeZone)

Returns a string of `option` tags for pretty much any timezone in the world. Supply a `TimeZone` name as selected to have it preselected. You can also supply an array of `TimeZone` objects as `priority_zones`, so that they will be listed above the rest of the (long) list. `TimeZone.us_zones` is a convenience method that gives you a list of the U.S. timezones only.

The `selected` parameter must be either `nil`, or a string that names a `TimeZone` (covered in the Appendix A, "ActiveSupport API Reference").

By default, the `model` is the `TimeZone` constant (which can be obtained in `ActiveRecord` as a value object). The only requirement is that the `model` parameter be an object that responds to `all`, returning an array of objects representing timezones.

FormTagHelper

The following helper methods generate HTML form and input tags based on explicit naming and values, contrary to the similar methods present in `FormHelper`, which require association to an `ActiveRecord` model instance. All of these helper methods take an `options` hash, which may contain special options or simply additional attribute values that should be added to the HTML tag being generated.

check_box_tag(name, value = "1", checked = false, options = {})

Creates HTML for a check box input field. Unlike its fancier cousin, `check_box` in `FormHelper`, this helper does not give you an extra hidden input field to ensure that a false value is passed even if the check box is unchecked.

```
>> check_box_tag('remember_me')
=> <input id="remember_me" name="remember_me" type="checkbox"
value="1"/>

>> check_box_tag('remember_me', 1, true)
=> <input checked="checked" id="remember_me" name="remember_me"
   type="checkbox" value="1" />
```

end_form_tag

Prior to Rails 2.0, the `end_form_tag` was used to output the HTML string `</form>` into your template, and was used in conjunction with `start_form_tag`. Nowadays, we use a block to wrap the content of a form and this method is no longer needed.

file_field_tag(name, options = {})

Creates a file upload field. Remember to set your HTML form to *multipart* or file uploads will mysteriously not work:

```
<%= form_tag { :action => "post" }, { :multipart => true } %>
  <label for="file">File to Upload</label>
  <%= file_field_tag :uploaded_data %>
  <%= submit_tag %>
<%= end_form_tag %>
```

The controller action will receive a `File` object pointing to the uploaded file as it exists in a tempfile on your system. Processing of an uploaded file is beyond the scope of this book. If you're smart, you'll use Rick Olson's excellent AttachmentFu[3] plugin instead of rolling your own handler code.

form_tag(url_for_options = {}, options = {}, *parameters_for_url, &block)

Starts a `FORM` tag, with its action attribute set to the URL passed as the `url_for_options` parameter. It is aliased as `start_form_tag`.

The `:method` option defaults to POST. Browsers handle HTTP GET and POST natively; if you specify "put," "delete," or any other HTTP verb is used, a hidden input field will be inserted with the name `_method` and a value corresponding to the `method` supplied. The Rails request dispatcher understands the `_method` parameter, which is the basis for the RESTful techniques you learned in Chapter 4.

The `:multipart` option allows you to specify that you will be including file-upload fields in the form submission and the server should be ready to handle those files accordingly.

```
>> form_tag('/posts')
=> <form action="/posts" method="post">

>> form_tag('/posts/1', :method => :put)
=> <form action="/posts/1" method="put">

>> form_tag('/upload', :multipart => true)
=> <form action="/upload" method="post" enctype="multipart/form-data">
```

You might note that all parameters to `form_tag` are optional. If you leave them off, you'll get a form that posts back to the URL that it came from—a quick and dirty solution that I use quite often when prototyping or experimenting. To quickly set up a controller action that handles post-backs, just include an `if/else` condition that checks the request method, something like this:

```
def add
  if request.post?
    # handle the posted params
    redirect_to :back
  end
end
```

Notice that if the request is a post, I handle the form `params` and then redirect back to the original URL (using `redirect_to :back`). Otherwise, execution simply falls through and would render whatever template is associated with the action.

hidden_field_tag(name, value = nil, options = {})

Creates a hidden field, with parameters similar to `text_field_tag`.

image_submit_tag(source, options = {})

Displays an image that, when clicked, will submit the form. The interface for this method is the same as its cousin `image_tag` in the `AssetTagHelper` module.

Image input tags are popular replacements for standard submit tags, because they make an application look fancier. They are also used to detect the location of the mouse cursor on click—the `params` hash will include x and y data.

password_field_tag(name = "password", value = nil, options = {})

Creates a password input field. This method is otherwise identical to `text_field_tag`.

radio_button_tag(name, value, checked = false, options = {})

Creates a radio button input field. Make sure to give all of your radio button options the same `name` so that the browser will consider them linked.

select_tag(name, option_tags = nil, options = {})

Creates a drop-down selection box, or if the `:multiple` option is set to true, a multiple-choice selection box. The `option_tags` parameter is an actual string of `option` tags to put inside the `select` tag. You should not have to generate that string explicitly yourself—use the helpers in `FormOptions` (covered in the previous section of this chapter), which can be used to create common select boxes such as countries, time zones, or associated records.

start_form_tag

Alias for `form_tag`.

submit_tag(value = "Save changes", options = {})

Creates a submit button with the text value as the caption. The option :disable_with can be used to provide a name for disabled versions of the submit button.

text_area_tag(name, content = nil, options = {})

Creates a multiline text input field (the TEXTAREA tag). The :size option lets you easily specify the dimensions of the text area, instead of having to resort to explicit :rows and :cols options.

```
>> <%= text_area_tag "body", nil, :size => "25x10" %>
=> <textarea name="body" id="body" cols="25" rows="10"></textarea>
```

text_field_tag(name, value = nil, options = {})

Creates a standard text input field.

> **Courtenay Says...**
>
> Many of these functions are fine for the new Rails programmer, but real coders write their HTML tags and Javascript by hand.

JavaScriptHelper

Provides helper methods to facilitate inclusion of JavaScript code in your templates.

button_to_function(name, function, html_options={}, &block)

Returns a button that will trigger a JavaScript function via the onclick handler. The function argument can be left out, if you provide an update_page block containing RJS-style code. The opts hash takes optional attributes for the button tag.

```
button_to_function "Greeting", "alert('Hello world!')"

button_to_function "Delete", "if (confirm('Really?')) do_delete()"
```

```
button_to_function "Details" do |page|
  page[:details].visual_effect :toggle_slide
end

button_to_function "Details", :class => "details_button" do |page|
  page[:details].visual_effect :toggle_slide
end
```

define_javascript_functions()

Includes the source code for all of your project's JavaScript libraries inside a single SCRIPT tag. The function first includes prototype.js and then its core extensions (determined by filenames starting with "prototype"). Afterward, any additional scripts in the public/javascripts will be included in undefined order.

It is much preferable to use the javascript_include_tag helper method of AssetTagHelper to create remote SCRIPT links.

escape_javascript(javascript)

Escapes line breaks, single and double quotes for JavaScript segments.

javascript_tag(content, html_options={})

Outputs a SCRIPT tag with the content inside. The html_options are added as tag attributes.

link_to_function(name, function, html_options={}, &block)

Returns a link that will trigger a JavaScript function using the onclick handler of the link. A return false; statement is added, so that the browser knows to stop processing the link click.

```
>> link_to_function "Greeting", "alert('Hello world!')"
=> <a onclick="alert('Hello world!'); return false;"
href="#">Greeting</a>

>> link_to_function(image_tag("delete"), "if (confirm('Really?'))
do_delete()")
>> <a onclick="if (confirm('Really?')) do_delete(); return false;"
```

```
href="#">
    <img src="/images/delete.png?" alt="Delete"/>
</a>
```

Just like `button_to_function`, you can omit the function parameter and provide JavaScript RJS-style in a code block.

```
>> link_to_function("Show me more", nil, :id => "more_link") do |page|
     page[:details].visual_effect  :toggle_blind
     page[:more_link].replace_html "Show me less"
   end

>> <a href="#" id="more_link" onclick="try {
       $('details').visualEffect('toggle_blind');
       $('more_link').update('Show me less');
     }...
```

NumberHelper

This module provides assistance in converting numeric data to formatted strings suitable for displaying in your view. Methods are provided for phone numbers, currency, percentage, precision, positional notation, and file size.

human_size(size, precision=1)

Alias for `number_to_human_size`.

number_to_currency(number, options = {})

Formats a number into a currency string. You can customize the format in the options hash.

- `:precision`   Sets the level of precision, defaults to 2
- `:unit`   Sets the denomination of the currency, defaults to "$"
- `:separator`   Sets the separator between the units, defaults to "."
- `:delimiter`   Sets the thousands delimiter, defaults to ","

```
>> number_to_currency(1234567890.50)
=> $1,234,567,890.50

>> number_to_currency(1234567890.506)
=> $1,234,567,890.51

>> number_to_currency(1234567890.506, :precision => 3)
=> $1,234,567,890.506

>> number_to_currency(1234567890.50, :unit => "&pound;",
=> :separator => ",", :delimiter => ""
=> &pound;1234567890,50
```

number_to_human_size(size, precision=1)

Formats the bytes in size into a more understandable representation. Useful for reporting file sizes to users. This method returns nil if size cannot be converted into a number. You can change the default precision of 1.

```
number_to_human_size(123)          => 123 Bytes
number_to_human_size(1234)         => 1.2 KB
number_to_human_size(12345)        => 12.1 KB
number_to_human_size(1234567)      => 1.2 MB
number_to_human_size(1234567890)   => 1.1 GB
number_to_human_size(1234567890123) => 1.1 TB
number_to_human_size(1234567, 2)   => 1.18 MB
```

This method is also aliased as human_size.

number_to_percentage(number, options = {})

Formats a number as a percentage string. You can customize the format in the options hash.

- :precision   Sets the level of precision, defaults to 3
- :separator   Sets the separator between the units, defaults to "."

```
number_to_percentage(100)      => 100.000%
number_to_percentage(100, {:precision => 0})    => 100%
number_to_percentage(302.0574, {:precision => 2})    => 302.06%
```

number_to_phone(number, options = {})

Formats a number as a U.S. phone number. You can customize the format in the options hash.

- :area_code   Adds parentheses around the area code
- :delimiter   Specifies the delimiter to use, defaults to "-"
- :extension   Specifies an extension to add to the end of the generated number
- :country_code   Sets the country code for the phone number

```
number_to_phone(1235551234)       => 123-555-1234
number_to_phone(1235551234, :area_code => true)    => (123) 555-1234
number_to_phone(1235551234, :delimiter => " ")     => 123 555 1234
```

number_with_delimiter(number, delimiter=",", separator=".")

Formats a number with grouped thousands using a delimiter. You can customize the format using optional delimiter and separator parameters.

- delimiter   Sets the thousands delimiter, defaults to ","
- separator   Sets the separator between the units, defaults to "."

```
number_with_delimiter(12345678)       => 12,345,678
number_with_delimiter(12345678.05)    => 12,345,678.05
number_with_delimiter(12345678, ".")   => 12.345.678
```

number_with_precision(number, precision=3)

Formats a number with the specified level of precision. The default level of precision is 3.

```
number_with_precision(111.2345)    => 111.235
number_with_precision(111.2345, 2) => 111.24
```

PaginationHelper

The `PaginationHelper` module was removed from Rails 2. Basically, it sucked and everyone hated it. As long as anyone can remember, the Rails way has been to *not* use the pagination helper and use something else instead.

Luckily, you don't have to roll your own pagination because there are a couple of pagination plugins that are worth their weight in gold. We don't cover them extensively here, but I will at least point you in the right direction.

> **Courtenay Says**
>
> The default paginator worked well enough, but it didn't really scale.

will_paginate

This plugin,[4] written by the guys behind the popular ERR the blog, is the pagination library of choice for most savvy Rails developers. Install it as a plugin using the following command:

```
$ script/plugin install svn://errtheblog.com/svn/plugins/will_paginate
```

In a nutshell, `will_paginate` works by adding a `paginate` class method to your `ActiveRecord` models that takes the place of `find`. In addition to `find`'s usual naming conventions, arguments, and options, it takes a `:page` parameter, for obvious reasons.

A query in the controller might look like this:

```
@posts = Post.paginate_by_board_id @board.id, :page => params[:page]
```

View template code is not impacted very much; it just gets fewer records to display. To render the pagination control, you just have to call `will_paginate` with the collection being rendered:

```
<%= will_paginate @posts %>
```

The plugin authors even give you a batch of CSS code so that you can make the pagination control look really pretty, as shown in Figure 11.1.

Figure 11.1 Pagination control formatted by CSS code

Users with search-engine optimization (SEO) concerns probably should go with `will_paginate` because it generates those individually numbered page links. Search robots see them as unique links and will keep clicking through and indexing their content. Conventional SEO wisdom is that search robots click next links only a few times before getting bored and moving on to more interesting sites.

paginator

This project,[5] by notable Rails expert Bruce Williams, is hosted on Rubyforge and might appeal to some because of its simplicity. It's a Rubygem, not a plugin, so you would type `sudo gem install paginator` to get your hands on it.

Instead of integrating tightly with `ActiveRecord`, the way that `will_paginate` does, the paginator library provides a neat little API to wrap the `find` invocation in your controller, as follows:

```
def index
  @pager = ::Paginator.new(Foo.count, PER_PAGE) do |offset, per_page|
    Foo.find(:all, :limit => per_page, :offset => offset)
  end
  @page = @pager.page(params[:page])
  ...
end
```

The view code, instead of relying on special helper methods, has the `@page` object at its disposal:

```
<% @page.items.each do |foo| %>
  <%# Show something for each item %>
<% end %>
<%= @page.number %>
<%= link_to("Prev", foos_url(:page => @page.prev.number)) if @page.prev? %>
<%= link_to("Next", foos_url(:page => @page.next.number)) if@page.next? %>
```

Paginating Find

If you're adventurous, check out http://svn.cardboardrocket.com/paginating_find for a simple pagination library that extends ActiveRecord's find method, instead of trying to replace it. As a project, I think it's much less mature than will_paginate or paginator, but looks promising.

RecordIdentificationHelper

This module, which wraps the methods of ActionController::RecordIdentifier, encapsulates a number of naming conventions for dealing with records, like ActiveRecord models or ActiveResource models or pretty much any other type of model object that you want to represent in markup code (like HTML) and which has an id attribute. These patterns are then used to try to elevate the view actions to a higher logical level.

For example, assume that you have map.resources :posts defined in your routes file, and code that looks like this in your view:

```
<% div_for(post) do %>
  <%= post.body %>
<% end %>
```

The HTML for the DIV element would thus be rendered like this:

```
<div id="post_45" class="post">
  What a wonderful world!
</div>
```

Notice the convention reflected in the id attribute. Now, for the controller, which has an AJAX-enabled destroy method. The idea is that it can be called to delete the record and make it disappear from the page without a reload operation:

```
def destroy
  post = Post.find(params[:id])
  post.destroy

  respond_to do |format|
    format.html { redirect_to :back }
    format.js do
      # Calls: new Effect.fade('post_45');
      render(:update) { |page| page[post].visual_effect(:fade) }
```

```
      end
    end
  end
```

As the preceding example shows, you can stop caring to a large extent what the actual id of the model is (the DIV element holding the model information, that is). You just know that one is being assigned and that the subsequent calls in RJS expect that same naming convention and allow you to write less code if you follow it. You can find more information on this technique in Chapter 12.

dom_class(record_or_class, prefix = nil)

The DOM class convention is to use the singular form of an object or class.

```
dom_class(post)   # => "post"
dom_class(Person) # => "person"
```

If you need to address multiple instances of the same class in the same view, you can prefix the dom_class:

```
dom_class(post, :edit)   # => "edit_post"
dom_class(Person, :edit) # => "edit_person"
```

dom_id(record, prefix = nil)

The DOM class convention is to use the singular form of an object or class with the id following an underscore. If no id is found, prefix with new_ instead.

```
dom_class(Post.new(:id => 45)) # => "post_45"
dom_class(Post.new)            # => "new_post"
```

If you need to address multiple instances of the same class in the same view, you can prefix the dom_id like this: dom_class(Post.new(:id => 45), :edit) results in edit_post_45.

partial_path(record_or_class)

Returns plural/singular for a record or class, which is very useful for automatically rendering partial templates by convention.

```
partial_path(post)   # => "posts/post"
partial_path(Person) # => "people/person"
```

RecordTagHelper

This module is closely related to `RecordIdentificationHelper` in that it assists in creation of HTML markup code that follows good, clean naming conventions.

content_tag_for(tag_name, record, *args, &block)

This helper method creates an HTML element with `id` and `class` parameters that relate to the specified `ActiveRecord` object.

For instance, assuming `@person` is an instance of a `Person` class, with an `id` value of `123` the following template code...

```
<% content_tag_for(:tr, @person) do %>
  <td><%=h @person.first_name %></td>
  <td><%=h @person.last_name %></td>
<% end %>
```

will produce the following HTML:

```
<tr id="person_123" class="person">
  ...
</tr>
```

If you require the HTML `id` attribute to have a prefix, you can specify it as a third argument:

```
>> content_tag_for(:tr, @person, :foo) do ...
=> <tr id="foo_person_123" class="person">...
```

The `content_tag_for` helper also accepts a hash of options, which will be converted to additional HTML attributes on the tag. If you specify a `:class` value, it will be combined with the default class name for your object instead of replacing it (since replacing it would defeat the purpose of the method!).

```
>> content_tag_for(:tr, @person, :foo, :class => 'highlight') do ...
=> <tr id="foo_person_123" class="person highlight">...
```

div_for(record, *args, &block)

Produces a wrapper DIV element with id and class parameters that relate to the specified ActiveRecord object. This method is exactly like content_tag_for except that it's hard-coded to output DIV elements.

TagHelper

This module provides helper methods for generating HTML tags programmatically.

cdata_section(content)

Returns a CDATA section wrapping the given content. CDATA sections are used to escape blocks of text containing characters that would otherwise be recognized as markup. CDATA sections begin with the string <![CDATA[and end with (and may not contain) the string]]>.

content_tag(name, content = nil, options = nil, &block)

Returns an HTML block tag of type name surrounding the content. Add HTML attributes by passing an attributes hash as options. Instead of passing the content as an argument, you can also use a block to hold additional markup (and/or additional calls to content_tag) in which case, you pass your options as the second parameter.

Here are some simple examples of using content_tag without a block:

```
>> content_tag(:p, "Hello world!")
=> <p>Hello world!</p>

>> content_tag(:div, content_tag(:p, "Hello!"), :class => "message")
=> <div class="message"><p>Hello!</p></div>

>> content_tag("select", options, :multiple => true)
=> <select multiple="multiple">...options...</select>
```

Here it is with content in a block (shown as template code rather than in the console):

```
<% content_tag :div, :class => "strong" do -%>
  Hello world!
<% end -%>
```

The preceding code produces the following HTML:

```
<div class="strong"><p>Hello world!</p></div>
```

escape_once(html)

Returns an escaped version of HTML without affecting existing escaped entities.

```
>> escape_once("1 > 2 &amp; 3")
=> "1 &lt; 2 &amp; 3"

>> escape_once("&lt;&lt; Accept & Checkout")
=> "&lt;&lt; Accept &amp; Checkout"
```

tag(name, options = nil, open = false)

Returns an empty HTML tag of type name, which by default is XHTML compliant. Setting open to true will create an open tag compatible with HTML 4.0 and below. Add HTML attributes by passing an attributes hash to options.

The options hash is used with attributes with no value like (disabled and readonly), which you can give a value of true in the options hash. You can use symbols or strings for the attribute names.

```
>> tag("br")
=> <br />

>> tag("br", nil, true)
=> <br>

>> tag("input", { :type => 'text', :disabled => true })
=> <input type="text" disabled="disabled" />

>> tag("img", { :src => "open.png" })
=> <img src="open.png" />
```

TextHelper

The methods in this module provide filtering, formatting, and string transformation capabilities.

auto_link(text, link = :all, href_options = {}, &block)

Turns all URLs and e-mail addresses inside the text string into clickable links. The link parameter is used to optionally limit what should be linked; pass it :email_addresses or :urls. You can add HTML attributes to the generated links using href_options.

If for whatever reason you are unhappy with the way that Rails is turning your e-mail addresses and URLs into links, you can supply a block to this method. Each address found is yielded and the return value of the block is used as the link text.

```
>> auto_link("Go to http://obiefernandez.com and say hello to
obie@obiefernandez.com")
=> "Go to <a
href="http://www.rubyonrails.org">http://www.rubyonrails.org</a> and
say hello to <a
href="mailto:obie@obiefernandez.com">obie@obiefernandez.com</a>"

>> auto_link("Welcome to my new blog at http://www.myblog.com/.  Please
e-mail me at me@email.com.", :all, :target => '_blank') do |text|
    truncate(text, 15)
  end
=> "Welcome to my new blog at <a href=\"http://www.myblog.com/\"
target=\"_blank\">http://www.m...</a>.
      Please e-mail me at <a
href=\"mailto:me@email.com\">me@email.com</a>."
```

concat(string, binding)

The preferred method of outputting text in your views is to use the <%= *expression* %> ERB syntax. The regular puts and print methods do not operate as expected in an eRuby code block; that is, if you expected them to output to the browser. If you absolutely must output text within a non-output code block like <% *expression* %>, you can use the concat method. I've found that this method can be especially useful in your own custom helper method implementations.

cycle(first_value, *values)

Creates a Cycle object whose to_s method cycles through elements of the array of values passed to it, every time it is called. This can be used, for example, to alternate classes for table rows.

Here's an example that alternates CSS classes for even and odd numbers, assuming that the @items variable holds an array with 1 through 4:

```
<table>
 <% @items.each do |item| %>
   <tr class="<%= cycle("even", "odd") -%>">
    <td>item</td>
   </tr>
 <% end %>
</table>
```

As you can tell from the example, you don't have to store the reference to the cycle in a local variable or anything like that; you just call the cycle method repeatedly. That's convenient, but it means that nested cycles need an identifier. The solution is to pass cycle a :name => cycle_name option as its last parameter. Also, you can manually reset a cycle by calling reset_cycle and passing it the name of the cycle to reset.

For example, here is some data to iterate over:

```
# Cycle CSS classes for rows, and text colors for values within each
row
@items = [{:first => 'Robert', :middle => 'Daniel', :last => 'James'},
          {:first => 'Emily', :last => 'Hicks'},
          {:first => 'June', :middle => 'Dae', :last => 'Jones'}]
```

And here is the template code. Since the number of cells rendered varies, we want to make sure to reset the colors cycle before looping:

```
<% @items.each do |item| %>
<tr class="<%= cycle("even", "odd", :name => "row_class")
  <% item.values.each do |value| %>
    <td style="color:<%= cycle("red", "green", :name => "colors") -%>">
```

```
      <%= value %>
      </td>
   <% end %>
   <% reset_cycle("colors") %>
 </tr>
 <% end %>
```

excerpt(text, phrase, radius = 100, excerpt_string = "...")

Extracts an excerpt from text that matches the first instance of phrase. The radius expands the excerpt on each side of the first occurrence of phrase by the number of characters defined in radius (which defaults to 100). If the excerpt radius overflows the beginning or end of the text, the excerpt_string will be prepended/appended accordingly. If the phrase isn't found, nil is returned.

```
>> excerpt('This is an example', 'an', 5)
=> "...s is an examp..."

>> excerpt('This is an example', 'is', 5)
=> "This is an..."

>> excerpt('This is an example', 'is')
=> "This is an example"

>> excerpt('This next thing is an example', 'ex', 2)
=> "...next t..."

>> excerpt('This is also an example', 'an', 8, '<chop> ')
=> "<chop> is also an example"
```

highlight(text, phrases, highlighter = '<strong class="highlight">\1</strong>')

Highlights one or more phrases everywhere in text by inserting it into a highlighter string. The highlighter can be specialized by passing highlighter as a single-quoted string with \1 where the phrase is to be inserted.

```
>> highlight('You searched for: rails', 'rails')
=> You searched for: <strong class="highlight">rails</strong>
```

```
>> highlight('You searched for: ruby, rails, dhh', 'actionpack')
=> You searched for: ruby, rails, dhh

>> highlight('You searched for: rails', ['for', 'rails'],
'<em>\1</em>')
=> You searched <em>for</em>: <em>rails</em>

>> highlight('You searched for: rails', 'rails', "<a
href='search?q=\1'>\1</a>")
=> You searched for: <a href='search?q=rails>rails</a>
```

markdown(text)

Returns the text with all the Markdown codes turned into HTML tags. This method
is only available if the BlueCloth gem is available.

```
>> markdown("We are using __Markdown__ now!")
=> "<p>We are using <strong>Markdown</strong> now!</p>"

>> markdown("We like to _write_ `code`, not just _read_ it!")
=> "<p>We like to <em>write</em> <code>code</code>, not just
<em>read</em> it!</p>"

>> markdown("The [Markdown
website](http://daringfireball.net/projects/markdown/) has more
information.")
=> "<p>The <a
href="http://daringfireball.net/projects/markdown/">Markdown
website</a> has more information.</p>"

>> markdown('![The ROR logo](http://rubyonrails.com/images/rails.png
"Ruby on Rails")')
=> '<p><img src="http://rubyonrails.com/images/rails.png" alt="The ROR
logo" title="Ruby on Rails" /></p>'
```

pluralize(count, singular, plural = nil)

Attempts to pluralize the singular word unless count is 1. If the plural is supplied, it
will use that when count is > 1. If the ActiveSupport Inflector is loaded, it will

use the `Inflector` to determine the plural form; otherwise, it will just add an "s" to the singular word.

```
>> pluralize(1, 'person')
=> "1 person"

>> pluralize(2, 'person')
=> "2 people"

>> pluralize(3, 'person', 'users')
=> "3 users"

>> pluralize(0, 'person')
=> "0 people"
```

reset_cycle(name = "default")

Resets a cycle (see the `cycle` method in this module) so that it starts cycling from its first element the next time it is called. Pass in a `name` to reset a named cycle.

sanitize(html)

Sanitizes the HTML by converting `<form>` and `<script>` tags into regular text, and removing all "on*" (e.g., `onClick`) attributes so that arbitrary JavaScript cannot be executed. It also strips `href` and `src` attributes that start with "`javascript:`". You can modify what gets sanitized by defining VERBOTEN_TAGS and VERBOTEN_ATTRS before this module is loaded.

```
>> sanitize('<script> do_nasty_stuff() </script>')
=> &lt;script> do_nasty_stuff() &lt;/script>

>> sanitize('<a href="javascript: sucker();">Click here for $100</a>')
=> <a>Click here for $100</a>

>> sanitize('<a href="#" onClick="kill_all_humans();">Click
here!!!</a>')
=> <a href="#">Click here!!!</a>

>> sanitize('<img src="javascript:suckers_run_this();" />')
=> <img />
```

> **Courtenay Says...**
>
> An even better way of sanitizing is Rick Olsen's Whitelist plugin at http://svn.techno-weenie.net/projects/plugins/white_list

simple_format(text)

Returns text transformed into HTML using simple formatting rules. Two or more consecutive newlines (\n\n) are considered to denote a paragraph and thus are wrapped in P tags. One newline (\n) is considered to be a line break and a BR tag is appended. This method does not remove the newlines from the text.

strip_links(text)

Strips all link tags from text leaving just the link text.

```
>> strip_links('<a href="http://www.rubyonrails.org">Ruby on
Rails</a>')
=> Ruby on Rails

>> strip_links('Please e-mail me at <a
href="mailto:me@email.com">me@email.com</a>.')
=> Please e-mail me at me@email.com.

strip_links('Blog: <a href="http://www.myblog.com/" class="nav"
target=\"_blank\">Visit</a>.')
=> Blog: Visit
```

strip_tags(html)

Strips all HTML tags from the HTML, including comments. This uses the html-scanner tokenizer and so its HTML parsing ability is limited by that of html-scanner.

```
>> strip_tags("Strip <i>these</i> tags!")
=> Strip these tags!

>> strip_tags("<b>Bold</b> no more!  <a href='more.html'>See more
here</a>...")
=> Bold no more!  See more here...
```

```
>> strip_tags("<div id='top-bar'>Welcome to my website!</div>")
=> Welcome to my website!
```

textilize(text)

This method is only available if the RedCloth gem is available. It returns text with all the Textile codes turned into HTML tags. Learn more about Textile syntax at http://hobix.com/textile/.

```
>> textilize("*This is Textile!*  Rejoice!")
=> "<p><strong>This is Textile!</strong>  Rejoice!</p>"

>> textilize("I _love_ ROR(Ruby on Rails)!")
=> "<p>I <em>love</em> <acronym title="Ruby on
Rails">ROR</acronym>!</p>"

>> textilize("h2. Textile makes markup -easy- simple!")
=> "<h2>Textile makes markup <del>easy</del> simple!</h2>"

>> textilize("Visit Rails website "here":http://www.rubyonrails.org/.)
=> "<p>Visit the Rails website <a
href="http://www.rubyonrails.org/">here</a>.</p>"
```

textilize_without_paragraph(text)

Returns the text with all the Textile codes turned into HTML tags, but without the bounding <p> tag that RedCloth adds.

truncate(text, length = 30, truncate_string = "...")

If text is longer than length, text will be truncated to the length specified and the last three characters will be replaced with the truncate_string:

```
>> truncate("Once upon a time in a world far far away", 4)
=> "Once..."

>> truncate("Once upon a time in a world far far away")
=> "Once upon a time in a world f..."
```

```
>> truncate("And they found that many people were sleeping better.",
15, "... (continued)")
=> "And they found... (continued)"
```

word_wrap(text, line_width = 80)

Wraps the text into lines no longer than `line_width`. This method breaks on the first whitespace character that does not exceed `line_width` (which is 80 by default).

```
>> word_wrap('Once upon a time', 4)
=> "Once\nupon\na\ntime"

>> word_wrap('Once upon a time', 8)
=> "Once upon\na time"

>> word_wrap('Once upon a time')
=> "Once upon a time"

>> word_wrap('Once upon a time', 1)
=> "Once\nupon\na\ntime"
```

UrlHelper

This module provides a set of methods for making links and getting URLs that depend on the routing subsystem, covered extensively in Chapters 3 through 5 of this book.

button_to(name, options = {}, html_options = {})

Generates a form containing a single button that submits to the URL created by the set of options. This is the safest method to ensure that links that cause changes to your data are not triggered by search bots or accelerators. If the HTML button does not work with your layout, you can also consider using the `link_to` method (also in this module) with the `:method` modifier.

The options hash accepts the same options as the `url_for` method (also part of this module).

The generated FORM element has a class name of button-to to allow styling of the form itself and its children. The :method and :confirm options work just like the link_to helper. If no :method modifier is given, it defaults to performing a POST operation. You can also disable the button by passing :disabled => true.

```
>> button_to "New", :action => "new"
=> "<form method="post" action="/controller/new" class="button-to">
      <div><input value="New" type="submit" /></div>
   </form>"

>> button_to "Delete Image", { :action => "delete", :id => @image.id },
:confirm => "Are you sure?", :method => :delete
=>  "<form method="post" action="/images/delete/1" class="button-to">
      <div>
        <input type="hidden" name="_method" value="delete" />
        <input onclick="return confirm('Are you sure?');"
value="Delete"
type="submit" />
      </div>
   </form>"
```

current_page?(options)

Returns true if the current request URI was generated by the given options. For example, let's assume that we're currently rendering the /shop/checkout action:

```
>> current_page?(:action => 'process')
=> false

>>current_page?(:action => 'checkout') # controller is implied
=> true

>> current_page?(:controller => 'shop', :action => 'checkout')
=> true
```

link_to(name, options = {}, html_options = nil)

One of the fundamental helper methods. Creates a link tag of the given name using a URL created by the set of options. The valid options are covered in the description of this module's url_for method. It's also possible to pass a string instead of an options hash to get a link tag that uses the value of the string as the href for the link. If `nil` is passed as a name, the link itself will become the name.

- `:confirm => 'question?'`   Adds a JavaScript confirmation prompt with the question specified. If the user accepts, the link is processed normally; otherwise, no action is taken.

- `:popup => true`   Forces the link to open in a pop-up window. By passing `true`, a default browser window will be opened with the URL. You can also specify a string of options to be passed to JavaScript's `window.open` method.

- `:method => symbol`   Specify an alternative HTTP verb for this request (other than GET). This modifier will dynamically create an HTML form and immediately submit the form for processing using the HTTP verb specified (`:post`, `:put`, `:delete`, or other custom string like "`HEAD`", and so on).

Generally speaking, GET requests should be *idempotent*, that is, they do not modify the state of any resource on the server, and can be called one or many times without a problem. Requests that modify server-side resources or trigger dangerous actions like deleting a record should not usually be linked to with a normal hyperlink, since search bots and so-called *browser accelerators* can follow those links while spidering your site, leaving a trail of chaos.

If the user has JavaScript disabled, the request will always fall back to using GET, no matter what `:method` you have specified. This is accomplished by including a valid `href` attribute. If you are relying on the POST behavior, your controller code should check for it using the `post?`, `delete?`, or `put?` methods of `request`.

As usual, the `html_options` will accept a hash of HTML attributes for the link tag.

```
>> link_to "Visit Other Site", "http://www.rubyonrails.org/",
:confirm => "Are you sure?"
=> "<a href="http://www.rubyonrails.org/" onclick="return confirm('Are
you sure?');">Visit Other Site</a>"

>> link_to "Help", { :action => "help" }, :popup => true
=> "<a href="/testing/help/" onclick="window.open(this.href);return
false;">Help</a>"

>> link_to "View Image", { :action => "view" }, :popup =>
['new_window_name', 'height=300,width=600']
```

```
=> "<a href="/testing/view/" onclick="window.open(this.href,
'new_window_name','height=300,width=600');return false;">View
Image</a>"

>> link_to "Delete Image", { :action => "delete", :id => @image.id },
:confirm => "Are you sure?", :method => :delete
=> <a href="/testing/delete/9/" onclick="if (confirm('Are you sure?'))
{
var f = document.createElement('form');
        f.style.display = 'none'; this.parentNode.appendChild(f);
f.method = 'POST'; f.action = this.href;
        var m = document.createElement('input'); m.setAttribute('type',
'hidden'); m.setAttribute('name', '_method');
        m.setAttribute('value', 'delete'); f.appendChild(m);f.submit();
};return false;">Delete Image</a>
```

link_to_if(condition, name, options = {}, html_options = {}, &block)

Creates a link tag using the same options as link_to if the condition is true; otherwise, only the name is output (or block is evaluated for an alternative value, if one is supplied).

link_to_unless(condition, name, options = {}, html_options = {}, &block)

Creates a link tag using the same options as link_to unless the condition is true, in which case only the name is output (or block is evaluated for an alternative value, if one is supplied).

link_to_unless_current(name, options = {}, html_options = {}, &block)

Creates a link tag using the same options as link_to unless the condition is true, in which case only the name is output (or block is evaluated for an alternative value, if one is supplied).

This method is actually pretty useful sometimes. Remember that the block given to link_to_unless_current is evaluated if the current action is the action given.

So, if we had a comments page and wanted to render a "Go Back" link instead of a link to the comments page, we could do something like this:

```
<%= link_to_unless_current("Comment", { :controller => 'comments',
    :action => 'new'}) do
      link_to("Go back", { :controller => 'posts', :action => 'index'
})
    end %>
```

mail_to(email_address, name = nil, html_options = {})

Creates a `mailto` link tag to the specified `email_address`, which is also used as the name of the link unless `name` is specified. Additional HTML attributes for the link can be passed in `html_options`.

The `mail_to` helper has several techniques for hindering e-mail harvesters and customizing the e-mail address itself by passing special keys to `html_options`:

- `:encode`   This key will accept the strings "`javascript`" or "`hex`". Passing "`javascript`" will dynamically create and encode the `mailto:` link and then `eval` it into the DOM of the page. This method will not show the link on the page if the user has JavaScript disabled. Passing "`hex`" will hex-encode the `email_address` before outputting the `mailto:` link.

- `:replace_at`   When the link name isn't provided, the `email_address` is used for the link label. You can use this option to obfuscate the `email_address` by substituting the @ sign with the string given as the value.

- `:replace_dot`   When the link name isn't provided, the `email_address` is used for the link label. You can use this option to obfuscate the `email_address` by substituting the "." in the email with the string given as the value.

- `:subject`   The subject line of the e-mail.

- `:body`   The body of the e-mail.

- `:cc`   Add cc recipients to the e-mail.

- `:bcc`   Add bcc recipients to the e-mail.

Here are some examples of usages:

```
>> mail_to "me@domain.com"
=> <a href="mailto:me@domain.com">me@domain.com</a>
```

```
>> mail_to "me@domain.com", "My email", :encode => "javascript"
=> <script type="text/javascript">eval(unescape('%64%6f%63...%6d%65'))
</script>

>> mail_to "me@domain.com", "My email", :encode => "hex"
=> <a href="mailto:%6d%65@%64%6f%6d%61%69%6e.%63%6f%6d">My email</a>

>> mail_to "me@domain.com", nil, :replace_at => "_at_", :replace_dot =>
"_dot_", :class => "email"
=> <a href="mailto:me@domain.com"
class="email">me_at_domain_dot_com</a>

>> mail_to "me@domain.com", "My email", :cc => "ccaddress@domain.com",
:subject => "This is an example email"
=> <a
href="mailto:me@domain.com?cc=ccaddress@domain.com&subject=This%20i
s%20an%20example%20email">My email</a>
```

url_for(options = {})

The url_for method returns a URL for the set of options provided and takes the same options as url_for in ActionController (discussed extensively in Chapter 3, "Routing").

Note that by default, the :only_path option is set to true so that you'll get the relative /controller/action instead of the fully qualified URL like http:// example.com/controller/action.

When called from a view, url_for returns an HTML-escaped URL. If you need an unescaped URL, pass :escape => false in the options.

Here is the complete list of options accepted by url_for:

- :anchor   Specifies an anchor name (#anchor) be appended to the end of the path.

- :only_path   Specifies a relative URL (omitting the protocol, host name, and port).

- :trailing_slash   Adds a trailing slash, as in "/archive/2005/". Note that this is currently not recommended since it breaks caching.

- :host   Overrides the default (current) host if provided.

- :protocol   Overrides the default (current) protocol if provided.

- :user   Inline HTTP authentication (requires :password option).

- :password   Inline HTTP authentication (requires :user option).

- :escape   Determines whether the returned URL will be HTML-escaped or not.

```
>> url_for(:action => 'index')
=> /blog/

>> url_for(:action => 'find', :controller => 'books')
=> /books/find

>> url_for(:action => 'login', :controller => 'members', :only_path =>
false, :protocol => 'https')
=> https://www.railsapplication.com/members/login/

>> url_for(:action => 'play', :anchor => 'player')
=> /messages/play/#player

>> url_for(:action => 'checkout', :anchor => 'tax&ship')
=> /testing/jump/#tax&amp;ship

>> url_for(:action => 'checkout', :anchor => 'tax&ship', :escape =>
false)
=> /testing/jump/#tax&ship
```

Relying on Named Routes

If you pass an ActiveRecord or ActiveResource model instance instead of a hash to any method in the UrlModule that takes url_for parameters, you'll trigger generation of a path for that record's named route (assuming that one exists). The lookup is based on the name of the class and is smart enough to call new_record? on the passed model to figure out whether to reference a *collection* or *member* route.

For example, passing a Timesheet object will attempt to use the timesheet_path route. If that object's route is nested within another route, you'll have to use a path helper method explicitly, since Rails won't be able to figure it out automatically.

```
>> url_for(Workshop.new)
=> /workshops

>> url_for(@workshop) # existing record
=> /workshops/5
```

Writing Your Own Helpers

As you develop an application in Rails, you should be on the lookout for opportunities to refactor duplicated view code into your own helper methods. As you think of these helpers, you add them to one of the helper modules defined in the `app/helpers` folder of your application.

There is an art to effectively writing helper methods, similar in nature to what it takes to write effective APIs. Helper methods are basically a custom, application-level API for your view code. It is difficult to teach API design in a book form. It's the sort of knowledge that you gain by apprenticing with more experienced programmers and lots of trial and error. Nevertheless, in this section, we'll review some varied use cases and implementation styles that we hope will inspire you in your own application design.

Small Optimizations: The Title Helper

Here is a simple helper method that has been of use to me on many projects now. It's called `page_title` and it combines two simple functions essential to a good HTML document:

- Setting the `title` of the page in the document's `head`
- Setting the content of the page's `h1` element

This helper assumes that you want the `title` and `h1` elements of the page to be the same, and has a dependency on your application template. The code for the helper is in Listing 11.6 and would be added to `app/helpers/application_helper.rb`, since it is applicable to all views.

Listing 11.6   The `title` Helper

```
def page_title(name)
  @title = name
  content_tag("h1", name)
end
```

First it sets the value of a variable named `@title` and then it outputs an h1 element containing the same text. I could have used string interpolation on the second line, such as `"<h1>#{name}</h1>"`, but in my opinion that would be sloppier than using the built-in Rails helper method `content_tag`.

My application template looks for a `@page_title` to be available, in which case it will prepend it to the site title, the name of the application:

```
<html>
  <head>
    <title><%= "#@page_title - " if @page_title %>Site Title</title>
```

As should be obvious, you call the `page_title` method in your view template where you want to have an h1 element:

```
<%= page_title "New User" %>
<%= error_messages_for :user %>
<% form_for(:user, :url => user_path) do |f| %>
  ...
```

Encapsulating View Logic: The `photo_for` Helper

Here's another relatively simple helper. This time, instead of simply outputting data, we are encapsulating some view logic that decides whether to display a user's profile photo or a placeholder image. It's logic that you would otherwise have to repeat over and over again throughout your application.

The dependency (or contract) for this particular helper is that the user object being passed in has a `profile_photo` associated to it, which is an attachment model based on Rick Olson's excellent `attachment_fu` Rails plugin.[3] The code in Listing 11.7 should be easy enough to understand without delving into the details of `attachment_fu`. Since this is a code example, I broke out the logic for setting `src` into an `if`/`else` structure; otherwise, this would be a perfect place to use Ruby's *ternary* operator.

Listing 11.7 The photo_for Helper, Encapsulating Common View Logic

```
def photo_for(user, size=:thumb)
  if user.profile_photo
    src = user.profile_photo.public_filename(size)
  else
    src = 'user_placeholder.png'
  end
  link_to(image_tag(src), user_path(user)
end
```

Smart View: The breadcrumbs Helper

Lots of web applications feature user-interface concepts called *breadcrumbs*. They are made by creating a list of links, positioned near the top of the page, displaying how far the user has navigated into a hierarchically organized application. I think it makes sense to extract breadcrumb logic into its own helper method instead of leaving it in a layout template.

The trick to our example implementation (shown in Listing 11.8) is to use the presence of instance variables, based on a convention specific to your application, to determine whether or not to add elements to an array of breadcrumb links.

Listing 11.8 breadcrumbs Helper Method for a Corporate Directory Application

```
 1 def breadcrumbs
 2   return if controller.controller_name == 'homepage'

 3   html = [link_to('Home', home_path)]

 4   # first level
 5   html << link_to('Companies', companies_path) if @companies ||
     @company
 6   html << link_to(@company, company_path(@company)) if @company

 7   # second level
 8   html << link_to('Departments', departments_path) if @depts || @dept
 9   html << link_to(@dept, department_path(@dept)) if @dept

10   # third and final level
11   html << link_to('Employees', employees_path) if @employees ||
     @employee
12   html << link_to(@employee.name, employee_path(@employee)) if
     @employee

13   html.join(' &gt; ')
14 end
```

Here's the line-by-line explanation of the code, noting where certain application-design assumptions are made:

On line 2, we abort execution if we're in the context of the application's `home-page` controller, since its pages don't ever need breadcrumbs. A simple return with no value implicitly returns `nil`, which is fine for our purposes—nothing will be output to the layout template.

On line 3 we are starting to build an array of HTML links, held in the `html` local variable, which will ultimately hold the contents of our breadcrumb trail. The first link of the breadcrumb trail always points to the home page of the application, which of course will vary, but since it's always there we use it to initialize the array. In this example, it uses a *named route* called `home_path`.

After the `html` array is initialized, all we have to do is check for the presence of the variables that make up the hierarchy (lines 4 to 12). It is assumed that if a department is being displayed, its parent company will also be in scope. If an employee is being displayed, both its department and company will be in scope as well. This is not just an arbitrary design choice—it is a common pattern in Rails applications that are modeled based on REST principles and using nested resource routes.

Finally, on line 13, the array of HTML links is joined with the > character, to give the entire string the traditional breadcrumb appearance.

Wrapping and Generalizing Partials

I don't think that partials (by themselves) lead to particularly elegant or concise template code. Whenever there's a shared partial template that gets used over and over again in my application, I will take the time to wrap it up in a custom helper method that conveys its purpose and formalizes its parameters. If appropriate, I'll generalize its implementation to make it more of a lightweight, reusable component.

Oh, the heresy! The word *component* is a dirty word among Rails cognoscenti, and Rails components are so out of favor that I do not cover them in this book and they've been removed from Rails 2.0. To be clear, I'm not talking about components in anything other than the sense of an easily reusable piece of user interface.

A `tiles` Helper

Let's trace the steps to writing a helper method that wraps what I consider to be a general-purpose partial. Listing 11.9 contains code for a partial for a piece of a user interface that is common to many applications, and generally referred to as a *tile*. It pairs a small thumbnail photo of something on the left side of the widget, with a linked name and description on the right.

Tiles can also represent other models in your application, such as users and files. As I mentioned, tiles are a very common construct in modern user interfaces and operating systems. So let's take the cities tiles partial and transform it into something that can be used to display other types of data.

> **NOTE**
>
> I realize that it's become passé to use HTML tables and I happen to agree that DIV-based layouts plus CSS are a lot more fun and flexible to work with. However, for the sake of simplicity in this example, and since the UI structure we're describing is tabular, I've decided to structure it using a table.

Listing 11.9   A Tiles Partial, Prior to Wrapping and Generalization

```
 1 <table class="cities tiles">
 2 <% cities.in_groups_of(columns) do |row| -%>
 3  <tr>
 4  <% row.each do |city| -%>
 5   <td id="<%= dom_id(city) %>">
 6    <div class="left">
 7     <%= image_tag city.main_photo.public_filename(:thumb) -%>
 8    </div>
 9    <div class="right">
10     <div class="title"><%= city.name %></div>
11     <div class="description"><%= city.description %></div>
12    </div>
13   </td>
14  <% end # row.each -%>
15  </tr>
16 <% end # in_groups_of -%>
17 </table>
```

Explanation of the Tiles Partial Code

Since we're going to transform this city-specific partial into a generalized UI component, I want to make sure that the code we start with makes absolute sense to you first. Before proceeding, I'm going through the implementation line by line and explaining what everything in Listing 11.9 does.

Line 1 opens up the partial with a table element and gives it semantically signifi-cant CSS classes so that the table and its contents can be properly styled.

Line 2 leverages a useful `Array` extension provided by Rails, called `in_groups_of`. It uses both of our local variables: `cities` and `columns`. Both will need to be passed into this partial using the `:locals` option of the `render :par-tial` method. The `cities` variable will hold the list of cities to be displayed, and `columns` is an integer number representing how many city tiles each row should con-tain. A loop iterates over the number of rows that will be displayed in this table.

Line 3 begins a table row using the `<tr>` element.

Line 4 begins a loop over the tiles for each row to be displayed, yielding a `city` for each.

Line 5 opens a `<td>` element and uses the `dom_id` helper method to autogener-ate an identifier for the table cell in the style of `city_98, city_99`, and so on.

Line 6 opens a `<div>` element for the left side of the widget, and is demarcated with the appropriate CSS class name needed so that it can be styled properly.

Line 7 calls the `image_tag` helper to insert a thumbnail photo of the city.

Skipping along, line 10 inserts the content for the `title` DIV element, in this case, the name and state of the city.

Line 11 directly invokes the `description` method and finally, the remainder of the lines in the listing simply close out the loops and container elements.

Calling the Tiles Partial Code

In order to use this partial, we have to call `render :partial` with the two required parameters specified in the `:locals` hash:

```
render :partial => "cities/tiles",
       :locals => { :collection => @user.cities, :columns => 3 }
```

I'm guessing that most experienced Rails developers have written some partial code similar to this and tried to figure out a way to include default values for some of the parameters. In this case, it would be really nice to not have to specify `:columns` all the time, since in most cases we want there to be three.

The problem is that since the parameters are passed via the `:locals` hash and become local variables, there isn't an easy way to insert a default value in the partial itself. If you left off the `:columns => ` n part of your partial call, Rails would bomb with an exception about columns not being a local variable or method. It's not the same as an instance variable, which defaults to `nil` and can be used willy-nilly.

Experienced Rubyists probably know that you can use the `defined?` method to figure out whether a local variable is in scope or not, but the resulting code would be very ugly. The following code might be considered elegant, *but it doesn't work!*[6]

```
<% columns = 3 unless defined? columns %>
```

Instead of teaching you how to jump through annoying Ruby idiom hoops, I'll show you how to tackle this challenge the Rails way, and that is where we can start discussing the helper wrapping techique.

Write the Helper Method

First, I'll add a new helper method to the `CitiesHelper` module of my application, like in Listing 11.10. It's going to be fairly simple at first. In thinking about the name of the method, it occurs to me that I like the way that `tiled(@cities)` will read instead of `tiles(@cities)`, so I name it that way.

Listing 11.10   The `CitiesHelper` Tiled Method

```
module CitiesHelper

  def tiled(cities, columns=3)
    render :partial => "cities/tiles",
           :locals => { :collection => cities, :columns => columns }
  end

end
```

Right from the start I can take care of that default columns parameter by giving the helper method parameter for columns a default value. That's just a normal feature of Ruby.

Now instead of specifying the `render :partial` call in my view template, I can simply write `<%= tiled(@cities) %>`, which is considerably more elegant and terse. It also serves to decouple the implementation of the tiled city table from the view. If I need to change the way that the tiled table is rendered in the future, I just have to do it in one place: the helper method.

Generalizing Partials

Now that we've set the stage, the fun can begin. The first thing we'll do is to move the helper method to the `ApplicationHelper` module so that it's available to all view templates. We'll also move the partial template file to `app/views/shared/_tiled_table.html.erb` to denote that it isn't associated with a particular kind of view, and to more accurately convey its use. As a matter of good code style, I also do a sweep through the implementation and generalize the identifiers appropriately. The reference to `cities` becomes `collection`. The block variable `item` becomes `item`. Listing 11.11 has the new partial code.

Listing 11.11   Tiles Partial Code with Revised Naming

```
 1 <table class="tiles">
 2  <% collection.in_groups_of(columns) do |row| -%>
 3   <tr>
 4   <% row.each do |item| -%>
 5    <td id="<%= dom_id(item) %>">
 6     <div class="left">
 7      <%= image_tag(item.main_photo.public_filename(:thumb)) %>
 8     </div>
 9     <div class="right">
10       <div class="title"><%= item.name %></div>
11       <div class="description"><%= item.description %></div>
12     </div>
13    </td>
14   <% end # row.each -%>
15   </tr>
16  <% end # in_groups_of -%>
17 </table>
```

There's still the matter of a contract between this partial code and the objects that it is rendering. Namely, they must respond to the following messages: `main_photo`, `name`, and `description`. A survey of other models in my application reveals that I need more flexibility. Some things have names, but others have titles. Sometimes I want the description to appear under the name of the object represented, but other times I want to be able to insert additional data about the object plus some links.

Lambda: the Ultimate

Ruby allows you to store references to anonymous methods (also known as *procs* or *lambdas*) and call them at will whenever you want.[7] Knowing this capability is there, what becomes possible? For starters, we can use lambdas to pass in blocks of code that will fill in parts of our partial dynamically.

For example, the current code for showing the thumbnail is a big problem. Since the code varies greatly depending on the object being handled, I want to be able to pass in instructions for how to get a thumbnail image without having to resort to big if/else statements or putting view logic in my model classes. Please take a moment to understand the problem I'm describing, and then take a look at how we solve it in Listing 11.12. Hint: The thumbnail, link, title, and description variables hold lambdas!

Listing 11.12   Tiles Partial Code Refactored to Use Lambdas

```
1    <div class="left">
2      <%= link_to thumbnail.call(item), link.call(item) %>
3    </div>
4    <div class="right">
5      <div class="title">
6        <%= link_to title.call(item), link.call(item) %>
7      </div>
8      <div class="description"><%= description.call(item) %></div>
9    </div>
```

Notice that in Listing 11.12, the contents of the left and right DIVs come from variables containing lambdas. On line 2 we make a call to link_to and both of its arguments are dynamic. A similar construct on line 6 takes care of generating the title link. In both cases, the first lambda should return the output of a call to image_tag and the second should return a URL. In all of these lambda usages, the item currently being rendered is passed to the lambdas as a block variable.

> **Wilson Says...**
>
> Things like link.call(item) could potentially look even sassier as link[item], except that you'll shoot your eye out doing it. (Proc#[] is an alias for Proc#call.)

The New Tiled Helper Method

If you now direct your attention to Listing 11.13, you'll notice that the tiled method is changed considerably. In order to keep my positional argument list down to a manageable size, I've switched over to taking a hash of options as the last parameter to the method. This approach is useful and it mimics the way that almost all helper methods take options in Rails.

One of the options, :link, will always be unique to whatever we're passing in, and cannot simply be guessed, so I make it required by checking for it on line 3. Default values are provided for all optional parameters, and they are all passed along to the partial via the :locals hash given to render :partial.

Listing 11.13   The Tiled Collection Helper Method with Lambda Parameters

```
 1   module ApplicationHelper

 2     def tiled(collection, opts={})
 3       raise 'link option is required' unless opts[:link]

 4       opts[:columns] ||= 3

 5       opts[:thumbnail] ||= lambda do |item|
 6         image_tag(item.photo.public_filename(:thumb))
 7       end

 8       opts[:title] ||= lambda {|item| item.to_s }
 9       opts[:description] ||= lambda {|item| item.description }

10       render :partial => "shared/tiled_table",
11               :locals => { :collection  => collection,
12                            :columns     => opts[:columns] || 3,
13                            :thumbnail   => opts[:thumbnail],
14                            :title       => opts[:title],
15                            :description => opts[:description] }
16     end
17   end
```

Finally, to wrap up this example, here's a snippet showing how to invoke our new tiled helper method from a template:

```
<%= tiled(@cities, :link => lambda {|city| city_path(city)}) %>
```

The city_path method is available to the lambda block, since it is a *closure*, meaning that it inherits the execution context in which it is created.

Conclusion

This long chapter served as a thorough reference of helper methods, both those provided by Rails and ideas for ones that you will write yourself. Effective use of helper methods lead to more elegant and maintainable view templates.

Before we fully conclude our coverage of ActionPack, (the name used to refer to `ActionController` and `ActionView` together), we'll jump into the world of Ajax and Javascript. Arguably, one of the main reasons for Rails's continued popularity is its support for those two crucial technologies of Web 2.0.

References

1. Josh Susser tells you how to cheat and provide default values to non-column model attributes at http://blog.hasmanythrough.com/2007/1/22/using-faux-accessors-to-initialize-values.

2. To read up on the "Form field helpers don't use object accessors saga" check http://dev.rubyonrails.org/ticket/2322.

3. The Attachment Fu plugin can be found at http://svn.techno-weenie.net/projects/plugins/attachment_fu.

4. The WillPaginate plugin can be found at http://require.errtheblog.com/plugins/browser/will_paginate, but you knew that already, since all Rails developers subscribe to Err the Blog.

5. The Paginator project's homepage is http://paginator.rubyforge.org/.

6. If you want to know why it doesn't work, you'll have to buy the first book in this series: *The Ruby Way, Second Edition*; ISBN: 0672328844.

7. If you're familiar with Ruby already, you might know that Proc.new and its alias proc are also ways to create anonymous blocks of code. I prefer lambda, because of subtle behavior differences. Lambda blocks check the *arity* of the argument list passed to them when call is invoked, and explicitly calling return in a lambda block works *correctly*.

CHAPTER 12

Ajax on Rails

Ajax isn't a technology. It's really several technologies, each flourishing in its own right, coming together in powerful new ways
—Jesse J. Garrett, who coined the term

Ajax is an acronym that stands for *Asynchronous JavaScript and XML*. It encompasses techniques that allow us to liven up web pages with behaviors that happen outside the normal HTTP request life cycle (without a page refresh).

Some example use-cases for Ajax techniques are

- Sending form data asynchronously

- Seamless navigation of web-presented maps, as in Google Maps

- Dynamically updated lists and tables, as in Gmail and other web-based email services

- Web-based spreadsheets

- Forms that allow in-place editing

- Live preview of formatted writing alongside a text input

Ajax is made possible by the `XMLHttpRequestObject` (or XHR for short), an API that is available in all modern browsers. It allows JavaScript code on the browser to exchange data with the server and use it to change the user interface of your application on the fly, without needing a page refresh. Working directly with XHR in a cross-browser-compatible way is difficult, to say the least, which is why the open-source ecosystem flourishes with Ajax JavaScript libraries.

Incidentally, Ajax, especially in Rails, has very little to do with XML, despite its presence there at the end of the acronym. The payload of those asynchronous requests going back and forth to the server can be anything. Often it's just a matter of form parameters posted to the server, and receiving snippets of HTML back, for dynamic insertion into the page's DOM. Many times it even makes sense for the server to send back data encoded in a simple kind of JavaScript called JavaScript Object Notation (JSON).

It's outside the scope of this book to teach you the fundamentals of JavaScript and/or Ajax. It's also outside of our scope to dive into the design considerations of adding Ajax to your application, elements of which are lengthy and occasionally controversial. Proper coverage of those subjects would require a whole book and there are many such books to choose from in the marketplace. Therefore, the rest of the chapter simply assumes that you understand what Ajax is and why you would use it in your applications.

Ruby on Rails makes adding Ajax to your application very simple, because of its smart integration with Prototype and Scriptaculous. We begin this chapter by examining the philosophy and implementation of those two important JavaScript libraries, and follow with a comprehensive reference section covering the relevant `ActionPack` helpers that enable Ajax on Rails. We also cover Rails' RJS feature, which allows you to invoke JavaScript with Ruby code based on the server.

To get the most benefit of this chapter, you should have at least a basic understanding of JavaScript programming.

Prototype

The Prototype library (located at http://prototype.conio.net) was written and is actively maintained by Sam Stephenson, a member of the Rails core team. Prototype is described by its creator as a "unique, easy-to-use toolkit for class-driven development and the nicest Ajax library around."

Prototype is distributed with Ruby on Rails and is copied into new Rails projects as `public/javascripts/prototype.js` by the Rails script. Its roughly 2000 lines of JavaScript are a powerful foundation for building all sorts of Ajax interaction with the server and visual effects on the client. In fact, despite its close connection to Ruby on Rails, Prototype is extremely successful in its own right as an Ajax library.

FireBug

FireBug,[1] an extremely powerful extension for Firefox, is a must-have tool for doing Ajax work. It lets you inspect Ajax requests and probe the DOM of the page extensively, even letting you change elements and CSS styles on the fly and see the results on your browser screen. It also has a very powerful JavaScript debugger that you can use to set watch expressions and breakpoints. See Figure 12.1.

Figure 12.1   FireBug is a must-have for doing Ajax work.

FireBug's DOM browser can be used to explore the Prototype library as it exists at runtime in your browser page. FireBug also has an interactive console, which allows you to experiment with JavaScript in the browser just as you would use `irb` in Ruby. In some cases, the code samples in this chapter are copied from the FireBug console, which has a >>> prompt.

For example, inspecting `Prototype` with the console yields the following output:

```
>>> Prototype
Object Version=1.5.0_rc2 BrowserFeatures=Object
```

As I've jokingly told many of my Ruby on Rails students when covering Ajax on Rails: "Even if you don't listen to anything else I say, use FireBug! The productivity gains you experience will make up for my fee very quickly."

The Prototype API

Having an understanding of the Prototype API and how it works is not strictly necessary to doing Ajax on Rails, but it will help tremendously when you want to move beyond the simple example cases and write your own JavaScript routines.

Much of `prototype.js` is code defining advanced object-oriented language constructs on top of what is already provided by JavaScript. For example, the `extend` function creates a way to do inheritance. Much of Prototype will be startlingly familiar to Ruby programmers, such as the `inspect` method on `Object` and the `gsub` method on `String`. Since JavaScript functions act as *closures*, just like Ruby blocks, Prototype follows the example of Ruby when it comes to array use and manipulation with iterators, and many other aspects of its API.

The overall flavor of Prototype code is very Rubyish, making it a comfortable and productive fit for Ruby and Rails hackers. You might even develop a liking for JavaScript (if you didn't have one already), which despite its humble origins and bad reputation, is actually an extremely powerful and expressive programming language. Never mind the function keyword everywhere in your code—it blends into the background eventually.

Top-Level Functions

The following functions are defined in the top-level context of Prototype:

`$(id[, id2...])`

The `$` function is a shortcut *and* extension of one of the most commonly used functions in all JavaScript browser programming: `document.getElementByID`. The name is so short because it is used so often, according to one of the main principles of effective API design.

You may pass `$()` one or more strings, to which it will return either one matching element or an array of them, assuming the supplied ID strings match elements present on the page. For convenience, `$` will not blow up if you pass it an element instance rather than a string in its parameters. It will simply pass the element back to you or add it to its results list.

ID parameters without matching elements will result in `undefined` return values, just like with the underlying `document.getElementByID` function. Trying to retrieve more than one element with the same ID will probably not work, and is dependent on the browser implementation. It's better to stick to well-formed markup and not have duplicate identifiers.

$$(expr[, expr2...])

The $$ function takes one or more CSS selector strings and returns an array of matching elements from the DOM. The ability to find elements by CSS selector is one of the most powerful features of Prototype.

$A(var)

The $A function is an alias for `Array.from`. It converts its parameter into an `Array` object, including the functions of `Enumerable`. (See the section "Enumerable" in this chapter.)

Inside Prototype, $A is mostly used for converting lists of arguments and DOM nodes into arrays. Note that the latest versions of Prototype mix enumerable functions right into JavaScript's native `Array` object, which makes this function of very little use.

$F(id)

The $F function is an alias for `Form.Element.getValue`. It returns the value of any form field on a page, by ID. It is a useful convenience method because it works regardless of whether you pass it a text input, a select input, or a text area.

$H(obj)

The $H function extends a plain JavaScript object with the functions of `Enumerable` and `Hash` making it resemble a hash in Ruby. (See the section "Hash" in this chapter.)

$R(start, end, exclusive)

The $R function is a shortcut for the `ObjectRange` constructor. (See the section "ObjectRange" in this chapter.)

Try.these(func1, func2[, func3...]

This is not exactly a top-level function, but it made the most sense to me to include it in this section, since `these` is the only function of the `Try` object.

When doing cross-browser-compatible operations, it's quite common to need to try a couple of different ways of doing something until one of them works. The `Try` object defines a `these` function, to which you pass a list of functions that should be attempted until one *doesn't* throw an exception.

A classic example, taken right from the Prototype codebase, is the way that you grab a reference to the `XMLHttpRequest` object, which varies significantly between Firefox and Internet Explorer:

```
var Ajax = {
  getTransport: function() {
    return Try.these(
      function() {return new XMLHttpRequest()},
      function() {return new ActiveXObject('Msxml2.XMLHTTP')},
      function() {return new ActiveXObject('Microsoft.XMLHTTP')}
    ) || false;
  },

  activeRequestCount: 0
}
```

Class

The `Class` object defines a `create` function, used to declare new instances of Ruby-like classes in the rest of the framework. Those classes can then declare an `initialize` function to serve as an constructor when `new` is invoked to create a new instance,

Here is the implementation of `ObjectRange` as an example:

```
ObjectRange = Class.create();
Object.extend(ObjectRange.prototype, Enumerable);
Object.extend(ObjectRange.prototype, {
  initialize: function(start, end, exclusive) {
    this.start = start;
    this.end = end;
    this.exclusive = exclusive;
  },

  ...
});

var $R = function(start, end, exclusive) {
  return new ObjectRange(start, end, exclusive);
}
```

First, a class is created for `ObjectRange` (which would look like `class ObjectRange` in Ruby). Next, the `prototype` object of `ObjectRange` is extended in order to establish instance methods. The functions of `Enumerable` are mixed in, followed by the anonymous JavaScript object defined by the curly braces, inside of which is the `initialize` function plus whatever other instance methods are needed.

Extensions to JavaScript's `Object` Class

One reason that Prototype code can be so clean and concise is that it mixes functions right into JavaScript's base classes, such as `Object`.

`Object.clone(object)`

Returns a copy of the `object` supplied as a parameter, by using it to extend a new `Object` instance:

```
clone: function(object) {
  return Object.extend({}, object);
}
```

`Object.extend(destination, source)`

The `extend` static function literally loops through every property of the supplied `source` object and copies them over to the `destination` object, including functions, thereby serving as an inheritance and cloning mechanism. (JavaScript doesn't have built-in support for inheritance.)

The source code is instructional and simple enough to include here:

```
Object.extend = function(destination, source) {
  for (var property in source) {
    destination[property] = source[property];
  }
  return destination;
}
```

`Object.keys(obj)` and `Object.values(obj)`

Objects in JavaScript behave almost exactly like associative arrays (or hashes) in other languages, and they're used extensively in that fashion in JavaScript code. The `keys` static function returns a list of the properties defined on an object. The `values` static function returns a list of property values.

`Object.inspect(param)`

If the parameter is undefined (which is different than null in JavaScript), the static `inspect` function returns the string `'undefined'`. If the parameter is null, it returns `'null'`. If an `inspect()` function is defined on the parameter, it is invoked; otherwise, `toString()` is called as a final resort.

Extensions to JavaScript's `Array` Class

The following methods are available on arrays in addition to those defined in `Enumerable`.

`array.clear()`

Removes all elements from the array and returns it. Interestingly enough, the implementation of this method simply sets the length of the array to zero:

```
clear: function() {
  this.length = 0;
  return this;
}
```

`array.compact()`

Removes all `null` and `undefined` elements from the array and returns it. Notice the use of `select` in the implementation:

```
compact: function() {
  return this.select(function(value) {
    return value != undefined || value != null;
  });
}
```

`array.first()` and `array.last()`

Returns the first and last elements of an array, respectively.

array.flatten()

Takes the array and recursively flattens its contents into a new array, which is returned. In other words, this function iterates over the elements of the source array, and for each element that is an array, it extracts its elements into the new array to be returned. Notice the use of inject in the implementation:

```
flatten: function() {
  return this.inject([], function(array, value) {
    return array.concat(value && value.constructor == Array ?
      value.flatten() : [value]);
  });
}
```

array.indexOf(object)

Returns the index of a particular element belonging to an array or returns -1 if the element is not found.

```
indexOf: function(object) {
  for (var i = 0; i < this.length; i++)
    if (this[i] == object) return i;
  return -1;
  });
}
```

array.inspect()

Overrides the default inspect and prints out the elements of the array delimited by commas.

```
indexOf: function() {
  return '[' + this.map(Object.inspect).join(', ') + ']';
}
```

array.reverse(inline)

Reverses the order of the array. The inline argument, which defaults to true, specifies whether to modify the receiving array or leave it in its original state.

`array.shift()`

Removes the first element of the array and returns it, causing the size of the array to shrink by 1.

`array.without(obj1[, obj2, ...])`

Removes (or subtracts) the elements specified as arguments from the receiver. Takes either an array or list of elements to be removed, which is easily accomplished by wrapping `arguments` in a call to `$A`. Notice the use of `select` in the implementation:

```
without: function() {
  var values = $A(arguments);
  return this.select(function(value) {
    return !values.include(value);
  });
}
```

Extensions to the document Object

The `document.getElementsByClassName(className [, parentElement])` method returns a lists of elements from the DOM that have the supplied CSS `className`. The optional `parentElement` parameter lets you limit the search to a particular branch of the DOM instead of searching the entire document, starting from the `body` element (default).

Extensions to the Event Class

The following list of constants is added to the `Event` class, for convenience.

```
Object.extend(Event, {
  KEY_BACKSPACE: 8,
  KEY_TAB:       9,
  KEY_RETURN:    13,
  KEY_ESC:       27,
  KEY_LEFT:      37,
  KEY_UP:        38,
  KEY_RIGHT:     39,
  KEY_DOWN:      40,
  KEY_DELETE:    46
});
```

The constants make it easy to define event handlers for keyboard events. In the following code example, we make use of a use of a `switch` statement inside of a simple `onKeyPress` event handler to detect when the user presses Escape.

```
onKeyPress: function(event) {
  switch(event.keyCode) {
    case Event.KEY_ESC:
      alert('Canceled');
      Event.stop(event);
  }
}
```

Event.element()
Returns the element that originated the event.

Event.findElement(event, tagName)
Traverses the DOM tree upward, starting from the element that originated the event. Returns the first element it finds that matches the `tagName` parameter (case-insensitive). If no matching parent element is found, this function returns the element that originated the event by default instead of erroring out, which can cause some confusion.

Event.isLeftClick(event)
Returns `true` if a click of the left mouse button caused the event to occur.

Event.observe(element, name, observer, useCapture) and Event.stopObserving(element, name, observer, useCapture)
The `observe` function wraps the browser's own `addEventListener` function, which is part of the DOM Level 2 specification. It establishes an observer relationship between the specified `element` and an `observer` function. The `element` parameter may refer to a string ID or the element itself, quite often `document` in the case of mouse and keyboard events.

The `stopObserving` function is essentially the same except that it disconnects the event handler, and wraps the `removeEventListener` method of the DOM.

The name parameter refers to a valid event name (as a string), as defined in the DOM specification for browsers (blur, click, and so on).[2]

The observer parameter should be a function *reference*, meaning the name of a function without parentheses (often a source of confusion!). In almost all cases, you will want to use the bindAsEventListener function in conjunction with observe, so that the event-handler function executes in the correct context. (See "Extensions to JavaScript's Function Class" in the next section.)

The useCapture option can be used to specify that the handler should be called in the capture phase instead of the bubbling phase, and defaults to false.

Here's an example of Event.observe taken from Scriptaculous' AutoCompleter object:

```
addObservers: function(element) {
  Event.observe(element, "mouseover",
this.onHover.bindAsEventListener(this));
  Event.observe(element, "click",
this.onClick.bindAsEventListener(this));
}
```

Event.pointerX(event) and Event.pointerY(event)

Returns *x* and *y* coordinates of the mouse pointer on the page when the event occurred.

Event.stop(event)

Halts propagation of an event and cancels its default behavior, whatever that might have been.

Extensions to JavaScript's Function Class

The following two functions are mixed into the native Function class.

function.bind(obj)

Used to bind a function into the context of the object passed as a parameter. That parameter is almost always inevitably the value this, the current object context, because the main use for bind is to take a function that was defined elsewhere and make sure that it will execute with the exact context where you want it to be executed.

For example, see the way that the `registerCallback` function of `PeriodicalExecuter` is implemented:

```
registerCallback: function() {
  setInterval(this.onTimerEvent.bind(this), this.frequency * 1000);
}
```

It is necessary to bind the `onTimerEvent` function to execute in the context of whatever object the callback is being registered on, rather than the prototype object of the `PeriodicalExecuter` object itself.

Use of `bind` is admittedly a difficult concept to grasp, unless you are an experienced JavaScript programmer or have an affinity for functional programming, so don't fret if you don't understand it immediately.

function.bindAsEventListener(obj)

Used to *attach* a function as a DOM event handler in such a way that the `event` object will get passed to the function as its parameter. Used in similar fashion to `bind` where you want to make sure that some method gets executed in the context of a particular instance, rather than the prototype class where it is defined. This method is not used by the Prototype library itself, but it is used extensively in Scriptaculous and in custom application JavaScript, whenever you want to create observer-style classes to contain event handlers bound to elements on a page.

The following code example is a custom class designed to alert you to changes in an input field with a customizable message:

```
var InputObserver = Class.create();
InputObserver.prototype = {
  initialize: function(input, message) {
    this.input = $(input);
    this.message = message;
    this.input.onchange = this.alertMessage.bindAsEventListener(this);
  },

  alertMessage: function(e) {
    alert(this.message + ' (' + e.type + ')');
  }
};

var o = new InputObserver('id_of_some_input_field', 'Input field');
```

Extensions to JavaScript's Number Class

The following three functions are mixed into the native Number class.

number.toColorPart()

Returns the hexadecimal representation of an integer RGB value.

```
toColorPart: function() {
  var digits = this.toString(16);
  if (this < 16) return '0' + digits;
  return digits;
},
```

Remember that numbers in JavaScript are not automatically *auto-boxed*, so to speak. You have to assign the number to a variable, wrap the value in a Number instance yourself, or simply put it in plain parentheses in order to be able to invoke functions on it. Not convinced? You can figure it out interactively using the FireBug console:

```
>>> 12.toColorPart();
missing ; before statement 12.toColorPart();
>>> n = new Number(12)
12
>>> n.toColorPart();
"0c"
>>> n = 12
12
>>> n.toColorPart();
"0c"
>>> (12).toColorPart();
"0c"
>>> 12.toColorPart
missing ; before statement 12.toColorPart
>>> (12).toColorPart
function()
```

number.succ()

Simply returns the next number:

```
succ: function() {
  return this + 1;
},
```

number.times()

Just like the `times` method available on numerics in Ruby, `number.times()` takes a block of code and invokes it a number of times (according to the value of the number it is called on). Notice the use of `$R` to easily create a range, and `each` to invoke the supplied `iterator` function.

```
times: function(iterator) {
  $R(0, this, true).each(iterator);
  return this;
}
```

Here's a simple example that will pop up an alert box five times. Remember that you can't invoke a JavaScript function directly on a *raw* number because it will confuse the parser, hence the extra parentheses are needed:

```
>>> (5).times(new Function("alert('yeah')"))
5
```

Extensions to JavaScript's String class

The following methods are mixed into the native `String` class.

string.camelize()

Turns dash-separated strings into lowerCamelCase.

```
>>> "about-to-be-camelized".camelize()
"aboutToBeCamelized"
```

`string.dasherize()`

Turns underscore-separated strings into dash-separated-strings.

```
>>> "about_to_be_dasherized".dasherize()
"about-to-be-dasherized"
```

`string.escapeHTML()` and `string.unescapeHTML()`

The `escapeHTML` instance function escapes all HTML and XML markup in the receiving string, by turning the angle brackets of tags into entities.

```
>>> '<script src="http://evil.org/bad.js"/>'.escapeHTML()
"&lt;script src="http://evil.org/bad.js"/&gt;"
```

The `unescapeHTML` function reverses the operation.

`string.evalScripts()` and `string.extractScripts()`

The `evalScripts` instance function executes any `<script>` tags found in the receiving string.

The `extractScripts` instance function returns an array of strings containing the text of all `<script>` tags found in the receiving string. Note that the opening and closing `<script>` tags themselves are omitted; only JavaScript code is extracted.

`string.gsub(pattern, replacement)` and `string.sub (pattern, replacement, count)`

The `gsub` instance function returns a *copy* of the receiving string, with all occurrences of `pattern` replaced with the value supplied in `replacement`. The receiving string is not modified. Pattern should be a literal JavaScript regular expression, delimited with "/" characters.

The `sub` function is similar to `gsub`, but only makes as many replacements as specified in the `count` parameter, which defaults to 1.

`string.scan(pattern, iterator)`

The `scan` instance function is very similar to `gsub`, except that it takes an iterator function instead of a replacement value.

`string.strip()`

The `strip` instance function removes leading and trailing whitespace. Notice the chained calls to `replace` in the implementation:

```
strip: function() {
  return this.replace(/^\s+/, '').replace(/\s+$/, '');
}
```

`string.stripScripts()` and `string.stripTags()`

The `stripScripts` instance function removes `<script>` tags (including their content) from the receiving string. The `stripTags` instance function removes all HTML and XML tags from the receiving string.

`string.parseQuery()` and `string.toQueryParams()`

Both functions turn a query string (URL request format) into a JavaScript object.

```
>>> "?foo=bar&da=da+do+la".toQueryParams()
Object foo=bar da=da+do+la
```

`string.toArray()`

Returns the characters of the receiving string as an array.

`string.truncate(length, truncationString)`

Works just like the `truncate` method that Rails mixes into strings. If the receiving string is longer than `length`, it will be truncated and the last three characters will be the `truncationString` (defaults to an ellipse, "`...`").

```
>>> "Mary had a little lamb".truncate(14)
"Mary had a ..."
```

`string.underscore()`

Practically a direct port of the `underscore` method mixed into strings in Rails. Turns camelCase strings into underscored form. Changes `::` to `/` to convert Ruby-style namespaces to paths.

```
>>> "ActiveRecord::Foo::BarCamp".underscore()
"active_record/foo/bar_camp"
```

The Ajax Object

The `Ajax` object has useful behavior and also serves as the root namespace for other Ajax-related objects in Prototype.

`Ajax.activeRequestCount`

Holds the number of Ajax requests executing at any given moment, and there may be more than one since they fire asynchronously. Primarily used when implementing activity indicators (a.k.a. "spinners"), those little animated icons let the user know when communication with the server is happening:

```
Ajax.Responders.register({
  onCreate: function() {
    if($('busy') && Ajax.activeRequestCount > 0)
      Effect.Appear('busy', { duration:0.5, queue:'end' });
  },

  onComplete: function() {
    if($('busy') && Ajax.activeRequestCount == 0)
      Effect.Fade('busy', {duration:0.5, queue:'end' });
  }
});
```

`Ajax.getTransport()`

Returns a reference to the `XMLHttpRequestObject` implementation provided by the browser. You don't normally have to use this function yourself—it's used internally by the other Ajax functions.

Ajax.Responders

The Responders object manages the list of event handlers interested in notification about Ajax-related events. The preceding code example shows Ajax.Responders used to register a pair of custom callback functions, onCreate and onComplete, which take care of showing and hiding a spinner graphic that indicates Ajax activity.

In addition to the static functions described in the following sections, Ajax.Responders extends Enumerable.

Ajax.Responders.register(responder)

Adds responder objects to the list of registered responders interested in receiving Ajax-related events. Responders are invoked in the order in which they were registered, and they should implement at least one of the following Ajax callbacks: onCreate, onComplete, or onException.

Ajax.Responders.unregister(responder)

Removes a responder from the list of registered responders.

Enumerable

The Enumerable object is used just as you would use the Enumerable module as a mixin in Ruby. It depends on the receiver having an _each function defined. Prototype mixes Enumerable into quite a number of other objects, including Array, Hash, ObjectRange, Ajax.Responders, and Element.ClassNames.

Just as in Ruby, you can mix Enumerable into your own custom JavaScript classes. Just provide an implementation of _each for Enumerable's functions to use.

```
// Provide your custom class with an _each function
var MyCustomClass = Class.create();
MyCustomClass.prototype = {
  _each: function(iterator) {
    for (var i = 0, length = this.length; i < length; i++) {
      iterator(this[i]);
    }
  }
}

// Mix in Enumerable's iterator functions
Object.extend(MyCustomClass.prototype, Enumerable);
```

JavaScript doesn't support private or protected functions; therefore, functions not intended for public use are prefixed with an underscore in Prototype.

The design of `Enumerable` varies from Ruby in that it provides you with a public each function, which uses _each under the covers. Apart from that, most of the iterator functions provided by `Enumerable` are very similar to their counterparts in Ruby.

enumerable.each(iterator)

The each function takes a function reference as its `iterator` parameter and invokes that function for each of its elements. The individual element is passed as the parameter to the iterator function.

Let's look at a simple example, which will alert three times:

```
function alerter(msg) {
  alert(msg);
}

["foo", "bar", "baz"].each(alerter)
```

The way to pass a function by reference in JavaScript is to simply refer to it by name, leaving off the parentheses.

Here are the rest of the enumerable functions. Most iterator are invoked with two parameters: `value` and `index`.

enumerable.all(iterator)

The `all` function passes each element of the `Enumerable` object to the iterator, and returns `true` if the `iterator` function never returns `false`. If the `iterator` parameter is omitted, each element itself is considered in a Boolean context. You can think of the `all` function as a big Boolean AND operation.

enumerable.any(iterator)

The any function passes each element of the `Enumerable` object to the iterator, and returns `true` if the `iterator` function ever returns `true`. If the `iterator` parameter is omitted, each element itself is considered in a Boolean context. You can think of the any function as a big Boolean OR operation.

enumerable.collect(iterator) and enumerable.map(iterator)

The `collect` function (aliased as `map`) returns the results of running the `iterator` function for each of the elements in an `Enumerable` object.

```
>>> $R(1,4).collect(Prototype.K) // K returns whatever you pass it
[1, 2, 3, 4]
>>> $R(1,4).collect(function(){return "cat"})
["cat", "cat", "cat", "cat"]
```

enumerable.detect(iterator) and enumerable.find(iterator)

The `detect` function (aliased as `find`) is used to find the first element of an enumerable that matches criteria defined in the `iterator` function.

```
>>> $R(1,100).detect(function(i){ return i % 5 == 0 && i % 6 == 0 })
30
```

enumerable.eachSlice(number[, iterator])

The `eachSlice` function splits the elements of the array into a number of *slices* as specified by the number parameter. Then it returns the results of calling `collect` with the optional `iterator` function, on the *list of resulting slices*, which effectively flattens the result back down into a single-dimension array.

```
>>> $R(1,10).eachSlice(5)
[[1, 2], [3, 4], [5, 6], [7, 8], [9, 10]]

>>> $R(1,10).eachSlice(2, function(slice) { return slice.first() })
[1, 3, 5, 7, 9]
```

enumerable.findAll(iterator) and enumerable.select (iterator)

The `findAll` function (aliased as `select`) is used to find all of the elements of an enumerable that match the criteria defined in the `iterator` function.

```
>>> $R(1,100).findAll(function(i){ return i % 5 == 0 && i % 6 == 0 })
[30, 60, 90]
```

enumerable.grep(pattern[, iterator])

The grep function returns all elements of an enumerable for which the regular expression passed as the pattern parameter matches with a non-null result.

The optional iterator function is invoked for any values that matched.

```
>>> quote = "The truth does not change according to our ability to
stomach it"
"The truth does not change according to our ability to stomach it"

>>> quote.split(' ').grep(/\w{5}/)
["truth", "change", "according", "ability", "stomach"]

>>> quote.split(' ').grep(/\w{5}/, function(val, i){ return i + ":" +
val })
["1:truth", "4:change", "5:according", "8:ability", "10:stomach"]
```

enumerable.include(obj) and enumerable.member(obj)

The include function (aliased as member) returns true if any member of the enumerable equals the obj parameter. The comparison is made using the == function.

```
>>> ['a','b','c'].include('a')
true
>>> ['a','b','c'].include('x')
false
```

enumerable.inGroupsOf(num[, filler])

The inGroupsOf function is kind of like eachSlice, but does not take an iterator. It always returns a two-dimensional array containing equal-sized groups, composed of the enumerable's elements. The optional filler parameter allows you to specify a value that should be used to *fill out* the remaining slots, if any, on the last group, and defaults to null.

```
>>> $R(1,10).inGroupsOf(3)
 [[1, 2, 3], [4, 5, 6], [7, 8, 9], [10, null, null]]
>>> $R(1,10).inGroupsOf(3, 0) // pad with zeros
[[1, 2, 3], [4, 5, 6], [7, 8, 9], [10, 0, 0]]
```

enumerable.inject(accumulator, iterator)

The `inject` function combines the elements of the enumerable, applying the `iterator` function to the `accumulator` and each element, in turn. At each iteration, the value of `accumulator` is set to the value returned by the `iterator` function. Unlike the Ruby version, Prototype's `inject` requires an initial value for `accumulator`.

```
>>> $R(1,5).inject(0, function(acc, e) { return acc + e })
15
```

enumerable.invoke(functionName[, arg1, arg2...])

The `invoke` function invokes the function named by `functionName` to each element of the enumerable and collects the results. The optional parameters will be passed as parameters to the invoked function.

```
>>> $R(1,5).inject(0, function(acc, e) { return acc + e })
15
```

enumerable.max([iterator]) and enumerable.min([iterator])

The `max` and `min` functions are very similar to each other, and return the elements of the enumerable of the highest and least values, respectively. An optional `iterator` function can be supplied to transform the value of the element that is used for comparison.

```
>>> $R(1,5).min()
1
>>> ["1","2","3"].max(function(val) { return Number(val) })
3
```

enumerable.partition([iterator])

The `partition` function returns a two-item array. The first is an array containing the enumerable's elements for which the optional `iterator` function returned `true`, and the second contains those elements for which it returned `false`. If an `iterator` is not supplied, the Boolean value of the element itself will be used.

```
>>> ["1",null,"2",null,null].partition()
[["1", "2"], [null, null, null]]
```

`enumerable.pluck(propertyName)`

The `pluck` function conveniently *plucks* a list of property values from an enumerable. This is essentially a convenience method similar to `collect`.

```
>>> $$('script').pluck('src')
["http://localhost:3000/javascripts/prototype.js?1165877878",
 "http://localhost:3000/javascripts/effects.js?1161572695",
"http://localhost:3000/javascripts/dragdrop.js?1161572695",
"http://localhost:3000/javascripts/controls.js?1161572695",
"http://localhost:3000/javascripts/application.js?1161572695", ""]
```

`enumerable.reject(iterator)`

The `reject` function returns elements of the enumerable for which the required iterator function returns `false`.

`enumerable.sortBy(iterator)`

The `sortBy` function returns the elements of `Enumerable` sorted according to the criteria returned by the required `iterator` function.

Incidentally, when I was coming up with an example for this function, I realized that because I'm used to coding Ruby, I quite often forget to say `return` in the body of the `iterator` function. Unfortunately, that won't usually cause the script to fail, and can be very confusing. Don't forget that JavaScript functions need an explicit `return` statement!

```
>>> linusQuote = "Software is like sex: It's better when it's free."
"Software is like sex: It's better when it's free."
>>> linusQuote.split(' ').sortBy(function(s,index) { return s.length })
["is", "it's", "sex:", "It's", "like", "when", "free.", "better",
"Software"]
```

`enumerable.toArray()` and `enumerable.entries()`

The `toArray` function (aliased as `entries`) returns the elements of the enumerable as an array.

enumerable.zip(enum1, enum2[, enum3...][, iterator])

The interesting `zip` function is modeled after the Ruby iterator of the same name. It has nothing to do with compression; rather, think of the behavior of a zipper on your clothing. The `zip` function merges the elements of each enumerable supplied as a parameter, such that the returned list has the same number of elements as the receiving enumerable does.

If the last (optional) parameter is a function, it is used as an `iterator` and invoked on each array element that will be returned. The easiest way to explain is probably to illustrate with an example, similar to the one presented in the "Pickaxe" book (*Programming Ruby*):

```
>>> a = [4, 5, 6]
[4, 5, 6]
>>> b = [7, 8, 9]
[7, 8, 9]
>>> [1, 2, 3].zip(a, b)
[[1, 4, 7], [2, 5, 8], [3, 6, 9]]
```

Hash

The `Object` class in JavaScript, which can be created on the fly with curly-brace literals, is very close to an associative array (a.k.a. hash) already. Without modification, it supports square-bracket notation for assignment and lookup.

Prototype gives us a `Hash` class that extends `Enumerable` and adds familiar functions similar to those available in Ruby hashes.

hash.keys() and hash.values()

The `keys` and `values` functions return lists of keys and values, accordingly.

hash.merge(another)

The `merge` function merges values passed in from `another` hash into the receiver. If any keys exist in both the receiver and passed-in hash, the value of the receiver's entry will be overwritten.

```
>>> $H({foo:'foo', bar:'bar'}).merge({foo:'F00', baz:'baz'})
Object foo=F00 bar=bar baz=baz
```

`hash.toQueryString()`

The `toQueryString` function formats the key/value pairs of a hash as a query string appropriate for appending to a URL. It comes in very handy, compared to trying to construct query strings yourself:

```
>>> $H(Prototype).toQueryString()
"Version=1.5.0_rc2&BrowserFeatures=%5Bobject%20Object%5D&ScriptFragment
=(%3F%3A%3Cscript.*%3F%3E)((%0A%7C%0D%7C.)*%3F)(%3F%3A%3C%2Fscript%3E)"
```

ObjectRange

`ObjectRange` provides an easy way to create JavaScript ranges. `ObjectRange` does provide a constructor but the more common way is to use `$R`. Prototype uses the `succ` method to figure out what the next value is in the range and Prototype provides such a method on `Number` and `String`. Prototype also mixes in `Enumerable`, making ranges much more usable.

```
>>> $A($R(1, 5)).join(', ')
'1, 2, 3, 4, 5'
>>> $R(1, 3).zip(['Option A', 'Option B', 'Option C'], function(tuple) {
  return tuple.join(' = ');
})
['1 = Option A', '2 = Option B', '3 = Option C']
```

Special care needs to be taken when using strings in ranges as `ObjectRange` does not use alphabetical boundaries but instead goes through the entire character table. This can create a huge array if not considered.

```
>>> $A($R('a', 'c'))
['a', 'b', 'c']
>>> $A($R('aa', 'ab'))
[..., 'ax', 'ay', 'az', 'a{', 'a|', 'a}', ...]  // A very large array
```

The `Prototype` Object

The `Prototype` object holds the version number of the library as the `Version` property, a regular expression snippet to match a script tag in HTML markup as `ScriptFragment`, and two very simple functions.

The `emptyFunction` is just that: empty. The `K` function has nothing to do with hyperfactorial or complex numbers; it simply returns the value that was passed into it as an argument and is used internally by Prototype.

The `PrototypeHelper` Module

When we covered helper modules in Chapter 11, we purposely left out `PrototypeHelper` and its companion, `Scriptaculous` helper. They provide an easy way to use the Prototype and Scriptaculous Javascript libraries (respectively) to add Ajax functionality to your application.

`link_to_remote`

Now that we've discussed the JavaScript functionality in Prototype, "All About Helpers," we can make a basic Ajax call. Rails minimizes the amount of JavaScript you need to write by hand. One of the most common helper methods is `link_to_remote`, which we'll use to fetch a random number from the controller in Listing 12.1. The controller follows RESTful principles and leverages the `respond_to` method to respond to callers that expect a JavaScript response.

Listing 12.1 A Controller Method to Call Using Ajax Techniques

```
Class RandomsController < ApplicationController
  def index
  end

  def new
    respond_to do |wants|
      wants.js { render :text => rand(1_000_000) }
    end
  end
end
```

We'll create only an index view since the new method only renders text. In the index view we'll use the `link_to_remote` helper to generate an Ajax link to our new method. The result of the request will be placed inside the `div` tag with the id of result. We define what to link to using the `url` parameter. It accepts the same values as the standard `link_to` method.

```
<html>
  <head>
    <%= javascript_include_tag :defaults %>
  </head>
  <body>
    <%= link_to_remote 'Random Number Please', :url =>
new_random_path,
:update => 'result' %>
    <br/><br/>
    <div id="result"></div>
  </body>
</html>
```

The rendered page will look like this:

```
<html>
  <head>
    <script src="/javascripts/prototype.js?1184547490"
            type="text/javascript"></script>
    <script src="/javascripts/effects.js?1184547490"
            type="text/javascript"></script>
    <script src="/javascripts/dragdrop.js?1184547490"
            type="text/javascript"></script>
    <script src="/javascripts/controls.js?1184547490"
            type="text/javascript"></script>
    <script src="/javascripts/application.js?1184547490"
            type="text/javascript"></script>
  </head>
  <body>
    <a href="#" onclick="new Ajax.Updater('result',
'http://localhost:3000/randoms/new', {asynchronous:true,
evalScripts:true}); return false;">Random Number Please</a>
    <br/>
    <br/>
    <div id="result"></div>
  </body>
</html>
```

The call to `javascript_include_tag :defaults` added the needed `script` tags. Rails appends a unique number to the URL to help prevent problems caused by the browser caching old versions of your JavaScript files.

The `link_to_remote` helper is highly customizable, which means that we can use it to retain all the random numbers we've received. We need to change the view to use an unordered list first and to not replace the contents of the `ul` tag each time we click on the Ajax link. Instead the result should be appended below the unordered list.

```
<html>
  <head>
    <%= javascript_include_tag :defaults %>
  </head>
  <body>
    <%= link_to_remote 'Random Number Please', :url =>
new_random_path,
:update => 'result', :position => :bottom %>
<br/><br/>
    <ul id="result"></ul>
  </body>
</html>
```

Next we change the controller to render a list item tag.

```
Class RandomsController < ApplicationController
  ...

  def new
    respond_to do |wants|
      wants.js { render :text => "<li>#{rand(1_000_000)}</li>" }
    end
  end
end
```

Now each time we click the link, the result will be placed below the last one. The position parameter takes for different options: `:before`, `:after`, `:top`, and `:bottom`. The `:before` and `:after` values refer to the element, whereas the `:top` and `:bottom` values refer to the children of the element. If we wanted the newest random number to appear first in the list, we just need to replace `:bottom` with `:top`.

If we replaced it with :before, though, we would insert our list items outside the unordered list like this:

```
...
    <br/><br/>
    <li>15416</li>
    <li>9871</li>
    <ul id="result"></ul>
...
```

What if a problem occurs during our Ajax request? The link_to_remote has a callback to handle these situations. To use it you just need to set the :failure parameter.

```
...
<%= link_to_remote 'Random Number Please', :url => new_random_path,
 :update => 'result', :position => :bottom, :failure => "alert('HTTP
Error ' + request.status + '!')" %>
...
```

The :failure parameter takes a JavaScript function or fragment as a value. The callback has access to the underlying XMLHttpRequest object. In this case, the status code is displayed but we could also display the complete response by calling request.responseText. There are a number of other callbacks described in Table 12.1.

Table 12.1 Callback Options for link_to_remote

Parameter	Description
:before	Called before request is initiated.
:after	Called immediately after request was initiated and before :loading.
:loading	Called when the remote document is being loaded with data by the browser.
:loaded	Called when the browser has finished loading the remote document.
:interactive	Called when the user can interact with the remote document, even though it has not finished loading.
:success	Called when the XMLHttpRequest is completed, and the HTTP status code is in the 2XX range.
:failure	Called when the XMLHttpRequest is completed, and the HTTP status code is not in the 2XX range.
:complete	Called when the XMLHttpRequest is complete (fires after success/failure if they are present).

If you need more control, you can set callbacks for specific status codes. The following example sets a callback for a 404 status code. Note that the status code is not a symbol but rather an integer.

```
...
<%= link_to_remote 'Random Number Please', :url => new_random_path,
  :update => 'result', :position => :bottom, :failure => "alert('HTTP
  Error ' + request.status + '!')", 404 => "alert('Not Found')" %>
...
```

The `link_to_remote` method has a number of parameters to customize the browser-side behavior. While Ajax is typically asynchronous, you can change this behavior to be synchronous by setting `:type => :synchronous`. This will cause the browser to block until the request is finished processing. You can also add a confirmation dialog by setting `:confirm => true`. If you need to perform your Ajax request conditionally, you can set the `:condition` parameter to a JavaScript expression of browser-side conditions.

remote_form_for

Just as `link_to` has `link_to_remote`, `form_for` has `remote_form_for`. It takes the same options and callbacks as `link_to_remote` but returns a form tag that submits the form elements using an `XMLHttpRequest` in the background. Just like the `form_for` method, `remote_form_for` will present its values in the standard `params` object. We can illustrate this by creating an Ajax form, which will create a new `Addition` model, add the attributes together, and return the result. The controller would look like this:

```
Class AdditionsController < ApplicationController
  def new
    @addition = Addition.new
  end

  def create
    @addition = Addition.new(params[:addition])
    respond_to do |wants|
      wants.js { render :text => @addition.sum_x_and_y}
    end
  end
end
```

In the new view we would have:

```
<html>
  <head>
    <%= javascript_include_tag :defaults %>
  </head>
  <body>
    <% remote_form_for :addition, @addition,
         :url => additions_path,
         :update => 'result' do |f| %>
      X: <%= f.text_field :x %>
      Y: <%= f.text_field :y %>
      <%= submit_tag 'Create' %>
    <% end %>
    <div id="result"></div>
  </body>
</html>
```

The preceding view is rendered as follows:

```
<html>
  <head>
    ...
  </head>
  <body>
    <form action="/additions/non_ajax_create" method="post"
          onsubmit="new Ajax.Updater('result', '/additions',
          {asynchronous:true,
evalScripts:true, parameters:Form.serialize(this)}); return false;">
X: <input id="addition_x" name="addition[x]" size="30" type="text" />
Y: <input id="addition_y" name="addition[y]" size="30" type="text" />
<input name="commit" type="submit" value="Create" />
    </form>
    <div id="result"></div>
  </body>
</html>
```

The `remote_form_for` can also take a "fall-through" target for browsers that don't support JavaScript. By default this is the same action as the one specified in the url parameter. To set it to something else, set the :action parameter in the html options, like this:

```
...
<% remote_form_for :addition, @addition, :url => additions_path,
  :update => 'result', :html => { :action => url_for(:controller =>
  'additions', :action => 'non_ajax_create') } do |f| %>
...
```

Another option for submitting a form via Ajax is to use a regular form_for and a submit_to_remote instead of a standard submit. The submit_to_remote takes all the same options as remote_form_for.

periodically_call_remote

A common Rails Ajax method is periodically_call_remote, which will call a URL every *n* number of seconds. It takes the same options and has the same callbacks as link_to_remote. It defaults to calling the URL every 10 seconds, though you can change that by setting the :frequency parameter. We can change the random number generator view in the previous example to fetch a new number every five seconds. We don't need to change the controller, just the view to it:

```
<html>
  <head>
    <%= javascript_include_tag :defaults %>
  </head>
  <body>
    <%= periodically_call_remote :url => new_random_path, :update =>
  'result', :frequency => 5 %>
<br/><br/>
    <div id="result"></div>
  </body>
</html>
```

observe_field

Whereas periodically_call_remote happens every *n* seconds, observe_field happens on every change in a particular form field. We can use this to display a list of possible area codes as a user enters one into a text field. To do this, we'll use the following index view.

```
<html>
  <head>
    <%= javascript_include_tag :defaults %>
  </head>
  <body>
    Area Code: <%= text_field_tag 'number' %>
    <br/>d
    <span id="area_code_results"></span>
    <%= observe_field 'number', :url => { :controller => 'area_codes',
 :action => 'show'}, :frequency => 0.25, :update => '
area_code_results', :with => 'number' %>
  </body>
</html>
```

In our numbers controller we'll modify our show method.

```
Class AreaCodesController < ApplicationController
  def show
    respond_to do |wants|
      wants.js {
        @area_codes = AreaCode.find_like(params[:number])
`if @area_codes.empty? || params[:number].blank?
          render :text => ' '
        else
          render :text => @area_codes.map(&:to_s).join('<br/>')
        end
      }
    end
  end
end
```

The observe_field method checks the DOM element identified by *number* every 0.25 seconds for any changes. If the field has changed, that is, more data has been entered into or removed from the field, an XMLHttpRequest is made. The request is sent to the action identified by the url parameter; in this case, show on the area codes controller. That method looks for all area codes that start with the numbers entered so far.

We can use the standard `params` object in the controller because we specified the `with` parameter in the `observe_field` method. If we hadn't used the `with` parameter, we would have to look at the actual request body using something like `request.body.read`. We could also send additional parameters by setting the `with` parameter to something like: `'number='+ escape($(''number'').value) + '&other_value=-1'`. We could then access `number` and `other_value` from the `params` object once again.

By default the `observe_field` method will trigger on changed events for text fields and text areas, and on clicks for radio buttons and check boxes. If you want to use a different event, simply set the on parameter to the appropriate handler like blur of focus. In the preceding example we make a request to a URL, but we could also have called a JavaScript function instead. To do this we would set the function parameter to the appropriate function like: `:function => 'update_results'`. Additionally, `observe_field` takes all the options that `link_to_remote` does.

observe_form

If you need to observe an entire form, `observe_form` may be a better choice than `observe_field`. The `observe_form` takes the DOM ID of a form and watches all elements of the form. It takes all the same options and behaves the same as `observe_field` except the default value of the `with` parameter is the serialized value of the form (the request string).

RJS—Writing Javascript in Ruby

Rails includes a feature called RJS, which arguably stands for Ruby JavaScript. The RJS API generates blocks of JavaScript code based on Ruby code, thus allowing you to manipulate a view or parts of a view from the server side.

In the area codes example of the preceding section, we rendered the result of an area code search using `render :text` like this:

```
render :text => @area_codes.map(&:to_s).join('<br/>')
```

What if we also wanted to prefix the results with the number found? We might just add that to the string we return, like this:

```
render :text => "Found #{area_codes.size} Results<br/>
                 #{@area_codes.map(&:to_s).join('<br/>')}"
```

That works, but what if we needed to show the results count somewhere else in the view— somewhere that a simple string concatenation like the one used in the preceding example wouldn't work.

We could start using RJS by structuring the view template like this:

```
<html>
  <head>
    <%= javascript_include_tag :defaults %>
  </head>
  <body>
    Area Code: <%= text_field_tag 'number' %>
    <span id="area_code_results_message"></span>
    <br/>
    <hr/>
    <span id="area_code_results"></span>
    <%= observe_field 'number', :url => { :controller => 'area_codes',
  :action => 'show'}, :frequency => 0.25, :with => 'number' %>
</body>
</html>
```

Now using RJS, the `respond_to` block in our controller might look like this:

```
wants.js {
  @area_codes = AreaCode.find_like(params[:number])
if @area_codes.empty?
    render :update do |page|
      page.replace_html 'area_code_results_message',
                        'No Results Found'
      page.replace_html 'area_code_results', ''
    end
  else
    render :update do |page|
      page.replace_html 'area_code_results_message',
                        "Found #{@area_codes.size} Results"
      page.replace_html 'area_code_results',
                        @area_codes.map(&:to_s).join('<br/>')
end
  end
}
```

Since we're using RJS, we no longer need to use the `update` parameter in the `observe_field` method. This is because `observe_field` and all the methods we've talked about so far will execute any JavaScript received.

In the controller we no longer render text. Instead, the call to `render :update` tells `ActionController` to render a block of JavaScript. Rails provides a number of helper methods that help us create JavaScript for rendering.

The preceding code uses one of those: `replace_html`, which replaces the inner HTML of the element identified in the first argument with the value of the second argument.

We can use FireBug to see the JavaScript sent back to the browser in the response body.

```
Element.update("area_code_results_message", "Found 41 Results");
Element.update("area_code_results", "301 - MD, W Maryland: Silver
Spring, Frederick, Camp Springs, Prince George's County (see
 240)\074br/\076302 - DE, Delaware\074br/\076303 - CO, Central
 Colorado:Denver (see 970, also 720 overlay)\074br/\076...
```

RJS Templates

We haven't been following sane best practices, because we're combining controller and view logic in one place. We can fix things up by geting RJS code out of our controller and into template files.

First we create a view called `show.js.rjs` that contains the following lines:

```
if @area_codes.empty? || params[:number].blank?
  page.replace_html 'area_code_results_message',
                    'No Results Found'
  page.replace_html 'area_code_results', ''
else
  page.replace_html 'area_code_results_message',
                    "Found #{@area_codes.size} Results"
page.replace_html 'area_code_results',
                  @area_codes.map(&:to_s).join('<br/>')
end
```

Now we can clean up our controller:

```
class AreaCodesController < ApplicationController
  def show
    @area_codes = AreaCode.find(:all,
      :conditions => ['number like ?', "#{params[:number]}%"])
  end
end
```

The `respond_to` construct is gone, and we instead rely on Rails' default behavior of picking a view that matches the request. In other words, Rails will choose to serve a JavaScript view if the request was from an `XMLHttpRequest`. RJS can also be used in helpers too.

Rails comes with a number of RJS methods, which are described in the following sections.

`<<(javascript)`

This method will write raw JavaScript to the page. This is useful if we have a custom method in `application.js` that we want to call. For example:

```
// application.js
function my_method() {
  alert('my_method called');
}

// my_controllers.rb
class MyControllers < Application
  def show
    ...
    render :update do |page|
      page << 'my_method();'
    end
    ...
  end
end
```

[](id)

This returns a reference of the element identified by id in the DOM. Further calls can then be made on this element reference like hide, show, and so on. This behaves just like the $(id) construct in Prototype.

```
render :update do |page|
  page['my_div'].hide # same thing as $('my_div').hide
end
```

alert(message)

This will display a JavaScript alert with the given message:

```
render :update do |page|
  page.alert('Something is not right here')
end
```

call(function, *arguments, &block)

Calls the JavaScript function with the given arguments if any. If a block is given, a new JavaScript generator will be created and all generated JavaScript will be wrapped in a function() { ... } and passed as the class final argument.

```
// application.js
function my_method() {
  alert('my_method called');
}

// my_controllers.rb
class MyControllers < Application
  def show
    ...
      render :update do |page|
        page.call('my_method)
      end
    ...
  end
end
```

delay(seconds = 1) { ... }

This will execute the given block after the given number of seconds have passed.

```
render :update do |page|
  page.delay(5) {
    page.visual_effect :highlight, 'results_div', :duration => 1.5
  }
end
```

draggable(id, options = {})

This creates a draggable element (draggable elements are discussed in the section "Drag and Drop."

drop_receiving(id, options = {})

This creates a drop receiving element, which is discussed in the section "Drag and Drop."

hide(*ids)

Hides the elements identified by the given DOM ids.

```
render :update do |page|
  page.hide('options_div')
  page.hide('options_form', 'options_message')
end
```

insert_html(position, id, *options_for_render)

Inserts HTML at the given position relative to the given element identified by the DOM id. Position can be any one of the values shown in Table 12.2.

Table 12.2 Options for `insert_html` Method

Parameter	Description
`:top`	HTML is inserted inside the element, before the element's existing content.
`:bottom`	HTML is inserted inside the element, after the element's existing content.
`:before`	HTML is inserted immediately preceding the element.
`:after`	HTML is inserted immediately following the element.

The `options_for_render` can be either a string of HTML to insert or options passed to `render`.

```
render :update do |page|
  page.insert_html :after, 'my_div', '<br/><p>My Text</p>'
  page.insert_html :before, 'my_other_div', :partial => 'list_items'
end
```

literal(code)

This is used to pass a literal JavaScript expression as an argument to another JavaScript generator method. The returned object will have a `to_json` method that will evaluate to code.

redirect_to(location)

Causes the browser to redirect to the given location.

```
render :update do |page|
  page.redirect_to 'http://www.berlin.de'
end
```

remove(*ids)

Removes the given elements identified by the DOM ids.

replace(id, *options_for_render)

Replaces the entire element (not just its internal HTML) identified by the DOM id with either a string or render options set in `options_for_render`.

```
render :update do |page|
  page.replace 'my_div', '<div>Message</div>'
  page.replace 'my_div', :partial => 'entry'
end
```

replace_html(id, *options_for_render)

Replaces the internal HTML identified by the DOM id with either a string or render options set in `options_for_render`.

select(pattern)

Obtains a collection of element references by finding it through a CSS pattern. You can use standard prototype enumerations with the returned collection.

```
render :update do |page|
  page.select('div.header p').first
  page.select('div.body ul li).each do |value|
    value.hide
  end
end
```

show(*ids)

Show the given hidden elements identified by the DOM ids.

sortable(id, options = {})

Creates a sortable element that is discussed in the section "Sortable."

`toggle(*ids)`

Toggles the visibility of the elements identified by the ids. In other words, visible elements will become hidden and hidden elements will become visible.

`visual_effect(name, id = nil, options = {})`

This will start the named effect on the element identified by the DOM id. From RJS you can call `appear`, `fade`, `slidedown`, `slideup`, `blinddown`, and `blindup`. Each of these effects results in an element showing or hiding on the page. You can also call `toggle_appear`, `toggle_slide`, and `toggle_blind` to toggle the effect. For a complete list of visual effects, not just the displaying of elements, and options they take, consult the Scriptaculous documentation. To fade an element, we would do the following:

```
render :update do |page|
  page.visual_effect :fade, 'my_div'
end
```

JSON

JavaScript Object Notation (JSON) is a simple way to encode JavaScript objects. Rails provides a `to_json` on every object. We can use JSON instead of RJS to accomplish similar results. The main difference is where the logic lives to handle the result. Using RJS, the logic lives in Rails. Using JSON, the logic lives in JavaScript.

To illustrate, let's change our recurring example controller to return JSON.

```
class AreaCodesController < ApplicationController
  def show
    respond_to do |wants|
      wants.json {
        @area_codes=
          AreaCode.find_all_by_number(params[:area_code][:number])
        render :json => @area_codes.to_json
      }
    end
  end
end
```

This will return the following:

```
[{attributes: {updated_at: "2007-07-22 20:47:18", number: "340", id:
"81", description: "US Virgin Islands (see also 809)", created_at:
"2007-07-22 20:47:18", state: "VI"}}, {attributes: {updated_at: "2007-
07-22 20:47:18", number: "341", id: "82", description: "(overlay on
510; SUSPENDED)", created_at: "2007-07-22 20:47:18", state: "CA"}},
{attributes: {updated_at: "2007-07-22 20:47:18", number: "345", id:
"83", description: "Cayman Islands", created_at: "2007-07-22
20:47:18", state: "—"}}, {attributes: {updated_at: "2007-07-22
20:47:18", number: "347", id: "84", description: "New York (overlay
for 718: NYC area, except Manhattan)", created_at: "2007-07-22
20:47:18", state: "NY"}}]
```

We now need to change our view to handle this returned JSON content.

```
<html>
  <head>
    <%= javascript_include_tag :defaults %>
  </head>
  <body>
    Area Code: <%= text_field_tag 'number' %>
    <span id="area_code_results_message"></span>
    <br/>
    <hr/>
    <span id="area_code_results"></span>
    <%= observe_field 'number',
          :url => { :controller => 'area_codes',:action => 'show'},
          :frequency => 0.25,
          :with => 'number',
          :complete => "process_area_codes(request)" %>
  </body>
</html>
```

The only change is the addition of a callback to the `process_area_codes`
JavaScript function which we'll define in `application.js`.

```
function process_area_codes(request) {
  area_codes = request.responseText.evalJSON();
  $('area_code_results').innerHTML = ' '
  area_codes.each(function(area_code, index) {
    new Insertion.Bottom("area_code_results", "<li>" +
      area_code.attributes.number + " - " +
```

```
        area_code.attributes.state + ", " +
        area_code.attributes.description + "</li>");
    });
}
```

Drag and Drop

Scriptaculous makes doing drag and drop less painful, and Rails provides a few helper methods to make it even more painless. We can illustrate this by making the returned list of area codes draggable to a drop area where it can be selected. First we need to change our view.

```
<html>
  <head>
    <%= javascript_include_tag :defaults %>
  </head>
  <body>
    Area Code: <%= text_field_tag 'number' %>
    <span id="area_code_results_message"></span>
    <hr/>
    Selected: <span id="selected" style="padding: 0 100px; width:
 200px; height: 200px; background-color: lightblue;"></span>
<%= drop_receiving_element 'selected', :onDrop =>
 "function(element) { $('selected').innerHTML = element.innerHTML; }",
 :accept=>'area_code' %>
    <hr/>
    <span id="area_code_results"></span>
    <%= observe_field 'number', :url => { :controller => 'area_codes',
 :action => 'show'}, :frequency => 0.25, :with => 'number' %>
  </body>
</html>
```

We've used a JavaScript helper called `drop_receiving_element` to make the element identified by the DOM ID `'selected'` receive draggable elements of the class `'area_code'`. We've further customized it by setting the `onDrop` parameter to a JavaScript function to copy the dragged element's HTML. With the drop element

defined, we need to change our show.js.rjs view to make each returned area code
a draggable element.

```
if @area_codes.empty? || params[:number].blank?
  page.replace_html 'area_code_results_message',
                    'No Results Found'
  page.replace_html 'area_code_results', ''
else
  page.replace_html 'area_code_results_message',
                    "Found #{@area_codes.size} Results"
page.replace_html 'area_code_results', ''

  @area_codes.each do |area_code|
    id = area_code.number.to_s
    page.insert_html :bottom,
                     'area_code_results',
                     content_tag(:div,
                                 area_code,
                                 :id => id, :class => 'area_code')
page.draggable id, :revert => true
  end
end
```

Here we iterated over the collection of area codes and made each one a draggable
div element. We set the id of the element to the area code number and set the class
to 'area_code'. The class is important as the drop element we created in the preceding example will only accept elements whose class is 'area_code'.

We can now refresh the page and drag an area code to the colored selected box.
This is nice, but what would be more useful is to send back to the server the area code
that was selected. We can accomplish this by changing the drop element:

```
<%= drop_receiving_element 'selected',
        :onDrop => "function(element) {$('selected').innerHTML =
                                        element.innerHTML; }",
        :accept => 'area_code',
        :url => { :controller => 'area_codes',
                  :action => 'area_code_selected' } %>
```

Now when an element is dropped, an XMLHttpRequest will be made to the
area_code_selected method. By default, the dragged element's id is sent to the

server, which is the area code number in this case. In our controller we can log the selected area code.

```
Class AreaCodesController < ApplicationController
  def area_code_selected
    area_code = AreaCode.find_by_number(params[:id])
    # do something with area_code
    render :nothing => true
  end
end
```

Sortable

Scriptaculous and Rails builds on top of the Drag and Drop to create sortable lists. We can use this to sort the area codes returned. First we need to change our view to use an unordered list since the sortable JavaScript expects this.

```
<html>
  ...
  <ul id="area_code_results"></ul>
  ...
</html>
```

In the show.js.rjs view we also know to change over to list items and make the list sortable. We also remove the draggable declaration since we get that behavior automatically when the list is declared as sortable.

```
if @area_codes.empty? || params[:number].blank?
  ...
else
  ...
  @area_codes.each do |area_code|
    id = area_code.number.to_s
    page.insert_html :bottom, 'area_code_results', content_tag(:li,
  area_code, :id => id, :class => 'area_code')
  end
  page.sortable 'area_code_results', :url => { :controller =>
  'area_codes', :action => 'sorted_area_codes' }
end
```

With this we can now sort the returned area code result by dragging and dropping within the list. Each time we drop an area code element an `XMLHttpRequest` is made to the `sorted_area_codes` method. We access the list order via `params[:area_code_results]`, which contains an array of area codes in sorted order using the DOM ID of the area codes. If an underscore is present in the DOM ID, only the last part of it will be serialized and sent to the server. For example, a sorted element with a DOM ID of '`string_1`' will be sent as '`1`'.

Autocompleter

While this functionality is slated for a plugin in Rails 2.0, it's still quite useful. Autocompleters are often used to suggest values as you enter characters into a text field.

To return to our recurring example, we can use an autocompleter to display possible matching area codes as you type. In other words, if I enter 6, an autocompleter will show me all area codes that start with 6. We'll start with a special text field:

```
<html>
  <head>
    <%= javascript_include_tag :defaults %>
  </head>
  <body>
    Area Code: <%= text_field_with_auto_complete :area_code, :number
%>
  </body>
</html>
```

This will create a text field and associate it with an `Ajax.Autocompleter` that will make an `XMLHttpRequest` on each keystroke to a method called `auto_complete _for_area_code_number`. By default, `text_field_with_auto_complete` looks for a method named `auto_complete_for_#{object_name}_#{field}`. This method in our controller looks like this:

```
class AreaCodesController < ApplicationController
  ...
  def auto_complete_for_area_code_number
    @area_codes = AreaCode.find_by_number(params[:area_code][:number])
render :inline => "<%=auto_complete_result(@area_codes, :number)%>"
  end
  ...
end
```

We render it as an inline because `auto_complete_result` is an `ActionView` helper and not directly available in the controller.

In-Place Editors

We can also use Rails and Scriptaculous to create in-place `XMLHttpRequest` editors. Again, this functionality will be removed from Rails core and become part of a plug-in in Rails 2.0. If we wanted to edit the descriptive text of an area code in this fashion, our view would look like this:

```
<html>
  <head>
    <%= javascript_include_tag :defaults %>
  </head>
  <body>
    Number: <%= in_place_editor_field :area_code, :number %><br/>
    State: <%= in_place_editor_field :area_code, :state%><br/>
    Description: <%= in_place_editor_field :area_code, :description %>
  </body>
</html>
```

The in-place editor fields will by default look for a method name `set_#{object_name}_#{field}`. In the case of number, this method would be `set_area_code_number`, which looks like this:

```
Class AreaCodesController < ApplicationController
  ...
  def set_area_code_number
   @area_code = AreaCode.find(params[:id])
   render :text => @area_code.number
  end
  ...
end
```

Conclusion

The success of Rails is often correlated to the rise of Web 2.0, and one of the factors linking Rails into that phenomenon is its baked-in support for Ajax. There are a ton of books about Ajax programming, including some that are specific to using Ajax and

Rails together. It's a big subject, but it's a big enough part of Rails that we felt the need to include it as part of The Rails Way.

In this chapter, you were encouraged to use the FireBug plugin for Firefox if you aren't doing so already. Then we provided a comple reference guide to the Prototype JavaScript library, essential for doing Ajax programming, along with a review of the functionality provided by the Rails `PrototypeHelper` module.

In the sections dealing with RJS, you learned how you can write JavaScript in Ruby, which may come in very handy sometimes.

Finally, you learned the built-in Rails helpers for Scriptaculous effects and controls.

References

1. The first step to getting the FireBug plugin for Firefox is to visit http://www.getfirebug.com/.

2. See http://www.quirksmode.org/dom/w3c_events.html for a comprehensive explanation of DOM events and how to use them.

CHAPTER 13

Session Management

I'd hate to wake up some morning and find out that you weren't you!
—Dr. Miles J. Binnell (Kevin McCarthy) in "Invasion of the Body Snatchers"
(Allied Artists, 1956)

HTTP is a stateless protocol. Without the concept of a session (a concept not unique to Rails), there'd be no way to know that any HTTP request was related to another one. You'd never have an easy way to know who is accessing your application! Identification of your user (and presumably, authentication) would have to happen on each and every request handled by the server.[1]

Luckily, whenever a new user accesses our Rails application, a new session is automatically created. Using the session, we can maintain just enough server-side state to make our lives as web programmers significantly easier.

We use the word *session* to refer both to the time that a user is actively using the application, as well as to refer to the persistent hash data structure that we keep around for that user. That data structure takes the form of a hash, identified by a unique *session id*, a 32-character string of random hex numbers. When a new session is created, Rails automatically sends a cookie to the browser containing the session id, for future reference. From that point on, each request from the browser sends the session id back to the server, and continuity can be maintained.

The Rails Way to design web applications dictates minimal use of the session for storage of stateful data. In keeping with the "share nothing" philosophy embraced by Rails, the proper place for persistent storage of data is the database, period. The bottom line is that the longer you keep objects in the user's session hash, the more problems you create for yourself in trying to keep those objects from becoming stale (in other words, out of date in relation to the database).

This chapter deals with matters related to session use, starting with the question of what to put in the session.

What to Store in the Session

Deciding what to store in the session hash does not have to be super-difficult, if you simply commit to storing as little as possible in it. Generally speaking, integers (for key values) and short string messages are okay. Objects are not.

The Current User

There is one important integer that most Rails applications store in the session, and that is the current_user_id. Not the current user object, but its id. Even if you roll your own login and authentication code (which you shouldn't do), don't store the entire User (or Person) in the session while the user is logged in. (See Chapter 14, "Login and Authentication," for more information about keeping track of the current user.) The authentication system should take care of loading the user instance from the database prior to each request and making it available in a consistent fashion, via a method on your ApplicationController. In particular, following this advice will ensure that you are able to disable access to given users without having to wait for their session to expire.

Session Use Guidelines

Here are some more general guidelines on storing objects in the session:

- They must be serializable by Ruby's Marshal API, which excludes certain types of objects such as a database connection and other types of I/O objects.

- Large object graphs may exceed the size available for session storage. Whether this limitation is in effect for you depends on the session store chosen and is covered later in the chapter.

- Critical data should not be stored in the session, since it can be suddenly lost by the user ending his session (by closing the browser or clearing his cookies).

- Objects with attributes that change often should not be kept in the session. Think of a situation where you store a model with counter cache attributes, and constantly refer to it out of the session rather than pulling it from the database. The counters would never be up-to-date.

- Modifying the structure of an object and keeping old versions of it stored in the session is a recipe for disaster. Deployment scripts should clear old sessions to prevent this sort of problem from occurring, but with certain types of session stores, such as the cookie store, this problem is hard to mitigate. The simple answer (again) is to just not keep objects in the session.

Session Options

A number of basic session options are available for use in controllers, via the `session` class method. Calls to `session` can be placed in `ApplicationController`, or at the top of specific controllers in your application.

For example, some applications do not need to track user sessions, in which case you can get a tremendous performance boost by turning off that part of Rails' request handling:

```
# turn off session management for all actions.
session :off
```

As with other configuration-type class methods in controllers, the `:except` and `:only` options are supported:

```
# turn off session management for all actions _except_ foo and bar.
session :off, :except => %w(foo bar)

# turn off session management for only the atom and rss actions.
session :off, :only => %w(atom rss)
```

The `:if` option is also available and is useful for things like checking to see if a particular request's attributes merit a session or not:

```
# the session will only be disabled for 'foo',
# and only if it is requested as a web service
session :off, :only => :foo, :if => lambda { |req| req.parameters[:ws]
}
```

Disabling Sessions for Robots

If you are running a public website, web-crawling and spidering agents (also known as *robots*) will eventually find you. Since they don't support cookies, every request they make causes a new session to be created, a totally unnecessary burden on your server.

Turning off sessions specifically for robots is pretty easy, since they identify themselves via the user agent header of the HTTP request. All you have to do is add `session :off` to your `ApplicationController` with a dynamic `:if` condition, as showing in Listing 13.1.

Listing 13.1   Disabling Sessions for Robots by Inspecting the User Agent String

```
class ApplicationController < ActionController::Base
  session :off, :if => lambda {|req| req.user_agent =~
/(Google|Slurp)/i}
```

A typical Googlebot identifies itself as: "Mozilla/5.0 (compatible; Googlebot/2.1; +http://www.google.com/bot.html)". Yahoo's robot identifies itself as: "Mozilla/5.0 (compatible; Yahoo! Slurp; http://help.yahoo.com/help/us/ysearch/slurp)". It's worth doing some research using your web server's access logs to determine which robots are visiting your site and which user agent strings you need to match. Then add those strings to the regular expression inside the lambda block.

There's one more aspect to this technique, having to do with testing. As of this writing, the `TestRequest` class does not have a `user_agent` method. This means that your controller tests or specs will blow up after adding a call to `req.user_agent` as shown in Listing 13.1. Thankfully, Ruby's open classes mean we can remedy the situation with ease. Just add the code in Listing 13.2 to your `test_helper.rb` or `spec_helper.rb` file.

Listing 13.2   Monkeypatching the `TestRequest` Class to include `user_agent`

```
class ActionController::TestRequest
  def user_agent
    "Mozilla/5.0"
  end
end
```

Selectively Enabling Sessions

Suppose you have a truly nonstateful application and have turned off sessions for the entire thing in your `ApplicationController`:

```
class ApplicationController < ActionController::Base
  session :off
```

You may still want to selectively enable sessions for certain controllers, for instance, an administrative console. You can't say `session :on` in a subclass of `ApplicationController`—it won't work, but surprisingly, you *can* say `session :disable => false`.

```
class AdminController < ApplicationController
  session :disable => false
```

Secure Sessions

Sometimes you need to set up your Rails app so that sessions only work with HTTPS:

```
# the session will only work over HTTPS
session :session_secure => true
```

The `:session_secure` option can also be used in conjunction with `:only`, `:except`, and `:if` options, to secure only specific parts of your application. Keep in mind that your web server will need to be set up to work securely in order for this option to work.

Storage Mechanisms

The mechanism via which sessions are persisted on your Rails server can vary and you should pick the one most suited to your particular needs. I estimate that 80% or more of production Rails deployments use the `ActiveRecord Session Store`.

ActiveRecord SessionStore

Rails' default behavior is to store session data as files in the `/tmp/sessions` folder of your project, which is fine for experimentation and very small applications. For larger applications, it is advisable to minimize the amount of interaction Rails does with the filesystem, and that includes sessions.

There are a number of options for optimizing session storage, but the most common is to use `ActiveRecord` so that session data is stored in the database. In fact, it's so common that the tools to switch over to this setup are already built into Rails.

The first step is to create the necessary migration, using a rake task provided for that very purpose, and run the migration to actually create the new table:

```
$ rake db:sessions:create
      exists  db/migrate
      create  db/migrate/009_add_sessions.rb

$ rake db:migrate
(in /Users/obie/prorails/time_and_expenses)
== AddSessions: migrating
================================================
-- create_table(:sessions)
   -> 0.0049s
-- add_index(:sessions, :session_id)
   -> 0.0033s
-- add_index(:sessions, :updated_at)
   -> 0.0032s
== AddSessions: migrated (0.0122s)
====================================
```

The second (and final) step is to tell Rails to use the new sessions table to store sessions, via a setting in `config/environment.rb`:

```
config.action_controller.session_store = :active_record_store
```

That's all there is to it.

PStore (File-Based)

The default session storage mechanism for Rails is to keep the session data as PStore-formatted files in a `tmp` directory. The files will contain the contents of session hashes in their native serialized form. You don't have to change any settings to use this option.

If you are running a high-traffic site, you definitely *do not* want to use this option! It's slow, because marshalling/unmarshalling data structures in Ruby is slow. The server will also suffer severe strainage from having to maintain thousands of session files in a single directory, possibly running out of file descriptors. I've seen (and blogged about) a live Rails site going offline because the partition holding their session files ran out of space!

DRb Session Storage

DRb is Ruby's remoting service. It lets Ruby processes easily share objects over the network. In order to use DRb session storage, you need to run a separate DRb server process that will serve as the session repository. When you start bringing additional processes into the picture, the entire deployment becomes more complicated to maintain properly. So unless you really need to consider this option for performance reasons, you're better off sticking with the `ActiveRecord Session Store`.

At the time I'm writing this, DRb session storage is really unpopular and according to some blogs, it doesn't even work properly. If you do want to experiment with DRb and Rails sessions, search for the `drb_server.rb` script in your Rails source code.

```
config.action_controller.session_store = :drb_store
```

If you think you're outgrowing the `ActiveRecord Session Store`, look into Stefan Kaes' extra-super-optimized version[2] or consider `memcache` session storage.

`memcache` Session Storage

If you are running an extremely high-traffic Rails deployment, you're probably already leveraging `memcache` in some way or another. `memcache` is a remote-process memory cache that helps power some of the most highly trafficked sites on the Internet.

The `memcache` session storage option lets you use your `memcache` server as the repository for session data and is blazing fast. It's also nice because it has built-in expiration, meaning you don't have to expire old sessions yourself. However, it is also much more complicated to set up and maintain.[3]

```
config.action_controller.session_store = :mem_cache_store
```

In order to get the `memcache` session storage working, you'll need to make sure that `memcache`'s settings are included in your `environment.rb` file:

```
require 'memcache'
memcache_options = {
  :c_threshold => 10_000,
```

```
    :compression => true,
    :debug => false,
    :namespace => :app-#{RAILS_ENV}",
    :readonly => false,
    :urlencode => false
}

CACHE = MemCache.new memcache_options
CACHE.servers = 'localhost:11211'

ActionController::Base.session_options[:expires] = 1800
ActionController::Base.session_options[:cache] = CACHE
```

The Controversial `CookieStore`

In February 2007, core-team member Jeremy Kemper made a pretty bold commit to
Rails. He changed the default session storage mechanism from the venerable `PStore`
to a new system based on a `CookieStore`. His commit message summed it up well:

> Introduce a cookie-based session store as the Rails default. Sessions typically con-
> tain at most a user_id and flash message; both fit within the 4K cookie size limit.
> A secure hash is included with the cookie to ensure data integrity (a user cannot
> alter his user_id without knowing the secret key included in the hash). If you
> have more than 4K of session data or don't want your data to be visible to the
> user, pick another session store. Cookie-based sessions are dramatically faster than
> the alternatives.

In order to use the `CookieStore`, you have to be running Rails 2.0 (where it is
the default) or add the following configuration to `environment.rb`:

```
config.action_controller.session = {
  :session_key => '_my_app_session',
  :secret      => 'some_really_long_and_hashed_key'
}
```

I describe the `CookieStore` as controversial because of the fallout over making it
the new default session storage mechanism. For one, it imposes a very strict size limit,
only 4K. A significant size constraint like that is fine if you're following the Rails way,
and not storing anything other than integers and short strings in the session. If you're
bucking the guidelines, well, you might have an issue with it.

Lots of people also complained about the inherent insecurity of storing session information, including the current user information on the user's browser. However, there are security measures in place that make the cookie store hard to crack. For instance, you'd need to be able to compromise SHA512, and that is somewhat difficult to do.

If you want better security[4], for instance, you can easily override the existing hashing code:

```
class CGI::Session::CookieStore
  def generate_digest(data)
    # replace this line with your own encryption logic
    Digest::SHA512.hexdigest "#{data}#{@secret}"
  end
end
```

Another problem with cookie-based session storage is its vulnerability to *replay attacks*, which generated an enormous message thread on the rails-core mailing list. S. Robert James kicked off the thread[5] by describing a replay attack:

Example:

1. User receives credits, stored in his session.
2. User buys something.
3. User gets his new, lower credits stored in his session.
4. Evil hacker takes his saved cookie from step #1 and pastes it back in his browser's cookie jar. Now he's gotten his credits back.

This is normally solved using something called nonce —each signing includes a once-only code, and the signer keeps track of all of the codes, and rejects any message with the code repeated. But that's very hard to do here, since there may be several app servers (mongrels).

Of course, we could store the nonce in the DB—but that defeats the entire purpose!

The short answer is: Do not store sensitive data in the session. Ever. The longer answer is that coordination of nonces across multiple servers would require remote process interaction on a per-request basis, which negates the benefits of using the cookie session storage to begin with.

The cookie session storage also has potential issues with replay attacks that let malicious users on shared computers use stolen cookies to log in to an application that the user thought he had logged out of. The bottom line is that if you decide to use the cookie session storage, please think long and hard about the implications of doing so.

Timing Out and Session Life Cycle

Quite often you are required to time out a user's session if they are idle for a certain length of time. Amazingly, this basic functionality is not available by default in Rails. Using built-in session options, you can set a specific expiry time; however, when your Rails application starts up in production mode, the expiry time will be set just once. That's fine if you are setting your expiry time far in the future (beyond the time that you are likely to restart your server processes).

What if you want to set your timeout in the near future? Say perhaps, 20 minutes from time of session creation? Would the following work?

```
class ApplicationController < ActionController::Base
  session :session_expires => 20.minutes.from_now
end
```

The problem is that 20 minutes from now (the time that the server process is started) will soon become a time in the past. When the session expiry date is in the past, every new request will cause a new session to be created, and much havoc and misery will transpire.

Session Timeout Plugin for Rails

Luckily, there is a well-proven plugin that solves our problem. It is written by Luke Redpath and is available at http://opensource.agileevolved.com/trac/wiki/SessionTimeout.

After installing the plugin in your application, there will be a `session_times_out_in` method available for use in `ApplicationController`. The first parameter is the duration in seconds after which the session should expire, and you can use Rails' convenience methods to keep your code very readable.

For example, let's implement that 20-minute timeout we were discussing a minute ago:

```
class ApplicationController < ActionController::Base
  session_times_out_in 20.minutes
end
```

The second (optional) parameter allows you to specify a callback method to be invoked when a request comes in that causes the session to be expired. It might be necessary to do some end-of-session cleanup, or redirect the user to a particular place, things of that nature.

As is common with Rails callbacks, the second parameter value can be a symbol, referring to a method:

```
class ApplicationController < ActionController::Base
  session_times_out_in 20.minutes, :after_timeout => :log_timeout_msg

  private

  def log_timeout_msg
    logger.info "Session expired"
  end
end
```

Or you can specify a `Proc` or `lambda`. It will be passed an instance of the current controller, which I've ignored in the example:

```
class ApplicationController < ActionController::Base
  session_times_out_in 20.minutes,
    :after_timeout => proc {|controller| logger.info "Session expired"
}
end
```

Elegant, isn't it?

Tracking Active Sessions

Quite often we want a way to display the number of active users of an application. If you are using `ActiveRecord Session Store`, this is very easy to accomplish. The `sessions` table gets created by default with an `updated_at` column. Assuming your definition of *active* is one hour, the code to count active users would look like this:

```
CGI::Session::ActiveRecordStore::Session.count :conditions =>
["updated_at > ?", 1.hour.ago ]
```

In fact, objects found using the `Session` class can be used just like any other `ActiveRecord` instance. The session contents are stored in the `data` attribute, serialized (in a non-human-readable way) into a text column, so it isn't possible (by default) to query sessions by their content. Want to see what it looks like?

```
>> CGI::Session::ActiveRecordStore::Session.find:first
=> #<CGI::Session::ActiveRecordStore::Session:0x26fe65c

@attributes={"updated_at"=>"2006-11-29 02:06:01",
"session_id"=>"73bb9cd7fd19a5c1cae8cd0fda0cb6bb", "id"=>"1",
"data"=>"BAh7BiIKZmxhc2hJQzonQWN0aW9uQ29udHJvbGxlcjo6Rmxhc2g6OkZsYXNo\nSG
FzaHsABjoKQHVzZWR7AA==\n"}>
```

So if you want to query for data contained *inside* the session data, say for instance, to display a list of names of the current users, then it's going to take a little bit more work. In a nutshell, you'd have to add another column to the `sessions` table and add an `after_filter` to your `ApplicationController` that stores the data you want on a per-request basis. (The full implementation is left as an exercise for the reader.)

Enhanced Session Security

Erik Elmore gives a very long and detailed description of how to write a "paranoid" session store on his blog.[6] Among other things, his implementation provides protection against session-fixation attacks (by capturing IP addresses as part of the session record), a facility for being able to see which users are "online," and the ability to administratively end sessions of troublemakers. It's also "lightning fast" because it uses the database directly instead of instantiating `ActiveRecord` objects. His article may not be entirely applicable to you, particularly since it is written for MySQL, but is definitely worth examination if you will be tackling advanced session work.

Cleaning Up Old Sessions

If you're using Luke Redpath's `session_timeout` plugin and `ActiveRecordStore`, cleaning up old sessions is really easy. Remember that the session timeout gives you an `:after_timeout` option?

You can also write your own little utilities for maintaining your sessions. Listing 13.3 is a class that you can add to your `/lib` folder and invoke from the production console or a script whenever you need to do so.

Listing 13.3   `SessionMaintenance` Class for Cleaning Up Old Sessions

```
class SessionMaintenance

  def self.cleanup(period=24.hours.ago)
    session_store = CGI::Session::ActiveRecordStore::Session
    session_store.destroy_all( ['updated_at < ?', period] )
  end

end
```

Cookies

This section is about using cookies, not the cookie session store. The *cookie container,* as it's known, looks like a hash, and is available via the `cookies` method in the scope of controllers. Lots of Rails developers use cookies to store user preferences and other small nonsensitive bits of data. Always be careful not to store sensitive data in cookies, since they can easily be read and modified by malicious users. The database is a more appropriate place to store sensitive data.

Contrary to what at least some developers might expect, the `cookies` container is not available by default in view templates or helpers. If necessary, and in accordance with proper model-view-controller practice, you should set an instance variable in your controller with the value of a cookie for use in your view:

```
@list_mode = cookies[:list_mode] or 'expanded'
```

If you are really intent on being able to access cookies in your helpers or views, there is a simple solution. Simply declare `cookies` to be a helper method:

```
class MyController < ActionController::Base
  helper_method :cookies
```

Reading and Writing Cookies

The cookie container is filled with cookies received along with the request, and sends out any cookies that you write to it with the response. Note that cookies are read by value, so you won't get the cookie object itself back, just the value it holds as a string (or as an array of strings if it holds multiple values). That's a limitation, but I'm not sure how severe of a limitation it is in practice.

To create or update cookies, you simply assign values using the brackets operator. You may assign either a single string value or a hash containing options, such as :expires, which takes a number of seconds before which the cookie should be deleted by the browser. Remember that Rails convenience methods for time are useful here:

```
# writing a simple session cookie
cookies[:list_mode] = params[:list_mode]

# specifying options, curly brackets are needed to avoid syntax error
cookies[:recheck] = {:value => "false", :expires => Time.now +
5.minutes}
```

I find the :path options useful in allowing you to set options specific to particular sections or even particular records of your application. The :path option is set to '1', the root of your application, by default.

The :domain option allows you to specify a domain, which is most often used when you are serving up your application from a particular host, but want to set cookies for the whole domain.

```
cookies[:login] = {:value => @user.security_token,
                   :domain => '.domain.com',
                   :expires => Time.now.next_year }
```

Cookies can also be written using the :secure option, and Rails will only ever transmit them over a secure HTTPS connection:

```
# writing a simple session cookie
cookies[:account_number] = { :value => @account.number, :secure =>
true }
```

Finally, you can delete cookies using the delete method:

```
cookies.delete :list_mode
```

Conclusion

Deciding how to use the session is one of the more challenging tasks that faces a web application developer. That's why we put a couple of sections about it right in the beginning of this chapter. We also covered the various options available for configuring sessions, including storage mechanisms and methods for timing out sessions and the session lifecycle.

Moving on, we'll continue with a related topic: login and authentication.

References

1. If you are really new to web programming and want a very thorough explanation of how web-based session management works, you may want to read the information available at http://www.technicalinfo.net/papers/WebBasedSessionManagement.html.

2. Find Stefan Kaes' super-optimized ActiveRecord SessionStore at http://railsexpress.de/blog/articles/2005/12/19/roll-your-own-sql-session-store.

3. Geoffrey Grosenbach has a fantastic tutorial on memcache basics at http://nubyonrails.com/articles/2006/08/17/memcached-basics-for-rails.

4. My fellow cabooser Courtenay wrote a great blog post about cookie session storage at http://blog.caboo.se/articles/2007/2/21/new-controversial-default-rails-session-storage-cookies.

5. If you want to read the whole thread (all 83 messages of it), simply search Google for "Replay attacks with cookie session." The results should include a link to the topic on the Ruby on Rails: Core Google Group.

6. http://burningtimes.net/articles/2006/10/15/paranoid-rails-session-storage

CHAPTER 14

Login and Authentication

"Thanks goodness, there's only about a billion of these because DHH doesn't think auth/auth belongs in the core."
—Comment at http://del.icio.us/revgeorge/authentication

I bet every web app you've ever worked on has needed some form of user security, and some people assume it makes sense to include some sort of standard authentication functionality in a "kitchen-sink" framework such as Rails.

However, it turns out that user security is one of those areas of application design that usually involves a bit more business logic than anyone realizes upfront.

David has clearly stated his opinions on the matter, to help us understand why Rails does not include any sort of standard authentication mechanism:

> Context beats consistency. Reuse only works well when the particular instances are so similar that you're willing to trade the small differences for the increased productivity. That's often the case for infrastructure, such as Rails, but rarely the case for business logic, such as authentication and modules and components in general.

For better or worse, we need to either write our own authentication code or look outside of Rails core for a suitable solution. It's not too difficult to write your own authentication code, to the extent that it isn't really that difficult to write *anything* in Rails. But why reinvent the wheel? That's not the Rails way!

As alluded to in the chapter quote, we have many different options out there to choose from. It seems that since authentication is one of the first features you add to a new application, it is also one of the first projects undertaken by many an aspiring plugin writer.

A multitude of options can be a good thing, but I contend that in this particular case it is not. A Google search for "rails authentication" turns up *over 5 million results!* Looking through the first page of results alone I can count at least ten different approaches to tackling this problem—and what the heck is a *salted password generator?*

No need to worry or be confused. It turns out that Rails pros agree that the two best authentication plugins are written by Rails core team member Rick Olson, a.k.a. *techno weenie*[1]. In this chapter, we take an in-depth look at both of them.

Acts as Authenticated

Acts as Authenticated is described by Rick as "a simple authentication generator plugin." It allows you to easily add *form-based authentication* to your application. It also provides a standard API for accessing information such as whether a user is logged in or authorized as an admin, as well as accessing the `User` object itself.

> **Courtenay Says...**
>
> Acts as Authenticated also works out-of-the-box with HTTP Basic Authentication (a.k.a. *ugly login box*) so you don't have to do anything extra to get a protected API for your RESTful applications. It even returns the right 401 Unauthorized response when necessary.

Installation and Setup

Install `acts_as_authenticated` as a plugin by invoking `script/plugin install acts_as_authenticated`. First you generate skeleton code for authentication using a Rails generator included in the plugin, and then you customize the basic implementation so that it behaves according to the needs of your particular application.

The code generator is invoked using `script/generate` and takes a couple of parameters: one for model and one for controller name. We'll invoke the generator, specifying `user` and `account` as our desired names for our authentication model and controller.

```
$ script/generate authenticated user account
      exists  app/models/
      exists  app/controllers/
```

```
exists   app/helpers/
create   app/views/account
exists   test/functional/
exists   test/unit/
create   app/models/user.rb
create   app/controllers/account_controller.rb
create   lib/authenticated_system.rb
create   lib/authenticated_test_helper.rb
create   test/functional/account_controller_test.rb
create   app/helpers/account_helper.rb
create   test/unit/user_test.rb
create   test/fixtures/users.yml
create   app/views/account/index.rhtml
create   app/views/account/login.rhtml
create   app/views/account/signup.rhtml
create   db/migrate
create   db/migrate/001_create_users.rb
```

Somewhat similar to the way scaffolding code is generated, we see that a number of files for a model and controller, migration, and associated tests are created. I'll walk you through use of the plugin and point out what we can learn from it with regard to our own application code.

The `User` Model

First let's take a look at the migration that was automatically created by the generator: `db/migrate/001_create_users.rb`.

```
class CreateUsers < ActiveRecord::Migration
  def self.up
    create_table "users", :force => true do |t|
      t.column :login,                    :string
      t.column :email,                    :string
      t.column :crypted_password,         :string, :limit => 40
      t.column :salt,                     :string, :limit => 40
      t.column :created_at,               :datetime
      t.column :updated_at,               :datetime
      t.column :remember_token,           :string
      t.column :remember_token_expires_at, :datetime
    end
  end
end
```

```
def self.down
  drop_table "users"
end
end
```

The standard columns should look pretty much like ones you'd associate with a `User` model. We'll cover the meaning of `crypted_password` and `salt` a little later on in the chapter. If you wanted additional columns, such as first and last names, just add them to this migration.

Now we'll open `app/models/user.rb` and see what our shiny new `User` model looks like in Listing 14.1.

Listing 14.1   The *User* Model Generated by Acts As Authenticated

```
require 'digest/sha1'

class User < ActiveRecord::Base
  # Virtual attribute for the unencrypted password
  attr_accessor :password

  validates_presence_of       :login, :email
  validates_presence_of       :password,
                              :if => :password_required?
  validates_presence_of       :password_confirmation,
                              :if => :password_required?
  validates_length_of         :password, :within => 4..40,
                              :if => :password_required?
  validates_confirmation_of   :password,
                              :if => :password_required?
  validates_length_of         :login,    :within => 3..40
  validates_length_of         :email,    :within => 3..100
  validates_uniqueness_of     :login, :email, :case_sensitive => false

  before_save :encrypt_password

  # Authenticates a user by their login name and unencrypted password,
  # returning the user or nil.
  def self.authenticate(login, password)
    u = find_by_login(login) # need to get the salt
    u && u.authenticated?(password) ? u : nil
  end

  # Encrypts some data with the salt.
  def self.encrypt(password, salt)
    Digest::SHA1.hexdigest("--#{salt}--#{password}--")
  end
```

```ruby
      # Encrypts the password with the user salt
      def encrypt(password)
        self.class.encrypt(password, salt)
      end

      def authenticated?(password)
        crypted_password == encrypt(password)
      end

      def remember_token?
        remember_token_expires_at &&
       (Time.now.utc < remember_token_expires_at)
      end

      # These create and unset the fields required
      # for remembering users between browser closes
      def remember_me
        self.remember_token_expires_at =
          2.weeks.from_now.utc
        self.remember_token =
          encrypt("#{email}--#{remember_token_expires_at}")
        save(false)
      end

      def forget_me
        self.remember_token_expires_at = nil
        self.remember_token           = nil
        save(false)
      end

    protected
      def encrypt_password
        return if password.blank?
        self.salt =
          Digest::SHA1.hexdigest("--#{Time.now}--#{login}--") if
  new_record?
        self.crypted_password = encrypt(password)
      end

      def password_required?
        crypted_password.blank? || !password.blank?
      end
  end
```

Whoa! That's certainly a lot more code than we're used to seeing in a Rails-generated class. Let's analyze the User model to see what we can learn.

Non-Database Attributes

Sometimes it makes sense to add non-database attributes to your `ActiveRecord` models. They're added using `attr_*` macros, which you should know about from practically every Ruby language primer in existence.

At the very top of `User`, notice that an attribute has been specified for `:password`. Does that seem a little weird? Doesn't the user's password need to be kept in the database?

It might make a little more sense if we consider that non-database attributes are often used in `ActiveRecord` models to hold *transient* data. The password exists in plaintext only during a request, when it is being submitted from an HTML form. Before saving, the plaintext password string needs to be encrypted, by the `encrypt_password` method.

```
def encrypt_password
  return if password.blank?
  if new_record?
    self.salt = Digest::SHA1.hexdigest("--#{Time.now.to_s}--#{login}--")
  end
  self.crypted_password = encrypt(password)
end
```

Notice that the `password` property is referenced in the call to `password.blank?` and `encrypt(password)`. Since non-database attributes exist outside the knowledge of `ActiveRecord`, when does the `password` attribute get set? Explicitly?

The fact that we have unit test coverage means we have a great way of seeing exactly where our `password` attribute is set. My gut says that most of the time these extra attributes are set via `ActiveRecord` constructor methods, but by using the `User` unit test I can prove it to you quite vividly.

What unit test? The plugin generated one. Before changing anything, let's run `rake test` to make sure we have passing tests to begin with.

```
$ rake
(in /Users/obie/time_and_expense)
/opt/local/bin/ruby -Ilib:test
"/opt/local/lib/ruby/gems/1.8/gems/rake-
0.7.1/lib/rake/rake_test_loader.rb" "test/unit/user_test.rb"
Loaded suite /opt/local/lib/ruby/gems/1.8/gems/rake-
0.7.1/lib/rake/rake_test_loader
```

```
Started
..........
Finished in 0.312914 seconds.

10 tests, 17 assertions, 0 failures, 0 errors

/opt/local/bin/ruby -Ilib:test
"/opt/local/lib/ruby/gems/1.8/gems/rake-
0.7.1/lib/rake/rake_test_loader.rb"
"test/functional/account_controller_test.rb"
Loaded suite /opt/local/lib/ruby/gems/1.8/gems/rake-
0.7.1/lib/rake/rake_test_loader

Started
..............
Finished in 0.479761 seconds.

14 tests, 26 assertions, 0 failures, 0 errors
/opt/local/bin/ruby -Ilib:test
"/opt/local/lib/ruby/gems/1.8/gems/rake-
0.7.1/lib/rake/rake_test_loader.rb"
```

Green bar—all tests passed! That means it's safe to do some experimentation. Remember we were wondering about how that `password` attribute is used. What will break if we change `attribute_accessor` to `attribute_reader`, thereby making `password` read-only?

```
class User < ActiveRecord::Base
  # Non-database attribute for the unencrypted password
  attr_reader :password
```

When we run the test suite again, it turns out that a whole bunch of tests broke, effectively pointing to every place in the codebase where the value of `password` is set. All of them are indeed `ActiveRecord` constructors.

For example, one of the errors occurs in the test for the `signup` method of `AccountController`.

```
4) Error:
test_should_require_pwd_confirmation_on_signup(AccountControllerTest):
NoMethodError: undefined method `password=' for #<User:0x2a45068>
    active_record/base.rb:1842:in `method_missing'
    active_record/base.rb:1657:in `attributes='
```

```
active_record/base.rb:1656:in `attributes='
active_record/base.rb:1490:in `initialize_without_callbacks'
active_record/callbacks.rb:225:in `initialize'
app/controllers/account_controller.rb:23:in `signup'
```

A quick look at the `signup` method confirms that the `password` attribute is getting passed into `User`'s constructor, bundled into the user parameters hash that is generated when the signup form is posted submitted from the view.

```
def signup
  @user = User.new(params[:user])
  return unless request.post?
  ...
end
```

Non-database attributes are significant because they can be leveraged to mask implementation choices from the view. In this case, it would present a security risk to expose the `salt` and `crypted_password` properties to the view.

Validations

Turning our attention back to the `User` model, we see that Rick has provided sensible defaults for password validation. Of course, you have the freedom to modify these to your heart's content to match your own requirements and purpose.

```
validates_presence_of      :password
                           :if => :password_required?
validates_presence_of      :password_confirmation,
                           :if => :password_required?
validates_length_of        :password, :within => 4..40,
                           :if => :password_required?
validates_confirmation_of  :password,
                           :if => :password_required?
```

Those validation rules should only execute under one condition, if the `crypted_password` attribute is blank and the `password` attribute is not. Without this condition in place, every update to the user model would reset the password.

```
def password_required?
  crypted_password.blank? || !password.blank?
end
```

Conditional Callbacks

Note the use of `:if` parameters used on the validation methods to specify a conditional callback. The symbol `:password_required?` identifies the method that should be invoked to determine whether or not to enable the validation.

At first glance, it looks as if this code could be a bit DRYer, since the clause `:if =>` `:password_required?` is repeated four times. Can we refactor it to be more concise?

```
# looks more DRY, but will it work?
if password_required?
  validates_presence_of      :password
  validates_presence_of      :password_confirmation
  validates_length_of        :password, :within => 4..40,
  validates_confirmation_of  :password
end
```

No! Think about the timing of the `if` clause: We need to check if `password_required?` during the validation step of the model's life cycle, not at the time that the `User` class is defined. It is possible to DRY up this code using Rails' `with_options` method, although this *might* be one of those cases where the reward does not quite justify the effort.

```
with_options :if => :password_required? do |u|
  u.validates_presence_of      :password
  u.validates_presence_of      :password_confirmation
  u.validates_length_of        :password, :within => 4..40
  u.validates_confirmation_of  :password
end
```

The `before_save` Callback

As covered in Chapter 2, "Working with Controllers," callbacks allow you to point at a method that should be invoked at a certain stage in the life cycle of an `ActiveRecord` object, like this:

```
before_save :encrypt_password
```

Getting back to the `User` model walk-through, notice that there is a need to encrypt the user's password before saving a new user record to the database. The

:encrypt_password symbol points to the protected method of the same name closer to the bottom of the class:

```
def encrypt_password
  return if password.blank?
  if new_record?
    self.salt = Digest::SHA1.hexdigest("--#{Time.now}--#{login}--")
  end
  self.crypted_password = encrypt(password)
end
```

This says: "First of all, if the password is blank, don't try to encrypt it. Otherwise,
calculate and capture the salt and crypted_password attributes for saving."

The salt column stores a one-time hashing key, which helps to make our
authentication system more secure than if a system-wide constant were used.

The authenticate Method

Moving along, the two-line authenticate method serves as a good example of a class
method for your application code. It is a generic bit of class logic, not associated with
any particular instance. However, its implementation might be somewhat dense and
cryptic unless you know Ruby really well. I'll try to dissect it for you.

```
# Authenticates a user by their login name and unencrypted password,
# returning the user or nil.
def self.authenticate(login, password)
  u = find_by_login(login) # need to get the salt
  u && u.authenticated?(password) ? u : nil
end
```

The first line attempts to find a user record using the login value supplied. If the
record does not exist, the finder will return nil, which will be assigned to u, causing
the && expression on line 2 to return false.

However, if a record user *is* found, then it is time to check the password. Rick's
comment succinctly says: "need to get the salt," because if we were not using a unique
salt value per user, then authentication could be done by simply querying the database
for username *and* the crypted password. Assuming that call to find_by_login
returned a user instance, the *ternary expression* on line 2 will invoke authenticated?
to determine whether to return the user instance or nil.

The `remember_token`

You know how a lot of web applications have a little check box under their login and password fields so that you don't have to authenticate manually every time? That is accomplished via a *shared secret* in the form of the `remember_token`. Whenever the `remember_me` method of `User` is invoked, an encrypted string is created to be stored as a cookie on the user's web browser. Rick's default implementation lasts two weeks before expiring, but you can change it to meet your need.

The `forget_me` method simply clears the attributes.

```
def remember_me
  self.remember_token_expires_at = 2.weeks.from_now.utc
  self.remember_token =
      encrypt("#{email}--#{remember_token_expires_at}")
  save(false)
end

def forget_me
  self.remember_token_expires_at = nil
  self.remember_token            = nil
  save(false)
end
```

NOTE

Here's a bit of Rails trivia about `save` with a Boolean argument, as seen in those last two methods. It means *save without running validations*. I call this a bit of trivia because the Rails API docs don't mention that `save` takes a Boolean argument. In fact that's because the normal implementation doesn't—*until you specify validations on your model*—meaning that the method signature of `save` changes dynamically at runtime.

The `remember_token?` method checks to see whether we have an unexpired token to check. Notice that by default it works with UTC, not local time.

```
def remember_token?
  remember_token_expires_at && (Time.now.utc <
remember_token_expires_at)
end
```

That does it for our walk-through of the `acts_as_authenticated` plugin-generated `User` model. Of course you can add additional application code to `User` to represent your own user-related business logic.

The Account Controller

Now, let's open up `app/controllers/account_controller.rb` and examine the actions that were generated for us by the plugin, in Listing 14.2.

Listing 14.2 The `AccountController` Class

```
class AccountController < ApplicationController

  # Be sure to include AuthenticationSystem in Application Controller
  # instead of here
  include AuthenticatedSystem

  # If you want "remember me" functionality, add this before_filter
  # to Application Controller
  before_filter :login_from_cookie

  # say something nice, you goof!  something sweet.
  def index
    redirect_to(:action => 'signup') unless logged_in? || User.count > 0
  end

  def login
    return unless request.post?
    self.current_user =
      User.authenticate(params[:login], params[:password])
    if current_user
      if params[:remember_me] == "1"
        self.current_user.remember_me
        cookies[:auth_token] =
          { :value => self.current_user.remember_token,
            :expires => self.current_user.remember_token_expires_at }
      end

      redirect_back_or_default(:controller => '/account',
                               :action => 'index')

  flash[:notice] = "Logged in successfully"
    end
  end

  def signup
    @user = User.new(params[:user])
    return unless request.post?
```

```
      @user.save!
      self.current_user = @user
      redirect_back_or_default(:controller => '/account',
                                  :action => 'index')
  flash[:notice] = "Thanks for signing up!"
    rescue ActiveRecord::RecordInvalid
      render :action => 'signup'
    end

  def logout
    self.current_user.forget_me if logged_in?
    cookies.delete :auth_token
    reset_session
    flash[:notice] = "You have been logged out."
    redirect_back_or_default(:controller => '/account',
                                :action => 'index')
  end
  end
```

Note the important instructions given in the comments near the top of the file. There are a couple of lines of code there that we should move to our application controller.

```
class ApplicationController < ActionController::Base
  include AuthenticatedSystem
```

First of all, we should include the `AuthenticatedSystem` module in our `ApplicationController` so that its methods are available to all the controllers in our system. The `AuthenticatedSystem` module gives us reader and writer methods in our controllers for `current_user` (as stored in the session). It also gives us a very useful `logged_in?` method. We can use these methods in the header of our application layout, for example, to display login and logout links based on whether the user is logged in or not:

```
<div id="login_message">
 <% if logged_in? -%>
  <%= "Logged in as <strong>#{current_user.name}</strong>" %> |
  <%= link_to "Logout", :controller => 'account', :action => 'logout' %>
 <% else -%>
  <%= link_to "Logout", :controller => 'account', :action => 'login' %>
 |
```

```
   <%= link_to "Signup", :controller => 'account', :action => 'signup' %>
 <% end -%>
</div>
```

This brings up a very interesting and potentially puzzling question: How is it that you can access `current_user` and `logged_in?` from the view? `Controller` methods (which these are, via the `AuthenticatedSystem` module). They should only be available from the view if they're declared as helper methods. Taking a quick look at `application.rb`, we notice that there isn't a call to `helper_method` in sight.

The answer lies near the middle of `authenticated_system.rb` in the `self.included` method:

```
# Inclusion hook to make #current_user and #logged_in?
# available as ActionView helper methods.
def self.included(base)
  base.send :helper_method, :current_user, :logged_in?
end
```

Aha! Personally, I don't like putting `included` hooks anywhere except the top of the modules because it can cause a bit of confusion if you don't see them right away.

To explain, what is happening here is that when `AuthenticatedSystem` is included into another class, this hook will be invoked in the *class context* of the object doing the inclusion, and thus the `helper_method` will happen exactly as if it had been hard-coded into the original class. A bit of metaprogramming magic? No, just proper use of Ruby's modules functionality and very much part of the Rails way.

Login from Cookie

Second, there's the optional filter that enables logging in using a browser cookie, which gives us the so-called "Remember me" functionality. For now, let's assume that we do intend to let users stay logged in to our application, so we move `before_filter` `:login_from_cookie` to `ApplicationController` also. Let's take a peek under the covers at what the `login_from_cookie` method of `AuthenticatedSystem` actually does:

```
# When called with before_filter :login_from_cookie will check for an
# :auth_token cookie and log the user back in if apropriate
def login_from_cookie
```

```
    return unless cookies[:auth_token] && !logged_in?
    user = User.find_by_remember_token(cookies[:auth_token])
    if user && user.remember_token?
      user.remember_me
      self.current_user = user
      cookies[:auth_token] = {
        :value => self.current_user.remember_token,
        :expires => self.current_user.remember_token_expires_at
      }
      flash[:notice] = "Logged in successfully"
    end
  end
```

This code reads fairly well, but let's do a quick walk-through as another example of idiomatic Ruby and Rails code, as well as usage of the `cookies` object.

The first line of the method demonstrates proper use of Ruby's optional `return` keyword, bailing out unless there is an `:auth_token` cookie and we're not already logged in. It's important to not burn too many cycles before bailing out, since this line will get executed during each request in the system.

Next step is to use the `:auth_token` from the cookie to look up the user from the database. The way that the `if` clause is structured is a very common idiom. The `&&` will short-circuit and return false if `user` is `nil`, which prevents the `NoMethodError` from occurring if `remember_token` was invoked on `nil`. You'll see this particular idiom over and over again in Rails code and you should learn to use it in your own coding.

If the condition passes, we call `remember_me` on the user object, and set it as the current user (which is effectively what accomplishes the "login"). Finally, updated cookie values are set and a "Logged in successfully" message is placed in flash storage for display to the user.

The Current User

My Java-addled brain has occasionally found lines such as `self.current_user = user` confusing. "Why on earth would we be setting the current user as an *instance variable on the controller*!?!?" The thing is that the implementation of the `current_user` reader and writer methods are more than just pedestrian *getters* and *setters!* They actually have quite a bit of logic in them, albeit written in somewhat terse Ruby code.

```
# Accesses the current user from the session.
def current_user
  @current_user ||=
  (session[:user] && User.find_by_id(session[:user])) || :false
end

# Store the given user in the session.
def current_user=(new_user)
  session[:user]=
    (new_user.nil? || new_user.is_a?(Symbol)) ? nil : new_user.id
@current_user = new_user
end
```

Wilson Says...

Apparently Rick's text editor charges him by the line.

Once you interpret that code, you might be surprised to realize that the current user's id is what's being stored in the session, never the actual user instance. Storing the id of an object and looking it up when needed rather than storing the object itself is considered a Rails best-practice, because of the problems inherent with serializing objects and having to keep them synchronized.

Additionally, the idiomatic use of ||= ensures that the current user is only read once from the database per request—after the first time, it is cached as an instance variable on the controller. By the way, new controller instances are created by the Rails dispatcher for each incoming request, so you don't have to worry about that current_user instance variable becoming a security issue.

Based on experience, I can tell you that the current_user method returning :false when nobody is logged in is a pain in the butt. Think I'm being harsh? You try maintaining all the if logged_in? checks that you'll need to keep non-authenticated users from blowing up a large application with all sorts of NoMethodErrors.

One of the first things you should do to avoid that kind of pain is to override AuthenticatedSystem's version of current_user on your ApplicationController. The implementation can look mostly the same, but return a sensible GuestUser *null object* instead of :false.

```
# Accesses the current user from the session.
def current_user
  @current_user ||=
  (session[:user] && User.find_by_id(session
:user])) || GuestUser.new
end
```

Your own implementation of GuestUser will vary depending on the needs of your application. You might be inclined to mimic the interface of a real User object, except with empty attributes.

A different approach would be to give your GuestUser a method_missing callback that raises a LoginRequiredError to be rescued by the authentication system. The idea is to automatically prompt for a login before access to a given resource can continue, instead of having to code the particular case explicitly or even worse, cause a server error.

Logging In During Testing

Rick also gives us a Ruby module named AuthenticatedTestHelper that we can mix into TestUnit in our test_helper.rb file so that its methods are always available in our test cases.

```
class Test::Unit::TestCase
  include AuthenticatedTestHelper
```

The most important method in that module is login_as, which you can call from a setup method or a test case to establish a session. Pass it a User object to log in; or (this is where your user fixtures come in pretty handy), login_as knows to reference the user fixtures (test/fixtures/users.yml) when you pass it a symbol instead:

```
def setup
  login_as(:quentin) # quentin was added by acts_as_authenticated
```

AuthenticatedTestHelper also gives you a method named authorize_as that simulates HTTP basic authentication, instead of simply assigning the user you identify as the `current_user` for the session. You can use `authorize_as` to test controller actions that will be serving web services and other users that will authenticate via HTTP, instead of logging in via a form.

Finally, the `assert_requires_login` and `assert_http_authentication_required` test helper methods take blocks and allow you to verify that given controller actions actually force the user to log in or use basic authentication.

Conclusion

Almost every Rails application needs some sort of login and access control functionality. That's why it's so convenient to learn how to use the Acts as Authenticated plugin, the main subject of this chapter. In addition to the plugin's code generator and user class, we also looked at the account controller it generates, how to log in from a cookie, and how to access the current user from the rest of our application code.

References

1. Rick's website is http://techno-weenie.net/.

CHAPTER 15

XML and `ActiveResource`

Structure is nothing if it is all you got. Skeletons spook people if they try to walk
around on their own. I really wonder why XML does not.
—Erik Naggum

XML doesn't get much respect from the Rails community. It's "enterprisey." In the
Ruby world, that other markup language, YAML (Yet Another Markup Language),
gets a heck of a lot more attention. However, use of XML is a fact of life for many
applications, especially when it comes to interoperability with other systems. Luckily,
Ruby on Rails gives us some pretty good functionality-related to XML.

This chapter examines how to both generate and parse XML in your Rails applications, starting with a thorough examination of the to_xml method that all objects
have in Rails.

The `to_xml` Method

Sometimes you just want an XML representation of an object, and `ActiveRecord`
models provide easy, automatic XML generation via the to_xml method. Let's play
with this method in the console and see what it can do.

I'll fire up the console for my book-authoring sample application and find an
`ActiveRecord` object to manipulate.

```
>> Book.find(:first)
=> #<Book:0x264ebf4 @attributes={"name"=>"Professional Ruby on Rails
Developer's Guide", "uri"=>nil, "updated_at"=>2007-07-02T13:58:19-
```

```
05:00, "text"=>nil, "created_by"=>nil, "type"=>"Book", "id"=>"1",
"updated_by"=>nil, "version"=>nil, "parent_id"=>nil, "position"=>nil,
"state"=>nil, "created_at"=>2007-07-02T13:58:19-05:00}>
```

There we go, a `Book` instance. Let's see that instance as its generic XML representation.

```
>> Book.find(:first).to_xml
=> "<?xml version=\"1.0\" encoding=\"UTF-8\"?>\n<book>\n  <created-at
type=\"datetime\">2007-07-02T13:58:19-05:00</created-at>\n  <created-by
type=\"integer\">\n  </created-by>\n  <id type=\"integer\">\n1  </id>\n
<name>Professional Ruby on Rails Developer's Guide</name>\n  <parent-id
type=\"integer\">\n  </parent-id>\n  <position type=\"integer\">\n
</position>\n  <state></state>\n  <text>Empty</text>\n  <updated-at
type=\"datetime\">2007-07-02T13:58:19-05:00</updated-at>\n  <updated-by
type=\"integer\">\n  </updated-by>\n  <uri></uri>\n  <version
type=\"integer\">\n  </version>\n</book>\n"
```

Ugh, that's ugly. Ruby's `print` function might help us out here.

```
>> print Book.find(:first).to_xml
<?xml version="1.0" encoding="UTF-8"?>
<book>
  <created-at type="datetime">2007-07-02T13:58:19-05:00</created-at>
  <created-by type="integer"></created-by>
  <id type="integer">1</id>
  <name>Professional Ruby on Rails Developer's Guide</name>
  <parent-id type="integer"></parent-id>
  <position type="integer"></position>
  <state></state>
  <text>Empty</text>
  <updated-at type="datetime">2007-07-02T13:58:19-05:00</updated-at>
  <updated-by type="integer"></updated-by>
  <uri></uri>
  <version type="integer">
  </version>
</book>
```

Much better! So what do we have here? Looks like a fairly straightforward serialized representation of our `Book` instance in XML.

Customizing to_xml Output

The standard processing instruction is at the top, followed by a tag name corresponding to the class name of the object. The properties are represented as subelements, with nonstring data fields including a type attribute. Mind you, this is the default behavior and we can customize it with some additional parameters to the to_xml method.

We'll strip down that XML representation of a book to just a name and URI using the only parameter. It's provided in a familiar options hash, with the value of the :only parameter as an array:

```
>> print Book.find(:first).to_xml(:only => [:name,:uri])
<?xml version="1.0" encoding="UTF-8"?>
<book>
  <name>Professional Ruby on Rails Developer's Guide</name>
  <uri></uri>
</book>
```

Following the familiar Rails convention, the only parameter is complemented by its inverse, except, which will exclude the specified properties.

What if I want my book title and URI as a snippet of XML that will be included in another document? Then let's get rid of that pesky instruction too, using the skip_instruct parameter.

```
>> print Book.find(:first).to_xml(:skip_instruct => true, :only =>
[:name,:uri])
<book>
  <name>Professional Ruby on Rails Developer's Guide</name>
  <uri></uri>
</book>
```

We can change the root element in our XML representation of Book and the indenting from two to four spaces by using the root and indent parameters respectively.

```
>> print Book.find(:first).to_xml(:root => 'textbook', :indent => 4)

<?xml version="1.0" encoding="UTF-8"?>
<textbook>
    <created-at type="datetime">2007-07-02T13:58:19-05:00</created-at>
    <created-by type="integer"></created-by>
```

```
    <id type="integer">1</id>
    <name>Professional Ruby on Rails Developer's Guide</name>
    <parent-id type="integer"></parent-id>
    <position type="integer"></position>
    <state></state>
    <text>Empty</text>
    <updated-at type="datetime">2007-07-02T13:58:19-05:00</updated-at>
    <updated-by type="integer"></updated-by>
    <uri></uri>
    <version type="integer">
    </version>
</textbook>
```

By default Rails converts CamelCase and underscore attribute names to dashes as in created-at and parent-id. You can force underscore attribute names by setting the dasherize parameter to false.

```
>> print Book.find(:first).to_xml(:dasherize => false, :only =>
[:created_at,:created_by])

<?xml version="1.0" encoding="UTF-8"?>
<book>
  <created_at type="datetime">2007-07-02T13:58:19-05:00</created_at>
  <created_by type="integer"></created_by>
</book>
```

In the preceding output, the attribute type is included. This too can be configured using the skip_types parameter.

```
>> print Book.find(:first).to_xml(:skip_types => true, :only =>
[:created_at,:created_by])

<?xml version="1.0" encoding="UTF-8"?>
<book>
  <created-at>2007-07-02T13:58:19-05:00</created-at>
  <created-by></created-by>
</book>
```

Associations and `to_xml`

So far we've only worked with a base `ActiveRecord` and not with any of its associations. What if we wanted an XML representation of not just a book but also its associated chapters? Rails provides the `:include` parameter for just this purpose. The `:include` parameter will also take an array or associations to represent in XML.

```
>> print Book.find(:first).to_xml(:include => :chapters)
<?xml version="1.0" encoding="UTF-8"?>
<book>
  <created-at type="datetime">2007-07-02T13:58:19-05:00</created-at>
  <created-by type="integer"></created-by>
  <id type="integer">1</id>
  <name>Professional Ruby on Rails Developer's Guide</name>
  <parent-id type="integer"></parent-id>
  <position type="integer"></position>
  <state></state>
  <text>Empty</text>
  <updated-at type="datetime">2007-07-02T13:58:19-05:00</updated-at>
  <updated-by type="integer"></updated-by>
  <uri></uri>
  <version type="integer">
  </version>
  <chapters>
    <chapter>
      <name>Introduction</name>
      <uri></uri>
    </chapter>
    <chapter>
      <name>Your Rails Decision</name>
      <uri></uri>
    </chapter>
  </chapters>
</book>
```

The `to_xml` method will also work on any array so long as each element in that array responds to `to_xml`. If we try to call `to_xml` on an array whose elements don't respond to `to_xml`, we get this result:

```
>> [:cat,:dog,:ferret].to_xml
RuntimeError: Not all elements respond to to_xml
        from /activesupport/lib/active_support/core_ext/array/
```

```
conversions.rb:48:in `to_xml'
from (irb):6
```

Unlike arrays, Ruby hashes are naturally representable in XML, with keys corresponding to tag names, and their values corresponding to tag contents. Rails automatically calls to_s on the values to get string values for them.

```
>> print ({:pet => 'cat'}.to_xml)
<?xml version="1.0" encoding="UTF-8"?>
<hash>
  <pet>cat</pet>
</hash>
```

Both Array and Hash objects take the same to_xml method arguments, except :include.

Advanced to_xml

By default, ActiveRecord's to_xml method only serializes persistent attributes into XML. However, there are times when transient, derived, or calculated values need to be serialized out into XML form as well. For example, our Book model could have a method that gives the average pages per chapter.

```
class Book < ActiveRecord::Base

  def pages_per_chapter
    self.pages / self.chapters.length
  end

end
```

To include the result of this method when we serialize the XML, we use the :methods parameter:

```
>> print Book.find(:first).to_xml(:methods => :pages_per_chapter)
<?xml version="1.0" encoding="UTF-8"?>
<book>
  <created-at type="datetime">2007-07-02T13:58:19-05:00</created-at>
  <created-by type="integer"></created-by>
  <id type="integer">1</id>
  <name>Professional Ruby on Rails Developer's Guide</name>
```

```
    <parent-id type="integer"></parent-id>
    <position type="integer"></position>
    <state></state>
    <text>Empty</text>
    <updated-at type="datetime">2007-07-02T13:58:19-05:00</updated-at>
    <updated-by type="integer"></updated-by>
    <uri></uri>
    <version type="integer"></version>
    <pages-per-chapter>45</pages-per-chapter>
</book>
```

We could also set the `methods` parameter to an array of method names to be called.

Dynamic Runtime Attributes

In cases where we want to include extra elements unrelated to the object being serialized, we can use the `:procs` option. Just pass one or more `Proc` instances. They will be called with `to_xml`'s option hash, through which we access the underlying `XmlBuilder`. (`XmlBuilder` provides the principal means of XML generation in Rails, and is covered later in this chapter in the section "The XML Builder.")

```
>> copyright = Proc.new {|opts|
opts[:builder].tag!('copyright','2007')}

>> print Book.find(:first).to_xml(:procs => [copyright])

<?xml version="1.0" encoding="UTF-8"?>
<book>
  <created-at type="datetime">2007-07-02T13:58:19-05:00</created-at>
  <created-by type="integer"></created-by>
  <id type="integer">1</id>
  <name>Professional Ruby on Rails Developer's Guide</name>
  <parent-id type="integer"></parent-id>
  <position type="integer"></position>
  <state></state>
  <text>Empty</text>
  <updated-at type="datetime">2007-07-02T13:58:19-05:00</updated-at>
  <updated-by type="integer"></updated-by>
  <uri></uri>
  <version type="integer"></version>
  <color>blue</color >
</book>
```

Unfortunately, the :procs technique is hobbled by a puzzling limitation: The record being serialized is not exposed to the procs being passed in as arguments, so only data external to the object may be added in this fashion.

To gain complete control over the XML serialization of Rails objects, you need to override the to_xml method and implement it yourself.

Overriding `to_xml`

Sometimes you need to do something out of the ordinary when trying to represent data in XML form. In those situations you can create the XML by hand.

```
class Book < ActiveRecord::Base

  def to_xml(options = {})
    xml = options[:builder] ||= Builder::XmlMarkup.new(options)
    xml.instruct! unless options[:skip_instruct]
    xml.book do
      xml.tag!(:color, 'red')
    end
  end
  ...
end
```

This would give the following result:

```
>> print Book.find(:first).to_xml
<?xml version="1.0" encoding="UTF-8"?><book><color>red</color></book>
```

Learning from `Array`'s `to_xml` Method

Array's to_xml method is a good example of the power and elegance possible when programming with Ruby. Let's take a look at the code, which exists as part of Rails extensions to Ruby's Array class, located in the ActiveSupport's core_ext/array/conversions.rb.

```
def to_xml(options = {})
  raise "Not all elements respond to to_xml" unless all? { |e|
    e.respond_to? :to_xml }
```

See how close the first line is to English? The way that the to_xml method checks the elements of the array is a beautiful example of the readability achievable when programming in Ruby and the level of elegance you should be shooting for in your own code.

Moving on, we see how Rails figures out what to name the container tag.

```
options[:root]||= all? { |e|
  e.is_a?(first.class) && first.class.to_s != "Hash" } ?
  first.class.to_s.underscore.pluralize : "records"
```

First of all, the short-circuiting OR assignment ||= either uses the provided value for options[:root] or calculates it. This style of conditional assignment is a very common idiom in Ruby code and one you should get accustomed to using. If options[:root] is nil, a bit of logic takes place, starting with a check to see if all of the elements are instances of the same class (and that those instances are not hashes).

If that condition is true, that is, if all the elements are of the same type as the first element of the array, then the following expression generates our container tag name: first.class.to_s.underscore.pluralize.

Otherwise, the container tag will default to the constant "records", a fact that is not mentioned in the Rails API documentation. When I was looking through this code, I asked myself, "What does that first variable refer to?"

Then I remembered that this code executes in the context of an Array instance, so first is actually a method call that returns the first element of the array.

Cool. Let's move ahead to the next line of the to_xml method, which governs the name used for the tags of the array's elements: options[:children] ||= options[:root].singularize.

That was easy. Unless it's configured explicitly, Rails will simply use the singular inflection of the container tag. One of the first things we learn in the Rails world is how ActiveRecord automatically figures out plural and singular forms in relation to class names and database tables. What many of us don't usually realize until much later is the importance of the Inflector class and how widely it is used in the rest of the Rails codebase. Hopefully this walk-through is reinforcing the importance of cooperating with the Rails Inflector instead of working against it by configuring names manually.

What about the indentation? It defaults to two spaces: options[:indent] ||= 2.

Now things start getting a little more interesting. As we can see in the next line, the `to_xml` method uses `Builder::XmlMarkup` to do its XML generation.

```
options[:builder]  ||=
  Builder::XmlMarkup.new(:indent => options[:indent])
```

The `:builder` option allows us to pass in an existing `Builder` instance instead of using a new one, and the importance of this option will become clearer later on in the chapter when we discuss how to integrate the use of the `to_xml` method into more specialized XML generation routines.

```
root = options.delete(:root).to_s
children = options.delete(:children)
```

We're going to need those values for root and children tag names, so we capture them at the same time that we remove them from the options hash. This is our first hint that the options hash is going to get reused for another call (when it comes time to generate XML for our child elements).

```
if !options.has_key?(:dasherize) || options[:dasherize]
  root = root.dasherize
end
```

The `:dasherize` option defaults to `true`, which makes sense since conventions in the XML world dictate that compound tag names are delimited by dashes. It's hard to overemphasize how much of Rails' code elegance comes from the way that its libraries build on each other, as demonstrated by this use of the whimsically named `dasherize`.

Moving on, we come to our `:instruct` parameter, discussed earlier in the chapter. `Builder` has an `instruct!` method, which causes the XML instruction line to be inserted. Of course, once it's inserted, we don't want to insert it again, which is why the options hash that we will use recursively now gets its `:skip_instruct` parameter hard-coded to `true`.

```
options[:builder].instruct! unless options.delete(:skip_instruct)
opts = options.merge({:skip_instruct => true, :root => children })
```

Finally, we invoke `tag!` on our XML builder to actually write the container XML, followed immediately by a recursive call (via the `each` method) that calls `to_xml` on our child elements.

```
    options[:builder].tag!(root) { each { |e| e.to_xml(opts) } }
  end
```

The XML Builder

As introduced in the previous section, `Builder::XmlMarkup` is the class used internally by Rails when it needs to generate XML. When `to_xml` is not enough and you need to generate custom XML, you will use `Builder` instances directly. Fortunately, the Builder API is one of the most powerful Ruby libraries available and is very easy to use, once you get the hang of it.

The API documentation says: "All (well, almost all) methods sent to an `XmlMarkup` object will be translated to the equivalent XML markup. Any method with a block will be treated as an XML markup tag with nested markup in the block."

That is actually a very concise way of describing how `Builder` works, but it is easier to understand with some examples, again taken from `Builder`'s API documentation. The `xm` variable is a `Builder::XmlMarkup` instance:

```
xm.em("emphasized")              # => <em>emphasized</em>
xm.em { xm.b("emp & bold") }     # => <em><b>emph &amp; bold</b></em>

xm.a("foo", "href"=>"http://foo.org")
                                 # => <a href="http://foo.org">foo</a>

xm.div { br }                    # => <div><br/></div>

xm.target("name"=>"foo", "option"=>"bar")
                                 # => <target option="foo" name="bar"\>

xm.instruct!                     # <?xml version="1.0" encoding="UTF-8"?>

xm.html {                        # <html>
  xm.head {                      #   <head>
    xm.title("History")          #     <title>History</title>
  }                              #   </head>
```

```
  xm.body {                          #    <body>
    xm.comment! "HI"                 #      <!-- HI -->
    xm.h1("Header")                  #      <h1>Header</h1>
    xm.p("paragraph")                #      <p>paragraph</p>
  }                                  #    </body>
}                                    #  </html>
```

A common use for using `Builder::XmlBuilder` is to render XML in response to a request. Previously we talked about overriding `to_xml` on `ActiveRecord` to generate our custom XML. Another way, though not as recommended, is to use an XML template.

We could alter our `BooksController` show method to use an XML template by changing it from

```
def BooksController < ApplicationController
  ...
  def show
    @book = Book.find(params[:id])
    respond_to do |format|
    format.html
    format.xml { render :xml => @book.to_xml }
  end
  ...
end
```

to:

```
def BooksController < ApplicationController
  ...
  def show
    @book = Book.find(params[:id])
    respond_to do |format|
    format.html
    format.xml
  end
  ...
end
```

Now Rails will look for a file called `show.xml.builder` in the `RAILS_ROOT/views/books` directory. That file contains `Builder::XmlMarkup` code like this:

```
xml.book {
  xml.title @book.title
  xml.chapters {
    @book.chapters.each { |chapter|
      xml.chapter {
        xml.title chapter.title
      }
    }
  }
}
```

In this view the variable `xml` is an instance of `Builder::XmlMarkup`. Just as in ERb views, we have access to the instance variables we set in our controller, in this case `@book`. Using the `Builder` in a view can provide a convenient way to generate XML.

Parsing XML

Ruby has a full-featured XML library named REXML, and covering it in any level of detail is outside the scope of this book. If you have basic parsing needs, such as parsing responses from web services, you can use the simple XML parsing capability built into Rails.

Turning XML into Hashes

Rails lets you turn arbitrary snippets of XML markup into Ruby hashes, with the `from_xml` method that it adds to the `Hash` class.

To demonstrate, I'll throw together a string of simplistic XML and turn it into a hash:

```
>> xml = <<-XML
<pets>
  <cat>Franzi</cat>
  <dog>Susie</dog>
  <horse>Red</horse>
</pets>
XML

>> Hash.from_xml(xml)
=> {"pets"=>{"horse"=>"Red", "cat"=>"Franzi", "dog"=>"Susie"}}
```

There are no options for from_xml. You can leave off the argument, pass it a string of XML, or pass it an IO object. If you pass nothing, the from_xml method looks for a file named *scriptname*.xml (or more correctly $0.xml). This isn't immediately useful in Rails, but can be handy if you use this functionality in your own scripts outside of Rails HTTP request handling.

A more common use is to pass a string into from_xml as in the preceding example or to pass it an IO object. This is particularly useful when parsing an XML file.

```
>> Hash.from_xml(File.new('pets.xml')
=> {"pets"=>{"horse"=>"Red", "cat"=>"Franzi", "dog"=>"Susie"}}
```

XmlSimple

Under the covers, Rails uses a library called XmlSimple to parse XML into a Hash.

```
class Hash

  ...

  def from_xml(xml)
    typecast_xml_value(undasherize_keys(XmlSimple.xml_in(xml,
          'keeproot'     => true,
          'forcearray'   => false,
          'forcecontent' => true,
          'contentkey'   => '__content__')
      ))
  end
  ...
end
```

Rails sets four parameters when using XmlSimple. The first parameter, :keeproot, tells XmlSimple not to discard the root element, which it would otherwise do by default.

```
>> XmlSimple.xml_in('<book title="The Rails Way" />', :keeproot =>
true)
=> { 'book' => [{'title' => 'The Rails Way'}]

>> XmlSimple.xml_in('<book title="The Rails Way" />', :keeproot =>
false)
=> {'title' => 'The Rails Way'}
```

The second parameter Rails sets is :forcearray, which forces nested elements to be represented as arrays even if there is only one. XmlSimple's default is to set this to true. The difference is shown in the following example:

```
>> XmlSimple.xml_in('<book><chapter index="1"/></book>', :forcearray =>
true)
=> {"chapter"=>[{"index"=>"1"}]}

>> XmlSimple.xml_in('<book><chapter index="1"/></book>', :forcearray =>
false)
=> {"chapter" => {"index"=> "1"}}
```

The third parameter that's set to true is :forcecontent, which ensures that a content key-value pair is added to the resulting hash even if the element being parsed has no content or attributes. By setting this parameter to true, sibling elements are normalized, which makes the resulting hash a heck of a lot more usable, as you should be able to deduce from the following snippet.

```
>> XmlSimple.xml_in('<book>
                        <chapter index="1">Words</chapter>
                        <chapter>Numbers</chapter>
                     </book>', :forcecontent => true)

=> {"chapter" => [{"content"=>"Words", "index"=>"1"},
{"content"=>"Numbers"}]}

>> XmlSimple.xml_in('<book>
                        <chapter index="1">Words</chapter>
                        <chapter>Numbers</chapter>
                     </book>', :forcecontent => false)

=> {"chapter" => [{"content"=>"Words", "index"=>"1"}, "Numbers"]}
```

The final parameter is :contentkey. XmlSimple by default uses the key string '"content" to represent the data contained within an element. Rails changes it to "__content__" to lessen the likelihood of name clashes with actual XML tags named "content".

Typecasting

When we use `Hash.from_xml`, the resulting hash doesn't have any "`__content__`" keys. What happened to them? Rails doesn't pass the result of `XmlSimple` parsing directly back to the caller of `from_xml`. Instead it sends it through a method called `typecast_xml_value`, which converts the string values into proper types. This is done by using a `type` attribute in the XML elements. For example, here's the auto-generated XML for a `Book` object.

```
>> print Book.find(:first).to_xml
<?xml version="1.0" encoding="UTF-8"?>
<book>
  <created-at type="datetime">2007-07-02T13:58:19-05:00</created-at>
  <created-by type="integer"></created-by>
  <id type="integer">1</id>
  <name>Professional Ruby on Rails Developer's Guide</name>
  <parent-id type="integer"></parent-id>
  <position type="integer"></position>
  <state></state>
  <text>Empty</text>
  <updated-at type="datetime">2007-07-02T13:58:19-05:00</updated-at>
  <updated-by type="integer"></updated-by>
  <uri></uri>
  <version type="integer">
  </version>
</book>
```

As part of the `to_xml` method, Rails sets attributes called `type` that identify the class of the value being serialized. If we take this XML and feed it to the `from_xml` method, Rails will typecast the strings to their corresponding Ruby objects:

```
>> Hash.from_xml(Book.find(:first).to_xml)
=> {"book"=>{"name"=>"Professional Ruby on Rails Developer's Guide",
"uri"=>nil, "updated_at"=>Mon Jul 02 18:58:19 UTC 2007,
"text"=>"Empty", "created_by"=>nil, "id"=>1, "updated_by"=>nil,
 "version"=>0, "parent_id"=>nil, "position"=>nil, "created_at"=>Mon Jul
02 18:58:19 UTC 2007, "state"=>nil}}
```

ActiveResource

Web applications often need to serve both users in front of web browsers and other systems via some API. Other languages accomplish this using SOAP or some form of XML-RPC, but Rails takes a simpler approach. In Chapter 4, "REST, Resources, and Rails," we talked about building RESTful controllers and using `respond_to` to return different representations of resources. By doing so we could connect to http://localhost:3000/auctions.xml and get back an XML representation of all auctions in the system. We can now write a client to consume this data using `ActiveResource`.

`ActiveResource` is a standard part of the Rails package, having replaced `ActionWebService` (which is still available as a plugin). `ActiveResource` has complete understanding of RESTful routing and XML representation. A minimal `ActiveResource` for the previous auctions example is

```
class Auction < ActiveResource::Base
  self.site = 'http://localhost:3000'
end
```

To get a list of auctions we would call its `find` method:

```
>> auctions = Auction.find(:all)
```

`ActiveResource` is designed to look and feel much like `ActiveRecord`.

Find

`ActiveResource` has the same `find` methods as `ActiveRecord`, as seen in Table 15.1. The only difference is the use of `:params` instead of `:conditions`.

Table 15.1 Find methods for `ActiveResource`

ActiveRecord	**ActiveResource**	URL
Auction.find(:all)	Auction.find(:all)	GET http://localhost:3000/auctions.xml
Auction.find(1)	Auction.find(1)	GET http://localhost:3000/auctions/1.xml
Auction.find(:first)	Auction.find(:first)	GET http://localhost:3000/auctions.xml *gets a complete list than calls first on the returned list

continues

Table 15.1 Continued

ActiveRecord	**ActiveResource**	URL
`Auction.find(:all,` `:conditions =>` `{ :first_name =>` `'Matt')`	`Auction.find(:all,` `:params =>` `{ :first_name =>` `'Matt')`	GET http://localhost:3000/ auctions.xml?first_name=Matt
`Item.find(:all,` `:conditions =>` `{ :auction_id =>` `6 })`	`Item.find(:all,` `:params =>` `{ :auction_id =>` `6 })`	GET http://localhost:3000/ auctions/6/items.xml
`Item.find(:all,` `:conditions =>` `{ :auction_id =>` `6, :used => true })`	`Item.find(:all,` `:params =>` `{ :auction_id =>` `6, :used => true })`	GET http://localhost:3000/auctions/ 6/items.xml?used=true

The last two examples in Table 15.1 show how to use `ActiveResource` with a nested resource. We could also create a custom `used` method in our `items` controller like this:

```
class ItemController < ActiveResource::Base

  def used
    @items = Item.find(:all,
                :conditions => {:auction_id => params[:auction_id],
                                :used => true })

    respond_to do |format|
      format.html
      format.xml { render :xml => @items.to_xml }
    end
  end
end
```

In our `routes.rb` file we would add to our `items` resource like this:

```
map.resources :items, :member => {:used => :get }
```

With this in place we now have the following URL:

```
http://localhost:3000/auctions/6/items/used.xml
```

We can now access this URL and the data behind it using `ActiveResource` with the following call:

```
>> used_items = Item.find(:all, :from => :used)
```

This custom method returns a collection of items and hence the `:all` parameter. Suppose we had a custom method that returned only the newest item, as in the following example:

```
class ItemController < ActiveResource::Base

  def newest
    @item = Item.find(:first,
                :conditions => {:auction_id => params[:auction_id]},
                :order => 'created_at DESC',
                :limit => 1)

    respond_to do |format|
      format.html
      format.xml { render :xml => @items.to_xml }
    end
  end
end
```

We could then make the following call:

```
>> used_items = Item.find(:one, :from => :newest)
```

What's important to note is how a request to a nonexistent item is handled. If we tried to access an item with an id of `-1` (there isn't any such item), we would get an HTTP 404 status code back. This is exactly what `ActiveResource` receives and raises a `ResourceNotFound` exception. `ActiveResource` makes heavy use of the HTTP status codes as we'll see throughout this chapter.

Create

`ActiveResource` is not limited to just retrieving data; it can also create it. If we wanted to place a new bid on an item via `ActiveResource`, we would do the following:

```
>> Bid.create(:username => 'me', :auction_id => 3, :item_id => 6,
:amount => 34.50)
```

This would create an HTTP POST to the URL: http://localhost:3000/auctions/6/items/6.xml with the supplied data. In our controller, the following would exist:

```
class BidController < ActiveResource::Base
  ...
  def create
    @bid = Bid.new(params[:bid])
    respond_to do |format|
      if @bid.save
        flash[:notice] = 'Bid was successfully created.'
        format.html { redirect_to(@bid) }
        format.xml  { render :xml => @bid, :status => :created,
:location => @bid }
      else
        format.html { render :action => "new" }
        format.xml  { render :xml => @bid.errors, :status =>
:unprocessable_entity}
      end
    end
  end
  ...
end
```

If the bid is successfully created, the newly created bid is returned with an HTTP 201 status code and the Location header is set pointing to the location of the newly created bid. With the Location header set, we can determine what the newly created bid's `id` is. For example:

```
>> bid = Bid.create(:username => 'me', :auction_id => 3, :item_id =>
6, :amount => 34.50)
>> bid.id # => 12
>> bid.new? # => false
```

If we tried to create the preceding bid again but without a dollar amount, we could interrogate the errors.

```
>> bid = Bid.create(:username => 'me', :auction_id => 3, :item_id => 6)
>> bid.valid? # => false
>> bid.id # => nil
>> bid.new? # => true
>> bid.errors.class # => ActiveResource::Errors
>> bid.errors.size # => 1
>> bid.errors.on_base # => "Amount can't be blank"
>> bid.errors.full_messages # => "Amount can't be blank"
>> bid.errors.on(:amount) # => nil
```

In this case a new `Bid` object is returned from the `create` method, but it's not valid. If we try to see what its `id` is we also get a nil. We can see what caused the `create` to fail by calling the `ActiveResources.errors` method. This method behaves just like `ActiveRecord.error` with one important exception. On `ActiveRecord` if we called `Errors.on`, we would get the error for that attribute. In the preceding example, we got a nil instead. The reason is that `ActiveResource`, unlike `ActiveRecord`, doesn't know what attributes there are. `ActiveRecord` does a SHOW FIELDS FROM <table> to get this, but `ActiveResource` has no equivalent. The only way `ActiveResource` knows an attribute exists is if we tell it. For example:

```
>> bid = Bid.create(:username => 'me', :auction_id => 3, :item_id =>
6, :amount => nil)
>> bid.valid? # => false
>> bid.id # => nil
>> bid.new? # => true
>> bid.errors.class # => ActiveResource::Errors
>> bid.errors.size # => 1
>> bid.errors.on_base # => "Amount can't be blank"
>> bid.errors.full_messages # => "Amount can't be blank"
>> bid.errors.on(:amount) # => "can't be blank"
```

In this case we told `ActiveResource` that there is a title attribute through the `create` method. As a result we can now call `Errors.on` without a problem.

Update

Editing an ActiveResource follows the same ActiveRecord pattern.

```
>> bid = Bid.find(1)
>> bid.amount # => 10.50
>> bid.amount = 15.00
>> bid.save # => true
>> bid.reload
>> bid.amount # => 15.00
```

If we set the amount to nil, ActiveResource.save would return false. In this case we could interrogate ActiveResource::Errors for the reason, just as we would with create. An important difference between ActiveResource and ActiveRecord is the absence of the save! and update! methods.

Delete

Removing an ActiveResource can happen in two ways. The first is without instantiating the ActiveResource:

```
>> Bid.delete(1)
```

The other way requires instantiating the ActiveResource first:

```
>> bid = Bid.find(1)
>> bid.destroyAuthorization
```

ActiveResource comes with support for HTTP Basic Authentication. As a quick reminder, Basic Authentication is accomplished by setting an HTTP header, and as such can be easily snooped. For this reason, an HTTPS connection should be used. With a secure connection in place, ActiveResource just needs a username and password to connect.

```
Class MoneyTransfer < ActiveResource::Base
  self.site = 'https://localhost:3000'
  self.username = 'administrator'
  self.password = 'secret'
end
```

ActiveResource will now authenticate on each connection. If the username and/or password is invalid, an ActiveResource::ClientError is generated. We can implement Basic Authentication in our controller using a plugin.

```
$ ./script/plugin install http_authentication
```

Next we need to set up our controller:

```
class MoneyTransferController < ApplicationController
  USERNAME, PASSWORD = "administrator", "secret"

  before_filter :authenticate

  ...
  def create
    @money_transfer = Bid.new(params[:money_transfer])
    respond_to do |format|
      if @ money_transfer.save
        flash[:notice] = 'Money Transfer was successfully created.'
        format.html { redirect_to(@money_transfer) }
        format.xml  { render :xml => @ money_transfer, :status =>
:created, :location => @ money_transfer }
      else
        format.html { render :action => "new" }
        format.xml  { render :xml => @ money_transfer.errors, :status
=> :unprocessable_entity}
      end
    end
  end
  ...

  private
    def authenticate
      authenticate_or_request_with_http_basic do |username, password|
        username == USERNAME && password == PASSWORD
      end
    end
end
```

Headers

`ActiveResource` allows for the setting of HTTP headers on each request too. This can be done in two ways. The first is to set it as a variable:

```
Class Auctions< ActiveResource::Base
  self.site = 'http://localhost:3000'

  @headers = { 'x-flavor' => 'orange' }
end
```

This will cause every connection to the site to include the HTTP header: HTTP-X-FLAVOR: orange. In our controller we could use the header value.

```
class AuctionController < ActiveResource::Base
  ...
  def show
      @auction = Auction.find_by_id_and_flavor(params[:bid],
request.headers['HTTP_X_FLAVOR'])    respond_to do |format|
      format.html
      format.xml { render :xml => @auction.to_xml }
    end
  end
  ...
end
```

The second way to set the headers for an `ActiveResource` is to override the headers method.

```
Class Auctions< ActiveResource::Base
  self.site = 'http://localhost:3000'

  def headers
    { 'x-flavor' => 'orange' }
  end
end
```

Customizing

`ActiveResource` assumes RESTful URLs, but that doesn't always happen. Fortunately, you can customize the URL prefix and `collection_name`. Suppose we assume the following `ActiveResource`:

```
Class OldAuctionSystem < ActiveResource::Base
  self.site = 'http://s60:3270'

  self.prefix = '/cics/'
  self.collection_name = 'auction_pool'
end
```

The following URLs will be used:

`OldAuctionSystem.find(:all)` GET http://s60:3270/cics/auction_pool.xml
`OldAuctionSystem.find(1)` GET http://s60:3270/cics/auction_pool/1.xml
`OldAuctionSystem.find(1).save` PUT http://s60:3270/cics/auction_pool/1.xml
`OldAuctionSystem.delete(1)` DELETE http://s60:3270/cics/auction_pool/1.xml
`OldAuctionSystem.create(...)` POST http://s60:3270/cics/auction_pool.xml

We could also change the element name used to generate XML. In the preceding `ActiveResource`, a `create` of an `OldAuctionSystem` would look like the following in XML:

```
<?xml version=\"1.0\" encoding=\"UTF-8\"?>
  <OldAuctionSystem>
    <title>Auction A</title>
    ...
  </OldAuctionSystem>
```

The element name can be changed with the following:

```
Class OldAuctionSystem < ActiveResource::Base
  self.site = 'http://s60:3270'

  self.prefix = '/cics/'
  self.element_name = 'auction'
end
```

which will produce:

```
<?xml version=\"1.0\" encoding=\"UTF-8\"?>
<Auction>
  <title>Auction A</title>
  ...
</Auction>
```

One consequence of setting the `element_name` is that `ActiveResource` will use the plural form to generate URLs. In this case it would be 'auctions' and not 'OldAuctionSystems'. To do this you will need to set the `collection_name` as well.

It is also possible to set the primary key field `ActiveResource` uses with

```
Class OldAuctionSystem < ActiveResource::Base
  self.site = 'http://s60:3270'

  self.primary_key = 'guid'
end
```

Hash Forms

The methods `Find`, `Create`, `Save`, and `Delete` correspond to the HTTP methods of GET, POST, PUT, and DELETE respectively. `ActiveResource` has a method for each of these HTTP methods too. They take the same arguments as `Find`, `Create`, `Save`, and `Delete` but return a hash of the XML received. For example:

```
>> bid = Bid.find(1)
>> bid.class # => ActiveRecord::Base
>> bid_hash = Bid.get(1)
>> bid_hash.class # => Hash
```

Conclusion

In practice, the `to_xml` and `from_xml` methods meet the XML handling needs for most situations that the average Rails developer will ever encounter. Their simplicity masks a great degree of flexibility and power, and in this chapter we attempted to explain them in sufficient detail to inspire your own exploration of XML handling in the Ruby world.

As a pair, the `to_xml` and `from_xml` methods also enabled the creation of a framework that makes tying Rails applications together using RESTful web services drop-dead easy. That framework is named `ActiveResource`, and this chapter gave you a crash-course introduction to it.

CHAPTER 16

ActionMailer

It's a cool way to send emails without tons of code
— Jake Scruggs[1]

Integration with e-mail is a crucial part of most modern web application projects. Whether it's support for retrieving lost passwords or letting users control their accounts via e-mail, you'll be happy to hear that Rails offers great support for both sending and receiving e-mail, thanks to its `ActionMailer` framework.

In this chapter, we'll cover what's needed to set up your deployment to be able to send and receive mail with the `ActionMailer` framework and by writing *mailer models*, the entities in Rails that encapsulate code having to do with e-mail handling.

Setup

By default, Rails will try to send e-mail via SMTP (port 25) of localhost. If you are running Rails on a host that has an SMTP daemon running and it accepts SMTP e-mail locally, you don't have to do anything else in order to send mail. If you don't have SMTP available on localhost, you have to decide how your system will send outbound e-mail.

When not using SMTP directly, the main options are to use *sendmail* or to give Rails information on how to connect to an external mail server. Most organizations have SMTP servers available for this type of use, although it's worth noting that due to abuse many hosting providers have stopped offering shared SMTP service.

Mailer Models

Now that we have the mail system configured, we can go ahead and create a mailer model that will contain code pertaining to sending and receiving a class of e-mail. Rails provides a generator to get us started rapidly.

To demonstrate, let's create a mailer for sending late notices to users of our time-and-reporting sample application:

```
$ script/generate mailer LateNotice
      exists   app/models/
      create   app/views/late_notice
      exists   test/unit/
      create   test/fixtures/late_notice
      create   app/models/late_notice.rb
      create   test/unit/late_notice_test.rb
```

A view folder for the mailer is created at `app/views/late_notice` and the mailer itself is stubbed out at `app/models/late_notice.rb`:

```
class LateNotice < ActionMailer::Base
end
```

Kind of like a default `ActiveRecord` subclass, there's not much there at the start. What about the test? See Listing 16.1.

Listing 16.1 An `ActionMailer` Test

```
require File.dirname(__FILE__) + '/../test_helper'

class LateNoticeTest < Test::Unit::TestCase

  FIXTURES_PATH = File.dirname(__FILE__) + '/../fixtures'
  CHARSET = "utf-8"

  include ActionMailer::Quoting

  def setup
    ActionMailer::Base.delivery_method = :test
    ActionMailer::Base.perform_deliveries = true
    ActionMailer::Base.deliveries = []
```

```
    @expected = TMail::Mail.new
    @expected.set_content_type "text", "plain", { "charset" => CHARSET }
    @expected.mime_version = '1.0'
  end

  private
    def read_fixture(action)
      IO.readlines("#{FIXTURES_PATH}/late_notice/#{action}")
    end

    def encode(subject)
      quoted_printable(subject, CHARSET)
    end
end
```

Whoa! There's quite a lot more setup involved for this test than what we're used to seeing, which reflects the greater underlying complexity of working with a mail subsystem.

Preparing Outbound Email Messages

You work with `ActionMailer` classes by defining public *mailer* methods that correspond to types of e-mails that you want to send. Inside the public method, you set the options for the message and assign any variables that will be needed by the mail message template.

Continuing with our example, let's write a `late_timesheet` mailer method that takes `user` and `week_of` parameters. Notice that it sets the basic information needed to send our notice e-mail (see Listing 16.2).

Listing 16.2   A `mailer` method

```
def late_timesheet(user, week_of)
  recipients user.email
  subject "[Time and Expenses] Late timesheet notice"
  from "system@timeandexpenses.com"
  body :recipient => user.name, :week => week_of
end
```

Here is a list of all the mail-related options that you can set inside of mailer methods.

`attachment`

Specify a file attachment. Can be invoked multiple times to make multiple file attachments.

`bcc`

Specifies blind recipient (Bcc:) addresses for the message, either as a string (for a single address) or an array for multiple addresses.

`body`

Defines the body of the message. Takes a hash (in which case it specifies the variables to pass to the template when it is rendered), or a string, in which case it specifies the actual text of the message.

ActionMailer automatically *normalizes lines* for plain-text body content, that is, it ensures that lines end with \n instead of a platform-specific character.

`cc`

Specifies carbon-copy recipient (Cc:) addresses for the message, either as a string (for a single address) or an array for multiple addresses.

`charset`

The character set to use for the message. Defaults to the value of the `default_charset` setting specified for `ActionMailer::Base`.

`content_type`

Specifies the content type for the message. Defaults to `text/plain`.

`from`

Specifies the from address for the message as a string (required).

`headers`

Specifies additional headers to be added to the message as a hash.

`implicit_parts_order`

An array specifying the order in which the parts of a multipart e-mail should be sorted, based on their MIME content-type. Defaults to the value of the `default_implicit_parts_order` setting specified on `ActionMailer::Base` and defaults to ["text/html", "text/enriched", "text/plain"].

`mailer_name`

Overrides the mailer name, which defaults to an inflected version of the mailer's class name and governs the location of this mailer's templates. If you want to use a template in a nonstandard location, you can use this to specify that location.

`mime_version`

Defaults to "1.0", but may be explicitly given if needed.

`part`

Enables sending of multipart email messages by letting you define sets of content-type, template, and body variables. Note that you don't usually need to use this method, because `ActionMailer` will automatically detect and use multipart templates, where each template is named after the name of the action, followed by the content type.

On the other hand, this method is needed if you are trying to send HTML messages with inline attachments (usually image files). See the section "MultiPart Messages" a little further along in the chapter for more information, including the part method's special little API.

`recipients`

The recipient addresses for the message, either as a string (for a single address) or an array (for multiple addresses). Remember that this method expects actual address *strings* not your application's user objects.

```
recipients users.map(&:email)
```

`sent_on`

An optional explicit sent on date for the message, usually passed `Time.now`. Will be automatically set by the delivery mechanism if you don't supply a value.

`subject`

The subject line for the message.

`template`

Specifies the template name to use for the current message. Since the template defaults to the name of the mailer method, this option may be used to have multiple mailer methods share the same template.

The body of the e-mail is created by using an `ActionView` template (regular ERb) that has the content of the body hash parameter available as instance variables. So the corresponding body template for the mailer method in Listing 16.2 could look like this:

```
Dear <%= @recipient %>,

Your timesheet for the week of <%= @week %> is late.
```

And if the recipient was David, the e-mail generated would look like this:

```
Date: Sun, 12 Dec 2004 00:00:00 +0100
From: system@timeandexpenses.com
To: david@loudthinking.com
Subject: [Time and Expenses] Late timesheet notice


Dear David Hansson,

Your timesheet for the week of Aug 15th is late.
```

HTML Email Messages

To send mail as HTML, make sure your view template generates HTML and set the content type to html in your mailer method, as shown in Listing 16.3.

Listing 16.3 An HTML Mailer Method

```
class MyMailer < ActionMailer::Base

  def signup_notification(recipient)
    recipients    recipient.email_address_with_name
    subject       "New account information"
    body          "account" => recipient
    from          "system@example.com"
    content_type "text/html"
  end

end
```

Other than the different `content_type` value, the process is exactly the same as sending plaintext email. Want to *embed* images in the HTML that will go along with the email (as inline attachments) and display to the end user? At the time of this writing there is an outstanding issue with `ActionMailer` that makes it difficult to do so. See http://dev.rubyonrails.org/ticket/2179 for more information and a patch that provides a workaround.[2]

Multipart Messages

The `part` method is a small API in and of itself for creating multipart messages. Using the `part` method, you can compose email messages made up of distinct kinds of content. A popular technique (as demonstrated in Listing 16.4) uses multiparts to send a plaintext part along with an HTML email message, so that recipients who can only read plaintext are not left in the dark.

Listing 16.4 A Multipart Signup Notification Mailer Method

```
class ApplicationMailer < ActionMailer::Base

  def signup_notification(recipient)
    recipients      recipient.email_address_with_name
    subject         "New account information"
    from            "system@example.com"

    part :content_type => "text/html",
```

```
          :body => render_message("signup_as_html", :account =>
    recipient)

      part "text/plain" do |p|
        p.body = render_message("signup_as_plain", :account =>
    recipient)
        p.transfer_encoding = "base64"
      end
    end

  end
```

Part Options

The `part` method accepts a variety of options, either as a hash or via block initialization. (Both types of initialization are demonstrated in Listing 16.4.)

- `:body` Represents the body of the part, *as a string!* This *should not be a hash* (like `ActionMailer::Base`.) If you want a template to be rendered into the body of a subpart you can do it using the mailer's `render` or `render_template` methods and assign the result to this option (like in Listing 16.4).

- `:charset` Specify the charset for this subpart. By default, it will be the charset of the containing part or mailer (e.g. UTF8).

- `:content_type` The MIME content type of the part.

- `:disposition` The content disposition of this part, typically either "inline" or "attachment."

- `:filename` The filename to use for this subpart, usually attachments. The value of this option is the filename that users will see when they try to save the attachment and has nothing to do with the name of files on your server.

- `:headers` Specifying additional headers to include with this part as a hash.

- `:transfer_encoding` The transfer encoding to use for this subpart, like "base64" or "quoted-printable".

Implicit Multipart Messages

As mentioned earlier in the chapter, multipart messages can also be used implicitly, without invoking the `part` method, because `ActionMailer` will automatically detect and use multipart templates, where each template is named after the name of the action, followed by the content type. Each such detected template will be added as separate part to the message.

For example, if the following templates existed, each would be rendered and added as a separate part to the message, with the corresponding content type. The same body hash is passed to each template.

- signup_notification.text.plain.erb

- signup_notification.text.html.erb

- signup_notification.text.xml.builder

- signup_notification.text.x-yaml.erb

File Attachments

Attachments can be added by using the attachment method in conjunction with the `File.read` method of Ruby, or application code that generates file content. See Listing 16.5.

Listing 16.5   Adding Attachments to an Email

```
class ApplicationMailer < ActionMailer::Base
  def signup_notification(recipient)
    recipients      recipient.email_address_with_name
    subject         "New account information"
    from            "system@example.com"

    attachment :content_type => "image/jpeg",
      :body => File.read("an-image.jpg")

    attachment "application/pdf" do |a|
      a.body = generate_your_pdf_here()
    end
  end
end
```

```
end
```

The `attachment` method is really just a convenience wrapper around the `part` API. The first attachment of Listing 16.5 could have been done (just a little less elegantly) with the following code:

```
part :content_type => "image/jpeg",
     :disposition => "inline",
     :filename => "an-image.jpg",
     :transfer_encoding => "base64" do |attachment|
  attachment.body = File.read("an-image.jpg")
end
```

We've now talked extensively about preparing email messages for sending, but what about actually sending them to the recipients?

Actually Sending an Email

Don't ever try to actually call the instance methods like `signed_up` directly. Instead, call one of the two class methods that are generated for you based on the instance methods defined in your mailer class. Those class methods are prefixed with `deliver_` and `create_`, respectively. Really, the main one that you care about is `deliver`.

For example, if you wrote a `signed_up_notification` instance method on a class named `ApplicationMailer`, using it would look like the following example:

```
# create a tmail object for testing
ApplicationMailer.create_signed_up_notification("david@loudthinking.com")

# send the signed_up_notification email
ApplicationMailer.deliver_signed_up("david@loudthinking.com")

# wrong!
ApplicationMailer.new.signed_up("david@loudthinking.com")
```

Receiving E-Mails

`TMail` is a Ruby library for email processing that dates back to 2003. It comes bundled in Rails as an included dependency of `ActionMailer`. There's really only one

TMail class that you care about as a Rails developer, and that is the TMail::Mail class.

To receive e-mails, you need to write a public method named receive on one of your application's ActionMailer::Base subclasses. It will take a Tmail object instance as its single parameter. When there is incoming email to handle, you call a *class method* named receive on your Mailer class. The raw email string is converted into a Tmail object automatically and your receive method is invoked for further processing. You don't have to implement the receive *class* method yourself, it is inherited from ActionMailer::Base.

That's all pretty confusing to explain, but simple in practice. Listing 16.6 shows an example.

Listing 16.6   The Simple MessageArchiver Mailer Class with a Receive Method

```
class MessageArchiver < ActionMailer::Base

  def receive(email)
    person = Person.find_by_email(email.to.first)
    person.emails.create(:subject => email.subject, :body =>
email.body)
  end

end
```

The receive *class* method can be the target for a Postfix recipe or any other mail-handler process that can pipe the contents of the email to another process. The Rails runner script makes it easy to handle incoming mail:

```
./script/runner 'MessageArchiver.receive(STDIN.read)'
```

That way, when a message is received, the receive *class* method would be fed the raw string content of the incoming email via STDIN.

TMail::Mail API Reference

Since the object representation of the incoming email message is an instance of TMail::Message, I think it makes sense to have a reference to at least the basic attributes of that class that you will be using. The online documentation for all of TMail is at http://i.loveruby.net/en/projects/tmail/doc/, but the following list of methods gives you pretty much everything you need.

attachments

An array of `TMail::Attachment` objects associated with the message object. `TMail::Attachment` extends Ruby's own `StringIO` class and adds `original_filename` and `content_type` attributes to it. Other than that, you use it exactly as you would use any other `StringIO` (See Listing 16.7 for example).

body

The body text of the email message, assuming it's a plain text single-part message. Multipart messages will return the *preamble* when `body` is called.

date

A `Time` object corresponding to the value of the `Date:` header field.

has_attachments?

Returns `true` or `false` based on whether the message contains an attachment.

multipart?

Returns `true` if the message is a MIME-multipart email message.

parts

An array of `TMail::Mail` objects, one for each part of the MIME-multipart email message.

subject

The subject line of the email message.

to

An *array* of strings representing the `To:` addresses associated with the message. The `cc`, `bcc`, and `from` attributes function similarly for their respective address fields.

Handling Attachments

Processing files attached to incoming email messages is just a matter of using the `attachments` attribute of `TMail`, as in Listing 16.7. This example assumes that you have a `Person` class, with a `has_many` association to an `attachment_fu` object named `photos`.

```
class PhotoByEmail < ActionMailer::Base

  def self.receive(email)
    from = email.from.first
    person = Person.find_by_email(from)
    logger.warn("Person not found [#{from}]") and return unless person

    if email.has_attachments?
      email.attachments.each do |file|
        person.photos.create(:uploaded_data => file)
      end
    end
  end
end
```

There's not much more to it than that, except of course to wrestle with the configuration of your mail-processor (outside of Rails) since they are notoriously difficult to configure.[3] After you have your mail-processor calling the Rails runner script correctly, add a `crontab` so that incoming mail is handled about every five minutes or so, depending on the needs of your application.

Configuration

Most of the time, you don't have to configure anything specifically to get mail sending to work, because your production server will have `sendmail` installed and `ActionMailer` will happily use it to send emails.

If you don't have sendmail installed on your server, you can try setting up Rails to send email directly via SMTP. The `ActionMailer::Base` class has a hash named `smtp_settings` (`server_settings` prior to Rails 2.0) that holds configuration information. The settings here will vary depending on the SMTP server that you use.

The sample (as shown in Listing 16.7) demonstrates the SMTP server settings that are available (and their default values). You'll want to add similar code to your `config/environment.rb` file:

Listing 16.7   SMTP Settings for `ActionMailer`

```
ActionMailer::Base.smtp_settings = {
  :address => 'smtp.yourserver.com',    # default: localhost
  :port => '25',                        # default: 25
  :domain => 'yourserver.com',          # default:
localhost.localdomain
  :user_name => 'user',                 # no default
  :password => 'password',              # no default
  :authentication => :plain             # :plain, :login or :cram_md5
}
```

Conclusion

In this chapter, we learned how Rails makes sending and receiving email easy. With relatively little code, you can set up your application to send out email, even HTML email with inline graphics attachments. Receiving email is even easier, except perhaps for setting up mail-processing scripts and cron jobs. We also briefly covered the configuration settings that go in your `config/environment.rb` file related to mail.

References

1. http://jakescruggs.blogspot.com/2007/02/actionmailer-tips.html

2. Note that a Google search on the topic of inline image attachments will usually lead you to http://blog.caboo.se/articles/2006/02/19/how-to-send-multipart-alternative-e-mail-with-inline-attachments, which purports to give you an easy solution to the problem, but doesn't actually work.

3. Rob Orsini, author of O'Reilly's *Rails Cookbook* recommends getmail, which you can get from http://pyropus.ca/software/getmail.

CHAPTER 17

Testing

It's not that Rails encourages you to do test-driven development, it's that it makes it difficult for you to not do test-driven development.
—Brian Eng, interviewed on the Rails podcast

Automated tests allow us to verify the functionality of our application, prevent regression (introduction of new and previously fixed bugs), and help us to keep our code flexible. Test coverage refers to the quality and number of automated tests that we have in relation to production code. When our test coverage is deficient, there is no proof that the system works as intended. We could change something that breaks the application, and not notice the failure until much time has passed, when it will be much more difficult to diagnose and to fix.

The importance of testing your Ruby code cannot be overstated. Without a compiler, there is no way of knowing that the code you've written is even free of syntax errors! You must assume that your code is broken until you put it through its paces. Do you want that to happen on your development machine, under your control, where you can diagnose problems? Or would you rather find out about errors when your deployed application bombs the server and aggravates your bosses, colleagues, and end users? It's a serious issue.

David and everyone on the Rails core team are all true believers in high-quality automated testing and they lead the community by example: Rails itself has an extraordinary amount of test coverage. Patches, even for small fixes, are not accepted unless they are accompanied by working test cases. From the beginning, testing has been an integral and essential part of the Rails way, which sets Rails apart from the majority of other frameworks out there.

When you make a habit of driving your development with testing, you end up clarifying and elaborating your project requirements up front, instead of after your work has been through the QA department a few times. So the act of developing tests during coding is essentially a kind of specification activity. RSpec is a Ruby library that takes the concept of driving development with specifications literally, and you can use it with Rails *instead* of testing. Unfortunately, RSpec is not yet a mainstream choice for Rails developers, and since this chapter's title is "Testing," we'll hold off talking about RSpec until Chapter 18, "RSpec on Rails."

Realistically, the topics included in this chapter could fill a (large) book of their own. It's been a real challenge to organize the material in such a way that it makes sense for the majority of readers. It's also been really difficult to decide on the appropriate level of detail to include.

Since *The Rails Way* is primarily a reference work, I've tried to not to go off on too many philosophical tangents related to testing, and limit the discussion to the following topics:

- Rails testing terminology

- A review of `Test::Unit`, Ruby's unit-testing framework and how it relates to Rails

- Fixtures, for managing testing data and analysis of why everyone hates them

- Unit, functional, and integration testing with `Test::Unit`

- Rake tasks related to testing

- Acceptance testing and Selenium

Rails Testing Terminology

Before we go any further, I need to clarify something that tends to be very confusing to Rails newcomers who are familiar with unit-testing orthodoxy. The standard directories of your application's `test` folder are shown in Figure 17.1.

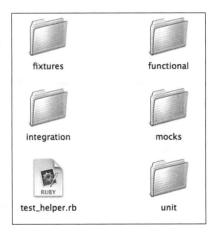

Figure 17.1   Standard directories in a Rails `test` folder

The terms *fixtures, functional, integration, mocks,* and *unit* all have their own special meanings in Rails, which are either slightly different or completely divergent from commonly accepted definitions in the greater world of software engineering. The resulting cognitive dissonance makes Rails testing one of my least favorite aspects of the overall framework.

So Much for Isolation...

Both unit and functional tests in Rails use the Fixtures API, which interacts with the database. In fact, it takes quite a bit of hacking to make unit tests in Rails *not* involve the database. Given that normal Rails tests never test isolated units of Ruby code, they can't possibly be (true) unit tests; they must all be functional tests, by traditional definitions of the term. Wait a minute—if they're all functional tests, why is there a `unit` folder? Ah, you see the conflict.

I'm afraid there isn't a particularly good defense of the chosen nomenclature. Tests that live in the `unit` folder are in fact functional tests of models that happen to be oriented toward testing of individual methods, in the traditional unit-test way. Tests that live in the `functional` folder are indeed functional tests of controllers that happen to be oriented toward testing of individual controller actions. We give both types full sections in this chapter.

Rails Mocks?

The `mocks` folder is treated specially during test runs. Classes in it are loaded last, meaning that they can override behavior of other classes in your system. That ability is particularly useful when you depend on classes that do things that shouldn't be done during a test run, such as

- Interaction with external systems, such as payment gateways, geocoders, or other web services

- Execution of forked or long-running processes

- Alteration of the state of the system in an unrecoverable way

Using Ruby's open classes, you can write your own *mock* versions of methods that you don't want to actually execute during your test run. For instance, assume that you have code that submits transactions for processing via a `PaymentGateway` class. Your production code invokes the `process` method. Unless you mock it out, whenever you run a test, a transaction will be sent to the *actual* payment gateway, which is probably bad.

However, you can solve that problem if you *monkeypatch*[1] `PaymentGateway` with your own implementation of `process`, which does not actually talk to the real payment gateway. You could add a class like the following to your `mocks` directory.

```
class PaymentGateway
  def process(transaction)
    # In ur gateway, mocking ur transactions!
  end
end
```

The concept is somewhat reminiscent of traditional test mocking, yet has nothing to do with it. (It's actually a form of *stubbing*—you are stubbing out the real functionality of the class.) Now, if you were doing a mock payment gateway this way for real, you would probably give it some state, to be able to check later that `process` was actually called.

```
class PaymentGateway
  attr :processed_transaction
```

```
  def process(transaction)
    # In ur gateway, mocking your transactions!
    @processed_transaction = transaction
  end
end
```

You see, if you didn't check to see if `process` was called, you would never know if your code is working correctly. I'm not going to go any further with this example, or with coverage of Rails mocks in this sense. As far as I'm concerned, you should delete the `mocks` directory. Nobody uses it. In fact, many of us consider this feature of Rails an abomination that should have never seen the light of day.[2]

Real Mocks and Stubs

The `Mocha` library[3] should be your choice for adding mocking to your Rails tests. It's actually included inside Rails as a dependency of Rails' own test suite. However, Mocha is a RubyGem, and you should get a copy of the latest version for yourself using the usual gem install magic:

```
sudo gem install mocha
```

Mocha provides a unified, simple, and readable syntax for both traditional mocking and for mocking with real objects. A *traditional* mock is an object that you can script with expectations about which of its methods will be called during a test. If those expectations are not met, the mock object causes the test to fail.

Mocha also gives you the ability to do *stubbing*, which is the act of overriding existing methods to return known values. It even lets you mock and stub methods on real (non-mock) classes and instances. For example, you can stub `ActiveRecord` instance methods like `find` or association accessors and reduce dependence on complicated fixture setups.

For example, here's a real example of using Mocha to mock behavior that we really don't want to *actually* trigger during a test run—that of the Google Geocoder service. Not only would it be slow, but we would never be able to run this test successfully unless we were online:

```
class SearchControllerTest < Test::Unit::TestCase

  def test_should_geolocate_zip_codes_to_return_cities_result
    res = mock('response')
```

```
    res.stubs(:lat => 40, :lng => 50)
    GoogleGeocoder.expects(:geocode).with('07601').returns(res)

    place = mock('place')
    Place.expects(:new).with(:lat => 40, :lng => 50).returns(place)

    hackensack = mock('city')
    City.expects(:near).with(place, 10.miles).returns([hackensack])
    post :index, :text => '07601'

    assert_include hackensack, assigns(:places)
  end
end
```

In case it isn't obvious, this test checks to make sure that the search controller invokes the geolocation service to help it find cities near a supplied zip code.

The mock method creates a new mock response object. The actual type of the object doesn't matter, thanks to *duck typing*. The stubs method tells the mock which methods should simply return specified values if invoked, using a nice hash syntax.

I'll stop talking about Mocha now, so we don't get totally derailed from the overall subject of the chapter, which is, of course, testing. However, throughout the chapter I've included some examples on how using Mocha makes your Rails testing tasks easier.

Integration Tests

Rails integration tests were introduced in Rails 1.1 and are probably closest to the actual meaning of their name in the software engineering world. They engage the entire stack of Rails components and allow you to chain together multiple requests to test large-scale interactions of application code.

```
class AdvancedTest < ActionController::IntegrationTest
  fixtures :people, :forums

  def test_login_and_create_forum
    login_as :admin
    get '/forums'
    assert_response :success

    post '/forums', :forum => {:name => 'a new forum'}
    assert_response :redirect
    follow_redirect!
```

```
    assert_select 'div#topics div.title:last-of-type', 'a new forum'
  end
end
```

Integration tests are kind of like functional tests on steroids. You won't need too many of them in your projects, and you won't want too many of them either because they're slow. However, they will prove their worth in helping you flush out hard-to-find interaction bugs. There's a whole section on integration tests later in the chapter ("Rails Integration Tests").

Dealing with the Confusion

Is Rails testing nomenclature confusing? *Yes, clearly.* Is it going to be fixed anytime soon? *Nope.*[4]

Are there options? Of course! It wouldn't be Ruby otherwise. However, I warn you that going down these roads means leaving the Rails way, and your mileage may vary.

Here's a quick rundown of your options as I see them:

- My favorite option: scrap Rails testing altogether and use RSpec instead. (Make sure to take a quick look at the section about fixtures and integration tests in this chapter, then skip over to the next chapter.")

- Rename your test directories to `models`, `controllers`, `views`, and so on. The resulting changes to Rake tasks are left as an exercise to the reader.

- Prohibit database access from unit tests, using advice from Jay Fields at http://blog.jayfields.com/2006/06/ruby-on-rails-unit-tests.html.

The one option that you should never take is to ditch testing altogether. Delivering Rails applications without automated test coverage is irresponsible and unprofessional.

> **Wilson Says...**
> Writing applications without tests makes you a bad person, incapable of love.

Test::Unit

All standard tests in Rails extend Ruby's built-in testing framework called Test::Unit, which is considered part of the *xUnit family*. Similar frameworks exist for all other major programming languages. If you've used Java's JUnit or .NET's NUnit before, you should be familiar with the major concepts involved. If not, the following review of xUnit concepts may prove valuable.

A test case is made by subclassing the Test::Unit::TestCase and populating it with a collection of test methods that stress some aspect of your application. This is what a test case looks like in Rails:

```
require File.dirname(__FILE__) + '/../test_helper'

class UserTest < Test::Unit::TestCase

  fixtures :models

  def setup
    # code to be run before all test methods
  end

  def test_some_bit_of_functionality
    # logic and assertions
  end

  def teardown
    # code to be run after all test methods
  end
end
```

A *test* is a single public method of a test case, whose name begins with the prefix test_ and whose body contains code that proves the correct operation of some small part of your program. Test method names should be descriptive and describe the intention of the test in an explicit manner. A long name such as test_only_authorized _user_may_be_associated_as_approver is great, but a short name such as test_works is considered bad form. It should be easy to read the test and quickly figure out what the code under test is supposed to do. To that end, keep test methods bodies short and to the point.

An *assertion* is the comparison of an expected value with the result of an expression. For example, in a test you may set an attribute on a model in a way that should fail validation, and then use an `assert` statement to ensure that the error message produced is what it should be.

A *setup* method runs before each and every test method. A *teardown* runs after each method. Setup methods are very common in Rails tests, while teardown methods are not.

A successful test is one that executes without assertion failures or exceptions raised. Tests have two unsuccessful modes, *failure* and *error*. A test failure means that an assertion failed, while a test error means that an exception or runtime error halted execution of the test.

Sometimes we call a successful test run a *green bar* and a failing test run a *red bar*. That's based on the traditional behavior of unit-testing GUIs. When you run tests from the command prompt, you see a series of dots appear, signaling the execution of the individual test methods being run. The characters F and E in the series of dots indicate *failure* and *error* status, respectively.

Test *suites* are collections of test cases, and in other languages they are often defined by the developer. Standard Rails projects do not have the notion of developer-defined test suites. Instead, collections of tests are kept in three subdirectories of the test folder: functional, integration, and unit and are executed with rake tasks.

Running Tests

Because of the way that `Test::Unit` classes work, simply executing a test file from the command line with the Ruby interpreter will run all of its test methods. It is also possible to run a single test method, by supplying its name with an -n command-line option:

```
$ ruby test/unit/timesheet_test.rb -n
  test_only_authorized_user_may_be_associated_as_approver

Loaded suite test/unit/timesheet_test
Started
.
Finished in 1.093507 seconds.

1 tests, 2 assertions, 0 failures, 0 errors
```

Most of the time, we run the entire test suite for our application by simply typing `rake test` at the command prompt in our project directory. Even just `rake` will do, since `test` is the default task. Later on in the chapter we cover all of the test-related Rake tasks.

Fixtures

> The ability to get a named reference to a particular chunk of a known object
> graph is completely killer.
> —Michael Koziarski, Rails core team

In manufacturing, *fixtures* are used to build and test everything from circuit boards, to electronic devices, to raw materials and finished goods. As specifically applied to software engineering, fixtures are a mechanism for defining the baseline state of a system prior to running tests on it.

Whenever you use Rails code generation, default fixture files for new models are created inside the `test/fixtures` directory of your project and have contents that look like Listing 17.1.

The file has a `.yml` extension, indicating that it is a YAML (Yet Another Markup Language) file.[5] YAML is primarily a data serialization language and has no direct relationship to XML. Its indentation-based scoping is reminiscent of Python.

Listing 17.1   A Simple YAML Fixture File Example: `test/fixtures/users.yml`

```
quentin:
  id: 1
  email: quentin@example.com
  created_at: <%= 6.months.ago.to_s(:db) %>
newbie:
  id: 2
  email: newbie@domain.com
  crypted_password: <%= Digest::SHA1.hexdigest("password") %>
  created_at: <%= 1.minute.ago.to_s(:db) %>
```

The indentation of fields in your fixture must be consistent, or the YAML parser will balk. Also, the indentation *must not contain any tab characters*. According to the YAML spec, the amount of indentation is a presentation detail used exclusively to delineate structure and is otherwise ignored. My advice is to stick with the two-space indentation scheme common to the Ruby world.[6]

Take another look at the fixture in Listing 17.1. The file contains the contents of the users database table, as it should exist in your test database when you run your test. In case it's not immediately obvious, the mapping from fixture file to database table is based on the name of the file.

Fixtures are essentially two-dimensional serialized hashes. In our sample, the tag `quentin:` is the key (name) that is used to uniquely identify the hash of properties corresponding to the first record of our test users database table. Make it a goal to name your fixture records in an informative and semantically meaningful way whenever possible. You use the key to be able to quickly get a reference to a fixture object in your test, without having to load it via `ActiveRecord`.

The second-level keys (`:id`, `:email`, `:created_at`, etc.) must correspond to column names in the user table. As you can see in the example, it is not necessary to add keys for every column of the mapped table; in fact you should make it a practice to add only the minimum amount of data that you need for your testing purposes. The `:id` field is always needed, and often you'll run into problems by messing up the sequence of ids in a way that your database will get quite upset about. We'll cover a technique to avoid that hassle when we talk about dynamic fixture data later on in this section.

CSV Fixtures

Fixtures can also be formatted as comma-separated values (known as CSV). In case you haven't heard of it, CSV is an old, portable text file format that is best-known nowadays as the best way to get data in and out of Microsoft Excel in a cross-platform-compatible fashion.

Here's the same (yet much harder to read) fixture as before, but formatted as CSV:

```
id, email, crypted_password, created_at
1, quentin@example.com, , <%= 6.months.ago.to_s(:db) %>
2, newbie@domain.com, <%= Digest::SHA1.hexdigest("password") %>,
<%= 1.minute.ago.to_s(:db) %>
```

Ugh, that's ugly. Depending on the nature of your sample data, managing it with a spreadsheet tool like Excel might make sense. However, YAML is by far a more popular choice, because it's much more readable, and easier to edit by hand.

Accessing Fixture Records from Tests

The fact that records in a YAML fixture file are keyed with meaningful names is another factor that makes YAML a better choice. To access a record from your fixture file, you need to specify use of the fixture in the class context of your test. Then from inside methods you invoke a method with the same name as your fixture file and pass the name of the fixture record as its parameter, for example: `users(:quentin)` or `timesheets(:first)`. It's a quick and easy way to access your sample data, and the fact that you can choose the names means that you can give them rich semantic meaning.

```
fixtures :users

def test_can_access_quentin_fixture
  assert(users(:quentin) != nil)
end
```

On the other hand, names for records in CSV fixtures are automatically generated, created by deriving the class name of the fixture file and adding an incrementing number to the end. In our example, the first fixture would be called `:user_1` and the next would be called `:user_2`, and so on. There's no semantic meaning in those names, other than knowing that we're dealing with a user instance.

Dynamic Fixture Data

Before loading the records of a fixture into the test database, Rails runs its textual content through the ERb template parser. It means you can embed actual Ruby code in your fixture files using `<% %>` and `<%= %>` markup, just as you do in your view templates. That dynamic behavior can be leveraged to really streamline the work involved in using fixtures effectively.

The preceding examples have dynamic content. `<%= Digest::SHA1.hexdigest ("password") %>` saves us from having to actually do the encryption ourselves and manually copy in an unreadable and error-prone string like `00742970dc9e6319f8019fd54864d3ea740f04b1`.

Another example is how the date values are populated, by letting Rails take care of formatting the dates the way the database expects them: `<%= 5.days.ago.to_s(:db) %>`

Use of dynamic content in fixtures is not limited to conversion and formatting of values, though. You can also use looping constructs to create lots of fixture data easily. The example given in the Rails documentation demonstrates the basic technique:

```
<% for i in 1..1000 %>
fix_<%= i %>:
  id: <%= i %>
  name: guy_<%= 1 %>
<% end %>
```

Don't forget that you can put any valid Ruby inside those ERb tags, which includes defining new helper methods and including modules.

One of my biggest annoyances with fixture files used to be having to manually maintain the id numbers in proper sequence. Then I realized I can just add an `auto_increment` method to the fixture file (I shortened the fixture records themselves for brevity):

```
<%
  def auto_increment
    @id ||= 0; @id += 1
  end
%>
quentin:
  id: <%= auto_increment %>
  login: quentin
aaron:
  id: <%= auto_increment %>
  login: aaron
```

If you want to make methods such as `auto_increment` in the preceding example available to *all* of your fixture files, define them in a Ruby file called `fixture_helpers.rb`. Place it in your project's `/lib` directory, and make sure they're available by adding the line `require 'fixture_helpers'` at the top of `test/test_helper.rb`.

Using Fixture Data in Development Mode

After spending much time carefully crafting sample data for testing an application, it's not unusual to want to dump your fixture records into the development database so that you can use that sample data interactively via your browser or console.

The default Rails rake configuration includes a target that does exactly that. Invoke `rake db:fixtures:load` from the command line to import fixture records into the current environment. That rake target lets you pick a subset of fixtures to load, by adding the variable expression `FIXTURE=table1,table2` at the end of the command line.

> **NOTE**
>
> If you're using fixture helper methods as described in the previous section, keep in mind that the `db:fixtures:load` task doesn't require `test_helper.rb`, so you will probably need to put the `require 'fixture_helpers'` at the bottom of `config/environments/development.rb` instead.

Generating Fixtures from Development Data

By the same token, if your application has complicated relationships or you're just too lazy[7] to manually craft your fixture files, you might be inclined to automatically generate your fixture files from data in the development database. Assuming you have a working application already, you would be able to just point and click your way to sample data. All you need is a way to get data out of the database and into the right YAML format.

For whatever reason, dumping data to fixtures is *not* a part of core Rails.[8] Considering that Rails gives you a `to_yaml` method on `ActiveRecord` models and `Hash` objects, it wouldn't be too hard to write your own Rake task. However, it's not necessary to do so because of a well-proven plugin written by Geoff Grosenbach. It's called `ar_fixtures` and you can install it with the following command:

```
$ script/plugin install http://topfunky.net/svn/plugins/ar_fixtures
```

Once the plugin is installed, dumping a fixture is a simple matter of invoking a new rake task called `rake db:fixtures:dump`. Unlike the built-in loading rake task, this one takes a `MODEL` parameter with the name of the `ActiveRecord` class that you want to dump data for:

```
$ rake db:fixtures:dump MODEL=BillingCode
```

No feedback is provided, so check the fixtures file to verify what happened:

```
--
billing_code_00001:
  code: TRAVEL
  client_id:
  id: 1
  description: Travel expenses of all sorts
billing_code_00002:
  code: DEVELOPMENT
  client_id:
  id: 2
  description: Coding, etc.
```

Frankly, I'm not too thrilled about the way that the data is dumped with this plugin, but it's only because I'm picky about wanting my id column to appear first, and things like that. I also don't like to have entries for nil columns. Nevertheless, this plugin might be a good starting point for your purposes.

By the way, you don't need to worry about the `--` characters at the top of the file. They just indicate the beginning of a YAML document and can be safely deleted.

Fixtures Options

The `use_transactional_fixtures` option, present along with explanatory documentation in the standard `test/test_helper.rb` file of your project, governs whether Rails will try to accelerate your tests by wrapping each test method in a transaction that's rolled back on completion. The rollback speeds up execution of the test suite, since the fixture data doesn't have to be reloaded into the database for each test. The default setting for this option is `true`.

Using transactional fixtures is important for more than just performance. Rolling back changes after each test method ensures that you don't write test methods that are coupled to each other by depending on database changes that happened outside of their scope. Interlinked test methods are notoriously difficult to debug and a horrible practice to fall into.

The `use_instantiated_fixtures` setting, which is set by default to `false`, is another option present in the standard `test_helper.rb` file. Turning on this setting will make instance variables available automatically for each fixture record, at the cost of severely degraded performance of your tests. It dates back to the earliest versions of Rails, and as far as I can tell, has really fallen out of favor.

Everybody Hates Fixtures

During Railsconf 2006, one of the speakers asked, "Who in the audience *likes* fixtures?"

I was standing in the back of the room, mind wandering a bit, and I'm the type of person who doesn't hesitate to raise his hand in public situations. As such, I found myself in the awkward position of being one of the only people to answer affirmatively.

Why *do* so many experienced Rails people hate fixtures? There are various answers to that question—all of them multifaceted. Here are my interpretations of the most popular reasons to hate fixtures, followed by my own feelings on the Rails way to use fixtures.

Fixtures Make My Test Suite Slow

This one is true. Fixtures engage the database layer, and will make large test suites bog down in a thick soup of frenzied I/O activity. Leave fixtures out of the equation and it's not uncommon to have test suites with thousands of test cases that take only a few seconds to execute. This reason is popular with the unit-testing "purist" crowd.

As a general rule, don't include fixtures that you don't need in your tests. If you can manage testing using objects created "from scratch" or using only mocks and stubs with a library such as Mocha, then it's even better.

Fixtures Allow Invalid Data

If you're the sort of person who stresses the importance of valid data in the database, you probably think fixtures are downright evil. Why? Because there is no validation that takes place when data from fixtures gets shoved into the database. Rails doesn't care whether you define a single column's data on a fixture object, or all of them. It will happily populate a row in the database with any data you give it. Pretty much the only requirement is that the column type is compatible with what you're trying to stick in it. That's pure evil.

The thing is, if you feel that strongly about not having invalid data in your database, *don't write fixtures with invalid data*. Problem solved.

On a related note, if this reason for hating fixtures strikes a chord with you, you might believe in using database foreign-key constraints. Fixtures don't work well with foreign-key constraints, since it's difficult to consistently define the order in which they are loaded into the database.

Maintainability Challenges

This reason is one of the more globally applicable ones. If you try to keep a lot of data in fixtures, you will eventually start having problems keeping it all properly maintained. It's just too difficult to manage large datasets in the fixtures format... that's why we keep data in databases!

It's also difficult to maintain foreign-key relationships between objects stored in fixtures. Most of our brains are just not very good at remembering relationships based on nothing but small integers.

In all my time doing Rails, I haven't found any good reasons to keep more than a few representative instances of model objects in fixture files. Go beyond a few at your own peril.

Fixtures Are Brittle

Yet another good reason to hate fixtures is that they are *brittle*. Brittleness is a term that denotes your code's resistance to changes (or lack thereof). If any little change in your fixtures breaks a bunch of tests, they are brittle. If you have too many brittle tests, you will stop testing altogether, and when you die you will definitely go to hell. You see, fixtures *are* evil!

Seriously, there are some good strategies for keeping fixtures unbrittle. I'll reiterate my advice to keep your set of fixtures down to a manageable size. That will reduce the pain of having to make changes. There are also plugins available that let you define discrete sets of fixtures,[9] representing different testing scenarios, instead of having to cram all possibilities into one global set.

Also, the `fixtures_references` plugin[10] gives you another interesting solution to the brittleness problem, by allowing you to reference fixtures from within fixtures. Yes, that's right, you won't have to cross-reference foreign keys by memory any more if you use this plugin. Just reference the related fixture record using the same syntax you would use in your test:

```
<% fixtures :employees %>

packaging:
  id: 1
  name: Packaging
  manager_id: <%= employees(:bob)['id'] %>
```

Fixtures Really Aren't That Bad

I've proven to myself on my projects that when you use a mocking framework like Mocha, you can cut your usage of fixtures down to where they aren't nearly as painful as we've described in the preceding section.

Sometimes you can get away with using no fixtures at all, and that's great. Other times, they're convenient. The key, I believe, is to keep the number of fixtures you have to maintain down to a handful of representative cases, and stub them together as needed.

Incidentally, there are situations where fixtures are downright crucial (unless you want to create a bunch of model objects from scratch and save them to the database inside your test, which I hate doing). The one situation that comes to mind immediately is testing usages of `find_by_sql` in your model. Since you're writing SQL, you definitely want to run that against a real database and make sure that it works. There's no way of unit-testing it purely unless you parse the SQL yourself!

The bottom line: You don't need to *hate* fixtures; just try to be smart about how you use them.

Assertions

Assertion methods are the mechanism with which you actually perform verification in your test methods. Assertion methods always take an optional (last) parameter specifying a failure message. Use failure messages as insurance against confusion when someone (perhaps even you) is trying to figure out a test failure in the future.

Basic Assertions

The `Test::Unit::Assertions` module (part of Ruby itself) gives you a variety of basic assertion methods that you can use in all of your Rails tests. To preserve space, the following list combines assertions with `not` variants under the same heading. I also left out a couple that are not relevant for Rails programming.

`assert` and `deny`

If assertions were hand tools, `assert` and `deny` would be sledgehammers—blunt, to the point, and not much use in detail-oriented work. Give `assert` or `deny` basic Boolean expressions and they're happy. More than any other assertions, plain-old assert and deny deserve explicit failure messages. Otherwise you get frustrating results like "false should be true."

```
assert @user.valid?, "user was not valid"
```

```
deny @user.valid?, "user was valid"
```

If you use assert, by all means make sure you are passing it a Boolean value. Remember that nil is considered false in a Boolean context. If you are purposely checking whether an expression evaluates to nil or not, then use assert_nil or assert_not_nil to communicate your intention.

assert_block

Check that the final return value of a block of Ruby code is true.

```
assert_block "Failed because couldn't do the thing" do
  # do some processing required to do_the_thing
  do_the_thing
end
```

assert_empty

Check that a collection is empty?.

```
assert_empty @collection
```

assert_equal and assert_not_equal

Takes two parameters to check for equality (or not), using the equal? method. The first parameter is the reference value. The second is the expression to check.

```
assert_equal "passed", @status
```

`assert_in_delta` and `assert_in_epsilon`

Checks that a float value is within a certain tolerance. The Ruby docs say that `assert in_epsilon` is "like `assert_in_delta` but better dealing with errors proportional to the sizes of [the parameters]."

```
assert_in_delta(expected, actual, 0.01, message="exceeded tolerance")
```

`assert_include`

Checks that an item is included in a collection.

```
assert_include item, @collection
```

`assert_instance_of`

Checks that an object is an instance of a class (not module). The `of` part of the name should help you remember that the class is the first parameter.

```
assert_instance_of Time, @timestamp
```

`assert_kind_of`

Checks that an object is a `kind_of?` class *or* module. Again, the `of` part of the name indicates that the class or module to check comes first.

```
assert_instance_of Enumerable, @my_collection
```

`assert_match` and `assert_no_match`

Checks that a regular expression matches a given value (or not). The regular expression comes first.

```
assert_match /\d{5}(-\d{4})?/, "78430-9594"
```

`assert_nil` and `assert_not_nil`

Checks that a reference is nil (or not).

```
assert_not_nil User.find(:first)
```

`assert_same` and `assert_not_same`

Checks that two references point to the same object (or not).

```
assert_same "foo".intern, "foo".intern
```

`assert_raise` and `assert_nothing_raised`

Checks that exceptions are raised in the block provided (or not). I love the example given in the Ruby docs.

```
assert_raise RuntimeError, LoadError do
  raise 'Boom!!!'
end
```

`assert_respond_to`

Checks that an object `respond_to?` a given message. The object comes first, followed by the message.

```
assert_respond_to @playlist, :shuffle
```

`flunk`

Fails the test with the supplied message.

```
flunk "REDO FROM START"
```

It's easy to make the mistake of using `fail` (belonging to the `Kernel` class, and therefore available everywhere) instead of `flunk`. The `fail` method causes a runtime error to be raised, which will stop your test, but with an error condition instead of a failure.

Rails Assertions

Rails adds a number of assertions that supplement the ones provided by `Test::Unit`.

- `assert_difference` and `assert_no_difference`
- `assert_generates`, `assert_recognizes`, and `assert_routing`
- `assert_response` and `assert_redirected_to`
- `assert_tag` (deprecated) and `assert_select`
- `assert_template`
- `assert_valid`

The only ones in the list that are general purpose are `assert_difference` and `assert_no_difference`. All are covered in the following sections, with code examples and as they apply to testing specific parts of Rails.

One Assertion per Test Method

> I'd rather know the first time I run the suite that 10 things are failing, not that 5 are failing and a few others may or may not be failing.
> —Jay Fields

I like to make my tests as elegant and expressive as possible. The idea of limiting each test method to one assertion is usually attributed to TDD guru Dave Astels, and has been popularized in the Rails community by Jay Fields[11] and others.

If you are following the one-assertion guideline, then rather than a single test method that looks like this...

```
def test_email_address_validation
  u = users(:sam)
  u.email = "sam"
  assert ! u.valid?
  u.email = "johh.doe@google.com"
  assert u.valid?
  u.email = "johh_doe@mail.mx.1.google.com"
  assert u.valid?
  u.email = "johh_doe+crazy-iness@mail.mx.1.google.com"
  assert u.valid?
  u.email = "sam@@colgate.com"
  assert ! u.valid?
end
```

you would have instead written at least five test methods, each with a better description of the behavior being tested. For convenience, I would also move the assignment of a short variable for users(:sam) up to a setup method:

```
def setup
  @sam = users(:sam)
end

def test_email_validation_fails_with_simple_string_name
  @sam.email = "sam"
  assert not @sam.valid?  # prefer not over ! for readability
end

def
test_email_validation_should_succeed_for_valid_email_containing_dot
  @sam.email = "johh.doe@google.com"
  assert @sam.valid?
end

... # you get the picture, I hope
```

The main advantage to following the guideline is to increase maintainability of your tests, but there are also other important benefits, such as

- You are forced to spell out the meaning of your tests in the test name, which is output to the test results on failure. Otherwise, the intention of the assertion would be hidden in a comment, or not present in the test at all.

- You get a more accurate picture of *how* broken a test is. When there are multiple (potentially unrelated) assertions in a single test method, all it takes is for the first assertion to break and the rest will not get executed.

- Jay also claims that following the one-assertion guideline helps him think more critically about the design of his domain model: "Often the methods of my domain model end up with a single responsibility."

Let's talk some more about testing the domain model of your Rails app, its ActiveRecord models.

Testing Models with Unit Tests

As we've mentioned earlier in the chapter, a Rails unit test is actually a functional test of an `ActiveRecord` model. It's not necessary to test the operation of built-in methods such as `find`, since those are adequately covered by the tests supplied with Rails itself.

For example, the following test might be instructional in some way, but is altogether useless for your Rails project:

```
def test_find
  @user = User.create(:name => "John Foster")
  assert_equal @user, User.find_by_name("John Foster")
end
```

Why is it useless? It tests native functionality of Rails, which already has adequate test coverage. Unless you hand-coded a `find_by_name` method, you haven't proven anything about *your* code, only that Rails behaves as expected.

It's worth mentioning that besides instance methods, our `ActiveRecord` models are also filled with declarative *macro-style* code at the top of their files. It's easy to mess up that code, so make sure to give them some test coverage too.

Model Testing Basics

Whenever you use a generator to create an `ActiveRecord` model, Rails automatically creates a skeleton unit test in the `test/unit` directory of your project. It looks something like this:

```
require File.dirname(__FILE__) + '/../test_helper'

class BillableWeekTest < Test::Unit::TestCase
  fixtures :billable_weeks

  # Replace this with your real tests.
  def test_truth
    assert true
  end
end
```

> **Wilson Says...**
>
> The average Rails app would be 120% better if the default test generated for the model was `flunk "write me"` instead of `assert true`.

Traditionally, a unit test limits itself to testing one public method of an object and nothing more.[12] When we're testing an `ActiveRecord` model in Rails, we usually include multiple test methods for each public method, to make sure that we verify behavior thoroughly.

Listing 17.2 contains a couple of test methods from the `TimesheetTest` of our recurring sample application.

Listing 17.2 The Timesheet Model Test from the Time & Expenses Sample App

```
 1 class TimesheetTest < Test::Unit::TestCase
 2
 3   fixtures :users
 4
 5   def test_authorized_user_may_be_associated_as_approver
 6     sheet = Timesheet.create
 7     sheet.approver = users(:approver)
 8     assert sheet.save
 9   end
10
11   def test_non_authorized_user_cannot_be_associated_as_approver
12     sheet = Timesheet.create
13     begin
14       sheet.approver = users(:joe)
15       flunk "approver assignment should have failed"
16     rescue UnauthorizedApproverException
17       # expected
18     end
29   end
20 end
```

As we covered earlier in the chapter, we can leverage the fixtures system to have objects ready for testing. (Line 3 invokes `fixtures :users`.) You can use as many fixtures as necessary, and the names are always plural. I didn't load the timesheet fixtures because I don't need them. A basic, newly created `Timesheet` instance suits my needs just fine (lines 6 and 12).

If I wanted to use even more idiomatic Ruby in this test example, I would probably refactor lines 13–18 to use `assert_raises`.

Deciding What to Test

The implementation that determines whether a user is an authorized approver or not is hidden from view in this test. That may or may not be a bad thing in your case. I'm of the opinion that it's a good thing. This is after all a timesheet test, not a user or authorization test. All I wanted to verify when I wrote this test case was that one assignment succeeded, and the other didn't. The logic for authorization is not relevant in this test case.

Testing Controllers with Functional Tests

Whenever you use a generator to create an `ActiveRecord` controller, Rails automatically creates a functional test for it. Functional tests let you verify that your controllers exhibit the correct behavior in handling requests that come their way. Since the functional test subsystem also invokes the view code for the actions invoked, functional tests can include assertions on the content of the response.

Structure and Setup

Functional tests follow certain conventions, which most new Rails developers are introduced to when they first open up a scaffolding-generated functional test. Let's use a functional test from an open-source bulletin board package for Rails named Beast for our main examples.[13]

The top line is similar to a unit test in that it requires the common `test_helper` file. Next, the controller under test is required:

```
require File.dirname(__FILE__) + '/../test_helper'
```

Normally, any errors raised during controller execution are rescued so that the appropriate error page can be displayed to the user. But during testing, you want those errors to rise all the way to the top where the test framework can register that they happened. In a great example of how useful open classes are in Ruby, the solution for our functional tests is simply to override the `rescue_action` method of `ActionController`.

```
require 'forums_controller'
# Re-raise errors caught by the controller.
class ForumsController; def rescue_action raise e end; end
```

Semicolons, which are optional line delimiters in Ruby, are used to keep the line length of the file minimal.

Next up is the opening of the functional test class itself, which by naming convention, starts with the name of the controller it is testing. If the test uses fixtures, they are usually specified on the following line:

```
class ForumsControllerTest < Test::Unit::TestCase
  fixtures :forums, :posts, :users
```

Functional tests always have a setup method like the following one. It sets three required instance variables for the test, and will be run prior to each test method invocation:

```
def setup
  @controller = ForumsController.new
  @request    = ActionController::TestRequest.new
  @response   = ActionController::TestResponse.new
end
```

You can use the `@request` and `@response` objects, but additional convenience accessors for `session`, `flash`, and `cookies` are also provided. You can access those structures at any time in your test method, whether to set values to them or make assertions about how their state changed due to the controller action execution.

Functional Test Methods

Normally, you should have at least a couple of test methods per controller action, to verify handling of *happy path* and error conditions. The general workflow of a functional test method is to put any necessary preconditions into place, and then call a method on the test itself (such as GET, POST, PUT, DELETE, or HEAD) corresponding to the HTTP request desired. An `xhr` method is also provided, which lets you simulate an `XMLHttpRequest` interaction, as would occur if the browser made an Ajax request.

The first parameter to the request method is a symbol corresponding to the name of the action method to be tested, followed by a hash of parameters.

The following example tests that a GET request to `/forums/edit/1` is successful.

```
def test_should_get_edit_form
  login_as :aaron
```

```
  get :edit, :id => 1
  assert_response :success
end
```

Common Assertions

The following sorts of assertions are the most common for functional tests. You may come up with your own, but remember that controllers shouldn't be doing much more than invoking business logic on your models, and setting up an environment for the view to render properly.

Assert That Variables Were Assigned Properly for Use by Templates

One of the main behaviors of controller actions that render a template is the setting of instance variables to be used in the view. There are a variety of different ways to make assertions of that type, but all revolve around the fact that after invoking the controller action, the `assigns` method returns a hash of instance variables set for the template.

The scaffolding code has gotten a lot of people in the habit of asserting that assigned variables are not nil. That's not as safe as actually making assertions about the contents of those assigned variables.

```
def test_that_users_are_assigned_properly

  # lame assertion
  assert_not_nil assigns(:users)

  # getting better
  assert_equal 3, assigns(:users).size

  # best, check the contents of users but get a sane error on failure
  assert_equal %w(Bobby Sammy Jonathan), assigns(:users).map(&:login)

end
```

As alluded to in the final comment and assertion, we'll get a "sane error on failure" by doing a little magic with the `map` method, in order to check an array of names instead of an array of objects. The thing is, when `assert_equal` fails, the output will be an `inspect` dump of the objects that didn't match, which for a big `ActiveRecord` model can be a big multiline jumble of code that isn't very readable.

Assert the HTTP Status Code of a Response and Its MIME Content Type

The `assert_response` method of functional tests is a convenience method that asserts that the response is one of the following types:

- `:success`　Status code was 200.

- `:redirect`　Status code was in the 300–399 range.

- `:missing`　Status code was 404.

- `:error`　Status code was in the 500–599 range.

```
def test_should_get_index_successfully
  get :index
  assert_response :success
end
```

You can also pass an explicit status number like `assert_response(501)` or its symbolic equivalent[14] `assert_response(:not_implemented)`.

Assert the MIME Content Type of a Response (or Other Header Values)

The `@response` object is packed with information. (Just try adding `puts` `@response.inspect` after processing a request if you want a look.) Among the attributes of a response is the headers hash, which can be used to verify things like MIME content type and character encoding.

```
XML_UTF8 = "application/xml; charset=utf-8"

def test_should_get_index_with_xml
  request.env['Content-Type'] = 'application/xml'
  get :index, :format => 'xml'
  assert_response :success
  assert_equal XML_UTF8, @response.headers['Content-Type']
end
```

Assert Rendering of a Particular Template

The `assert_template` method makes it simple to test whether a particular template was rendered by the action under test:

```
def test_get_index_should_render_index_template
  get :index
  assert_template 'index'
end
```

Assert Redirection to a Specified URL

By the same token, the `assert_redirected_to` method makes it easy to verify that the redirection options passed in match those of the redirect called in the latest action. This match can be partial, such that `assert_redirected_to(:controller =>` "weblog") will also match the redirection of `redirect_to(:controller =>` "weblog", `:action =>` "show") and so on.

```
def test_accessing_protected_content_redirects_to_login
  get :protected
  assert_redirected_to :controller => "session", :action => "new"
end
```

The `follow_redirect` method is supposed to allow you to continue making assertions for a second action on the same controller.[15] Trying to follow a redirect to another controller will raise an error. See the section "Rails Integration Tests" later in this chapter to learn more about making more than one request per test method.

Assert Setting of Flash Messages

The `flash` convenience method gives you direct access to the flash hash of the user's session.

```
def test_accessing_protected_content_redirects_to_login
  post :create ... # bad attributes

  assert_equal "Problem saving. Check form and try again.",
flash[:error]
end
```

Assert Database Changes Resulting from Actions

The `assert_difference` method provides an easy way to check controller actions that cause records to be added to the database.

```
assert_difference 'Article.count' do
  post :create, :article => {...}
end
```

Positive or negative differences can be specified. The default is +1, but if we specify -1 then we have an easy way of testing delete operations.

```
assert_difference 'Article.count', -1 do
  delete :destroy, :id => ...
end
```

An array of expressions can also be passed in and evaluated.

```
assert_difference [ Report.count', 'AuditLog.entries.size' ], +2 do
  post :create, :article => {...}
end
```

By the way, that +2 is legal (albeit somewhat rare) Ruby syntax. While it happens to be unnecessary in this usage, it does convey the idea of this assertion quite eloquently. Make readability of your code an important goal of your day-to-day coding activities, especially in tests.

If you want to make sure that records were not added or removed from the database, you can use the `assert_no_difference` method:

```
assert_no_difference 'Article.count' do
  post :create, :article => {...}  # invalid_attributes
end
```

Assert Validity of a Model

The `assert_valid` method ensures that the passed record is valid by `ActiveRecord` standards and outputs error messages if it fails.

```
def test_create_should_assign_a_valid_model
  post :create ... # good attributes
  assert_valid assigns(:post)
end
```

Asserting View Output

The Rails way of testing view template output is to do so within the scope of controller test methods. Triggering a controller action causes the entire rendering chain to occur, and HTML (or other type) output to be set to `response.body`. Rails has a powerful API for making assertions on that output: `assert_select`. If you're looking through older Rails code, you might find usages of an older view assertion method named `assert_tag`—it was deprecated in favor of `assert_select`.

Testing Views with Functional Tests

The `assert_select` method uses CSS selector syntax for asserting contents of HTML or XML markup. It's extraordinarily flexible and powerful, because CSS selection is very flexible and powerful. If you already understand CSS selector syntax (and as a web application developer, you probably do), then `assert_select` should definitely be your preferred method of testing the contents of your views.[16]

Here are some examples, inspired by the documentation, showing how you can test that selected element(s) exist, have specific text content, test number, and order of elements, and more:

```
def test_page_has_right_title
  get :index
  assert_select "title", "Welcome"
end

def test_form_includes_four_input_fields
  get :new
  assert_select "form input", 4
end

def test_show_does_not_have_any_forms_in_it
  get :show, :id => 1
  assert_select "form", false, "Show page must contain no forms"
end

def page_has_one_link_back_to_user_page
  get :show, :id => 1
  assert_select "a[href=?]",
                url_for(:controller=>"user", :id=>user_id),
                :count => 1, :text => "Back to page"
end
```

The `assert_select` method comes in two variants, and has one of the most complicated APIs of any other Rails method that I know. It's unusual in that the first parameter is optional. In both forms, the `value`, `equality`, and `message`, as well as block parameters are optional.

`assert_select(selector, [*values, equality, message, &block])`

The first (most common) form uses the CSS `selector` string to select elements from the response in the context of a functional test.

`assert_select(element, selector, [*values, equality, message, &block])`

The second form, which I believe is rarely used by most developers, takes an explicit instance of `HTML::Node` as the `element` parameter, and selects all matching elements starting from (and including) that element and all its children in depth-first order.

Optional Block Parameter

Calling `assert_select` inside an `assert_select` block will automatically run the assertion for each element selected by the enclosing assertion, as in the following examples, which have the exact same behavior:

```
assert_select "ol > li" do |elements|
  elements.each do |element|
    assert_select element, "li"
  end
end

# use the shorter version

assert_select "ol > li" do
  assert_select "li"
end
```

Selector Reference

The `assert_select` method understands the set of CSS selector formats listed in Table 17.1. Combine them to identify one or elements for assertion.

Table 17.1   CSS Selector Reference

Selector	Behavior
`E`	An element with the tag name `E`. (For example "`DIV`" matches the first `DIV`[17] element encountered.)
	In the subsequent table entries, `E` may refer either to a tag name or any other legal CSS expression identifying one or more elements to be matched.
`E F`	Element `F` present anywhere in the child hierarchy of element `E`.
`E > F`	Element `F` as an immediate child of element `E`.
	Example: Verify the title of a Login page:
	`assert_select "html:root > head > title", "Login"`
`E ~ F`	Element `F` as preceded by element `E`.
	Example: Ensure that sponsored content in a list is before unsponsored content:
	`assert_select 'LI.sponsored ~ LI:not(.sponsored)'`
`E + F`	Element `F` as immediately preceded by element `E`.
	Example: Assert that your content `DIV` immediately follows your header `DIV` with nothing in between:
	`assert_select 'DIV#header + DIV#content'`

`E.class`
`E.class.`
`otherclass`
	Elements attributed with a CSS class named `class`.

`E#myid`	Elements attributed with an ID equal to `myid`.
`E[attribute]`	Elements with a specified attribute name.
`E[attribute=` `"value"]`	Elements with an `attribute` matching `value` exactly.
`E[attribute~=` `"value"]`	Elements with an `attribute` containing space-delimited values, one of which matches `value` exactly.
`E[attribute^=` `"start"]`	Elements with an `attribute` value that begins with `start`.
`E[attribute$=` `"end"]`	Elements with an `attribute` value that ends with `end`.

Table 17.1 CSS Selector Reference

Selector	Behavior
`E[attribute*=` `"str"]`	Elements with an *attribute* value containing the substring *str*.
`E[attribute|=` `"value"]`	Elements with an *attribute* containing a hyphen-separated list of values beginning with *value*.
`E:root`	An element that is the root element of the document.
`E:first-child`	The first child element of *E*. Note: This and other selectors like it will match multiple elements if *E* matches multiple elements.
`E:last-child`	The last child element of *E*.

`E:nth-child(n)`
`E:nth-last-`
`child(n)`
	The *n*-th child of an *E* element starting with the first. (In CSS, *n* is always 1-indexed.)
	
	The `last-child` variant counts up from the last child.

`E:first-of-type`	The first sibling of type *E*. Example: Assert that all drop-down selection boxes in a given document always include a blank option at the top: `assert_select('SELECT OPTION:first-of-type','')`
`E:last-of-type`	The last sibling(s) of type *E*.

`E:nth-of-type(n)`
`E:nth-last-`
`of-type(n)`
	The *n*-th sibling(s) of its type. The `last-of-type` variant counts up from the last sibling.
	Example: Assert the order and content of the `OPTION` tags for the following `SELECT` markup:
	
	`<SELECT id="filter">`
	
	`  <OPTION>None</OPTION>`
	
	`  <OPTION>Businesses</OPTION>`
	
	`  <OPTION>People</OPTION>`
	
	`</SELECT>`
	
	`assert_select('SELECT#filter option:nth-of-type(1)',`
	`'None')`
	
	`assert_select('SELECT#filter option:nth-of-type(2)',`
	`'Businesses')`
	
	`assert_select('SELECT#filter option:nth-of-type(3)',`
	`'People')`

Table 17.1   CSS Selector Reference

Selector	Behavior
`E:only-child`	Elements that are the only child of its parent matching *E*.
`E:only-of-type`	Elements that are the only sibling of their type matching *E*.
	Example: Ensure that only one external JavaScript file is ever included on the page. (A rule sometimes enforced for performance reasons…)
	`assert_select('HEAD SCRIPT[src]:only-of-type')`
`E:empty`	Elements that have no children (includes text nodes).
`E:not(selector)`	Elements that do not match the *selector* string provided.

Sometimes you want to use a substitution value, instead of matching for the existence or count of the CSS selector string defined. In that case, you can use the ? character as a placeholder. Works with class names (`.?`, *classname*), identifier attributes (`#?`, *id*), and regular attributes (`[attr=?]`, *string*, or *regexp*).

```
assert_select "form[action=?]", url_for(:action=>"login") do
  assert_select "input[type=text][name=username]"
  assert_select "input[type=password][name=password]"
end
```

Equality Tests

The equality parameter is optional and can be one of the values listed in Table 17.2. The default value is `true`, which means that at least one element was found matching the CSS selector. If you wish to supply only one criterion for the matched elements, use the singular form. Otherwise, pass the criteria as a hash.

Table 17.2   Options for the `equality` Parameter of `assert_select`

Singular Form	Hash Form	Explanation
true	:minimum => 1	At least one element matched
false	:count => 0	No elements matched.
"something"	:text => "something"	All elements matched have the text content.
/^[a-z]{2}$/i	:text => /^[a-z]{2}$/i	All elements matched match the regular expression.
n	:count => *n*	Exactly *n* elements matched.
	:minimum => *n*	At least *n* elements matched.
	:maximum => *n*	At most *n* elements matched
n..m	:minimum => *n*, :maximum => *m*	Number of elements matched falls in the supplied `Range`.

Testing RJS Behavior

Variants of `assert_select_rjs` are used in functional tests to check RJS-style manipulation of the view by your controllers.

`assert_select_rjs(*args, &block)`

Leaving off the `args` asserts simply that one or more elements were updated or inserted via RJS. With all variants of `assert_select_rjs`, nested `assert_select` statements can be used to verify the HTML payload of the update or insertion:

```
# Check that RJS inserts or updates a list with four items.
assert_select_rjs 'my_list' do
  assert_select "ol > li", 4
end
```

`assert_select_rjs(id)`

Same as `assert_select_rjs(*args, &block)`, but specifies a particular *id* that is being updated or inserted.

`assert_select_rjs(operation, id)`

Same as `assert_select_rjs(*args, &block)`, but specifies the *operation* applied to a particular *id* as `replace`, `chained_replace`, `replace_html`, `chained_replace_html`, or `insert_html`.

`assert_select_rjs(:insert, position, id)`

Again same as `assert_select_rjs(*args, &block)`, but specifies that the RJS operation is an `:insert` and the *position* is one of `:top`, `bottom`, `before`, or `after`.

Other Selection Methods

Rounding out the `assert_select` code are methods for checking e-mail and encoded HTML, as well a the `css_select` method, which is useful in conjunction with the version of the `assert_select` that takes an HTML node as its first parameter.

`assert_select_email(*args, &block)`

Assertions on the (HTML) body of the delivered e-mail.

`assert_select_encoded(*args, &block)`

For operating on encoded HTML such as RSS item descriptions.

`css_select(selector, *values)` and `css_select(element, selector, *values)`

Return arrays of selected elements that are empty if no elements selected.

Testing Routing Rules

Rails provides a set of assertions for use in functional tests that allow you to check that your routing file is configured as you expect it to be.

**assert_generates(expected_path, options, defaults={},
extras = {}, message=nil)**

Asserts that the provided options can be used to generate the provided path, which is the inverse behavior of assert_recognizes.

```
assert_generates("/items", :controller => "items",
                  :action => "index")

assert_generates("/items/list", :controller => "items",
                  :action => "list")

assert_generates("/items/list/1", :controller => "items",
                  :action => "list", :id => "1")
```

**assert_recognizes(expected_options, path, extras={},
message=nil)**

Asserts that the routing of the given path was handled correctly and that the parsed options match, which is the inverse behavior of assert_generates.

```
# check the default action
assert_recognizes({:controller => 'items', :action => 'index'},
'items')

# check a specific action
assert_recognizes({:controller => 'items', :action => 'list'},
'items/list')

# check an action with a parameter
assert_recognizes({:controller => 'items', :action => 'list',
 :id => '1'}, 'items/list/1')
```

Pass a hash in the second argument to specify the request method. This is useful for routes requiring a specific HTTP method. The hash should contain a :path with the incoming request path and a :method containing the required HTTP verb.

```
# assert that POSTing to /items will call create on ItemsController
assert_recognizes({:controller => 'items', :action => 'create'},
                  {:path => 'items', :method => :post})
```

You can also pass in "extras" with a hash containing parameters that would normally be present in the query string. This can be used to assert that URL query parameters are added to the params hash correctly. To test query strings you must use the extras argument; appending the query string on the path the way that you normally do in your application code will not work.

```
# assert that a path of '/items/list/1?view=print' returns correct
options
assert_recognizes({:controller => 'items', :action => 'list',
                   :id => '1', :view => 'print'},
                 'items/list/1', { :view => "print" })
```

assert_routing(path, options, defaults={}, extras={},

message=nil)

Asserts that path and options match both ways; in other words, the URL generated from options is the same as path, and also that the options recognized from path are the same as options. This essentially combines assert_recognizes and assert_generates into one step.

Rails Integration Tests

Rails 1.1 introduced a built-in *integration test* API as a "logical progression in the existing series of available tests."[18]

Integration tests differ from functional tests in that they verify interactions across multiple browser requests, spanning any number of controllers and actions. In addition to validating functionality of the application, well-written integration tests should help flush out whatever bugs may be lurking in your use of routing and user sessions. When used in this way, Rails integration tests *might* be suitable acceptance tests for your project.

Basics

Integration tests are kept as files in the test/integration directory. They are executed via the rake target test:integration, or just like other Rails tests, by invoking the file directly with the Ruby interpreter.

You don't have to write the skeleton code for an integration test yourself, since a generator is provided. Give the generator an integration test name as its argument in CamelCase or under_score format.

```
$ script/generate integration_test user_groups
      exists  test/integration/
      create  test/integration/ user_groups_test.rb
```

The generator will create an integration test template ready for editing, such as the following:

```
require "#{File.dirname(__FILE__)}/../test_helper"

  class UserGroupsTest < ActionController::IntegrationTest
    # fixtures :your, :models

    # Replace this with your real tests.
    def test_truth
      assert true
    end
  end

end
```

So far the process is very similar to how we write tests for models and controllers, but in order to proceed, we have to make some decisions on how we want to implement the feature to be tested. In this sense, writing the integration test prior to implementation of a feature serves as a design and specification tool. Before going any further with our example, let's take a quick look at the API methods available for coding our integration tests.

The Integration Test API

The `get` and `post` methods take a string path as their first argument and request parameters as the second argument, as a hash. To use the familiar controller/action hash for the first parameter instead of a literal URL string, use the `url_for` method.

The `follow_redirect!` method instructs your test to follow any redirect initiated by the last request. The `status` method returns the HTTP status code of the last request. When asserting a redirect, the `redirect?` method asserts that the status code of the last request is equal to 300.

`ActionController::Assertions::ResponseAssertions` is a module containing the assertions that we use in our integration tests. Remember that all assertion methods in Rails have an optional message parameter displayed when the assertion fails during a test run.

`assert_redirected_to(options = {}, message = nil)`

Asserts that the redirection options passed in match those of the redirect called in the latest action. This match can be partial, such that `assert_redirected_to` `(:controller => "weblog")` will also match the redirection of `redirect_to(:controller => "weblog", :action => "show")`, and so on.

`assert_response(type, message = nil)`

Asserts that the HTTP response status code matches the supplied criteria. The following list of symbols can be used in place of an actual integer value such as `assert_response(501)`.

- `:success`   Status code was 200.
- `:redirect`   Status code was in the 300–399 range.
- `:missing`   Status code was 404.
- `:error`   Status code was in the 500–599 range.

`assert_template(expected = nil, message = nil)`

Asserts that the request was rendered with the appropriate template file.

Working with Sessions

An integration `Session` instance represents a set of requests and responses performed sequentially by some virtual user. Because you can instantiate multiple sessions and run them side by side, you can also mimic (to some limited extent) multiple simultaneous users interacting with your system.

Typically, you will instantiate a new session using `IntegrationTest#open_session`, rather than instantiating `Integration::Session` directly.

Rake Tasks Related to Testing

The default Rakefile for Rails projects includes 10 tasks related to testing, as shown in Table 17.3.

Table 17.3   Rake Testing Tasks

Target	Description
rake db:test:clone	The clone task re-creates the test database from the current environment's database schema.
rake db:test: clone_structure	The clone_structure task re-creates the test database using the structure of the development database. Similar to db:test:clone, except that it only copies over the schema of the database and not the contents. You shouldn't need to invoke either of these tasks during everyday work, because they are dependencies of other testing tasks.
rake db:test:prepare	Prepares the test database for a test run and loads the current development schema into it. If you are running a test directly after having made schema changes to your database, you have to run this task first or your test will fail.
rake db:test:purge	Empties the test database.
rake test	The test target is marked as the default in standard Rails rakefiles, meaning you can run it simply by typing rake at the command line. It runs all tests in test/units and test/functionals folders.
rake test:functionals	Run only the tests in the test/functionals folder.
rake test:integration	Run only the tests in the test/integration folder.
rake test:units	Run only the tests in the test/units folder.
rake test:recent	Run only tests that have been modified in the last 10 minutes.
rake test:uncommitted	Run only the tests that are modified according to Subversion.

Acceptance Tests

A well-written acceptance test suite is an essential ingredient in the success of any complex software project, particularly those run on Agile principles and methodologies such as extreme programming. In fact, one of the best definitions that I've run across for *acceptance test* is from the Extreme Programming official website:

> The customer specifies scenarios to test when a user story has been correctly implemented. A story can have one or many acceptance tests, what ever it takes to ensure the functionality works.[19]

Stated simply, acceptance tests let us know that we are done implementing a given feature, or user story, in XP lingo. Traditionally, acceptance tests consist of test scripts—a list of actions taken by a tester (or encoded into a testing tool) to ensure that the application works correctly. Nowadays, relying on manual acceptance testing to verify web applications is considered a worst practice. It is slow, error-prone, and expensive.

An individual acceptance test is useful to the developer who writes it as a design and tasking tool. A whole suite of automated acceptance tests covering the desired functionality of our application is a useful and continuous indicator of the state of your project's completion.

Acceptance Test First?

As a Rails developer working on a given user story or feature, having an automated acceptance test keeping me focused on the task at hand helps keep my productivity at optimal levels. The same principles of test-driven development (TDD) apply, just at a higher conceptual level than unit tests. It's so easy to do most stuff in Rails that you might find it hard to limit yourself to working on a particular task at a time, and that's a dangerous habit to get into.

Also, experience has shown that most Rails applications (and Web 2.0 apps in general) are data and UI-heavy. They simply don't have a lot of business logic driving a critical need for extensive unit tests. However, you can't just leave parts of your application without test coverage—in an interpreted language like Ruby, that's a recipe for disaster.

That's where automated acceptance tests come in: Encode the acceptance criteria for a given user story or feature prior to implementing it. Requirements not clear? Seek clarity. Not sure how your application's models and controllers need to be designed? Go for it. Make some initial decisions and use those as the basis for your test.

Prior to working on the implementation, your acceptance test will fail near its beginning. As you code the implementation, run the acceptance test over and over again and watch the red bars turn into green bars. Once the whole test is green, you're done! In the process you've created an automated regression suite that yields a multitude of benefits down the road.

Luckily, since so many Rails developers are fans of Agile, there are strong options available that let you quickly and easily create acceptance test suites for your own Rails projects.

This chapter covers the most significant options available, starting with an open-source product called Selenium on Rails, continuing with a look at the acceptance-testing capabilities built into Rails itself, and finishing off with descriptions of other useful acceptance-testing tools for Rails.

Selenium

Selenium is the name of a family of testing tools featuring tests that run directly in the web browser, exactly replicating the actions of a real user. Selenium was developed by a team of programmers and testers at ThoughtWorks, and is designed specifically for the acceptance testing requirements of Agile teams.

Basics

A Selenium script consists of a series of commands that manipulate and verify the state of the web browser. There are three kinds of Selenium commands: actions, accessors, and assertions. In the beginning, you will mostly be using actions and assertions. Most commands take two parameters: *target* and *value*.

Some commands wait for a condition to become true, which allows Selenium to test page transitions and Ajax functionality. Such commands will succeed immediately if the condition is already true, but they will fail and halt the test if a timeout value is exceeded before the condition does become true.

Actions and Assertions

Actions are commands that generally manipulate the state of the application. They do things like "open a URL" and "click a specific hyperlink." When an action fails or errors out, execution of the test stops.

Actions with the "AndWait" suffix, such as `click_and_wait`, tell Selenium that the action will cause the browser to make a call to the server, and that Selenium should wait for a new page to load or an Ajax call to complete.

Assertions are used to verify that the state of the application conforms to what is expected. Examples include "make sure the page title is X" and "verify that this check box is checked." All Selenium assertions can be used in three modes: `assert`, `verify`, and `wait_for`. For example, you can `assert_text`, `verify_text`, and `wait_for_text`.

When an `assert` fails, the test stops execution. When a `verify` fails, the test will log the failure, but continue executing. Therefore, use `asserts` to check state that is necessary in order to continue testing, and `verifies` to check things like form-field values, which don't necessarily mean you need to halt the test.

Locators

You target Selenium actions and assertions at some HTML element on the page under test using element locators. There are various kinds of locator strings with their own conventions in Selenium, but the most common are automatically understood by the engine. Locators starting with `document.` are treated as a DOM traversal expression in JavaScript. Locators starting with `//` are treated as a DOM traversal expression in XPath. Any other locator string (unless prefixed) is treated as an identifier (`id` attribute of an element).

Patterns

Patterns are used to specify expected values of arbitrary text on the page, form field values, specific nodes in the markup, element attributes, and so on. Selenium supports various types of pattern including regular expressions, but most of the time your pattern will simply be a text string.

Selenium Reference

A complete Selenium reference is available online.[20] This chapter introduces the use of Selenium commands, but does not provide an exhaustive usage guide for them.

Getting Started

Selenium on Rails[21] is the name of the Selenium product crafted specifically for Rails developers and is distributed as a Rails plugin. It has been designed to work seamlessly with the Rails testing environment and fixtures.

It's easy to install Selenium on Rails and get started.

1. Install the core Selenium files needed by the plugin: `gem install selenium`

2. Install the Selenium on Rails plugin for a given project: `script/plugin install` http://svn.openqa.org/svn/selenium-on-rails/selenium-on-rails/

3. Generate the test directory and a test script: `script/generate selenium first.rsel`

4. Start your Rails server in its test environment: `server -e test`

5. Open the Selenium Test Runner in your browser: http://localhost:3000/selenium

If your installation and setup succeeded, you see the Selenium Test Runner in your browser. You should also know that Selenium tests can be run from the command line and integrated into an automated suite of tests, but for demonstration purposes we will use the built-in web interface to execute our tests.

First Test

Go ahead and click the All button in the Execute Tests control panel. Selenium will execute the First test script, displayed in the center-top panel of the interface. Unless the title of the page at the base URL of your Rails application reads "Home," the test will fail.

The first two commands of the test have a light green background color. This indicates that they executed correctly. However, the header cell and the row containing the `assertTitle` command have light red backgrounds indicating failure. The control panel in the top-right pane of the interface shows the status of the test run.

To make the test pass, open the file `test/selenium/first.rsel`, and edit the `assert_title` command so that it checks the actual contents of the title element for your site. In my case, I changed it to check for "Ruby on Rails: Welcome aboard."

```
setup
open '/'
assert_title 'Ruby on Rails: Welcome aboard'
```

I flip back over to the browser and refresh the page so that my changes are picked up. Now when I run the test, it should pass successfully and turn green, the color of progress!

RSelenese

Selenium on Rails scripts are written in Ruby, using an API that the authors have nick-named RSelenese. It is a direct port of the Selenium command language, except that commands are Ruby-fied—lowercase and underscore-delimited rather than CamelCase. The Selenium on Rails engine looks for RSelenese tests in the `test/selenium` directory tree in files ending with the `.rsel` extension.

Selenium on Rails also understands HTML-formatted scripts, and will execute any that it finds in files with an `.sel` extension. However, in practice you are better off keeping as much of your application written in Ruby as possible, and tests are not necessarily an exception to that rule. Also, since RSelenese is just plain Ruby, you can use normal language constructs such as conditionals and loops for extra expressive power whenever needed.

The example shows use of an iterator in RSelenese to successively open 10 pages:

```
(1..10).each do |num|

  open :controller => 'user', :action => 'list', :page => num
end
```

Partial Scripts

Quite often, there are parts of your acceptance test suite that will appear identically in each test case. To keep things DRY, you can define script partials and include them inside test scripts. If you have some common actions you want to do in several test cases you can put them in a separate partial test case and include them in your other test cases.

A partial test case is just like a normal test case except that its filename starts with an underscore.

```
#_login.rsel
open '/login'
type 'name', 'john'
type 'password', 'password'
click 'submit'
```

To include a partial test case in a RSelenese test case, use `include_partial`:

```
include_partial 'login'
```

The ability to pass variables to partials makes them even more useful. For instance, let's assume that we want to use the `_login` partial for more than just the `john` user. Within the partial, put local variable placeholders for the parameters...

```
#_login.rsel with params
open '/login'
type 'name', name
type 'password', password
click 'submit'
```

...and then pass values for those parameters in the call to `include_partial` as a hash.

```
include_partial 'login', :name => 'jane', :password => 'foo'
```

Conclusion

This chapter has turned out to be one of the most difficult to write in the whole book, probably because the material in it merits a book of its own. We've learned quite a bit about Rails testing, and how in order for it to be hassle-free, we have to be smart about our use of fixtures and use third-party mocking libraries such as Mocha. We also discussed the differences between unit, functional, integration, and acceptance tests in Rails, covering a lot of reference material along the way that will be helpful to you in your day-to-day coding.

It turns out that many Rails developers have opted to drop Rails testing entirely and adopt a slightly different way of thinking about how they verify their projects. The philosophy is called *behavior-driven development* and the library they use is called *RSpec*.

References

1. Snooty Pythonistas hate the term "monkeypatching," which is used to describe changing implementation of classes that you didn't write thanks to open classes. Hardcore Rubyists dislike it as well, because they don't think the practice is unusual enough to merit a special term. Adam Keys suggests the term "duck-punching" is now in vogue. I simply think one word is preferable to the mouthful: "altering the behavior of an existing class or object thanks to Ruby's open classes."

2. I admit that's hyperbole. When I ran this paragraph by Rick Olson, he implicitly defended the core team by telling me "Mocha wasn't around then."

3. Learn more about Mocha at http://mocha.rubyforge.org/.

4. I asked David to explain why they are categorized the way they are, and he said, "Unit tests were chosen to imply that these tests were about dealing with individual methods of the models or services while functional tests would deal with compositions of more elements (both controllers and models). In practice, there's much bleeding going on and today it could just as well have been called models and controller tests. It's not an area of great importance to us."

5. See http://yaml.org for more information about YAML.

6. It is not uncommon to accidentally mess up the indentation of fixture files. Luckily, the error message that Rails will spit out when you have a bad fixture is usually informative.

7. Hey, as a programmer it's actually a compliment, not an insult, to be called lazy.

8. When I asked in #caboose, Courtenay said: "It's about whether anyone in core ever wanted to dump their fixtures to a file." It's probably as simple as that.

9. Improve your fixtures experience with http://thatswhatimtalkingabout.org/news/2006/8/31/fixture-sets-for-rails.

10. Improve your fixtures experience even more with http://www.pluginaweek.org/2007/04/07/14-fix-your-fixtures-with-fewer-foreign-key-ids/.

11. Jay has one of the best explanations for why you should limit the number of assertions in a single test at http://blog.jayfields.com/2007/06/testing-one-assertion-per-test.html.

12. If dependencies external to the object under test are required in order to write a unit test, they should be mocked or stubbed so that the correct operation of those external dependencies does not become part of this particular test case. We'll talk about mocks and stubs later.

13. Beast is a "small, lightweight forum in Rails with a scary name and a goal of around 500 lines of code." Visit http://beast.caboo.se/ for more information.

14. Browse `ActionController::StatusCodes` in the Rails source code for a full list of response symbols.

15. At the time of this writing, the `follow_redirect` method for functional tests is broken. See http://dev.rubyonrails.org/ticket/7997 for more information and status of this bug.

16. Incidentally, `assert_select` is evidence of the Rails plugin philosophy in action. It started out as a plugin authored by Assaf Arkin and was found to be so useful that the core team rolled it into the release of Rails 1.2 in January 2007.

17. CSS tag selectors are case-insensitive. Throughout this book we generally set off HTML tag names in caps just for clarity's sake.

18. Jamis has a good introduction at http://jamis.jamisbuck.org/articles/2006/03/09/integration-testing-in-rails-1-1.

19. Definition of acceptance testing is at http://www.extremeprogramming.org/rules/functionaltests.html.

20. Selenium reference is available at http://release.openqa.org/selenium-core/nightly/reference.html.

21. For the Selenium on Rails plugin see http://openqa.org/selenium-on-rails/.

CHAPTER 18

RSpec on Rails

I do not think there is any thrill that can go through the human heart like that
felt by the inventor as he sees some creation of the brain unfolding to success.
—Nikola Tesla

RSpec is a Ruby domain-specific language for specifying the desired behavior of a
Ruby application. Its strongest appeal is that RSpec scripts tend to be very readable,
letting the authors express their intention with greater readability and fluidity than is
achievable using `Test::Unit`'s methods and assertions.

RSpec on Rails, a drop-in replacement for the Rails testing subsystem, was released
by the RSpec team in late 2006. It supplies verification, mocking, and stubbing features customized for use with Rails models, controllers, and views. I'm happy to say
that I've been using the *RSpec* plugin for my Rails projects every day since it was
released, and have never needed to touch `Test::Unit` for anything significant again.[1]
RSpec is simply that good.

Introduction to RSpec

Since RSpec scripts (or specs) are so readable, I can't really think of a better way of
introducing you to the framework than to dive into some actual specs. Along the way,
I'll highlight the key concepts that you need to know.

Listing 18.1 is part of a real-world RSpec script defining the behavior of a
`CreditCard` model class.

Listing 18.1 A Description Block from Monkeycharger's `CreditCard` Spec[2]

```
 1  describe "A valid credit card" do
 2    before(:each) do
 3      @credit_card = generate_credit_card
 4    end
 5
 6    it "should be valid after saving" do
 7      @credit_card.save
 8      @credit_card.should be_valid
 9    end
10  end
```

RSpec scripts are collections of *behaviors*, which in turn have collections of examples. Line 1 uses the `describe` method to create a `Behavior` object under the covers. The behavior sets the context for a set of specification examples, and you should pass it a sentence fragment that accurately describes the context you're about to specify.

The `before` method on line 2 (and its companion `after`) are akin to the `setup` and `teardown` methods of xUnit frameworks like `Test::Unit`. They are used to set up the state as it should be prior to running an example, and if necessary, to clean up the state after the example has run. This particular behavior did not require an `after` block. (For brevity, the source of the `generate_credit_card` method on line 3 is not included in this listing. It is simply a factory method that returns instances of `CreditCard` preset with known and overridable attribute values. We'll learn more about using helper methods to write more readable spec code later in the chapter.)

The `it` method on line 6 is used to create an `Example` object, and you also give it a description. The idea is to complete the thought that was started in the `describe` method, so that it forms a complete sentence. Our example reads "A valid credit card should be valid after saving." See it?

Should and Expectations

Moving on, line 7 of Listing 18.1 invokes `save` on the credit card object, and since it's an `ActiveRecord` model, we know that will get it validated. So all we have left is to verify that the credit card instance is valid. Rather than xUnit-style assertions, RSpec introduces some funky DSL-ish syntax to do verification, based on a pair of methods called `should` and `should_not`.

RSpec mixes `should` and `should_not` into the base Ruby `Object` class at run-time so that they are available on all objects. They expect to receive `Matcher` objects, which you generate using RSpec expectation syntax.

```
@credit_card.should be_valid
```

There are several ways to generate expectation matchers and pass them to `should` (and `should_not`):

```
receiver.should(matcher)                    # the simplest example
# Passes if matcher.matches?(receiver)

receiver.should == expected #any value
# Passes if (receiver == expected)

receiver.should === expected #any value
# Passes if (receiver === expected)

receiver.should =~ regexp
# Passes if (receiver =~ regexp)
```

The process of learning to write expectations is probably one of the meatier parts of the RSpec learning curve. One of the most common idioms is "should equal," akin to `Test::Unit`'s `assert_equal` assertion. This is how you would rewrite the "credit card should be valid" assertion using should equal syntax:

```
@credit_card.valid?.should == true
```

The `valid?` method returns `true` or `false` and according to our spec, it should be `true`. Now, why didn't we write the expectation that way to begin with? Simply because that question-mark-and-period combo is ugly. It works, but it's not as elegant or readable as saying: `should be_valid`. There is no predefined `be_valid` method in RSpec—it is an *arbitrary predicate*.

Predicates

Thanks to the magic of `method_missing`, RSpec can support arbitrary predicates, that is, it understands that if you invoke something that begins with `be_`, then it should use the rest of the method name as a pointer to a Boolean attribute of the target object.

The simplest hard-coded predicate-style matchers are used to assert Boolean and nil target values:

```
target.should be_true
target.should be_false
target.should be_nil
target.should_not be_nil
```

The arbitrary predicate matchers can assert against any Boolean target, and even support parameters!

```
collection.should be_empty #passes if target.empty?
target.should_not be_empty          # passes unless target.empty?
target.should_not be_under_age(13) # passes unless
target.under_age?(13)
```

As an alternative to prefixing arbitrary predicate matchers with be_, you may choose from the indefinite article versions be_a_ and be_an_, making your specs read much more naturally:

```
"a string".should be_an_instance_of(String)
3.should be_a_kind_of(Fixnum)
3.should be_a_kind_of(Numeric)
3.should be_an_instance_of(Fixnum)
3.should_not be_instance_of(Numeric) #fails
```

The cleverness (madness?) doesn't stop there. RSpec will even understand have_ prefixes as referring to predicates like has_key?:

```
{:foo => "foo"}.should have_key(:foo)
{:bar => "bar"}.should_not have_key(:foo)
```

RSpec has a number of expectation matchers for working with classes that implement module Enumerable. You can specify whether an array should include a particular element, or if a string contains a substring.

```
[1, 2, 3].should include(1)
[1, 2, 3].should_not include(4)
```

```
"foobar".should include("bar")
"foobar".should_not include("baz")
```

You get a slick bit of syntactic sugar for testing the length of collections:

```
[1, 2, 3].should have(3).items
```

What if you want to specify the length of a `has_many` collection? "Schedule.days.should have(3).items" is admittedly quite ugly. RSpec gives us some more sweetness here as well.

```
schedule.should have(3).days   # passes if schedule.days.length == 3
```

Custom Expectation Matchers

When you find that none of the stock expectation matchers provide a natural-feeling expectation, you can very easily write your own. All you need to do is write a Ruby class that implements the following four methods (only two are required):

```
matches?(actual)
failure_message
negative_failure_message #optional
description #optional
```

The example given in the RSpec API documentation is a game in which players can be in various zones on a virtual board. To specify that a player `bob` should be in zone 4, you could write a spec like this:

```
bob.current_zone.should eql(Zone.new("4"))
```

However, it's more expressive to say one of the following, using the custom matcher in Listing 18.2:

```
bob.should be_in_zone("4") and bob.should_not be_in_zone("3")
```

Listing 18.2 `BeInZone` Custom Expectation Matcher Class

```
class BeInZone
  def initialize(expected)
    @expected = expected
  end
  def matches?(target)
    @target = target
    @target.current_zone.eql?(Zone.new(@expected))
  end

  def failure_message
    "expected #{@target.inspect} to be in Zone #{@expected}"
  end

  def negative_failure_message
    "expected #{@target.inspect} not to be in Zone #{@expected}"
  end

end
```

In addition to the matcher class you would also need to write the following method so that it'd be in scope for your spec.

```
def be_in_zone(expected)
  BeInZone.new(expected)
end
```

This is normally done by including the method and the class in a module, which is then included in your spec.

```
describe "Player behaviour" do
  include CustomGameMatchers
  ...
end
```

Or you can include helpers globally in a `spec_helper.rb` file required from your spec file(s):

```
Spec::Runner.configure do |config|
  config.include(CustomGameMatchers)
end
```

Note that you don't have to worry about `Behavior` and `Example` object instances while you're writing RSpec scripts. (They are only used internally by the framework.)

Multiple Examples per Behavior

The Monkeycharger example presented in Listing 18.1 is pretty simple and only has one example, but only because I wanted a simple introduction to the most basic concepts of RSpec.

A behavior usually has more than one example in it. It's easiest to just show you some more code from Monkeycharger. Listing 18.3 is the next `describe` block of that `CreditCard` spec and has five examples.

Listing 18.3   Another Description Block from Monkeycharger's `CreditCard` Spec

```
describe CreditCard do
  it "should have a valid month" do
    card = generate_credit_card(:month => 'f')
    card.errors.on(:month).should == "is not a valid month"
  end

  it "should have a valid year" do
    card = generate_credit_card(:year => 'asdf')
    card.errors.on(:year).should == "is not a valid year"
  end

  it "date should not be in the past" do
    past_month = (Date.today << 2)
    card = generate_credit_card(:year  => past_month.year,
                                :month => past_month.month)
    card.should_not be_valid
  end

  it "should have two words in the name" do
    card = generate_credit_card(:name => "Sam")
    card.errors.on(:name).should == "must be two words long."
  end

  it "should have two word last_name if name is three words long" do
    card = generate_credit_card(:name => "Sam Van Dyk")
    card.last_name.should == "Van Dyk"
  end

  it "should have one word first_name if name is three words long" do
    card = generate_credit_card(:name => "Sam Van Dyk")
    card.first_name.should == "Sam"
  end

end
```

Even if you don't know much about credit cards (or RSpec for that matter), you should still be able to read through this spec without too much of a problem.

Plain old RSpec scripts usually need a string passed to the `describe` method. The spec in Listing 18.3 happens to be an `ActiveRecord` model spec based on the RSpec on Rails plugin, so it's okay to pass it an `ActiveRecord` model class instead of a description string. (More on that later when we get into Rails specifics. Right now we're still just getting through the basics of RSpec.)

Shared Behaviors

Often you'll want to specify multiple behaviors that share a lot of the same behavior. It would be silly to type out the same code over and over. Most programmers will extract the common code into individual methods. However, the problem is that an RSpec behavior contains many pieces:

- `before(:all)`
- `before(:each)`
- `after(:each)`
- `after(:all)`
- all of the expectations
- any included modules

Even with good refactoring, you'll end up with lots of duplication. Fortunately RSpec lets us take advantage of shared behaviors. Shared behaviors aren't run individually, but rather are included into other behaviors. We do this by passing the `:shared => true` option to describe.

Let's say we want to specify two classes, `Teacher` and `Student`. In addition to their unique behavior, they have some common behavior that we're interested in. Instead of specifying the same behavior twice, we can create a shared behavior and include it in each class's specification.

```
describe "people in general", :shared => true do
  it "should have a name" do
    @person.name.should_not be_nil
  end
```

```
  it "should have an age" do
    @person.age.should_not be_nil
  end
end
```

Where does the `@person` instance variable come from? We never assigned it anywhere. It turns out this spec won't run because there's nothing to run yet. Shared behaviors are just used to factor out common behavior specifications. We need to write another spec that uses the shared behavior.

```
describe Teacher do
  before(:each) do
    @person = Teacher.new("Ms. Smith", 30, 50000)
  end

  it_should_behave_like "people in general"

  it "should have a salary" do
    @person.salary.should == 50000
  end
end
```

The `it_should_behave_like` takes a string argument. RSpec then finds the shared behavior with that name and includes it into the `Teacher` specification.

We can do the same thing with `Student`.

```
describe Student do
  before(:each) do
    @person = Student.new("Susie", 8, "pink")
  end

  it_should_behave_like "people in general"

  it "should have a favorite color" do
    @person.favorite_color.should == "pink"
  end
end
```

Passing —`format specdoc` (or -`f s` in abbreviated form) to the `spec` command shows that the shared behavior is indeed included in the individual class specifications.

```
Teacher
- should have a name
- should have an age
- should have a salary

Student
- should have a name
- should have an age
- should have a favorite color
```

It's important to note that, as of this writing, RSpec runs the `before` and `after` methods in the order they're defined in the spec. You can see this by adding an output statement to each one.

```
describe "people in general"
  before(:each) do
    puts "shared before()"
  end

  after(:each) do
    puts "shared after()"
  end
  ...
end

describe Teacher do
  before(:each) do
    puts "teacher before()"
    @person = Teacher.new("Ms. Smith", 30, 50000)
  end

  after(:each) do
    puts "teacher after()"
  end

  it_should_behave_like "people in general"
  ...
end
```

This will give us the following output:

```
teacher before()
shared before()
teacher after()
shared after()
.
```

Move the `it_should_behave_like` statement to the beginning of the spec and notice how the shared behavior's `before` method runs first.

RSpec's Mocks and Stubs

In Chapter 17, "Testing," we introduced the concepts of mocks and stubs in association with the Mocha library. RSpec relies heavily on mocking and stubbing.[3] It's possible to use Mocha together with RSpec, but in our examples we'll use RSpec's own mocking and stubbing facilities, which are equally powerful. Actually, they are almost the same—mostly the method names change a little bit.

Mock Objects

To create a mock object, you simply call the `mock` method anywhere in a spec, and give it a name as an optional parameter. It's a good idea to give mock objects a name if you will be using more than one of them in your spec. If you use multiple anonymous mocks, you'll probably have a hard time telling them apart if one fails.

```
echo = mock('echo')
```

Remember that you set expectations about what messages are sent to your mock during the course of your spec—mocks will cause a spec to fail if their expectations are not met. Where you would say `expects` in Mocha to set an expectation on that mock that a message will be passed, in RSpec we say `should_receive` or `should_not_receive`.

```
echo.should_receive(:sound)
```

Both frameworks have a chained method called `with` used to set expected parameters, and where in Mocha we would say `returns` to set the return value, in RSpec we say `and_return`. It's close enough that you should be able to switch between frameworks pretty easily, if you need to do so.

```
echo.should_receive(:sound).with("hey").and_return("hey")
```

Null Objects

Occasionally you just want an object for testing purposes that accepts any message passed to it—a pattern known as *null object*. It's possible to make one using the `mock` method and the `:null_object` option.

```
null_object = mock('null', :null_object => true)
```

Stub Objects

You can easily create a *stub object* in RSpec via the `stub` factory method. You pass `stub` a name (just like a mock) and default attributes as a hash.

```
yodeler = stub('yodeler', :yodels? => true)
```

By the way, there's no rule that the name parameter of a mock or stub needs to be a string. It's pretty typical to pass `mock` or `stub` a class reference corresponding to the real type of object.

```
yodeler = stub(Yodeler, :yodels? => true)
```

The `stub` factory method is actually just a convenience—what you get back is a `Mock` object, with predefined method stubs, as you can see from its implementation shown in Listing 18.4:

Listing 18.4   File `rspec/lib/spec/mocks/spec_methods.rb`, Line 22

```
def stub(name, stubs={})
  object_stub = mock(name)
  stubs.each { |key, value| object_stub.stub!(key).and_return(value) }
  object_stub
end
```

Partial Mocking and Stubbing

See the `stub!` method in Listing 18.4? You can use it to install or replace a method on any object, not just mocks—a technique called partial mocking and stubbing.

A *partial* is RSpec's way of describing an instance of an existing class that has some mocked or stubbed behavior set on it. Even though RSpec's authors warn us about the practice in their docs, the ability to do partial mocking and stubbing is actually really crucial to RSpec working well with Rails, particularly when it comes to interactions involving `ActiveRecord`'s `create` and `find` methods.

To see RSpec mocking and stubbing in action, let's go back and take a look at another Monkeycharger model spec, this time for the `Authorizer` class. It talks to a payment gateway and specifies how credit card transactions are handled.

You might recall that back in Chapter 17, in the "Rails Mocks?" section, we touched on how external services need to be mocked, so that we don't end up sending test data to a real service. Listing 18.5 shows you this technique in action, using RSpec mocks and stubs.

Listing 18.5   Monkeycharger's `Authorizer` Model Spec

```
describe Authorizer, "processing a non-saved card" do

  before(:each) do
    @card = CreditCard.new(:name => 'Joe Van Dyk',
                           :number => '4111111111111111',
                           :year => 2009, :month => 9,
                           :cvv => '123')
  end

  it "should send authorization request to the gateway" do
    $gateway.should_receive(:authorize)
        .with(599, @card).and_return(successful_authorization)

    Authorizer::authorize!(:credit_card => @card, :amount => '5.99')
  end

  it "should return the transaction id it receives from the gateway" do
    $gateway.should_receive(:authorize)
        .with(599, @card).and_return(successful_authorization)

    Authorizer::authorize!(:credit_card => @card, :amount => '5.99')
```

```
        .should == successful_authorization.authorization
    end

  it "authorize! should raise AuthorizationError on failed authorize" do
    $gateway.should_receive(:authorize)
        .with(599, @card).and_return(unsuccessful_authorization)

      lambda {
        Authorizer::authorize!(:credit_card => @card, :amount =>
'5.99')
      }.should raise_error(AuthorizationError,
                            unsuccessful_authorization.message)
  end

  private

  def successful_authorization
    stub(Object, :success? => true, :authorization => '1234')
  end

  def unsuccessful_authorization
    stub(Object, :success? => false, :message => 'reason why it
failed')
  end
end
```

Running Specs

Specs are executable documents. Each example block is executed inside its own object instance, to make sure that the integrity of each is preserved (with regard to instance variables, etc.).

If I run the credit card specs from Listings 18.1 and 18.2 using the `spec` command that should have been installed on my system by RSpec, I'll get output similar to that of `Test::Unit`—familiar, comfortable, and passing… just not too informative.

```
$ spec spec/models/credit_card_spec.rb
.........

Finished in 0.330223 seconds

9 examples, 0 failures
```

Bye-Bye `Test::Unit`

In case it wasn't obvious by now, when we're using RSpec, we don't have to use `Test::Unit` any more. They serve similar, mutually exclusive functions: to specify and verify the operation of our application. Both can be used to drive the design of an application in an evolutionary manner according to the precepts of test-driven development (TDD).

There's a project called test/spec that implements Behavior-Driven Development (BDD) principles on top of `Test::Unit`, but at the time that I'm writing this, it's far behind RSpec and doesn't seem to have much momentum.

RSpec is capable of outputting results of a spec run in many formats. The traditional dots output that looks just like `Test::Unit` is called *progress* and, as we saw a moment ago, is the default.

If we add the `-fs` command-line parameter to `spec`, we can cause it to output the results of its run in a very different and much more interesting format, the *specdoc* format. It surpasses anything that `Test::Unit` is capable of doing on its own "out of the box."

```
$ spec -fs spec/models/credit_card_spec.rb

A valid credit card
- should be valid

CreditCard
- should have a valid month
- should have a valid year
- date should not be in the past
- should have two words in the name
- should have two words in the last name if the name is three words
long
- should have one word in the first name if the name is three words
long
```

```
We only take Visa and MasterCard
- should not accept amex
- should not accept discover

Finished in 0.301157 seconds

9 examples, 0 failures
```

Nice, huh? If this is the first time you're seeing this kind of output, I wouldn't be surprised if you drifted off in speculation about whether RSpec could help you deal with sadistic PHB-imposed documentation requirements.

We can also do Ruby RDoc-style output:

```
$ spec -fr spec/models/authorization_spec.rb
# Authorizer a non-saved card
# * the gateway should receive the authorization
# * authorize! should return the transaction id
# * authorize! should throw an exception on a unsuccessful
authorization

Finished in 0.268268 seconds

3 examples, 0 failures
```

And perhaps the most beautiful output of all, color-coded HTML output, which is what TextMate pops up in a window whenever I run a spec in the editor.

Figure 18.1 shows a successful spec run. If we had failing examples, some of those bars would have been red. Having these sorts of self-documenting abilities is one of the biggest wins you get in choosing RSpec. It actually compels most people to work toward better coverage of their project. I also know from experience that development managers tend to really appreciate RSpec's output, even incorporating it into their project deliverables.

Besides the different formatting, there are all sorts of other command-line options available. Just type **spec --help** to see them all.

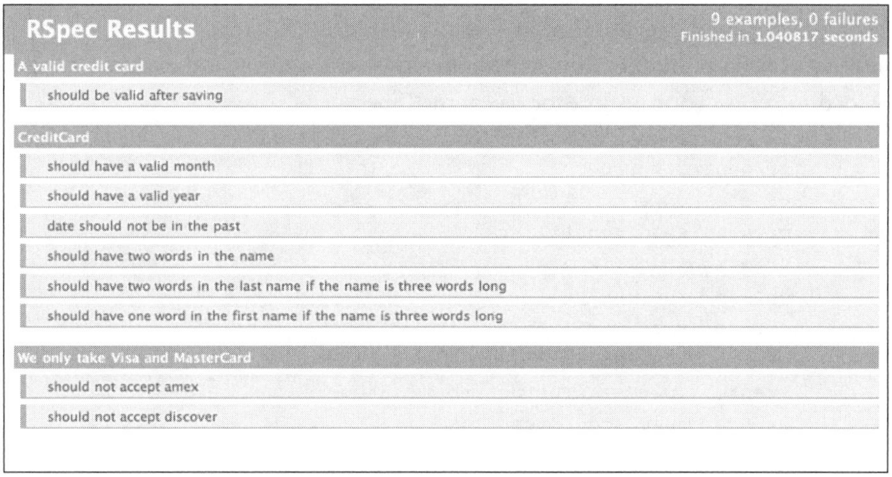

Figure 18.1   RSpec HTML-formatted results

Installing RSpec and the RSpec on Rails Plugin

To get started with RSpec on Rails, you need to install the main RSpec library gem. Then install the RSpec on Rails plugin[4] into your project:

```
sudo gem install rspec

script/plugin install
    svn://rubyforge.org/var/svn/rspec/tags/CURRENT/rspec_on_rails
```

The project leads actually advise you to install RSpec as a Rails plugin also, so that you can have different versions on a per-project basis.

That does it for our introduction to RSpec. Now we'll take a look at using RSpec with Ruby on Rails.

The RSpec on Rails Plugin

The RSpec on Rails plugin provides four different contexts for specs, corresponding to the four major kinds of objects you write in Rails. Along with the API support you need to write Rails specs, it also provides code generators and a bundle of Rake tasks.

Generators

Assuming you have the plugin installed already, you should run the `rspec` generator provided to set up your project for use with RSpec.

```
$ script/generate rspec
      create  spec
      create  spec/controllers
      create  spec/fixtures
      create  spec/helpers
      create  spec/models
      create  spec/views
      create  spec/spec_helper.rb
      create  spec/spec.opts
      create  previous_failures.txt
      create  script/spec_server
      create  script/spec
```

A `spec` directory is created, containing subdirectories for each of the four types of specs. A bunch of additional support files are also created, which we'll look at in detail later on.

Model Specs

Model specs help you design and verify the domain model of your Rails application, both `ActiveRecord` and your own classes. RSpec on Rails doesn't provide too much special functionality for model specs, because there's not really much needed beyond what's provided by the base library.

An `rspec_model` generator is provided, which can be used in place of the default `model` generator that's included in Rails. It functions almost the same as its default counterpart, except that it creates a stubbed-out spec in the `models` directory instead of a stubbed-out test in the `test` directory. Pass it a class name (capitalized) and pairs of *attribute_name*:*type* values. The `datetime` columns (`updated_at`/`created_at`) are automatically added to the migration; no need to specify them.

```
$ script/generate rspec_model Schedule name:string
      exists  app/models/
      exists  spec/models/
      exists  spec/fixtures/
      create  app/models/schedule.rb
      create  spec/fixtures/schedules.yml
```

```
create  spec/models/schedule_spec.rb
exists  db/migrate
create  db/migrate/001_create_schedules.rb
```

The generated `Schedule` class is empty and not very interesting. The skeleton `spec/models/schedule.rb` looks like this:

```
require File.dirname(__FILE__) + '/../spec_helper'

describe Schedule do
  before(:each) do
    @schedule = Schedule.new
  end

  it "should be valid" do
    @schedule.should be_valid
  end
end
```

Assume for a moment that the `Schedule` class has a collection of day objects.

```
class Schedule < ActiveRecord::Base
  has_many :days
end
```

Let's specify that we should be able to get a roll-up total of hours from schedule objects. Instead of fixtures, we'll mock out the `days` dependency.

```
require File.dirname(__FILE__) + '/../spec_helper'

describe Schedule do
  before(:each) do
    @schedule = Schedule.new
  end

  it "should calculate total hours" do
    days_proxy = mock('days')
    days_proxy.should_receive(:sum).with(:hours).and_return(40)
    @schedule.stub!(:days).and_return(days_proxy)
    @schedule.total_hours.should == 40
  end
end
```

Here we've taken advantage of the fact that association proxies in Rails are rich objects. `ActiveRecord` gives us several methods for running database aggregate functions. We set up an expectation that `days_proxy` should receive the `sum` method with one argument—`:hours`—and return `40`.

We can satisfy this specification with a very simple implementation:

```
class Schedule
  has_many :days

  def total_hours
    days.sum :hours
  end
end
```

One valid criticism of this approach is that it makes our code harder to refactor. Our spec would fail if we changed the implementation of `total_hours` to use `Enumerable#inject`, even though the external behavior doesn't change. Specifications are not only about describing the visible behavior of objects, but the interactions between an object and its associated objects as well. Mocking the association proxy in this case lets us clearly specify how a `Schedule` should interact with its `Days`.

A huge benefit of mocking the `days` proxy is that we no longer rely on the database[5] in order to write our specifications and implement the `total_hours` method. Our specs will run very quickly, and we don't have any messy fixtures to deal with!

Leading mock objects advocates see mock objects as a temporary design tool. You may have noticed that we haven't defined the `Day` class yet. So another benefit of using mock objects is that they allow us to specify behavior in true isolation, and during design-time. There's no need to break our design rhythm by stopping to create the `Day` class and database table. This may not seem like a big deal for such a simple example, but for more involved specifications it is really helpful to just focus on the design task at hand. After the database and real object models exist, you can go back and replace the mock `days_proxy` with calls to the real deal. This is a subtle, yet very powerful message about mocks that is usually missed.

Quick Mock `ActiveRecord` Models

```
mock_model(model_class, stubs = {})
```

The `mock_model` method creates mocks with autogenerated numeric ids and a number of certain common methods stubbed out:

- `id`   Returns the autogenerated `id` value
- `to_param`   Returns the `id` value as a string
- `new_record?`   Returns `false`
- `errors`   Returns a stub errors collection that will report a 0 error count
- `is_a?`   Returns `true` if the parameter matches `model_class`
- `class`   Returns `model_class`

You should pass in any additional stubbed method values via the `stubs` hash argument or set them in a block using the yielded mock instance.

Controller Specs

RSpec gives you the ability to specify your controllers either in isolation from their associated views or together with them, as in regular Rails tests. According to the API docs:

> Controller Specs use `Spec::Rails::DSL::ControllerBehaviour`, which supports running specs for Controllers in two modes, which represent the tension between the more granular testing common in TDD and the more high-level testing built into rails. BDD sits somewhere in between: we want to achieve a balance between specs that are close enough to the code to enable quick fault isolation and far enough away from the code to enable refactoring with minimal changes to the existing specs.

The `Controller` class is passed to the `describe` method like this:

```
describe MessagesController do
```

An optional second parameter can provide additional information, or you can explicitly use the `controller_name` method inside a `describe` block to tell RSpec which controller to use.

```
describe "Requesting /messages using GET" do
  controller_name :messages
  fixtures :people
```

I typically group my controller examples by action and HTTP method. Fixtures are available if needed, like any other Rails test or spec. This example requires a logged-in user, so I stub my application controller's `current_person` accessor to return a fixture.

```
    before(:each) do
      controller.stub!(:current_person, people(:quentin))
```

Next, I create a mock `Message` object using the `mock_model` method. I want this mock message to be returned whenever `Message.find` is called during the spec.

```
    @message = mock_model(Message)
      Message.stub!(:find).and_return([@message])
    end
```

Now I can start specifying the behavior of actions (in this case, the `index` action). The most basic expectation is that the response should be successful, HTTP's 200 OK response code.

```
    it "should be successful" do
      get :index
      response.should be_success
    end
```

I also want to specify that the `find` method of `Message` is called with the proper arguments.

```
    it "should find all the messages" do
      Message.should_receive(:find).with(:all).and_return [@message]
      get :index
    end
```

Additional expectations that should be done for most controller actions include the template to be rendered and variable assignment.

```
it "should render index.rhtml" do
  get :index
  response.should render_template(:index)
end

it "should assign the found messages for the view" do
  get :index
  assigns[:messages].should include(@message)
end
```

Previously we saw how to stub out a model's association proxy. It would be nice not to have to use fixtures in the controller specs. Instead of stubbing the controller's `current_person` method to return a fixture, we can have it return a mock person.

```
@mock_person = mock_model(Person, :name => "Quentin")
controller.stub!(:current_person).and_return @mock_person
```

Isolation and Integration Modes

By default, RSpec on Rails controller specs run in *isolation mode*, meaning that view templates are not involved. The benefit of this mode is that you can spec the controller in complete isolation of the view, hence the name. Maybe you can sucker someone else into maintaining the view specs? (The next heading in the chapter is all about spec'ing views.)

Actually, that "sucker" comment is facetious. Having separate view specs is not as difficult as it's made out to be sometimes. It also provides much better fault isolation, which is a fancy way of saying that you'll have an easier time figuring out what's wrong when something fails.

If you prefer to exercise your views in conjunction with your controller logic inside the same controller specs, just as traditional Rails functional tests do, then you can tell RSpec on Rails to run in *integration* mode using the `integrate_views` macro. It's not an all-or-nothing decision—you can specify modes on a per-behavior basis.

```
describe "Requesting /messages using GET" do
  integrate_views
```

When you run integrated, the controller specs will be executed once with view rendering turned on.

Specifying Errors

Ordinarily, Rails rescues exceptions that occur during action processing, so that it can respond with a 501 error code and give you that great error page with the stack trace and request variables, and so on. In order to directly specify that an action should raise an error, you have to override the controller's `rescue_action` method, by doing something like this:

```
controller.class.send(:define_method, :rescue_action) { |e| raise e }
```

If you don't mind just checking that the response code was an error, you can just use the `be_an_error` predicate or `response_code` accessor of the `response` object:

```
it "should return an error in the header" do
  response.should be_an_error
end

it "should return a 501" do
  response.response_code.should == 501
end
```

Specifying Routes

One of Rails' central components is routing. The routing mechanism is the way Rails takes an incoming request URL and maps it to the correct controller and action. Given its importance, it is a good idea to specify the routes in your application. You can do this with the `route_for` method in a controller spec.

```
describe MessagesController, "routing" do
  it "should map { :controller => 'messages', :action => 'index' } to
  /messages" do
    route_for(:controller => "messages", :action => "index").should ==
  "/messages"
  end

  it "should map { :controller => 'messages', :action => 'edit',
  :id => 1 }
```

```
  to /messages/1;edit" do
    route_for(:controller => "messages", :action => "edit",
  :id => 1).should == "/messages/1;edit"
  end
end
```

View Specs

Controller specs let us integrate the view to make sure there are no errors with the view, but we can do one better by specifying the views themselves. RSpec will let us write a specification for a view, completely isolated from the underlying controller. We can specify that certain tags exist and that the right data is outputted.

Let's say we want to write a page that displays a private message sent between members of an internet forum. RSpec creates the spec/views/messages directory when we use the rspec_controller generator. The first thing we would do is create a file in that directory for the show view, naming it show_rhtml_spec.rb. Next we would set up the information to be displayed on the page.

```
describe "messages/show.rhtml" do
  before(:each) do
    @message = mock_model(Message, :subject => "RSpec rocks!")
    sender = mock_model(Person, :name => "Obie Fernandez")
    @message.stub!(:sender).and_return(sender)
    recipient = mock_model(Person, :name => "Pat Maddox")
    @message.stub!(:recipient).and_return(recipient)
```

If you want to be a little more concise at the cost of one really long line of code that you'll have to break up into multiple lines, you can inline the creation of the mocks like this:

```
describe "messages/show.rhtml" do
  before(:each) do
    @message = mock_model(Message,
      :subject => "RSpec rocks!",
      :sender => mock_model(Person, :name => "Obie Fernandez"),
      :recipient => mock_model(Person, :name => "Pat Maddox"))
```

Either way, this is standard mock usage similar to what we've seen before. Again, mocking the objects used in the view allows us to completely isolate the specification.

Assigning Instance Variables

We now need to assign the message to the view. The `rspec_on_rails` plugin gives us a familiar-looking `assigns` method, which you can treat as a hash.

```
    assigns[:message] = @message
  end
```

Fantastic! Now we are ready to begin specifying the view page. We'd like to specify that the message subject is displayed, wrapped in an `<h1>` tag. The `have_tag` expectation takes two arguments—the tag selector and the content within the tag. It wraps the `assert_select` functionality included with Rails testing, which we covered extensively in Chapter 17.

```
it "should display the message subject" do
  render "messages/show"
  response.should have_tag('h1', 'RSpec rocks!')
end
```

HTML tags often have an ID associated with them. We would like our page to create a `<div>` with the ID `message_info` for displaying the sender and recipient's names. We can pass the ID to `have_tag` as well.

```
it "should display a div with id message_info" do
  render "messages/show"
  response.should have_tag('div#message_info')
end
```

What if we want to specify that the sender and recipient's names should appear in `<h3>` tags within the `div`?

```
it "should display sender and recipient names in div#message_info" do
  render "messages/show"
  response.should have_tag('div#message_info') do
    with_tag('h3#sender', 'Sender: Obie Fernandez')
    with_tag('h3#recipient', 'Recipient: Pat Maddox')
  end
end
```

Stubbing Helper Methods

Note that the view specs do not mix in helper methods automatically, in order to preserve isolation. If your view template code relies on helper methods, you need to mock or stub them out on the provided `template` object.

The decision to mock versus stub those helper methods should depend on whether they're an active player in the behavior you want to specify, as in the following example:

```
it "should truncate subject lines" do
  template.should_receive(:truncate).exactly(2).times
  render "messages/index"
end
```

If you forget to mock or stub helper method calls, your spec will fail with a `NoMethodError`.

Helper Specs

Speaking of helpers, it's really easy to write specs for your custom helper modules. Just pass `describe` to your helper module and it will be mixed into the spec class so that its methods are available to your example code.

```
describe ProfileHelper do
  it "profile_photo should return nil if user's photos is empty" do
    user = mock_model(User, :photos => [])
    profile_photo(user).should == nil
  end
end
```

It's worth noting that in contrast to view specs, all of the framework-provided `ActionView::Helper` modules are mixed into helper specs, so that they're available to your helper code. All dynamically generated routes helper methods are added too.

Scaffolding

Rails comes with the `scaffold_resource` generator to easily create RESTful controllers and the underlying models. The `rspec_on_rails` plugin provides the `rspec_scaffold` generator, which does the same thing using RSpec instead of `Test::Unit`.

Play around with `rspec_scaffold` when you have some free time—the generated specs are another source of very good example spec code for all three MVC layers. It generates specs that cover the Rails-generated code 100%, making it a very good learning tool.

RSpec Tools

There are several open-source projects that enhance RSpec's functionality and your productivity. (None of these tools are unique to RSpec. In fact they all were originally written for `Test::Unit`.)

Autotest

The Autotest project is part of the ZenTest suite[6] created by Ryan Davis and Eric Hodel. As the name implies, it automatically runs your test suite for you. Each time you save a file in your project, Autotest will run any spec files that may be affected by the change. This is an excellent tool for getting in a solid red-green-refactor rhythm because you won't have to switch windows to manually run the tests. In fact you don't even need to run any command! Just `cd` to your project's directory and type `autospec` to kick things off.

RCov

RCov is a code coverage tool for Ruby.[7] You can run it on a spec file to see how much of your production code is covered. It provides HTML output to easily tell what code is covered by specs and what isn't. You can RCov individually on a spec file, or the `rspec_on_rails` plugin provides the `spec:rcov` task for running all of your specs under RCov. The results are outputted into a directory named `coverage` and contain a set of HTML files that you can browse by opening `index.html` (as shown in Figure 18.2):

Heckle is part of the Seattle Ruby Brigade's awesome collection of projects,[8] and is another code coverage tool. Instead of simply checking the scope of your tests, Heckle helps you measure the effectiveness of your specs. It actually goes into your code and scrambles things like variable values and `if` statements. If none of your specs break, you're missing a spec somewhere.

The current versions of RSpec have Heckle support built-in. Just experiment with the `--heckle` option and see what happens.

C0 code coverage information

Generated on Thu Sep 06 14:59:20 -0400 2007 with rcov 0.8.0

Name	Total lines	Lines of code	Total coverage	Code coverage
TOTAL	630	391	89.5%	83.6%
app/controllers/application.rb	45	29	91.1%	86.2%
app/controllers/assets_controller.rb	105	62	94.3%	90.3%
app/controllers/session_controller.rb	30	25	100.0%	100.0%
app/controllers/user_assets_controller.rb	24	14	87.5%	78.6%
app/controllers/users_controller.rb	90	64	93.3%	90.6%
app/helpers/application_helper.rb	8	5	50.0%	40.0%
app/helpers/assets_helper.rb	2	2	100.0%	100.0%
app/helpers/user_assets_helper.rb	6	5	100.0%	100.0%
app/helpers/users_helper.rb	2	2	100.0%	100.0%
app/models/asset.rb	26	7	100.0%	100.0%
app/models/authenticated_base.rb	87	61	100.0%	100.0%
app/models/user.rb	44	17	81.8%	58.8%
lib/ar_extensions.rb	41	36	85.4%	83.3%
lib/authenticated_system.rb	120	62	75.8%	53.2%

Generated using the rcov code coverage analysis tool for Ruby version 0.8.0.

Figure 18.2   A sample RCov coverage reportHeckle

Conclusion

You've gotten a taste of the different testing experience that RSpec delivers. At first it may seem like the same thing as Test::Unit with some words substituted and shifted around. One of the key points of TDD is that it's about design rather than testing. This is a lesson that every good TDDer learns through lots of experience. RSpec uses a different vocabulary and style to emphasize that point. It comes with the lesson baked in so that you can attain the greatest benefits of TDD right away.

References

1. Well, other than to write Chapter 17, which has full coverage of `Test::Unit`.

2. You can grab a copy of the Monkeycharger project at http://monkeycharger.googlecode.com/.

3. Confused about the difference between mocks and stubs? Read Martin Fowler's explanation at http://www.martinfowler.com/articles/mocksArentStubs.html.

4. If you have firewall trouble with that plugin because of the `svn://` address, please follow the instructions at http://rspec.rubyforge.org/documentation/rails/install.html.

5. Actually that's not quite true. `ActiveRecord` still connects to the database to get the column information for Schedule. However, you could actually stub that information out as well to completely remove dependence on the database.

6. http://rubyforge.org/projects/zentest/.

7. http://rubyforge.org/projects/rcov.

8. http://rubyforge.org/projects/seattlerb/.

CHAPTER 19

Extending Rails with Plugins

Once again, when we come to the creation of things by people, the form this unfolding takes, always, is step by step to please yourself. We cannot perform the unfolding process without knowing how to please ourselves.
—Christopher Alexander

Even though the standard Ruby on Rails APIs are very useful, sooner or later you'll find yourself wishing for a particular feature not in Rails core or that a bit of standard Rails behavior were different. That's where plugins come into play, and this book has already described many useful plugins that you will use on a day-to-day basis to write your Rails applications.

What about plugins as a way to accomplish reuse with our own code? Would learning how to write plugins help us write more modular applications and better understand how Rails itself is implemented? Absolutely!

This chapter covers the basic topics of managing plugins in your project, including the use of a tool that some consider indispensable for the task: Piston. We'll also supply you with enough information to get you started writing your own Rails plugins.

Managing Plugins

Rails 1.0 introduced a plugin system that lets developers easily add new functionality into the framework. An official mechanism makes it feasible to extract some of the novel, useful features you've come up with in your individual applications and share those extracted solutions with other developers, as a single self-contained unit that is easy to both maintain and share.

Plugins aren't only useful for sharing new features: As Rails matures, more and more focus is being placed on the use of plugins to test alterations to the Rails framework itself. Almost any significant new piece of functionality or patch can be implemented as a plugin and road-tested easily by a number of developers before it is considered for inclusion in the core framework. Whether you find a bug in Rails and figure out how to fix it or you come up with a significant feature enhancement, you will want to put your code in a plugin for easy distribution and testing.

Of course, changing significant core behavior of the framework demands a solid understanding of how Rails works internally and is beyond the scope of this book. However, some of the techniques demonstrated will help you understand the way that Rails itself is implemented, which we trust will help you start patching core behavior the day that you need to do so.

Reusing Code

Our jobs as programmers require us to be abstract problem solvers. We solve problems that range from searching databases to updating online to-do lists to managing user authentication. The product of our labor is a collection of solutions, usually in the form of an application, to a particular set of problems that we've been asked to solve.

However, I doubt that many of us would *still* be programmers if we had to solve exactly the same problems repeatedly, day after day. Instead, we are always looking for ways to reapply existing solutions to the problems we encounter. Your code represents the abstract solution to a problem, and so you are often striving to either reuse this abstraction (albeit in slightly different contexts), or refine your solution so that it *can* be reused. Through reuse, you can save time, money, and effort, and give yourself the opportunity to focus on the interesting and novel aspects of the particular problem you're currently trying to solve. After all, it's coming up with interesting and novel solutions to problems that makes us really succeessful.

The Plugin Script

Using the `script/plugin` command is often the simplest and easiest way to install plugins. It should be run from the root directory of the application you are developing.

Before getting into gory details, here is an example of `script/plugin` in action:

```
$ cd /Users/obie/time_and_expenses
$ script/plugin install acts_as_taggable
+./acts_as_taggable/init.rb
+./acts_as_taggable/lib/README
+./acts_as_taggable/lib/acts_as_taggable.rb
+./acts_as_taggable/lib/tag.rb
+./acts_as_taggable/lib/tagging.rb
+./acts_as_taggable/test/acts_as_taggable_test.rb
```

Checking the `vendor/plugins` directory after running this script, you can see that a new directory has appeared named `acts_as_taggable`.

Where did these files come from? How did `script/plugin` know where to go to download `acts_as_taggable`? To understand what's really going on under the hood here, let's examine the plugin script's commands a bit more closely.

In the following sections, we cover each command in depth:

`script/plugin list`

Finding a list of all the available plugins is simple, using the `list` command:

```
$ script/plugin list
account_location
http://dev.rubyonrails.com/svn/rails/plugins/account_location/
acts_as_taggable
http://dev.rubyonrails.com/svn/rails/plugins/acts_as_taggable/
browser_filters
http://dev.rubyonrails.com/svn/rails/plugins/browser_filters/
continuous_builder
http://dev.rubyonrails.com/svn/rails/plugins/continuous_builder/
deadlock_retry
http://dev.rubyonrails.com/svn/rails/plugins/deadlock_retry/
exception_notification
http://dev.rubyonrails.com/svn/rails/plugins/exception_notification/
localization
http://dev.rubyonrails.com/svn/rails/plugins/localization/
...
```

This command returns a list of available plugins, along with the URL where that plugin can be found. If you take a closer look at the list of URLs, it should be clear that groups of plugins are often located under the same base URL: http://dev.rubyonrails.com/svn/rails/plugins, for instance. This URL is called a source, and the `list` command uses a collection of these when searching for plugins.

For example, when running `script/plugin install acts_as_taggable` earlier, the command checked each source in turn for one that contains a directory of the name specified—in this case, `acts_as_taggable`. The script found one under the source URL http://dev.rubyonrails.com/svn/ rails/plugins, and downloaded that directory to your local machine, giving you a copy of the `acts_as_taggable` plugin.

script/plugin sources

You can examine the list of all the plugin sources Rails will currently search when looking for plugins by using the `sources` command:

```
$ script/plugin sources
http://dev.rubyonrails.com/svn/rails/plugins/
http://svn.techno-weenie.net/projects/plugins/
http://svn.protocool.com/rails/plugins/
http://svn.rails-engines.org/plugins/
http://lesscode.org/svn/rtomayko/rails/plugins/
...
```

Note that you may see more or fewer URLs than this; don't worry, that's perfectly normal. This list is stored in a file on your local machine, and can be examined directly by opening it in any text editor. On Mac OS X and Linux, the file is located at: `~/.rails-plugin-sources`

script/plugin source [url [url2 [...]]]

It's possible to add a new plugin source manually, using the `source` command:

```
$ script/plugin source http://www.our-server.com/plugins/
Added 1 repositories.
```

The URL for the source includes everything up to but not including the name of your plugin itself. You can verify this by running `script/plugin  sources` afterward; the added URL should be there at the end of the list.

When this command fails, the URL specified has probably already been added as a source. In fact, that's one of its only failure modes, which conveniently brings us to the unsource command.

script/plugin unsource [url/url2 [...]]]

Imagine that you've added a plugin source with the following command:

```
$ script/plugin source http:///www.our-server.com/plugins/
 Added 1 repositories.
```

The triple slash (///) between http and www means that this URL isn't going to work properly, so you need to remove this source and add a corrected version. The source command's destructive twin, unsource, removes URLs from the list of active plugin sources:

```
$ script/plugin unsource http:///www.our-server.com/plugins/
 Removed 1 repositories.
```

You can ensure that the source has been removed by using `script/plugin sources` again. For both the `source` and `unsource` commands, multiple URLs can be given and each will be added (or removed) from the source list.

script/plugin discover [url]

The `discover` command checks via the Internet for any new plugin, and lets you add new sources for plugins to your collection. These sources are actually found by scraping the "Plugins" page on the Rails wiki[1] for the string "plugin" on any HTTP or Subversion URL. As you can see, each of the URLs returned matches this pattern:

```
$ script/plugin discover
Add http://opensvn.csie.org/rails_file_column/plugins/? [Y/n] y
Add http://svn.protocool.com/rails/plugins/? [Y/n] y
Add svn://rubyforge.org//var/svn/laszlo-plugin/rails/plugins/? [Y/n] y
Add http://svn.hasmanythrough.com/public/plugins/? [Y/n] y
Add http://lesscode.org/svn/rtomayko/rails/plugins/? [Y/n] y
...
```

You can supply your own plugin source page for `script/plugin discover` to scrape. Supplying the URL as an argument causes the `discover` command to use your page, rather than the Rails wiki, when it attempts to discover new plugin sources:

```
$ script/plugin discover http://internaldev.railsco.com/railsplugins
```

This can be especially effective if you maintain a list of sources you find useful and wish to share them with all of the developers on your team, for instance.

script/plugin install [plugin]

We've already seen this command in action, but `install` still has some tricks up its sleeve that will prove very useful. When using the `install` command, typically you supply it with a single argument, specifying the name of the plugin to download and install, for example:

```
$ script/plugin install simply_restful
```

As seen earlier, this command relies on the plugin being available from the list of sources you've manually added or discovered. On many occasions, you will bypass the source list and install a plugin directly from a known URL, by supplying it as an argument to the command:

```
$ script/plugin install
http://www.pheonix.org/plugins/acts_as_macgyver
+./vendor/plugins/acts_as_macgyver/init.rb
+./vendor/plugins/acts_as_macgyver/lib/mac_gyver/chemistry.rb
+./vendor/plugins/acts_as_macgyver/lib/mac_gyver/swiss_army_knife.rb
+./vendor/plugins/acts_as_macgyver/assets/toothpick.jpg
+./vendor/plugins/acts_as_macgyver/assets/busted_up_bike_frame.html
+./vendor/plugins/acts_as_macgyver/assets/fire_extinguisher.css
```

By specifying the direct URL explicitly, you can install the plugin without searching the list of sources for a match. Perhaps most usefully, avoiding a search through the list of sources can save a lot of time.

This isn't the end of the `install` command's talents, but those more advanced features are discussed later in the section "Subversion and `script/plugin`."

`script/plugin remove [plugin]`

Quite appropriately, this command performs the opposite of install: It removes the plugin from `vendor/plugins`:[2]

```
$script/plugin -v remove acts_as_taggable
Removing 'vendor/plugins/acts_as_taggable'
```

A quick inspection of your `vendor/plugins` directory shows that the `acts_as_taggable` folder has indeed been removed completely.

Running the `remove` command will also run the plugin's `uninstall.rb` script, if it has one.

`script/plugin update [plugin]`

Intuitively you might expect that running a command like `$ script/plugin update acts_as_taggable` will update your version of `acts_as_taggable` to the latest release, should any update exist, but that isn't quite the case, unless you have used one of the Subversion installation methods covered in the following section.

If you have installed your plugin using the simple, standard methods described so far, you can update the plugin in place by using the `install` command with the force flag:

```
$ script/plugin -f install my_plugin
```

The inclusion of the `-f` flag will force the plugin to be removed and then reinstalled.

Subversion and `script/plugin`

As mentioned earlier, most of the plugin sources you encounter will actually be Subversion repositories. Why is this useful for plugin users? Most importantly, because you don't have to be a developer contributing to a repository to receive updates from it; you can maintain a copy of a plugin that can be easily (or even automatically) updated when the plugin author adds new features, fixes bugs, and generally updates the central plugin code.

Before you can use Subversion, you need to ensure that it has been installed on your local systems. The Subversion project can be found at http://subversion.tigris.org, where they maintain a number of binary distributions of the Subversion tools. If you're running on Linux or Mac OS X, chances are that you already have it installed, but Windows users will almost certainly need to use one of the prebuilt installers available on the Subversion web site.

Checking Out a Plugin

When you run the install command without any options, it will produce a direct copy of the plugin files and place them in a folder under vendor/plugins. You will have to check the plugin's files into your own Subversion repository, and there will not be any direct link between the plugin's files and where they came from, except your memory and any documentation the author may have supplied, which can get somewhat problematic when you want to update this plugin with bug fixes or new features.

A possibly better option is to use Subversion to check out a copy of the code to your application and keep additional information that can be used to determine the current version of the plugin and where the plugin came from. This information can also be used to automatically update the plugin to the latest version from the repository.

To install a plugin by checking it out via Subversion, add the -o flag when running the install command:

```
$ script/plugin install -o white_list
A  t_and_e/vendor/plugins/white_list/test
A  t_and_e/vendor/plugins/white_list/test/white_list_test.rb
A  t_and_e/vendor/plugins/white_list/Rakefile
A  t_and_e/vendor/plugins/white_list/init.rb
A  t_and_e/vendor/plugins/white_list/lib
A  t_and_e/vendor/plugins/white_list/lib/white_list_helper.rb
A  t_and_e/vendor/plugins/white_list/README
Checked out revision 2517.
```

In the example, the white_list plugin is now checked out to my working directory, beneath the plugins folder, but it isn't linked in any way to my project or my own source control.

script/plugin update

When you're using Subversion to download your plugins, the update command becomes useful. When you run the update command against a plugin installed with the -o flag, the plugin script instructs Subversion (via the svn command) to connect to that plugin's Subversion repository and download any changes, updating your copy to the latest version. As with the `install -o` command, you can use the `-r` parameter to specify a specific revision to update to.

SVN Externals

While using Subversion with the `install -o` command is somewhat useful, it may cause you some grief when you try deploying your application. Remember that other than the existence of that plugin's files in your local working directory, it isn't linked to your project in any way. Therefore, you will need to install each of the plugins manually on the target server all over again when you attempt to deploy. Not good.

What we really need is some way of stating, as part of our application, that version X of plugin Y is needed wherever the application is expected to run. One way to achieve that outcome is to use a somewhat advanced feature of Subversion named externals.

When you set `svn:externals` properties on source-controlled folders of your application, you are effectively telling Subversion, "Whenever you check out or update this code, also check out or update this plugin from this other repository."

The `plugin install` script takes an `-x` parameter that tells it to do just that.

```
$ script/plugin install -x continuous_builder
A  t_and_e/vendor/plugins/continuous_builder/tasks
A  t_and_e/vendor/plugins/continuous_builder/tasks/test_build.rake
A  t_and_e/vendor/plugins/continuous_builder/lib
A  t_and_e/vendor/plugins/continuous_builder/lib/marshmallow.rb
A  t_and_e/vendor/plugins/continuous_builder/lib/builder.rb
A  t_and_e/vendor/plugins/builder/README.txt
Checked out revision 5651.
```

Running `svn propget svn:externals` allows you to see the properties that have been set for a given source-controlled directory. We'll run it on the `vendor/plugins` directory of our application:

```
$ svn propget svn:externals vendor/plugins/ continuous_builder
   http://dev.rubyonrails.com/svn/rails/plugins/continuous_builder
```

Because we installed the continuous builder plugin using the `-x` option, whenever you check out your application from the repository (including on a production server), that plugin will automatically be checked out also. However, it's still not an ideal solution, because the version that will be checked out is the latest HEAD revision of the plugin, not necessarily one that we've proven works correctly with our application.

Locking Down a Specific Version

As with the `install -o` and `update` commands, you can specify a specific revision to link via `svn:externals` by using the `-r` flag with a version number. When the `-r` flag is used, the specified plugin version will be used even when the plugin author releases a new version.

If you think about the chaos that could ensue from dependencies of your application being updated to new, potentially unstable versions without your explicit knowledge, you'll understand why it's a good practice to lock down specific revisions of your plugins. However, there's an even simpler way to manage plugin dependencies.

Using Piston

The free open-source utility Piston (http://piston.rubyforge.org/) makes managing the versions of libraries in your project's `vendor` folder (Rails, Gems, and Plugins) much less time-consuming and error-prone than working directly with Subversion.

Piston imports copies of dependent libraries into your own repository instead of linking to them via `svn:externals` properties. However, Piston also keeps metadata having to do with the source and revision number of the dependency as Subversion properties associated with the imported content. Piston's hybrid solution works out quite well in practice.

For example, since the plugin code becomes part of your source code repository, you can make changes to it as needed. (Local changes are not possible when using `svn:externals`.) When the day comes that you want to update the plugin to a newer version, in order to pick up bug fixes or new features, Piston will automatically merge your compatible local changes with the updated versions.

Installation

Piston is distributed as a RubyGem. Installation is as simple as typing `gem install piston`:

```
$ sudo gem install -include-dependencies piston
Need to update 13 gems from http://gems.rubyforge.org
```

```
. . . . . . . . . . . .
complete
Successfully installed piston-1.2.1
```

After installation, a new executable named `piston` will be available on your command line, with the following commands:

```
$ piston
Available commands are:
   convert        Converts existing svn:externals into Piston managed
folders
   help           Returns detailed help on a specific command
   import         Prepares a folder for merge tracking
   lock           Lock one or more folders to their current revision
   status         Determines the current status of each pistoned
directory
   unlock         Undoes the changes enabled by lock
   update         Updates all or specified folders to the latest revision
```

Importing a Vendor Library

The `import` command tells Piston to add a vendor library to your project. For example, let's use Piston to make our sample project run *EdgeRails*, meaning that Rails is executed out of the `vendor/rails` folder instead of wherever it is installed as a RubyGem:

```
$ piston import http://dev.rubyonrails.org/svn/rails/trunk
vendor/rails
Exported r5731 from 'http://dev.rubyonrails.org/svn/rails/trunk' to
'vendor/rails'
```

Piston does not commit anything to Subversion on its own. To make Piston changes permanent, you need to check in the changes yourself.

```
$ svn commit -m "Importing local copy of Rails"
```

Also, don't forget that unlike Rails' own plugin script, Piston takes a second argument specifying the target directory to install the library into (and if you leave the parameter off, it will default to the current directory).

For example, here's how you would install Rick Olsen's excellent `white_list` plugin, from the projects directory:

```
$ piston import
  http://svn.techno-
weenie.net/projects/plugins/white_list/vendor/plugins/white_list
Exported r2562 from
'http://svn.techno-weenie.net/projects/plugins/white_list' to
'vendor/plugins/white_list'
```

Converting Existing Vendor Libraries

If you've already been using `svn:externals` to link plugins into the source code of your project, the first thing you should do is to convert those over to Piston, by invoking the `piston convert` command from your project directory:

```
$ piston convert
Importing 'http://macromates.com/svn/Bundles/trunk/Bundles/
Rails.tmbundle/Support/plugins/footnotes' to vendor/plugins/footnotes
(-r 6038)
Exported r6038 from 'http://macromates.com/svn/Bundles/trunk/Bundles/
Rails.tmbundle/Support/plugins/footnotes' to 'vendor/plugins/footnotes'

Importing 'http://dev.rubyonrails.com/svn/rails/plugins/
continuous_builder' to vendor/plugins/continuous_builder (-r 5280)
Exported r5280 from 'http://dev.rubyonrails.com/svn/rails/plugins/
continuous_builder' to 'vendor/plugins/continuous_builder'

Done converting existing svn:externals to Piston
```

Again, remember that it's necessary to check in the resulting changes to your project files after running Piston.

Updating

When you want to get the latest changes from a remote repository for a library installed with Piston, use the `update` command:

```
$ piston update vendor/plugins/white_list/
Processing 'vendor/plugins/white_list/'...
   Fetching remote repository's latest revision and UUID
   Restoring remote repository to known state at r2562
   Updating remote repository to r2384
   Processing adds/deletes
   Removing temporary files / folders
   Updating Piston properties
   Updated to r2384 (0 changes)
```

Locking and Unlocking Revisions

You can prevent a local Piston-managed folder from updating by using the `piston lock` command. And once a folder is locked, you can unlock it by using the `piston _unlock` command. Locking functionality is provided as an extra precaution available to teams of Rails developers. If you know that updating a plugin will break the application, you can lock it and other developers will get an error if they try to update without unlocking.

Piston Properties

If we use `svn proplist` to examine the properties for `vendor/plugins/continuous _builder`, we'll see that Piston stores its own properties for each plugin folder rather than on the `plugins` folder itself:

```
$ svn proplist —verbose vendor/plugins/continuous_builder/

Properties on 'vendor/plugins/continuous_builder':

  piston:root :
http://dev.rubyonrails.com/svn/rails/plugins/continuous_builder

  piston:local-revision : 105
  piston:uuid : 5ecf4fe2-1ee6-0310-87b1-e25e094e27de
  piston:remote-revision : 5280
```

Writing Your Own Plugins

At some point in your Rails career, you might find that you want to share common code among similar projects that you're involved with. Or if you've come up with something particularly innovative, you might wonder if it would make sense to share it with the rest of the world.

Rails makes it easy to become a plugin author. It even includes a plugin generator script that sets up the basic directory structure and files that you need to get started:

```
$ script/generate plugin my_plugin
      create   vendor/plugins/my_plugin/lib
      create   vendor/plugins/my_plugin/tasks
      create   vendor/plugins/my_plugin/test
      create   vendor/plugins/my_plugin/README
      create   vendor/plugins/my_plugin/MIT-LICENSE
      create   vendor/plugins/my_plugin/Rakefile
      create   vendor/plugins/my_plugin/init.rb
      create   vendor/plugins/my_plugin/install.rb
      create   vendor/plugins/my_plugin/uninstall.rb
      create   vendor/plugins/my_plugin/lib/my_plugin.rb
      create   vendor/plugins/my_plugin/tasks/my_plugin_tasks.rake
      create   vendor/plugins/my_plugin/test/my_plugin_test.rb
```

The generator gives you the entire set of possible plugin directories and starter files, even including a /tasks folder for your plugin's custom rake tasks. The install.rb and uninstall.rb are optional one-time setup and teardown scripts that can do anything you want them to do. You don't have to use everything that's created by the plugin generator.

The two defining aspects of a plugin are the presence of the init.rb file and of a directory in the plugin called lib. If neither of these exists, Rails will not recognize that subdirectory of vendor/plugins as a plugin. In fact, many popular plugins consist only of an init.rb script and some files in lib.

The init.rb Hook

If you pop open the boilerplate init.rb file that Rails generated for you, you'll read a simple instruction.

```
# insert hook code here
```

Hook code means code that hooks into the Rails initialization routines. To see a quick example of hook code in action, just go ahead and generate a plugin in one of your projects and add the following line to its `init.rb`:

```
puts "Current Rails version: #{Rails::VERSION::STRING}"
```

Congratulations, you've written your first simple plugin. Run the Rails console and see what I mean:

```
$ script/console
Loading development environment.
Current Rails version: 1.2.3
>>
```

Code that's added to `init.rb` is run at startup. (That's any sort of Rails startup, including server, console, and `script/runner`.) Most plugins have their `require` statements in `init.rb`.

A few special variables are available to your code in `init.rb` having to do with the plugin itself:

- **name**—The name of your plugin (`'my_plugin'` in our simple example).

- **director**—The directory in which the plugin exists, which is useful in case you need to read or write nonstandard files in your plugin's directory.

- **loaded_plugins**—A `Set` containing all the names of plugins that have already been loaded, including the current one being initialized.

- **config**—The configuration object created in `environment.rb`. (See Chapter 1, "Rails Environments and Configuration," as well as the online API docs for `Rails::Configuration` to learn more about what's available via `config`.)

Our simple example is just that, simple. Most of the time you want a plugin to provide new functionality to the rest of your application or modify the Rails libraries in more interesting ways than printing out a version number on startup.

The `lib` Directory

The `lib` directory of your plugin is added to Ruby's load path before `init.rb` is run. That means that you can `require` your code without needing to jump through hoops specifying the load path:

```
require File.dirname(__FILE__) + '/lib/my_plugin' # unnecessary
```

Assuming your `lib` directory contains a file named `my_plugin.rb`, your `init.rb` just needs to read:

```
require 'my_plugin'
```

Simple. You can bundle any class or Ruby code in a plugin's lib folder and then load it in `init.rb` (or allow other developers to optionally load it in `environment.rb`) using Ruby's require statement. This is the simplest way to share Ruby code among multiple Rails applications.

It's typical for plugins to alter or enhance the behavior or existing Ruby classes. As a simple example, Listing 19.1 is the source of a plugin that gives ActiveRecord classes a cursorlike iterator. (Please note that a smarter implementation of this technique might incorporate transactions, error-handling, and batching. See http://weblog.jamisbuck.org/2007/4/6/faking-cursors-in-activerecord for more on the subject.)

Listing 19.1   Adding `Each` to `ActiveRecord` Classes

```ruby
# in file vendor/plugins/my_plugin/my_plugin.rb

class ActiveRecord::Base

  def self.each
    ids = connection.select_values("select id from #{table_name}")
    ids.each do |id|
      yield find(id)
    end
    ids.size
  end

end
```

In addition to opening existing classes to add or modify behavior, there are at least three other ways used by plugins to extend Rails functionality:

- Mixins, which describes inclusion of modules into existing classes

- Dynamic extension through Ruby's callbacks and hooks such as `method_missing`, `const_missing`, and `included`

- Dynamic extension using runtime evaluation with methods such as `eval`, `class_eval`, and `instance_eval`

Extending Rails Classes

The way that we re-open the `ActiveRecord::Base` class in Listing 19.1 and simply add a method to it is simple, but most plugins follow a pattern used internally in Rails and split their methods into two modules, one each for class and instance methods. We'll go ahead and add a useful `to_param` instance method to all our ActiveRecord objects too[3].

Let's rework `my_plugin` so that it follows that style. First, after requiring 'my_plugin' in `init.rb`, we'll send an include message to the ActiveRecord class itself:

```
ActiveRecord::Base.send(:include, MyPlugin)
```

There's also another way of accomplishing the same result, which you might encounter when browsing through the source code of popular plugins[4]:

```
ActiveRecord::Base.class_eval do
  include MyPlugin
end
```

Now we need to write a `MyPlugin` module to house the class and instance variables with which we will extend `ActiveRecord::Base`. See Listing 19.2.

Listing 19.2   Extensions to `ActiveRecord::Base`

```
module MyPlugin
  def self.included(base)
    base.extend(ClassMethods)
    base.send(:include, InstanceMethods)
  end

  module ClassMethods
    def each
      ids = connection.select_values("select id from #{table_name}")
      ids.each do |id|
        yield find(id)
      end
      ids.size
    end
  end

  module InstanceMethods
    def to_param
      has_name? ? "#{id}-#{name.gsub(/[^a-z0-9]+/i, '-')}" : super
    end

    private

    def has_name?
      respond_to?(:name) and not new_record?
    end

  end
end
```

You can use similar techniques to extend controllers and views.[5] For instance, if you want to add custom helper methods available in all your view templates, you can extend `ActionView` like this:

```
ActionView::Base.send(:include, MyPlugin::MySpecialHelper)
```

Now that we've covered the fundamentals of writing Rails plugins (`init.rb` and the contents of the `lib` directory), we can take a look at the other files that are created by the plugin generator script.

The README and MIT-LICENSE File

The first thing that developers do when they encounter a new plugin is to take a look in the README file. It's tempting to ignore this file, but at the very least, you should add a simple description of the what the plugin does, for future reference. The README file is also read and processed by Ruby's RDoc tool, when you generate documentation for your plugin using the doc:: Rake tasks. It's worth learning some fundamentals of RDoc formatting if you want the information that you put in the README file to look polished and inviting later.

Rails is open-sourced under the extremely liberal and open MIT license, as are most of the popular plugins available. In his keynote address to Railsconf 2007, David announced that the plugin generator will auto-generate an MIT license for the file, to help to solve the problem of plugins being distributed without an open-source license. Of course, you can still change the license to whatever you want, but the MIT license is definitely considered *the Rails way.*

The install.rb and uninstall.rb Files

This pair of files is placed in the root of the plugin directory along with init.rb and README. Just as the init.rb file can be used to perform a set of actions each time the server starts, these files can be used to ensure that prerequisites of your plugin are in place when the plugin is installed using the script/plugin install command and that your plugin cleans up after itself when it is uninstalled using script/ plugin remove.

Installation

For example, you might develop a plugin that generates intermediate data stored as temporary files in an application. For this plugin to work, it might require a temporary directory to exist before the data can be generated by the plugin—the perfect opportunity to use install.rb. See Listing 19.3.

Listing 19.3 Creating a Temporary Directory During Plugin Installation

```
require 'fileutils'
FileUtils.mkdir_p File.join(RAILS_ROOT, 'tmp', 'my_plugin_data')
```

By adding these lines to your plugin's install.rb file, the directory tmp/my_plugin_data will be created in any Rails application in which the plugin is installed.

This fire-once action can be used for any number of purposes, including but not limited to the following:

- Copying asset files (HTML, CSS, and so on) into the public directory
- Checking for the existence of dependencies (for example, RMagick)
- Installing other requisite plugins (see Listing 19.4)

Listing 19.4 Installing a Prerequisite Plugin

```
# Install the engines plugin unless it is already present
unless File.exist?(File.dirname(__FILE__) + "/../engines")
  Commands::Plugin.parse!(['install',
    'http://svn.rails-engines.org/plugins/engines'])
end
```

Listing 19.4 demonstrates how with creativity and a little digging through the Rails source code, you can find and reuse functionality such as the `parse!` directive of `Commands::Plugin`.

Removal

As mentioned, the `script/plugin remove` command checks for the presence of a file called `uninstall.rb` when removing a plugin. If this file is present, it will be evaluated just prior to the plugin files actually being deleted. Typically, this is useful for reversing any actions performed when the plugin was installed. This can be handy for removing any directories or specific data files that your plugin might have created when installed, or while the application was running.

Common Sense Reminder

What might not be so obvious about this scheme is that it isn't foolproof. Users of plugins often skip the installation routines without meaning to do so. Because plugins are almost always distributed via Subversion, it is trivial to add a plugin to your project with a simple checkout:

```
$ svn co http://plugins.com/svn/whoops vendor/plugins/whoops # no install
```

Or perhaps even more common is to add a plugin to your project by copying it over from another Rails project using the filesystem. I know I've done this many times. Same situation applies to plugin removal—a developer that doesn't know any better might uninstall a plugin from his project simply by deleting its folder from the vendor/plugins directory, in which case the uninstall.rb script would never run.

If as a plugin writer you are concerned about making sure that your install and/or uninstall scripts are actually executed, it's probably worthwile to stress the point in your announcements to the community and within the plugin documentation itself, such as the README file.

Custom Rake Tasks

It is often useful to include Rake tasks in plugins. For example, if your plugin stores files in a temporary directory (such as /tmp), you can include a helpful task for clearing out those temporary files without having to dig around in the plugin code to find out where the files are stored. Rake tasks such as this should be defined in a .rake file in your plugin's tasks folder (see Listing 19.5).

Listing 19.5 A Plugin's Cleanup Rake Task

```
# vendor/plugins/my_plugin/tasks/my_plugin.rake

namespace :my_plugin do

  desc 'Clear out the temporary files'
  task :cleanup => :environment do
    Dir[File.join(RAILS_ROOT, 'tmp', 'my_plugin_data')].each do |f|
      FileUtils.rm(f)
    end
  end

end
```

Rake tasks added via plugins are listed alongside their standard Rails brothers and sister when you run rake -T to list all the tasks in a project. (In the following snippet, I limited Rake's output by passing a string argument to use for matching task names):

```
$ rake -T my_plugin
rake my_plugin:cleanup    # Clear out the temporary files
```

The Plugin's Rakefile

Generated plugins get their own little Rakefile, which can be used from within the plugin's directory to run its tests and generate its RDoc documentation (see Listing 19.6).

Listing 19.6   A Generated Plugin Rakefile

```
require 'rake'
require 'rake/testtask'
require 'rake/rdoctask'

desc 'Default: run unit tests.'
task :default => :test

desc 'Test the my_plugin plugin.'
Rake::TestTask.new(:test) do |t|
  t.libs << 'lib'
  t.pattern = 'test/**/*_test.rb'
  t.verbose = true
end

desc 'Generate documentation for the my_plugin plugin.'
Rake::RDocTask.new(:rdoc) do |rdoc|
  rdoc.rdoc_dir = 'rdoc'
  rdoc.title    = 'MyPlugin'
  rdoc.options << '--line-numbers' << '--inline-source'
  rdoc.rdoc_files.include('README')
  rdoc.rdoc_files.include('lib/**/*.rb')
end
```

While we're on the subject, I'll also mention that Rails has its own default rake tasks related to plugins, and they're fairly self-explanatory:

```
$ rake -T plugin

rake doc:clobber_plugins        # Remove plugin documentation
rake doc:plugins                # Generate docs for installed plugins
rake test:plugins               # Run the plugin tests in
                                  vendor/plugins/*/**/test
                                  (or specify with PLUGIN=name)
```

Before closing this section, let's make the distinction between a plugin's `Rakefile` and any `.rake` files in the `tasks` folder clear:

- Use Rakefile for tasks that operate on the plugin's source files, such as special testing or documentation. These must be run from the plugin's directory.
- Use `tasks/*.rake` for tasks that are part of the development or deployment of the application itself in which the plugin is installed. These will be shown in the output of `rake -T`, the list of all Rake tasks for this application.

Testing Plugins

Last, but not least, after you've written your plugin, it's essential that you provide tests that verify its behavior. Writing tests for plugins is for the most part identical to any testing in Rails or Ruby and for the most part the methods used to test both are the same. However, because plugins cannot often predict the exact environment in which they are run, they require extra precautions to ensure that the test behavior of your plugin code is isolated from the rest of the application.

There is a subtle distinction between running plugin tests using the global `test:plugins` rake task and via the plugin's own `Rakefile`. Although the former can test all installed plugins at the same time, the internal `Rakefile` can and should be exploited to add any specific tasks your plugin requires to be tested properly.

Techniques used in testing plugins properly include bootstrapping a separate database for testing plugins in complete isolation. This is particularly useful when a plugin augments ActiveRecord with additional functionality, because you need to test the new methods in a controlled environment, minimizing the interaction with other plugins and the application's own test data.

As you can imagine, testing of plugins is a lengthy topic that is primarily of interest to plugin authors. Unfortunately, I must leave further analysis of the subject out of this book for reasons of practicality and overall length.

Conclusion

You have now learned about all the basic aspects of Rails plugins. You learned how to install them, including use of the Piston tool to help you manage plugin versions. You also learned the fundamentals of writing your own plugins—probably enough to get you started.

To cover everything related to Rails plugins would require its own book and would go beyond the needs of most Rails developers. To that end, we did not cover testing plugins or the more advanced techniques employed by plugin developers. We also did not discuss topics related to the life of a plugin beyond its initial development.

For in-depth learning about extending Rails with plugins, I strongly recommend the Addison-Wesley publication *Rails Plugins* by James Adam, who is considered the world's top expert on the subject.

References

1. http://wiki.rubyonrails.org/rails/pages/Plugins

2. The -v flag turns on verbose mode, and is only present in the example because the `remove` command does not normally give any feedback; without -v, it would be difficult to demonstrate that anything had actually happened.

3. See http://www.jroller.com/obie/entry/seo_optimization_of_urls_in for an explanation of how smart use of the `to_param` method can help your search engine optimization efforts on public-facing websites.

4. Jay Fields has a good blog post about the motivations behind using the various types of code extension at http://blog.jayfields.com/2007/01/class-reopening-hints.html.

5. Alex Young's http://alexyoung.org/articles/show/40/a_taxonomy_of_rails_plugins covers a variety of different kinds of Rails plugins, including a useful explanation of how to handle passed-in options for runtime-configuration.

CHAPTER 20

Rails Production Configurations

Persons grouped around a fire or candle for warmth or light are less able to pursue independent thoughts, or even tasks, than people supplied with electric light. In the same way, the social and educational patterns latent in automation are those of self-employment and artistic autonomy.
—Marshall McLuhan

One frequently overlooked aspect of building a Rails application is, believe it or not, launching and running it in production. In some cases you may not be responsible for this part of your project, but it is important to understand how a modern web application operates in a production environment. In this chapter we're going to show you how to build a simple production "stack," and how to get your Rails application running on it. Many concerns play a role in how you design your production stack. We are going to stick with a basic, common configuration so that you can understand the key components and best practices. We will review some of the common concerns that require more complex configurations, which will be helpful if this is your first production deployment.

Even if you have run a Rails app in a production environment before, you will probably find this chapter worth reading, as we discuss some simple ways to automate your production system and keep its configuration clean and simple.

A Brief History of Rails In Production

Fortunately it has become a relatively straightforward procedure to get a Rails application running in a production environment, but that has not always been the case. Many of the time-saving design philosophies and best practices that are essential to Rails, including the well-known maxims like "convention over configuration" and "don't repeat yourself," have also made their way into production configurations and deployment practices as well. Another way of saying this would be that automation is key. Rails enables developers to focus on the unique behavior of their application and automates the rest of the application behavior for you. In the same vein, tools like Mongrel, Mongrel Cluster, and Capistrano simplify and automate the tedious parts of running an application in production. Many of the lessons that have been learned about running a Rails app in production have been baked into tools like Capistrano, Mongrel, and Mongrel Cluster.

When Rails first came out, your options for running it behind a real web server like Apache were limited to CGI, Apache's `mod_ruby`, or FastCGI (aka FCGI), all of which had their shortcomings. Scripts in your Rails script directory like `spawner` and `reaper` were just workarounds for FastCGI issues.

In 2006 Zed Shaw wrote a production-capable, mostly Ruby HTTP web server called Mongrel. Mongrel was designed from the start to replace the existing options while staying small and simple. Instead of forcing a front-facing web server like Apache to convert an incoming HTTP request to CGI just in order to load the Ruby environment, Mongrel,[1] as an HTTP-speaking Ruby process, could speak to Apache directly. In doing so, Mongrel cut out two middlemen (converting the request from HTTP to CGI, and loading Ruby), reduced the number of moving parts, increased the reliability and predictability of the production environment, and sped up the performance. It also provided a fast web server for local development.

Some Basic Prerequisites

In order to successfully set up the production stack we're going to build, you'll need at least the following:

- A working understanding of Unix

  By a large margin most Rails applications in production are running on some variant of Unix (FreeBSD, OSX, Solaris, any Linux distro, etc.). Unless you have some severe production environment constraints (i.e., you work at a big company and are trying to sneak Rails through the back door), you should be setting your application up on Unix too. We'll assume that you understand how to use the command-line interface, and you can execute basic commands, install packages, start/stop services, and so on. The examples we list in this chapter will be through the Bash shell.[2]

- Access to a fresh server with sudo access

  We'll be installing everything onto one server, so you'll need to have access to one and be able to install software and perform deployments onto it. We'll list the specific applications and types of access in the section "The Stack Checklist." There are hosting options we'll list as well, in case you weren't able to find any via your favorite search engine.

- Respect for the production environment and a strong desire to learn

  Hopefully, your Rails application will live a long, healthy life in production. If you are not usually the person who is responsible for handling the production life cycle of an application, it's critical to understand how important this part is. You should avoid thinking about the setup and maintenance of your production environment as a chore. These tasks may not be as fun as writing an application, but they are at least as important. Like any technology (e.g., cars, ships, etc.), after your app is out in the open it will take on a different set of concerns. This is particularly important for modern web applications, which undergo frequent changes and iterative development cycles. Your production life cycle will feed back into your development life cycle, and so on.

  If you have ever run or maintained an application in production before, you understand how many of the peskier bugs arise here, and that this is the last place you want cluttered, poorly organized logs and configuration files getting in your way when you are the one getting up at 4 a.m. if something blows up. Respecting the importance and cleanliness of your production environment will inevitably save many headaches down the line, and many of the best practices you'll find here (and in the tools and libraries we recommend) are the product of learning how to avoid them.

- Willingness to shed old habits and learn new ones

  One key concept in production environments is *automation*. Automate everything! All of the deployments and configurations make your life simple by doing all of the work for you. If you like to tweak files by hand or modify deployments already on the server, you will need to break those old habits. These kinds of behaviors (which we have seen in developers and sysadmins alike) will make your production environment brittle, unpredictable, and otherwise doomed.

  The ability to operate a heavily automated production system requires you to use it as much as possible and remove any chance of manual human interference. You may think it's faster to make a quick change by hand by editing some file on the live production server, but those habits result in death by a thousand cuts. They are difficult to track over time, and automated systems do not respond well to manual changes.

- Willing suspension of disbelief

  This is somewhat of a corollary to the preceding point. Sometimes developers and system administrators like to complicate things, especially when they think they have a better way. If you are one of these people (even if you think you aren't) and read this chapter and think our approach is wrong, overly simplified, or whatever, just take it easy. Most simple Rails applications run on environments just like this, and the packages we recommend are among the most heavily used by professional Rails hosting environments. For example, some people don't like the idea of using any web server other than Apache, usually because it's been around for years and it's the only thing they know. Don't be afraid of Nginx; you might actually like it after you see how simple and fast (and bug-free) it is.

The Stack Checklist

Before we get into the details of the software you'll need, we'll cover the general assumptions about what kind of configuration we're going to build. As we said earlier, there are many ways to build a production stack, so we're sticking with a simple, proven configuration that will work well for many Rails applications.

The following sections describe the key components for the production stack we'll be building. You will notice that in addition to the standard Web, Application, and Database tiers we also discuss two other critical parts that are frequently left out of discussion: the server and network environment and monitoring components.

Server and Network Environment

Of course, we need to run our application somewhere…

Standalone/Dedicated Server or VPS Slice

Since we are going to run everything from one server, you will need to have access to either a dedicated server, or a VPS slice. Some VPS hosting services are already tailored for hosting Rails applications and will take care of all the dirty work for you (e.g., Rails Machine, EngineYard, or Slicehost). For our purposes we're going to start from a naked server and work our way up, though ultimately the configuration will largely be the same.

Fresh OS Install

A fresh install of any popular Linux distro should work. We prefer Debian, Gentoo, CentOS, or RedHat. Some of us have personal preferences for other distros, but these are usually the ones hosting companies prefer to use.

Depending on your comfort level or preference, you can install the required packages using your favorite package manager or you can compile them from source. In our examples we'll compile from source or install precompiled binaries (e.g., MySQL), for the sake of staying simple.

As we mentioned at the beginning of the chapter, you'll need to have a user with sudo privileges (or just root). If you don't have this, it's not impossible to get a Rails app running, but you'll need to coordinate with the sysadmin who does have sudo access to make sure everything can be installed correctly.

Network Access

We are running everything from one server, but you'll still need to get to it for administration, and since it's a web site, your users will need to get to it through a browser. You will need SSH access, and ports 80 and 443 open. If your server is running behind a firewall, the firewall will need to keep those open. We strongly recommend running SSH on a nonstandard port, just to avoid some common security attacks. See the security section for more details on ports.

Web Tier

The current best practice for running your Rails application in production is to use a fast "static" web server like Apache or Nginx running in the front that points to a cluster of mongrels running in the back. The fast web server will receive an incoming request and reverse-proxy it to one of the available Mongrel processes when appropriate (e.g., you can set up the rules so it will serve static assets or cached files directly). This approach is used by most professional Rails hosting companies and in many production clusters and is much more reliable than FastCGI, SCGI, or any of the previous approaches.

Apache 2.2.x and Nginx are the two preferred web servers to run in the front. We're going to use Nginx here, because it is fast, stable, far less complicated than Apache, and it has a tiny memory footprint. It's relatively new to the Western hemisphere, but the Nginx site states that about one-fifth of Russian websites are running on it.[3] One critical reason we prefer it to Apache is that its reverse-proxying is less error-prone. Apache is still a good solution, but if you only prefer it because you already know it, we suggest giving Nginx a chance. You'll be happily surprised. If you *must* use Apache, the Mongrel site has some excellent resources about how to set up `mod_proxy_balancer` to talk to your Mongrel Cluster.[4]

Application Tier

The tools that you need to run at the application tier are minimal. Ruby, RubyGems, Rails, and their dependent gems will be enough to get you going. We'll list the specific gems needed for running the stack in the "Installations" section, but you should know which gems your own application is dependent upon.

Our configuration will be based on the deployment of a simple, single Rails application. If you have more complex requirements, such as a BackrounDRb process, or cron jobs, and so on, you will have to handle those details yourself. Keep in mind that if you have a more complex configuration you'll need to make sure your Capistrano tasks are all set up properly. You can read more about Capistrano in the next chapter.

Database Tier

Most Rails applications use a single database. In a simple production configuration like ours we will run the database on the same server. In more complex configurations you can set up your database to address redundancy, failover, or performance concerns. As long as you're doing a simple database server setup, this won't change much from your local development environment.

We recommend the MySQL version 5.x branch; however, version 4.x is largely interchangeable and will work well for most projects. You will know your own application's database requirements, so if you prefer another database, make sure you have reviewed Rails support for it.

Monitoring

Monitoring tools are not technically required in order to run a production environment, but in the interest of best practices we're making them required here. Running your Rails application without them will be like driving a car without any gauges. Since this is a production environment, you'll probably want to know when the site becomes unavailable, or when someone uploads a file and it pegs the CPU or MySQL processes.

Version Control

We recommend Subversion for version control. You will likely already have your application in version control (and if you don't, now is a good time to start). We also recommend storing other important files in version control, which we discuss later in the section "Configurations."

Installations

In this section we're going to install all of the necessary applications and tools before you can perform a deployment. Before you begin you should make sure you meet the requirements described in the preceding section, or know enough to work within your own constraints.

In this section we're installing the tools directly from source, but you can install them using your favorite package manager if you prefer. In some cases the package managers make it easier to maintain subsequent updates, but they tend to be a few revisions behind what are sometimes important updates to tools.

Note

Everyone has their preferences about where to store libraries on their systems. If you prefer to install into different paths than what you see here, feel free. We're going to install into `/usr/local` and will be putting the application in `/var/www/apps/railsway/`, which you will see referenced in some of the configurations.

Ruby

The current recommended version of Ruby is the 1.8.5 branch. There have been some problems reported with Ruby 1.8.6, so unless you are fully confident that 1.8.6 works fine in your development and staging environments, we recommend sticking with the latest patch release from the 1.8.5 branch. As of this writing, the latest patch release is 52.

The following commands will download and install Ruby from source.

```
$ curl -O ftp://ftp.ruby-lang.org/pub/ruby/1.8/ruby-1.8.5-p52.tar.gz
$ tar zxvf ruby-1.8.5-p52.tar.gz
...
$ cd ruby-1.8.5-p52
$ ./configure —prefix=/usr/local
$ make
$ sudo make install
```

RubyGems

The current version of RubyGems is 0.9.4. Once you install this, all other Ruby-related libraries can be installed by installing gems. The following commands will download and install RubyGems from source. Once it is installed, RubyGems can upgrade itself when new versions are released.

```
$ curl -O http://files.rubyforge.mmmultiworks.com/rubygems/rubygems-
0.9.4.tgz
$ tar zxvf rubygems-0.9.4.tgz
...
$ cd rubygems-0.9.4
$ sudo ruby setup.rb
...
```

Rails

We are working on the latest 1.2.x version, which at the time of this writing is 1.2.3. The `-y` switch here is the equivalent of `—include-dependencies`. The following command will install the Rails gems (one for each subframework) into your system gems.

```
$ sudo gem install rails -y
```

Mongrel

We are using Mongrel 1.0.1, which is the version most widely used in production environments. On your local development machine you usually call the `mongrel_rails` (or `script/server`) command directly. Once we set up the `init` scripts later in the chapter, you will use that to control the start, stop, and restart of the cluster. The following command installs the Mongrel gem and its dependencies.

```
$ sudo gem install mongrel -y
```

Mongrel Cluster

Mongrel Cluster is a gem that allows you to run a set of mongrel processes with a common configuration so they can be proxied to from Nginx. We are using version 1.0.2.

The following command will install the `mongrel_cluster` gem, which will allow you to configure and run mongrels in a "pack." When we set up the static web server we will point to a configured `mongrel_cluster` configuration. Mongrel Cluster's commands will automatically be available to you through Mongrel's `mongrel_rails` command.

```
$ sudo gem install mongrel_cluster -y
```

Nginx

Nginx is the fast, simple, static web server that will sit at the front of your production environment. It will be responsible for handling incoming HTTP requests, either on its own (such as for static assets on disk already) or by proxying the requests to one of

the mongrel processes running in the mongrel cluster. The following commands will
download and compile the source for the current stable 0.5.x branch of Nginx.

```
$ curl -O http://sysoev.ru/nginx/nginx-0.5.28.tar.gz
$ tar zxvf nginx-0.5.28.tar.gz
$ cd nginx-0.5.28
$ ./configure --sbin-path=/usr/local/sbin --with-http_ssl_module
...
$ make
...
$ sudo make install
```

Subversion

Version control should be part of your standard arsenal. You can use other version
management systems with Capistrano but Subversion is the preferred default. The following commands will download and install Subversion and some of its additional
dependencies from source:

```
$ curl -O http://subversion.tigris.org/downloads/subversion-
1.4.4.tar.gz
$ curl -O http://subversion.tigris.org/downloads/subversion-deps-
1.4.4.tar.gz
$ tar zxvf subversion-1.4.4.tar.gz
$ tar zxvf subversion-deps-1.4.4.tar.gz
$ cd subversion-1.4.4
$ ./configure --prefix=/usr/local --with-openssl --with-ssl --with-zlib
...
$ make
...
$ sudo make install
```

MySQL

MySQL 5.x can be installed using your package manager, from source, or from the
precompiled binaries for your platform. The way you install it depends on your preferences and constraints. For our purposes we'll install the generic binaries.

You can find the appropriate package at http://dev.mysql.com/downloads/
mysql/5.0.html.

We strongly recommend that you lock down your MySQL installation by setting a root password and limiting access to the local machine. You can find out more about MySQL at http://www.securityfocus.com/infocus/1726.

Monit

Monit[5] is an excellent monitoring tool for managing processes and keeping tabs on your resource usage. Monit is highly configurable and can be set up to notify you based on many key metrics (CPU usage, disk usage, and so on). The following commands will download and install Monit from source files.

```
$ curl -O http://www.tildeslash.com/monit/dist/monit-4.9.tar.gz
$ tar zxvf monit-4.9.tar.gz
...
$ cd monit-4.9
$ ./configure
...
$ make
...
$ sudo make install
...
```

Capistrano

You do not need to install Capistrano on the server, only on your local machine. We are using the latest version of Capistrano, which right now is 2.x. We cover Capistrano thoroughly in Chapter 21, "Capistrano." The following command will download and install the Capistrano Ruby gem and its dependencies:

```
$ sudo gem install capistrano -y
```

Configurations

Now that we have everything installed, we're going to set up the configurations for each of the tools. For most straightforward Rails applications you will only need to configure a few things: Mongrel Cluster, Nginx, and Monit.

One technique for simplifying and automating your system is to keep a `deploy` directory right in your `config/` directory of your app, and use a separate subdirectory for each of the deployments you have (e.g., `dev`, `staging`, `production`). Each subdirectory will have its own copy of `mongrel_cluster.yml`, `database.yml`, `nginx.conf`, `railsway.conf`, and so on. In your post-deploy Capistrano tasks you can push these files into `/var/www/railsway/shared/config` and symlink to them from where they are expected (e.g., `/etc/nginx/nginx.conf   ->  /var/www/railsway/shared/config/nginx.conf`).

Configuring Mongrel Cluster

We're going to generate a basic `mongrel_cluster` config file using the mongrel cluster gem's `configure` command. You can always write and edit this configuration by hand, but it's convenient to generate at least the initial version. You can do this like so:

```
$ mongrel_rails cluster::configure -p 8000 -e production \
-a 127.0.0.1 -N 2 --user deploy --group deploy \
-P /var/www/apps/railsway/shared/pids/mongrel.pid \
-c /var/www/apps/railsway/current
```

That will produce the file `mongrel_cluster.yml`, whose contents are shown in the following listing. You can store it in the shared directory of your Capistrano deployment tree (e.g., `/var/www/railsway/shared/config/mongrel_cluster.yml`).

```
--
cwd: /var/www/apps/railsway/current
port: '8000'
user: deploy
group: deploy
environment: production
address: 127.0.0.1
pid_file: /var/www/apps/railsway/shared/pids/mongrel.pid
servers: 2
```

Configuring Nginx

We're going to split the total Nginx configuration into two separate files: `nginx.conf` and `railsway.conf`. This pattern is a simple way to keep the application-specific details out of the global config file.

`nginx.conf`

This is your primary Nginx configuration file. It sets up the pid, basic logging, gzip compression, and mime-types. Notice at the bottom that it includes the `railsway.conf` file. You could just as easily paste the contents of `railsway.conf` in its place, but by keeping it separate it will be easier to read and change over time. This approach also works well when you have multiple applications running on the same server.

```
# user and group to run as
user deploy deploy;
# number of nginx workers
worker_processes  4;
# pid of nginx master process
pid /var/run/nginx.pid;
error_log  /var/log/nginx/default.error.log debug;
# Number of worker connections. 1024 is a good default
events {
  worker_connections  8192;
  use epoll; # linux only!
}
# start the http module where we config http access.
http {
  # pull in mime-types. You can break out your config
  # into as many include's as you want to make it cleaner
  include /etc/nginx/mime.types;
  # set a default type for the rare situation that
  # nothing matches from the mime-type include
  default_type  application/octet-stream;
  # configure log format
  log_format main '$remote_addr - $remote_user [$time_local] '
                  ''$request' $status  $body_bytes_sent
'$http_referer' '
                  ''$http_user_agent' '$http_x_forwarded_for'';
  # no sendfile on OSX
  sendfile on;
  # These are good default values.
```

```
tcp_nopush          on;
tcp_nodelay         on;
# output compression saves bandwidth
gzip                on;
gzip_http_version 1.0;
gzip_comp_level 2;
gzip_proxied any;
gzip_types          text/plain text/html text/css application/
x-javascript text/xml application/xml application/xml+rss text/
javascript;
access_log  /var/log/nginx.default.access.log  main;
error_log  /var/log/nginx.default.error.log  info;
# Hosted applications
include /etc/nginx/railsway.conf;
}
```

railsway.conf

This is your specific application's config file. It will be included inside the main
nginx.conf in the preceding listing. Just as in Apache, when you have SSL set up,
you need to basically copy the set of configuration details. We include an example of
an SSL config here, but if you don't need SSL you can just remove it.

```
upstream railsway {
  server 127.0.0.1:8000;
  server 127.0.0.1:8001;
}
server {
  # port to listen on. Can also be set to an IP:PORT
  listen 80 default;
  # Set the max size for file uploads to 50Mb
  client_max_body_size 50M;
  # sets the domain[s] that this vhost server requests for
  server_name railsway.com;
  # doc root
  root /var/www/apps/railsway/current/public;
  # vhost specific logs
  access_log  /var/www/apps/railsway/shared/log/railsway.access.log
main;
  error_log  /var/www/apps/railsway/shared/log/railsway.error.log
  notice;
```

```
# this rewrites all the requests to the maintenance.html
# page if it exists in the doc root. This is for capistrano's
# disable web task
if (-f $document_root/system/maintenance.html) {
  rewrite  ^(.*)$  /system/maintenance.html last;
  break;
}
# Block access to paths containing .svn
location ~* ^.*\.svn.*$ {
  internal;
}
location / {
  index  index.html index.htm;
  # Forward the user's IP address to Rails
  proxy_set_header          X-Real-IP $remote_addr;
  # needed for HTTPS
  proxy_set_header          X_FORWARDED_PROTO https;
  proxy_set_header          X-Forwarded-For
$proxy_add_x_forwarded_for;
  proxy_set_header          Host $http_host;
  proxy_redirect            false;
  proxy_max_temp_file_size  0;
  location ~ ^/(images|javascripts|stylesheets)/ {
    expires 10y;
  }
  if (-f $request_filename) {
    break;
  }
  if (-f $request_filename/index.html) {
    rewrite (.*) $1/index.html break;
  }
  if (-f $request_filename.html) {
    rewrite (.*) $1.html break;
  }
  if (! -f $request_filename) {
    proxy_pass http://railsway;
    break;
  }
}
error_page   500 502 503 504   /500.html;
location = /500.html {
  root /var/www/apps/railsway/current/public;
}
```

```
}
server {
  # port to listen on. Can also be set to an IP:PORT
  listen 443 default;
  # Set the max size for file uploads to 50Mb
  client_max_body_size 50M;
  # sets the domain[s] that this vhost server requests for
  server_name railsway.com;
  # SSL certificate configuration
  ssl                on;
  ssl_certificate    /etc/nginx/ssl/railsway.cert;
  ssl_certificate_key /etc/nginx/ssl/railsway.key;
  keepalive_timeout  70;
  add_header         Front-End-Https    on;
  # doc root
  root /var/www/apps/railsway/current/public;
  # vhost specific logs
  access_log  /var/www/apps/railsway/shared/log/railsway.access.log
main;
  error_log   /var/www/apps/railsway/shared/log/railsway.error.log
   notice;
  # this rewrites all the requests to the maintenance.html
  # page if it exists in the doc root. This is for capistrano's
  # disable web task
  if (-f $document_root/system/maintenance.html) {
    rewrite  ^(.*)$  /system/maintenance.html last;
    break;
  }
  # Block access to paths containing .svn
  location ~* ^.*\.svn.*$ {
    internal;
  }
  location / {
    index  index.html index.htm;
    # Forward the user's IP address to Rails
    proxy_set_header        X-Real-IP $remote_addr;
    # needed for HTTPS
    proxy_set_header        X_FORWARDED_PROTO https;
      proxy_set_header        X-Forwarded-For
  $proxy_add_x_forwarded_for;
    proxy_set_header        Host $http_host;
    proxy_redirect          false;
    proxy_max_temp_file_size 0;
```

```
location ~ ^/(images|javascripts|stylesheets)/ {
  expires 10y;
}
if (-f $request_filename) {
  break;
}
# Rails page caching, part 1
# Add '/index.html' to the end of the current request's path
in the URL
# and look for that file on the file system.
if (-f $request_filename/index.html) {
  rewrite (.*) $1/index.html break;
}
# Rails page caching, part 2
if (-f $request_filename.html) {
  rewrite (.*) $1.html break;
}
if (! -f $request_filename) {
  proxy_pass http://railsway;
  break;
}
}
error_page   500 502 503 504   /500.html;
location = /500.html {
  root /var/www/apps/railsway/current/public;
}
}
```

You can test the configs by running the following command against them:

```
$ sudo /usr/local/sbin/nginx -t -c config/nginx.conf
```

Configuring Monit

Monit's configuration file is quite easy to read. This fairly extensive configuration example will check the key processes on your server in one-minute intervals and alert you if any of the conditions you specify are met. You can check system- or process-level usage of disk, CPU, and average load. You can check whether processes are running, and you can even see if a process has been restarted a certain number of times within a given number of intervals. You can find more examples of useful Monit configurations in the example `monitrc` included with the tool's source.

```
set daemon 60 # Poll at 1-minute intervals
set logfile /var/log/monit.log

set alert monit-alerts@railsway.com

set mail-format {
       from: monit@railsway.com
    subject: $SERVICE service - $EVENT
    message: $ACTION $SERVICE on $HOST: $DESCRIPTION
  }

set httpd port 1380
    allow localhost   # Allow localhost to connect

check system railsway.com
    alert monit-alerts@railsway.com but not on { instance }
    if loadavg(1min) > 4 for 3 cycles then alert
    if loadavg(5min) > 3 for 3 cycles then alert
    if memory usage > 80% for 3 cycles then alert
    if cpu usage (user) > 70% for 5 cycles then alert
    if cpu usage (system) > 30% for 5 cycles then alert
    if cpu usage (wait) > 20% for 5 cycles then alert

check process nginx with pidfile /var/run/nginx.pid
    start program = "/etc/init.d/nginx start"
    stop program = "/etc/init.d/nginx stop"
    if 2 restarts within 3 cycles then timeout
    if failed host localhost port 80 protocol http then restart
    if failed host localhost port 443 then restart

check process sendmail with pidfile /var/run/sendmail.pid
    start program = "/etc/init.d/sendmail start"
    stop program = "/etc/init.d/sendmail stop"

check process mysql with pidfile /var/run/mysqld/mysqld.pid
    start program = "/etc/init.d/mysqld start"
    stop program = "/etc/init.d/mysqld stop"

check process mongrel_8000 with pidfile /var/www/railsway/shared/pids/
mongrel.8000.pid
```

```
      start program = "/usr/bin/mongrel_rails cluster::start -C
/var/www/railsway/shared/config/mongrel_cluster.yml --clean --only
8000"
      stop program = "/usr/bin/mongrel_rails cluster::stop -C
/var/www/railsway/shared/config/mongrel_cluster.yml --clean --only
8000"

    if failed port 8000 protocol http
      with timeout 10 seconds
      then restart

    if totalmem is greater than 128 MB for 4 cycles then restart
        # eating up memory?
    if cpu is greater than 60% for 2 cycles then alert
        # send an email to admin
    if cpu is greater than 90% for 5 cycles then restart
        # hung process?
    if loadavg(5min) greater than 10 for 8 cycles then restart
        # bad, bad, bad
    if 3 restarts within 5 cycles then timeout
        # something is wrong, call the sys-admin
    group mongrel

check process mongrel_8001 with pidfile /var/www/railsway/shared/
pids/mongrel.8001.pid
start program = "/usr/bin/mongrel_rails cluster::start -C /var/www/
railsway/shared/config/mongrel_cluster.yml --clean --only 8001"
stop program = "/usr/bin/mongrel_rails cluster::stop -C /var/www/
railsway/shared/config/mongrel_cluster.yml --clean --only 8001"

    if failed port 8001 protocol http
      with timeout 10 seconds
      then restart

    if totalmem is greater than 128 MB for 4 cycles then restart
        # eating up memory?
    if cpu is greater than 60% for 2 cycles then alert
        # send an email to admin
    if cpu is greater than 90% for 5 cycles then restart
        # hung process?
    if loadavg(5min) greater than 10 for 8 cycles then restart
        # bad, bad, bad
    if 3 restarts within 5 cycles then timeout
        # something is wrong, call the sys-admin
    group mongrel
```

Configuring Capistrano

Capistrano will play an essential role in your complete production system. See the next chapter for details on how you can set up your deployment configuration to work with your application and production environment.

Configuring `init` Scripts

As we mentioned earlier in this chapter, many of the time- and cost-saving benefits of setting up your production environment the way we are recommending are based on *automation*. Process management is a good candidate for heavy automation. This is done using `init` scripts, which serve two purposes: They are run on system startup (when your server boots), and they are run either through the shell (by you, manually when necessary) or when you execute Capistrano commands when running start/stop/restart tasks. We include code samples for Mongrel, Monit, and Nginx, though the last two are shell scripts and are OS-specific. The Mongrel `init` script is written in Ruby and is generic enough for general use.

Nginx `init` Script

You will want to find an Nginx `init` script so you can start, stop, or reconfigure Nginx. You should find one (using your friendly search engine) that is specific to the OS you are using. The following example is for CentOS. This file should be named `/etc/init.d/nginx`.

```
#!/bin/sh
# v1.0
# nginx - Start, stop, or reconfigure nginx
#
# chkconfig: - 60 50
# description: nginx [engine x] is light http web/proxy server
#              that answers incoming ftp service requests.
# processname: nginx
# config: /etc/nginx/nginx.conf
# pidfile: /var/run/nginx.pid

# Source function library.
. /etc/rc.d/init.d/functions

# Source networking configuration.
```

```
. /etc/sysconfig/network

# Check that networking is up.
[ ${NETWORKING} = "no" ] && exit 0

BINARY=/usr/sbin/nginx
CONF_FILE=/etc/nginx/nginx.conf
PID_FILE=/var/run/nginx.pid
[ -x $BINARY ] || exit 0

RETVAL=0
prog="nginx"

start() {
  # Start daemons.
  if [ -e $BINARY ] ; then

    echo -n $"Starting $prog: "
    $BINARY -c $CONF_FILE
    RETVAL=$?
    [ $RETVAL -eq 0 ] && {
    touch /var/lock/subsys/$prog
    success $"$prog"
  }
  echo
else
  RETVAL=1
fi
return $RETVAL
}

stop() {
  # Stop daemons.
  echo -n $"Shutting down $prog: "
  kill -s QUIT `cat $PID_FILE 2>/dev/null`
  RETVAL=$?
  echo
  [ $RETVAL -eq 0 ] && rm -f /var/lock/subsys/$prog
  return $RETVAL
}

# See how we were called.
case "$1" in
```

```
  start)
    start
    ;;
  stop)
    stop
    ;;
  reconfigure)
    if [ -f /var/lock/subsys/$prog ]; then
      kill -s HUP `cat $PID_FILE 2>/dev/null`
      RETVAL=$?
    fi
    ;;
  status)
    status $prog
    RETVAL=$?
    ;;
  *)
    echo $"Usage: $0 {start|stop|reconfigure|status}"
    exit 1
esac

exit $RETVAL
```

Mongrel init Script

This Ruby script goes in /etc/init.d/mongrel (your OS may have a different place
to store init scripts). You can use it to start, stop, and restart mongrel processes. If you
place this script in init.d, it will be run when the server boots.

```
#! /usr/bin/env ruby
#
# mongrel        Startup script for Mongrel clusters.
#
# chkconfig: 345 85 00
#
# description: mongrel_cluster manages multiple Mongrel
  processes for use \
#              behind a load balancer.
#
MONGREL_RAILS = '/usr/bin/mongrel_rails'
CONF_FILE     = '/etc/railsway/mongrel_cluster.yml'
```

```
SUBSYS          = '/var/lock/subsys/mongrel'
SUDO            = '/usr/bin/sudo'
case ARGV.first
  when 'start'
    '#{MONGREL_RAILS} cluster::start -C #{CONF_FILE}'
    '#{SUDO} touch #{SUBSYS}'
  when 'stop'
    '#{MONGREL_RAILS} cluster::stop -C #{CONF_FILE}'
    '#{SUDO} rm -f #{SUBSYS}'
  when 'restart'
    '#{MONGREL_RAILS} cluster::restart -C #{CONF_FILE}'
  when 'status'
    '#{MONGREL_RAILS} cluster::status -C #{CONF_FILE}'
  else
    puts 'Usage: /etc/init.d/mongrel {start—stop—restart—status}'
    exit 1
end
exit $?
```

Monit Configuration

You will also want to have your `init` script for Monit. If you use Monit to manage your processes, then Monit will actually call the other scripts in the Capistrano tasks. You will want to make sure that Monit is responsible for starting, stopping, and restarting tasks, because if you stop the process manually, Monit will discover at the next specified interval that the process is not running and will start it back up. This behavior is sometimes exactly what you *do not* want to happen if you are having issues on your production server and need to stop a process.

As with the Nginx `init` script previously, this script is specific to CentOS. You can find one specific to your OS online.

```
#! /bin/sh
#
# monit          Monitor Unix systems
#
# Author:        Clinton Work,  <work@scripty.com>
#
# chkconfig:     2345 98 02
# description:   Monit is a utility for managing and monitoring
processes,
```

```
#                     files, directories and devices on a Unix system.
# processname:  monit
# pidfile:      /var/run/monit.pid
# config:       /etc/mcommons/monitrc

# Source function library.
. /etc/rc.d/init.d/functions

# Source networking configuration.
. /etc/sysconfig/network

MONIT=/usr/local/bin/monit
CONFIG=/etc/monitrc

# Source monit configuration.
if [ -f /etc/sysconfig/monit ] ; then
        . /etc/sysconfig/monit
fi

[ -f $MONIT ] || exit 0

RETVAL=0

# See how we were called.
case "$1" in
  start)
        echo -n "Starting monit: "
        daemon $NICELEVEL $MONIT -c $CONFIG
        RETVAL=$?
        echo
        [ $RETVAL = 0 ] && touch /var/lock/subsys/monit
        ;;
  stop)
        echo -n "Stopping monit: "
        killproc monit
        RETVAL=$?
        echo
        [ $RETVAL = 0 ] && rm -f /var/lock/subsys/monit
        ;;
  restart)
        $0 stop
        $0 start
        RETVAL=$?
```

```
        ;;
    condrestart)
        [ -e /var/lock/subsys/monit ] && $0 restart
        ;;
    status)
        status monit
        RETVAL=$?
        ;;
    *)
        echo "Usage: $0 {start|stop|restart|condrestart|status}"
        exit 1
esac

exit $RETVAL
```

Deployment and Launch

Now that you have your server running, you should be ready to try deploying to it. We are going to defer to Chapter 21 for instructions in setting up your application for deployments. You can see from the directory structure we've referred to that we are expecting to run the application from the base directory of /var/www/apps/railsway, and that we expect you to use monit to control your process management.

You should be aware of where the logs will be stored for your application, for the Mongrels, for Nginx, for Monit, and so on. These are often the first place you need to look when troubleshooting. You can use curl to hit your site quickly without needing to use a browser.

Other Production Stack Considerations

The following kinds of concerns should always be factored into how you design your production environment. Each of these topics on their own can result in huge labor and hardware costs, depending on your level of priority and, in some cases, paranoia. Be aware that addressing these concerns is always a compromise of time, money, and efficiency.

Redundancy and Failover

What happens if the database goes down, or if a disk fails? Redundancy and failover concerns deal with your ability to react to a failure at one or more levels of software or hardware. We are not going to cover these topics here, as there are many levels of redundancy and failover at each level of your production stack.

Caching

Caching is intended to improve the performance of your system by storing the results of common requests and making them easier and faster to access than processing the entire request from scratch. Common ways to cache include storing previous HTTP responses as HTML files on disk (aka page caching), storing them in memory (e.g., Memcache), and so on. There are many ways to cache at each level of your production configuration. You can read an excellent tutorial on caching in Rails at http://www.railsenvy.com/2007/2/28/rails-caching-tutorial.

Performance and Scalability

The terms "performance" and "scaling" are often used interchangeably, and although they are related, they represent different concerns and have different solutions. Performance is a measure of the behavior of a given "unit" of resources. For example, you can benchmark the performance of the login system receiving 20,000 requests for the login page within one minute, running on a single web server and database connection. Repeated benchmarks across various parts of the application stack will establish the baseline performance you can expect from a single "unit" of resources.

Scalability, on the other hand, refers to how efficiently the system architecture can grow in proportion to increasing demand. In other words, it is a measure of change in the ratio between units of demand and units of resources as the units of demand increase. For example, let's say you have a three-server stack, with one box each for web, app, and database tiers. If that stack can handle 1,000 req/sec based on your performance measurements, how much hardware will you need to handle 2,000 req/sec? Ideally an architecture should be able to scale "horizontally" (i.e., proportionately), meaning that you could add more "units" of resources without reducing the performance of the entire system. In the preceding example, that would mean we just double the hardware, but it is not always that simple.

In practical production environments, your ability to scale easily will depend on a number of factors. Some aspects of scaling behavior depend on the overall behavior of your application. For example, write-heavy applications (i.e., those that perform a lot of database INSERTs)—such as social networks or financial transaction applications—will require more complex database cluster solutions than read-heavy applications such as blog or news aggregators. Another factor in scaling behavior is that different parts of your application may scale at different rates. Vendor or third-party integration points—such as a mail delivery vendor, an e-commerce payment gateway, or external asset storage service—will often scale at different rates than the rest of your application.

You can read more about these at http://en.wikipedia.org/wiki/Scalability. Scaling a stack is far too intricate a topic to be able to cover with any depth in this chapter, but you can find some excellent resources online by searching for presentations and blog posts that deal with it. Rails uses "share-nothing architecture" similar to its LAMP-stack predecessors, which has proven to be an effective, low-cost way to structure an application. This approach has evolved as the web industry has matured over the past decade or so, and works well for many applications. Many of the veterans of the "share-nothing architecture" earned their badges with LAMP, but you can apply most of their wisdom to Rails without losing much value. Because our production stack is simple, it will not be difficult to change into more complex configurations later.

Security

It is largely impossible to address security here with any degree of depth, but it is probably worth noting the following simple steps to at least protect yourself from obvious attacks.

Application Security

You can lock down your server and network and bury the hardware in an old missile silo, but that won't keep you safe if your application is open for attacks. Fortunately, Rails' tools and methods will make it easy to keep your application relatively safe out of the box, and by employing some best practices you can avoid the most common attacks, such as SQL injection and Cross-Site Scripting (XSS). You can find out more from the ROR security blog at http://www.rorsecurity.info.

Lock Down Your Ports

You should lock down your ports so that you can only access 80, 443, and your nonstandard SSH port. If you have a firewall and can configure it yourself, this should be done at the firewall level. If you do not have access to the firewall you can lock down these ports at the server level using `iptables`.[6]

Maintainability

After you actually launch your application, you'll want to keep tabs on it and generally keep your system clean. You'll also want it to be pretty straightforward to hunt down problems and troubleshoot them when they happen. All kinds of odd things happen in production environments that are tough or impossible to reproduce on your local development machine.

Conclusion

Setting up your production environment is not as daunting an endeavor as it used to be. Developers and sysadmins tend to stick to what they know, which is understandably all too easy in our age of specialties. Rails, for its part, has helped to chip away at this tendency by encouraging developers to crawl out of their holes and play DBA, sysadmin, or "front-end designer" by simply putting them within reach. In general, the web as a production, publication, and distribution medium has vastly simplified the skills and efforts required to get ideas, products, and services out into the open. Rails and the wealth of libraries and tools that developers have created to support it have served this paradigm well by simplifying even the most mundane areas of web development such as deployments and system administration.

In this chapter we have reviewed the key technical and philosophical components of setting up a modern production environment. There are, of course, millions of possible permutations, a few of which will be most suitable for your needs. Even if you use PostgreSQL, FreeBSD, and Perforce, you should be able to adapt our recommended configuration for your own system easily. You should always seek the advice of your peers, especially if this is your first production environment setup, but you can consider the approach that we're recommending as the generally accepted best practices, at least for Rails applications.

The big remaining step of getting your application into production is the actual configuration of your application with Capistrano, so it can be deployed to your fancy new production environment. We cover this in the next chapter.

References

1. Mongrel project homepage: http://mongrel.rubyforge.org

2. Information about the Bash shell: http://en.wikipedia.org/wiki/Bash

3. Nginx project homepage: http://nginx.net

4. Instructions for setting up Apache to talk to a Mongrel Cluster using `mod_proxy_balancer`: http://mongrel.rubyforge.org/docs/apache.html

5. iptables project homepage: http://www.netfilter.org/projects/iptables/index.html

6. Monit project homepage: http://www.tildeslash.com/monit/

CHAPTER 21

Capistrano

"When we .NET developers say that getting into Rails is tough, this is the kind of stuff we're talking about. [...] It's the Linux shell, server applications, and other things we're not used to that trip us up."
—Brian Eng http://www.softiesonrails.com/2007/4/5/the-absolute-moron-s-guide-to-capistrano

Need being the great mother of invention, the story goes that in his work for 37signals, Jamis created Switchtower (later renamed to Capistrano[1]) when Basecamp grew to be hosted on more than one production server. It's a tool for automating tasks on remote servers.

Although Capistrano is now firmly established as the standard solution to Rails deployment challenges, its multiserver transactional approach to running remote commands lends it to a fairly broad range of deployment scenarios.

This chapter delves into Capistrano (version 2[2]), clearly showing how it works out of the box to solve tricky and time-consuming activities. We also show what it doesn't do for you and how you can extend it by crafting your own deployment recipes to customize Capistrano's capabilities. In conclusion, we'll explore a few great recipes created by the Capistrano community that have gained broad acceptance.

Overview of Capistrano

We'll start with a high-level overview of Capistrano. The first stop on that journey is to take stock of Capistrano's domain-specific terminology.

Terminology

Capistrano has its own vocabulary that distinguishes it from simply being an extension of Rake, on which it is based:

- One or many *deployment machines* are the computers to which we will deploy.

- *Recipes* are what tasks are to Rake. Whether they represent a single task or more, a recipe provides a desirable solution. Recipes are made up of tasks.

- *Tasks* are atomic units of functionality, and exist to be called directly by an end user, or internally by another task. Tasks sit within namespaces.

- A Capistrano *namespace* groups tasks logically. In this way a task name may be repeated within another namespace and are a great way for contributing authors to add recipes without the fear of task-name collisions.

- Roles such as `:app` and `:db` are means by which we can group task execution— we can target the running of a task within a role—so that the task runs only against that role. You can think of them as a task qualifier where the qualifier is generally a class of deployment machine such as `:app`, `:db`, or `:web` for which the task will run.

- `Variables` are global variables available to the rest of the script.

The Basics

The first time I sat down to use Capistrano, I asked myself: What do I need to do to use Capistrano? What does it expect of my app? Of my server? And when a deployment is finished, what has Capistrano done and what hasn't it?

The following sections answer these questions and should set in place the larger view of Capistrano in your project development workflow.

What Do I Need to Do to Use Capistrano?

First, it's important to note that Capistrano is only installed on your development (or "deploy from") computer. Capistrano has no requirements to be installed on the deployment machine itself. It operates solely on its core requirements and assumptions of the deployment machine, and executes commands to the deployment machines through an established and secure SSH infrastructure.

So, the short answer is to consider the assumptions and requirements and address them. You'll likely find your first few deployments are a little rough—trial and error. But over time I bet you'll find Capistrano to be your key deployment ally.

What Does Capistrano Expect?

Some requirements are mandatory and some are baseline assumptions that can be overridden. This core philosophy encourages best practices while not locking you in to them.

Capistrano's *core* requirements are that

- You are using SSH to access the remote machine.

- The deployment machine has a POSIX[3]-compatible shell.

- If you're using passwords, that all deployment machines have the same password (PKI is the recommended solution). [4]

The following assumptions are *overridable:*

- You want to deploy a Rails application.

- You're using Subversion to manage source code.

- You've got your production environment already built (operating system, Ruby, Rails, other gems, database, web/app/db servers).

- Passwords are the same for your deployment machine and your `svn` repository.

- You've created the deployment database plus a user that can access it.

- You have all config files in subversions ready to run in your production environment (which includes user/passwords for the aforementioned deployment database).

- Your migrations will run from 0 to 100 (`deploy:migrate`).

- Your web/app servers are configured with a `spin` script to start/stop/restart the web app.

As mentioned, these requirements and assumptions are the defaults. If they don't suit you, stay tuned, because we'll show you how to build tasks and callbacks to customize Capistrano to suit your specific needs.

What Has Capistrano Done and What Hasn't It?

When you're done getting Capistrano and its requirements addressed (either directly or through customization), you're left in deployment Nirvana. Okay, that's a little strong, but your code will be deployed from your repository, migrations run, Apache and your app server (Mongrel, fastcgi) will be booted, and well... now you're deployed, and ready for that next deployment event.

So now you can start doing great things like updating your servers with the latest svn check-in using `cap deploy:update`, or go full out and update to the latest release and restart your app servers using `cap deploy`. You can even put up a maintenance page during extended downtime using `cap deploy:web:disable`, and roll back when you mess up a deployment, using `cap deploy:rollback`.

If you've got multiple servers to manage, the commands don't change, just your setup. Just a little config-file tweaking and you're using `cap deploy` and `cap deploy:invoke` to run arbitrary commands on all servers simultaneously.

Getting Started

Now that we've taken seen the view from 10,000 feet, we're now going to get on the ground. For the sake of this first exercise, we're going to take for granted that all of Capistrano's expectations as described in the last section have been met.

Installation

To get started, let's install Capistrano:

```
$ sudo gem install capistrano
Install required dependency net-ssh? [Yn]
Install required dependency net-sftp? [Yn]
Install required dependency highline? [Yn]

Successfully installed capistrano-2.0
```

Running `cap` with the `--tasks` switch will tell us what tasks Capistrano knows about.

```
$ cap --tasks
cap invoke #Invoke a single command on the remote servers.
cap shell   #Begin an interactive Capistrano session.
```

```
Learn more about each with the explain switch(-e):
cap -e command #ie. cap -e deploy:pending:diff
```

Both of these are general-purpose, built-in tasks that allow you to run one or more commands on the deployment machines. The `invoke` task will run a single command, while `shell` opens up an `irb`-like command-prompt where you can issue multiple commands. But where are all the great things you can do with Capistrano?

"Capify" Your Rails Application

In order to prepare your project for deployment, Capistrano provides us with the `capify` command, which builds the basic configuration files, and with a little bit of editing on our part our app will be ready to deploy. Taking `my_project`, previously configured as per Capistrano's assumptions, we'll create two files:

```
$ cd my_project
$ capify .
[add] writing `./Capfile'
[add] writing `./config/deploy.rb'
 [done] capified!
```

Now before we look at the two files created, let's run `cap --tasks` again.

```
$ cap --tasks
cap deploy                    #Deploys your project.
cap deploy:check              #Test deployment dependencies.
cap deploy:cleanup            #Clean up old releases.
cap deploy:cold               #Deploys and starts a 'cold' application.
cap deploy:migrate            #Run the migrate rake task.
cap deploy:migrations         #Deploy and run pending migrations.
cap deploy:pending            #Displays the commits since your last deploy.
cap deploy:pending:diff       #Displays the diff' since your last deploy.
cap deploy:restart            #Restarts your application.
cap deploy:rollback           #Rolls back to a previous version and restarts.
cap deploy:rollback_code      #Rolls back to the previously deployed version.
cap deploy:setup              #Prepares one or more servers for deployment.
cap deploy:start              #Start the application servers.
cap deploy:stop               #Stop the application servers.
cap deploy:symlink            #Updates the symlink to the deployed version.
cap deploy:update             #Copies your project and updates the symlink.
cap deploy:update_code        #Copies your project to the remote servers.
```

```
cap deploy:upload          #Copy files to the currently deployed version.
cap deploy:web:disable     #Present a maintenance page to visitors.
cap deploy:web:enable      #Makes the application web-accessible again.
cap invoke                 #Invoke a single command on the remote servers.
cap shell                  #Begin an interactive Capistrano session.
```

Now that's more like it! But where did these new tasks come from? For that answer, we'll look at Capfile:

```
$ cat Capfile
require 'capistrano/version'
load 'deploy' if respond_to?(:namespace) # cap2 differentiator
load 'config/deploy'
```

It's short! As you can see, the cap command loads up recipes by reading the Capfile in the present directory. Just like Rake, Capistrano will search up the directory tree until it finds a Capfile, which means you can run cap in a subdirectory of your project.

The Capfile built by capify loads up a bunch of standard Capistrano recipes in deploy, plus it also loads up your project-specific recipes in config/deploy:

```
my_project> $ cat config/deploy.rb

set :application, "set your application name here"
set :repository,  "set your repository location here"

# If you aren't deploying to /u/apps/#{application} on the target
# servers (which is the default), you can specify the actual location
# via the :deploy_to variable:
# set :deploy_to, "/var/www/#{application}"

# If you aren't using Subversion to manage your source code, specify
# your SCM below:
# set :scm, :subversion

role :app, "your app-server here"
role :web, "your web-server here"
role :db,  "your db-server here", :primary => true
```

Configuring the Deployment

Minor edits to the boilerplate `config/deploy.rb` file are all that's required to pre-pare your app for deployment. The `deploy.rb` file describes your application deployment in simple-to-read language.

Name Your Application

The first basic setting is the name of your application:

```
set :application, "set your application name here" # used as a folder
name
```

Although the help text in `deploy.rb` has spaces in the application name, you probably don't want them, because the application name will be used as a directory name on the deployment machine.

Repository Info

Next, we need to tell Capistrano where to find the source code for your application:

```
set :repository,  "set your repository location here"
```

Assuming a Subversion server, set `:repository` to a Subversion URL (whether HTTP, svn, or svn+ssh). Another built-in assumption is that the username and password for the Subversion account are the same as those of your deploy user. The login name of the user running Capistrano will be used to connect to svn, and you will be prompted if your svn server requires authentication.

Define Roles

Next we're going to point Capistrano at the domain name or IP address of your deployment machine(s). Capistrano will SSH to this address to perform the actions that you script. For this easy case, all three Roles (or classes) of machines will be the same.

```
role :app, "my_deployment_machine" #or you can use an IP address
role :web, "my_deployment_machine"
role :db,  "my_deployment_machine", :primary => true
```

Roles are a powerful means by which we can target execution of specific tasks on a class of machines. For instance, we can use `deploy shell` to run a `grep` on all `:app` machines.

Extra Role Properties

In our example, the `:db` role is marked with the option `:primary => true`. This attribute indicates the primary database server. Certain tasks, such as database migrations, will only run on the primary database server, since the most common database-clustering scenario calls for slaves to synch up with the primary. You can also specify that a given role is a slave (using `:slave => true`) so that you can target certain types of tasks, such as backups. Think of these attributes as qualifiers of the Role for finer grain control, and although there are standard qualifiers provided by Capistrano, you can define your own.

That's it! Once the name of the application, the source-control information, and roles are defined, you are done with configuration.

A Little Spin, Please...

After a successful deploy, Capistrano is going to try to start (spin) your application. By default, it will look for `./script/spin`, expecting that file to contain a script to start your application servers. It's your job to write that script (since Rails doesn't come with one), starting the app server of your choice. The easiest approach is to have your spin script talk to the spawner script, provided by Rails, since it knows how to fire up both FCGI and Mongrel.

You can read about the spawner tool easily; just type **script/process/spawner --help** at the console. A simple spin script to call spawner to start Mongrel[5] will look like this:

```
/deploy_to/current/script/process/spawner -p 8256 -i 2
```

Add that line of code as `./script/spin` to your repository, and upon a successful deploy, Capistrano will start two Mongrel instances, listening on ports 8256 and 8257. The distinct advantage of using the standard Rails spawner is that it will track the process ids, which means other standard Rails scripts are available. This includes `script/reaper`, used for restarting, monitoring, and stopping application server instances.

If you decide to step outside the tightly integrated spin solution, perhaps because you want to roll in some background process management, or you want to use a third-party startup script such as `mongrel_cluster`, then you'll have to override the standard deploy tasks. Later on in the chapter, in Baking Exercise #2, we'll show you how to do just that.

Set Up the Deployment Machine

Now that we've got our default configuration in place, and all assumptions are covered, we can ask Capistrano to set up our deployment machine. What does setup mean? The `deploy:setup` task essentially creates the directory structure that holds your application deployments.

```
$ cap deploy:setup
```

Deployment Directory Structure

After running `deploy:setup`, SSH over to your deployment server, and peruse the directory structure that was created. The default is `/var/www/apps/application_name`, containing the following subdirectories:

```
releases
current
shared
shared/log
shared/system
shared/pids
```

This structure bears some discussion. Whenever you deploy, Capistrano checks out (or exports) your project from `svn`, and places the files in the `releases` folder, *each in its own release folder named based on the current date and time.* After this happens successfully, Capistrano builds a link from the `releases` folder to *application_name/*`current`, where your currently deployed web application is found.

Symbolic Links

Capistrano also makes the following symbolic links on each deployment:

- *application_name*/shared/log is linked to your current project's log directory, so that logs persist across releases.

- *application_name*/shared/pids is linked to your current project's tmp/pids
  directory.

- *application_name*/shared/system is linked to your current projects pub-
  lic/system directory. This is where Capistrano stores HTML files that show
  your project in maintenance mode. (See cap deploy:web:disable/enable.)

Checking a New Deployment Setup

Before we move on to our first deploy, Capistrano provides us with the
deploy:check task to verify that all assumptions and pieces are in place:

```
cap --quiet deploy:check # quiet shuts out the verbosity
```

In addition to the default permissions checking, utilities (svn), and others
required, deploy:check also provides a means to verify application-specific dependencies. These can be nicely declared within your deploy.rb, and that works for both
local and remote dependencies:

```
depend :remote, :gem, "runt", ">= 0.3.0"
depend :remote, :directory, :writeable, /var/www/current/config
depend :remote, :command, "monit"
depend :local, :command, "svn"
```

When a dependency fails during the deploy:check task, you'll see a message like
the following one:

```
The following dependencies failed. Please check them and try again:
--> gem `runt' >= 0.3.0 could not be found (my_deployment_machine)
```

Deploy!

If you've done everything correctly up to now in setting up your application's `deploy.rb` script and you have set up the remote machines, then you're ready to actually do a deployment.

On a first deploy of this app, we'll run `cap deploy:cold` —otherwise we'd run the default task `cap deploy`. The only difference between these two is that `cap deploy` will try to shut down your server first, which won't work since it isn't running yet.

```
$ cap deploy:cold # cold will "svn co", run migrations, link this
release
                  # to the current and start your servers
```

In most cases, you will be asked to enter the password to your `svn` server. This is a case where it is extremely handy to have set up SSH keys on the local and client machine so that you authenticate automatically with certificates instead of having to enter passwords multiple times.

If all went well, you shouldn't see any error messages, and a browser session will show your app is up. If not, read the verbose output, go over the assumptions, and start again.

Overriding Capistrano Assumptions

Now that we've learned how to use Capistrano with its standard assumptions, we'll take a look at scenarios in which they need to be worked around. Some scenarios involve simply setting additional Capistrano variables, while others involve overriding existing tasks or hooking into callback functions. Some scenarios require entirely new tasks to be defined.

Using a Remote User Account

To use a remote user account other than the currently logged-in user, just set the `:user` variable to the desired remote user account name.

```
set :user, "deploy"
```

That was simple, and also makes an important point. Capistrano tries to simplify working outside the stated assumptions. Another example would be changing the source-control system to something other than Subversion.

Customizing the SCM System Used by Capistrano

Although the default SCM system is Subversion, Perforce, Bzr, and Darcs are also supported.

```
set :scm, :subversion # default. :perforce, :bzr, :darcs
```

You can also customize the deployment strategy, and we do not recommend that you stick with the default, which is :checkout, since it is very inefficient. All those little .svn directories chew up disk space like crazy! Instead, try the :export option, which will do an svn export of your codebase into the release directory. The :remote_cache performs well also, since it makes a copy of the last release, and then executes svn up to get the latest code, but we like :export best.

```
set :deploy_via, :checkout        # default
set :deploy_via, :export
set :deploy_via, :remote_cache # copies from cache, then svn up
```

Working without SCM Access from the Deployment Machine

Sometimes, particularly for security reasons, you don't have (or want) access to SCM on your deployment machine. For these cases, Capistrano provides a means to deploy_via :copy. The :copy strategy tars and gzips your project before using SFTP to upload it to the release directory on the remote machine. In the rare case that your local machine does not have the required binaries, you can tell Capistrano to use Ruby's internal zip library.

```
set :deploy_via, :copy        # local scm check out.
                    # Cap will tar/gzip sftp to deployment machine

set :copy_strategy, :export # changes deploy_via :copy to :export
                    # instead of default scm check out

set :copy_compression, :zip    # if you don't have tar/gzip binaries,
                    # Cap will zip for you
```

Hopefully you are noticing that although Capistrano's assumptions are good defaults, you have a great deal of flexibility in specifying alternatives, without having to write your own tasks.

What If I Don't Store `database.yml` in My SCM Repository?

People sometimes leave configuration files such as `database.yml` out of the repository for a number of reasons, among them security concerns. We don't advise this practice, since it complicates distributed development and local config requirements. However, learning how to work around the challenge posed by nonversioned configuration files provides us a valuable and realistic opportunity to teach you how to move beyond basic understanding of Capistrano.

Note that out of the following three options, there is only one that is really good in our opinion. However, you stand to learn from all three.

Option A: Version It Anyway, but with a Different Name

In this option, you add a file like `production.database.yml` to the repository, and then rename it to `database.yml` automatically on deployment. We might have gotten to this challenge because we didn't want passwords in our repository to begin with, but at least some Rails developers will feel this is a legitimate solution. After all, the more popular reason to leave `database.yml` out of the repository is so that each developer on a team can have their own local database connection configuration.

- **Pros**   Easy solution. No default configuration; just create the additional task and add a file named `production.database.yml` to the repository.

- **Cons**   Plaintext passwords in the repository, which could be a big problem in some shops.

To implement this option, add a file named `production.database.yml` to the repository and give it your production database details. Then add the task definition (as shown in Listing 21.1) to `config/deploy.rb`.

Listing 21.1   Copying a `production.database.yml` Configuration after Code Update

```
task :after_update_code, :roles => :app do
  run "cp #{release_path}/config/production.database.yml
       #{release_path}/config/database.yml"
end
```

Tasks named `:after_update_code` function as callbacks, invoked after the code for the new release is updated. Here we also see demonstrated the `run` command, which gives you an idea of how easy it is to run commands remotely.

Option B: Store Production-Ready `database.yml` in the `shared/config` Folder

Here's another solution, but take heed that it isn't the best one either. We're giving it to you mainly to demonstrate the `:after_symlink` callback.

- Pros   No username and password information stored in your repository.

- Cons   Requires manually copying configuration files to the deployment machine.

To implement this option, add the following task to `config/deploy.rb`:

```
task :after_symlink, :roles => :app do
    run "cp #{shared_path}/config/database.yml
            #{release_path}/config/database.yml"
end

then...
 a. cap setup
 b. copy production-ready database.yml file to the shared/config
 folder
 c. cap cold_deploy
```

Option C: The Best Option: Autogenerate `database.yml`

This one just sounds so right that we hope you don't even consider the other two. You autogenerate `database.yml` (as shown in Listing 21.2) and put it in the shared config directory on the remote machine. Then you link it to your release's config folder.

- **Pros**   Easy reuse, flexibility, and no passwords in the repository.

- **Cons**   A little harder to code, but we only do this once.[6]

Listing 21.2 Create `database.yml` in Shared Path Based on Template

```
require 'erb'

before "deploy:setup", :db
after "deploy:update_code", "db:symlink"

namespace :db do
  desc "Create database yaml in shared path"
  task :default do
    db_config = ERB.new <<-EOF
    base: &base
      adapter: mysql
      socket: /tmp/mysql.sock
      username: #{user}
      password: #{password}

    development:
      database: #{application}_dev
      <<: *base

    test:
      database: #{application}_test
      <<: *base

    production:
      database: #{application}_prod
      <<: *base
    EOF

    run "mkdir -p #{shared_path}/config"
    put db_config.result, "#{shared_path}/config/database.yml"
  end

  desc "Make symlink for database yaml"
  task :symlink do
    run "ln -nfs #{shared_path}/config/database.yml
        #{release_path}/config/database.yml"
  end
end
```

Then to use your new `.yml` file, execute the following commands:

```
$ cap deploy:setup
$ cap deploy:update
```

What If My Migrations Won't Run from 0 to 100?

The Capistrano recipe `deploy:migrations` expects a `database.yml` production-specified database, does a deployment as usual, and runs any pending migrations. Unfortunately, it is pretty common to get yourself into a situation where your whole suite of migrations won't run without an error.

One possible solution is to create a task that sets up your database using `db/schema.rb`, a Ruby script that (using the Migrations API) handily stores the most recently migrated version of your database schema (DDL). The Capistrano task in Listing 21.3 loads the schema.

Listing 21.3   Load Database Schema Remotely Using `schema.rb`

```
namespace :deploy do
  desc "runs 'rake db:schema:load' for current release"
  task :load_schema, :roles => :db do

    rake = fetch(:rake, "rake")
    rails_env = fetch(:rails_env, "production")

    run "cd #{current_release}; #{rake} RAILS_ENV=#{rails_env}
db:schema:load"
  end
end
```

Run the task in two steps: `cap  deploy:cold` followed by `cap deploy:load_schema`.

Useful Capistrano Recipes

One of the greatest things about Capistrano is the ease with which we can roll our own recipes. But before we do, there are some things we need to clear up about variables.

Variables and Their Scope

There are two ways we can specify variables. One is from the recipe definitions (as we've already seen in this chapter). The other is from the command line.

From the command line we can set variable values using either an `-s` or `-S` switch. Typing `cap -s foo=bar` is equivalent to having `set :foo, "bar"` *after* all your recipes are loaded, and `cap -S foo=bar` does so *before* recipes are loaded.

As with Rake, you can also specify variables within the OS environment. As this is a little tougher in Windows, Capistrano command-line switches are a better cross-platform solution.

Whenever possible, I prefer to create specific Capistrano tasks that set common variables rather than depend on shell scripts or command-line operations. This keeps the deployment knowledge within Capistrano, and not spread around your environment.

A topic that deserves a little investigation at this time is the scoping of Capistrano variables. Are variables local to the task? Local to the namespace? Or global to Capistrano in general? To figure out this bit of undocumented Capistrano, we're going to write some tasks (Listing 21.4) to play with the possibilities. We'll start by creating two namespaces (:one and :two) and assign identically named variables (:var_one) to them. Then we'll set and get those values from a third namespace. The resulting values should teach us much about Capistrano's scoping rules.

Listing 21.4   Exploring Scoping of Capistrano Variables

```
namespace :one do
  task :default do
    set :var_one, "var_one value"
  end
end

namespace :two do
  task :default do
    set :var_one, "var_two value"
  end
end

namespace :three do
  task :default do
    puts "!!!! one.var_one == #{one.var_one}"
    puts "!!!! global name space var_one == #{var_one}"

    two.default

    puts "!!!! one.var_one == #{one.var_one}"
    puts "!!!! two.var_one == #{two.var_one}"
    puts "!!!! global name space var_one == #{var_one}"
  end
end

before "deploy:update", :one
before "deploy:update", :two
after "deploy:update", :three

$cap deploy:update
```

Running the code in Listing 21.4 dumps the following output to the console:

```
  * executing `three' # run one
!!!! one.var_one == var_one value
!!!! global name space var_one == var_one value

  * executing `two' # run two
!!!! one.var_one == var_two value
!!!! two.var_one == var_two value
!!!! global name space var_one == var_two value
```

What does this mean? First we can see that referencing one.var_one and (the global) var_one returns the same value; looks as if they're one and the same. Taking a second kick at it, in the second run we call task two.default. Setting only two.var_one confirms that there isn't a local variable namespace—but simply one global namespace for variables.

In the preceding tester code you may have noticed the *funny* two.default call in the example—this is simply the way to call namespaced tasks. In the case of default, we use the explicit name (merely two won't resolve as it does in the namespace syntax shortcut :two).

In summary, we have shown that variables aren't scoped by namespace; referencing them by namespace will always return the global value and will probably confuse you and others down the line. But be aware that scoped variables are planned for a future version of Capistrano.

Exercise #1: Staging

A particularly useful trick with Capistrano is the ability to initialize a starting configuration for tasks. A great use for such preinitialization is for setting up the environment for which we will be deploying.

We can do this in two ways; first, using the -S switch to set an initial value:

```
$ cap -S app_server=the_rails_way.com,secure_ssh_port=8256 deploy
```

The deploy task will be run with the app_server and secure_ssh_port parameters set. This strategy rapidly gets out of hand as we need new parameters. Do we need an additional shell script to hold those parameters? Yuck! Capistrano can be a powerful friend, especially if you don't distribute your deployment logic.

The second, and much more DRY, method is to code tasks that define each of your staging environments, so that you can say something like `cap production deploy`, letting the `production` task setup the needed variables, just as we show you in Listing 21.5.

Listing 21.5   Production and Staging Environment Tasks

```
desc "deploy to the production environment"
task :production do
  set :tag, "release-1.0" unless variables[:tag]
  set :domain, "the-rails-way.com"
  set :repository, "http://svn.nnovation.ca/svn/the-rails-
way/tags/#{tag}"
  set :rails_env, "production"
  set :app_server, "the-rails-way.net"
  set :secure_ssh_port, 8256

  role :app, "#{app_server}:#{secure_ssh_port}"
  role :web, "#{app_server}:#{secure_ssh_port}"
  role :db,  "#{app_server}:#{secure_ssh_port}", :primary => true
end

desc "deploy to the staging environment"
task :staging do
  set :domain, "staging.the-rails-way.com"
  set :repository, "http://svn.nnovation.ca/svn/the-rails-way/trunk"
  set :rails_env, "development"
  set :app_server, "staging.the-rails-way.com"
  set :secure_ssh_port, 8256

  role :app, "#{app_server}:#{secure_ssh_port}"
  role :web, "#{app_server}:#{secure_ssh_port}"
  role :db,  "#{app_server}:#{secure_ssh_port}", :primary => true
end
```

Thus, we can deploy very concisely and without worrying about command-line parameters.

```
$ cap staging deploy    # trunk to staging
$ cap production deploy # tags/release-1.0 to production
```

Now I don't know about you, but those repetitive role assignments smell a little. How about we just move them out of the tasks, perhaps below the two task definitions? We tried, and learned an important lesson when Capistrano reported that `app_server` and `secure_ssh_port` weren't understood. Is it a matter of scoping? Is our execution order off?

The answer is that both scoping and execution order are coming into play. When you move the role assignments out of the task's `do..end` blocks into the main body of the script, you are changing the timing of their evaluation. Those lines will in fact execute prior to the code that is inside of the task definition. So in this particular case, the role assignments would get executed before an `app_server` value is set.

Luckily for us, the solution is pretty simple and simplifies our code nicely. We'll do a Capistrano version of an *extract method* refactoring, except with an additional task instead of a method.

Define a task named `:finalize_staging_init`, and then add a call to it at the end of the `staging` and `production` tasks.

```
task :staging do
  set :domain, "staging.the-rails-way.com"
  set :repository, "http://svn.nnovation.ca/svn/the-rails-way/trunk"
  set :rails_env, "development"
  set :app_server, "staging.the-rails-way.com"
  set :secure_ssh_port, 8256

  finalize_staging_init
end

task :production do
  set :tag, "release-1.0" unless variables[:tag]
  set :domain, "the-rails-way.com"
  set :repository, "http://svn.nnovation.ca/svn/the-rails-
way/tags/#{tag}"
  set :rails_env, "production"
  set :app_server, "the-rails-way.net"
  set :secure_ssh_port, 8256

  finalize_staging_init
end

task :finalize_staging_init do
  role :app, "#{app_server}:#{secure_ssh_port}"
  role :web, "#{app_server}:#{secure_ssh_port}"
  role :db,  "#{app_server}:#{secure_ssh_port}", :primary => true
end
```

Exercise #2: Managing Other Services

A typical Rails deployment scenario involves a cluster of Mongrels, and perhaps some additional processes such as backgroundrb, memcache, and search engine daemons.

The canned deploy:start, :stop, and :start take care of a single Mongrel instance fronted by Apache. In this exercise, as shown in Listing 21.6, we're going to override the default tasks, and insert our own to manage a Mongrel cluster and a BackgrounDRb installation; however, note that this recipe doesn't manage Apache, as I rarely bring it up or down. At this point you should know enough about Capistrano to understand the recipe and easily bake in Apache support.

Listing 21.6 A Comprehensive Deploy Task

```
namespace :deploy do

  desc "Restart the Mongrel cluster and backgroundrb"
  task :restart, :roles => :app do
    stop
    start
  end

  desc "Start the mongrel cluster and backgroundrb"
  task :start, :roles => :app do
    start_mongrel
    start_backgroundrb
  end

  desc "Stop the mongrel cluster and backgroundrb"
  task :stop, :roles => :app do
    stop_mongrel
    stop_backgroundrb
  end

  desc "Start Mongrel"
  task :start_mongrel, :roles => :app do
    begin
      run "mongrel_cluster_ctl start -c #{app_mongrel_config_dir}"
    rescue RuntimeError => e
      puts e
      puts "Mongrel appears to be down already. "
    end
  end

  desc "Stop Mongrel"
  task :stop_mongrel, :roles => :app do
    begin
      run "mongrel_cluster_ctl stop -c #{app_mongrel_config_dir}"
```

```ruby
    rescue RuntimeError => e
      puts e
      puts "Mongrel appears to be down already. "
    end
  end

  desc "Start the backgroundrb server"
  task :start_backgroundrb , :roles => :app do
    begin
      puts "starting brb in folder #{current_path}"
      run "cd #{current_path} && RAILS_ENV=#{rails_env} nohup
./script/backgroundrb start > /dev/null 2>&1"
    rescue RuntimeError => e
      puts e
      puts "Problems starting backgroundrb - running already?"
    end
  end

  desc "Stop the backgroundrb server"
  task :stop_backgroundrb , :roles => :app do
    begin
      puts "stopping brb in folder #{current_path}"
      run "cd #{current_path} && ./script/backgroundrb stop"
    rescue RuntimeError => e
      puts e
      puts "Backgroundrb appears to be down already."
    end
  end
end
```

Multiserver Deployments

Things are going great on your one server. But as life would have it, business is booming and you decide to build out a *cluster* of servers. Some are specialized to serve your application, while others are specialized to run the web server, and one is specifically for running asynchronous processing, and so forth. A booming business sure is nice, but traditional deployment is not fun at all. Deploying to 10 machines? Well, might you be tempted to call in sick on deployment day?

Not with Capistrano! It was built right from the beginning to handle multiserver deployments. Jamis really wanted to make deploying to 100 machines as easy as deploying to one. In fact, many people claim that is exactly where Capistrano shines brightest.

Capistrano succeeds so well in its multiserver handling that you won't notice the difference either from the command line or in writing the task definitions. The secret sauce to multiserver deployments lies in the `role`[7] command, by which we can assign one or more deployment machines per task. When a task with many machines qualifies for simultaneous execution, each server assigned to the role will have the task executed—in parallel!

```
role :app, "uno.booming-biz.com", "dos.booming-biz.com"
role :db,  "kahuna.booming-biz.com", :primary => true
```

Adding a second (or third) server to our deployment means it will automatically be executed by all qualifying tasks. More specifically this means that all referenced tasks will execute on your newly added server—all tasks that either specifically require the :app role plus all tasks that don't indicate a qualifying role.

```
namespace :monitor
  task :exceptions :roles => :app do
    run "grep 'Exception' #{shared_path}/log/*.log"
  end
end
```

As an example, running `cap monitor:exceptions` will run against the entire :app role of machines you throw at it. Capistrano will `grep` all log files in parallel, streaming a merged result back to your terminal.

Capistrano's adherence to the DRY principle means that you can scale your physical deployment with zero impact on deployment rules and very little impact on your deployment configuration.

What about the impact on your deployment process? More machines means that mistakes and unexpected errors have bigger negative consequences, right? Not necessarily, since Capistrano has a feature that is usually associated with databases, not deployment systems: Transactions!

Transactions

Although a failed or incomplete install on one deployment machine can be tough to restore, consider when you have many more, each with their own particular flavor of install failure. Capistrano provides tasks with a transaction infrastructure that wraps and protects key deployment commands. It also has unique `on_rollback` handlers to ensure that we can recover from a disastrous deployment scenario with as little collateral damage as possible.

For example, look at the code for the :update_code and :symlink tasks—both have on_rollback blocks that clean up their respective actions, if necessary. This bears some similarity to the up-and-down migration methods of ActiveRecord.

```
namespace :deploy do
task :update do
  transaction do
    update_code
    symlink
  end
end

task :update_code do
  on_rollback { run "rm -rf #{release_path}" }
  strategy.deploy!
  finalize_update
end

task :symlink, :except => { :no_release => true } do
  on_rollback do
    run "rm -f #{current_path}"
    run "ln -s #{previous_release} #{current_path}; true"
  end

  run "rm -f #{current_path} && ln -s #{release_path} #{current_path}"
end
end
```

The preceding example is yanked right from Capistrano's source code[8]—the :update task uses your SCM strategy of choice to update the deployed codebase, and then sets up the symbolic links of the newly installed application to the ./current folder.

But what if our app failed to deploy at strategy.deploy!, perhaps because of problems connecting to the Subversion server? Would the deploy continue creating symlinks? Or perhaps the subversion deploy worked, but the symlinks failed to happen? Either scenario would leave our application in a fractured state. The problem would be compounded if we deployed successfully to one deployment machine, but failed on the second—problems would not necessarily be apparent right away!

```
task :update_code do
  on_rollback { run "rm -rf #{release_path}" }
  strategy.deploy!
  finalize_update
end
```

To mitigate the risks of failure and handle the greatest number of reasons for possible failure, the :update task is wrapped in a transaction. If a fault condition were to occur, each and every on_rollback block would be called, in reverse. That's why each on_rollback block should be designed to algorithmically reverse the current task's operation.

For example, the preceding on_rollback block removes all files possible created by both strategy.deploy! and finalize_update, correcting a potentially fractured deployment.

The transaction system employed by Capistrano isn't like any that you may have encountered before. For example, it doesn't keep track of local or remote object changes. The simple but effective transaction system puts *you* in control of the rollback. It should also be said that Capistrano doesn't place migrations under transaction—DDL transactions aren't widely supported by databases,[9] which makes it very difficult to roll back a failed migration.

Proxied Access to Deployment Machines

Real-world deployments often protect application servers through the use of secure proxies and firewalls. The result is that we won't be able to SSH directly to the deployment machine. However, don't let that stop you from using Capistrano, thanks to its support for proxied access to deployment machines using the :gateway setting:

```
set :gateway, 'gateway.booming-biz.com'
role :app, "192.168.1.100", "192.168.1.101"
role :db, "192.168.1.200", :primary => true
```

Setting a :gateway will cause all requests to tunnel securely to your roled machines through the specified gateway proxy machines. The assumption made by Capistrano is that the roled hosts are not directly accessible, and so to access them it must first establish a connection to `gateway.booming-biz.com` and establish SSH tunnels from there.

It's magical—well, the magic of port forwarding anyway.[10] Other than making sure that the roled machines can be reached through TCP/IP, there's very little you need to do to support the gateway capability. In fact if you're using passwords to authenticate there's nothing else—you will be prompted. But if you're using PKI, you'll have to add the public key of your gateway server to your nonpublic roled servers.

Conclusion

This chapter gave you a crash course in using Capistrano to automate your Rails deployment tasks. It should have also pointed you in the right direction to begin using Capistrano as your systems administration helper, given its ability to reliably automate tasks and execute tasks in parallel across one or dozens of remote servers.

References

1. Switchtower, the original name, was changed to Capistrano in response to a trademark violation. For details see http://weblog.rubyonrails.org/2006/3/6/switchtower-is-now-capistrano.

2. Since it is well documented on the web, but now obsolete, we omit coverage of Capistrano 1.x. The site capify.org provides ample upgrade instructions for developers wanting to migrate to the latest versions of Capistrano.

3. This means "you," Windows, although some have had success with cygwin.

4. This probably doesn't need to be said, but please, please consider PKI—you're gonna seriously reduce the possibility of break-ins.

5. Although Mongrel is today's best-of-show choice, fastcgi can be as easily configured.

6. http://shanesbrain.net/articles/2007/05/30/database-yml-management-with-capistrano-2-0

7. You can also use the `:host` qualifier for a task, but rolling host assignments up to the role will simplify your life when you roll out more servers.

8. Use `gem environment` to find the gem source, and pore over Capistrano's source code. This is a great way to learn.

9. MySQL doesn't, but I understand that Postgres may support DDL transactions.

10. For all the gory details, read Jamis Buck's post: http://weblog.jamisbuck.org/2006/9/26/inside-capistrano-the-gateway-implementation.

CHAPTER 22

Background Processing

Waiting for railsapplication.com…
—The status bar of your user's web browser

On the web, your users find out that your application is working at exactly one time—when your program responds to a request. The classic example of this is credit card processing. Which would you prefer to use: a site that says "Now processing your transaction" alongside a soothing animation, or one that shows a blank page?

In addition to such *user experience* situations, your application may have requirements that simply cannot be satisfied in a few seconds. Perhaps you run a popular site that allows users to upload video files and share them with others. You'll need to convert various types of video content into Flash. No server you can buy is fast enough to perform this work while the user's web browser waits.

Do either of these scenarios sound familiar? If so, it is probably time to think about performing work in the background of your application. In this chapter, *background* refers to anything that happens outside of the normal HTTP request/response cycle. Most developers will need to design and implement background processing at some point. Luckily, Rails and Ruby have several libraries and techniques for background processing, including:

- `script/runner`—Built into Rails

- DRb—A proven distributed processing library by Masatoshi Seki

- BackgrounDRb—A plugin written by Ezra Zygmuntowicz and maintained by Skaar

• Daemons—Makes it easy to create long-running system services. Written by Thomas Uehlinger

With these tools, you can easily add background processing to your Rails applications. This chapter aims to teach you enough about each one that you can decide which makes sense for your particular application.

script/runner

Rails comes with a built-in tool for running tasks independent of the web cycle. The runner script simply loads the default Rails environment and then executes some specified Ruby code. Popular uses include

• Importing "batch" external data

• Executing any (class) method in your models

• Running intensive calculations, delivering e-mails in batches, or executing scheduled tasks

Usages involving `script/runner` that you should avoid at all costs are

• Processing incoming e-mail

• Tasks that take longer to run as your database grows

Getting Started

For example, let us suppose that you have a model called "Report." The Report model has a class method called `generate_rankings`, which you can call from the command line using

```
$ ruby script/runner 'Report.generate_rankings'
```

Since we have access to all of Rails, we can even use the `ActiveRecord` finder methods to extract data from our application:[1]

```
$ ruby script/runner 'User.find(:all).map(&:email).each { |e| \
puts "<#{e}>"}'
```

```
<charles.quinn@highgroove.com>
<me@seebq.com>
<bill.gates@microsoft.com>
# ...
<obie@obiefernandez.com>
```

This example demonstrates that we have access to the `User` model and are able to execute arbitrary Rails code. In this case, we've collected some e-mail addresses that we can now spam to our heart's content. (Just kidding!)

Usage Notes

There are some things to remember when using `script/runner`. You must specify the production environment using the `-e` option; otherwise, it defaults to development. The `script/runner` help option tells us:

```
$ script/runner -h

Usage: script/runner [options] ('Some.ruby(code)' or a
filename)

    -e, --environment=name    Specifies the environment for the
runner
                              to operate in (test/development/
production)

                              Default: development
```

You can also use `runner` as a shebang line for your scripts like this:

```
#!/usr/bin/env /path/to/script/runner
```

Using `script/runner`, we can easily script any batch operations that need to run using `cron` or another system scheduler.

For example, you might calculate the most popular or highest-ranking product in your e-commerce application every few minutes or nightly, rather than make an expensive query on every request:

```
$ script/runner —e production 'Product.calculate_top_ranking'
```

A sample `crontab` to run that script might look like this:

```
0 */5 * * *   root  /usr/local/bin/ruby \
/apps/exampledotcom/current/script/runner -e production \
'Product.calculate_top_ranking'
```

The script will run every five hours to update the `Product` model's top rankings.

script/runner Considerations

On the positive side: It doesn't get any easier and there are no additional libraries to install. That's about it.

As for negatives: The `script/runner` process loads the entire Rails environment. For some tasks, particularly short-lived ones, that can be quite wasteful of resources.

Also, nothing prevents multiple copies of the same script from running simultaneously, which can be catastrophically bad, depending on the contents of the script.

> **Wilson Says...**
>
> Do not process incoming e-mail with `script/runner`.
> This is a Denial of Service attack waiting to happen.
> Use Fetcher (or something like it) instead:
> http://slantwisedesign.com/rdoc/fetcher/

The bottom line is, use `script/runner` for short tasks that need to run infrequently.

DRb

You might already know that you can use DRb as a session container for Rails with a little bit of configuration, but out of the box, it comes ready to process simple TCIP/IP requests and perform some background heavy lifting.

> DRb literally stands for "Distributed Ruby." It is a library that allows you to send and receive messages from remote Ruby objects via TCP/IP. Sound kind of like RPC, CORBA, or Java's RMI? Probably so. This is Ruby's simple as dirt answer to all of the above.—Chad Fowler's Intro to DRb
> (http://chadfowler.com/ruby/drb.html)

A Simple DRb Server

Let's create a DRb server that performs a simple calculation. We will run this server on localhost, but keep in mind that it could be run on one or more remote servers to distribute the load or provide fault tolerance.

Create a file named `distributed_server.rb` and give it the contents of Listing 22.1.

Listing 22.1   A Simple DRb Calculation Service

```
#!/usr/bin/env ruby -w
# DRb server

# load DRb
require 'drb'

class DistributedServer
 def perform_calculation(num)
  num * num
 end
end

DRb.start_service("druby://localhost:9000",
DistributedServer.new)
puts "Starting DRb server at: #{DRb.uri}"

DRb.thread.join
```

After making this file executable (`chmod +x`, or equivalent), run it so that it listens on port 9000 for requests:

```
$./distributed_server
Starting DRb server at: druby://localhost:9000
```

Using DRb from Rails

Now, to call this code from Rails, we can require the DRb library at the top of a controller where we plan to use it:

```
require 'drb'
class MessagesController < ApplicationController
```

To add an action in the controller to invoke a method on our distributed server, you would write an action method such as this one:

```
def calculation
  DRb.start_service
  drb_client = DRbObject.new(nil, 'druby://localhost:9000')
  @calculation = drb_client.perform_calculation(5)
end
```

We now have access to a @calculation instance variable that the distributed server actually processed for us. This is a trivial example, but it demonstrates how simple it is to farm out processes to a distributed server.

This code will still be executed as part of the normal Rails request/response cycle. Rails will wait for the DRb perform_calculation method to complete before processing any view templates or sending any data to the user agent. We may be able to leverage the power of several other servers by using this technique, but it's still not precisely what most people mean by background processing. To complete our journey to the dark side, we need to implement some kind of job control to wrap around this code.

The good news is that it's easy to do, but the better news is that someone's already done it. More on that in the next section, "BackgrounDRb."

DRb Considerations

On the positive side: DRb is part of the Ruby Standard Library, so there is nothing extra to install. Extremely reliable. Suitable for persistent processes that can return results quickly to the caller.

On the negative side: DRb is a relatively "low-level" library and does not provide any job control or configuration file support. Using it directly requires you to invent your own conventions for port numbers, class names, and so on.

Use DRb when you need to implement your own load balancing, or when no other solution offers enough control.

Resources

For a more in-depth understanding of how DRb operates, and what is going on in these code samples, see the following web articles:

- An Introduction to DRb by Eric Hodel at http://segment7.net/projects/ruby/drb /introduction.html

- Intro to DRb by Chad Fowler at http://chadfowler.com/ruby/drb.html

- Distributed Ruby in a Nutshell by Frank Spychalski at http://amazing-development.com/archives/2006/03/16/rails-and-distributed-ruby-in-a-nutshell/

BackgrounDRb

BackgrounDRb is a "Ruby job server and scheduler" available at http://backgroundrb. devjavu.com/. The principal use case for the BackgrounDRb plugin for Rails is "divorcing long-running tasks from the Rails request/response cycle."[2]

In addition to supporting asynchronous background processing, BackgrounDRb (along with Ajax code in your Rails application) is commonly used to support status updates and indicators. BackgrounDRb is frequently used to provide progress bars during large file uploads.

BackgrounDRb received a major rewrite for the 0.2.x branch that completely altered the previous version's job creation and execution. Job processing now uses multiple processes instead of a single, threaded process. Results are also stored in a `Result` worker, to allow each job its own process from which to store and retrieve results. It has an active community, and an open source repository with good test/rspec coverage.

Getting Started

BackgrounDRb can be run standalone or as a Rails plugin. It has two package dependencies, installable as gems: Slave 1.1.0 (or higher) and Daemons 1.0.2 (or higher). Install it into an existing Rails application by running the following command:

```
svn co http://svn.devjavu.com/backgroundrb/tags/release-0.2.1
vendor/plugins/backgroundrb
```

Note that using the following command

```
script/plugin install svn://rubyforge.org//var/svn/backgroundrb
```

installs the older, single-process version of BackgrounDRb, which *you don't want*. We'll cover the newer 0.2.x version only, since current documentation and development occurs there.

Verify that the tests run by visiting the `plugin` directory. You will need the RSpec gem installed if you wish to do this.

```
$ rake
(in /Users/your_login/your_app/vendor/plugins/backgroundrb)
/usr/local/bin/ruby -Ilib:lib "test/backgroundrb_test.rb"
"test/scheduler_test.rb"
Loaded suite /usr/local/lib/ruby/gems/1.8/gems/rake-
0.7.1/lib/rake/rake_test_loader
Started
.................
Finished in 3.107323 seconds.

18 tests, 26 assertions, 0 failures, 0 errors
```

Assuming that all tests pass, change back to your RAILS_ROOT and run `rake backgroundrb:setup` to install BackgrounDRb's configuration file, scripts, and directories for tasks and workers.

Configuration

The default `config/backgroundrb.yml` file will look like this:

```
---                    .
:rails_env: development
:host: localhost
:port: 2000
```

The default BackgrounDRb server runs in the development environment, and listens on the localhost server on port 2000. A move to production requires you to update this `rails_env` variable. The official BackgrounDRb documentation included with the distribution has more details.

Understanding BackgrounDRb

The heart of BackgrounDRb is the `MiddleMan` class, which facilitates the creation of *workers*, keeps track of them, and provides access to their results.

BackgrounDRb allows us to define workers, which are classes containing the code that we would like to execute in the background. By default they will be stored in the `lib/workers` directory of your Rails project.

These workers will be subclasses of one of two base classes provided by the plugin:

- `BackgroundDRb::Worker::Base`—Simple workers needing minimal environmental setup

- `BackgroundDRb::Worker::RailsBase`—Workers that need access to a fully configured Rails environment

Workers that subclass `RailsBase` will consume more resources than `Base` workers, so if you do not need access to `ActiveRecord` models or other Rails facilities, try to use the simple worker class.

If workers need to return their output to our application, we can use their `results` method when we invoke them. It operates like a normal `Hash` object, but behind the scenes it is a special `Result` worker. We can also create log messages via the BackgrounDRb `logger` method.

Each worker needs to define a `do_work` method that accepts a single `args` parameter. BackgrounDRb will automatically call this method when a worker is initialized. Typically this method should be kept simple, and will call other methods you define in order to perform its work.

Using the `MiddleMan`

Let's create a worker in our new `lib/workers` directory. We'll use the provided generator to create the base class:

```
$script/generate worker Counter
```

We'll add some code to make it count to 10000, to simulate a long-running task. Real-life examples include processing an uploaded file, converting an image, or generating and sending a report. In Listing 22.2, we will shove all of the code into the do_work method, but in your own code you will want to adhere to normal model design principles and factor out your code appropriately.

Listing 22.2 CounterWorker Class Counts Up to 10,000

```
class CounterWorker < BackgrounDRb::Worker::RailsBase
 def do_work(args)
  logger.info 'Starting the CounterWorker'
  1.upto 10_000 do |x|
   results[:count] = x
   logger.info "Count: #{x}"
  end
  logger.info 'Finished counting to 10,000'
 end

end

CounterWorker.register
```

With a worker ready to go, we can fire up the BackgrounDRb server:

```
$ ruby script/backgroundrb start
```

Check to see that the BackgrounDRb processes are running by using the `ps` command:[3]

```
$ps aux | grep background
you    617  0.6 -0.2   3628 ?? R    4:20PM  0:00.23
backgroundrb
you    618  0.0 -0.7  14640 ?? S    4:20PM  0:00.10
backgroundrb_logger
you    619  0.0 -0.7  14572 ?? S    4:20PM  0:00.09
backgroundrb_results
```

Now, we can trigger the worker from a controller action. The `new_worker` class method of `MiddleMan` instantiates a new worker and returns a "key" that will allow us to refer to it later.

Here we create a new `CounterWorker` and store its key in the session for later use:

```
def start_counting
  session[:key] = MiddleMan.new_worker(:class =>
:counter_worker)
  redirect_to :action => 'check_counter'
end
```

We'll go ahead and create another action to check the status of the worker. We must use the key that we saved moments ago to fetch the running worker, and then use the `results` method to access the current value of the counter:

```
def check_counter
  count_worker = MiddleMan.worker(session[:key])
  @count = count_worker.results[:count]
end
```

The corresponding view (for `check_counter`) could be this simple:

```
<p>We're currently counting. We're at <%= @count %>.</p>
```

Inside the `start_counting` action, the `new_worker` method immediately calls the `do_work` method we defined in the `CounterWorker` class. This is a nonblocking call, and our web application happily continues along and redirects us, while the worker chugs along counting.

If we hit the Refresh button on the `check_counter` action to reload the results of the worker, it will show the `@count` variable increasing, as the background process progresses with its job.

Caveats

Unfortunately, changes to the workers require BackgrounDRb to be restarted. They are loaded once and then cached, just like your `ActiveRecord` models in production mode.

If you get an error like this

```
/usr/local/lib/ruby/site_ruby/1.8/rubygems/custom_require.rb:
27:in `gem_original_require': no such file to load — slave
(LoadError)
```

remember that BackgrounDRb depends on the `slave` and `daemons` gems.

If the backgroundrb process should exit or die, the process ID files will need to be cleaned up. You'll know that it happened if subsequent attempts to start the service result in

```
ERROR: there is already one or more instance(s) of the program
running
```

To remove the `log/backgroundrb.pid` and `log/backgroundrb.ppid`, we can use the convenient, built-in `zap` command:

```
$ script/backgroundrb zap
```

BackgrounDRb should start normally after the old files are zapped.

BackGrounDRb Considerations

On the positive side:

- Provides job control and asynchronous invocation right out of the box.

- Popular, with many code samples posted on the web.

- Optimal for "event-based" tasks, such as those that occur every time a user hits a particular action.

As for negatives:

- The current version is considered "experimental" by the maintainers. You may end up needing to change your worker or action code as the API evolves.

- Support for scheduled tasks is new, and may not be as stable as the rest of the codebase.

- Some configuration options are *baked in* and may be difficult to customize if your production environment is unusual.

All things considered, BackgrounDRb seems perfect for tasks that need to be initiated from a controller action or a model callback.

Daemons

The website http://daemons.rubyforge.org/ offers an excellent Ruby library that lets you "daemonize" your script for easy management and maintainability.

Usage

The script in Listing 22.3 is a simple example of how to use the `daemons` library to run a scheduled task.

Listing 22.3   A Simple Use of Daemons to Update RSS Feeds in the Background

```
require 'daemons'

class BackgroundTasks
 include Singleton
 def update_rss_feeds
  loop do
   Feed.update_all
   sleep 10
  end
 end
end

Daemons.run_proc('BackgroundTasks') do
 BackgroundTasks.instance.update_rss_feeds
end
```

The script defines a simple task, `update_rss_feeds`, and runs it in a loop. If you save it as `background_tasks.rb` and run it without any options like this:

```
script/runner background_tasks.rb
```

it will show you all options provided by the daemons library:

```
Usage: BackgroundTasks <command> <options> -- <application
options>

* where <command> is one of:
  start     start an instance of the application
  stop      stop all instances of the application
  restart    stop all instances and restart them afterwards
  run       start the application and stay on top
```

```
zap        set the application to a stopped state
```

* and where <options> may contain several of the following:

```
-t, --ontop             Stay on top (does not daemonize)
-f, --force             Force operation
```

```
Common options:
 -h, --help              Show this message
    --version            Show version
```

You can control your background task process using simple commands.

The Daemon library also guarantees that only one copy of your task is running at a time, which prevents the need for control logic that tends to creep into script/runner or cron scripts.

Introducing Threads

The preceding example demonstrates the control that the Daemons library provides. However, as written, it doesn't do much. Let's modify the script to make it fetch e-mails from an external server as well (as shown in Listing 22.4). Since fetching e-mail happens to use the network, we'll use threads to get more work done in less time.

Listing 22.4 The Threaded E-mail Fetcher

```
require 'thread'
require 'daemons'

class BackgroundTasks
 include Singleton

 def initialize
  ActiveRecord::Base.allow_concurrency = true
 end

 def run
  threads = []
  [:update_rss_feeds, :update_emails].each do |task|
   threads << Thread.new do
    self.send task
   end
  end
  threads.each {|t| t.join }
 end
```

Listing 22.4   The Threaded E-mail Fetcher

```
  protected
  def update_rss_feeds
   loop do
    Feed.update_all
    sleep 10
   end
  end

  def update_emails
   loop do
    User.find(:all, :conditions => "email IS NOT NULL").each do
 |user|
     user.fetch_emails
    end
    sleep 60
   end
  end
end

Daemons.run_proc('BackgroundTasks') do
 BackgroundTasks.instance.start
end
```

An important thing to notice about the code in Listing 22.4 is that we added

```
ActiveRecord::Base.allow_concurrency = true
```

to the `initialize` method. That is a critical step for using `ActiveRecord` concurrently in multiple threads. Among other things, the setting gives each thread its own database connection. Forgetting this step can lead to data corruption and other horrors. *Consider yourself warned!*

> **Wilson Says...**
>
> If your concurrent `ActiveRecord` code has bugs, you may face the indignity of running out of database connections. You should be careful about exception handling while using threads.
>
> You may also want to call `ActiveRecord::Base.verify_active_connections!` as part of your processing loop to clear out any stale connections. This method is moderately expensive to execute, but is fairly essential if you enable `ActiveRecord` concurrency.

The daemon we have just written has only the most trivial scheduling support. Your application may need something more robust than `sleep 60`. If this is the case, you may want to consider using the unfortunately named OpenWFEru library available at http://openwferu.rubyforge.org/scheduler.html, which provides a wide variety of scheduling possibilities.

Daemon Considerations

Daemons are the most *cost-effective* way to implement background-processing code that needs to run continuously, and they offer precise control over which libraries you load, and which settings you configure.

Daemons are also easy to manage with monitoring tools like `monit`: http://www.tildeslash.com/monit/.

On the negative side, setting up daemons is not as *automatic* as BackgrounDRb or as simple as `script/runner`. (Fundamentalist programmers might be scared to work on them too.)

Consider using Daemons whenever you need something to run continuously.

Conclusion

In this chapter, our final one of the book, we've covered extending Rails with behavior that runs in a context external to normal request processing, that is *in the background*. The topic runs deep, and we've just skimmed across the surface of what is possible.

References

1. Be careful to escape any characters that have specific meaning to your shell.

2. http://backgroundrb.rubyforge.org/

3. Windows users can use the `tasklist` command to get similar results.

Appendix A

ActiveSupport API Reference

`ActiveSupport` is a Rails library containing utility classes and extensions to Ruby's built-in libraries. It usually doesn't get much attention on its own—you might even call its modules the supporting cast members of the Rails ensemble.

However, `ActiveSupport`'s low profile doesn't diminish its importance in day-to-day Rails programming. To ensure that this book is 100 percent useful as a programming companion, here is a complete, enhanced version of the Rails `ActiveSupport` API reference, supplemented where appropriate with real-life example usages and commentary.

Direct extensions of Ruby classes and modules are listed under headings according to class or module name. Extensions made via mixin module appear under headings according to their `ActiveSupport` module name.

> **NOTE**
> This API reference was prepared based on revision 7360 of Edge Rails (prior to Rails 2.0). A few obscure methods have been judged inconsequential and omitted because they are old and currently unused in the Rails codebase.

Array

Rails only adds one method directly to the `Array` class: `blank?`.

Public Instance Methods

blank?

Returns `true` if the array is empty.

Array::Conversions (in ActiveSupport::CoreExtensions)

Provides methods for converting Ruby arrays into other formats.

Public Instance Methods

to_formatted_s(format = :default)

Two formats are supported, `:default` and `:db`.

The `:default` format delegates to the normal `to_s` method for an array, which simply concatenates the contents into one mashed-up string.

The much more interesting `:db` option returns "`null`" if the array is empty, or concatenates the `id` fields of its member elements into a comma-delimited string like this:

```
collect { |element| element.id }.join(",")
```

to_param

Converts its string elements into a slash-delimited string (used to generate URL paths).

```
>> ["riding","high","and","I","want","to","make"].to_param
=> "riding/high/and/I/want/to/make"
```

`to_sentence(options = {})`

Converts the array to a comma-separated sentence in which the last element is joined by the connector word.

```
>> %w(alcohol tobacco firearms).to_sentence
=> "alcohol, tobacco, and firearms"
```

The following options are available for `to_sentence`:

- `:connector`—The word used to join the last element in arrays with two or more elements (default: "and").

- `:skip_last_comma`—Set this option to `true` to return "a, b and c" instead of "a, b, and c."

`to_xml(options = {}) {|xml if block_given?| ...}`

As covered in Chapter 15, "XML and ActiveResource," the `to_xml` method on `Array` can be used to create an XML collection by iteratively calling `to_xml` on its members, and wrapping the entire thing in an enclosing element.

All of the array elements must respond to `to_xml`.

```
>> ["riding","high"].to_xml
RuntimeError: Not all elements respond to to_xml
```

The preceding example yields the `Builder` object to an optional block so that arbitrary markup can be inserted at the bottom of the generated XML, as the last child of the enclosing element.

The following code

```
{:foo => "foo", :bar => :bar}.to_xml do |xml|
    xml.did_it "again"
end
```

outputs the following XML:

```
<?xml version="1.0" encoding="UTF-8"?>
<hash>
  <bar:bar/>
```

```
  <foo>foo</foo>
  <did_it>again</did_it>
</hash>
```

The options for to_xml are:

- :builder—Defaults to a new instance of Builder::XmlMarkup. Specify explicitly if you're calling to_xml on this array as part of a larger XML construction routine.

- :children—Sets the name to use for element tags explicitly. Defaults to singularized version of the :root name by default.

- :dasherize—Whether or not to turn underscores to dashes in tag names (defaults to true).

- :indent—Indent level to use for generated XML (defaults to two spaces).

- :root—The tag name to use for the enclosing element. If no :root is supplied and all members of the array are of the same class, the dashed, pluralized form of the first element's class name is used as a default. Otherwise the default :root is records.

- :skip_instruct—Whether or not to generate an XML instruction tag by calling instruct! on Builder.

- :skip_types—Whether or not to include a type="array" attribute on the enclosing element.

Array::ExtractOptions (in ActiveSupport::CoreExtensions)

Provides a method for extracting Rails-style options from a variable-length set of argument parameters.

Public Instance Methods

extract_options!

Extracts options from a variable set of arguments. It's a bang method because it removes and returns the last element in the array if it's a hash; otherwise, it returns a blank hash and the source array is unmodified.

```
def options(*args)
  args.extract_options!
end

options(1, 2)           # => {}
options(1, 2, :a => :b) # => {:a=>:b}
```

Array::Grouping (in ActiveSupport::CoreExtensions)

Provides a couple of methods used for splitting array elements into logical groupings.

Public Instance Methods

in_groups_of(number, fill_with = nil) {|group| ...}

A true Rails superstar, the in_groups_of method splits an array into groups of the specified number size, padding any remaining slots. The fill_with parameter is used for padding and defaults to nil.

If a block is provided, it is called with each group; otherwise, a two-dimensional array is returned.

```
>> %w(1 2 3 4 5 6 7).in_groups_of(3)
=> [[1, 2, 3], [4, 5, 6], [7, nil, nil]

>> %w(1 2 3).in_groups_of(2, ' ') {|group| puts group }
[1, 2]
[3, " "]
```

```
>> %w(1 2 3).in_groups_of(2, false) {|group| puts group }
[1, 2]
[3]
```

The in_groups_of method is particularly useful for batch-processing model objects and generating table rows in view templates.

split(value = nil, &block)

Divides an array into one or more subarrays based on a delimiting value:

```
[1, 2, 3, 4, 5].split(3)   #=> [[1, 2], [4, 5]]
```

or the result of an optional block:

```
(1..8).to_a.split { |i| i % 3 == 0 } # => [[1, 2], [4, 5], [7, 8]]
```

CachingTools::HashCaching (in ActiveSupport)

Provides a method that simplifies the caching of method invocations using nested default hashes. According to the API docs, "This pattern is useful, common practice in Ruby, and unsightly when done manually."

That may be the case, but this module appears to be somewhat useless, since its sole method, hash_cache, is not automatically accessible in any Rails context, and examination of the Rails codebase reveals that it is not used internally (except in its unit tests).

Public Instance Methods

hash_cache(method_name, options = {})

Dynamically creates a nested hash structure used to cache calls to *method_name*. The cache method is named *method_name*_cache unless :as => :*alternate_name* is given.

For example, the following slow_method

```
def slow_method(a, b)
 a ** b
end
```

can be cached by calling `hash_cache :slow_method`, which will define the method `slow_method_cache`.

We can then calculate (and cache) the result of a `**` b using this syntax:

```
slow_method_cache[a][b]
```

The hash structure is created using nested calls to `Hash.new` with initializer blocks, so the hash structure returned by `slow_method_cache` for the example looks like this:

```
Hash.new do |as, a|
  as[a] = Hash.new do |bs, b|
    bs[b] = slow_method(a, b)
  end
end
```

The implementation of `hash_cache` uses heavy Ruby metaprogramming. Generated code is compressed into a single line to maintain sensible backtrace signatures in the case of exceptions.

Class

Rails extends Ruby's `Class` object with a number of methods.

Public Instance Methods

cattr_accessor(*syms)

Defines one or more class attribute reader and writer methods in the style of the native `attr*` accessors for instance attributes. Used extensively throughout the Rails codebase to save option settings. Values are shared by reference with subclasses, which is very different than `class_inheritable_accessor`.

cattr_reader(*syms)

Defines one or more class attribute reader methods.

cattr_writer(*syms)

Defines one or more class attribute writer methods.

class_inheritable_accessor(*syms)

Allows attributes to be shared within an inheritance hierarchy, but each descendant gets a copy of its parents' attributes, instead of just a pointer to the same. This means that the child can add elements to, for example, an array without those additions being shared with either its parent, siblings, or children, which is unlike the regular class-level attributes, which are shared across the entire hierarchy.

class_inheritable_array

Convenience method that sets up an inheritable reader and writer and defaults it to an empty array so that you don't have to initialize it yourself.

class_inheritable_hash

Convenience method that sets up an inheritable reader and writer and defaults it to an empty hash so that you don't have to initialize it yourself.

class_inheritable_reader(*syms)

Defines one or more inheritable class attribute writer methods.

class_inheritable_writer(*syms)

Defines one or more inheritable class attribute writer methods.

const_missing(class_id)

The const_missing callback is invoked when Ruby can't find a specified constant in the current scope, which is what makes Rails autoclassloading possible. See the Dependencies module for more detail.

remove_class(*klasses)

Removes the constant associated with the specified classes so that they effectively become inaccessible and unusable.

remove_subclasses

Removes all subclasses of this class.

subclasses

Returns all subclasses of this class.

CGI::EscapeSkippingSlashes (in ActiveSupport::CoreExtensions)

Public Instance Methods

escape_skipping_slashes(str)

Takes a string to be used as a URL and escapes any non-letter or non-number characters in it (except for slashes).

```
>> CGI.escape_skipping_slashes "/amc/shows/mad men on thursday nights"
=> "/amc/shows/mad+men+on+thursday+nights"
```

Date::Behavior (in ActiveSupport::CoreExtensions)

Public Instance Methods

acts_like_date?

Simply returns `true` to enable more predictable duck-typing on `Date`-like classes.

```
>> Date.today.acts_like_date?   #=> true
```

Date::Calculations (in ActiveSupport::CoreExtensions)

Enables the use of calculations with `Date` objects.

Public Instance Methods

+ (other)

Rails extends the existing + operator so that a `since` calculation is performed when the `other` argument is an instance of `ActiveSupport::Duration` (the type of object returned by methods such as `10.minutes` and `9.months`).

```
>> Date.today + 1.day == Date.today.tomorrow
=> true
```

advance(options)

Provides precise `Date` calculations for years, months, and days. The `options` parameter takes a hash with any of these keys: `:months`, `:days`, `:years`.

```
>> Date.new(2006, 2, 28) == Date.new(2005, 2, 28).advance(:years => 1)
=> true
```

ago(seconds)

Converts `Date` to a `Time` (or `DateTime` if necessary) with the time portion set to the beginning of the day (0:00) and then subtracts the specified number of seconds.

```
>> Time.local(2005, 2, 20, 23, 59, 15) == Date.new(2005, 2, 21).ago(45)
=> true
```

at_beginning_of_day, at_midnight, beginning_of_day, and midnight

Converts `Date` to a `Time` (or `DateTime` if necessary) with the time portion set to the beginning of the day (0:00).

```
>> Time.local(2005,2,21,0,0,0) == Date.new(2005,2,21).beginning_of_day
=> true
```

at_beginning_of_month and beginning_of_month

Returns a new DateTime representing the start of the month (1st of the month; time set to 0:00).

```
>> Date.new(2005, 2, 1) == Date.new(2005,2,21).beginning_of_month
=> true
```

at_beginning_of_quarter and beginning_of_quarter

Returns a new Date/DateTime representing the start of the calendar-based quarter (1st of January, April, July, and October).

```
>> Date.new(2005, 4, 1) == Date.new(2005, 6, 30).beginning_of_quarter
=> true
```

at_beginning_of_week, beginning_of_week, and monday

Returns a new Date (or DateTime) representing the beginning of the week. (Calculation is Monday-based.)

```
>> Date.new(2005, 1, 31) == Date.new(2005, 2, 4).beginning_of_week
=> true
```

at_beginning_of_year and beginning_of_year

Returns a new Date/DateTime representing the start of the calendar year (1st of January).

```
>> Date.new(2005, 1, 1) == Date.new(2005, 2, 22).beginning_of_year
=> true
```

at_end_of_month and end_of_month

Returns a new Date/DateTime representing the last day of the calendar month.

```
>> Date.new(2005, 3, 31) == Date.new(2005,3,20).end_of_month
=> true
```

change(options)

Returns a new `Date` where one or more of the elements have been changed according to the options parameter.

The valid options are `:year`, `:month`, and `:day`.

```
>> Date.new(2007, 5, 12).change(:day => 1) == Date.new(2007, 5, 1)
=> true

>> Date.new(2007, 5, 12).change(:year => 2005, :month => 1) == ➡
Date.new(2005, 1, 12)
=> true
```

end_of_day()

Converts `Date` to a `Time` (or `DateTime` if necessary) with the time portion set to the end of the day (23:59:59).

```
>> Time.local(2005,2,21,23,59,59) == Date.new(2005, 2, 21).end_of_day
=> true
```

in(seconds) and since(seconds)

Converts `Date` to a `Time` (or `DateTime` if necessary) with the time portion set to the beginning of the day (0:00) and then adds the specified number of seconds.

```
>> Time.local(2005, 2, 21, 0, 0, 45) == Date.new(2005, 2, 21).since(45)
=> true
```

last_month()

Syntax sugar for `months_ago(1)`.

last_year()

Syntax sugar for `years_ago(1)`.

months_ago(months)

Returns a new Date (or DateTime) representing the time a number of specified months ago.

```
>> Date.new(2005, 1, 1) == Date.new(2005, 3, 1).months_ago(2)
=> true
```

months_since(months)

Returns a new Date (or DateTime) representing the time a number of specified months into the past or the future. Supply a negative number of months to go back to the past.

```
>> Date.today.months_ago(1) == Date.today.months_since(-1)
=> true
```

next_month()

Syntax sugar for months_since(1).

next_week(day = :monday)

Returns a new Date (or DateTime) representing the start of the given day in the following calendar week. Default day of the week may be overridden with a symbolized day name.

```
>> Date.new(2005, 3, 4) == Date.new(2005, 2, 22).next_week(:friday)
=> true
```

next_year()

Syntax sugar for years_since(1).

tomorrow()

Convenience method that returns a new Date (or DateTime) representing the time one day in the future.

```
>> Date.new(2007, 3, 2) == Date.new(2007, 2, 28).tomorrow.tomorrow
=> true
```

years_ago(years)

Returns a new `Date` (or `DateTime`) representing the time a number of specified years ago.

```
>> Date.new(2000, 6, 5) == Date.new(2007, 6, 5).years_ago(7)
=> true
```

years_since(years)

Returns a new `Date` (or `DateTime`) representing the time a number of specified years into the future.

```
>> Date.new(2007, 6, 5) == Date.new(2006, 6, 5).years_since(1)
=> true
```

yesterday()

Convenience method that returns a new `Date` (or `DateTime`) representing the time one day ago.

```
>> Date.new(2007, 2, 21) == Date.new(2007, 2, 22).yesterday
=> true
```

Date::Conversions (in ActiveSupport::CoreExtensions)

This module mixes methods into `Date` that are useful for getting dates in different convenient string representations and as other objects.

Constants

The `DATE_FORMATS` constant holds a hash of formats used in conjunction with the `to_formatted_s` method.

```
DATE_FORMATS = {
  :short        => "%e %b",
  :long         => "%B %e, %Y",
```

```
  :db            => "%Y-%m-%d",
  :long_ordinal => lambda {|date| date.strftime("%B ➥
#{date.day.ordinalize}, %Y") }, # => "April 25th, 2007"
  :rfc822        => "%e %b %Y" }
```

Public Instance Methods

to_date

Used in order to keep Time, Date, and DateTime objects interchangeable in conversions.

to_datetime

Converts a Date object into a Ruby DateTime object. The time is set to beginning of day.

to_formatted_s(format = :default)

Converts a Date object into its string representation, according to the predefined formats in the DATE_FORMATS constant. (Aliased as to_s. Original to_s is aliased as to_default_s.)

```
def test_to_s
  date = Date.new(2005, 2, 21)
  assert_equal "2005-02-21",           date.to_s
  assert_equal "21 Feb",               date.to_s(:short)
  assert_equal "February 21, 2005",    date.to_s(:long)
  assert_equal "February 21st, 2005",  date.to_s(:long_ordinal)
  assert_equal "2005-02-21",           date.to_s(:db)
  assert_equal "21 Feb 2005",          date.to_s(:rfc822)
end
```

to_time(timezone = :local)

Converts a Date object into a Ruby Time object; time is set to beginning of day. The time zone can be :local or :utc.

```
>> Time.local(2005, 2, 21) == Date.new(2005, 2, 21).to_time
=> true
```

xmlschema

Returns a string that represents the time as defined by XML Schema (also known as iso8601):

```
CCYY-MM-DDThh:mm:ssTZD
```

If the `Date` object is a UTC time, Z is used as TZD. Otherwise `[+-]`*hh*`:`*mm* is used to indicate the hours offset.

DateTime::Calculations (in ActiveSupport::CoreExtensions)

Enables the use of time calculations within `DateTime` itself.

Public Instance Methods

at_beginning_of_day, at_midnight, beginning_of_day, midnight

Convenience methods that all represent the start of a day (00:00). Implemented simply as `change(:hour => 0)`.

advance(options)

Uses `Date` to provide precise `Time` calculations for years, months, and days. The `options` parameter takes a hash with any of the keys `:months`, `:days`, and `:years`.

ago(seconds)

Returns a new `DateTime` representing the time a number of seconds ago. The opposite of `since`.

change(options)

Returns a new `DateTime` where one or more of the elements have been changed according to the `options` parameter. The valid date options are `:year`, `:month`, `:day`. The valid time options are `:hour`, `:min`, `:sec`, `:offset`, and `:start`.

end_of_day

Convenience method that represents the end of a day (23:59:59). Implemented simply as `change(:hour => 23, :min => 59, :sec => 59)`.

seconds_since_midnight

Returns how many seconds have passed since midnight.

since(seconds)

Returns a new `DateTime` representing the time a number of seconds since the instance time. The opposite of `ago`.

DateTime::Conversions (in ActiveSupport::CoreExtensions)

Public Instance Methods

readable_inspect

Overrides the default inspect method with a human-readable one that looks like this:

```
Mon, 21 Feb 2005 14:30:00 +0000
```

to_date

Converts `self` to a Ruby `Date` object, discarding time data.

to_datetime

Returns `self` to be able to keep `Time`, `Date`, and `DateTime` classes interchangeable on conversions.

to_formatted_s(format=:default)

See the options on `to_formatted_s` of the `Time` class.

`to_time`

Attempts to convert `self` to a Ruby `Time` object. Returns `self` if out of range of Ruby `Time` class. If `self.offset` is 0, will attempt to cast as a UTC time; otherwise, will attempt to cast in local timezone.

Dependencies (in **ActiveSupport**)

Contains the logic for Rails' automatic classloading mechanism, which is what makes it possible to reference any constant in the Rails varied loadpaths without ever needing to issue a `require` directive.

This module extends *itself*, a cool hack that you can use with modules that you want to use elsewhere in your codebase in a functional manner:

```
module Dependencies
  extend self
```

As a result, you can call methods directly on the module constant, à la Java static class methods, like this:

```
Dependencies.search_for_file('.erb')
```

You shouldn't need to use this module in day-to-day Rails coding—it's mostly for internal use by Rails and plugins. On occasion, it might also be useful to understand the workings of this module when debugging tricky class-loading problems.

Module Attributes

Several of these attributes are set based on `Configuration` settings declared in your various environment files, as described in Chapter 1, "Rails Environments and Configuration."

`autoloaded_constants`

An array of qualified constant names that have been loaded. Adding a name to this array will cause it to be unloaded the next time `Dependencies` are cleared.

`clear`

Clears the list of currently loaded classes and removes unloadable constants.

constant_watch_stack

An internal stack used to record which constants are loaded by any block.

explicitly_unloadable_constants

An array of constant names that need to be unloaded on every request. Used to allow arbitrary constants to be marked for unloading.

history

The Set of all files *ever* loaded.

load_once_paths

The Set of directories from which automatically loaded constants are loaded only once. All directories in this set must also be present in +load_paths+.

load_paths

The Set of directories from which Rails may automatically load files. Files under these directories will be reloaded on each request in development mode, unless the directory also appears in load_once_paths.

loaded

The Set of all files *currently* loaded.

log_activity

Set this option to true to enable logging of const_missing and file loads. (Defaults to false.)

mechanism

A setting that determines whether files are loaded (default) or required. This attribute determines whether Rails reloads classes per request, as in development mode.

warnings_on_first_load

A setting that determines whether Ruby warnings should be activated on the first load of dependent files. Defaults to true.

Public Instance Methods

`associate_with(file_name)`

Invokes `depend_on` with `swallow_load_errors` set to `true`. Wrapped by the `require_association` method of `Object`.

`autoload_module!(into, const_name, qualified_name, path_suffix)`

Attempts to autoload the provided module name by searching for a directory matching the expected `path suffix`. If found, the module is created and assigned to `into`'s constants with the name +const_name+. Provided that the directory was loaded from a reloadable base path, it is added to the set of constants that are to be unloaded.

`autoloadable_module?(path_suffix)`

Checks whether the provided `path_suffix` corresponds to an autoloadable module. Instead of returning a Boolean, the autoload base for this module is returned.

`autoloaded?(constant)`

Determines if the specified `constant` has been automatically loaded.

`depend_on(file_name, swallow_load_errors = false)`

Searches for the `file_name` specified and uses `require_or_load` to establish a new dependency. The `swallow_load_errors` argument specifies whether `LoadError` should be suppressed. Wrapped by the `require_dependency` method of `Object`.

`load?`

Returns `true` if `mechanism` is set to `:load`.

`load_file(path, const_paths = loadable_constants_for_path(path))`

Loads the file at the specified `path`. The `const_paths` is a set of fully qualified constant names to load. When the file is loading, `Dependencies` will watch for the addition of these constants. Each one that is defined will be marked as autoloaded, and will be removed when `Dependencies.clear` is next called.

If the second parameter is left off, `Dependencies` will construct a set of names that the file at `path` may define. See `loadable_constants_for_path` for more details.

load_once_path?(path)

Returns `true` if the specified `path` appears in the `load_once_path` list.

load_missing_constant(mod, const_name)

Loads the constant named `const_name`, which is missing from `mod`. If it is not possible to load the constant from `mod`, try its parent module by calling `const_missing` on it.

loadable_constants_for_path(path, bases = load_paths)

Returns an array of constants, based on a specified filesystem `path` to a Ruby file, which would cause `Dependencies` to attempt to load the file.

mark_for_unload(constant)

Marks the specified `constant` for unloading. The constant will be unloaded on each request, not just the next one.

new_constants_in(*descs) {...}

Runs the provided block and detects the new constants that were loaded during its execution. Constants may only be regarded as *new* once. If the block calls `new_constants_in` again, the constants defined within the inner call will not be reported in this one.

If the provided block does not run to completion, and instead raises an exception, any new constants are regarded as being only partially defined and will be removed immediately.

qualified_const_defined?(path)

Returns `true` if the provided constant path is `defined?`

qualified_name_for(parent_module, constant_name)

Returns a qualified path for the specified `parent_module` and `constant_name`.

remove_unloadable_constants!

Removes the constants that have been autoloaded, and those that have been marked for unloading.

require_or_load(file_name, const_path = nil)

Implements the main classloading mechanism. Wrapped by the `require_or_load` method of `Object`.

search_for_file(path_suffix)

Searches for a file in `load_paths` matching the provided `path_suffix`.

will_unload?(constant)

Returns `true` if the specified constant is queued for unloading on the next request.

Deprecation (in ActiveSupport)

This module provides Rails core and application developers with a formal mechanism to be able to explicitly state what methods are deprecated. (Deprecation means to *mark for future deletion*.) Rails will helpfully log a warning message when deprecated methods are called.

All you do to mark a method as deprecated is to call `deprecate` and pass it the name of the method as a symbol. Make sure to add your call to `deprecate` *after the method definition*.

```
deprecate :subject_of_regret
```

The `deprecate` method is mixed into Ruby's `Module` class so that it's available everywhere.

Deprecation::Assertions (in ActiveSupport)

This module provides assertions that allow testing deprecation of methods.

Public Instance Methods

assert_deprecated(match = nil) { ... }

Asserts that the code in the block triggered a deprecation warning. The optional `match` argument allows the assertion to be more specific to a given method name. Just supply a regular expression to use in matching the name of the method(s) expected to be deprecated.

```
def test_that_subject_of_regret_is_deprecated
  assert_deprecated do
    subject_of_regret
  end
end
```

assert_not_deprecated { ... }

Asserts that the code in the block does not use any deprecated methods.

Duration (in ActiveSupport)

Provides accurate date and time measurements using the `advance` method of `Date` and `Time`. It mainly supports the methods on `Numeric`, such as in this example:

```
1.month.ago # equivalent to Time.now.advance(:months => -1)
```

Public Instance Methods

+ (other)

Adds another `Duration` or a `Numeric` to this `Duration`. `Numeric` values are treated as seconds.

- (other)

Subtracts another `Duration` or a `Numeric` to this `Duration`. `Numeric` values are treated as seconds.

ago(time = Time.now)

Calculates a new `Time` or `Date` that is as far in the past as this `Duration` represents.

```
birth = 35.years.ago
```

from_now(time = Time.now)

Alias for `since`, which reads a little bit more naturally when using the default `Time.now` as the `time` argument.

```
expiration = 1.year.from_now
```

inspect

Calculates the time resulting from a `Duration` expression and formats it as a string appropriate for display in the console. (Remember that IRB and the Rails console automatically invoke `inspect` on objects returned to them. You can use that trick with your own objects.)

```
>> 10.years.ago
=> Sun Aug 31 17:34:15 -0400 1997
```

since(time = Time.now)

Calculates a new `Time` or `Date` that is as far in the future as this `Duration` represents.

```
expiration = 1.year.since(account.created_at)
```

until(time = Time.now)

Alias for `ago`. Reads a little more naturally when specifying a `time` argument instead of using the default value, `Time.now`.

```
membership_duration = created_at.until(expires_at)
```

Enumerable

Extensions to Ruby's built-in `Enumerable` module, which gives arrays and other types of collections iteration abilities.

Public Instance Methods

group_by(&block)

Collects an enumerable into sets, grouped by the result of a block. Useful, for example, for grouping records by date like this:

```
latest_transcripts.group_by(&:day).each do |day, transcripts|
  puts "[#{day}] #{transcripts.map(&:class).join ', '}"
end

"[2006-03-01] Transcript"
"[2006-02-28] Transcript"
"[2006-02-27] Transcript, Transcript"
"[2006-02-26] Transcript, Transcript"
"[2006-02-25] Transcript"
"[2006-02-24] Transcript, Transcript"
"[2006-02-23] Transcript"
```

Uses Ruby's own `group_by` in versions 1.9 and above.

sum(default = 0, &block)

Calculates a sum from the elements of an enumerable, based on a block.

```
payments.sum(&:price)
```

It's easier to understand than Ruby's clumsier `inject` method:

```
payments.inject { |sum, p| sum + p.price }
```

Use full block syntax (instead of the `to_proc` hack) to do more complicated calculations:

```
payments.sum { |p| p.price * p.tax_rate }
```

Also, `sum` can calculate results without the use of a block:

```
[5, 15, 10].sum # => 30
```

The default *identity* (a fancy way of saying, "the sum of an empty list") is 0. However, you can override it with anything you want by passing a `default` argument:

```
[].sum(Payment.new(0)) { |i| i.amount } # => Payment.new(0)
```

index_by

Converts an enumerable to a hash, based on a block that identifies the keys. The most common usage is with a single attribute name:

```
>> people.index_by(&:login)
=> { "nextangle" => <Person ...>, "chad" => <Person ...>}
```

Use full block syntax (instead of the `to_proc` hack) to generate more complex keys:

```
>> people.index_by { |p| "#{p.first_name} #{p.last_name}" }
=> {"Chad Fowler" => <Person ...>, "David Hansson" => <Person ...>}
```

Exception

Extensions to Ruby's `Exception` class.

Public Instance Methods

application_backtrace

Returns the backtrace of an exception without lines pointing to files in the following directories: `generated`, `vendor`, `dispatch`, `ruby`, or `script`.

blame_file!(file)

Used to blame a particular file as being the source of the exception.

blamed_files

Returns the array of files that have been blamed as the source of an exception.

copy_blame!(other)

Copies an array of blamed files from one exception to another.

framework_backtrace

The opposite of `application_backtrace`: returns the backtrace of an exception with *only* lines pointing to files in the following directories: `generated`, `vendor`, `dispatch`, `ruby`, or `script`.

FalseClass

Remember that everything in Ruby is an object, even the literal `false`, which is a special reference to a singleton instance of the `FalseClass`.

Public Instance Methods

blank?

Always returns `true`.

File

Provides an `atomic_write` method to Ruby's `File` class.

Public Instance Methods

atomic_write(file_name, temp_dir = Dir.tmpdir)

Writes to a file atomically, by writing to a temp file first and then renaming to the target `file_name`. Useful for situations where you need to absolutely prevent other processes or threads from seeing half-written files.

```
File.atomic_write("important.file") do |file|
  file.write("hello")
end
```

If your `temp` directory is not on the same filesystem as the file you're trying to write, you can provide a different temporary directory with the `temp_dir` argument.

```
File.atomic_write("/data/something.imporant", "/data/tmp") do |f|
  file.write("hello")
end
```

Hash

Hashes are used throughout Rails, yet ActiveSupport only adds one extra method directly to their class.

Public Instance Methods

blank?

Aliased to `empty?` and returns `true` if the hash has no elements.

Hash::ClassMethods (in ActiveRecord::CoreExtensions)

Provides a `from_xml` method that can quickly turn properly formatted XML into a nested hash structure.

Public Class Methods

from_xml(xml)

Parses arbitrary strings of XML markup into nested Ruby arrays and hashes. Works great for quick-and-dirty integration of REST-style web services.

Here's a quick example in the console with some random XML content. The XML only has to be well-formed markup.

```
>> xml = %(<people>
  <person id="1">
    <name><family>Boss</family> <given>Big</given></name>
    <email>chief@foo.com</email>
```

```
    </person>
    <person id="2">
      <name>
       <family>Worker</family>
       <given>Two</given></name>
      <email>two@foo.com</email>
    </person>
</people>)
=> "<people>...</people>"

>> h = Hash.from_xml(xml)
=> {"people"=>{"person"=>[{"name"=>{"given"=>"Big", "family"=>"Boss"},
"id"=>"1", "email"=>"chief@foo.com"}, {"name"=>{"given"=>"Two",
"family"=>"Worker"}, "id"=>"2", "email"=>"two@foo.com"}]}}
```

Now you can easily access the data from the XML:

```
>> h["people"]["person"].first["name"]["given"] => "Big"
```

Hash::Conversions (in ActiveSupport::CoreExtensions)

Provides methods for transformations of hashes into other forms.

Constants

The XML_TYPE_NAMES hash shows how Ruby classes are mapped to XML schema types.

```
XML_TYPE_NAMES = {
  "Fixnum"     => "integer",
  "Bignum"     => "integer",
  "BigDecimal" => "decimal",
  "Float"      => "float",
  "Date"       => "date",
  "DateTime"   => "datetime",
  "Time"       => "datetime",
  "TrueClass"  => "boolean",
  "FalseClass" => "boolean"
}
```

The XML_FORMATTING hash contains the set of procs that are used to convert certain kinds of Ruby objects to XML string value representations.

```
XML_FORMATTING = {
  "date"     => Proc.new { |date| date.to_s(:db) },
  "datetime" => Proc.new { |time| time.xmlschema },
  "binary"   => Proc.new { |binary| Base64.encode64(binary) },
  "yaml"     => Proc.new { |yaml| yaml.to_yaml }
}
```

The XML_PARSING hash contains the set of procs used to convert XML string values into Ruby objects.

```
XML_PARSING = {
  "date"         => Proc.new  { |date| ::Date.parse(date) },
  "datetime"     => Proc.new  { |time| ::Time.parse(time).utc },
  "integer"      => Proc.new  { |integer| integer.to_i },
  "float"        => Proc.new  { |float| float.to_f },
  "decimal"      => Proc.new  { |number| BigDecimal(number) },
  "boolean"      => Proc.new  do |boolean|
    %w(1 true).include?(boolean.strip)
  end,
  "string"       => Proc.new  { |string|  string.to_s },
  "yaml"         => Proc.new  { |yaml| YAML::load(yaml) rescue yaml },
  "base64Binary" => Proc.new  { |bin|    Base64.decode64(bin) },
  "file"         => Proc.new do |file, entity|
    f = StringIO.new(Base64.decode64(file))
    eval "def f.original_filename()
      '#{entity["name"]}' || 'untitled'
    end"
    eval "def f.content_type()
      '#{entity["content_type"]}' || 'application/octet-stream'
    end"
    f
  end
}

XML_PARSING.update(
  "double"   => XML_PARSING["float"],
  "dateTime" => XML_PARSING["datetime"]
)
```

Public Instance Methods

to_query

Collects the keys and values of a hash and composes a URL-style query string using ampersand and equal-sign characters.

```
>> {:foo => "hello", :bar => "goodbye"}.to_query
=> "bar=goodbye&foo=hello"
```

to_xml(options={})

Collects the keys and values of a hash and composes a simple XML representation.

```
>> print ({:greetings => {
             :english => "hello",
             :spanish => "hola"}}).to_xml

<?xml version="1.0" encoding="UTF-8"?>
<hash>
  <greetings>
    <english>hello</english>
    <spanish>hola</spanish>
  </greetings>
</hash>
```

See the description of the `Array::Conversions` to_xml method for a full list of options.

Hash::Diff (in ActiveSupport::CoreExtensions)

Provides a method for getting the difference between one hash and another.

Public Instance Methods

diff(hash2)

A method for getting the difference between one hash and another. Returns the difference between a hash and the one passed in as a parameter.

A quick example in the console:

```
>> {:a => :b}.diff({:a => :b})
=> {}
>> {:a => :b}.diff({:a => :c})
=> {:a=>:b}
```

Hash::Except (in ActiveSupport::CoreExtensions)

Returns a hash that includes everything but the given keys. Useful for quickly excluding certain key values from a hash like this:

```
@person.update_attributes(params[:person].except(:admin))
```

Public Instance Methods

except(*keys)

Returns a new hash without the specified keys, leaving the original unmodified.

except!(*keys)

Destructively removes the specified keys from the hash.

Hash::Keys (in ActiveSupport::CoreExtensions)

Provides methods that operate on the keys of a hash. The `stringify` and `symbolize` methods are used liberally throughout the Rails codebase, which is why it generally doesn't matter if you pass option names as strings or symbols.

You can use `assert_valid_keys` method in your own application code, which takes Rails-style option hashes.

Public Instance Methods

assert_valid_keys(*valid_keys)

Raises an `ArgumentError` if the hash contains any keys not specified in `valid_keys`.

```
def my_method(some_value, options={})
  options.assert_valid_keys(:my_conditions, :my_order, ...)
  ...
end
```

stringify_keys

Returns a new copy of the hash with all keys converted to strings.

stringify_keys!

Destructively converts all keys in the hash to strings.

symbolize_keys and to_options

Returns a new hash with all keys converted to symbols.

symbolize_keys! and to_options!

Destructively converts all keys in the hash to symbols.

Hash::ReverseMerge (in ActiveSupport::CoreExtensions)

Allows for reverse merging where it's the keys in the calling hash that win over those in the other_hash. This is particularly useful for initializing an incoming option hash with default values like this:

```
def setup(options = {})
  options.reverse_merge! :size => 25, :velocity => 10
end
```

In the example, the default :size and :velocity are only set if the options passed in don't already have those keys set.

Public Instance Methods

reverse_merge(other_hash)

Returns a merged version of two hashes, using key values in the other_hash as defaults, leaving the original hash unmodified.

reverse_merge!(other_hash) and reverse_update

Destructive versions of reverse_merge; both modify the original hash in place.

Hash::Slice (in ActiveSupport::CoreExtensions)

Methods to slice a hash to include only the specified keys. Useful for limiting an options hash to valid keys before passing to a method, like this:

```
def search(criteria = {})
  assert_valid_keys(:mass, :velocity, :time)
end

search(options.slice(:mass, :velocity, :time))
```

Public Instance Methods

`slice(*keys)`

Returns a new hash containing only the specified `keys`.

`slice!(*keys)`

Destructive version of `slice`; modifies the original hash in place, removing any keys not specified in `keys`.

HashWithIndifferentAccess

A subclass of `Hash` used internally by Rails. As stated in the source file:

> This class has dubious semantics and we only have it so that people can write `params[:key]` instead of `params['key']`.

Inflector::Inflections (in ActiveSupport)

The `Inflections` class transforms words from singular to plural, class names to table names, modularized class names to ones without, and class names to foreign keys. The default inflections for pluralization, singularization, and uncountable words are kept in `activesupport/lib/active_support/inflections.rb`.

A singleton instance of `Inflections` is yielded by `Inflector.inflections`, which can then be used to specify additional inflection rules in your `config/environment.rb` file.

Here are some examples:

```
Inflector.inflections do |inflect|
  inflect.plural /^(ox)$/i, '\1en'
  inflect.singular /^(ox)en/i, '\1'
  inflect.irregular 'octopus', 'octopi'
  inflect.uncountable "equipment"
end
```

New rules are added at the top. So in the example, the irregular rule for octopus will now be the first of the pluralization and singularization rules that are checked when an inflection happens. That way Rails can guarantee that your rules run before any of the rules that may already have been loaded.

Public Instance Methods

This API reference lists the inflections methods themselves in the modules where they are actually used: `Numeric::Inflections` and `String::Inflections`.

`irregular(singular, plural)`

Specifies a new irregular that applies to both pluralization and singularization at the same time. The `singular` and `plural` arguments must be strings, not regular expressions. Simply pass the irregular word in singular and plural form.

```
irregular 'octopus', 'octopi'
irregular 'person', 'people'
```

`plural(rule, replacement)`

Specifies a new pluralization rule and its replacement. The `rule` can either be a string or a regular expression. The `replacement` should always be a string and may include references to the matched data from the rule by using backslash-number syntax, like this:

```
Inflector.inflections do |inflect|
  inflect.plural /^(ox)$/i, '\1en'
end
```

`singular(rule, replacement)`

Specifies a new singularization rule and its replacement. The `rule` can either be a string or a regular expression. The `replacement` should always be a string and may include references to the matched data from the rule by using backslash-number syntax, like this:

```
Inflector.inflections do |inflect|
  inflect.singular /^(ox)en/i, '\1'
end
```

uncountable(*words)

Adds uncountable words that should not be inflected to the list of inflection rules.

```
uncountable "money"
uncountable "money", "information"
uncountable %w( money information rice )
```

Integer::EvenOdd (in ActiveSupport::CoreExtensions)

Methods to check whether an integer is even, odd, or a multiple of another number.

Public Instance Methods

even?

Returns true if the integer is even. Zero is considered even.[1]

```
1.even? # => false
```

multiple_of?(number)

Returns true if the integer is a multiple of number.

```
9.multiple_of? 3 # => true
```

odd?

Returns true if the integer is odd.

```
1.odd? # => false
```

`Integer::Inflections` (in `ActiveSupport::CoreExtensions`)

Provides an ordinal inflection to Ruby's integers.

Public Instance Methods

`ordinalize`

Turns an integer into an *ordinal* string used to denote the position in an ordered sequence such as 1st, 2nd, 3rd, 4th.

```
1.ordinalize    # => "1st"
2.ordinalize    # => "2nd"
1002.ordinalize # => "1002nd"
1003.ordinalize # => "1003rd"
```

JSON (in `ActiveSupport`)

JSON stands for "JavaScript Object Notation," and can be used to serialize data. It is more lightweight than XML and can be easily parsed by JavaScript interpreters, since it is JavaScript's object literal format.

```
{ drink: "too much", smoke: "too much" }
```

Ruby might get better built-in support for JSON in versions 1.9 and above, since literal hash notation that looks exactly like JavaScript's is being added to the language.

```
{ :drink: "too much", :smoke: "too much" } # valid hash in Ruby 1.9
```

Lately JSON has become a popular data transport for Ajax applications. Chapter 12, "Ajax on Rails," has a section specifically about JSON.

Constants

The following words will cause problems if you try to use them as identifiers in your JSON-encoded data, because they are reserved words in JavaScript.

```
RESERVED_WORDS = %w(
    abstract      delete       goto          private       transient
    boolean       do           if            protected     try
    break         double       implements    public        typeof
    byte          else         import        return        var
    case          enum         in            short         void
    catch         export       instanceof    static        volatile
    char          extends      int           super         while
    class         final        interface     switch        with
    const         finally      long          synchronized
    continue      float        native        this
    debugger      for          new           throw
    default       function     package       throws
)
```

Module Attributes

unquote_hash_key_identifiers

When this attribute is set to true, the to_json method on Hash will omit quoting string or symbol keys, provided that the resulting keys are valid JavaScript identifiers. Note that this is technically improper JSON (all object keys are supposed to be quoted), so if you need strict JSON compliance, set this option to false.

```
ActiveSupport::JSON.unquote_hash_key_identifiers = false
```

Class Methods

decode(json)

Converts a JSON string into a Ruby object. Decoding is accomplished via intermediate conversion to YAML, which is very close to JSON, syntactically speaking.

Raises ParseError if invalid JSON is provided.

encode(object)

Converts a Ruby object into a string of JSON.

```
>> print ActiveSupport::JSON.encode(:drink => "too much")
{drink: "too much" }
```

In practice, it can be quite difficult to encode ActiveRecord models as JSON because associations lead to circular dependencies:

```
ActiveSupport::JSON::CircularReferenceError: object references itself
```

A probable solution is to write custom Ruby classes that contain only the data that you need to serialize.

reserved_word?(word)

Returns true if the word is a reserved word in JavaScript and will cause problems if used in JSON-encoded data.

valid_identifier?(str)

Returns true if str is a valid JSON identifier (including reserved word check).

Kernel

Methods added to Ruby's Kernel class are available in all contexts.

Public Instance Methods

daemonize

Turns the current script into a daemon process that detaches from the console. It can be shut down with a TERM signal.

The source provides pretty much all the explanation you need:

```
def daemonize
  exit if fork                # Parent exits, child continues
  Process.setsid              # Become session leader
  exit if fork                # Zap session leader
```

```
    Dir.chdir "/"                # Release old working directory
    File.umask 0000              # Ensure sensible umask
    STDIN.reopen "/dev/null"     # Free file descriptors and...
    STDOUT.reopen "/dev/null", "a" # point them somewhere sensible.
    STDERR.reopen STDOUT         # TODO: better to go to a logfile

    trap("TERM") { exit }
end
```

debugger

Starts a debugging session if `ruby-debug` has been loaded. Calls `script/server –debugger` to start Mongrel with the debugger (Rails 2.0 only).

enable_warnings {...}

Sets $VERBOSE to true for the duration of the block and back to its original value afterward.

require_library_or_gem

Requires a library with fallback to RubyGems. Warnings during library loading are silenced to increase signal/noise for application warnings.

silence_stream(stream) { ... }

Silences any stream for the duration of the block.

```
silence_stream(STDOUT) do
  puts 'This will never be seen'
end

puts 'But this will'
```

silence_warnings { ... }

Sets $VERBOSE to false for the duration of the block and back to its original value afterward.

`suppress(*exception_classes) { ... }`

A method that should be named `swallow`. Suppresses raising of any exception classes specified inside of a block. Use with caution.

Logger

Extensions to the built-in Ruby logger, accessible via the `logger` property in various Rails contexts such as `ActiveRecord` models and controller classes. Always accessible via the constant `RAILS_DEFAULT_LOGGER`. Use of the logger is explained in Chapter 1.

To use the default log formatter as defined in the Ruby core, you need to set a formatter for the logger as in the following example:

```
logger.formatter = Formatter.new
```

You can then specify properties such as the datetime format, for example:

```
logger.datetime_format = "%Y-%m-%d"
```

Public Instance Methods

`around_debug(start_message, end_message) { ... }`

Streamlines the all-too-common pattern of wrapping a few lines of code in comments that indicate the beginning and end of a routine, as follows:

```
logger.debug "Start rendering component (#{options.inspect}): "
result = render_component_stuff(...)
logger.debug "\n\nEnd of component rendering"
result
```

The same code would be written with `around_debug` like this:

```
around_debug "Start rendering component (#{options.inspect}):",
             "End of component rendering" do
  render_component_stuff(...)
end
```

around_error, **around_fatal**, and **around_info**

See as `around_debug` except with a different log-level.

datetime_format

Gets the current logging datetime format. Returns `nil` if the formatter does not support datetime formatting.

datetime_format=(datetime_format)

Sets the format string passed to `strftime` to generate the log's timestamp string.

formatter

Gets the current formatter. The Rails default formatter is a `SimpleFormatter`, which only displays the log message.

silence(temporary_level = Logger::ERROR)

Silences the logger for the duration of a block provided.

```
RAILS_DEFAULT_LOGGER.silence do
  # some particularly verbose (or secret) operation
end
```

Module

Extensions to Ruby's `Module` class, available in all contexts.

Public Instance Methods

alias_attribute(new_name, old_name)

This super-useful method allows you to easily make aliases for attributes, including their reader, writer, and query methods.

In the following example, the `Content` class is serving as the base class for `Email` using STI, but e-mails should have a subject, not a title:

```
class Content < ActiveRecord::Base
  # has column named 'title'
```

```
end

class Email < Content
  alias_attribute :subject, :title
end
```

As a result of the `alias_attribute`, you can see in the following example that the `title` and `subject` attributes become interchangeable:

```
>> e = Email.find(:first)

>> e.title
=> "Superstars"

>> e.subject
=> "Superstars"

>> e.subject?
=> true

>> e.subject = "Megastars"
=> "Megastars"

>> e.title
=> "Megastars"
```

alias_method_chain(target, feature)

Encapsulates the following common pattern:

```
alias_method :foo_without_feature, :foo
alias_method :foo, :foo_with_feature
```

With `alias_method_chain`, you simply do one line of code and both aliases are set up for you:

```
alias_method_chain :foo, :feature
```

Query and bang methods keep the same punctuation. The following syntax

```
alias_method_chain :foo?, :feature
```

is equivalent to

```
alias_method :foo_without_feature?, :foo?
alias_method :foo?, :foo_with_feature?
```

so you can safely chain foo, foo?, and foo!.

as_load_path

Returns the load path string corresponding to this module.

attr_accessor_with_default(sym, default = nil, &block)

Declares an attribute accessor with an initial default return value.

To give attribute :age the initial value 25, you would write the following:

```
class Person
  attr_accessor_with_default :age, 25
end
```

To give attribute :element_name a dynamic default value, evaluated in scope of self, you would write

```
attr_accessor_with_default(:element_name) { name.underscore }
```

attr_internal

Alias for attr_internal_accessor.

attr_internal_accessor(*attrs)

Declares attributes backed by *internal* instance variables names (using an @_ naming convention). Basically just a mechanism to enhance controlled access to sensitive attributes.

For instance, Object's copy_instance_variables_from will not copy internal instance variables.

attr_internal_reader(*attrs)

Declares an attribute reader backed by an internally named instance variable.

attr_internal_writer(*attrs)

Declares an attribute writer backed by an internally named instance variable.

const_missing(class_id)

The const_missing callback is invoked when Ruby can't find a specified constant in the current scope, which is what makes Rails autoclassloading possible. See the Dependencies module for more detail.

delegate(*methods)

Provides a delegate class method to easily expose contained objects' methods as your own. Pass one or more methods (specified as symbols or strings) and the name of the target object as the final :to option (also a symbol or string). At least one method and the :to option are required.

Delegation is particularly useful in conjunction with ActiveRecord associations:

```
class Greeter < ActiveRecord::Base
  def hello
    "hello"
  end

  def goodbye
    "goodbye"
  end
end

class LazyFoo < ActiveRecord::Base
  belongs_to :greeter
  delegate :hello, :to => :greeter
end
```

Multiple delegates to the same target are allowed:

```
class Foo < ActiveRecord::Base
  belongs_to :greeter
  delegate :hello, :goodbye, :to => :greeter
end
```

deprecate(*method_names)

Declares that a method has been deprecated. See Deprecation for more information and usage instructions.

included_in_classes

Returns a list of classes in which this module is included, using Ruby's ObjectSpace.

local_constants

Returns the constants that have been defined locally by this object and not in an ancestor. This method may miss some constants if their definition in the ancestor is identical to their definition in the receiver.

mattr_accessor(*syms)

Defines one or more module attribute reader and writer methods in the style of the native attr* accessors for instance attributes.

mattr_reader(*syms)

Defines one or more module attribute reader methods.

mattr_writer(*syms)

Defines one or more module attribute writer methods.

parent

Returns the module that contains this one; if this is a root module, such as ::MyModule, then Object is returned.

parents

Returns all the parents of this module, ordered from nested outward. The receiver is not contained within the result.

unloadable(const_desc = self)

Marks a given constant as unloadable, to be removed each time dependencies are cleared. See unloadable in Object for additional details.

MissingSourceFile

The `LoadError` raised by Rails when its name-based classloading mechanism fails to find a class. An explanation of how Rails looks for and loads classes is in Chapter 1, in the "Rails, Modules, and Auto-Loading Code" section.

Multibyte::Chars (in ActiveSupport)

The `chars` proxy enables you to work transparently with multibyte encodings in the Ruby `String` class without having extensive knowledge about encoding.

A `Chars` object accepts a string upon initialization and proxies `String` methods in an encoding-safe manner. All the normal `String` methods are proxied through the `Chars` object, and can be accessed through the `chars` method. Methods that would normally return a `String` object now return a `Chars` object so that methods can be chained together safely.

```
>> "The Perfect String".chars.downcase.strip.normalize
=> "the perfect string"
```

`Chars` objects are perfectly interchangeable with `String` objects as long as no explicit class checks are made. If certain methods do explicitly check the class, call `to_s` before you pass `Chars` objects to them, to go back to a normal `String` object:

```
bad.explicit_checking_method("T".chars.downcase.to_s)
```

The actual operations on the string are delegated to handlers. Theoretically handlers can be implemented for any encoding, but the default handler handles UTF-8. This handler is set during initialization.

Note that a few methods are defined on `Chars` instead of the handler because they are defined on `Object` or `Kernel` and `method_missing` (the method used for delegation) can't catch them.

Class Methods

handler=(klass)

If you want to implement your own handler or use a third-party one, you can set it on the `Chars` class manually:

```
ActiveSupport::Multibyte::Chars.handler = MyHandler
```

Look at the `UTF8Handler` source for an example of how to implement your own handler. If you implement your own handler to work on anything but UTF-8, you probably also want to override the `handler` on `Chars`.

Public Instance Methods

`<=> (other)`

Returns -1, 0, or +1 depending on whether the `Chars` object is to be sorted before, equal to, or after the object on the right side of the operation. In other words, it works exactly as you would expect it to.

`=~ (other)`

Like `String`'s version, only this method returns the character offset (in codepoints) instead of a byte offset.

`gsub(*a, &b)`

Works exactly the same as `gsub` on a normal string.

`handler`

Returns the proper handler for the contained string depending on `$KCODE` and the encoding of the string. This method is used internally by Rails to always redirect messages to the proper classes depending on the context.

`method_missing(m, *a, &b)`

Tries to forward all undefined methods to the designated handler. When a method is not defined on the handler, it sends it to the contained string instead. Also responsible for making the bang (`!`) methods destructive, since a handler doesn't have access to change an enclosed string instance.

`respond_to?(method)`

Makes duck-typing with `String` possible.

split(*args)

Works just like the normal String's split method, with the exception that the items in the resulting list are Chars instances instead of String, which makes chaining calls easier.

string

The contained String instance. You shouldn't need to do anything with it via the Chars object.

NilClass

Remember that everything in Ruby is an object, even nil, which is a special reference to a singleton instance of the NilClass.

Besides blank?, the extensions to nil try to raise more descriptive error messages, to help Rails newbies. The aim is to ensure that when developers pass nil to methods unintentionally, instead of NoMethodError and the name of some method used by the framework, they'll see a message explaining what type of object was expected. The behavior was named *whiny nil* as an inside joke.

Method missing magic is used to capture the method that was erroneously invoked on nil. The method name is looked up in a hash containing method names indexed to Rails classes, so that a helpful suggestion can be attempted.

If you've done any amount of Rails programming, you're probably familiar with the output of this error-helping process, as the description of a NoMethodError:

> You have a nil object when you didn't expect it! You might have expected an instance of *class_name*. The error occurred while evaluating nil.*method_name*.

The whiny nil behavior can be controlled in the individual environment configurations with the following line:

```
config.whiny_nils = true
```

Rails has it set to true by default in development and test modes, and false in production mode.

Public Instance Methods

blank?

Always returns `true`.

id

Raises a message along the lines of: `Called id for nil, which would mistakenly be 4 -- if you really wanted the id of nil, use object_id`.

Numeric

As with `Hash`, ActiveSupport only adds the `blank?` method directly to the `Numeric` class.

Public Instance Methods

blank?

Always returns `false`.

Numeric::Bytes (in ActiveSupport::CoreExtensions)

Enables the use of byte calculations and declarations, like `45.bytes + 2.6.megabytes`.

Public Instance Methods

byte and bytes

Returns the value of `self`.

kilobyte and kilobytes

Returns `self * 1024`.

megabyte and megabytes

Returns `self * 1024.kilobytes`.

gigabyte and gigabytes

Returns `self * 1024.megabytes`.

terabyte and terabytes

Returns `self * 1024.gigabytes`.

petabyte and petabytes

Returns `self * 1024.terabytes`.

exabyte and exabytes[2]

Returns `self * 1024.petabytes`.

Numeric::Time (in ActiveSupport::CoreExtensions)

Syntax sugar that enables the use of seconds-based time calculations and declarations directly on numbers, like this:

```
1.minute + 45.seconds == 105.seconds #=> true
```

The methods in this module use `Time`'s `advance` method for precise date calculations as well as adding or subtracting their results from a `Time` object:

```
# equivalent to Time.now.advance(:months => 1)
1.month.from_now

# equivalent to Time.now.advance(:years => 2)
2.years.from_now

# equivalent to Time.now.advance(:months => 4, :years => 5)
(4.months + 5.years).from_now
```

While these methods provide precise calculation when used as in the example, care should be taken concerning loss of precision when typecasting them to integral values. Ruby's core `Date` and `Time` classes should be used for high-precision date and time arithmetic.

Public Instance Methods

ago and until

Appends to a numeric time value to express a moment in the past.

```
10.minutes.ago
```

day and days

A duration equivalent to `self * 24.hours`.

fortnight and fortnights

A duration equivalent to `self * 2.weeks`.

from_now(time = Time.now) and since(time = Time.now)

An amount of time in the future, from a specified time (which defaults to `Time.now`).

hour and hours

A duration equivalent to `self * 3600.seconds`.

minute and minutes

A duration equivalent to `self * 60.seconds`.

month and months

A duration equivalent to `self * 30.days`.

second and seconds

A duration in seconds equal to `self`.

week and weeks

A duration equivalent to `self * 7.days`.

year and years

A duration equivalent to `self * 365.25.days`.

Object

Rails mixes quite a few methods into the `Object` class, meaning they are available via every other object at runtime.

Public Instance Methods

` (command)

Makes backticks behave (somewhat more) similarly on all platforms. On `win32` `` `nonexistent_command` `` raises `Errno::ENOENT`; on UNIX, the spawned shell prints a message to `STDERR` and sets `$?`. Emulates UNIX on the former but not the latter, by making `win32` print a message to `STDERR`.

acts_like?(duck)

A duck-type assistant method, with a really simple implementation:

```
def acts_like?(duck)
  respond_to? "acts_like_#{duck}?"
end
```

ActiveSupport extends `Date` to define an `acts_like_date?` method, and extends `Time` to define `acts_like_time?`. As a result, we can do `x.acts_like?(:time)` and `y.acts_like?(:date)` to do duck-type-safe comparisons, since classes that we want to act like `Time` simply need to define an `acts_like_time?` method that returns `true`.

blank?

An empty string (`""`), a string with only whitespace (`"    "`), `nil`, an empty array (`[]`), and an empty hash (`{}`) are all considered blank.

Works by calling `strip` (to remove whitespace) if that method is available, and then calling `empty?`. If no `empty?` method is available, simply returns the negation of self.

copy_instance_variables_from(object, exclude = [])

Useful to copy instance variables from one object to another.

extended_by

Returns an array of modules that are in the `ancestors` of a given object.

To illustrate, here's a list of modules included in a `Person` class belonging to one of my real projects. Is the list bigger than you might expect?

```
>> Person.find(:first).extended_by.sort_by(&:name)
=> [ActiveRecord::Acts::List, ActiveRecord::Acts::NestedSet,
ActiveRecord::Acts::Tree, ActiveRecord::Aggregations,
ActiveRecord::Associations, ActiveRecord::AttributeMethods,
ActiveRecord::Calculations, ActiveRecord::Callbacks,
ActiveRecord::Locking::Optimistic, ActiveRecord::Locking::Pessimistic,
ActiveRecord::Observing, ActiveRecord::Reflection,
ActiveRecord::Timestamp, ActiveRecord::Transactions,
ActiveRecord::Validations, ActiveRecord::XmlSerialization, Base64,
Base64::Deprecated, ERB::Util, GeoKit::ActsAsMappable, LatLongZoom,
PP::ObjectMixin, PhotosMixin, Reloadable::Deprecated,
ScottBarron::Acts::StateMachine, UJS::BehaviourHelper, UJS::Helpers,
UJS::JavascriptProxies, WhiteListHelper, WillPaginate::Finder]
```

extend_with_included_modules_from(object)

Invokes `extend` on an object with each module included by the `object` argument, with a really simple implementation:

```
def extend_with_included_modules_from(object)
  object.extended_by.each { |mod| extend mod }
end
```

instance_exec(*arguments, &block)

The `instance_exec` method allows you to (somewhat efficiently) take a block of Ruby code and execute it in the context of another object.

```
>> t = Tag.find(:first)
=> #<Tag id: 1, name: "politics">
>> t.instance_exec { name }
=> "politics"
```

instance_values

Returns instance variables of an object as a hash.

```
>> Tag.find(:first).instance_values
=> {"attributes" => {"name" => "politics", "id" => "1"}}
```

load(file, *extras)

Rails overrides Ruby's built-in `load` method to tie it into the `Dependencies` subsystem.

require(file, *extras)

Rails overrides Ruby's built-in `require` method to tie it into the `Dependencies` subsystem.

require_association(file_name)

Used internally by Rails. Invokes `Dependencies.associate_with (file_name)`.

require_dependency(file_name)

Used internally by Rails. Invokes `Dependencies.depend_on(file_name)`.

require_or_load(file_name)

Used internally by Rails. Invokes `Dependencies.require_or_load(file_name)`.

returning(value) { ... }

A Ruby-ized realization of the K combinator, courtesy of Mikael Brockman. Simplifies the idiom where you know you will want to return a certain object; you just want to do a couple of things to it first, like this:

```
def foo
  returning values = [] do
    values << 'bar'
    values << 'baz'
  end
end


foo # => ['bar', 'baz']
```

A slightly more elegant way to access the returning value is via block variable. Here is the same example again, but with a block variable for values:

```
def foo
  returning [] do |values|
    values << 'bar'
    values << 'baz'
  end
end


foo # => ['bar', 'baz']
```

unloadable(const_desc)

Marks the specified constant as *unloadable*. Unloadable constants are removed each time dependencies are cleared.

Note that marking a constant for unloading need only be done once. Setup or init scripts may list each unloadable constant that will need unloading; constants marked in this way will be removed on every subsequent Dependencies.clear, as opposed to the first clear only.

The provided constant descriptor const_desc may be a (nonanonymous) module or class, or a qualified constant name as a string or symbol.

Returns true if the constant was not previously marked for unloading, false otherwise.

with_options(options)

An elegant way to refactor out common options.

```
with_options(:class_name => 'Comment', :order => 'id desc') do |post|
  post.has_many :approved, :conditions => ['approved = ?', true]
  post.has_many :unapproved, :conditions => ['approved = ?', false]
  post.has_many :all_comments
end
```

Can also be used with an explicit receiver, which will be passed as a block parameter:

```
map.with_options :controller => "people" do |people|
  people.connect "/people",      :action => "index"
  people.connect "/people/:id", :action => "show"
end
```

OrderedHash (in ActiveSupport)

A hash implementation as a subclass of Ruby `Array`. Preserves ordering of its elements, in contrast to normal Ruby hashes. It's namespaced to prevent conflicts with other implementations. You can assign it to a top-level namespace if you don't want to constantly use the fully qualified name:

```
OrderedHash = ActiveSupport::OrderedHash
```

The normal square bracket operators are implemented, but otherwise, it's an `Array`.

```
>> oh = ActiveSupport::OrderedHash.new
=> []
>> oh[:one] = 1
=> 1
>> oh[:two] = 2
=> 2
>> oh[:three] = 3
=> 3
>> oh
=> [[:one, 1], [:two, 2], [:three, 3]]
```

OrderedOptions (in ActiveSupport)

A subclass of OrderedHash that adds a method-missing implementation so that hash elements can be accessed and modified using normal attribute semantics, dot-notation:

```
def method_missing(name, *args)
  if name.to_s =~ /(.*)=$/
    self[$1.to_sym] = args.first
  else
    self[name]
  end
end
```

Rails trivia: The initializer.rb file contains an exact duplicate of this class, except in the Rails namespace. The reason? It's needed before ActiveSupport is loaded, as part of the startup process.

Proc

Extensions to Ruby's Proc class that make instance_exec magic possible.

Public Instance Methods

bind(object) { ... }

Facilitates binding of a proc to an arbitrary object, so that it executes in that object's context when it is called. This technique makes the instance_exec method of Object possible.

To demonstrate in the following example, we first verify that name is not defined in the current context. Then we create a Proc object that invokes name, and show that it still generates a NameError when we call it.

```
>> name
NameError: undefined local variable or method `name' ...

>> p = Proc.new { name }
=> #<Proc:0x031bf5b4@(irb):15>

>> p.call
NameError: undefined local variable or method `name' ...
```

Now, we use the `bind` method to easily call our proc in the context of two separate objects that do define `name`:

```
>> p.bind(Person.find(:first)).call
=> "Admin"

>> p.bind(Tag.find(:first)).call
=> "politics"
```

The clever implementation works by first defining a new method on the target object using a generated unique name and the body of the proc. Then a reference to the new `Method` instance is saved, and it is removed from the target object using `remove_method`. Finally, the target object is bound to the new method and returned, so that `call` executes the proc in the context of the target object.

Range

Extensions to Ruby's `Range` class.

Constants

The `DATE_FORMATS` constant holds a single proc used to convert a range into a SQL expression:

```
DATE_FORMATS = {
  :db => Proc.new {|start, stop|
    "BETWEEN '#{start.to_s(:db)}' AND '#{stop.to_s(:db)}'"
  }
}
```

Public Instance Methods

`to_formatted_s(format = :default)`

Generates a formatted string representation of the range.

```
>> (20.days.ago..10.days.ago).to_formatted_s
=> "Fri Aug 10 22:12:33 -0400 2007..Mon Aug 20 22:12:33 -0400 2007"
>> (20.days.ago..10.days.ago).to_formatted_s(:db)
=> "BETWEEN '2007-08-10 22:12:36' AND '2007-08-20 22:12:36'"
```

String

Extensions to Ruby's `String` class.

Public Instance Methods

at(position)

Returns the character at `position`, treating the string as an array (where 0 is the first character). Returns `nil` if the position exceeds the length of the string.

```
"hello".at(0)  # => "h"
"hello".at(4)  # => "o"
"hello".at(10) # => nil
```

blank?

Returns the result of `empty?` (stripping whitespace, if needed).

first(number)

Returns the first `number` of characters in a string.

```
"hello".first     # => "h"
"hello".first(2)  # => "he"
"hello".first(10) # => "hello"
```

from(position)

Returns the remaining characters of a string from the `position`, treating the string as an array (where 0 is the first character). Returns `nil` if the position exceeds the length of the string.

```
"hello".at(0)  # => "hello"
"hello".at(2)  # => "llo"
"hello".at(10) # => nil
```

last(number)

Returns the last number of characters in a string.

```
"hello".last      # => "o"
"hello".last(2)   # => "lo"
"hello".last(10)  # => "hello"
```

to(position)

Returns the beginning of the string up to the position treating the string as an array (where 0 is the first character). Doesn't produce an error when the position exceeds the length of the string.

```
"hello".at(0)   # => "h"
"hello".at(2)   # => "hel"
"hello".at(10)  # => "hello"
```

to_date

Uses ParseDate.parsedate to turn a string into a Date.

to_datetime

Uses ParseDate.parsedate to turn a string into a DateTime.

to_time(form = :utc)

Uses ParseDate.parsedate to turn a string into a Time either using either :utc (default) or :local.

String::Inflections (in ActiveSupport::CoreExtensions)

String inflections define new methods on the String class to transform names for different purposes.

For instance, you can figure out the name of a database from the name of a class:

```
"ScaleScore".tableize => "scale_scores"
```

If you get frustrated by the limitations of Rails inflections, try the most excellent Linguistics library by Michael Granger at http://www.deveiate.org/projects/ Linguistics. It doesn't do all of the same inflections as Rails, but the ones that it does do, it does better. (See `titleize` for an example.)

Public Instance Methods

camelize(first_letter = :upper)

By default, `camelize` converts strings to UpperCamelCase. If the argument to `camelize` is set to `:lower`, then `camelize` produces lowerCamelCase. The `camelize` method will also convert "/" to "::", which is useful for converting paths to namespaces.

```
"active_record".camelize #=> "ActiveRecord"
"active_record".camelize(:lower) #=> "activeRecord"
"active_record/errors".camelize #=> "ActiveRecord::Errors"
"active_record/errors".camelize(:lower) #=> "activeRecord::Errors"
```

classify

Creates a class name from a table name; used by `ActiveRecord` to turn table names to model classes. Note that the `classify` method returns a string and not a `Class`. (To convert to an actual class, follow `classify` with `constantize`.)

```
"egg_and_hams".classify #=> "EggAndHam"
"post".classify #=> "Post"
```

constantize

The `constantize` method tries to find a declared constant with the name specified in the string. It raises a `NameError` if a matching constant is not located.

```
"Module".constantize #=> Module
"Class".constantize #=> Class
```

`dasherize`

Replaces underscores with dashes in the string.

```
"puni_puni" #=> "puni-puni"
```

`demodulize`

Removes the module prefixes from a fully qualified module or class name.

```
>> "ActiveRecord::CoreExtensions::String::Inflections".demodulize
=> "Inflections"

"Inflections".demodulize #=> "Inflections"
```

`foreign_key(separate_class_name_and_id_with_ underscore = true)`

Creates a foreign key name from a class name.

```
"Message".foreign_key #=> "message_id"
"Message".foreign_key(false) #=> "messageid"
"Admin::Post".foreign_key #=> "post_id"
```

`humanize`

Capitalizes the first word of a string, turns underscores into spaces, and strips _id. Similar to the `titleize` method in that it is intended for creating pretty output.

```
"employee_salary" #=> "Employee salary"
"author_id" #=> "Author"
```

`pluralize`

Returns the plural form of the word in the string.

```
"post".pluralize #=> "posts"
"octopus".pluralize #=> "octopi"
```

```
"sheep".pluralize #=> "sheep"
"words".pluralize #=> "words"
"the blue mailman".pluralize #=> "the blue mailmen"
"CamelOctopus".pluralize #=> "CamelOctopi"
```

singularize

The reverse of `pluralize`; returns the singular form of a word in a string.

```
"posts".singularize #=> "post"
"octopi".singularize #=> "octopus"
"sheep".singluarize #=> "sheep"
"word".singluarize #=> "word"
"the blue mailmen".singularize #=> "the blue mailman"
"CamelOctopi".singularize #=> "CamelOctopus"
```

tableize

Creates a plural and underscored database table name based on Rails conventions. Used by `ActiveRecord` to determine the proper table name for a model class. This method uses the `pluralize` method on the last word in the string.

```
"RawScaledScorer".tableize #=> "raw_scaled_scorers"
"egg_and_ham".tableize #=> "egg_and_hams"
"fancyCategory".tableize #=> "fancy_categories"
```

titlecase

Alias for `titleize`.

titleize

Capitalizes all the words and replaces some characters in the string to create a nicer-looking title. The `titleize` method is meant for creating pretty output and is not used in the Rails internals.

```
>> "The light on the beach was like a sinus headache".titleize
=> "The Light On The Beach Was Like A Sinus Headache"
```

It's also not perfect. Among other things, it capitalizes words inside the sentence that it probably shouldn't, like "a" and "the." It also has a hard time with apostrophes:

```
>> "Her uncle's cousin's record albums".titleize
=> "Her Uncle'S Cousin'S Record Albums"
```

The Linguistics gem mentioned in the beginning of this section has an excellent proper_noun method that in my experience works much better than titleize:

```
>> "Her uncle's cousin's record albums".en.proper_noun
=> "Her Uncle's Cousin's Record Albums"
```

underscore

The reverse of camelize. Makes an underscored form from the expression in the string. Changes "::" to "/" to convert namespaces to paths.

```
"ActiveRecord".underscore #=> "active_record"
"ActiveRecord::Errors".underscore #=> active_record/errors
```

String::Iterators (in ActiveSupport::CoreExtensions)

Contains a custom string iterator that can be used to operate on each character of a string sequentially, in a Unicode-safe fashion.

Public Instance Methods

each_char { |char| ... }

Yields a single-character string for each character in the string. When $KCODE equals 'UTF8', multibyte characters are yielded appropriately.

String::StartsEndsWith (in ActiveSupport::CoreExtensions)

Provides String with additional condition methods.

Public Instance Methods

starts_with?(prefix)

Returns true if the string starts with the specified prefix.

ends_with?(suffix)

Returns true if the string ends with the specified suffix.

String::Unicode (in ActiveSupport::CoreExtensions)

Defines methods for handling Unicode strings.

Public Instance Methods

chars

The chars method returns an instance of the ActiveSupport::Multibyte::Chars class, a Unicode-safe proxy encapsulating the original string. Unicode versions of all the String methods are defined on the chars proxy, which gives you assurance that you won't end up with garbled or ruined string data.

Undefined methods are forwarded to String, so all of the string overrides can also be called through the chars proxy with confidence.

Here are some examples:

```
name = 'Claus Müller'
name.reverse #=> "rell??M sualC"   # garbled!!
name.length #=> 13                 # wrong!!

name.chars.reverse.to_s #=> "rellüM sualC"
name.chars.length #=> 12
```

All the methods on the chars proxy that normally return a string will return a chars proxy object instead. This allows method chaining on the result of any of these methods without a problem.

```
name.chars.reverse.length #=> 12
```

The `Char` proxy class tries to be as interchangeable with `String` as possible: sorting and comparing between `String` and `Chars` objects work as expected. The bang (!) methods change the internal string representation in the `Chars` object. Interoperability problems should be resolved easily with a `to_s` call.

For more information about the methods defined on the `Chars` proxy, see `Multibyte::Chars` and `Multibyte::Handlers::UTF8Handler`.

is_utf8?(suffix)

Returns `true` if the string has UTF-8 semantics, versus strings that are simply being used as byte streams.

Symbol

Extensions to Ruby's built-in `Symbol` class.

Public Instance Methods

to_proc

Infamous Rails syntax sugar. Turns a symbol into a simple proc, which is especially useful for enumerations.

```
# The same as people.collect { |p| p.name }
people.collect(&:name)

# The same as people.select { |p| p.manager? }.collect { |p| p.salary }
people.select(&:manager?).collect(&:salary)
```

Test::Unit::Assertions

Rails adds a number of assertions to the basic ones provided with `Test::Unit`.

Public Instance Methods

`assert_difference(expressions, difference = 1, message = nil, &block)`

Tests whether a numeric difference in the return value of an expression is a result of what is evaluated in the yielded block. (Easier to demonstrate than to explain!)

The following example eval's the expression `Article.count` and saves the result. Then it yields to the block, which will execute the `post :create` and return control to the `assert_difference` method. At that point, `Article.count` is eval'd again, and the difference is asserted to be `1` (the default difference).

```
assert_difference 'Article.count' do
  post :create, :article => {...}
end
```

Any arbitrary expression can be passed in and evaluated:

```
assert_difference 'assigns(:article).comments(:reload).size' do
  post :create, :comment => {...}
end
```

Arbitrary difference values may be specified. The default is +1, but negative numbers are okay too:

```
assert_difference 'Article.count', -1 do
  post :delete, :id => ...
end
```

An array of expressions can also be passed in—each will be evaluated:

```
assert_difference [ 'Article.count', 'Post.count' ], +2 do
  post :create, :article => {...}
end
```

A error message can be specified:

```
assert_difference 'Article.count', -1, "Article should be destroyed" do
  post :delete, :id => ...
end
```

assert_no_difference(expressions, message = nil, &block)

Tests that the return value of the supplied expression does *not* change as a result of what is evaluated in the yielded block.

```
assert_no_difference 'Article.count' do
  post :create, :article => invalid_attributes
end
```

Time::Calculations (in ActiveSupport::CoreExtensions)

Extensions to Ruby's built-in Time class.

Class Methods

days_in_month(month, year = nil)

Returns the number of days in the given month. If a year is given, February will return the correct number of days for leap years. Otherwise, this method will always report February as having 28 days.

local_time(*args)

Wraps the class method time_with_datetime_fallback with utc_or_local argument set to :local.

time_with_datetime_fallback(utc_or_local, year, month=1, day=1, hour=0, min=0, sec=0, usec=0)

Returns a new Time if the requested year can be accommodated by Ruby's Time class. The range of the Time class is either 1970..2038 or 1902..2038, depending on the host system's architecture. Years outside the supported range will return a DateTime object.

utc_time(*args)

Wraps the class method `time_with_datetime_fallback` with `utc_or_local` argument set to `:utc`.

Public Instance Methods

+ (other)

Implemented by the `plus_with_duration` method. It allows addition of times like this:

```
expiration_time = Time.now + 3.days
```

- (other)

Implemented by the `minus_with_duration` method. It allows addition of times like this:

```
two_weeks_ago = Time.now - 2.weeks
```

advance(options)

Provides precise `Time` calculations. The `options` parameter takes a hash with any of the keys `:months`, `:days`, `:years`, `:hour`, `:min`, `:sec`, and `:usec`.

ago(seconds)

Returns a new `Time` representing the time a number of seconds into the past; this is basically a wrapper around the `Numeric` extension of the same name. For the best accuracy, do not use this method in combination with `x.months`; use `months_ago` instead!

at_beginning of_day

Alias for `beginning_of_day`.

at_beginning of_month

Alias for `beginning_of_month`.

at_beginning of_week

Alias for `beginning_of_week`.

at_beginning of_year

Alias for `beginning_of_year`.

at_end of_day

Alias for `end_of_day`.

at_end of_month

Alias for `end_of_month`.

at_end of_week

Alias for `end_of_week`.

at_end of_year

Alias for `end_of_year`.

beginning of_day

Returns a new `Time` representing the "start" of the current instance's day, hard-coded to 00:00 hours.

beginning of_month

Returns a new `Time` representing the start of the month (1st of the month, 00:00 hours).

beginning_of_quarter

Returns a new `Time` representing the start of the calendar quarter (1st of January, April, July, October, 00:00 hours).

beginning of_week

Returns a new Time representing the "start" of the current instance's week, hard-coded to Monday at 00:00 hours.

beginning of_year

Returns a new Time representing the start of the year (1st of January, 00:00 hours).

change(options)

Returns a new Time where one or more of the elements have been changed according to the options parameter. The valid date options are :year, :month, :day. The valid time options are :hour, :min, :sec, :offset, and :start.

end_of_day

Returns a new Time representing the end of the day (23:59:59).

end_of_month

Returns a new Time representing the end of the month (last day of the month, 00:00 hours).

last_month

Convenience method for months_ago(1).

last_year

Convenience method for years_ago(1).

monday

Alias for beginning of_week.

months_ago(months)

Returns a new Time representing the time a number of specified months into the past.

`months_since(months)`

The opposite of `months_ago`. Returns a new `Time` representing the time a number of specified `months` into the future.

`next_month`

Convenience method for `months_since(1)`.

`next_year`

Convenience method for `years_since(1)`.

`seconds_since_midnight`

Returns the number of seconds that have transpired since midnight.

`since(seconds)`

Returns a new `Time` representing the time a number of `seconds` into the future starting from the instance time. This method is basically a wrapper around the `Numeric` extension of the same name. For best accuracy, do not use this method in combination with **x**`.months`; use `months_since` instead!

`tomorrow`

Convenience method for `self.since(1.day)`.

`years_ago(years)`

Returns a new `Time` representing the time a number of specified `years` into the past.

`years_since(years)`

The opposite of `years_ago`. Returns a new `Time` representing the time a number of specified `years` into the future.

`yesterday`

Convenience method for `self.ago(1.day)`.

Time::Conversions (in ActiveSupport::CoreExtensions)

Extensions to Ruby's Time class to convert time objects into different convenient string representations and other objects.

Constants

The DATE_FORMATS hash holds formatting patterns used by the to_formatted_s method to convert a Time object into a string representation:

```
DATE_FORMATS = {
  :db           => "%Y-%m-%d %H:%M:%S",
  :time         => "%H:%M",
  :short        => "%d %b %H:%M",
  :long         => "%B %d, %Y %H:%M",
  :long_ordinal => lambda { |time|
    time.strftime("%B #{time.day.ordinalize}, %Y %H:%M") },
  :rfc822       => "%a, %d %b %Y %H:%M:%S %z"
}
```

Public Instance Methods

to_date

Returns a new Date object based on a Time, discarding time data.

to_datetime

Returns a new DateTime object based on a Time, preserving the utc offset. Basically a wrapper around the DateTime.civil factory method:

```
DateTime.civil(year, month, day, hour, min, sec, Rational(utc_offset,
86400), 0)
```

to_formatted_s(format = :default)

Converts a `Time` object into a string representation. The `:default` option corresponds to the `Time` object's own `to_s` method.

```
>> Time.now.to_formatted_s(:long_ordinal)
=> "August 31st, 2007 15:00"
```

to_time

Returns `self`.

TimeZone

A *value object* representing a timezone. A timezone is simply a named offset (in seconds) from GMT. Note that two timezone objects are only equivalent if they have both the same offset and the same name.

When you have users spread out across the world, you generally want to store times on the server as UTC time, and store the user's timezone offset in association with their user accounts. That way, whenever you display a time for a user, you can adjust the time stored on the server to their local timezone.

Peter Marklund has a concise tutorial on the technique that you'll want to read at http://www.marklunds.com/articles/one/311. Pay attention to his advice to use the `TZInfo` Ruby library—it understands how to deal with Daylight Savings Time, whereas the Rails version does not.

Peter's tutorial covers everything from setting up `TZInfo` to adding timezone data to your `User` class with `composed_of`, and UI issues such as collecting the user's time zone setting using a Rails `time_zone_select` helper method.

Constants

`US_ZONES` is a regular expression that matches the names of all timezones in the USA.

```
US_ZONES = /US|Arizona|Indiana|Hawaii|Alaska/
```

Class Methods

[] (arg)

Locates a specific timezone object. If the argument is a string, it is interpreted to mean the name of the timezone to locate.

```
>> TimeZone['Dublin']
=> #<TimeZone:0x3208390 @name="Dublin", @utc_offset=0>
```

If it is a numeric value it is either the hour offset, or the second offset, of the timezone to find. (The first one with that offset will be returned.)

Returns `nil` if no such timezone is known to the system.

all

Returns an array of all `TimeZone` objects. There are multiple `TimeZone` objects per timezone (in many cases) to make it easier for users to find their own timezone.

This is the full array of timezone data included in the `TimeZone` class:

```
[[-43_200, "International Date Line West" ],
 [-39_600, "Midway Island", "Samoa" ],
 [-36_000, "Hawaii" ],
 [-32_400, "Alaska" ],
 [-28_800, "Pacific Time (US & Canada)", "Tijuana" ],
 [-25_200, "Mountain Time (US & Canada)", "Chihuahua", "La Paz",
          "Mazatlan", "Arizona" ],
 [-21_600, "Central Time (US & Canada)", "Saskatchewan",
   "Guadalajara",
          "Mexico City", "Monterrey", "Central America" ],
 [-18_000, "Eastern Time (US & Canada)", "Indiana (East)", "Bogota",
          "Lima", "Quito" ],
 [-14_400, "Atlantic Time (Canada)", "Caracas", "La Paz", "Santiago" ],
 [-12_600, "Newfoundland" ],
 [-10_800, "Brasilia", "Buenos Aires", "Georgetown", "Greenland" ],
 [ -7_200, "Mid-Atlantic" ],
 [ -3_600, "Azores", "Cape Verde Is." ],
 [      0, "Dublin", "Edinburgh", "Lisbon", "London", "Casablanca",
          "Monrovia" ],
```

```
[  3_600, "Belgrade", "Bratislava", "Budapest", "Ljubljana", "Prague",
          "Sarajevo", "Skopje", "Warsaw", "Zagreb", "Brussels",
          "Copenhagen", "Madrid", "Paris", "Amsterdam", "Berlin",
          "Bern", "Rome", "Stockholm", "Vienna",
          "West Central Africa" ],
[  7_200, "Bucharest", "Cairo", "Helsinki", "Kyev", "Riga", "Sofia",
          "Tallinn", "Vilnius", "Athens", "Istanbul", "Minsk",
          "Jerusalem", "Harare", "Pretoria" ],
[ 10_800, "Moscow", "St. Petersburg", "Volgograd", "Kuwait",
   "Riyadh",
          "Nairobi", "Baghdad" ],
[ 12_600, "Tehran" ],
[ 14_400, "Abu Dhabi", "Muscat", "Baku", "Tbilisi", "Yerevan" ],
[ 16_200, "Kabul" ],
[ 18_000, "Ekaterinburg", "Islamabad", "Karachi", "Tashkent" ],
[ 19_800, "Chennai", "Kolkata", "Mumbai", "New Delhi" ],
[ 20_700, "Kathmandu" ],
[ 21_600, "Astana", "Dhaka", "Sri Jayawardenepura", "Almaty",
          "Novosibirsk" ],
[ 23_400, "Rangoon" ],
[ 25_200, "Bangkok", "Hanoi", "Jakarta", "Krasnoyarsk" ],
[ 28_800, "Beijing", "Chongqing", "Hong Kong", "Urumqi",
          "Kuala Lumpur", "Singapore", "Taipei", "Perth", "Irkutsk",
          "Ulaan Bataar" ],
[ 32_400, "Seoul", "Osaka", "Sapporo", "Tokyo", "Yakutsk" ],
[ 34_200, "Darwin", "Adelaide" ],
[ 36_000, "Canberra", "Melbourne", "Sydney", "Brisbane", "Hobart",
          "Vladivostok", "Guam", "Port Moresby" ],
[ 39_600, "Magadan", "Solomon Is.", "New Caledonia" ],
[ 43_200, "Fiji", "Kamchatka", "Marshall Is.", "Auckland",
          "Wellington" ],
[ 46_800, "Nuku'alofa" ]]
```

create(name, offset)

Creates a new `TimeZone` instance with the given name and offset.

```
>> TimeZone.create("Atlanta", -5.hours)
=> #<TimeZone:0x31e6d44 @name="Atlanta", @utc_offset=-18000 seconds>
```

new(name)

Returns a `TimeZone` instance with the given name, or `nil` if no such `TimeZone` instance exists. This method exists to support the use of this class with the `composed_of` macro-style method on `ActiveRecord` models, like this:

```
class Person < ActiveRecord::Base
  composed_of :tz, :class_name => 'TimeZone',
              :mapping => %w(time_zone name)
end
```

us_zones

A convenience method for returning a collection of `TimeZone` objects for timezones in the USA.

```
>> TimeZone.us_zones.map(&:name)
=> ["Hawaii", "Alaska", "Pacific Time (US & Canada)", "Arizona",
"Mountain Time (US & Canada)", "Central Time (US & Canada)", "Eastern
Time (US & Canada)", "Indiana (East)"]
```

Public Instance Methods

<=> (other)

Compares this timezone to the parameter. The two are compared first based on their offsets, and then by name.

adjust(time)

Adjusts the given time to this timezone.

```
>> TimeZone['Fiji'].adjust(Time.now)
=> Sat Sep 01 10:42:42 UTC 2007
```

formatted_offset(colon = true)

Returns the offset of this timezone as a formatted string, in the format HH:MM. If the offset is zero, this method will return an empty string. If colon is false, a colon will not be inserted into the output.

initialize(name, utc_offset)

This constructor is used via TimeZone.create. Instantiates a new TimeZone object with the given name and offset. The offset is the number of seconds that this timezone is offset from UTC (GMT). Seconds were chosen as the offset unit because that is the unit that Ruby uses to represent timezone offsets (see Time's utc_offset method).

now

Returns Time.now adjusted to this timezone.

```
>> Time.now
=> Fri Aug 31 22:39:58 -0400 2007
>> TimeZone['Fiji'].now
=> Sat Sep 01 14:40:00 UTC 2007
```

to_s

Returns a textual representation of this timezone.

```
TimeZone['Dublin'].to_s   #=> "(GMT) Dublin"
```

today

Returns the current date in this timezone.

```
>> Date.today.to_s
=> "2007-08-31"
>> TimeZone['Fiji'].today.to_s
=> "2007-09-01"
```

TrueClass

Remember that everything in Ruby is an object, even `true`, which is a special reference to a singleton instance of the `TrueClass`.

Public Instance Methods

blank?

Always returns `false`.

References

1. For an interesting summary of why zero is considered by many to be an even number, read http://ask.yahoo.com/20020909.html.

2. Bytes Trivia: According to an IDC study commissioned by storage vendor EMC, 161 exabytes of digital information were created and copied in 2006. One exabyte equals a billion gigabytes. By 2010, IDC expects the volume of annual data created and copied to rise sixfold to 988 exabytes.

APPENDIX B
Rails Essentials

Chances are you learned about Rails from watching one of David's screencasts or one of the many tutorials available on the web. You might even have worked your way through *Agile Web Development with Rails*, which has sold so many copies that it is racing to the top of the list of most successful programming books of all time.

This appendix is a potpourri of essential bits of knowledge and tools that you need to be an effective, professional Rails developer—crucial information that all those introductions and tutorials *do not* tell you.

Edge Rails

Edge is the term used by the community to refer to the latest revision of Rails kept in the repository, as maintained by DHH and the Rails core team. Most Rails pros run *on edge* so that they can stay in tune with the latest improvements and bugfixes to the codebase. As a result, a lot of the most useful Rails plugins require you to run on edge in order to work.

In order to use EdgeRails you include a copy of Rails within your application rather than using the version installed on your machine as a library. Doing so is as easy as typing `rake rails:freeze:edge` from your command line inside a Rails project directory. That `rake` task will use Subversion to check out Rails into the `vendor/rails` directory of your project. From that moment on, anything Rails-related that you do (console, server, etc.) in that project will use edge Rails rather than whatever version you have installed as a gem.

If you're an experienced developer, you might be questioning the wisdom of using the latest *unreleased* version of Rails as it exists in the HEAD branch of the Ruby on Rails repository. Isn't that dangerous to your productivity? What if changes to the repository actually break your application? It does happen occasionally, which is why you don't want to track the latest version of Rails with every update to your codebase.

The answer is to pick a particular revision number of edge that is considered relatively stable. You do that by passing a variable to the freeze edge rake task, as follows:

```
rake rails:freeze:edge REVISION=1234
```

Wait a minute—how are you supposed to figure out what the latest stable revision is? And if any of those revisions really were stable, why wouldn't they be released? I admit that I don't have particularly good answers for you. Figuring out which revision of edge to use is more of an art than a science, and it changes with each project depending on your needs. Most of the time I start with the latest revision available at the time that I bootstrap my project and leave it there, only upgrading to a more recent version if I need to do so.

The Rails core team follows very strict policies regarding test coverage, which means that very few commits actually "break the build." Even though edge tends to be fairly stable, official releases have tended to lag behind edge at least a few months or more. A number of continuous-integration servers are set up to automatically test each version of the Rails trunk codebase against different database adapters. They send their broken-build notifications to the rails-core mailing list, which you can subscribe to at http://lists.rubyonrails.org/mailman/listinfo/rails-core.

Environmental Concerns

No, I'm not about to go off on a tangent about carbon credits and global warming. As a Rails pro, you're going to spend a lot of time using the command line, so you might as well save yourself as much confusion and extra typing as possible. The following little tips and tricks should make your life easier and more enjoyable.

Aliases

At minimum you should add aliases for starting your Rails server and console to your shell's execution environment. Geoffrey Grosenbach suggests[1] `alias ss './script/server'` and `alias sc './script/console'`.

Color

PJ Hyett and Chris Wanstrath, authors of the blog Err,[2] have provided the community with valuable, colorful essentials. First install the color gem:

```
sudo gem install color —source require.errtheblog.com
```

Now it's a cinch to make any string appear a different color in the terminal window, because methods for ANSI colors have been added to the `String` class.

Redgreen

While we're at it, let's also make our test-run results show in red and green. Again we use an `Err` gem:

```
sudo gem install redgreen —source require.errtheblog.com
```

Then open `test_helper.rb` in your nearest Rails project. Add `require 'redgreen'` to it; right under `require 'test_help'` will do. Now when you run your test suite, successful runs will print in green and failures/errors in red.

Essential Plugins

Some plugins are so valuable that (arguably) they should be a part of the core Rails distribution. However, because of the "less is more" philosophy of the core team, the Rails core distribution is actually shrinking, not growing.

The following sections are a list of what I (and the readers of my blog) consider to be essential plugins for the Rails pro to be aware of and use on a regular basis.

For the complete list of suggestions submitted for this section, read the comments on my blog post at http://www.jroller.com/obie/entry/rails_plugins_worth_their_something.

`ActiveRecord` Defaults

`http://svn.viney.net.nz/things/rails/plugins/active_record_defaults`
This plugin allows you to easily specify default values for attributes on new model objects.

Debug View Helpers

`script/plugin install debug_view_helper`
This plugin makes it easy to add a button that will pop up a window with the following debugging information, which we are accustomed to seeing on development mode error screens:

- Request parameters

- Session variables

- Flash variables

- Assigned template variables

Exception Notification

`http://svn.rubyonrails.org/rails/plugins/exception_notification`
This plugin, written by Rails core team member Jamis Buck, automatically sends you an e-mail whenever exceptions are raised on your site. It makes a remarkably adequate QA department for those lower-budget internal projects that *can* afford to be unstable. Will save your ass on those projects that *can't*.

Exception Logger

`http://svn.techno-weenie.net/projects/plugins/exception_logger`
According to Bryan Helmkamp, "I'd recommend `exception_logger` over `exception_notification`. The feeds and web UI are killer features."

Has Finder

`gem install has_finder`
This plugin is an extension to `ActiveRecord` that makes it easy to create custom finder and count methods on your `ActiveRecord` models. Read all about it at http://www.pivotalblabs.com/articles/2007/09/02/hasfinder-its-now-easier-than-ever-to-create-complex-re-usable-sql-queries.

Has Many Polymorphs

http://blog.evanweaver.com/files/doc/fauna/has_many_polymorphs
An `ActiveRecord` plugin for self-referential and double-sided polymorphic associations. However, the simplest way to describe it is to say that `has_many_polymorphs` is like a `has_many :through` where the `belongs_to` target is a polymorphic association. Want to know more? Read Pratik's tutorial at http://m.onkey.org/2007/8/14/excuse-me-wtf-is-polymorphs.

Query Trace

https://terralien.devguard.com/svn/projects/plugins/query_trace
The Rails development log already captures SQL statements generated by `ActiveRecord`. This little plugin by well-known Rubyist Nathaniel Talbott appends a short backtrace to every one of those log statements. It doesn't seem like a big deal, until you're trying to find the source of a nasty N+1 select problem or attempting to debug anything related to caching.

Spider Tester

http://sample.caboo.se/plugins/court3nay/spider_test
SpiderTester is an automated integration-testing script written by Courtenay that iterates over every page in your application.

It performs a few valuable tasks for you:

- Parses the HTML of every page, so if you have invalid HTML, you will be warned.

- Finds every link within your site and follows it, whether static or dynamic.

- Finds every `Ajax.Updater` link and follows it.

- Finds every form and tries to submit it, filling in values where possible.

   This plugin is helpful in determining

- Missing static pages (.HTML).

- Poor code coverage—forgot to test a file? Don't wait for a user to find it.

- Simple fuzzing of form values.

- Automated testing of form paths. Often we have forms that point to incorrect locations, and until now this has been impossible to test in an automated fashion or without being strongly coupled to your code.

Other Plugins

Descriptions of other useful plugins are included throughout the book where appropriate.

Screencasts

Screencasts are videos distributed online that teach you a narrowly focused topic of interest by capturing actual screen output (hence the name) while the author explains concepts and writes code.

PeepCode Screencasts

`http://peepcode.com/`
Ruby on Rails Podcast producer Geoffrey Grosenbach describes his PeepCode screencasts as "a high-intensity way to learn Ruby on Rails website development."

In reality, he uses his extensive knowledge and soothing voice to *gently* guide viewers into some of the deeper areas of Rails know-how. A new hour-long video screencast is released each month. They cost 9 USD each, but are well worth the expense in my opinion.

Railcasts

`http://railscasts.com/`
Short on cash? Host Ryan Bates posts a new screencast almost every week for free. Episodes are shorter and more narrowly focused than the PeepCode ones, and targeted at intermediate Ruby on Rails developers.

Subversion

In the last several years, Subversion (SVN) has become the predominant source-control management (SCM) system, and for good reasons. It is fast, stable, and is a huge improvement over its predecessor, CVS.

The Rails world is wedded to Subversion in various ways, particularly with its plugin system, which depends on Subversion to pull down plugin files from repositories.

What to do if you're stuck having to use an evil SCM, such as ClearCase or StarTeam (and you can't move to a more sensible employer)? One strategy that has been successful at times is to establish an SVN repository that you control for day-to-day development, and only check in packaged releases of your application to the main SCM.

Rake Tasks for Subversion

A number of bloggers have suggested custom rake tasks that make working with Subversion more convenient. Create a `lib/tasks/svn.rake` file in your Rails project and add the following task definitions to it.

Listing B.1 is a task that automatically sets up a new Rails project with the proper subversion repository settings, including ignores.

Listing B.1   Configure Subversion for Rails Custom Rake Task

```
namespace :rails do
  desc "Configure Subversion for Rails"
  task :configure_for_svn do
    system "svn propset svn:ignore -R '.DS_Store' . --force"
    system "svn update"
    system "svn commit -m 'ignore all .DS_Store files'"
    system "svn remove log/* --force"
    system "svn commit -m 'removing all log files from subversion'"
    system "svn propset svn:ignore '*.log' log/ --force"
    system "svn update log/"
    system "svn commit -m 'Ignoring all files in /log/ ending in .log'"
    system "svn propset svn:ignore '*' tmp/sessions tmp/cache
tmp/sockets"
    system "svn commit -m 'Ignoring all files in /tmp/'"
    system "svn propset svn:ignore '*.db' db/ --force"
    system "svn update db/"
    system "svn commit -m 'Ignoring all files in /db/ ending in .db'"
    system "svn move config/database.yml config/database.example --
force"
    system "svn commit -m 'Moving database.yml to database.example to
provide a template for anyone who checks out the code'"
    system 'svn propset svn:ignore "locomotive.yml\ndatabase.yml"
config/ --force'
    system "svn update config/"
    system "svn commit -m 'Ignoring locomotive.yml and database.yml'"
    system "script/plugin install -x ➥
http://dev.rubyonrails.org/svn/rails/plugins/exception_notification/"
  end
end
```

Listing B.2 declares an `svn` namespace and five tasks related to checking status, adding and deleting working files, and checking in code.

Listing B.2   Useful Subversion Rake Tasks

```ruby
namespace :svn do
  task :st do
    puts %x[svn st]
  end

  task :up do
    puts %x[svn up]
  end

  task :add do
    %x[svn st].split(/\n/).each do |line|
      trimmed_line = line.delete('?').lstrip
      if line[0,1] =~ /\?/
        %x[svn add #{trimmed_line}]
        puts %[added #{trimmed_line}]
      end
    end
  end

  task :delete do
    %x[svn st].split(/\n/).each do |line|
      trimmed_line = line.delete('!').lstrip
      if line[0,1] =~ /\!/
        %x[svn rm #{trimmed_line}]
        puts %[removed #{trimmed_line}]
      end
    end
  end
end

desc "Run before checking in"
task :pc => ['svn:add', 'svn:delete', 'svn:up', :default, 'svn:st']
```

WorkingWithRails.com

A comprehensive survey and description of the Rails community online would take too much time to compile and get out of date quickly, but I do want to highlight workingwithrails.com (or WWR for short), an open database of all things related to the people and groups doing Rails development. It is lovingly crafted (with Rails) by Martin Sadler and his UK-based company DSC.

Over time, I've found that WWR is one of the most effective ways to get your name out there and identify yourself as a member of the professional Rails community, especially if you're soliciting work as an independent contractor. If you're hiring, or looking for good people to work with, WWR is also a fantastic resource for identifying popular members of the community and talented developers in your local area.

If you enjoyed this book and found it useful, please consider recommending its author, contributors, and principle reviewers:

http://www.workingwithrails.com/person/5391-obie-fernandez
http://www.workingwithrails.com/person/8048-matt-bauer
http://www.workingwithrails.com/person/5747-david-a-black
http://www.workingwithrails.com/person/5541-trotter-cashion
http://www.workingwithrails.com/person/1363-matt-pelletier
http://www.workingwithrails.com/person/4746-jodi-showers
http://www.workingwithrails.com/person/5137-james-adam
http://www.workingwithrails.com/person/848-pat-maddox
http://www.workingwithrails.com/person/582-sebastian-delmont
http://www.workingwithrails.com/person/5167-sam-aaron

Using Subversion Hooks

If you want to take your use of Subversion on Rails projects to the next level, check out the excellent article at http://railspikes.com/2007/8/20/subversion-hooks-in-ruby.

---

1.   http://nubyonrails.com/articles/2006/01/19/sxsw-aliases

2.   http://errtheblog.com/

AFTERWORD

What Is the Rails Way (To You)?

I love the Ruby community. It's vibrant, witty, and smart. Truly, our community is one of the best aspects of working with Rails and no small part of its success. As I was nearing completion of this book, I felt a strong urge to include the community in whatever way possible, to give readers a taste of what it's like, and then it hit me. We all know that there *is* a Rails way, and yet it *is* an intensely personal experience, subject to interpretation and joyful exposition. What better way to end the book than with a collection of *your thoughts!*

So I asked and boy, did you all respond. I hope you enjoy reading the following series of quotes, quips, and essays as much as I did.

Obie Fernandez, Jacksonville Beach (September 12, 2007)

My first thought was "The Rails way is happiness," but then I remembered a poem that I really like by Edgar Allen Poe. The poem *Eleonora* started off with him talking about madness and intelligence and how it might be that they are one and the same. He goes on to talk about and give a sense of pity for those who can only dream by night. I am glad I am one of the ones who can dream by day as well as by night. I know the secret!

Men have called me mad; but the question is not yet settled, whether madness is or is not the loftiest intelligence—whether much that is glorious—whether all that is profound—does not spring from disease of thought—from moods of mind exalted at the expense of the general intellect. They who dream by day are cognizant of many things which escape those who dream only by night. In their gray visions they obtain glimpses of eternity, and thrill, in awakening, to find that they have been upon the verge of the great secret.
—Edgar Allen Poe

Desi McAdam, my favorite Rails developer

The creators of Rails were so unhappy with every existing tool for developing web applications that they started from scratch. As should by now be clear by the length of this book, that was a serious undertaking. How much better would PHP be if they had contributed patches instead of writing Rails?

Perhaps a little, but probably not enough for outsiders to notice. To paraphrase the shopkeeper in *Whisper of the Heart*: "You could polish rough ore, but what you'd get would be worthless. The smaller gem inside is purer. It takes time and effort to find it." Rails teaches us that sometimes you must discard what you are used to seeing before you can find what you are looking for.

The Ruby way is to polish a stone until you find the jewel within it. Ruby and Rails, for all their power and elegance, cannot stop you from writing cluttered, unreadable code. Only you can decide when the code you have written is as polished as you can make it. Ruby asks us to challenge ourselves to create elegant systems that are pleasant to use and to look upon. Rails asks us to constantly test our assumptions, and to not be afraid to discard large sections of code if they displease us.

These two forces, discontent with the current state of affairs and constant self-criticism of your own work, are what have made Ruby and Rails such popular and powerful tools. If you can recognize these forces in yourself, you will write better code. If you can harness them, you will have found the Rails way, even if that leads you to write something better to replace Rails itself.

Wilson Bilkovich, Rails myrmidon and Rubinius core developer

When I'm working in Ruby on Rails, I feel like I'm sketching with well-sharpened pencils on quality paper, with a good eraser by my side. I'm able to rough out my idea very quickly to see if it has merit. If not, the application can be tossed without too much grief, because a minimal amount of effort was expended initially. If things are working out, I'm able to refine what I like and delete what I don't, building up the same application from prototype to production with the tightest design spirals I've ever experienced developing software.

Dan Gebhardt

The wise student hears of the Rails way and embraces it.
The average student hears of the Rails way and forgets it.
The foolish student hears of the Rails way and laughs aloud.
But if there were no laughter, there would be no Rails way.

Jon Larkowski, with apologies to Lao-Tzu

I have been a .NET developer for the past several years. I have spent every day with .NET in one form or the other but when asked why I do it, my usual response is, "it pays the bills." I don't say I love the technology but that it is a means to an end. I still do it every day until there is something better I can do every day.

I think I see a light at the end of the long tunnel that has been my career and it's Ruby and Ruby on Rails. When using them the experience is very satisfying, very Zen-like, almost to the extreme of being philosophical in nature. When I am asked by my peers as to what Rails brings to me I often find it hard to explain in words they may understand. I realize I explain it as finding a religion, where it is not just the text or the way it is delivered but includes those who share the experience, making it very whole.

The Rails way, or the experience, is about finding passion and the feeling you are doing the right thing. The technology makes it good but the community makes it great.

My involvement in Rails has only been the past year or so but having 20-plus years of software development experience, I have the insight to know when I have found something great.

Rob Bazinet, a software developer currently enjoying learning Ruby and Rails

---

The Rails way is M: Magical V: Velocity Focused C: Community Driven

Matt Margolis

Freeing yourself from decision-making; that is the Rails way. All the important choices have already been made for you, and instead of deciding which technology to adopt or what application structure you should adopt, you sit down and hack. As you experience the development process, you extend Rails, making plugins to fill the need. It is Zen development.

Ben Stiglitz

I'm fairly new to web development. I wasn't doing web dev with Perl CGI scripts, or PHP, or even much with J2EE. Rails was my introduction to serious web development. For me, Rails made web development something that I didn't have to try and avoid.

I can't help but compare Rails to C. I learned C fairly early in my lifelong love affair with programming. Raw power, expressiveness (I was previously using mainly assembly language), being able to do some cool stuff very quickly. Smalltalk gave me the same feeling all over again. Rails gives me that feeling again... Ruby, of course is a big part of that... the ability to accomplish much in very little time, with very little code.

To me the Rails way is about how it feels. Rampant productivity, flow, expressiveness, malleability, few hurdles or roadblocks...

The Rails way is like blasting down the coastal California highway on a sunny day in a Corvette convertible with the top down.

Dave Astels, author of TDD: A Practical Guide *and* Test Mercenary at Google, Inc.

The Rails way is ...

To go out of the way to help without expectation.

To embrace ideas both new and old.

To realize we all have better things to do.

Jim Remsik, a.Net Developer with a job change in the near future

---

OK, so what is this "Rails way" that people speak of? Is there, in fact, such a thing, and if so, is it actually definable? I believe that the "Rails way" is a subjective concept, and as such I'd like to explain what it means to me. If we ever meet, I'd love to know what it means to you.

Let's start with a simple, almost embarrassing analogy. Let's talk locomotives, carriages, trains, and railways. No, I'm not talking about the small models that your dad painstakingly paints and crafts in the garage. I'm talking about the real deal. Big huge powerful engines. Tracks laid for miles. Cargo. Passengers. The heavy, sooty smell of smoke, steam, and coal. Technology that powered the industrial revolution. Technology that people constantly challenged, improved, and reinvented. It's still happening today. For example, in terms of technology, the Transrapid Shanghai Maglev Train is a far cry from the steam locomotives that operated along the English railways during the early nineteenth century. Books similar to this one were written about the technology behind railways, for the people interested in or building with the technology. However, for the majority of people, the technology behind railways isn't their focus. It's what railways enable that is interesting: holidays to the seaside, visiting Gran, shipping goods to new markets, being able to live farther from work. Now, what I personally think is interesting about railways is the inherent limitations; the fact that they limit where you can travel. Your choice of destinations is essentially decided for you. The decisions were made when the tracks were laid and the stations were built. People decided that you'd want to travel from London to Newcastle.

"Gah, the gall!" you might cry. "I want complete control of where I can go," you might suggest. After all, choice is freedom, right?

Ruby on Rails is similarly limiting. It lays the tracks down for you. It tells you where to go. Of course, you're not strictly limited to following its direction—you can go where you want. However, I'm sure that riding a train over rough undulating terrain won't be the most comfortable journey you've ever had. This leads to an important question: "How do I know that Rails is taking me in the right direction?" Clearly this is a subjective question. The answer really depends on your own definition of "right." However, for me it was most certainly the right direction. Let me give you a little bit of context:

So, I was well into my Ph.D. studies. I had implemented a prototype in Java to evaluate my ideas. The only problem was that the Java system was a house of cards constantly falling over. Looking back in retrospect, I think that it was mostly to do with the fact that my ideas were in a state of flux: They were constantly changing. After all, I was researching. Unfortunately, the Java code base I had written became complicated and convoluted with all the changes. In an ideal imaginary world I would have just conjured up new ideas which, in order to be evaluated, would be magically implemented by some AI research bot. Clearly this wasn't the case, and I had to write my own code. However, with the Java implementation, the code started to control my ideas rather than the ideas controlling the code. For example, I'd find myself saying things like "It would be great to be able to do this, but that would be too hard, or take too long to implement." It caused me a great amount of frustration, followed by a fair amount of depression.

Now, I'm not trying to get all emo on you. Go and find someone who's done a Ph.D. and you'll see that each and every one of them had some kind of depression during the course of their research. I hope you'll excuse the mild tautology, but it's just a depressing reality of the nature of Ph.D.'s. In my case, my depression grew from being frustrated with my tools, and not knowing where to turn next to fix the big mess I was in. I was lost, and without direction.

Somehow, I stumbled across Rails. I'm not sure what attracted me to it. Perhaps it was because I had already been using and enjoying the simple wiki Instiki for a while (one of the first-ever Rails applications). Perhaps it was the strong sense of community. Perhaps it was the smart, interesting, and often funny blog posts. Perhaps it was the sheer excitement and thrill displayed by people using Rails. "Whoops," I forgot the fact that it could have also been the eye-opening screencasts. In fairness, it was probably a healthy dose of each of these things. Rails offered me a lot of what I was wanting: an intelligent, excited community of interesting people focusing on a framework that allowed useful things to be built remarkably quickly and effortlessly. I needed some of that!

The next year or so were lost years in terms of research; I hardly progressed. However, I learned a lot more about programming than I had done in any other similar period of time. I devoured blog posts and books like I had been starved of information. Learning Ruby really opened my mind to the interesting facets of programming languages. Suddenly I could see that programming didn't just have to be an engineering task; there were many other aspects. It was also an art, a craft, even a study of language itself. The philosophies behind Rails such as "Convention over Configuration" and "Don't Repeat Yourself" didn't just make sense; they were obviously sensible. My eyes were starting to open. Everything that the Rails community did and talked about seemed interesting. It's almost as if they acted as a wonderful filter of what to read and learn, and most importantly it was a filter I grew to trust.

Let's return to the discussion about trains and freedom: "Railways limit where you can travel," and "your choice of destinations is essentially decided for you." We discussed that possible retorts to these statements would be phrases like "I want complete control of where I can go," and "choice is freedom." Well, look at it from my context. I had complete choice and freedom of where I could go with my research. That wasn't my problem. My problem was that I didn't know which way to go, and so I was going nowhere. Having too many unclear and unknown options was essentially blinding my way.

After my Rails hiatus, I returned back to my research with renewed vigor and strength. I decided to scrap my implementation, and completely rebuild it using Ruby and Rails. I rebuilt it in a fraction of the time it took to implement the original, with a fraction of the original code-base. What's more, the new implementation was completely tested, so the house-of-cards scenario was no more, and get this, I actually enjoyed building it. I enjoyed working on something that had once been such a frustration and cause of depression. It turned out that using Rails as a filter on the set of possible implementation options didn't feel at all restrictive or imprisoning; it actually gave me clarity and direction. I believe that this is part of what people refer to as the Rails way, which for me is only the start of an exciting and promising journey.

Sam Aaron, who doesn't do short answers ☺

Ruby on Rails demonstrates that quick need not be dirty, and best practices need not be complex. It is the perfect example of the 80/20 principle in the modern world of web applications—Rails doesn't meet everyone's needs, but when it does it is a sweet solution indeed.

Gabe da Silveira, available at websaviour.com

Rails and Ruby, Ruby and Rails, what can I say?

I've been an object-oriented programmer for 30-odd years. I was one of the lucky guys who was part of the Smalltalk community in its heyday. I grudgingly took up Java work when "write once run anywhere" took over the world.

Then I retired and went back to playing with technology according to my own whims, and picked up the odd job every now and then to pick up a stray buck.

I played with various open source web apps, some good, others not so much. I run a wiki based in mediawiki, and was actively playing with that code for a while. It shows that well-written code can even be obtained in PHP. On the other hand a few consulting experiences reacquainted me with the horrors of what hacked-together code could produce.

Along the way, one of my buddies asked me if I'd played with Ruby, so I took a look. Somehow I felt strangely at home. Ruby took enough OO ideas from Smalltalk, sprinkled in some advanced ideas like modules and singleton methods, and added some, mostly good, stuff from Perl. I'd looked at python too, but Ruby just felt more complete and comfortable.

Then I got a Rails gig, adding some new features to an existing app. In comparison to an earlier similar job to try to extend a PHP mission-critical app, this was heaven. Instead of spending all my time just trying to figure out what the code was supposed to be doing, the Rails code was obvious both in the code and its structure. Best of all there were TEST CASES. A great boon to the new kid on a project.

Of course that code didn't get the way it was just because it was written using Rails, but it sure helped. Another thing which Ruby, and Rails in particular, shares with Smalltalk is that there is quite a lot of good code in the literature to read, understand, and use as a source of exemplars.

It's not that you can't write awful Rails code, but you have to work at it a little harder! If you trust your sense of smell when you find yourself working in Rails, you know that you are probably doing something wrong, and should look for examples of how others solved similar problems; and you're very likely to find those examples without much looking.

Rick DeNatale, retired IBM Smalltalk Guru, principal of DenHaven Consulting and Terralien crew member

---

At numerous sweet at the mid-night
I say I love Rails
The night also becomes thus beautiful
The stars cannot help but blinking eye
The beautiful Rails world
I love you
I asked myself over and over again
I don't love you to love who
I love you, Rails

Hackem, university student in China

In my experience, first as an employee, and now as a company owner, the Rails way can be summed up with Three Cs—collaboration, consistency, and contribution.

Collaboration: Doing things "the Rails way" means not only tighter collaboration between team members, but also tighter collaboration with our clients. Between team members, there's a tangible feeling of excitement in using Rails to its fullest potential, resulting in code reviews that are dynamic and educational, instead of mind-numbing or incomprehensible. In client interactions, it means more frequent release cycles, and feedback at earlier stages. We hit a lot closer to the moving target with Rails than we did with PHP.

Consistency: Coming from a background in a variety of languages and frameworks which did not take an opinionated stance, I'm all too familiar with how hard it can be to decipher another programmer's coding style. Embracing the Rails way has reduced the time we spend explaining ourselves to each other, and simply puts us all on the same page. This has been invaluable to us.

Contribution: By doing things the Rails way we're in a much better position to give back to the community. While I've been a consumer of open source software for at least the past dozen years, Ruby on Rails is the first open source project to which I've contributed patches (and felt the joy of seeing those patches merged into the Rails core). Contribution is possible at any level, too. Plugins, gems, documentation, blog entries about new discoveries, or even just volunteering to speak at local Rails events. The cooperative spirit that seems to emerge from the Rails way is one I've not seen paralleled in any other software project, and I'm excited to be a part of it.

Jared Haworth, founder of Alloy Code, a web development company based in Raleigh, NC

For me, the Rails way represents freedom. The freedom to concentrate on writing solutions and not compiler fodder. The freedom to learn one underlying language and not esoteric configuration file formats. The freedom to mold said language and solution like a lump of clay into an elegant piece of software and not be thwarted by language or API designers who feel they know best. The freedom to have fun, again, to not mind the long, hard hours put into crafting a beautiful piece of software. The freedom to return to the familiar land of dynamic languages.

Mel Riffe, former Smalltalk programmer

The Rails way is about finding the most beautiful answer to any problem. These solutions are not found by one-off hackery, but by building upon smart conventions and principles with other developers. It's about keeping the obscurists out and bringing the artists in. Viva la Rails way!

Hampton Catlin, self-proclaimed Ruby Prophet

Rails has taken me places that I had forgotten existed. I recall a time not so long ago when I sat up late at night slowly grasping the joy of software creation. College was a time for exploration, for pushing the limits of my mind and my capabilities.

Then Corporation and Comfort snatched me from Excitement and Growth. Education was pushed back in my mind as I was molded into a standards-based automaton. Work just enough to impress, but don't even attempt to wow. Good enough was great and great was a pipe dream.

The epiphany that I was whiling away my passion for a consistent paycheck arrived suspiciously close to the moment I discovered Rails. Rails led me away from Corporation and back toward Fulfillment. Ruby slapped me in the face and left me smiling at the sting.

Barry Hess, who can be found speaking in tongues at bjhess.com

---

Rails has strong opinions about a particular way of rapidly building end-to-end applications from the simple to the complex with minimal effort and tight integration. Each developer should experience the Rails way of building web applications so they can decide if that way can be their way, and to learn what they can from that approach to take forward into their own work.

Geoffrey Wiseman, software development generalist and writer/editor at large

---

The Rails way is being part of a community dedicated to helping each other work smarter, build better products, and have more fun doing it. It's about the freedom of not being beholden to any single company. The Rails way is a path beaten out by people who care about beauty and craftsmanship in software development, and when you walk it, you do your part to mark it for those who will follow.

Luke Melia, railing away in NYC

Rails—beauty in code
Creative, fun, and perfect
Future that is pure

David Parker, all you need to know at davidwparker.com

I started programming when I was 13—I remember that summer well; it was the end of playing outside and skinned knees for me. I found the BASIC Programming book for our TRS-80. My monitor was a TV, my files were saved on a cassette tape, and my printer contained 5-inch wide thermal paper. I was hooked on programming. Over time, I upgraded my computers as well as my programming skills, learning more versions of Basic and C/C++. After four years of Pascal and one semester of Java in college, I picked up a PHP book and learned PHP and landed my first job. As I grew as a developer and became more familiar with web development, I struggled with good design such as MVC, database rows to objects and templates. I tried to come up with a web framework and experimented with a few. None of them made it simple enough or even logical enough. The typical CRUD part of development wore on me because it was so tedious and repetitive. Web development for me became boring and such a drag! I entered into about two years of what I call "programmer depression" where I was not excited about anything code-related and I would come home from work and not even turn my computer on.

Programming communities are inspiring. In 2006, I reconnected with developer and friend Keith Casey after a few years where we had no contact. He was involved in some open source projects, including DotProject, a LAMP-based project management application. I did some contract work with him and got involved in the open source community and participating in the forums for projects by helping answer questions and discuss design. He encouraged me to attend local user group meetings in Chicago. I found the Chicago PHP group and met some Perl programmers (shh, don't tell anyone there were Perl people at a PHP meeting!) and started learning Perl, then later found the Ruby group. I was soon attending three user group meetings a month—Ruby, Perl, and PHP. Occasionally, I visited the Python group. I was learning new things and being around other programmers both in person and through open source projects. At that time, I was the only programmer in the company and I was starved for some geek conversation. PHP is nice for some applications because it's so easily supported on most web servers. Perl I loved because of its testing libraries and its flexibility and I learned a lot about design. Rails I loved because it made MVC make sense to me; `ActiveRecord` lets me map database rows to objects with ease. Scaffolding made getting basic CRUD done quickly, leaving me the time and freedom to work on the business logic of the application. Programming was fun again!

Rails is agile. As my growth as a developer continued, I learned the agile/scrum process and Rails was a natural fit. Scaffolding helps me to prototype quickly and get feedback from the customer early in the process. One day, a business analyst came to the developers needing an application and was trying to explain what he needed. We had a similar application already, but he just needed a few things changed, which would unfortunately require significant redesign. After hearing him talk for 15 minutes, I walked to my desk and with the help of Streamlined created a basic Rails application with a few controllers and models. I had created a nearly complete site within the hour. I showed it to him and after I customized the forms the way he wanted and added a few more features, I had a production-level application deployed in about 18 hours.

Rails allows rapid development. Another thing I've learned is that managers who are used to languages other than Ruby may have a hard time with the rapid development of Rails. In one case, I had some tasks for a project and was given a lecture about how it's too much work for the hours estimated. Further, I could not possibly be creating quality code if I did manage to get it done within that time frame. I knew I could do it and with quality code! I left that meeting with determination and even took the time to explain the process to a person new to Rails as I created my RESTful Rails site, used scaffolding, then customized the parts that were particular to my needs. I ran the tests (46 of 'em!) and it was done. Just in case there was criticism about my code being high quality I ran `rcov` (a test coverage tool) on my tests and had 100% test coverage. How ya like them apples?

Rails has given me confidence and boldness. Normally I am a very timid person and don't often initiate conversations with strangers. One day, I'm on my daily commute via train to Chicago when someone sat next to me with a Play Station Portable (PSP) in a unique case. I asked him about his case and talked about how I am going to steal my husband's PSP one of these days and put linux on it. He said he was a mainframe programmer and didn't like it at all. He wanted to get into web development. So I immediately start in about Rails, sharing the highlights of the framework and how much I like it. He started writing down notes. I told him what sites to go to for more info, what books to read, and I even let him watch the classic "Rails Blog in 15 Minutes" video on my laptop. I keep watching for him on the train to ask if he's tried it yet!

More than anything, I try to use the right tool for the job. I like multiple languages and Ruby with Rails is the one I choose for web development in most cases. I may choose PHP for a site if it has only one dynamic page or a site that just needs an email form. Perl is great for system tasks or data processing. Each of these languages has their strengths and I will not put anyone down who thinks otherwise. I think the biggest problem is the lack of community among developers across languages. It's usually someone trying to point out why X language is no good. Come on guys… that doesn't help anyone. You can learn from other languages even if it's not your primary language. Sometimes when I am programming in one language I think of how I would do it in another. Often, thinking "outside the box" like this will guide me to the right solution.

Rails has definitely inspired me and changed the way I think about web development. The community surrounding Ruby/Rails is outstanding and that makes me a better programmer.

Nola Stowe, Language Geek

The Rails way is pragmatic to its core, born from the twin forces of deep experience and the need to solve the real-world programming problems at hand. It dumps conventional wisdom on how things ought to be done and, instead, takes a fresh look at the mitigating the real impediments to developer productivity.

Curt Hibbs, author of the most successful online tutorials for Rails

---

Some days, I think it means expressive, iterative, simple, elegant web development.

Some days, I think it means ignoring decades of collective wisdom and inventing a wheel made of cornstarch—it's more lightweight, and we're probably not going too far, so why overengineer?

Some days, I think it means "F*** you."

It's one of those days.

Jay Levitt, former chief mail systems architect at America Online, lives in Boston, MA

The Rails way is all about making programmers happy. It's about automating, abstracting, and refactoring until a web application can be written in the fewest number of lines needed to get the job done. It's about making it easier to write the right kind of code than the wrong kind.

And when programmers are happy, they can focus on writing great applications that make the user happy, too!

Geoffrey Grosenbach, PeepCode Publishing and voice of the Ruby on Rails podcast

---

```
"c7Fd9uk3nu4ck0td8iv9oz1nv0ak5ljjSw2iv6mu9pz1ly3im0cq7il4ta2y".gsub(/\w\d/,
"").gsub('jj',' ')
```

Jeremy Hubert, being his silly self

Working with Rails feels like pair programming with a talented, experienced, and opinionated web developer. If you can swallow your pride and follow Rails' lead, great productivity gains await you. If you have strong opinions about web development and database design, there are going to be arguments, and your productivity will languish. Initially, developing the Rails way means humbling yourself, surrendering to the opinions of Rails, and seeing web development through Rails' eyes. But take heart! As you learn Ruby, your arguments with Rails will begin turning in your favor. Eventually, developing the Rails way means listening to Rails' opinions, picking your battles, and through the power of Ruby, bending Rails to your will.

Dave Hoover, software craftsman

There's a line at the beginning of the SICP lectures—a famous course on functional programming—where Harold Abelson is defining "computer science" for his class:

> "Computer science" is a terrible name for this business. First of all, it's not a science; it might be engineering, or it might be art... It's also not very much about computers, in the same sense that physics is not really about particle accelerators, and biology is not really about microscopes and Petri dishes, and geometry is not really about using surveying instruments.
>
> The reason that we think that computer science is about computers is pretty much the same reason that the Egyptians thought that measuring their plots after

the flooding of the Nile was about surveying instruments, and not geometry: When some field is just getting started, and you don't really understand it very well, it's very easy to confuse the essence of what you're doing with the tools that you use.

In the same way, my sense of "the Rails way" is not really about Rails, Ruby, or any of these new tools we're using. Its "essence" is an uncompromising drive to optimize for productivity and happiness. It's a hard-learned pragmatism: Processes for people who refuse to solve the same problem twice, who are annoyed enough by the speed bumps their tools sometimes introduce that they happily gas up the steamroller.

A necessary corollary to the idea that Rails' secret sauce is distinct from the code frozen to our vendor directories is that one day, a better instantiation of these practices will come along. I love Ruby, Rails, and their communities, but I know that we'll all move on at some point. When that day comes, and some new 10-minute screencast makes us squeal like kids, we should have the sense to jump into it head-first, with the same abandon with which we dropped all that stuff we *used* to do for a living.

Chris Kampmeier blogs at http://www.shiftcommathree.com

If DHH ain't doing it, you don't do it. (Seems every time some clever fellow gets into trouble it's because of that.)
Zed Shaw, author of Mongrel web server

Index

C

F

X-Y-Z